CONTEMPORARY MUSICIANS

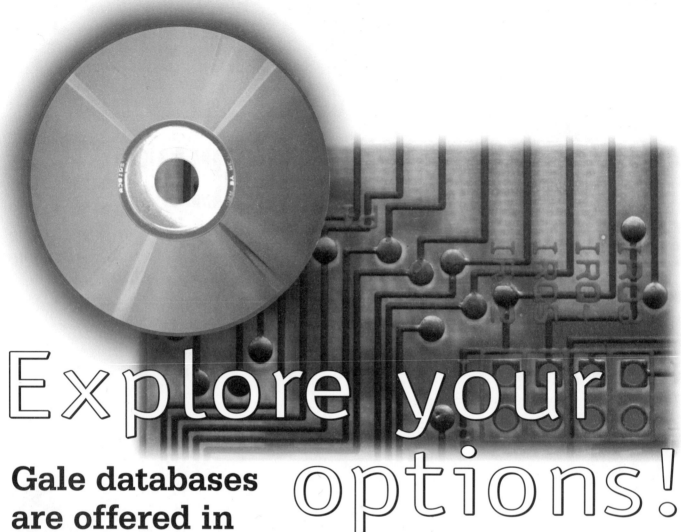

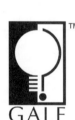

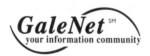

ISSN 1044-2197

CONTEMPORARY MUSICIANS

PROFILES OF THE PEOPLE IN MUSIC

LUANN BRENNAN, Editor
STACY A. McCONNELL, Contributing Editor

VOLUME 22
Includes Cumulative Indexes

GALE
DETROIT • LONDON

STAFF

Luann Brennan, *Project Editor*

McConnell,Terrie M. Rooney, *Contributing Editors*

Frank V. Castronova, Andrea K. Henderson, Bruce A. MacDonald, Katherine H. Nemeh, *Editorial Staff*

Mary Alice Adams, Bill Bennett, Carol Brennan, Gerald Brennan, John Cohassey, Ed Decker, Robert Dupuis, Shaun Frentner, Robert R. Jacobson, Mary Kalfatovic, Gretchen Monette, K. Michelle Moran, Christine Morrison, Sean Pollock, Jim Powers, Paula Pyzik-Scott, Sonya Shelton, Debra Reilly, B. Kim Taylor, *Sketchwriters*

Neil E. Walker, *Managing Editor*

Susan M. Trosky, *Permissions Manager*
Jessica L. Ulrich, *Permissions Associate*

Mary Beth Trimper, *Production Director*
Carolyn Fischer, *Production Assistant*
Cynthia Baldwin, *Product Design Manager*
Barbara J. Yarrow, *Graphic Services Supervisor*
Robert Duncan, Michael Logusz, *Imaging Specialists*
Randy Bassett, *Image Database Supervisor*
Pamela A. Reed, *Imaging Coordinator*
Gary Leach, *Graphic Artist*

Cover illustration by John Kleber

Printed in the United States of America

ISBN 0-7876-2090-4
ISSN 1044-2197

10 9 8 7 6 5 4 3 2 1

Contents

Introduction ix

Cumulative Subject Index 259

Cumulative Musicians Index 285

A-ha ... 1
Pretty boys of Oslo

Ace of Base ... 4
Studio masters

Aerosmith ... 8
Hard rock attitudes

Air Supply ... 13
Fare for softies

Rhett Akins ... 16
Rags to riches tale

The Alarm ... 19
Latter day punks

The Animals ... 22
Wild on stage

The Aquabats ... 26
Super human stage personas

Art of Noise ... 29
Electronic faceless wonders

Audio Adrenaline ... 32
Religion on the forefront

Aztec Camera ... 35
Soothing pop songs

Bad Company ... 38
No frills rock and roll

Bananarama ... 42
Top 40 girl group

The Bangles ... 45
Neo folkish act

Gato Barbieri ... 48
Tenor man with many lives

Black Flag ... 51
America's hard core punkers

Bluegrass Patriots ... 54
Bonded by bluegrass

Andrea Bocelli ... 57
Pop and opera superstar

Paul Brandt ... 60
Early starting country Canadian

Jim Brickman ... 63
New age pianist

Lisa Brokop ... 66
British Columbia's strong voice

Jeff Buckley ... 69
Tragic singer left large wake

Don Byron ... 73
Spicy jazz clarinetist

Joi Cardwell ... 75
Heartfelt R&B singer

Bob Carlisle ... 77
Definer of "Butterfly Kisses"

Regina Carter ... 81
Violin jazz fusion

Congo Norvell ... 84
Melodramatic gothic rock

Celia Cruz ... 87
Queen of salsa

The Dandy Warhols ... 91
Carrying the banner of psychedelia

Dead Milkmen ... 94
Punkers refuse to grow up

Chris de Burgh ... 96
Story-telling rock and roll

Deftones ... 99
Mosh pit madness

John Denver ... 103
Nurturing singer and naturalist

Dire Straits ... 107
"Sultans" of rock

Dubstar ... 111
Infectious electronic pop

The Faces ... 114
Band that launched Rod Stewart

Fairport Convention ... 117
Perennial British folk

Fatboy Slim ... 121
Electronic raver

Fine Young Cannibals ... 124
Link of punk and hip-hop

Flaming Lips ... 127
Twisted pop shenanigans

Kirk Franklin ... 130
Gospel hip-hop crossover

Fu Manchu ... 133
Fuzzy 70s retro rock

Julie Gold ... 136
She writes the songs

Teddy Harris ... 139
Player, producer, and teacher of bebop

Insane Clown Posse ... 143
Halloween rappers

Joe Jackson ... 146
Classically trained pop star

Wyclef Jean ... 150
Fugees guitar rapper

Ingrid Jensen ... 153
Soft trumpet sensibilities

Jimmie's Chicken Shack ... 156
Hard-driving mutt-rock

Carol Kaye ... 160
Pioneering session bassist

Kenny Wayne Shepherd ... 163
Louisiana blues prodigy

King Missile ... 166
Darlings of college radio

Less Than Jake ... 168
Horn laden punk pop

Letters to Cleo ... 171
Hard working punk

Charles Lloyd ... 175
Broke new ground for jazz

Aimee Mann ... 178
One of rock's best kept secrets

Master P ... 181
Balance of art and business

Eric Matthews ... 183
Inspired by the classics

Maxwell ... 185
Savior of soul

Mindy McCready ... 188
Charismatic country Miss

Brian McKnight ... 191
Romantic R&B crafter

Ron Miles ... 194
Self-styled trumpeter

Ronnie Montrose ... 196
"Thinking blue-collar man's guitar hero"

Peter Murphy ... 199
Godfather of goth-rock movement

Our Lady Peace ... 202
Rock on the fast-track

Portishead ... 205
Spacy trip-hop

Prodigy ... 208
Hip-hop electronica

Ma Rainey ... 212
Early blues entertainer

Oumou Sangare ... 215
Soulful Malian

The Shadows ... 217
Early Brit invaders

Carly Simon ... 221
Classy pop writer

Spice Girls ... 225
British bubblegum-pop

Spirit ... 229
West coast rock

Sugar Ray ... 232
Alternative's wise guys

Bernie Taupin ... 235
Elton John collaborator

Ralph Towner ... 239
Unconventional guitarist

Steve Turre ... 242
Trombone and conch shell maestro

Mike Watt ... 245
Influential pre-grunge rocker

Tomica Woods-Wright ... 248
Tough road to success

Maury Yeston ... 251
A master of the musical

Zhane ... 255
Multi-dimensional female duo

Introduction

Fills the Information Gap on Today's Musicians

Contemporary Musicians profiles the colorful personalities in the music industry who create or influence the music we hear today. Prior to *Contemporary Musicians,* no quality reference series provided comprehensive information on such a wide range of artists despite keen and ongoing public interest. To find biographical and critical coverage, an information seeker had little choice but to wade through the offerings of the popular press, scan television "infotainment" programs, and search for the occasional published biography or exposé. *Contemporary Musicians* is designed to serve that information seeker, providing in one ongoing source in-depth coverage of the important names on the modern music scene in a format that is both informative and entertaining. Students, researchers, and casual browsers alike can use *Contemporary Musicians* to meet their needs for personal information about music figures; find a selected discography of a musician's recordings; and uncover an insightful essay offering biographical and critical information.

Provides Broad Coverage

Single-volume biographical sources on musicians are limited in scope, often focusing on a handful of performers from a specific musical genre or era. In contrast, *Contemporary Musicians* offers researchers and music devotees a comprehensive, informative, and entertaining alternative. *Contemporary Musicians* is published three times per year, with each volume providing information on more than 80 musical artists and record-industry luminaries from all the genres that form the broad spectrum of contemporary music—pop, rock, jazz, blues, country, New Age, folk, rhythm and blues, gospel, bluegrass, rap, and reggae, to name a few—as well as selected classical artists who have achieved "crossover" success with the general public. *Contemporary Musicians* will also occasionally include profiles of influential nonperforming members of the music community, including producers, promoters, and record company executives. Additionally, beginning with *Contemporary Musicians 11,* each volume features new profiles of a selection of previous *Contemporary Musicians* listees who remain of interest to today's readers and who have been active enough to require completely revised entries.

Includes Popular Features

In *Contemporary Musicians* you'll find popular features that users value:

- **Easy-to-locate data sections:** Vital personal statistics, chronological career summaries, listings of major awards, and mailing addresses, when available, are prominently displayed in a clearly marked box on the second page of each entry.

- **Biographical/critical essays:** Colorful and informative essays trace each subject's personal and professional life, offer representative examples of critical response to the artist's work, and provide entertaining personal sidelights.

- **Selected discographies:** Each entry provides a comprehensive listing of the artist's major recorded works.

- **Photographs:** Most entries include portraits of the subject profiled.

- **Sources for additional information:** This invaluable feature directs the user to selected books, magazines, and newspapers where more information can be obtained.

Helpful Indexes Make It Easy to Find the Information You Need

Each volume of *Contemporary Musicians* features a cumulative Musicians Index, listing names of individual performers and musical groups, and a cumulative Subject Index, which provides the user with a breakdown by primary musical instruments played and by musical genre.

Available in Electronic Formats

Diskette/Magnetic Tape. *Contemporary Musicians* is available for licensing on magnetic tape or diskette in a fielded format. The database is available for internal data processing and nonpublishing purposes only. For more information, call (800) 877-GALE.

Online. *Contemporary Musicians* is available online as part of the Gale Biographies (GALBIO) database accessible through LEXIS-NEXIS, P.O. Box 933, Daton, OH 454012-0933; phone: (513)865-6800, toll-free:800-543-6862.

We Welcome Your Suggestions

The editors welcome your comments and suggestions for enhancing and improving *Contemporary Musicians*. If you would like to suggest subjects for inclusion, please submit these names to the editors. Mail comments or suggestions to:

The Editor
Contemporary Musicians
Gale Research
835 Penobscot Bldg.
Detroit, MI 48226-4094
Phone: (800) 347-4253
Fax: (313) 961-6599

A-ha

Pop band

Michael Ochs Archives

In their small snowy country of Norway, members of the 1980s super group A-ha are considered close to royalty. The pretty boys of Oslo were the first Norwegian band to make it big in pop-music. By the end of 1980s, they had amassed numerous awards and platinum albums.

Two of the band members, Magne Furuholmen and Pal Waaktaar, grew up in Oslo. Their first band together, Spider Empire—formed in 1977—was heavily influenced by the music of the Doors and Jimi Hendrix. Spider Empire evolved into another band called Bridges in 1979 and took on a bassist and drummer. Soon they released their first album, *Fakkeltog —Torchlight Procession*—on their own label, Vakenatt.The Bridges were working on their second album when Morten Harket entered the scene. Influenced by the falsetto of Freddy Mercury of Queen, Harket had been singing in other Oslo bands.

After deciding to work together, the band, with Harket on lead vocals and Furuholmen writing many of the lyrics, the band began tossing around ideas for a new name.They decided upon A-ha because, as Furuholmen explained, it was easily memorized and familiar exclamation in any language. "Originally, we were trying to find a Norwegian word that people would be able to say in English. Eventually Harket spotted a song called "a-ha" in Waaktaar's song notebook. It was a terrible song, but a great name. I mean, you say it, a-ha, all the time," Furuholmen said online.

In 1982, the band began changing its tune and started working on becoming a more commercial, synth-pop sounding band, like pop kings Duran Duran. The trio began looking toward England for a record label to offer them a contract. Even with their chiseled good looks and snappy sound, success would take a while.

1983 was to be the dawning for the Norwegian music marvels. After ringing in the new year by relocating to London in January, the trio managed to purchase some recording time at Rendezvous Studios. One demo, "Lesson One," caught the ear of John Ratcliff, manager of the recording studio. Ratcliff in turn played it for Terry Slater, a former record company executive who once worked with the Everly Brothers. Slater was so impressed with the band that he agreed to manage the trio immediately and arrange a series of influential auditions.

As a Christmas present for their families and compatriots, A-ha brought home a worldwide contract with Warner Bros. Records. The first album *Hunting High and Low,* included the single "Take On Me." Released in

For the Record . . .

Members include **Magne Furuholmen** (born November 1, 1962), keyboards, vocals; **Morten Harket** (born September 14, 1959), lead vocals; and **Pal Waaktaar** (born September 6, 1961), guitar, vocals.

Group formed in 1977 as Spider Empire, changed name to A-Ha in 1982. Released debut album *Hunting High and Low* on Warner Bros. Label, 1986; other releases on the Warner Bors. Labes include: *Scoundrel Days,* 1986; *Stay on These Roads,* 1988; *East of the Sun, West of the Moon,* 1991; *Headlines & Deadlines, The Hits of A-Ha,* 1991; *Memorial Beach,* 1993. Contributed "The Living Daylights" for soundtrack of the same name, 1987.

Awards: MTV Video Awards for Best New Concept Video, Best New Artist Video, Best Special Effects, Best Direction, Most Experimental and Viewers Choice Awards, all in 1986.

Address: *Record company*—Warner Bros. Records, 10907 Magnolia Blvd., Box 419, North Hollywood, CA.

early 1984, it was re-worked version of "Lesson One." The band experienced a successful Norwegian debut, but failed to reach audiences over in England and abroad. Only 300 copies of the album were sold outside its native Norway. In 1985, the band, at the urging of Slater, remixed and re-released the single.

During the summer of 1986, Warner Bros. Records decided to invest some money on a revolutionary video for the struggling band. "Take On Me," directed by SteveBarron, was a charcoal animation of the band members was a fore-runner in semi-animated video-market. At the third MTV Music Awards in 1986, the video won for Best New Concept Video, Best New Artist Video, Best Special Effects, Best Direction, Most Experimental and the Viewers Choice awards, among others awards. According to the *Encyclopedia of Rock Stars,* it was a record number of wins by one act for both the fledgling ceremony and band.

In 1986, A-ha released it's sophomore album, *Scoundrel Days.* Although less successful than *Hunting High And Low,* the album did include the hit single "Cry Wolf." A year later, the band was commissioned to create the theme song for the new James Bond movie, *The Living Daylights.* Their third album, *Stay on These Roads,* almost entirely written by guitarist Pal Waaktaar continued A-ha's popularity in England while marking its journey into obscurity in the United States. The album entered the English charts early in 1988 at number two.

After a two year holiday, A-ha released their fourth album, *East of the Sun, West of the Moon,* in November 1990. This new album shows a departure from the heavy synth-ladled albums of the past. In 1991, after a string of little noticed singles,, A-ha released a six year retrospective album entitled *Headlines and Deadlines, The Hits Of A-ha.*

During the fifth annual World Music Awards, the darlings of Norwegian pop music were named Best Selling Norwegian Artist of the Year two years in a row1992-93. In 1993, the band releases *Memorial Beach,* which featured the single "Dark Is the Night." More than previous A-ha albums, this album highlighted the talents of the other band members including new members bassist J.B. Bogeberg and Per Hillestad on drums. Much of the album reflects time spent in America.

Pursued Individual Artistic Challenges

After feeling "spent out" artistically, the band took a two year sabbatical according to an online interview at http://www.wwiv.com/a-ha/a-ha-faq.html. The trio decided to pursued individual artistic challenges. Furuholmen co-wrote the soundtrack for the Norwegian movie *Ten Knifes in the Heart,* which world premiered in 1994. He also created a wood carving for the cover design for the album *Songs from the Pocket,* a solo project of his fellow tour mate J.B Bogeberg. During this time apart, the band did regroup to record "Shapes That Go Together," theme song for the 1994 Special Olymics that were held in Lillehammer, Norway.

Harket recorded the Frankie Valli hit "Can't Take My Eyes Off Of You" for *the Coneheads* soundtrack in 1983. The movie was directed by Steve Baron, the gentleman behind the record shattering "Take On Me video." In 1995, Harket released *Wild Seed,* his first solo album with Warner Brothers Records International. In 1996, Pal Waaktaar also released an album with Warner Brothers Records International. With his band Savoy, he released *Mary is Coming* in early 1996 in Europe and the Unithed States writing all the songs on the album.

In 1997, A-ha decided toregroup and work on some new material. According to Furuholmen, in an online interview, "Yes, I am counting on returning to the studio as

A-ha now. We needed a break, we all agreed on that, but now the time has come again." His bandmate Harket agreed in the same interview: "The whole time, it was more or less obvious that we should do something more, because we feel A-ha is everything but a finished chapter. A large part still needs to be said and done."

Selected discography

Hunting High and Low (includes "Take On Me," "The Sun Always Shines on TV"), Warner Brothers, 1984
Scoundrel Days (includes "Cry Wolf") Warner Bros., 1986
(contributors) "The Living Daylights" (soundtrack), Warner Bros., 1987
Stay On These Roads (includes "Stay On These Roads"), Warner Bros., 1988
East of the Sun, West of the Moon (includes "I Call Your Name"), Warner Bros., 1991
Headlines & Deadlines, The Hits of a-ha, Warner Bros., 1991
Memorial Beach (includes "Dark is the Night" Warner Bros., 1993

Sources

Books

Rhyss, Dafydd and Luke Compton, eds., *Encyclopedia of Rock Stars,* DK, Publishing, NY, 1996

Online

http://warnerbros.com
http://www.wwiv.com/a-ha/news

—Gretchen Monette

Ace of Base

Pop band

Ace of Base launched into pop stardom at lightning speed. With their first album, they broke the world record for top-selling debut of all time. Hailing from Sweden, the group faced many comparisons to their 1970s counterpart quartet, ABBA, throughout their career. Keyboardist Ulf "Buddha" Ekberg described their sound to Glenn Kenny in *Rolling Stone* as "worldwide pop music with a Swedish taste." Armed with that style, Ace of Base conquered the airwaves across the globe with hits like "All That She Wants," "Don't Turn Around," and "Beautiful Life."

The members of Ace of Base included three siblings—singer Jenny Berggren, singer Linn Berggren, and keyboardist Jonas "Joker" Berggren—along with their close friend Ulf Ekberg. The Berggrens were born and raised in Gothenberg, Sweden. Their father Goran is a doctor and their mother Birgitta is a schoolteacher. Throughout their youth, the Berggren children were encouraged to study classical music. Jenny and Linn both sang in their hometown church choir before forming Ace of Base.

AP/Wide World Photos

For the Record . . .

Members include **Jenny Berggren** (born Jenny Cecilia Berggren, May 19, 1972, Gothenberg, Sweden), vocals; **Jonas "Joker Berggren,** (born Jonas Petter Berggren, March 21, 1967, Gothenberg, Sweden), keyboards; **Linn Berggren** (born Malin Sofia Katrina Berggren, October 31, 1970, Gothenberg, Sweden), vocals; **Ulf "Buddha" Ekberg** (born Ulf Gunnar Ekberg, December 6, 1970, Gothenberg, Sweden), keyboards.

Band formed in Gothenberg, Sweden, 1990; signed recording contract with Mega Records, 1992; *Happy Nation* released in Europe, 1993; signed U.S. record contract with Arista Records, 1993; *The Sign* released in North America, 1994; named to the *Guinness Book of World Records* as the best-selling debut, 1995.

Awards: 1993 Echo Award for Most Successful International Band; platinum certification for *Happy Nation,* 1994, *Billboard* for Top New Artist, 1994.

Addresses: *Record company*—Arista Records, 8370 Wilshire Blvd., 3rd Floor, Beverly Hills, CA 90211.

Ekberg's interest in music also bloomed at an early age. He was born in Gothenburg, but often traveled around with his tennis coach father, Mats Ekberg and his mother Monica. Unlike many musicians who began playing piano, guitar, or some other instrument as a child, Ekberg took a more modern route. At the age of 12, he began composing music on his Commodore 20 computer—although, as he got older, he became involved in gangs and violence. Then, he met Jonas Berggren, and his life turned around completely.

Ekberg played with a group that rehearsed in the same place as the Berggrens' group. One night in 1990, Ekberg's band opened for the Berggrens' group at a club in Gothenburg. One of the members of the Berggrens' band got stage fright just before they went on, so Ekberg volunteered to step in. From there, they decided to form a band called Tech Noir. The newly formed group aimed for a dark, aggressive style influenced by groups like Front 242 and Ministry.

As Jenny and Linn became more involved in the group, the music took on a brighter, rhythmic sound. As it developed, they used reggae influences with a dance pop foundation. "All of us love to go out and dance and party," Ekberg explained to Jeff Johnson in *DMA Magazine.* "That's why it's very natural for us to do dance music."

Sprouted into Swedish Sensations

The group changed its name to Ace of Base and performed their first show in August of 1990. Jonas Berggren described to Melissa W. Rawlins in *Entertainment Weekly* how they came up with their name. "Our base is our studio, and an ace is like a master," said Jonas. "So we are the aces of our studio." As the group took their music to the streets of Gothenburg, they aimed to create a sound that would crossover from dance clubs to the airwaves. "Some things work on the dance floor and not on the radio and vice versa," Jenny Berggren told Kenny, "but this sound has appeal in both places."

The following year, Ace of Base recorded a demo, which included the songs "All That She Wants" and "Wheel of Fortune." They sent it to ABBA's record label, Polar Records, in Stockholm, but received a rejection. Undaunted, the group sent the demo to Mega Record in Copenhagen, Denmark. The label signed them. Around the same time, producer Denniz PoP also became interested in Ace of Base. He received their demo tape and it got stuck in his car's cassette player. After having to listen to it every time he got in his car, he contacted them. He later produced their international hit, "All That She Wants."

Soon, their first two singles, "Wheel of Fortune" and "All That She Wants," became number one hits in Denmark. The latter went on to take over the top spot on the charts in Sweden, Norway, and Finland. The success got the attention of Metronome Music in Hamburg, Germany, which singed the band to a distribution deal for the rest of Europe and the Far East. Not long afterwards, "All That She Wants" reached number one in Germany.

Geared Up for World Domination

In 1993, the momentum of Ace of Base's hit single kept going. London Records in the U.K. agreed to distribute the group, and the single hit number one there, too. In June of that year, Ace of Base released their European debut, *Happy Nation,* which quickly soared to the top of the charts throughout Europe and Scandinavia. By November, interest in Ace of Base spread to the U.S. Arista Records signed the group, and "All That She Wants" reached platinum sales and number two on the

Billboard charts. As the group's notoriety spread throughout the world, Ace of Base had to compete with other bands covering their material. Rumors spread that groups like Age of Bass and Bass of Spades released singles in the U.S. before the real group had a chance to introduce themselves.

In March of 1994, Ace of Base received the 1993 Echo Award for Most Successful International Band in Frankfurt, Germany. The following month, Arista released *The Sign* in the U.S. The album included all the songs on *Happy Nation,* along with a few additional tracks. The title track topped *Billboard*'s Hot 100 singles chart almost immediately. The album grabbed the top spot and was certified platinum in the U.S. before the end of1994. Eclipsing the sensation ABBA created two decades earlier, Ace of Base became the first Swedish group to reach number one in the U.S.

Record-Breaking Successes

The year continued to bring in more awards for Ace of Base, including the World's Best-Selling Pop Newcomers of the Year and World's Best-Selling Scandinavian Recording Artists of the Year at the sixth annual World Music Awards in Monte Carlo, and Top New Artist and Top Pop Single at the *Billboard* Music Awards. Early in 1995, Ace of Base took home the American Music Awards for Best Band, Duo or Group/Pop Rock category and Best New Artist. The *Guinness Book of World Records* also named Ace of Base's *The Sign* as the best-selling debut album of all time. "We were all very surprised at how fast and how far the group has come since this whole thing began," Lasse Karlsson, Ace of Base's manager, told J.R. Reynolds in *Billboard.*

Despite all the awards, sales, and recognition, Ace of Base didn't slow down to enjoy the accolades. They jumped right back into their studio and recorded another album. *The Bridge* was released in December of 1995, along with the single "Beautiful Life." Jim Farber described the album in his *Entertainment Weekly* review. "Ace of Base provides the musical equivalent of a Mentos commercial: They're so deeply dorky, you have to love 'em.... But for sheer candied pop, this is one pleasurable way to rot your teeth." The following month, *The Bridge* was certified platinum for over a million copies sold. According to their record company biography, all of the members contributed to the songwriting process, instead of just Jonas Berggren and Ulf Ekberg. "It's nice to have different tempos, different moods," said Jonas.

After the release of *The Bridge,* Ace of Base set out once again on a worldwide tour, including South America and the Far East. Both albums were also released in China, adding another first to their list—the first Scandinavian artist to release recordings in China. The group also received their second award for World's Best-Selling Scandinavian Artist/Group of the year at the 1996 World's Music Awards.

By 1997, *Happy Nation* and *The Sign* had sold a cumulative 23 million copies worldwide, while *The Bridge* had sold five million. Finally, the group decided to take some time to enjoy their accomplishments. They began working on their next album with producer Charles Fisher late in 1997.

Despite their celebrity and accomplishments, Ace of Base still held fast to their roots. They maintained a studio in Gothenburg, and the Berggrens continued to live in their hometown. Jenny and Linn still sang in their hometown church choir when they were in town. For a few weeks each summer, the group took a break so Jenny could work at her volunteer job, where she helped disabled children in a Swedish summer camp. Although Ekberg moved to Marbella, Spain, he returned to Gothenburg to work with his bandmates. While the rest of the world showered Ace of Base with multiplatinum sales and adoration, the group refused to dismiss their humble beginnings.

Selected discography

The Sign, Arista Records, 1994.
The Bridge, Arista Records, 1995.

Sources

Books

Rees, Dafydd and Luke Crampton, eds., *Encyclopedia of Rock Stars,* DK Publishing, New York, 1996.

Periodicals

Billboard, August 14, 1993; February 12, 1994; June 4, 1994; December 17, 1994; December 24, 1994,; January 14, 1995; October 28, 1995; December 16, 1995.
Bop Magazine, August 1996.
DMA Magazine, January 1996.
Entertainment Weekly, January 14, 1994; June 17, 1994; November 24, 1995.
Esquire, September 1994, p. 196.
The Financial Times, January 1996.
People, February 28, 1994; May 23, 1994; December 4, 1995, p. 24.

Rolling Stone, August 11, 1994.
Spin, February 1996.

Online

http://www.aceofbase.net/biog/index.htm
http://www.aristarec.com/view2
http://www.eden.com/~wgunter/art/

Additional information for this profile was obtained from Arista Records and Mega Records promotional material, 1995-97.

—Sonya Shelton

Aerosmith

Rock band

Although many critics of the 1970s dismissed the band as merely a vulgar imitation of the Rolling Stones and other British blues/rock acts, Aerosmith proved one of the most popular acts of the decade and succeeded in conveying their hard-rock style and attitude to a new generation of fans and musicians into the 1980s. Originally labeled rock's "toxic Twins'" founding members Steven Tyler and Joe Perry defeated alcoholism and drug use in the 1980s while retaining their characteristic anti-establishment charm and attitude. Chris Norris commented in *Spin:* "Aerosmith is as close to Hollywood as rock-n-roll gets. In their 25 years, the Boston crew of Tyler, Perry, guitarist Brad Whitford, bassist Tom Hamilton, and drummer Joey Kramer have gone from being the definitive 1970s hard-rock band to a textbook on economy, surliness, and soul to the ultimate comeback band brought back almost literally from the dead in the mid 1980s to the most bankable act in popular music."

Aerosmith began on the east coast. Tyler was born Steven Tallarico, son of a second-generation Italian

AP/Wide World Photos

For the Record . . .

Band formed in 1970 in Boston; original members included **Tom Hamilton** (born December 31, 1951, in Colorado Springs, CO) bass; **Joey Kramer** (born June 21, 1950, in New York, NY), drums; **Joe Perry** (born September 10, 1950, in Boston, MA), lead guitar; **Steven Tyler** (real name, Tallarico; born March 26, 1948, in Yonkers, NY), lead vocals; and **Brad Whitford** (born February 23, 1952, in MA), rhythm guitar. Signed with Columbia Records executive Clive Davis and recorded self-titled debut LP *Aerosmith* in two weeks, which included their first hit single, "Dream On," 1972; released first platinum record, Toys in the Attic, 1976; became the undisputed top-venue rock act, 1979; replaced Perry with guitarist Jimmy Crespo and Whitford with Rick Dufay, 1979-80; band re-formed, 1984; achieved widespread success in the 1980s with such singles as "Dude (Looks Like a Lady)," "Angel," "Janie Got a Gun," and "Crazy."

Awards: MTV Music Awards for Best Group Video and Best Stage Performance in a Video, for "Dude Looks Like a Lady," 1988; MTV Music Awards for Best Metal/ Hard Rock Video and Viewers Choice Award for "Janie's Got A Gun," Grammy Award for "Janie's Got A Gun" 1990; MTV Music Award for Best Metal/Hard Rock Video for "The Other Side," 1991; MTV Music Viewer's Choice Award for "Livin' On The Edge," Grammy Award for Best Performance by a Duo or a Group for "Love in an Elevator" 1993; MTV Music Awards fornumber one All Time Favorite Video as voted by MTV viewers, Best Video, Best Group Video, and Viewer's Choice Award, for "Cryin'" 1994; Grammy Award for Best Performance By A Duo or Group with Vocal for "Crazy," 1996.

Addresses:*Management co.*—Collins/Barasso Mgmt., 215 1st St., Cambridge, Mass., 02142.

classical musician who played and taught music in Yonkers, New York. The Tallarico family also ran a resort in the Catskills in Lake Sunapee, New Hampshire where Tyler and Perry, whose family had a summer house there, first met. Tyler formed his first band, The Strangeurs, later changing the band's name to Chain Reaction. In 1966, Tyler recorded two singles with Chain Reaction. Meanwhile, Perry and future Aerosmith bass guitarist Hamilton formed a combo, Pipe Dream (later Jam Band), also in Sunapee.

In 1970, Perry, Tyler, and Hamilton (whose family also vacationed in Sunapee), formed Aerosmith, with Perry on guitar, Tyler on vocals, and Hamilton on bass guitar. Tyler commented of Perry's hard-edged guitar playing in a 1975 interview with *Circus Magazine:* "I loved Joe's style. He always played out of tune and real sloppy and I just loved it." In 1971, the trio recruited rhythm guitar player Brad Whitford and drummer Joey Kramer and began playing in the Boston area. The band cultivated a young audience following their first successful appearance at Nipmuc Regional High School in Mendon, Massachusetts.

Just Wanted It All

Aerosmith signed with Columbia Records in 1972. The same year the band entered Intermedia Sound Studios to record their debut album, *Aerosmith,* which was recorded in only two weeks. Although the album garnered little notice and achieved only modest financial success, *Aerosmith* garnered a generally positive critical response and introduced the band to the American public with their classic single "Dream On." "We weren't too ambitious when we started out," commented Tyler in Aerosmith Unwired. "We just wanted to be the biggest thing that ever walked the planet, the greatest rock band that ever was. We just wanted everything. We just wanted it all."

Aerosmith's second album, *Get Your Wings,* further cemented their growing reputation butreceived mixed reviews. The album, like its predecessor, fell short of achieving blockbuster status and provoked sarcastic comparisons to the Rolling Stones. Charley Walters of *Rolling Stone,* however, asserted that Aerosmith's second album "surges with pent-up fury yet avoids the excesses to which many peers succumb [the album] contains the vital elements of economy and ill-advised solo extravaganzas." *Get Your Wings* remained on the charts for a total of 86 weeks.

Between 1974 and 1976, Aerosmith released many of their biggest classic hit singles, including "Same Old Song and Dance," "Sweet Emotion," and "Walk This Way." The band toured heavily as their venues became larger and press coverage correspondingly increased. According to Phil Hardy and Dave Laing in their *Encyclopedia of Rock,* the band's third album, *Toys in the Attic,* "represented a milestone in the band's career and became their first album to represent the perfect distillation of the Aerosmith sound, a muscular but surprisingly agile rhythm section with the twin guitars howling and snapping around Tyler's vocal lines." *Toys in the Attic* stayed on the charts for almost two years.

"Coming after a brief era when rock-n-roll fans in their adolescence were bombarded with the exaggerated sexual ambiguity of Alice [Cooper], [David] Bowie, and [Lou] Reed, it must be reassuring to have a band that knows everything we've wanted to know about sex all along: that it's dirty," commented Wayne Robins of *Toys in the Attic,* in *Creem. Toys* became the band's first platinum record and spawned several underground classics, including "No More," and the title cut "Toys in the Attic". Tyler reminisced about the album's sweeping success in all media quarters in Aerosmith Unwired: "I remember reading in a newspaper, in like 1976, about how disgusting rock lyrics are, and they used "Walk This Way" as an example of how lyrics should be nice and wholesome. I couldn't believe it. Obviously, they didn't get the meaning of you ain't seen nothin' til you're down on your muffin."

Rocks followed the formula of *Toys in the Attic,* also achieving widespread critical and financial success. "Back in the Saddle," "Sick as a Dog," and "Last Child" remained prominent requests on classic rock stations well into the 1990s. "We were doing a lot of ... drugs by then, but you can hear that whatever we were doing, it was still working for us," Perry mentioned in Aerosmith Unwired. *Draw the Line,* released on Columbia Records in 19787, went platinum faster than any previous Aerosmith album. The band's Draw The Line Tour lasted through 1978 and early 1979, and their previously hectic recording schedule slowed for the first time in their career. In 1978, Aerosmith released one live album, *Live Bootleg,* and made their Hollywood debut with an appearance in Robert Stigwood's ill-received film *Sgt. Pepper's Lonely Hearts Club Band,* in which they covered the Beatles' "Come Together."

Drug Abuse of Legendary Proportions

During the two-year tour that followed *Draw the Line,* Aerosmith developed a reputation for drug abuse of legendary proportions, and deep personal animosities developed between the primary band members. Tensions between Perry and Tyler escalated, and during the making of 1979's *A Night in the Ruts,* Perry bowed out to pursue a solo career with his own group, The Joe Perry Project. The band's 1980 debut *Let the Music Do the Talking,* garnered Perry a minor hitwith its title cut, and Perry did not return. Guitarist Jimmy Crespo replaced Perry and the band continued recording, keeping several tracks that Perry had recorded. However, shortly after *A Night in the Ruts,* was completed, Brad Whitford left the band as well. In 1981, Aerosmith replaced Whitford with Rick Dufay.

In late 1981, Tyler was injured in a motorcycle accident in which he had been drinking. The accident took off his heel and put him in a hospital for over six months. By the time Aerosmith's next album, *Rock in a Hard Place,* appeared in 1982, Tyler found that the band's popularity had been eclipsed by a wide range of second-generation heavy metal bands.

Reformed in More Ways than One

In April of 1984, Aerosmith announced to the press that the original band would reunite and tour. "You should have felt the buzz the moment all five of us got together in the same room for the first time again," said Tyler. "We all started laughin, it was like the five years had never passed. We knew we'd made the right move." The band's members took their first steps toward defeating their various drug and alcohol addictions. After auditioning for Geffen Records, the band won a new contract.

For their 1986 comeback album, *Done with Mirrors,* Aerosmith recruited heavyweight producer Ted Templeman, who had worked with Van Halen on its first six albums. Recorded at the Power Station, the album was recorded quickly when, according to Perry, the band went in with some riffs and winged it. Some critics were skeptical about a sober Aerosmith, including a *Stereo Review* writer who suggested: A mediocre Aerosmith concert was two hours of imitation Stones. A great Aerosmith concert was a two-minute sound check punctuated by Steve Tyler hurling a bottle of Jack Daniels against Perry's amplifier, followed by ten minutes of pugilism, after which the band would stumble offstage." Although the album's sales were flat, possibly indicating that Aerosmith's once-loyal audience had lost faith, Aerosmith re-entered the charts for the first time in six years and successfully teamed with Run-DMC for a Rick Rubin-produced re-make of "Walk this Way." The cover was a hit and a new generation of young MTV viewers suddenly became interested in Aerosmith. Robert Christgau of the *Village Voice* asserted. Against all odds the old farts light one up: if you can stand the crunch, you'll find more get-up-and-go on the first side [of *Done with Mirrors*] than on any dozen random neogarage EP's."

In 1987, Aerosmith achieved undeniable success following the release of their album *Permanent Vacation.* The recording went triple platinum and sold more than two million copies, featuring several blockbuster hits, including "Dude (Looks Like a Lady)," "Rag Doll," and "Angel." The album also signaled Aerosmith's introduction to the video medium, initiating a tradition of releasing some of the most popular videos MTV ever aired.

Permanent Vacation drew largely positive comments from music reviewers. Deborah Frost commented in *Rolling Stone:* "[Aerosmith] has never worked with people so determined to turn it into Bon Jovi, Heart, or Starship. The good news is that it can't be done.... The raw, dirty edges of the Aerosmith of old slash through the power schmaltz.... The band has never sounded better or more charged."

Aerosmith continued to build upon their new, younger audience by touring with many of the groups they had helped to inspire, including Dokken, Guns-n-roses, and Poison. From 1987-88 the band produced two live albums, *Classics Live!* And *Classics Live II,* as well as a greatest hits compilation, *Gems.* In 1989, Aerosmith released their second chart-buster of the 1980s *Pump,* which went multi-platinum and garnered several MTV Awards as well as their first Grammy for "Janie's got a Gun," an uncharacteristically moral (at least in the traditional sense) song about child abuse.

Over the next seven years, Aerosmith garnered two more Grammys and many MTV Awards as they achieved increasing respectability for their ability to deliver high-charge rock while avoiding drugs during an era in which many rock stars succumbed to drug-related tragedies.

In late 1991, Sony signed Aerosmith away from Geffen, investing an estimated #30 million dollars in the band despite the fact that their contract would not begin until 1997. In 1993, the band released *Get a Grip,* which sold over five million copies and scored *Billboard* hits with such singles as "Livin on the Edge," "Cryin," "Crazy," and "Amazing." The video "Crazy" especially dominated the MTV airwaves. Produced by Bruce Fairburn, *Get a Grip* featured several songs written with outside collaborators and featured the mixing talents of Atlanta-based producer, Brendan O'Brien, who had formerly worked with the Black Crowes.

Nine Lives, Aerosmith's 1997 release for Sony, appeared amidst public allegations of drug relapse and a flurry of personnel changes. The trouble first started when the band fired their producer, John Kalodner, and replaced him with Glen Ballard, who had initially been hired as a songwriter. Next, drummer Joey Kramer temporarily left following his father's death. Kramer was replaced by studio drummer Steve Ferrone.

Well into the recording process, Sony communicated it's dissatisfaction with the rough cuts of *Nine Lives.* "I think they were right," commented Whitford. "I was listening to them and I just thought, Huey Lewis." Aerosmith replaced Ballard with producer Kevin Shirley of Silverchair and Journey fame. Tyler commented of Ballard's release from the band: "the general consensus of the band and the corporation was that, mixed with the fact Joey wasn't down there when we did it, it might be to our advantage to re-record it with someone who has a little more of a rock head and is into the Aerosmith that we all know and love."

Norris characterized *Nine Lives,* as "a rawly produced assertion of hard-rock supremacy, and attempt to fuse Aerosmith's 70s ragged glory with its 90s pop craft." The album failed to achieve the notoriety of previous major releases, but attracted some airplay with several cuts, including "Kiss Your Past Goodbye" and "Falling in Love (Is Hard on the Knees)." "The group certainly hasn't lost any of its bite on *Nine Lives,*" Gary Graff said in his Mr. Show Biz interview. "From the eastern touches of "Taste of India" to the industrial clangor of "Something's Gotta Give," and the flick-your-Bic power balladry of "Ain't That a Bitch" and "Fallen Angels," *Nine Lives* is a consistently strong effort and a message that those who wonder if the band is losing its edge can, well, dream on."

Selected discography

Aerosmith, Columbia, 1973.
Get Your Wings, Columbia, 1974.
Toys in the Attic, Columbia, 1975.
Rocks, Columbia, 1976.
Pure Gold, Columbia, 1976.
Draw the Line, Columbia, 1977.
Live Bootleg, Columbia, 1978.
A Night in the Ruts, Columbia, 1979.
Greatest Hits, Columbia, 1980.
Rock in a Hard Place, Columbia, 1982.
Done with Mirrors, Geffen, 1986.
Classics Live, Columbia, 1986.
Permanent Vacation, Geffen, 1987.
Classics! II, Columbia, 1987.
Gems, Columbia, 1989.
Pump, Geffen, 1989.
Pandora's Box, Columbia, 1991.
Get a Grip, Geffen, 1993.
Big Ones, Geffen, 1994.
Box of Fire, Geffen, 1994.
Nine Lives, Columbia/Sony, 1997.

Sources

Books

Clarke, Donald, editor, *The Penguin Encyclopedia of Popular Music,* Viking Press, New York, 1989.

Hardy, Phil, and Dave Laing, editors, *Encyclopedia of Rock,* Macdonald, 1987.

Morehead, Philip D., and Anne MacNeil, *The New American Dictionary of Music,* New York, Dutton, 1991.

Hitchcock, H. Wiley and Sadie, Stanley, eds., *The New Grove Dictionary of American Music,* London: Macmillan Press, 1986.

Pareles, Jon and Romanowski, Patricia, eds., *The Rolling Stone Encyclopedia of Rock & Roll,* Rolling Stone Press/summit Books, 1983.

Stambler, Irwin, *The Encyclopedia of Pop, Rock & Soul* (revised edition), St. Martin's Press, Nerw York, 1989.

Periodicals

Audio, April, 1980.

Boston Phoenix, September, 1989.

Circus Magazine, June, 1975.

Maclean's, July 21, 1997.

Music Wire, August, 1996.

People, January 21, 1980; October 19, 1987; February 22, 1988; March 31, 1997.

Rolling Stone, October 22, 1987; May 13, 1993; October 3, 1996.

Saturday Night, March 1997.

Spin, October, 1993; October, 1996; May, 1997.

Stereo Review, April, 1986.

Online

AeroSmith Unwired, http://www.geocities.com/SunsetStrip/Club/4385/frameaero.html)

http://web3/starwave.com/features/interviews/plus/aerosmith/html

—Sean Pollock

Air Supply

Pop band

When Graham Russell, a native of England, met up with Australian born Russell Hitchcock during an Australian production of Tim Rice's *Jesus Christ Superstar* in 1976, neither could have had an inkling of the success they would share together over the next 10 years. With the release of their first album, *Air Supply,* on Australian label Rainbow Records in 1976, Air Supply, named because both founding members have air zodiac signs,began a decade of controlling the pop album and single charts by releasing one hit after another. The collection of hits would earn them the awards only a few years later. But what really started them on their multi-million selling bonanza was being named opening act for Rod Stewart's worldwide "Footloose and Fancy Free" tour in 1978.

It was the sweet, whimsical and honeyed combination of Hitchcock's voice and Grahams overtly-romantic lyrics that launched them to the top of the adult contemporary charts. According to Detroit Free Press music critic Gary Graff, "Air Supply, after all, is regarded as fare for softies. Russell's best known works are syrupy love

AP/Wide World Photos

For the Record . . .

Members include **Russell Hitchcock,** (born June 15, 1949, Melbourne, Austrailia), vocals; **Graham Russell,** (born June 1, 1950, Nottinham UK), guitar and vocals; **Ralph Cooper,** drums; **Rex Goh**, guitar; **David Green,** bass; **David Moyse,** guitar; and **Frank Esler-Smith,** keyboards.

Formed in 1976 in Austrailia, Air Supply enjoyed almost a decade of Top Ten hits in America and the world. The band toured often and extensively. Both Russell and Hitchcock took time off for solo projects but rejoined and contined to release an album almost every year.

Awards: 1980 *Billboard* Top Adult Contemporary Single of the Year for "Here I Am"; American Music Awards Favorite Band, Duo or Group Pop/Rock, 1982; platinum certification for *Lost in Love,* The One *That You Love,* and *Now and Forever.*

Address: *Record company*—Giant Records, 8900 Wilshire Blvd., Ste. 200, Beverly Hills, CA, 90211, (310) 289-5500, fax (310) 289-5501.

songs that might even put a cavity in Barry Manilow's smile, filled with lush arrangements and harmonies." Not a bad comparison considering Manilow was an influence on the musicians, along with the Bee-Gees, Bread, and the Beatles. It was those syrupy love songs that enabled Air Supply to release nearly an album a year for almost 20 years and take command of the pop music charts for much of the 1980s.

The first of the duo's big hits came from their 1980 multi-platinum selling album *Lost in Love,* recorded with EMI Music Group. "Lost In Love," "Every Woman in the World," and "All out of Love," brought Air Supply international success and acclaim. "Lost In Love" became *Billboard*'s Top Adult Contemporary Single of 1980. Their second album, *The One That You Love,* released a year later, enjoyed similar success. The saccharine sweet plea "Here I Am" solidified the band's reputation for writing successful, albeit sappy, love songs. "People are ready to hear more songs about romance," Hitchcock explained to Bruce Britt in *the Detroit Free Press.* "People are waking up to the reality that love and romance are what it's all about. The recordings of Air Supply became a sound track for generations and elevators.

The band did not spend all their time in the recording studio though. Air Supply also toured the world extensively, crooning to a predominantly female crowd. The main attraction according to Britt was, "Hitchcock's voice, a ringing choirboy tenor, reminiscent of a male Barbara Streisand" Yet, argues Hitchcock in the same review, "We bring the album right to the stage. And every note I sing on record, I sing in concert." With Graham providing most of the lyrics and music, Air Supply enjoyed successful albums into the middle of the 1980s.

The 1982 Arista Records release *Now and Forever,* included the hit songs "Even the Nights Are Better," and "Two Less Lonely People in the World." In 1983, Air Supply released a greatest hits album filled with their signature heavy orchestrated ballads simply titled *Air Supply Greatest Hits in 1983.* The song "Making Love Out of Nothing All" was rereleased and made it to number two on the charts.

Sugar-Coated Love Songs

There was no doubt as to the sovereignty of Air Supply over the radio scene in the 1980s, especially in the United States. According to *Billboard* magazine, the first six singles Air Supply released entered the United States' music charts in the top five area. No other band had experienced such success since the heyday of the Jackson Five. As the decade progressed, a change came over the pop music scene. Rougher, synthesize-enhanced bands began to make a move on the position Air Supply held as sugar-coated love songs began to dissolve. Air Supply took two years off to consolidate ideas and songs for a second self-titled album for Arista. "It was clear that their audience was shrinking-the album was their first not to go platinum," wrote Stephen Thomas Erlewine, reviewing the band for the All-Music Guide web-site.

Another album in 1986, *Hearts In Motion,* brought the duo minimum success in the U.S. A year later *The Christmas Album* was released . It was the last album Air Supply would produce for Arista Records. An amiable separation between Hitchock and Russell took place in 1987 and Hitchcock went on to record a solo, self-titled album in 1990. Graham Russell rekindled a side project of his own, a rock opera entitled *Sherwood.* Russell, originally from Sherwood, England, wrote all the songs for the opera and Air Supply recorded the score.

Air Supply reunited in 1990 and, with a new contract from Giant Records, released *The Earth Is* in 1991. While well received in Europe and Japan, poor U.S. sales were further proof of Air Supply's waning American popularity.The same fate would befall the rest of their releases- *Vanishing Race,* 1993, *News From Nowhere,* 1995, *Now and Forever Live,* 1995, and *The Book of Love,* (1997). While Air Supply has not encountered the endearment from the U.S. they experienced in the mid-80s, Air Supply's popularity in other countries, especially Japan has increased dramatically. In 1993, a 20-track Air Supply karoake disk was released in Japan. During a tour of Asia, Air Supply recorded the 1995 album *Now and Forever-Live,* boasting a 16 piece string section. The tour made stops in Indonesia. Thailand, Singapore, Hong Kong and the Philippines.

Selected discography

Air Supply, Rainbow Records, 1976
Love and Other Bruises, Columbia, 1977
Lost in Love (includes "Lost in Love," "Every Woman in the World," and "All Out of Love), Arista, 1980
One That You Love (includes "Here I Am" and "The One that You Love"), Arista 1981
Now and Forever (includes "Even the Nights Are Better" and "Two Less Lonely Peoeple in the World"), Arista, 1982
Making Love- the Very Best of Air Supply, UK release, Arista, 1983
Air Supply, Arista, 1985
Hearts in Motion, Arista,1986
Christmas Album, Arista1987
The Earth Is.., Giant,, 1991
Vanishing Race, Giant 1993
News From Nowhere (includes "Someone"), Giant, 1995
Book of Love, Giant, 1997

Sources

Books

Clark, Donald, ed.,*The Penguin Encyclopedia of Popular Music,* Viking, 1989.
Rees, Dafydd and Luke Crampton, eds., *Encyclopeida of Rock Stars,* DK Publishing, New York, 1996.

Periodicals

Detroit Free Press, September 10, 1981; August 26, 1982; August 16, 1983
Detroit News, September 17, 1981

Online

http://airsupplymusic.com
All-Music Guide, http://www.amg.com

—Gretchen A. Monette

Rhett Akins

Country singer, songwriter

The story of country music star Rhett Akins's rise to fame seems the classic rags-to-riches tale. Akins first arrived on the scene in 1995 with his pithy honky-tonk lament, "That Ain't My Truck," and his plaintive vocal style quickly earned comparisons to established country icons like George Strait and Garth Brooks. Yet Akins was a relative newcomer to the music industry, a man whose first public performance came when he sang at a wedding—as an adult. "I always wanted be a musician," Akins admitted in an interview published on the *Houston Chronicle Interactive* Internet site, "but coming from a small town—and not knowing a soul who had ever gone on to be a singer—it was sort of like wanting to be an astronaut."

That small town was Valdosta, Georgia, where Akins was born in 1969. He was one of three sons of a local businessman, and football, not music, was his first love—Valdosta's pigskin season is an important part of the town's social fabric, and both his father and grandfather had been standout athletes. Akins was involved in the sport early childhood, and eventually played quarterback on the junior varsity team at the University of Georgia. It was an enlightening experience for him, and he left after a year there, knowing he would never play professionally. "I didn't think I could go any further with football," Akins told @Country's Craig Harris. "I had broken every bone in my body three times. I never had a summer vacation or a spring break. Football was year around, all the time. It was time to move on. I finally got burnt out."

Music, however, had played an increasing part in Akins's life as went through his teens. He began playing guitar at the age of fourteen, inspired by the heavy metal rock his older brothers listened to, and taught himself simply by picking out the right chords. It became an integral part of his life. "I even took my guitar to football camp at school," Akins said the *Houston Chronicle Interactive* interview. Hank Williams, Jr. and Lynyrd Skynyrd were favorites, but the coaches would tell Akins to knock it off. "They said, 'that guitar playing won't amount to nothing.'"

When Akins left college, he returned to Valdosta, took a job with his father's oil and gas company, and got married a woman he had known since junior high school. But he also faced what lay ahead—another several decades in Valdosta—and knew it was time to devote his energies to his true passion. A turning point came when he was sitting in a company truck and singing along to the radio; he vowed at that moment that he would be on the radio himself instead someday. He had never sang in public before, but managed to sing a Garth Brooks song at a wedding and realized he could do it. He began playing acoustic guitar locally at the Holiday Inn with a friend, and that led to gigs at Valdosta State University fraternity parties. "I really didn't know where I was headed in my life," Akins said of this time in his life in the interview with Harris. "That led me to start venting my feelings through writing songs. I wanted to write songs and play in public."

In 1992 Akins moved to Nashville, the nucleus of the country music industry. Songwriters and photogenic singing hopefuls were a dime a dozen, but Akins worked consistently to make contacts and find more established songwriters with whom he could collaborate. This led to a publishing deal with Sony Tree Publishing/Fire Hall Music, which enabled him to steadily proffer songwriting agents tunes he had written; sometimes they would give him songs by other writers to try out. Akins sent one of his demos to country music star Mark Chestnutt, who passed it on to his producer. That insider, Mark Wright, also worked with Clint Black and happened to be Decca Record's head of A&R. Wright brought Akins in to meet a company vice-president, and on the basis of his voice and songwriting capabilities he was signed.

Akins's debut on Decca, *A Thousand Memories,* was released in early 1995. Many of the ten songs—seven of which he wrote himself—reflected a less serious, youthful attitude. "I Brake for Brunettes," "She Said Yes," and

For the Record . . .

Born October 13, 1969, in Valdosta, GA; married Paige, c. 1989; children: Kasey Lee, Thomas Rhett

Began performing as part of a duo in Valdosta, GA; moved to Nashville, TN, 1992; signed publishing deal with Sony Tree Publishing/Fire Hall Music; signed to Decca Records, c. 1993; released first album, *A Thousand Memories* (includes "That Ain't My Truck"), January 1995; toured with Reba McEntire, 1995; released *Somebody New,* 1996, and *What Livin's All About,* Decca, 1998.

Awards: Named one of the Top Ten New Country Artists of the 1995 by *Country America* magazine.

Addresses: *Record company*—Decca Records, 60 Music Square East, Nashville, TN 37203.

its biggest hit, "That Ain't My Truck," all were representative of Akins' spirited personality and penchant for lovestruck laments. "When I moved to Nashville, I was twenty-one years old and didn't know what else to write about but the experiences I had growing up in Georgia," he told @Country's Harris. "That Ain't My Truck" became a huge country hit for the novice, reaching number three on the *Billboard* country charts. Written by Tom Shapiro, its lovelorn lyrics told the first-person tragedy of a man who is the loser in a love triangle; his girlfriend had told him she would be making a decision that night, and when he doesn't hear from her, he drives by her house.

Intricacies of a Country Singer

"That Ain't My Truck" helped Akins land a spot on *Country America* magazine's list of the top ten new country artists of 1995. *A Thousand Memories* also made a respectable showing on the country album charts, reaching number 45. More success came when he sang part of one of his songs, "Where Angels Live," in the 1995 movie *Something to Talk About,* a Julia Roberts/Dennis Quaid love story. Still, the new found stardom was a strange experience for the Valdosta native. "There's isn't any schooling you could have to prepare for having a record deal, having your songs on the radio and going out on tour," he told @Country's Harris. "I didn't realize all the little intricacies that go along with being a country singer, and how much of a business this really is."

For someone who had not sang before an audience until early adulthood, the adjustment may have been a difficult one, but in the competitive world of country music, Akins had little time to lose. For a good part of 1995, Akins played opening dates for country music star Reba McEntire. "I've played basically every type of situation you can play—from the smokiest bar in Texas to the largest indoor venue to Radio City Music Hall.... Overall, it's made me a much more versatile performer," he said in the *Houston Chronicle Interactive* article. When he was on the road with McEntire, Akins brought along songwriters to help him create material for his next album. Some of the songs were tested on live audiences, but Akins noted that crowd reaction is but one way to gauge a country hit. "...After that, I think it is just fate," he told Lydia Dixon Harden in *Music City News.* "If everybody knew what the audience wanted to hear, boy, we'd all have number ones every single time."

The tracks he eventually decided upon for his follow-up took him in a fresh musical direction, and *Something New* was chosen for a title. Released in June of 1996, *Something New* gave Akins a number one hit with "Don't Get Me Started," and the album itself reached number 13. Still, he remained somewhat dissatisfied with the image of himself as just another young buck in a ten-gallon hat. He began looking for songs that reflected a more mature side, with which someone like himself—married for years, with two young children—might identify. The results appeared on *What Livin's All About,* released on Decca in early 1998. Its first single, "More Than Anything," was a love song that soon became a standard for the wedding-ballad repertoire. "I think it's the best thing he's done in some time," one Los Angeles radio station executive, John Sebastian, told *Billboard*'s Deborah Evans Price.

Sebastian reflected that success for Akins was long overdue: "He's a great artist," the program director told *Billboard,* but stressed that the country music hit factory was heavily reliant upon solid, appealing songs—no matter who wrote or performed them. "You could almost be Garth Brooks and if you didn't have the songs, it's so competitive out there you would fall through the cracks," Sebastian told Price. Other tracks on *What Livin's All About* tapped into Akins's return to the basics. "I'll Be Right Here Loving You," "Happy As We Want to Be," "Love Rules," and "The Rest of Forever" evinced a more country, less rock feel, though not all the dozen tracks were serious heart-tuggers.

To promote his third record, Akins undertook an unusual whirlwind tour of his home state. He went through all 159 Georgia counties in just under ten days in the "Rhett Akins Across Georgia" tour. It tied in with the singer's fondness for his state, but also integrated his love of Civil War history (a fan site on the Internet divulged his favorite color as "Confederate Gray") as well as passion for collecting antique books and maps on the subject. "I've always wanted to travel to every single county in Georgia, hang out, and talk to people and find out the history," Akins told Billboard's Price. He remains philosophical about the road that brought him full-circle: "I want to be a big star, but not because I want to ride in limousines and have a jet airplane. The only reason is because I want more people to hear what I'm trying to say."

Selected discography

A Thousand Memories, Decca, 1995
Somebody New, Decca, 1996.
What Livin's All About, Decca, 1998.

Sources

Billboard, December 13, 1997.
Music City News, July 1996.

Online

http://www.decca-nashville.com
http://www.hsv.tis.net/mcn/issues/jul96/rhett.htm
http://webadv.chron.com./nonprof/house/chronicle/business/business/chronicle/hci/business/nation/interactive/c/country/NFrhett.html
http://www.nashville.net

Additional information for this profile was provided by Decca Records publicity materials, 1997.

—Carol Brennan

The Alarm

Rock band

The Alarm combined punk influences with acoustic guitars and political and sociological messages to become a notable rock band in the 1980s. Originating in Wales, the foursome of Eddie MacDonald on bass, Mike Peters on vocals and guitar, Dave Sharp on guitar, and Nigel Twist on drums, received unending comparisons to U2 throughout their career. Debby Miller described the Alarm in *Rolling Stone,* "With a fresh, muscular lineup of two acoustic guitars, bass, and drums, the Alarm are both hippies and latter-day punks, descendants of both Bob Dylan and the Clash." After a decade of recording and performing together, the members of the Alarm agreed to dissolve the group and pursue their individual interests.

The members of the Alarm had been friends since childhood. MacDonald and Peters met at the age of four in Rhyl, Clwyd, Wales, while Sharp and Twist became friends at the age of six in England. The latter two moved to Wales when they were 14 years old. Peters and Twist decided to form a punk band called the Toilets after seeing a Sex Pistols show in 1977. After a year, they

Michael Ochs Archives

For the Record . . .

Members include **Eddie MacDonald** (born November 1, 1959, Wales), bass; **Mike Peters** (born February 25, 1959, Wales), guitar, vocals; **Dave Sharp** (born January 28, 1959, Salford, England), guitar; **Nigel Twist** (born July 18, 1958, Manchester, England), drums.

Band formed as the Toilets and then Seventeen, before changing to the Alarm, 1981; signed recording contract with I.R.S. Records, 1982; released self-titled debut, 1983; *Declaration,* 1984; *Strength,* 1985; *Eye of the Hurricane,* 1987; *Electric Folklore Live,* 1988; *Change,* 1989; *Standards,* 1990; *Raw,* 1991; group disbanded, 1991.

Address: *Record company*—I.R.S. Records, 594 Broadway, Ste.901, New York, NY 10012; (212) 334-2170; fax (212) 334-2178.

recruited MacDonald and Sharp to join the group. The group later changed its name to Seventeen—after the Sex Pistols' song, and performed in Rhyl for four years. They recorded the single "Don't Let Go" backed with "Bank Holiday Weekend" on Vendetta Records. In 1981, Seventeen had the opportunity to tour with Dexy's Midnight Runners. After their first show, they got fired because the headlining band didn't think they were good enough to take on the road.

After a factory closed in Rhyl, many of its residents became unemployed. With work opportunities virtually impossible, the foursome decided to open a clothing shop called Riot, for which they made their own clothes. They also opened a nightclub called the Gallery, where they were able to hone their own musical talent.

Moved to London to Pursue Success

"Hard luck stories are one thing," Eddie MacDonald told Rick G. Karr in *Stereo Review,* "Doing something about it is something else. There was always sort of a scene in Wales, but no outlet. We made the outlets." When a fight broke out in the Gallery, demolishing its interior, the group decided to move to London, and changed their name to the Alarm. " Pretty early on, we found there wasn't much of an audience for music where we started out," Mike Peters told *Rock Express.* "So we moved down to London ... and started playing for anybody who'd listen."

The group recorded the single "Unsafe Building" backed with "Up for Murder," pressed 2,000 copies, and released them on their own White Cross label. They used the single as a demo and sold it at performances. In 1982, one of the members of U2 showed up at one of their shows in England. "We got talking and found out we had so much in common," Dave Sharp told Geoffrey Himes in *Musician.* "They're a passionate band and want to continue to be, and we're the same way.

After the two groups became friends, U2 invited the Alarm to open for them during a few of their shows in England. From there, they toured the U.S. together. Gaining interest from the press and music industry, the Alarm signed a record contract with I.R.S. Records. In September of 1982, they released their debut single, "Marching On." The following year, they released a self-titled EP and toured North America. Steve Pond described *The Alarm* in his *Rolling Stone* review as "simple, forceful music, rambling strings of earnestly poetic images and the conviction that speaking out just might change a few things."

In 1984, the Alarm returned to the studio and released the single "Where Were You Hiding When the Storm Broke" followed by the album *Declaration.* Again, the group continued to communicate their message. "What we try to do is inject hope into people, to show people that the individual is a creative force, that you have to make your own situation," Sharp told Himes. "We want to encourage people to turn around and look at themselves, and say, 'Yeah, we can do something.'"

Musical Direction Reexamined

After a year of reevaluating their direction, the Alarm returned to the studio with producer Mike Howlett to record *Strength.* "I think we've learned how to take control of our music a lot better," Peters told *Firework Fanzine,* "and we're learning to write better lyrics that have much more depth into the subject matter." The following year, the Alarm released a live concert video titled *Spirit of '86,* which was recorded in Los Angeles. In November of 1987, they returned with the release of *Eye of the Hurricane,* produced by John Porter. This time, the Alarm took their style in a slightly different direction in an effort to discover their musical definition. "We're not trying to ram things down people's throats like we did in the early days," Sharp told Jimmy Guterman in *Rolling Stone.* "The time for broad statements has long passed."

As part of their tour in 1988, the Alarm spent the summer in the opening slot for another of their musical influences—Bob Dylan. In November of the same year, they released their first live album, *Electric Folklore Live.* In 1989, their next release, *Change,* arrived in stores.

Returning to the roots of their home country, the Alarm also recorded a Welsh language version titled *Newid* ("change" in Welsh). The group also revisited their past with a remake of their earliest recording, called "Unsafe Building 1990" and a retrospective collection called *Standards.*

In 1991, Dave Sharp took a temporary detour from the band with a solo project. He released the album *Hard Travellin'* and played a limited acoustic tour in the Northeastern U.S. In May of the same year, the Alarm released their final album, *Raw.* The group had begun to have some difficulties. On June 30, 1991, the members of the Alarm had not yet decided to dissolve the band when they went on stage at London's Brixton Academy. Singer Mike Peters simply walked up to the microphone at the end of one of their songs and told the audience, "Thanks for coming to our final show." Although none of the other members anticipated it at that particular time, theyall knew it would happen eventually. "There was a time when it started becoming less fun," Peters told Rey Roldan in *Consummable.* "We all started to get egos. We all started feeling more superior than each other. I just felt like it was falling apart around me."

Peters went on to form the Poets of Justice, who released their debut, *Breathe,* in 1994. In 1996, he went on a solo tour called "Unalarmed," during which he resurrected the Alarm's material. "The 'Unalarmed' tour really put my faith back in music," Peters told Roldan. "I really loved hearing words which I once struggled to write being sung back to me. It's times like these when I feel like the luckiest man alive."

Selected discography

The Alarm, I.R.S. Records, 1983.
Declaration, I.R.S. Records, 1984.
Strength, I.R.S. Records, 1985.
Eye of the Hurricane, I.R.S. Records, 1987.
Electric Folklore Live, I.R.S. Records, 1988.
Newid (Change), I.R.S. Records, 1989.
Standards, I.R.S. Records, 1990.
Raw, I.R.S. Records, 1991.

Sources

Books

Rees, Dafydd and Luke Crampton, eds., *Encyclopedia of Rock Stars,* DK Publishing, New York, 1996.

Periodicals

Billboard, July 9, 1983; November 30, 1985; December 28, 1985; April 5, 1986; July 12, 1986.
Consummable, October 25, 1996.
Musician, May 1984, June 1984.
Rock Express, January 1988.
Rolling Stone, July 7, 1983; November 10, 1983; March 29, 1984; April 10, 1986; January 28, 1988.
Stereo Review, July 1984, May 1990.

Online

http://www.wheatmedia.com/alarm/firework.html

—*Sonya Shelton*

The Animals

Rock band

In the 1960s, the Animals became a part of what became known as the British invasion. Contemporaries of the Beatles and the Rolling Stones, the band was an influence and inspiration for decades after their peak. After the band began to disintegrate, singer Eric Burdon took over the name and continued the group as Eric Burdon & the Animals. The band's songs were later covered by such artists as Grand Funk Railroad, Tom Petty and the Heartbreakers, and Bruce Springsteen.

Despite the group's initial success, the Animals never reached the same level as the Beatles or the Rolling Stones. They gleaned the inspiration for their sound from the rawness and toughness of American blues and rhythm and blues (R&B). One reviewer wrote in *Rolling Stone,* "If the Beatles were the British Invasion's models of youthful optimism, the Animals were its pissed off proles, working-class rebels without a cause.. perpetually on the outside looking in."

The Animals grew from keyboardist Alan Price's band, the Alan Price Trio, which also included bassist Chas

AP/Wide World Photos

For the Record . . .

Members include **Alan Price** (born April 19, 1941, Fairfield, Durham, England), organ, piano; **Eric Burdon** (born May 11, 1941, Walker, Northumberland, England), vocals; **Chas Chandler** (born Byran Chandler, December 18, 1938, Heaton, Northumberland, England; died July 17, 1996, in Newcastle-upon-Tyne, England), bass; **John Steel** (born February 4, 1941, Gateshead, Northumberland, England), drums; **Hilton Valentine** (born May 21, 1943, North Shields, Northumberland, England), guitar

Other members include: **Vic Briggs** (born February 14, 1945, Twickenham, Surrey, England), guitar; **Barry Jenkins** (born December 22, 1944, Leicester, England), drums; **Danny McCullough** (born July 18, 1945, London, England), bass; **Tom Parker**, organ, piano; **Dave Rowberry** (born December 27, 1943, Newcastle, England), organ, piano; **John Weider** (born April 21, 1947, London, England), guitar.

Band formed as the Alan Price Combo, 1962; changed name to the Animals, 1962; released self-titled debut album, 1964; Price left the band, 1965; Steel left the band, 1966; the Animals disbanded, 1966; Eric Burdon & the Animals formed and released *Animalization,* 1966; band relocated to California, 1967; Burdon dissolved band, 1968; reunited for *Before We Were So Rudely Interrupted,* 1976; reunited for *Ark* and *Rip It To Shreds: The Animals Greatest Hits Live,* 1983-84.

Chandler and drummer John Steel in 1960. In 1962, Burdon joined the group to form the Alan Price Combo. They soon renamed themselves the Animals. According to the members, the moniker originally started as a nickname from their fans in Newcastle, England. "The name was probably an association with the kind of music we play—earthy and gutty," Burdon told Frank Ruppio in *Billboard.* "It's sort of an animal sound, and on stage we can be pretty wild."

In 1963, the Animals recorded a demo EP and pressed 500 copies to sell to their fans. The EP made its way to London and into the hands of manager/producer Mickie Most. Most began working with the band within the year, and the Animals moved to London. They signed a recording contract with EMI Records and released their first single, "Baby Let Me Take You Home." The band toured the U.K. and Japan with Chuck Berry, the Swinging Blue Jeans, and others.

Sound Migrated to the U.S.

In July of 1964, the Animals released one of the most popular singles of their career, "House of the Rising Sun." The record company almost refused to release it because of its length, over four minutes, which at the time was extraordinarily long for a single. Two months later, the Animals had signed a recording contract with MGM Records in the U.S., and released "House of the Rising Sun" in America, followed by their first U.S. tour. In November of the same year, they released their self-titled debut album, followed by the single "I'm Crying." They wrapped up the year with a nine-day tour of the former Union Soviet Union.

The Animals released a string of hit singles in 1965 as well, including a cover of John Lee Hooker's "Boom Boom," "Don't Let Me Be Misunderstood," "Don't Bring Me Down," "See See Rider," and "We've Gotta Get Out of This Place." By the end of the year, the band had had six Top Ten singles and two albums, *The Animals on Tour* and *Animal Tracks.*

In the middle of this streak of success, Price left the band to form another configuration of his solo band called the Alan Price Set, which recorded some of Randy Newman's first songs. Price left the band for several reasons. First and foremost, he and Burdon had begun to have a growing number of disagreements. Price also did not like flying in airplanes, which led to touring problems. The group replaced him with Dave Rowberry, formerly of Mike Cotton Sound.

Burdon Took the Reins

Price's departure was followed by a constant series of lineup changes and difficulties for the Animals. In February of 1966, Steel was replaced by ex-Nashville Teens drummer Barry Jenkins. The group released *The Best of the Animals,* followed by *Animalisms.* Burdon and the other members of the group began to have an increasing number of disagreements. Burdon had become heavily involved in drugs, while the rest of the members had not. At the end of the Animals' U.S. tour, they completely disbanded.

Like several of their contemporaries, the members of the Animals didn't see very much of the money they earned from their success. When they broke up, Steel sold his publishing rights for 4,000 pounds, and was the only member to leave the band with any money. "We all came out of the Animals relatively sane, because, although we were manipulated, we were never sheltered and protected like the Beatles," Burdon told Bob Hart in *Rolling Stone*.

Drummer Jenkins and singer Burdon decided to form a new version of the Animals within a few months. They quickly recruited bassist Danny McCullough and organist Tom Parker. In October of 1966, they released *Animalization* on MGM Records. The following year, they all moved to California and added guitarist Vic Briggs. But before their next album was recorded, Parker left the group.

Burdon recorded a solo album called *Eric Is Here* that same year. In addition, the latest version of Eric Burdon & the Animals released *Help Me Girl, Winds of Change* and *The Best of Eric Burdon & the Animals, Volume 2.* As their material progressed, the band left their original R&B style behind and moved toward a psychedelic hard rock sound.

Film Influences Led to Dissolution

After the release of *The Twain Shall Meet* in May of 1968, Briggs and McCullough left the band. They were replaced by keyboardist Zoot Money and guitarist Andy Summers (who later joined the Police). Burdon changed the name of the band to Eric Burdon & the New Animals. In September, they released *Every One of Us* and embarked on a high-tech tour, which included an extravagant light show and four films. "I can't get it out of my head every time I make a record that I'm making a documentary movie, and records you can only listen to," Burdon told Jerry Hopkins in *Rolling Stone.* "You can't see them. What we really are, right now, is a stage act."

Burdon's interest in film didn't end there, however. After they played a Christmas concert in his hometown of Newcastle, he announced that he was ending the group in order to pursue a career in film. "There are so many good groups now," Burdon told *Rolling Stone,* "that I just feel old and frustrated. I can't get much satisfaction out of me [sic] music anymore." MGM released two compilation albums the following year, *Love Is* and *The Greatest Hits of Eric Burdon & the Animals.*

Burdon returned to his music career in 1970 with the band War. His term was short-lived since he had to quit in the middle of the group's European tour because of exhaustion. Former bassist Chandler became Jimi Hendrix's first manager and later managed the English rock band Slade. Price spent the next two decades as a performer and composer of film, television, and stage musicals.

Two Brief Reunions

In 1976, Chandler and Price were both dealing with disintegrating marriages, while Burdon faced major financial problems. Along with Steel, they ended up in London at the same time, and decided to reunite to record an album together called *Before We Were So Rudely Interrupted* on Chandler's Barn Records. "When we play together, there's no sense of struggle," Burdon told Hart. "I might be able to fool my old lady, but I could never fool these guys." Due to Burdon's contractual obligations, the band could not release the album until the following year.

Following the brief reunion, the members of the Animals went their separate ways once again. But they got together one last time in July of 1983. This time, they recorded *Ark* and embarked on an extensive and lucrative world tour. On the road, tensions ran high, with the potential for another conclusion at any time. "It's the strangest thing," Steel told Steve Pond in *Rolling Stone.* "You're never really sure that the next gig is going to come off, never absolutely sure someone isn't going to run out. But that's good for the music." In 1984, the Animals released a live album from the tour called *Rip It To Shreds: The Animals Greatest Hits Live.*

Other collection albums followed over the next 10 years, including *Best of Eric Burdon & the Animals (1966-1968)* and *Animal Tracks: Heavy Hits.* Burdon published his autobiography, entitled *I Used to Be an Animal, But I'm Alright Now,* in 1986. He pursued a solo career apart from any Animals configuration, and toured with ex-Doors guitarist Robbie Krieger in 1990 and keyboardist Brian Auger in 1992.

The Animals were inducted into the Rock and Roll Hall of Fame in 1994 by Soul Asylum singer Dave Pirner. The original members joined together once again as the music industry recognized them for their musical contributions. Two years later, on July 17, 1996, Chandler died in Newcastle, England. However, the influence of all of the incarnations of the Animals continued to live on. Throughout its history, rock and roll has relied on the inspiration of its working-class roots. As many groups recorded cover versions of the Animals' material, their ever-struggling, American-inspired sounds endured.

Selected discography

The Animals, MGM Records, 1964.
The Animals on Tour, MGM Records, 1965.
Animal Tracks, MGM Records, 1965.
The Best of the Animals, MGM Records, 1966.

Animalisms, MGM Records, 1966.
Animalization, MGM Records, 1966.
Help Me Girl, MGM Records, 1967.
The Best of Eric Burdon & the Animals, Vol. 2, MGM Records, 1967.
Winds of Change, MGM Records, 1967.
The Twain Shall Meet, MGM Records, 1968.
Every One of Us, MGM Records, 1968.
Love Is, MGM Records, 1969.
The Greatest Hits of Eric Burdon & the Animals, MGM Records, 1969.
Before We Were So Rudely Interrupted, Barn Records, 1976.
Ark, I.R.S. Records, 1983.
Rip It To Shreds: The Animals Greatest Hits Live, I.R.S. Records, 1984.
The Best of Eric Burdon & the Animals (1966-1968), Polydor Records, 1986.
Animal Tracks: Heavy Hits, Special Music, 1994.

Sources

Books

Helander, Brock, editor, *The Rock Who's Who,* Schirmer Books, New York, 1996.
Rees, Dafydd and Luke Crampton, editors, *Encyclopedia of Rock Stars,* DK Publishing, New York, 1996.

Periodicals

Billboard, August 8, 1964; December 28, 1968.
People, December 26, 1983.
Rolling Stone, September 14, 1968; December 21, 1968; May 20, 1976; October 27, 1983; February 24, 1994.
Stereo Review, November 1983.
Time, July 29, 1996.

—*Sonya Shelton*

The Aquabats

Ska, rock band

An eight-member ensemble playing cheerful tunes on a wide variety of instruments including saxophone, organ, and Moog synthesizer, the Aquabats are often grouped with other "third wave ska" bands coming out of Southern California. Ska, a calypso-tinged twist on American rhythm and blues, began in Jamaica in the early 1960s. After years in decline, ska enjoyed a resurgence in the late 1970s. The most recent ska movement, developed in the late 1980s and dubbed "Third Wave Ska."

While there is an undeniable ska element in the music of the Aquabats, the band members, their devotees, and many commentators consider the ska label too narrow a description of the Aquabats style. "Though the Aquabats are too weird to be ska, their music is frequently ska-driven. Though they're too melodic to be punk, you'll hear that too—alongside rockabilly and doo-wop," wrote Paul Lamont in *OC Weekly.*

Another thing that separates the Aquabats from typical ska groups is the strong element of performance art in their stage shows and their outrageous matching costumes including skin-tight lycra suits, helmets, and goggles. The band has been likened to Devo, the robotic, uniform-wearing art rock group of the 1980s. Indeed, the Aquabats list Devo among their many influences. "We're huge fans of Devo and Oingo Boingo, but then everyone in the band has their individual tastes. Some band members like punk rock, some like surf rock of the Ventures and '50s and '60s rock 'n' roll," Aquabat guitarist Courtney Pollock explained to Jeff Niesel of the *Orange County Register.*

The Aquabats were founded in Orange County, California in 1994 by Christian Jacobs, Chad Larson, and Boyd Terry, all of whom attended the same Mormon church. After discovering a mutual interest in playing in a rock band and a brief rehearsal period, the Aquabats played their first engagement at a party in August of 1994. Attracted to the idea of matching outfits, they adapted costumes from items found at the surf-equipment manufacturing company owned by Terry's brother in Newport Beach. "The first performance we did as a joke. We weren't trying to be a band. We were trying to have fun," bassist Chad Larson told Mike Boehm of the *Los Angeles Times.* The Aquabats tightened their sound when guitarist Courtney Pollock, horn player Adam Diebert, and guitarist Charles Grey were recruited from an established ska band, the Goodwin Club. Two other members — drummer Travis Barker and saxophonist James Briggs — joined later, further expanding the band's sound.

The Aquabats do not talk much about their real beginnings. "It's not very interesting, really," Christian Jacobs told the *Riverside Press-Enterprise.* Instead, they speak of coming from a South Pacific island called "Aquabania." According to publicity material on the *Heckler Magazine* home page — "One day a dark and evil force descended upon the island and took it over. So the strongest men of the tribe set sail in a log to find help and gain the powers needed to overthrow the island.... The log finally beached in front of a mad professor's house in North Newport Beach. He found them and took them in. He did experiments on them while they learned magic powers from him in return. Although with different motives, they joined forces to take over the world. The professor knew that the only way to take over the world these days was through MTV, so he got them addicted to saccharine, high fructose corn syrups and other high-energy sweeteners and set them up as a rock group."

All eight Aquabat members have stage personas — The Bat Commander (Jacobs), Crash McLarson (Larson), Catboy (Boyd), Baron Von Tito (Barker), Jaime the Robot (Briggs), Chainsaw: The Prince of Karate (Pollock), Ultra Kyu (Grey), and Prince Adam (Diebert). Jacobs' brother Parker sometimes joins in stage appearances as the character of the Mad Professor. In performances, they pantomime battles with enemies such as the Powdered Milk Man. Marshmallow, Cheez-Whiz, and Silly String

For the Record . . .

Members include **Rod Arellano** (Roddy B, former member), drums and back up; **Travis Landon Barker** (The Baron Von Tito), drums and percussion; **Ben Bergeson** (The Brain, former member), guitar; **James Randall Briggs** (Jaime the Robot), saxophone, clarinet, flute, piano, vocals; **Adam Warren Deibert** (Prince Adam), trumpet, vocals; **Charles Wallace Grey** (Ultra Kyu), guitar, finger cymbals, piano, ebow, violin, sitar, mellotron, synthesizer, vocals; **Christian Richard Jacobs** (The Bat Commander), vocals; **Parker Jacobs** (The Mad Professor, ocassional member); **Chad Albert Larson** (Crash McLarson), bass guitar, organ, vocals; **Chad Parkin** (Nacho, former member), organ; **Courtney Adam Pollock** (Chainsaw: The Prince of Karate), guitar, samples and scratching, vocals; **Boyd Terry** (Catboy), trumpet, coronet, Sousaphone, vocals.

Band formed in Orange County, CA in 1994; released *The Return of the Aquabats,* 1995 and *The Fury of the Aquabats,* 1997.

Addresses: *Home*—Huntington Beach, CA. *Business*—Goldenvoice Records, Orange County, CA (national distribution through Time Bomb Recordings, a BMG affiliate, Laguna Beach, CA).

are also sprayed about the audience. The band's most loyal followers call themselves "Aquabat cadets."

The Aquabats unique style impressed Bill Fold, a leading Southern California concert promoter. "I'd seen them early on and it was pretty much joking around. But it became a real band. They were all in sync, and they really sparked my attention," Fold told Mike Boehm of *Los Angeles Times.* Fold and his partner Bill Hardie became managers of the Aquabats.

The band's 1995 debut CD, *The Return of the Aquabats*, sold well for a local group on a small label. Additional earnings were made from Aquabats merchandise such as T-shirts, goggles, and helmets. The Aquabats have increased their nationwide visibility by touring as the opening act for No Doubt, the Mighty, Mighty Bosstones, and the Red Hot Chili Peppers

Their second CD, called *The Fury of the Aquabats,* was released in 1997. "With the recent popularity of ska music, it is becoming difficult to tell the difference between hundreds of upbeat, blacktie-wearing skankers from Southern California. But if creativity is what you're looking for, there is a group of superhumans on the way to light up your musical life.... The Aquabats are all about having fun, and although not every song is an instant classic, *The Fury of the Aquabats* will definitely make you smile," wrote Ben Clark of the *Whitworthian.*

Though the Aquabats gain new followers wherever they tour, some problems may make their rise to the top somewhat hazardous. According to Fold, some people in the music industry are apprehensive towards bands associated with ska. Fold told the *Los Angeles Times* that "ska has less credibility for some reason, maybe because it's oriented to a younger crowd. Radio stations play it, but they complain about it, like they don't want to play it. Maybe it's geared to a younger crowd than their advertisers want."

In her review of an October 1997 Aquabats performance in Humboldt County, California, Monica Topping wrote in *Rhythmic* — "These guys had all of the essential elements of a really good live band. They had the obvious element of music, but most of all the Aquabats had perfect stage presence. Not only did they have cool costumes and special guests, like the Powdered Milk Man, who was the 'root of all that is evil', they had a special hold on the audience. What other band could make a whole entire room full of people sit down on the floor so the Commander could tell a story about the Martian Girl of his dreams, or get the audience to join them in a heartfelt chorus of 'The Star Spangled Banner'.... This was not just a group of musicians it was a group of entertainers."

It seems unlikely that the fantastical antics the Aquabats will ever draw widespread interest from the over twenty-one crowd. More probable is their following in the footsteps of earlier pre-teen fantasy phenomenons such as Kiss, Alice Cooper, and the Monkees. Indeed, an ambition of the Aquabats is to have a television show similar to the series the Monkees had in the 1960s. The Aquabats are not the kind of band that draws casual followers. Either one gets them or one doesn't. As Christian Jacobs told the *Riverside Press-Enterprise*—"Every so often you'll get kids who yell, 'You guys are stupid!' It's kind of like, the joke's on you, guy, we are stupid."

Selected discography

The Return of the Aquabats, 1995.
The Fury of the Aquabats, 1997

Sources

Periodicals

Los Angeles Times (Orange County edition), May 24, 1996, p.F23; October 28, 1997, p.F1.
OC Weekly (Orange County, CA), January 17, 1997, p.20; November 21, 1997, p.24.
Orange County Register, November 21, p.F55.
Rhythmic (Humboldt County, CA), November 1997.
Riverside Press-Enterprise, November 21, 1997, p.AA13.
The Whitworthian (Whitworth College, Brookhaven, MS), November 18, 1997.

Online

Heckler Magazine home page (www.heckler.com/4.4/bats.html).
In Music We Trust (on-line magazine) issue number 4, December 1996 - January 1997 (http://members.aol.com./zinepres).

— *Mary Kalfatovic*

Art of Noise

Rock band

Developing on their experience as studio musicians and producers, the members of Art of Noise created a group almost completely based on the electronic technology that moved into the mainstream in the 1980s. Their style influenced future trends in dance music well into the next decade. "In the early 80s, Art of Noise forged an eclectic mix of club grooves, atmospheric soundscapes, and rock panache that prefigured 90s techno and ambient," wrote Matt Diehl in *Entertainment Weekly*.

Anne Dudley, Jonathan "J.J." Jeczalik, and Gary Langan met through their work with noted 1980s producer Trevor Horn. They worked as musicians and producers for many film soundtracks and for other artists, such as Frankie Goes to Hollywood, ABC, Malcolm McLaren, Wham!, Billy Idol, and Paul McCartney. Following a grueling recording session with the band Yes, Horn and the trio decided to form a faceless band that would compose mostly instrumental collages of sound. "The reason we don't show our faces is that there is a tendency for the music industry to sign haircut-and-faces bands with no regard for the music," Dudley

Corbis

For the Record . . .

Members include **Anne Dudley** (born May 7, 1956, London, England), keyboards; **Jonathan "J.J." Jeczalik** (born May 11, 1955), keyboards, programmer; **Gary Langan**, engineer.

Band formed after a studio session with Yes, and signed with ZTT Records, 1984; released debut *(Who's Afraid of) The Art of Noise,* 1984; signed with China Records, 1985; released *In Visible Silence,* 1986; released *In No Sense? Nonsense!,* 1987; released *The Best of the Art of Noise,* 1988; and *Below the Waste,* 1990; group disbanded, 1990.

Address: *Record company*—Discovery Records, 2052 Broadway, Santa Monica, CA 90404; phone (310) 828-1033; fax (310) 828-1584.

explained to Jeff Burger in *Keyboard.* "We simply want people to listen to the music!"

Each member of Art of Noise added their own musical experiences and influences to the group. Langan was a fan of heavy rock, and brought an edge to their sound. Jeczalik loved classical music, especially Bach and Mahler. Dudley also enjoyed classical music, but also enjoyed pop, which brought more of a dance style to the mix. Dudley had also received a formal music education from London's Royal College of Music. "I'm extraordinarily lucky to have received classical training," Dudley told Bob Doerschuk in *Keyboard.* "Yet I'm also lucky to have worked with brilliant people in the pop world, such as Trevor Horn, who encouraged me to express myself and to be more creative and more daring than I would have ever imagined I could be."

After forming in 1984 and in search of a name, Paul Morely of ZTT (Zang Tuum Tumb) Records, Horn's label, suggested Art of Noise. He remembered the name from Russolo's *Futurist Manifesto,* in which he distinguished the music of the machine in the 1910s. Art of Noise signed a recording contract with ZTT/Island a few months later and released their debut single "Beat Box," which soared to number ten on *Billboard*'s R&B charts. By the end of 1984, they had released their debut album, *(Who's Afraid of) The Art of Noise.*

The following year, their single, "Close to the Edit," won the awards for Best Editing and Most Experimental at the second annual MTV Video Music Awards in New York. By the end of 1985, Art of Noise had split with Trevor Horn and left ZTT Records. They signed a new recording contract with China Records, and began working on their next album.

In July of 1986, Art of Noise released *In Visible Silence* on China/Chrysalis and the single, "Legs." Mark Peel described the album in *Stereo Review* as, "an awesome demonstration of the state of the recording art," declaring it, "the epitome of what, for better or worse, is happening to pop music in the electronic age." The album included some collaboration as well. On "Paranoimia," Art of Noise joined with the computerized television character Max Headroom. They were also joined by guitarist Duane Eddy, the "King of Twang," for a cover version of Henry Mancini's 1959 classic, "Peter Gunn." The following year, Art of Noise's "Peter Gunn" won Best Rock Instrumental Performance for an Orchestra, Group, or Soloist at the Grammy Awards. Mancini had won two Grammy awards for the same song in 1959.

Movies Boosted Popularity

The group headed back into the studio for their 1987 release, *In No Sense? Nonsense!,* continuing their mix of electronics, soundscapes, and musical instruments that resulted in their own style of "noise." In describing the album for *People Weekly,* reviewer David Hiltbrand said, "Art of Noise have mixed sound effects (wind chimes, footsteps, voices), studio synthetics, and sporadic snippets of music into a jumble that could come from a Martian beat box."

Art of Noise branched out into film music the next year, recording the main theme for *Dragnet,* starring Dan Ackroyd and Tom Hanks, as "Dragnet '88." They also contributed to the soundtrack for the comedy *Disorderlies,* starring fellow musicians the Fat Boys. Their big hit of the year, however, came from yet another collaborative remake. The group hooked up with singer Tom Jones for a cover version of Prince's 1986 song "Kiss." The single climbed the charts to number five in the UK and number 31 in the U.S. The track appeared as the new song on their 1988 collection *The Best of the Art of Noise.*

Art of Noise released their next single in 1989 called "Yebo," which featured the African group, Malathini & the Mahotella Queens. The song was remixed and reissued in 1995 by Ollie J. and Arkana, five years after the group released *Below the Waste,* the final album of the band's career.

In July of 1990, the members decided to break up and go their own ways. While Anne Dudley and former Killing

Joke singer Jaz Coleman collaborated to release *Songs from the Victorious City*, Jeczalik and Langan continued their own careers as producers and composers. Dudley followed suit within the year. All three members of the Art of Noise, though, had never completely left their own individual careers. They often worked on film soundtracks or with other artists, as well as their Art of Noise commitments.

The influence of the Art of Noise's music lived on for years past the groups demise. In 1994, Off Beat Records released a revised version of *The Best of the Art of Noise*, with post-1988 music and without the ZTT tracks. In 1997, China/Discovery Records, released three *The Best of the Art of Noise* collections: *The Ambient Collection*, *Drum and Bass Collection*, and *The FON Mixes*. The latter featured Art of Noise songs that were remixed by various producers. Althoughthe group performed together for less than a decade, their offbeat exploration into electronic and nonmusical sounds inspired techno and dance artists well into the 1990s.

Selected discography

(Who's Afraid of) The Art of Noise, ZTT/Island Records, 1984.
In Visible Silence, China/Chrysalis Records, 1986.
In No Sense? Nonsense!, China/Chrysalis Records, 1987.
The Best of the Art of Noise, China/Polygram Records, 1988.
Below the Waste, China/Polygram Records, 1990.
The Best of the Art of Noise, Off Beat Records, 1994.
The Best of the Art of Noise: The Ambient Collection, China/Discovery Records, 1997.
The Best of the Art of Noise: Drum and Bass Collection, China/Discovery Records, 1997.
The Best of the Art of Noise: The FON Mixes, China/Discovery Records, 1997.

Sources

Books

Rees, Dafydd and Luke Crampton, eds. *Encyclopedia of Rock Stars*, DK Publishing, New York, 1996.

Periodicals

Audio, May 1988.
Down Beat, September 1986.
Entertainment Weekly, January 17, 1997.
Guitar Player, October 1986.
Keyboard, September 1986, February 1989, April 1990.
People Weekly, May 5, 1986; December 7, 1987.
Rolling Stone, August 30, 1984.
Seventeen, August 1986.
Stereo Review, August 1986, December 1987.

—Sonya Shelton

Audio Adrenaline

Christian alternative rock group

Audio Adrenaline has created waves in the Christian alternative rock realm, and has seamlessly shifted from funk and rap music to alternative rock without losing equilibrium or devoted fans.The band worked with the mega Christian group D.C. Talk for more than two years on and off the tour circuits, and eventually altered their musical style to create more of a distinct sound separate from D.C. Talk. Aaron Brinley wrote of the band's music on Squares Music Online, "great alternative rock...that jumps right into your lap with a grunge crispness that revitalizes your soul." Audio Adrenaline meshes punk, thrash, ballads, and grunge in a fast, high-octane delivery, but they also create easy listening music and thoughtful, sincere ballads. The band consists of vocalist Mark Stuart from Owensboro, KY, guitarist/keyboard player Bob Herdman from Lynchburg, OH, bassist Will McGinniss from Caledonia, OH, drummer Ben Cissell from St. Louis, MO, and guitarist Tyler Burkum, a relative newcomer to the band.

Band members grew up listening to rock and 1970s-funk music. The Nashville-based quartet formed Audio Adrenaline in 1991 while Stuart and McGinniss studied at Kentucky Christian College in Grayson, Kentucky, and played in a local band. They met Herdman there and former band guitarist Barry Blair, who was replaced by Burkum in 1996. Herdman had written the song "DC-10" and he thought the band might want to perform it, which eventually led to his writing the single "My God" and the band's first record deal. The songs were a cross between speed metal and rap with a bold religious message. The band members were education and religion majors and planning on becoming chemistry teachers. They had no desire to make music for a living—but their musical success led them to believe they were chosen to be musicians.

Their college enlisted their assistance to recruit prospective students at youth conventions across the country, sponsoring the band and giving them equipment and a van in return for saying something positive about the school. They built up a following from this early touring, a loyal grassroots fan base primarily located throughout the Midwest, and also managed to sell a good amount of independent records as well.

In 1991 the band left college to sign with Forefront Records in Tennessee. On Audio Adrenaline's first major tour, they were teamed with fellow Forefront artists Geoff Moore & The Distance as the opening act. They were also the roadies; Stuart told *HotStar* magazine, "It was pretty hard but it was a good time because we were just starting off. It was our first time to experience the whole country."

They released their debut album, *Audio Adrenaline,* in 1992 but later felt the album didn't reflect their true musical perspective, citing the fact that their producers molded them into an adrenaline-charged style. Two of the singles from their debut album were in the punk rock vein: "DC-10" and "My God". The band released *Don't Censor Me* shortly after in 1993, which had more of a pop and contemporary music tone than their previous work and sold more than 300,000 units. The single "Big House" from the album received Dove Award nominations for rock song and video of the year, and a *Billboard* Music Award nomination for Best Christian Video. The single was also used in youth camps as a praise song and some churches used it in their services.

The band released *Live Bootleg* in 1995. *BloOm* was released in 1996, which contained more straight-ahead rock music than their other albums and sometimes bordered on easy-listening, serene music. It was produced by John Hampton, whose resume included production work with the Gin Blossoms. *BloOm* was an attempt to put religion in the forefront and to minimize their role in their success; the first single on the release was titled, "Never Gonna Be As Big As Jesus". *BloOm* produced seven Top five singles, four of them reaching the number one mark.

Some Kind of Zombie was released in 1997. The single "Some Kind of Zombie" is a reference to Colossians

For the Record . . .

Members include **Tyler Burkum,** guitar; **Ben Cissell** (born in St. Louis, MO), durms; **Bob Herdman** (born in Lynchburg, OH), guitar, keyboard, and vocals; **Will McGinniss** (born in Caledonia, OH), guitar, keyboard, and vocals; and **Mark Stuart** (born in Owensboro, KY),bass.

Band formed in 1991 while Stuart and McGinniss were studying at Kentucky Christian College in Grayson, KY, and playing in a local band; in 1991 the band left college to sign with Forefront Records; toured with D.C. Talk and Geoff Moore & The Distance as the opening act; released *Audio Adrenaline,* in 1992; *Don't Censor Me,* 1993 ; *Live Bootleg,* in 1995; *BloOm,* 1996, *Some Kind of Zombie,* 1997; published the book, *Some Kind of Journey: On the Road with Audio Adrenaline—7 Days, 7issues, 7 Souls,* by Standard Publishing on AVCD in 1997.

Address: *Record company*—Forefront Records, 201 Seaboard Lane, Franklin, TN 37067; (615) 771-2900. *Online*—www.forefrontrecords.com

Chapter 3, where a life is given over to God. The material was inspired by lead singer Mark Stuart's experiences living with his missionary parents in Haiti—where voodoo was conceived—the message being that you can be dead to your old self after becoming a new person through religion. *Some Kind of Zombie* utilized new sounds for the band: horns, strings, synthesizers, samples, and loops, and broadened their musical base.

Leap to Headliner

After the release of *Some Kind of Zombie,* Mark Rider—president of Nashville-based Just Radio, a production and programming company—told *Billboard*'s Deborah Evans Price, "I think this is the best rock record out right now....It's a real departure from their previous sound, more raw, and kids love it." Evans Price wrote, "Audio Adrenaline is poised to take the leap from promising new act to headliner with the release of *Some Kind of Zombie.*"

The album was slated to be released simultaneously with the book, *Some Kind of Journey: On the Road with Audio Adrenaline—7 Days, 7issues, 7 Souls,* published by Standard Publishing.The book chronicles the experiences of seven young people who journeyed seven days with the band and discussed pertinent cultural issues along the way. It is a cross between MTV's "Real Life" and "Road Rules". Topics covered include struggling through pain, marriage and sexuality, and life in the church. It was intended to be a tool for youth pastors to guide those who have been sheltered from the real world. The book and album were released on enhanced CD format (AVCD), featuring four audio tracks, two videos, interviews, and devotional segments.

The possibility of mainstream success doesn't spur band members on to greater glory, as they remain devoted to their original ideal of serving God and recruiting new Christians, particularly the young. Herdman told *Contemporary Christian Music*'s Brian Quincy Newcomb, "When we first started the band, the goal was ministry first, music second. We put on a killer show, so when we say music is second, it's not that we don't take it seriously. But we take ministry more seriously. Our number one goal is to spread the gospel."

Censored by Radio

The band intends to start their own label in the future. They play primarily at churches and county or state fairs when touring, which serves to keep them out of the mainstream venues.Stuart told J. Warner Soditus of *The Lighthouse,* "The Christian groups that are really selling well would be on the Top-40 *Billboard* but they don't recognize the Christian bookstores.... I think that's censorship. Another way we're being censored is radio stations and MTV won't play music or videos that are created by Christian labels. They're afraid of Christianity." Stuart continued to say that he felt Christianity was a generation away from extinction, which is the most compelling reason for the band to take their ministry to heart. He told Soditus, "We like to say, 'We're all Gods' kids.' We try not to have any barriers in our music. It's a lot of fun." Forefront Records' Ron Griffin described Audio Adrenaline to Soditus as, "The heart of a pastor with the energy of a sixteen year old."

Selected discography

Audio Adrenaline, Forefront, 1992.
Don't Censor Me, Forefront, 1993.
Live Bootleg, Forefront, 1995.
BloOm, forefront, 1996.
Some Kind of Zombie (AVCD single), Forefront, 1997.
Some Kind of Zombie, Forefront, 1997.

Sources

Periodicals

Billboard, November 15, 1997.
Contemporary Christian Music Magazine, February 1998.
HotStar, April 27, 1998.
Iowa State Daily, May 3, 1996.
The Lighthouse, July/August, 1993.

Online

http://www.audioa.com
http://www.forefrontrecords.com
http://www.iias.com/melanie/aa.html (Mel's Music)
http://205.186.189.2/cg/amg.exe'sql=2P_IDP

—B. Kimberly Taylor

Aztec Camera

Rock band

Michael Ochs Archives

As founder, musical leader, and sometimes sole member of Aztec Camera, Scottish-born Roddy Frame has created soothing pop songs that have created a long-standing niche in the indie music world, where bands and performer's careers are often short-lived. A somewhat confessional songwriter, Frame is known as a competent poetic craftsman, if at times a bit too idealistic in outlook and naive in imagery, with a particular penchant for love songs. While never a huge success in the U.S. as compared to the UK, Frame and company have been making music since 1980.

Born in East Kilbride, Scotland on January 29, 1964, Frame had his musical introduction at the age of 15 with a punk band called the Neutral Blue, which he left to create Aztec Camera. He modeled the band after the Byrds and the Velvet Underground. After signing with the independent label Postcard in 1981, they started playing in local pubs and began to kindle the flames of success. The first step to becoming successful was leaving the Postcard label. "On Postcard, the whole charm was the groups couldn't tune their own guitars," sniffed Frame to *Melody Maker*'s Steve Sutherland. "I didn't see that as charming—I thought it was crap."

The next year the band relocated to London and signed with Rough Trade Records. Drummer Dave Ruffy replaced Mulholland and with the addition of Bernie Clarke on keyboards, the band set out to record their debut album, *High Land, Hard Rain,* in 1983. The first endeavor won Aztec Camera critical praise and the album made it to number 22 on the U.K. charts. It also attracted the attention of Sire Records, who signed the band to a U.S. contract, and Elvis Costello, who praised Frame's songwriting and invited the band to open for him on an eight-week tour of America. Frame, only 19 years-old at the time, often had to lie about his age in states where the band performed.

Aztec Camera's second album, *Knife,* was released in 1984 and was produced by Dire Straits frontman Mark Knopfler. More polished and enhanced then the debut album, the addition of horns and studio musicians lent a different quality to Frame's delicate lyrics, a sound that Frame is both proud of and ambivalent towards. "I would have preferred it to sound much more like the original demos, sparser, with more room to breathe," Frame admitted to Paul Mathur of *Melody Maker.* "But it was interesting to come at things from a totally different perspective." Peter Anderson of London's *New Musical Express* echoed Frame declaring, "*Knife* has good songwriting, Roddy's best, the dashes of brilliance that are the mark of one with real talent, but it's all too smooth, too polished." Shortly thereafter, the band then began an extensive world tour to support the album.

For the Record . . .

Members have included **Roddy Frame**, (born January 29, 1964, Scotland) guitarist, lyricist, and singer; **Tommy Barlow** (1987), saxophone; **Yolanda Charles** (1995—), bass; **Bernie Clarke** (1982), keyboards; **Mark Edwards** (1993—), keyboards; **Craig Gannon** (1983), guitar; **Ruby James** (1987) vocals **Sylvia James** (1987), vocals; **Clare Kenny** (1989-93), bass; **Eddie Kulak** (1984-89) keyboards; **Dave Mulholland** (1980-82), drums; **Campbell Owens** (1981-86),bass; **Paul Powell** (1987-89), bass; **Malcolm Ross** (1984-85), guitar; **Dave Ruffy** (1982-88), drums; **Gary Sanford** (1987-93), guitar;**Gary Sanctuary** (1989-91), keyboards; **Steve Sidelnyk** (1987-93), percussion; **Jeremy Stacy** (1995—), drums; **Frank Tontoh** (1989-93), drums; **Alan Welsh** (1980-81), bass.

Formed in Scotland in 1980; first single, "Just Like Gold," released on Glasgow independent label, Postcard, 1981; signed to Sire Records in the U.S., released *High Land, Hard Rain,* 1983, *Knife,* 1984, *Aztec Camera* (EP), 1985, *Backwards and Forward* (EP), 1985, *Love,* 1987, *Stray,* 1990, and *Dreamland,* 1993; signed multi-album contract with WEA records in the UK, 1983, released *New, Live and Rare,* 1995; records version of Cole Porter's "Do I Love You?" for the AIDS awareness album, *Red Hot + Blue,* 1990.

Address: *Record company*—Reprise Records, 75 Rockefeller Plaza, New York, NY 10016. *Fan club*—Aztec Camera Fan Club, P.O. Box 321, London SW7 2JU, England. *Online*—www.aoinfo.com/aztec/html.

By 1986 Aztec Camera was almost completely a solo endeavor by Frame, backed by hired hands instead of full-fledged band members. The rotating roster of musicians in Aztec Camera has had much to do with the rather mercurial temper of Frame. "I find it quite hard to get along with people for a long time," he explained to Sutherland. "Some people are a bit stupid. Just to be around them,in a dressing room, in a hotel with them ... they have to go." In whatever incarnation, it took three years for Frame to release the third album, *Love,* and it was this record which received the greatest commercial attention. The album also boasted many well known producers including Tommy LiPuma, David Frank, and Russ Titelman. Some seven months after the album's release, the single "Somewhere In My Heart" reached to number three in the U.K. and re-ignited interest in the album, which reached number ten in the U.K. and gained platinum certification.

"In a half-light [*Love*] could slip past the entrance trying to pass itself off as Contemporary Rock fodder," Mathur wrote "but whip away the false beard and you're left with an admirably naked celebration." For Frame, the record was a highly personal one, written with an open, albeit guarded, heart. "There's words on the record that I look at and they seem really naive," he confessed to Mathur, "but at the same time, it was the way I was feeling when I wrote it. There had to be an honesty there to make it worth doing.... If someone hears the record, they know something about me, but not everything, not by a long way."

Aztec Camera: "A Nice Kind of Umbrella"

After spending time in America in an ill-fated attempt to write new songs, Frame returned to London where the tunes came quickly. The result was the 1990 eclectic album, *Stray.* A mix of jazz, pop, soul, and punk, Frame told Scott Isler of *Musician* that the record, "is the most spontaneous album I've ever made. A lot of songs I didn't even demo. I would just play them in rehearsal or in the studio; we'd change them as we went along, and then put them down." Frame calls the album one of bewilderment with a little anger thrown in, a decidedly different tone than his previous albums.

The record also has a lot to do with his adopted country. "When I looked at the lyrics to this album, it occurred to me it was all about Britain," Frame told Sutherland, "but I didn't want to call it *Good Morning, Britain* [a song on the album], because that's a stupid name. So I just decided to call it *Stray* because that's what it is really, just a kind of stray through all kinds of musical territories and different vibes." The song Frame mentions, "Good Morning Britain," was, in fact, a raucous feature of the album, a full-blown politically-irate punk duet with Mick Jones of the Clash and Big Audio Dynamite. Frame also found time to contribute the Cole Porter classic, "Do I Love You," for the *Red Hot + Blue* AIDS awareness album.

Following a tour to support *Stray,* Frame again took some time off to write and do occasional shows. In 1993, Frame emerged with *Dreamland,* a collaboration with composer/musician Ryuichi Sakamoto, creating a pairing that raised more than a few eyebrows. "The record company thought [Ryuichi] was going to be some kind of academic professor of electronic music," Frame explained to *Billboard*'s Craig Rosen. "But his approach was incredibly human. It's a strange pairing. I like to think of it as country and Eastern."

Frame also explained to Rosen his insistence on continuing to use the group name although he is essentially the only member. "The band isn't basically me," he told Rosen. "When I make records with other people, it's a collaboration. As soon as I get around other people it's a democracy." Besides, he says, Aztec Camera is, "a nice kind of umbrella. I like to think of it as kind of a brand name, but we're not as tight as Levi's and not as sweet as Coca-Cola."

In 1995 Frame released the sixth Aztec Camera album, *Frestonia,* to somewhat mixed reviews. In a review that celebrated Frame's long-standing career, Paul Lester of *Melody Maker* decided that while Frestonia has few surprises, he's not about to write off Frame, who has spent, "a decade and a half celebrating the romance of pain and the pain of romance." Scott Schinder of *Pulse!* echoed Lester, claiming Frame undercuts his smooth vocals and compassionate songwriting with "too-smooth studio technique." One rave was from David Roberts of *Q,* who declared, "Frame has put the soul back into the heart of his music ... with glorious melodies, subtly superb fretwork, and lyrics of instant, effortless articulacy—all sung in a voice which has lost none of its quiet poignancy."

After a short tour to support *Frestonia,* Frame learned that WEA had opted not to renew his recording contract. As he set off to write a new album and search for a new label—his new record is due in 1998—it's clear that Frame will continue on in the same way he's had since he was a 16 year-old Scottish kid who started a band. "Y'know, I don't really have the answers to anything but what I do have, I think is the power to express myself," he told Sutherland in 1990. "I hope I've got the power to put something on a record that can be sent off around the world and actually touch people. And maybe the things that I write in my bedroom can touch someone in their bedroom in Tokyo. That's the bottom line really."

Selected discography

High Land, Hard Rain, Sire, 1983.
Knife, Sire, 1984.
Aztec Camera (EP), Sire, 1985.
Backwards and Forward (EP), Sire, 1985.
Love, Sire, 1987.
Stray, Sire, 1990.
Dreamland, Sire, 1993.
New, Live and Rare, WEA, 1995.
Live on the Test, Windsong, 1995.
Frestonia, Reprise, 1995.

Sources

Books

Hardy, Phil and David Laing, eds. *Encyclopedia of Rock,* MacDonald, 1987.
Rhyss, Dafydd and Compton,Luke, eds. *Encyclopedia of Rock Stars,* DK Publishing, New York, 1996.

Periodicals

Billboard, June 19, 1993.
Chicago Tribune, June 20, 1993.
Melody Maker, August 22, 1981; October 31, 1981; September 4, 1982; October 13, 1984; February 13, 1988; June 9, 1990; November 11, 1995.
Musician, November 1990.
New Musical Express, October 20, 1984.
Pulse, December 1995.
Q, November, 1995.
Rolling Stone, September 1, 1983; September 30, 1993.

Online

www.aoinfo.com/aztec/html/
www.allmusicguide.com.

—Gretchen A. Monette

Bad Company

Rock band

Beginning as a rock supergroup in the 1970s, Bad Company set out to create a style stripped down to a simplistic four-piece rock band. The band shot to the top of the charts with their debut album, broke up in the mid-1980s, then resurfaced three years later. After more than two decades of recording in various configurations, Bad Company continued to modify and reform their no-frills rock and roll approach.

In August of 1973, drummer Simon Kirke and singer Paul Rodgers, both formerly of Free, decided to start a new group. They hooked up with Mick Ralphs, who had recently left Mott the Hoople, to play guitar. The trio named the band Bad Company after a 1972 western film starring Jeff Bridges and directed by Robert Benton. In November, Boz Burrell, who had played bass with King Crimson, completed the lineup.

Bad Company performed their first show in March of 1974 in Newcastle-upon-Tyne, England. Since each of the members had come from successful bands, they were quickly labeled a "supergroup." But instead of

AP/ Wide World Photos

For the Record . . .

Members include **Boz Burrell** (born Raymond Burrell, August 1, 1946, Lincoln, England), **David Colwell** (joined in 1991), guitar; **Robert Hart**, vocals **Brian Howe** (joined in 1986), **Simon Kirke** (born July 28, 1949, Shrewsbury, England), drums; **Mick Ralphs** (born March 31, 1944, Hereford, England), guitar; **Paul Rodgers** (born December, 17, 1949, Middlesbrough, England), **Rick Wills,** bass.

Band formed in England, 1973; signed to Swan Song Records, 1974; released six albums, 1974-83; reformed with new singer Brian Howe, 1986; released five albums, 1986-93; returned with singer Robert Hart and signed to EastWest Records, 1995.

Addresses: *Record company* — EastWest Records, 75 Rockefeller Plaza, New York, NY 10019.

taking a flamboyant, no-holds-barred rock and roll approach, Bad Company wanted to pursue a more sparse, mood-oriented direction. As John Swenson wrote in *Rolling Stone,* "For a supergroup, Bad Company is spectacularly understated." Rodgers told Bob Kirsch in *Billboard.*"[T]here is more subtlety than just hammering the hell out of people.... We grab the audience and then take them somewhere. The idea is to combine mood and excitement, with subtlety as the third ingredient."

Island Records and Swan Song

Bad Company began capturing the attention of fans and the music industry almost immediately. Led Zeppelin manager Peter Grant signed a management contract with them, and helped the group land a recording contract with Island Records in the U.K. and Led Zeppelin's Swan Song label in the U.S. By June of 1974, they had released their self-titled debut, which included hit singles like "Can't Get Enough" and "Ready for Love." The album soared to the top of the U.S. charts, resulting in a rise from opening act to headliner before the end of their first tour.

Bad Company returned to the studio right away to record their next release, *Straight Shooter.* They produced the album themselves, and it reached number three on the charts in both the U.K. and the U.S. Songs like "Good Lovin' Gone Bad" and "Feel Like Makin' Love" took over the radio airwaves. Ed Naha reviewed the album in *Rolling Stone:* "*Straight Shooter* is a fine example of contemporary rock & roll but, more than that, it is an exciting second step forward by a fledgling band that looks like it may be around for a long time to come."

Bad Company continued with its non-stop schedule, touring and recording *Run with the Pack* in 1976 and *Burnin' Sky* in 1977. When they took a break in 1978, rumors began to travel that the band was on the verge of breaking up. They squashed those rumors with the release of *Desolation Angels* in 1979, named after a Jack Kerouac novel. It included the popular singles "Rock 'n' Roll Fantasy" and "Gone, Gone, Gone." Ken Tucker noted a slight difference in the band's material in his *Rolling Stone* review: "*Desolation Angels* reveals qualities about these guys that their earlier work didn't hint at: wry world-weariness and a bemusement toward the tension between the sexes, plus a ouerulous, queasy feeling about their own place in all this."

Temporary Break-Up in Early 1980s

In 1980, the break-up rumors began to reach fruition. Rodgers began to consider leaving the group. However, he stayed to record the 1982 release *Rough Diamonds,* which included the single "Electricland," as well as perform the follow-up tour. In July of 1983, Bad Company announced they had officially disbanded. Rodgers recorded a solo album and went on to form the Firm with former Led Zeppelin guitarist Jimmy Page. From there, he performed with the band the Law, then formed Paul Rodgers & Company. Guitarist Ralphs toured with Pink Floyd and went on to perform his own material. Kirke formed a fleeting band called Wildlife, while Burrell also formed a short-lived rock band.

In 1986, Atlantic Records released *10 from 6,* a compilation of ten Bad Company hits from their six albums. Atlantic Records approached the group with the idea of a reformation. They decided to go ahead and returned with singer Brian Howe, who formerly worked with Ted Nugent. Bassist Steve Price filled in for Burrell in the studio, since Burrell had already committed to tour of Ireland.

Before they released their next album, they had to decide on a name. "We were having a terrible time picking a name—we had the lineup, and the record was in the can, but we didn't have a name," Kirke told Sharon Liveton in *Billboard.* Paul Cooper, the head of Atlantic on the West Coast, suggested they keep the name Bad

Company. "Until then, it hadn't even crossed my mind," said Kirke.

Resurfaced with Revolving Roster

With everything in place, the newly reformed Bad Company returned with the album *Fame and Fortune,* produced by Keith Olson. The album veered away slightly from the band's original simplistic style, adding the popular, electronic synthesizer sound. The group purposely wanted to start back up slowly, in order to avoid the madness that accompanied shooting to the top in 1974.

In 1988, Bad Company left the synthesizers behind on *Dangerous Age.* The album was an attempt to return to their original theme. As J.D. Constantine wrote in *Musician,* "*Dangerous Age* delivers all the bluesy punch of the first Bad Company albums without any of the excess that eventually drove the band to strutting self-parody."

The next decade brought a series of member changes for the group. In 1990, Burrell decided to leave the band, and Ralphs took an extended sabbatical to spend time with his family. Kirke and Howe recruited bassist Paul Cullen and guitarist Geoffrey Whitehorn as replacements. The new lineup recorded *Holy Water,* which included the tune "If You Needed Somebody." They followed up the release with a lengthy 203-show tour with Damn Yankees. In June of 1991, the fourth leg of the tour had yet another lineup, which included Kirke, Howe, the return of Ralphs, and the addition of bassist David Colwell. "Bad Company as a whole has always been more important than any individual in it," Ralphs said in the band's biography. It was a statement they proved again and again throughout the 1990s.

The following year, Bad Company released *Here Comes Trouble* on Atco Records, which included the single "How About That." After the release of the album, Colwell was replaced by bassist Rick Wills, who had played with Foreigner. In 1993, they released the live album *The Best of Bad Company Live ... What You Hear Is What You Get.* In his *Entertainment Weekly* review, Tom Sinclair wrote, "The playing is rock solid, all the hits ("Can't Get Enough," "Feel Like Makin' Love") are here, and singer Brian Howe does a fine imitation of the departed Paul Rodgers."

Reverted to Simplistic Style

Bad Company continued its series of member changes in 1995. Howe left the band and was replaced by singer Robert Hart. The new formation released their first studio album in three years called *Company of Strangers* on EastWest Records. "It's like we're a band again now," Colwell said in the band's biography. "We all write songs, we all co-wrote songs with each other, we went in and rehearsed like a real band.... That record really helped us get back the band's original vibe."

After the release of *Company of Strangers,* Bad Company played a successful, extensive tour with co-headliner Ted Nugent. With the spark of teamwork in place, they returned to the studio the following year for the release of *Stories Told & Untold,* the first album the band ever recorded in the U.S. This release brought Bad Company's past to the forefront. The changes, struggles, and challenges returned them to the outlook they started with in the mid-1970s. "What doesn't kill you makes you stronger.... It's come full circle now—this music could have been played 20 years ago," Kirke stated in the band's biography. "It's worth all the trials and tribulations we've gone through over the years. More than worth it."

Selected discography

Bad Company, Swan Song, 1974.
Straight Shooter, Swan Song, 1975.
Run with the Pack, Swan Song, 1976.
Burnin' Sky, Swan Song, 1977.
Desolation Angels, Swan Song, 1979.
Rough Diamonds, Swan Song, 1982.
10 from 6, Atlantic Records, 1986.
Fame and Fortune, Atlantic Records, 1986.
Dangerous Age, Atlantic Records, 1988.
Holy Water, Atco Records, 1990.
Here Comes Trouble, Atco Records, 1992.
The Best of Bad Company Live ... What You Hear Is What You Get, Atco Records, 1993.
Company of Strangers, EastWest Records, 1995.
Stories Told & Untold, EastWest Records, 1996.

Sources

Books

Rees, Dafydd and Luke Crampton, editors, *Encyclopedia of Rock Stars,* DK Publishing, New York, 1996.

Periodicals

Amusement Business, May 22, 1995.
Billboard, September 7, 1974; December 27, 1986; July 14, 1990; October 3, 1992.

Entertainment Weekly, November 5, 1993; June 23, 1995.
Musician, December 1988.
Rolling Stone, August 29, 1974; June 5, 1975; July 3, 1975; April 8, 1976; May 19, 1977; October 6, 1977; May 3, 1979; September 30, 1982; August 24, 1995.
Stereo Review, December 1982.

Online

http://www.elektra.com/rock_club/badco/badco.html

—Sonya Shelton

Bananarama

Pop trio

The success of Bananarama, the British female trio, is reflected in record sales rather than press clippings. Reviled by more serious-minded critics, the group has produced an impressive number of hit songs. In fact, Bananarama made the *Guinness Book of World Records* for being second only to the Supremes among "girl groups" with Top 40 hits. Debuting with a single cover of Black Blood's "Aie A Mwana"—a song in Swahili—in 1981, the group became a London club favorite; subsequently hits including "Cruel Summer" and "Venus" lifted them to international star status. The music was lighthearted and catchy, presumably the kind of material that makes for hits but not a lengthy career.

When Bananarama toured the United States in 1989, they felt they had proven to doubters—particularly the press—that they were a legitimate musical entity. As member Sarah Dallin told the *Washington Times,* "People originally thought we wouldn't last. They thought we'd be one-hit wonders.... I think seven years' success has proved everybody wrong. We've finally got the success we deserve."

Michael Ochs Archives

For the Record . . .

Members included **Sarah Dallin** (born December 17, 1961, in Bristol, England), vocals; **Siobhan Fahey** (born September 10, 1957, in London, England), vocals; **Jacqui Sullivan** (born August 7, 1960, 1988-91); and **Keren Woodward** (born April 2, 1961, in Bristol), vocals.

Sang unaccompanied in clubs beginning in 1981; recorded first single that same year; debut album *Deep Sea Skiving* was released in 1983; band attempted lip sync performances in the United States in the early 1980s and was booed; released *Bananarama,* 1984; released *True Confessions,* 1986; released *Greatest Hits Collection,* 1988; returned with new lineup on a 1989 tour, doing truly live performances for the first time; in 1991, founding members Dallin and Woodward split with Sullivan to record as a duo; released *Pop Life,* 1991; released *Ultra-Violet,* 1996.

Addresses: *Record company*—MCG/CURB RECORDS, 47 Music Square East, Nashville, TN 37203.

Founding Bananarama members Sarah Dallin, Keren Woodward, and Siobhan Fahey were roommates before forming their singing trio. Dallin and Woodward were former schoolmates from Bristol, England, who joined up with Fahey in London. All three were 18 years old, had little money, and were devoted to the club scene. Woodward had a job with the British Broadcasting Corporation (BBC), Fahey worked for the Decca Records press office, and Dallin was a student at the London College of Fashion. They dreamed of becoming famous singers and practiced together in front of a mirror. In 1981, the young women began performing unaccompanied in pubs and clubs, and they recorded a demo. A deal with Demon Records resulted in their single "Aie A Mwana," which they recorded with former Sex Pistol—and neighbor—Paul Cook as producer. Taking a tropical cue of this first recording and the title of a favorite Roxy Music song, "Pajamarama," the trio created the name Bananarama.

In 1982 the trio was recruited to sing backup for Fun Boy Three on "It Ain't What You Do, It's The Way That You Do It." This catchy tune was a springboard for Bananarama, and was quickly followed by their own Top five hits "He Was Really Sayin' Something" and "Shy Boy." In early 1983 the group continued their hit string with a cover of Steam's "Na Na Hey Hey (Kiss Him Goodbye)" and "Cruel Summer," tracks from their debut album *Deep Sea Skiving.* Susan Whitall described the unpretentious appeal of Bananarama during the early 1980s in the *Detroit News,* saying "Their voices were thinner than their lithe figures, but somehow the combination of flash English clothes, cocky club kid attitude and those wickedly insistent melodies managed to introduce a welcome party mood to the drab post-punk England music scene." Whitehall continued to explain the attraction of songs such as "Venus" and "Really Saying Something" when she remarked, "Both are shallow—even vanilla-flavored, but there's something hypnotic about three identical girlish voices singing in unison."

The group bolstered their popularity with videos and public performances. *Melody Maker* writer Caroline Sullivan noted, "Their ramshackle conception coincided with the dawn of video and it turned out to be a sublime match. Video was the only medium suitable for conveying theshambling savoir vivre that was the essence of Bananarama." U.S. audiences were rather shocked, however, when Bananarama lip-synced during an early New York gig; in fact, the women were booed off the stage. *New York Times* critic Jon Pareles disapproved of a similar if less wholesale technique used during a 1989 performance. He marveled, "It didn't seem to bother anyone but a lone, cranky critic that the drum kit was untouched until five songs into the set, or that the backup vocals (and it seemed, some of the lead vocals as well) were on tape along with the beat." This kind of response has diminished Bananarama's appeal to American concert goers, but is more accepted by audiences elsewhere. That explained why the 1989 tour featured a five-piece band, elaborate costumes, and dancers, elements that seemed out of place in the rather small U.S. venues where Bananarama performed; in other countries the trio played big concert halls. Woodward explained in the *Detroit News,* "in England and the rest of the world, it doesn't matter if you're a studio band."

Reviewers have questioned whether the driving force behind Bananarama is its members or their producers. Such criticism has resulted in a rocky relationship between the band and the press. The charge angers Woodward, who told the *Detroit News* "it's easier to be taken as brainless if you're even remotely attractive. It took us years before anyone would take us seriously." While the group has done its share of covers, the women do write their own songs, with Dallin serving as the main lyric writer. Perhaps in an effort to be taken more seriously, the group recorded message songs such as "Rough Justice" and "Hotline to Heaven" in the mid-1980s. The detour was short-lived, and the group returned to producing upbeat pop music.

The 1989 Bananarama tour featured a new lineup, following the departure of Fahey, who married Eurythmics member Dave Stewart and moved to Los Angeles. Fahey was replaced by Jacqui Sullivan, an old friend of Woodward and Dallin. When Fahey formed a new band, Shakespeare's Sister, and received some critical plums, it initially caused hard feelings among the former roommates. Woodward remarked in *Melody Maker,* "I think for a while [Siobhan] tried to forget her past and everything that went with it, socially and careerwise. In a way, she tried to justify what she was doing by trivialising what we stood for." In 1991, replacement Sullivan left the band, and Dallin and Woodward now record as a duo.

The remaining members of Bananarama sound as if they are coming to terms with being a popular if not critical success. They seem confident without taking themselves too seriously. Dallin commented in the *Washington Times* "I'm a talented entertainer, but I don't have the best voice in the world. I love to entertain people." With 14 Top 40 hits, Bananarama certainly has entertained an enormous audience. As Caroline Sullivan summarized in *Melody Maker,* "Bananarama are enshrined in the consciousness of a generation. They've got a huge hit-catalogue that defines the term purest pop. They've got wit, flair and great shoulders. What they haven't got is credibility." The credibility gap, however, isn't stopping Dallin and Woodward from continuing to make their own brand of infectious pop. A *Billboard* review of a 1995 single showed that Bananarama's appeal really hasn't changed, describing "Every Shade of Blue" as perfect fare for Bananarama fans and a "guilty pleasure" for others.

Selected discography

Deep Sea Skiving, London, 1983.
Bananarama, London, 1984.
True Confessions, 1986, Razor & Tie, reissued, 1995.
Greatest Hits Collection, London, 1988.
Pop Life, PGD/Polygram, 1991.
Ultra-Violet, WEA/Atlantic/Curb, 1996.

Sources

Periodicals

Detroit News, March 27, 1989, pp. B1-B2.
Melody Maker, July 1990, pp. 42-43.
New York Times, April 9, 1989.
Washington Times, April 23, 1989, p. E1.

Online

Curb Records Web site at www.curb.com.

—Paula Pyzik Scott

The Bangles

New-wave group

At the height of their fame, the Bangles appeared on the cover of *Rolling Stone* and opened for Queen; ten years later, they had faded into relative obscurity and remain synonymous with eighties new-wave pop stardom. Originally a neo-folkish Southern California act, the Bangles rose to prominence with a passel of songs written for them that they were savvy enough to brand with their own stamp. The doe-eyed prettiniess and solo ambitions of lead singer Susanna Hoffs spelled doom for the ensemble, however, and they disbanded before the decade ended.

The Bangles formed in 1981 when Hoffs, a recent University of California at Berkeley graduate, answered a classified ad in a Los Angeles-area newspaper for musicians interested in the Beatles, Byrds, and Buffalo Springfield. Hoffs had done some experimental music while studying art in college, and found when she met the two sisters who had placed the ad, Debbi and Vicki Peterson, that they had much in common. All three, plus a bass player named Annette Zilinskas, were products of suburban Southern California and shared a love of girl-group harmonies combined with sharp, melodic guitars. The called themselves the Supersonic Bangs, then changed it to the Bangs, and put out a single on a label they formed themselves.

Another group was already using the "Bangs" name, so the quartet metamorphed once more into the Bangles. Vicki Peterson's guitar talent emerged as the glue behind their sound, a style she had honed in the late 1970s playing in a band called the Fans. Initially the Bangles mixed some early songwriting forays with covers of Sixties classics for their live shows, but it was the novelty of an all-female act that attracted rabid fans, not their versions of Bob Dylan songs. Young men used to follow them into the bathroom so they could watch them change. Things improved somewhat when they signed a management deal with Miles Copeland of IRS Records, and were booked to open for the Beat (later known as the English Beat). Faulty Products, an IRS subsidiary that soon went under, released the EP *The Bangles* in June of 1982. Despite the business setback, the EP helped the band secure a deal with CBS/Columbia Records in 1983. They were considered part of the "Paisley Revival," a reflowering of the flower-power era that was sweeping the Southern California music scene.

Bassist Zilinskas dropped out around 1983, and was replaced by Michael Steele, formerly with the seminal punk band the Runaways. The Bangles' first full-length album was released in August of 1984, and the big money behind their label meant a big-money producer, David Kahne (responsible, among other million-sellers, for Sugar Ray's 1997 hit "Fly"). *All Over the Place* sold a respectable number of copies and was roundly praised by critics. The *Trouser Press Record Guide* asserted it had "everything a pop album needs: exceptional harmony vocals, catchy, memorable and intelligent tunes and a full dose of rock 'n' roll guitar energy."

The Bangles' follow-up, however, would place them in chart history. The Artist FormerlyKnown as Prince liked their sound so much he sent them a tape, and the band recorded one of its tracks and released it as a single in March of 1986. "Manic Monday" soon hit number two on the U.S. singles charts, and the album it was included on, *Different Light* also reached the number two spot on the album charts. Another single, "If She Knew What She Wants," written for them by Jules Shear, also charted, though not as spectacularly as its predecessor. "When we approach a song we didn't write, we want to Banglesize it," Vicki Peterson told *Time*'s Jay Cocks, who then explained to readers that to "Banglesize" involves "working out an arrangement that rocks hard but falls short of a sonic mugging, then concentrating on a vocal sounds that seems to have floated from a car radio lost somewhere in the `60s ozone." Not all critics found *Different Light* to their liking, however: *People* reviewer David Hiltbrand skewered *Different Light*—in comparison to their first record—and declared that it provides evidence that the quartet "have neither the talent nor the density of expression to get away with a very weighty approach."

For the Record . . .

Members include **Susanna Hoffs** (born January 17, 1957, Newport Beach, CA; daughter of Joshua [a psychoanalyst] and Tamar Simon [a screenwriter and film director] Hoffs; received degree in art from the University of California at Berkeley, 1980; married M. Jay Roach [a television producer]; children: Jackson), rhythm guitar, lead vocals; **Debbi Peterson** (born August 22, 1961, Los Angeles, CA), drums, vocals; **Vicki Peterson** (born January 11, 1958, Los Angeles, CA; daughter of an aerospace engineer and a homemaker; attended the University of California at Los Angeles for two years), lead guitar, vocals; **Annette Zilinskas** (born November 6, 1964, Van Nuys, CA), bass; Zilinskas was replaced by **Michael Steele** (born June 2, 1954; daughter of a businessperson and homemaker) in 1983, bass and vocals.

Formed in 1981 as the Supersonic Bangs; changed name to Bangs; released "Getting Out of Hand" on Downkiddie, December 1981; changed name to Bangles, January 1982; signed with IRS subsidiary Faulty Products and were booked to open for the English Beat; signed to CBS/Columbia Records, 1983; "Manic Monday" reached number two on U.S. singles charts in 1986; released final LP *Everything,* December 1988; disbanded September 1989.

Awards: BRIT Award for Best International Group, 1987.

Address: Record company—Columbia Records, 2100 Colorado Ave., Santa Monica, CA 94040, (310) 449-2100.

Despite the sniping, the Bangles were an instant success with the media: simultaneously quip-worthy and photogenic. Meanwhile, their male fan base had swelled to international proportions. "We're the female version of Wham!" Steele told *People* magazine in 1986; that same year *Time* magazine devoted an entire page to the Bangles, where Cocks praised them for "a sensual appeal that is insinuating and disarming at once." Yet their final coup on *Different Light* came in late 1986 with a third single, "Walk Like an Egyptian." It was a song that Toni Basil (of 1982 "Mickey" fame) had turned it down. Done by the Bangles, it spent four weeks at number one on the U.S. charts.

The Bangles' fall from grace began in the spring of 1987 with the release of *The Allnighter,* a B-movie written, produced, and directed by Tamar Simon Hoffs, Susanna's mother. Scenes of the Bangles lead singer cavorting naked in one scene brought snickers from the music establishment, and the film bombed at the box-office despite its star attraction. Yet once more, the band found success with a song they had not written, the Simon & Garfunkel classic "Hazy Shade of Winter." It was a single released on the Def Jam label, and was part of the soundtrack to the 1987 film *Less Than Zero,* adapted from the novel of the same name about jaded California youth. The Bangles' version hit number two in February of 1988. Later that year, their final LP, *Everything,* was released with nowhere near the success of its predecessor. One song co-written by Hoffs, "In Your Room," did well on the charts, as did "Eternal Flame," which she also co-wrote.

Enshrined as Eighties Icons

In the summer of 1989, the group released the compilation *Greatest Hits,* then called it quits. It was widely assumed that Hoffs' wish to pursue a solo career was behind the split, but she has enjoyed little success since. In 1991 she released *When You're a Boy* (a nod to the 1979 David Bowie song "Boys Keep Swinging"), which did somewhat better on the British charts (number 56) than it did on the U.S. (number 83), later contributed a cut to the soundtrack to the film *Buffythe Vampire Slayer,* and released *Susanna Hoffs* in 1996. Like her first effort, it was overwhelmingly ignored, though *Entertainment Weekly* did call Hoffs "a throat lozenge in a world of jagged little pills."

The other Bangles members are still involved in the music industry. Vicki Peterson plays in the Continental Drifters, and took Charlotte Caffey's place in the 1994 Go-Go reunion tour. Her sister Debbi recorded with Kindred Spirit and Siobhan Maher. Steele has been involved in a musical project called Eyesore. Hoffs has since married a television producer and in 1995 the couple had a son, Jackson. The Bangles have no plans to reunite.

Selected discography

"Getting out of Hand" (single), Downkiddie, 1981.
Bangles (EP), Faulty, 1982.
All Over the Place, Columbia, 1984.
Different Light, Columbia, 1985.
Everything, Columbia, 1988.
The Bangles Greatest Hits, Columbia, 1990.

Sources

Books

Rees, Dafydd and Luke Crampton, *Encyclopedia of Rock Stars,* DK Publishing, 1996.

Weisbard, Eric with Craig Marks (editors), *Spin Alternative Record Guide,* Vintage Books, 1995.

Periodicals

Entertainment Weekly, September 27, 1996, p. 30.

People, February 10, 1986, p. 22; April 28, 1986, pp. 52-54; June 8, 1987, pp. 46-47.

Time, April 14, 1986, p. 98.

Online

http://ubl.com (The Ultimate Band List)

http://www.banglesfan.demon.co.uk

http://www.trouserpress.com

—Carol Brennan

Gato Barbieri

Jazz musician, saxophone

AP/Wide World Photos

By combining the experimental jazz styles of the 1960s and his own Latin roots, Gato Barbieri has etched a place for himself in the music world as an individual character well known in Europe and the Americas. Critics have compared Barbieri with both John Coltrane and his contemporary Pharoah Sanders; but the tenorman would prefer to be likened to the rock group Santana and Motown R&B singer Marvin Gaye instead. "When I play, I try to sing without words," says the man made internationally famous for his score on the controversial film *Last Tango In Paris.* Barbieri has always seen himself as different from the rest of his contemporaries—as an intense yet mercurial creature, whereby he derived his Spanish nickname which means "cat". And as a cat, he's lived many lives as a musician during his long career, having moved from being an avant garde youth, to a cultural/political figure, to a thriving pop jazz artist in his recent comeback.

Gato was born Leandro Barbieri in 1934 in Rosario, Argentina into a musical family. He began his own artistic journey as a child by taking up the clarinet at age twelve, after hearing "Now's The Time" by jazz legend Charlie "Bird" Parker. At the age of thirteen, Barbieri's family moved to Buenos Aires, after which the young musician moved on to alto saxophone. Initially rejecting the music of his native land, Barbieri followed the influences of the American greats John Coltrane and Charlie Parker; whose methods reached the fledgling South American jazz scene.

Barbieri soon managed to join the roster of Lalo Schifrin's popular band, at first playing alto saxophone. After developing his own feeling and proficiency from his gigs with the band, Barbieri switched from alto to tenor sax; with that solid change in order he departed from Schifrin's ensemble and subsequently began his own. He spent a few years playing in Argentina, often with visiting American artists, and then decided to leave when the jazz scene fizzled out in his native land. This oscillation between the U.S. and his home country would soon become a pattern for Barbieri, paralleling his many changes in adoption of musical styles.

With his Italian-bred wife, Michelle, Barbieri packed up his sax and moved to Rome, Italy in 1962. His reputation began to grow there as he became a fixture of the city's chic club circuit, but Barbieri and his wife were far less than happy in this new environment. Many of Barbieri's contemporaries held the prejudiced assumption that a "real" jazz performer had to be a black man, and with his Italian last name and white skin, Barbieri was not well received by many other musicians who told him that he'd never make it. Not one to let such

For the Record . . .

Born **Leandro Barbieri** November 28, 1934, Rosario, Argentina; wife Michelle' nicknamed "Gato", Spanish for cat. Considered a political activist for the Latin American albums on Impulse! Records. Resided in Argentina, New York and Rome. Education: Studied clarinet at age 12; private lessons for alto sax, composition and clarinet for five years before switching to tenor sax.

Member of Lalo Schifrin's Band in Argentina (alto/tenor sax) at age 20; member of Don Cherry Band in Europe (tenor sax) 1963-65; released first solo album *In Search of Mystery,* 1967; released *Third World,* 1970 and *Fenix,* 1971 on Flying Dutchman Records; *Last Tango In Paris* soundtrack released, 1972; well-received *Latin America* "Chapters" fused South American rhythms with modern jazz; best selling album *Caliente* released, produced by Herb Alpert brought crossover to smooth jazz, 1976; makes his "comeback" recording *Que Pasa?,* 1997.

Awards: Grammy for 1972's *Last Tango In Paris* soundtrack.

Addresses: *Record company*—Columbia Records, 51 West 52nd Street, New York, NY, 10019.

affronts affect him, Barbieri continued to bolster his confidence and style until band leader Don Cherry turned the tide by adding the Argentine to his group in 1963.

Don Cherry was a well-known trumpeter and free form band leader playing in Paris whose group worked to break the old views of "black jazz" by incorporating an assortment of cultural backgrounds into one band. The cosmopolitan status of Cherry's outfit testifies to such a strategy, as it comprised one German member, one Italian, the Argentine Barbieri, and a French bass player. Barbieri quickly made Europe his home, as did many jazz-loving expatriates at the time, and adopted Cherry as his personal mentor for a few formative free-style years, which resulted in two albums that came out in 1966. Barbieri played tenor sax on Cherry's *Symphony for Improvisers* along with Pharoah Sanders, with whom he has constantly been compared to ever since, and followed up with Cherry's *Complete Communion.* Both albums have been regarded to be classics in improvisational recordings, marked by a sound that merges discord with an underlying understanding of harmony.

While the working relationship with Cherry did not end on a sour note, the restless Barbieri and his wife moved to New York City in 1965 to pursue his solo career. Following the social reform movements going on within black culture of this time, Barbieri began to embrace his own roots and incorporate the sounds of his native South America into his stylings. "So slowly, slowly, I changed," Barbieiri says of his blending. His tenor reached warmer textures, thicker coloring, smoothing out the shrieking intensity of earlier practice. "Many people are concerned about technique but I'm concerned about sound," he told *Downbeat* magazine. To wit, Barbieri's approach to sound is just as unique as the experimental and native roots he ties together. He prefers to use a tight mouthpiece, a Berg Larson 105 instead of the open 130 Otto Link that Coltrane used, and plays on a one and a half or number two reed instead of the usual four or five.

In 1967 Barbieri's first solo album *In Search of Mystery* was released on ESP records. In keeping with the experimental jazz of the times, the album has been called by one critic "screechy ... not necessarily a bad thing," and eschewed the more pop oriented, listener-friendly quality found in the works of earlier Coltrane albums, for example. After the fairly inauspicious release of *Mystery,* Barbieri appeared playing guest spots on a number of avant-garde styled big band albums before signing on to the Flying Dutchman label in 1969. Here he found his true voice on the record *Third World* which brought into fruition the Latin American impulses Gato had recently embraced, partly inspired by the behest of Brazilian filmmaker Glauber Rocha. Enriched by the collaboration of established jazz artists Charlie Haden and Roswell Rudd, this album has been ranked as one of Barbieri's essential works.

Following *Third World*'s creative success , Barbieri returned to Argentina to continue studying the sounds of his roots, and by 1971 his Flying Dutchman release *Fenix* demonstrates a rounding out of the Barbieri style, filled with Brazilian and Caribbean sounds. However, once again Barbieri was pulled away from working in his homeland toward Europe, and the success he found there nearly eradicated his newly found roots sensibility, and in retrospect *Third World* seems like a nostalgic farewell to traditional Argentinian rhythms.

Although Barbieri was well aware of the controversial nature of the project, he was quick to accept Italian film director Bernardo Bertolucci's invitation to score his movie *Last Tango In Paris.* Although he had done a few soundtracks in Argentina and Europe before the 1972 film, Bertolucci's risqué movie achieved enough fame for Barbieri to be heard by a larger audience, and consequently made him an "overnight success." The *Last Tango* soundtrack blended the traditional Argentinian tango with a shimmering, European flavor which perfectly captured the doomed romantic essence of the story and images it underscores. The album snared Barbieri a Grammy Award for Best Original Soundtrack, and soon popular artists such as Herb Alpert and Willie Mitchell were adding the film's theme to their repertoires. However, partly due to the fleeting nature of public taste and partly to yet another disenchantment with the European scene, Barbieri's status as a celebrity was relatively short lived.

Became a Radio-Friendly Artist

In 1973 Gato returned again to South America, first to Buenos Aires, then to Rio de Janeiro, Brazil. He recorded a series of four albums he calls "chapters" for ABC Impulse—his style having become outside the realm of the more conservative Flying Dutchman—which utilized native musicians and instruments, and reflected the tumultuous air that characterized the politically charged South America of the 1970s. "There was an almost overloaded thickness to the music," said a *Downbeat* critic of this period, "a texture of electric and acoustic, ancient, and modern instruments." But it was his 1976 pop and jazz hybrid album *Caliente* that brought him back to the pubic eye. Flying Dutchman and Impulse went out of business and popular horn-virtuoso Herb Alpert, founder of A&M Records, picked up the tenorman to play Santana and Marvin Gaye songs on his label. In yet another shift of milieu, Barbieri quickly moved from being an eclectic synthesizer of styles to a radio friendly artist. *Caliente* sold 225,000 copies, and became his most popular-selling album.

Barbieri would remain known throughout the eighties as a jazz pop artist, and during the years 1982-97 Gato took time off from creating in order to re-evaluate his style and identity. Since his move into the pop terrain, Barbieri had lost much of his critical viability, and this creative hiatus may in part be seen as a reaction to this, but more likely reflects personal issues. Suddenly, in 1995, only several months after the death of his wife and manager Michelle, Barbieri had a heart attack. Barbieri and his wife had been inseparable, and kept each other company in a life they had called "self-contained" and "insulated". Deeply bereaved, he returned to the only other constant in his life, his saxophone, to initiate a comeback with the release of the 1997 album *Que Pasa?.* Blending in perfectly alongside a new generation of popular "smooth jazz" artists Barbieri's earlier helped engender, *Que Pasa?,* in the words of *Billboard* magazine's Jim Macnie, "stresses the hallmark of Barbieri's work: a fervent attack and commitment to melody." Gato is a name the artist took to describe his intensity, but the name takes on new meaning when looking back on his career from the vantage point of his return to recording. Cats have seven lives for Argentineans and nine for Americans, and Barbieri's penchant for reinvention has indeed allowed a similar longevity.

Selected discography

Symphony For Improviser (with Don Cherry), Blue Note, 1966.
Complete Communion, (with Don Cherry) Blue Note, 1966.
In Search of Mystery, ESP Records, 1967.
Third World, Flying Dutchman, 1970.
Fenix, Flying Dutchman, 1971.
Last Tango In Paris (soundtrack), United Artists, 1972.
Chapter 1: Latin America, Impulse!, 1973.
Chapter 2: Latin America, Impulse!, 1973.
Chapter 3: Viva Emiliano Zapata, Impulse!, 1974.
Chapter 4: Alive In New York, Impulse!, 1975.
Que Pasa, 1997, Colombia/Sony.

Sources

Periodicals

Billboard, April 12, 1997.
Downbeat, May 1974; April, 1977
Essence, August 1978.

Online

http://members.aol.com/ilebaba/adeleke/barbieri.html

—Shaun Frentner

Black Flag

Punk band

AP/wide World Photos

Hailed as America's first hardcore punk band, Black Flag developed its aggressive Sex Pistols-inspired sound into an in-your-face, experimental rock band. The group formed its own record label, SST Records, and helped other similarly styled bands rise to success in the genre. Black Flag dissolved in 1986, yet several of the members continued their careers in music with various groups.

The seeds of Black Flag were planted in 1976, when guitarist Greg Ginn formed a band called Panic with singer Keith Morris. They set out to perform music far from the mainstream style of the time. "I felt that the pop music world was just people trying to make three-minute commercials," Ginn told Robin Tolleson in *Down Beat,* "and I didn't have much use for that." The following year, they recruited Chuck Dukowski on bass and Brian Migdol on drums, and began performing. In 1978, the group found out that another band already had the name Panic. So Ginn's brother Ray suggested the name Black Flag and proceeded to design their logo.

After they faced repeated rejection from record labels, the members of Black Flag decided to release their music through their own label, SST Records. The label grew to sign other bands, and became a well-known independent label that lasted for years past the demise of Black Flag. In 1978, the band released their first EP called *Nervous Breakdown.* By the end of that year, Morris had left the band and went on to form another punk rock band called the Circle Jerks. (On the *Everything Went Black* recordings, Black Flag credited Morris under the name Johnny "Bob" Goldstein.)

Ron Reyes, former singer for the Happy Tampons, joined the group as the new singer, but used the name Chavo Pederast. Not long after, Migdol left the group and was replaced by Robo on drums. The new lineup released the *Jealous Again* EP in 1980, followed by an extensive tour. Reyes quit the band at one of their shows, two songs into the set. Black Flag went several months without a singer, until they found Dez Cadena. With another lineup in place, they recorded and released the *EP Six Pack.*

Once again plagued with member changes, Cadena decided to step down as the group's singer when his voice became too strained on the road. He stayed with the group as a rhythm guitarist, and set out to help find his replacement. Henry Rollins, singer for the band S.O.A., met with the band and audition in New York. He became the final lead singer for Black Flag.

The band released their first full-length album, *Damaged,* and headed out on tour. During most of their shows,

For the Record . . .

Members include **Chuck Dukowski** (born February 1, 1954, Los Angeles, California), replaced by **Kira Roessler** (born August 13, 1962, New Haven, Connecticut), bass; **Greg Ginn** (born June 8, 1954, Phoenix, Arizona), guitar; **Anthony Martinez,** drums (replaced Bill Stevenson); **Henry Rollins** (born Henry Garfield, February 13, 1961, Washington, D.C.), vocals; **Bill Stevenson** (born September 10, 1963, Torrance, California), drums.

Band formed as Panic, 1976; changed name to Black Flag, 1978; formed SST Records and released debut EP, *Nervous Breakdown,* 1978; released first full-length album, *Damaged,* 1981; recorded eight more albums, 1984-1986; appeared in the documentary *Decline of Western Civilization,* 1985; disbanded, 1986.

Address: *Record company*—SST Records, Box 1, Lawndale, CA; phone (310) 430-7687; fax (310) 430-7286.

Rollins performed without a shirt, displaying his many tattoos. He soon became known as the "illustrated man of rock." Because of Black Flag's aggressive style and appearance, the group was often stereotyped as violent, over-the-top rebelrockers. Yet a closer look at the band uncovered the fact that Rollins and Ginn didn't drink alcohol or take any drugs. Ginn was also a vegetarian. "Our whole thing has been made out to be brutal, fascistic, and violent," Rollins told Michael Goldberg in *Rolling Stone.* "Those are three things that we're very much not into at all. We're not violent. We're not evil. We don't like to see anybody hurt at any time."

After the release of *Damaged,* Black Flag embarked on another long tour. As they were getting ready to leave for a series of concerts in the U.K., Robo was detained by customs and not allowed to accompany the band on the tour. At the last minute, the group asked Descendants' drummer Bill Stevenson to take Robo's place in the U.K. When Black Flag returned to the U.S., Robo had decided to leave the group and join the Misfits.

Before their next release, the group went through two more drummers — Emil and Chuck Biscuits — in as many years. Biscuits was dismissed from the band for undisclosed reasons, but went on to join Samhain and then Danzig. In 1983, Stevenson became Black Flag's new drummer. The 1983 retrospective collection *Everything Went Black* included songs from 1978 to 1981, through the groups various incarnations. The member roster hadn't quite solidified yet, however. Cadena left the group to form DC3, and Dukowski split with the band to form SWA. Dukowski did continue to work for SST Records, and later became Black Flag's manager.

Developed New Sound and Image

In 1984, the band began its prolific period. Ginn played bass in the studio under the name Dale Nixon, until they could find another bass player. They released another collection called *The First Four Years* before embarking on a marathon of recording and touring. With *My War,* they changed both their appearance with longer haircuts and musical style to slightly slower tempos, shocking many of their fans. The shift resulted in an expansion of their popularity and recognition.

Before their next 1984 release, they had enlisted Kira Roessler (the sister of 45 Grave keyboardist Paul Roessler) as their new bass player. This lineup became the most recognized member roster of Black Flag after their conclusion. Before the end of the year, the group released three more albums, *Slip It In, Family Man,* and *Live '84.* Rollins had begun to establish himself as a spoken word artist and poet. (He often did readings with Exene from the band X.) On *Family Man,* Rollins read his poetry on one side of the album, and the group recorded all instrumental tracks on the other. In 1984, Rollins also established his own book publishing company named after his birthdate 2.13.61.

Besides releasing multiple albums in 1984, Black Flag also performed 200 shows across the U.S. They toured the country in a beat-up van. After they paid their road crew expenses, the members usually ended up living on about $12.50 a day. Undaunted by the hardships and lack of compensation that went along with their tours, the group continued a grueling schedule. "We are the hungriest band I've ever seen," Rollins told Michael Goldberg in *Rolling Stone.* "I've neverseen a band who would go to any lengths to play like we will."

The group continued their fast pace through 1985. They appeared in Penelope Spheeris' *The Decline of Western Civilization,* a documentary on the rise of the Los Angeles punk rock scene. They went on to release three albums that year: *Loose Nut, The Process of Weeding Out,* and *In My Head.* The group experimented with an all-instrumental format on *The Process of Weeding Out,* which didn't include Rollins. Charles M. Young described the 1985 Black Flag approach in *Playboy,*

"These guys just look at how dismal your life is and promise to kill you for it.... The trick in listening is just to go with it, and pretty soon, you'll be angry about your dismal life, instead of merely depressed."

By the end of the year, Ginn had asked Stevenson to leave the band because of musical differences. Stevenson rejoined the Descendants, which later became the band All. In the meantime, Black Flag recruited drummer Anthony Martinez. In 1986, they released their final album, *Who's Got the 10 ½?* Not long afterward, Black Flag disbanded. Ginn said he had decided that punk rock no longer fit in to the music scene.

Ginn had already begun working with another band called Gone when Black Flag dissolved. He continued to run SST Records, and recorded solo albums into the 1990s. Rollins formed the Rollins Band and continued his publishing company and spoken word career. He also pursued acting and appeared in movies like *Johnny Mnemonic, The Chase,* and *Heat.* SST Records released two more Black Flag albums after the group broke up: *Wasted ... Again,* a compilation of Black Flag favorites, in 1987, and *I Can See You,* which included unreleased tracks from the 1984-85 era, in 1989.

In spite of Black Flag's volatility with so many member changes, the group managed to make its mark in rock music. They helped define the American genre of hardcore, and inspired many of the rebellious, hard-edged bands that followed—in the 1980s and beyond.

Selected discography

Nervous Breakdown, EP, SST Records, 1978.
Jealous Again, EP, SST Records, 1980.
Six Pack, EP, SST Records, 1980.
Damaged, SST Records, 1981.
Everything Went Black, SST Records, 1983.
The First Four Years, SST Records, 1984.
My War, SST Records, 1984.
Slip It In, SST Records, 1984.
Family Man, SST Records, 1984.
Live '84, SST Records, 1984.
Loose Nut, SST Records, 1985.
The Process of Weeding Out, SST Records, 1985.
In My Head, SST Records, 1985.
Who's Got the 10 ½?, SST Records, 1986.
Wasted ... Again, SST Records, 1987.
I Can See You, SST Records, 1989.

Sources

Books

Rees, Dafydd, and Luke Crampton, eds. *Encyclopedia of Rock Stars,* DK Publishing, New York, 1996.

Periodicals

Down Beat, December 1984, May 1988.
Guitar Player, June 1989.
Musician, January 1987.
Playboy, November 1985.
Rolling Stone, July 18, 1985.
Whole Earth Review, Spring 1989.

Online

http://www.ipass.net/~jthrush/flagline.htm

—*Sonya Shelton*

Bluegrass Patriots

Bluegrass band

The five members of the Bluegrass Patriots have been together since 1980 and remain passionately devoted to bluegrass music eighteen years after they formed their band. The band is comprised of baritone singer and banjo player Ken Seaman, baritone/lead singer and bass/Dobro/guitar player Rick Bradstreet, lead/tenor and bass player Dan Rogers, lead singer and guitarist Glenn Zankey, and lead/harmonies singer and mandolin player Willie McDonald. Joe Ross of *Bluegrass Unlimited* wrote, "Energy, enthusiasm, tasteful instrumentation, and good singing—the Bluegrass Patriots have developed a show incorporating these elements of a successful bluegrass band."

The band's members share a common love for bluegrass music, which is what has kept them happily together for almost two decades. They all sing and work outside of the band. Zankey and Bradstreet are carpenters, McDonald owns a house-painting business, Rogers is a former bar-owner who owns a carpet cleaning business, and Seaman teaches grades four through eight in a small mountain elementary school in Red Feather Lakes, Colorado.

Seaman, born and raised in the Ozark Mountain community of Eminence, Missouri, was influenced by Bill Monroe in the late 1940s and 1950s. He told Ross, "His music spun around in my head for days. I soon bought a guitar." Other musical influences for Seaman include Flatt and Scruggs, Jimmy Martin, Don Brown and the Ozark Mountain Trio, the Dillards, and Reno and Smiley. Seaman used to cut afternoon classes at Eminence High School in order to drive his father's '51 Buick to a local hill high enough to bring in a bluegrass radio show called the "Hickory Hollar Show," broadcasting out of Salem, Missouri in the late 1950s. Seaman founded the Ozark Mountain Bluegrass Festival held in Eminence, on the 4th of July before moving to Colorado in 1975.

Zankey, originally from Pittsburgh, Pennsylvania, didn't hear much bluegrass until the late 1960s; he cites Doc Watson, the Monroe Doctrine, City Limits, the Lee Brothers, Everybody and His Brother, the bluegrass Cardinals, Doyle Lawson and Quicksilver, Tim O'Brien, Ricky Scaggs, Del McCoury, and the Highstrung String Band as influences. Zankey's unique, "high lonesome" singing is a band trademark, and it was this distinctive bluegrass style of singing that initially attracted him to bluegrass.

Bradstreet, born in Sioux City, Iowa, and moved to Emporia, Kansas, as a teenager. He started playing banjo when he was fifteen, and is considered to be the group's most adept multi-instrumental musician—although all band members can play five or six bluegrass instruments. Bradstreet is a self-taught musician who loves to flatpick. His musical influences include Doc Watson, Norman Blake, Dan Crary, Bob Wills, Sonny Terry, Brownie McGee, Spike Jones, Homer and Jethro, the Geezenslaw Brothers, the Red Clay Ramblers, and the Allman Brothers. Bradstreet, a.k.a. "Ranger Rick," won the Colorado State Flatpicking Championship in both 1980 and 1981and has contributed material to commercials.

Willie McDonald, a songwriter from Burlington, Vermont, cites the Johnson Mountain Boys, the Bluegrass cardinals, Quicksilver, Larry Sparks, Herschel Sizemore, and J.D. Crowe as musical influences. Danny Rogers, a native of Fort Collins, CO, sings tenor or high leads with the band and plays bass. He sang hymns and church music as a child, learned to play the guitar by time he was 13, and was in a high school band—as the guitar player and singer—called The Torquays. His musical influences include Del McCoury who, he told Ross, "typifies the friendly, down-home feeling that is at the very roots of bluegrass." Other influences were the Country Blueboys, the Country Gazette, Ralph Stanley, the Country Gentlemen, Tim O'Brien, Keith Whitley, Doyle Lawson, the Johnson Mountain Boys, Red Knuckles and the Trailblazers, and the Monroe Doctrine.

The current group was formed in the fall of 1980—Zankey is the only leftover from the original band from

For the Record . . .

Members include **Rick Bradstreet** (Sioux City, IA), bass, Dobro, guitar and vocals; **Dan Rogers** (born Fort Collins, CO), bass and vocals; **Ken Seaman** (born Eminence, MS), banjo, vocals; **Glen Zankey** (born Pittsburgh, PA), guitar, vocals. All band members live in Fort Collins, CO;

Willie McDonald; Zankey and Bradstreet are carpenters, McDonald owns a house-painting business, Rogers is a former bar-owner who owns a carpet cleaning business, and Seaman teaches grades four through eight in a small mountain elementary school in Red Feather Lakes; CO.

Slowly began booking Midwestern festivals in 1981, by 1982 most of their summer weekends were spent performing; released their self-titled debut album 1984; released *Someone New*, 1986; *When You and I Were Young, Maggie,* 1990; released *The Last Waltz,* in 1993; *E Pluribus Bluegrass,* 1996.

Awards: Rick Bradstreet was the Colorado State Flatpicking Champion in 1980 and 1981; *The Last Waltz* made the National Bluegrass Survey in 1996.

Address: *Manager*— Patriot Management, 1807 Essex Drive, Fort Collins, CO 80526; (970) 482-0863. *E-mail*—MCS@riverside.com. *Website*—http://www.banjo.com/Profiles/BluegrassPatriots.html

1979-80. The band played only at weddings, local parties, and pubs for over a year. They slowly began booking Midwestern festivals in 1981 and by 1982 most of their summer weekends were spent performing. The Bluegrass Patriots released their self-titled debut album in 1984, which included numerous lesser-known traditional bluegrass songs, as well as two originals by mandolinist Willie McDonald. Two years later they released *Someone New,* which also featured original material. Their second release highlighted their musical diversity, with a nod to the influences of Jim Orchard and Don and Bessie Brown. The band released *When You and I Were Young, Maggie* in 1990 after an inspiring and overwhelmingly successful trip to Ireland. *The Last Waltz* was released three years after in 1993 and made the National Bluegrass Survey, and *E Pluribus Bluegrass* was released in 1996. McDonald told Frank Overstreet of *Bluegrass Music News,* "We have a good mix between the old and new songs....we all write songs for our records, but of equal importance is finding those obscure "chestnuts," such as "When You and I Were Young, Maggie" and "The Last Waltz".

It's this respect for the tried-and-true standards combined with the ability to pen enduring original material that underscores the band's success. Ross wrote, "The music played by the Bluegrass Patriots appeals to young and old alike ... the band has not compromised it's traditional sound to appeal to a different market." Seaman told Ross, "Diversity is the strength of bluegrass music. There is plenty of room for innovation and new directions in the music, but I hope that bluegrass always remains acoustic with basically the same instrumentation as we have had since its inception."

Performing Is a Labor of Love

By the time the band had released their fourth album, the Bluegrass Patriots relied mostly upon their own material—but when they presented bluegrass standards in concert, they infuse them with their own distinctive sound. The band is noted for emphasizing close harmonies combined with instrumental zeal, and when performing live, they sometimes include offbeat stage embellishments during songs—such as charts, stomping, and group theatrics. The groups tours festivals throughout the U.S. in a van each summer, and reserve the winter for rekindling their creativity. They begin working on new material in the spring, and by the time summer rolls around, the band's members all relish the prospect of a new festival tour. Seaman told Ross, "We like to camp in tents, pick until 3 a.m., and meet new friends," and he told Overstreet, "We want to continue to travel, spread and promote bluegrass wherever we can, and continue to play as long as it's fun." In an interview with *Bluegrass Unlimited,* Seaman told Nancy Cardwell, "People that are in the business know that part of the value isn't money. It's just flying up the road and going into a new town and meeting new people. It's that excitement there—that's what keeps us all doing it. It's in our blood, and what else can I say?"

Selected discography

Bluegrass Patriots, Bluegrass Patriots Records, 1982.
Someone New, Red Feather Records, 1986.
When You and I Were Young, Maggie, Red Feather Records, 1990.
The Last Waltz, Turquoise Records, 1996.
E Pluribus Bluegrass, Red Feather Records, 1996.

Sources

Periodicals

Bluegrass Music News, Spring 1994.
Bluegrass Unlimited, February 1996; April 1989.

Online

http://www.banjo.com/Profiles/BluegrassPatriots.html

Additional source material was provided by band members.

—B. Kimberly Taylor

Andrea Bocelli

Opera singer

AP/Wide World Photos

Multi-platinum-selling Italian tenor Andrea Bocelli reached a mainstream pop audience with his beautiful opera renditions after a film of his live concert in Pisa titled *Romanza in Concert: A Night in Tuscany* was aired on a PBS fund-raising special at the end of 1997. Bocelli aptly caters to both the pop and operatic worlds, appealing to ardent fans of both types of music with his remarkably lovely voice. According to the *Boston Herald*'s Stephen Schaefer, Bocelli has been dubbed the fourth tenor, the leading Tower of Pisa, the singing Tower of Pisa, and "the most beautiful voice in the world."

Bocelli was a best-selling pop artist in Europe with more than 10 million copies sold of his debut album, *Romanza*, and after his exposure through the PBS special, his success in the U.S. skyrocketed. The PBS production was slated to run only once, but due to its popularity it ran three times. Bocelli's debut album, *Romanza,* ranked alongside the *Titanic* soundtrack as one of the two best-selling holiday albums in 1997, and his second album, *Viaggio Italiano,* was on top of the *Billboard* classical charts in early 1998. His roster of fans includes such luminaries as Pope John Paul II, Luciano Pavarotti, Isabella Rossellini, Cecilia Bartoli, Julie Andrews, and Madonna. By 1998, Bocelli had performed for Pope John Paul II on four different occasions.

Bocelli was born on September 22, 1958, in the rural farming town of Lajatico, located about 20 miles from Pisa in Italy's Tuscany region. His parents sold farm equipment and grew olives and wine grapes. His family's farm was home to a small vineyard, from which his father, Sandro, still produces Chianti Bocelli. His family members were not especially musical, but they were encouraging when Bocelli displayed an interest in opera music as early as age six. He received piano, flute, and saxophone lessons as a boy. He became totally blind at the age of 12 after hitting his head during a soccer game with friends—Bocelli suffered a brain hemorrhage which resulted in blindness a few days later, yet his sight was already impaired from glaucoma at birth. He told Celestine Bohlen of the *New York Times,* "I know what colors look like and I have an idea of the world.... I believe we all have a destiny that we can perceive. Mine was singing. I always sang for my friends at school, for birthdays, so I knew inside what my destiny was." Bocelli feels too many people focus on his blindness; he doesn't consider it tragic, and he skis, enjoys horseback riding, and reaches for his own coffee.

Bocelli went to the University of Pisa and studied law instead of music, but he sang professionally in piano bars while a law student, which is where he met his wife, Enrica. She was seventeen when they met and has told

For the Record . . .

Born September 22, 1958, in Lajatico, Italy; father named Sandro; a farm equipment retailer and grower of olives and wine grapes; married Erica Bocelli in 1992; children Amos and Matteo. *Education:* Law degree from the University of Pisa; worked as a lawyer for a year after college; studied opera under Luciano Betterani and Franco Corelli.

First career break was the 1992 recording "Miserere (Pity)" with the Italian rock star Zucchero Fornaciari; released the single "Con Te Partiro," 1995; *Romanza,* 1997, which ranked alongside the *Titanic* soundtrack as one of the two best-selling holiday albums in 1997; released *Viaggio Italiano,* 1997; released *Aria: The Opera Album,* 1998; performed for Pope John Paul II four times.

Awards: First prize at the San Remo Music Festival in 1994 for "Il Mare Calmo Della Sera."

Address: *Record company*—Philips Music Group, a division of Polygram Classics, Worldwide Plaza, 825 Eighth Avenue, New York, NY 10019 (212) 333-8237.

reporters that she first fell in love with Bocelli's voice before falling in love with him. They married in 1992 and had two sons, Amos and Matteo, within five years.

Played in Piano Bars

To finance singing lessons, Bocelli continued to play in piano bars, and worked as a lawyer for a year after college. In 1992 Bocelli had his first career break when presented with the opportunity to record "Miserere (Pity)" with the Italian rock star Zucchero Fornaciari, who had originally written the material for Luciano Pavarotti. Bocelli told Bohlen that Pavarotti later heard the recording and, "said some nice things about my voice, and since then a lot has happened." The two men became friends, and Bocelli even spent a week at Pavarotti's home. In 1994 Bocelli won first prize at the San Remo Music Festival, viewed by one in every three people in Italy and the exposure was fortuitous. According to the *Wall Street Journal*'s Matthew Gurewitsch, Bocelli's winning entry, "Il Mare Calmo Della Sera," "rose from an intimate, half-murmured rasp to a refrain like a ringing anthem."

In 1995 Bocelli released the single, "Con Te Partiro," which was immensely popular in Europe. He later rerecorded the single with Sarah Brightman as a duet in English. It wasn't a commercial song, but when the public finally embraced it, its success spread rapidly.

Bocelli prefers singing opera to pop and studied under Luciano Betterani and Franco Corelli, former trainers for Maria Callas and Luciano Pavarotti. When Alan Niester of the Toronto *Globe and Mail* asked Bocelli if he enjoyed singing pop music, Bocelli replied, "Not very much, honestly, but I think it's important for many reasons. The first is that pop music has a big, big audience ... if one wants to have great popularity ... he has to sing these songs. And through the songs it's possible to bring people into the theatres who might not have come any other way." Bocelli has featured pop and canonized material on the same release; in *Romanza* he included several contemporary songs along with the classical standards "La Donna E Mobile" and "Nessun Dorma".

Part of Bocelli's appeal is his romantic appearance; he's tall with broad shoulders, a hint of a beard, a gentle, almost self-effacing manner, and a handsome profile. He appears shy when led on stage, and he doesn't take his resounding success seriously. He also has confessed in interviews to having a terror of live performances.

Bocelli's music is a hardy blend of opera and popular music. It follows the path cleared in 1990 by the Three Tenors—Luciano Pavarotti, Placido Domingo, and Jose Carreras; the only difference being that Pavarotti, Domingo, and Carreras began in the classical world of opera and moved into the more accessible realm of pop. On the other hand, Bocelli, began in piano bars and moved into classical concert halls. During his career, Bocelli has performed at Hampton Court Palace near London with Dame Kiri Te Kanawa and at the Royal Albert Hall with Sarah Brightman.

Sang for Pope with Bob Dylan

The Roman Catholic Church sponsored a concert pairing Bocelli with Bob Dylan in Bologna, Italy, which was attended by Pope John Paul II, and Bocelli has also performed with Bryan Adams. Bocelli's international agent, Craig Stanley, told Bohlen, "[He] can sing both operatic arias and love ballads with sensitivity. The bedrock is talent, but he also sings with emotion, from the heart ... pure, lyrical, good singing." Bocelli has what has been described as a phonogenic voice: a voice best suited for operettas and light songs.

Accepted Talent as Preordained Destiny

He told Bohlen, "You can't explain success. Success lives by mysterious rules: it comes when it wants and leaves when it wants." As for his future, he told *Billboard*'s Paul Verna and Mark Dezzani, "I have no precise idea what will happen. Each person has his own destiny, and destiny cannot be changed. I hope to arrive at some point in my life where I can sing exactly what I like, but this requires a lot of training." What elates Bocelli most about his success is the fact that there are often young children in the audience listening to his opera music. He told the *Boston Herald*'s Stephen Schaefer, "Of this, I am very proud." On the PBS special that was aired in the U.S., Bocelli was on horseback when he said that having a great voice is like owning a great horse, and that great horses come with great problems. He told Gurewitsch, "I have no more dreams. Reality has overtaken my dreams."

Selected discography

Romanza, Philips Music Group, 1997.
Viaggio Italiano, Philips Music Group, 1997.
Aria: The Opera Album, Philips Music Group, 1998.

Sources

Billboard, September 13, 1997; December 20, 1997.
Boston Herald, January 27, 1998.
Elle, November 1997.
Gavin, October 3, 1997.
New York Daily News, January 19, 1998.
New York Observer, October 13, 1997.
New York Times, October 4, 1997.
People, November 10, 1997.
Globe and Mail (Toronto), October 18, 1997.
USA Today, October 8, 1997; January 13, 1998.
Wall Street Journal, December 8, 1997.

—B. Kimberly Taylor

Paul Brandt

Country singer, songwriter

AP/Wide World Photos

After entering the country music scene in the early 1990s, Canadian Paul Brandt captured the hearts of country music fans throughout North America and Europe with his melodious baritone voice and touching, rock-edged lyrics. His 1996 debut album, *Calm Before The Storm*, mesmerized the country music world and reached gold status in the United States by April of 1997. During those two years, Brandt won numerous music awards and produced a second critically-acclaimed album entitled *Outside The Frame.*

Brandt was born Paul Rennée Belobersycky on July 21, 1972, to parents Claude and Edith, outside of Calgary, Alberta, in the small town of Airdrie. With his two sisters, Jenny and Sunny, he grew up amidst oil refineries and cattle ranches. His earliest exposure to music was hearing gospel hymns in church, and his first performances—with his sisters—were done there as well, singing in an *a cappella* trio and in choir. Brandt recalled in an interview with *Country Magazine,* "Secular music was not allowed in our household." He also explained that his interest in music was inherited from his Russian great grandfather who had been a musician and opera singer in Russia during the 1920s and 1930s.

While in the ninth grade, Brandt took up playing the guitar. His mother encouraged him by providing classical guitar lessons, and Brandt showed an exceptionally fine ear for music and taught himself as well. Until he was about 13 years old, the family had no television. Rather than feeling deprived, the situation provided Brandt with a wonderful opportunity to develop his artistic imagination. As a teenager he began writing poetry, which ultimately he would combine with his music. By the time he performed in front of an audience, they were hearing the total Brandt package—with lyrics and music written by the young man.

Brandt has said that he initially played folk music resembling the style of Four Strong Winds. He was part of a vocal/jazz ensemble. At the same time he started to connect his poems to music. He was also being strongly influenced by popular country artists, including Buck Owens, Dwight Yoakam, Clint Black, and George Strait. Brandt also appreciated The Mavericks, as he explained in an online interview with cable network Great American Country, because they were, "the artists who were traditional, yet managed to push the envelope." This was the beginning of Brandt's development of a country style with a rock edge.

During his final years in high school, Brandt began entering local talent contests for songwriters, singers, and performers. He entered the Calgary Stampede Contest three years in a row. The first year he placed in

For the Record . . .

Born Paul Rennée Belobersycky, July 21, 1972, in Airdrie, Alberta, Canada; son of Claude and Edith Belobersycky; married Elizabeth Peterson, February 22, 1997. *Education:* Attended nursing school.

Worked as a pediatric nurse in Alberta, Canada, c. 1991-93; gained attention of Reprise Records executives after winning Best Original Canadian Country Song in the 1993 National Talent Contest sponsored by the Canadian organization, SOCAN; signed with Reprise Records/Warner Bros. in 1994; recording debut *Calm Before The Storm* came in 1996; headlined first tour in 1997.

Awards: Calgary Stampede Talent Showcase, first place for songwriting, 1992; SOCAN National Talent Contest, Best Original Canadian Country Song, 1993 for "Calm Before The Storm;" Canadian Country Music Awards, Song of the Year 1996, for "My Heart Has A History;" Juno Award for Country Male Vocalist of the Year, 1997; Big Country Awards, Song of the Year and Video of the Year, for "My Heart Has A History," Album of the Year, Male Artist of the Year, and Canadian Country Artist of the Year, all 1997; Canadian Country Music Awards, SOCAN Song of the Year and Video of the Year, for "I Do," and Male Vocalist of the Year, all 1997.

Addresses: *Home*—Nashville, TN. *Record company*—Warner Bros., 1815 Division St., P.O. Box 120897, Nashville, TN 37212; Reprise Records, 3300 Warner Blvd., Burbank, CA 91505. *Fan Club*—P.O. Box 57144, Sunridge Postal Outlet, 2525 35th Street N.E., Calgary, Alberta T1Y 5T0, Canada.

the top ten, the second year he didn't place in any category, but by the third year—1992—he won first prize for songwriting and second prize for his performance.

This contest would prove to be the beginning of a new road for Brandt professionally. Although he had always enjoyed music, he was something of a reluctant performer and it hadn't occurred to him to pursue it as a career. After high school, Brandt went to college to become a registered nurse. In a way, he was following in his parents' footsteps: his father was a paramedic and his mother had returned to nursing school at the same time as her son. However, Brandt's fascination with music persisted during his time in nursing school. He spent all of his extra time and money entering contests, recording demos, and performing around the Calgary area.

New Professional Direction Beckoned

In 1993, Brandt won a national talent contest sponsored by the Canadian performance society SOCAN, when his tune "Calm Before The Storm" was named Best Original Canadian Country Song. This honor gained him the attention of Warner Music's Reprise label. Many powerful record executives had been in Hamilton, Ontario, for the competition and for the Country Music Week happening at the same time. After the contest, Warner Music Canada's Kim Cooke got in touch with Brandt and forwarded his demo tape to Nashville. Brandt then received a call from Warner vice-president Paige Levy, who sent representatives to Canada to see him perform. Shortly afterwards Levy signed the young man to a recording contract.

Having spent two years as a pediatric nurse for the Children's Hospital in Alberta, it was now clear that a new professional path lay ahead of Brandt. Nevertheless, he had found considerable fulfillment in his medical career. Speaking in the *Calgary Sun* of his experiences nursing sick children, Brandt said, "It was difficult, but it was also rewarding. When you have a chance to see kids get better, everything makes it all worth it. All I wanted was to try to make a difference in my life and have a legacy in some way, but for something I had done in someone else's life." As a nurse, Brandt hoped to make a difference in children's lives, and now he hopes to use music in the same way. The singer-songwriter's work with sick and dying children exposed him to the rawest of human emotions and showed him individuals in their most vulnerable moments. He shared the joy of new parents and felt the pain of those who lost a child. These experiences probably explain why, as a young man, Brandt has often seemed wise beyond his years.

Earned Early Acclaim

The reluctant country star first became a commercial success in Canada, with *Calm Before The Storm* going platinum by November of 1996 and double platinum by March of 1997. Later in 1997, *Calm Before The Storm* was certified "Gold" in the United States after sales exceeded 500,000 albums. Brandt now had the attention of country music lovers in both the United States and

Canada. *The Record* magazine reported in July of 1996 that his first single, "My Heart Has A History," was the "most played song on Canadian country radio." The cut "I Do" was Brandt's first number one hit single in the United States, according to *Billboard Magazine* in October of 1996.

In June of 1997, Brandt won five awards at the Big Country Awards. The tune "My Heart Has A History" earned Song of the Year and Video of the Year. The music industry newcomer also won Album of the Year, Male Artist of the Year, and Canadian Country Artist of the Year. The following month, Brandt returned to Calgary for a benefit performance. He was greeted enthusiastically by more than 13,000 fans at the Canadian Airlines Saddledome for his first concert in his hometown since releasing *Calm Before The Storm.* The concert's proceeds—some $250,000—were donated to Alberta's Children's Hospital.

In September of 1997, Brandt took four out of five honors that he was nominated for at the Canadian Country Music Awards. He took three prizes for the cut "I Do": Single of the Year, SOCAN Song of the Year, and Video of the Year. He also won Male Vocalist of the Year.

Thrived in Nashville

Brandt's award-winning style is based on a country stance supplemented with a modern edge. His rich baritone voice dives deep into a well of human emotion, singing about love, passion, and regret. While recording his first two albums at Emerald Studios in Nashville, Tennessee, Brandt worked with producer Josh Leo. His second album, *Outside The Frame,* was released to critical acclaim and included vocals by Kathy Mattea on "We Are The One." Brandt dedicated this album to his new wife. On February 22, 1997, he married Elizabeth Peterson—now known as Liz Brandt—who also sings backup on *Outside The Frame.* Many of the songs on the album speak of his marital bliss and his feelings towards his wife. While some of *Outside The Frame*'s cuts are rocking, like "Chain Reaction," Brandt slows the pace down on the introspective, "A Little In Love." A reviewer from *Entertainment Weekly* stated, "Brandt comes to his second album with driving, testosterone-fueled rhythm songs . . . his generally upbeat lyrics bring new dazzle to country's rhinestone heart."

Young, intelligent, and known as "Mr. Nice Guy," Brandt has shown the ability to bring audiences to tears. This phenomenon is explained by his approach to music, which he described to Great American Country: "The whole process of growing as a musician is a constant struggle to get to that place where there's nothing between what's in your heart and what's in your music." Brandt's combination of songwriting skills, gifted voice, and ability to project heartfelt emotion all point to a very bright future. On this subject, critic Jane Stevenson of the *Toronto Sun* noted, "My prediction is that Brandt is destined to become the next big thing in country music."

Selected discography

Calm Before The Storm, Reprise/Warner, 1996.
Outside The Frame, Warner Bros., 1997.
(With others) *The Way in a Manger: Country Christmas,* Warner Bros., 1997.

Sources

Periodicals

Calgary Sun, September 4, 1996; July 28, 1997.
Country Magazine, March 1996.
Entertainment Weekly, November 14, 1997, p. 93.
Heart of the Country, March 1996.
Record, July 1996.
Toronto Sun, September 14, 1997.

Online

http://paddle4.canoe.ca/JamAlbumsB/brandt_p_frame.html
http://paddle4.canoe.ca/JamMusicPaulBrandt/brandt_sept496.html
http://www.1200ckxm.com/1997ccmaawards.html
http://www.allmusic.com/
http://www.canoe.ca/JamConcertsA2D/brandt_p_270797.html
http://www.cduniverse.com
http://www.country105.com/artist/brandt/html
http://www.countrystars.com/artists/pbrandt.html
http://www.peermusic.com/country/paulbrandt.html
http://www.warnermusic.ca/
http://www.young-country.com/PaulBrandt.html

—Debra Reilly

Jim Brickman

Composer, pianist

In an era of increasing fragmentation of musical styles and genres, New Age solo instrumentalist, Jim Brickman's pop savvy, which was honed and perfected from years spent writing commercial jingles, managed to strike a responsive chord in the hearts and ears of rather diverse, and sometimes diametrically opposed, segments of the adult music, buying public in America. "Rocket to the Moon" from his debut album, *No Words*, became the first solo instrumental recording to ever make an appearance on the adult contemporary singles chart. His follow-up album, *By Heart*, yielded three songs that made the unprecedented leap from the top of the New Age chart to the top of the adult contemporary chart. Steve Vining, the president of Brickman's record label, Windham Hill, remarked to *Billboard*'s Gina Van Der Vliet that "the album [*Picture This*, Brickman's third release] has just exploded and we're all thrilled. This is one of those rare instances where someone who operates in a solo piano kind of New Age genre is able to break out of that area and go pop mainstream with massive radio play and record sales.... We've tapped into something pretty special here, and I think it's just the beginning of a long, long career."

The Cleveland, Ohio native, did not intend to embark on a career as a solo instrumental new age pianist, let alone to pursue a rather lucrative recording career. He was pursuing studies in business at Cleveland's Case Western Reserve University and was enrolled in classical composition courses at the Cleveland Institute of Music when he decided to undertake a career as a composer of music for advertising jingles. The 19 year-old Brickman's choice of a professional pursuit earned him the distinction of being the "black sheep of the conservatory." The "break the rules kind of guy" was quoted in the Lifetime web site as saying that, "everybody was putting their studies to use in a very classical sense, but I was applying it to the mainstream. That's what came naturally to me. Pop song writing."

He set up his own company, Brickman Arrangements, to publish the commercial jingles he was writing. He explained his reasons for pursuing a career as a jingle writer to *Shoot*'s Robert Goldrich, "I got into commercials to make a personal connection with people through my music—to affect people when they heard my work, and for me, instruments and real people performances are the only way to do that." Throughout the 1980s and early 1990s, Brickman and his company, Brickman Arrangements, worked on such prestigious and famous advertising accounts as Standard Oil, Purina Puppy Chow, the Gap, Mc Donald's, Pontiac, 7-Up, AT&T, Revlon, Miller Beer, and Walt Disney World. He was also instrumental in composing music for the children's television program *Sesame Street* and for various projects for the Henson Associates. Brickman also collaborated on projects with such popular vocalists as Whitney Houston, Luther Vandross, Richard Marx, and Michael Bolton.

By 1993, Brickman was beginning to lose interest in his career as a commercial jingle writer as he related in Windham Hill web site, "Eventually, I got bored doing jingles, and it became creatively limiting because I had to fake being trendy much of the time. I realized that I never sat down at the piano, except for work. I wanted to make music that was more personal, more real and from the heart." Further commenting on this subject to Goldrich, Brickman said that, "I purposely took a break from commercials, because while I was getting a lot of work, my clients weren't getting the best part of me creatively. In commercials, I was starting to move into a keyboards-and-synthesizer direction, which to me wasn't real music." About this same time, he signed to the Windham Hill Record label and started to embark on his new career as a solo instrumental pianist.

The six song demo of Brickman's musical interludes formed and shaped the sound of his debut release *No Words*. *No Words*, which was released in 1994, deftly married the catchy musical hooks of contemporary pop with romantic lyricism. According to the Windham Hill web site, this pop savvy earned him good sales for his debut album and widespread radio airplay on adult

For the Record . . .

Born James Brickman, c. 1962, in Cleveland, OH; attended Case Western Reserve University; the Cleveland Institute of Music.

Started working as a commercial jingle writer in the early 1980s; signed to Windham Hill in 1993; released *No Words,* 1994; *By Heart,* 1995; *Picture This,* 1997; *The Gift,* 1997.

Addresses: *Record company*—Windham Hill Records, Beverly Hills, CA 90210. *Management*—Edge Management, 11288 Ventura Blvd., Ste. 408B, Studio City, CA 91604. *Internet*—brickpiano@aol.com.

contemporary radio stations. Brickman started to develop a devoted fan base, due in no small part to the tremendous success of the single, "Rocket to the Moon." "Rocket to the Moon" earned the distinction of being the first solo instrumental song to ever place on the adult contemporary chart.

The following year, Brickman released the follow-up to *No Words.* It was called *By Heart* and its success even managed to outshine its predecessor. *By Heart* spawned two top ten adult contemporary hits: "Angel Eyes," which peaked at number eight, and "If You Believe," which made it to number ten.

Endless Noise

In 1996, Brickman signed an exclusive contract with the music and sound design collective known as Endless Noise. The contract was for the exclusive rights for the commercial representation of Brickman in all of his advertising music writing endeavors. Brickman still maintained his business, Brickman Arrangements, although its focus was now on maintaining and promoting Brickman's career as a solo recording artist. Explaining the impetus behind taking up jingle writing again and signing with Endless Noise, Brickman told Goldrich that "the attraction [of jingle writing] to me is very different than it was three years ago. I think people will think of me more for what I do best—performing on the piano and composing an organic, acoustic style of music. That's my specialty. And my music as a performer/composer might serve as a point of reference for agencies who want a score that sounds like a cut from one of my CDs."

Brickman's third album, the 1997 release *Picture This,* served to further solidify his position as the New Age/adult contemporary cross over king. The tremendous sales of *Picture This* were in excess of 100,000 its first month of release, thanks to the first single, a duet with country singer Martina Mc Bride. The duet was entitled "Valentine" and received airplay from not only adult contemporary stations but country ones as well. "Valentine" managed to crack the top 100 country singles chart besides easily making it in to the adult contemporary top ten. *Picture This,* the album the single was culled from, hit number 30 on Billboard's top album chart and debuted at number one on the top New Age album chart. In speaking about the phenomenal success of "Valentine," Mc Bride commented to Van Der Vliet that, "this just shows that good music of any kind can really transcend formats. I've sung all kinds of music in my life, including Top 40. It was fun to get to sing something a little different."

Brickman explained his appeal and success to Van Der Vliet as "I knew that a lot of the right things were in place. If you believe enough in what you're doing and how you're doing it, then it's very welcome. So, it's not terribly surprising, but I feel very fortunate that it's happening."

Later that same year, Brickman released his first Christmas album, *The Gift.* Like its predecessors, it was received warmly and with a good deal of acclaim. In the Windham Hill web site, Brickman offered his interpretation of why he has struck such a nerve with his audience. He said that "everyone has a different concept of what my music means to them, so they can paint their own pictures ... Also, there's my desire to reach those listeners and say 'O, come see what I'm doing, let me share a part of myself with you.' Again, the key is to be pure and honest."

Selected discography

No Words (includes "Rocket to the Moon"), Windham Hill, 1994.
By Heart (includes "Angel Eyes" and "If You Believe"), Windham Hill, 1995.
Picture This (includes "Valentine"), Windham Hill, 1997.
The Gift, Windham Hill, 1997.

Sources

Periodicals

Billboard, December 28, 1996; March 8, 1997.
Shoot, February 2, 1996.

On-line

"Weddings of a lifetime," http://www.lifetimetv.com/connections/weddings/jim_brickman.html (January 22, 1998).
"Jim Brickman," http://www.windham.com/artists/Jim_Brickman.html (January 22, 1998).

—Mary Alice Adams

Lisa Brokop

Singer, songwriter

Photo by Ken Settle

A youthful veteran in the country music business, Lisa Brokop has been called one of the most overlooked talents in Nashville. The Canadian native's impressive, husky voice seems ready to make it big. At the age of 24, Brokop had three albums, a wealth of singles, and many music awards, and a solid fan base around the world.

Brokop was born on June 6, 1973 in Surrey, British Columbia to parents Herb and Ann Brokop. At the age of four, Brokop became mesmerized when her favorite song, "Rhinestone Cowboy," played on the radio. Insisting that everyone be quiet, she sang along and hit all the notes. By the time she was seven, Brokop had made her first public appearance, singing the Canadian national anthem at a campground in British Columbia. Soon afterwards, her mother organized a family band; she played accordion, Lisa sang, and son Dean played drums. The trio appeared at church and community events, performed at hospitals, and entertained senior citizens. In a little while, Brokop began accompanying herself on guitar and commenced with voice and guitar lessons.

A few years later, Brokop was performing with top Canadian Country artists, making radio and television appearances, and winning contests. At the tender age of 15, Brokop turned professional. With the help of a special school program for performing artists, she continued her studies while touring Canada with the Marty Gillan Band. She joined the Vancouver-based road band as singer, rhythm guitarist, and keyboardist. Her first major concert was an opening gig for Willie Nelson at the Pacific Coliseum in 1988. The next year, the young singer made her first national television appearance on *The Tommy Hunter Show,* a Canadian showcase for country music performers. Subsequently, Brokop organized her own band, continued touring, and began releasing singles in Canada. Her first single was "Daddy Sing To Me."

In 1991, Brokop won the Nashville Songwriter's Contest sponsored by Vancouver radio station CKWX, giving her the opportunity to co-write with Peter McCann. Shortly thereafter, McCann produced her first album, *My Love,* which was released on the independent label Libre in 1991. The album included four of Brokop's earlier singles and six McCann compositions. The album sold extremely well for an independent label release, with over 25,000 copies purchased. It was also popular with country radio listeners.

After winning several awards from 1990-92, Brokop was cast in the movie *Harmony Cats.* This exposure, coupled with her independent record release, brought her to

For the Record . . .

Born June 6, 1973, in Surrey, British Columbia, Canada; daughter of Herb and Ann Brokop.

Became a professional performer at age 15, touring Canada as singer, rhythm guitarist, and keyboardist for the Marty Gillan Band; appeared on *The Tommy Hunter Show,* 1989; won contest to co-write with Peter McCann, who produced Brokop's first album *My Love,* 1991; signed with Capitol (Liberty/Patriot) records in 1993; moved to Sony Music, 1997.

Awards: British Columbia Country Music Association (BCCMA), Horizon Award winner for Best Newcomer and Gospel Performer of the Year, 1990; BCCMA Female Vocalist, 1993-95, International Achievement Award, 1993-95; Canadian Country Music Association, Vocal Collaboration of the Year, for "Two Names On An Overpass" with Duane Steele, 1997.

Addresses: *Record Company*—Sony Music, 34 Music Sq. E., Nashville, TN 37203-4323. *Fan Club*—Brokop Entertainment Ltd., Box 123-7101C 120 Street, Delta, BC, Canada, V4E 2A0. *Agent*—William Carter Career Management Co., 1028B 18th Ave. South, Nashville, TN 37212. *Website*—www.lisabrokop.org.

the attention of Liberty Records and resulted in a 1993 record contract. Brokop also moved to Nashville in 1993. Here she was riding high and won many awards during 1993-95, before Capitol's Liberty label went out of business. After the record company reorganized, Brokop felt it was time for a change and sought a new manager and label. She proceeded to release *Every Little Girl's Dream* in 1994 and *Lisa Brokop* in 1996. Both albums did well resulting in three singles each.

Voice of a Star

While Brokop had gained international acclaim with her singles, she had run into some problems trying to straddle the U.S.-Canadian border. With fans in both places, some songs ran into bureaucratic snags in her home country because of rules imposed by the Canadian Radio-Television and Telecommunications Commission. Their rules state that two out of four elements of a song—production, artist, music, and lyrics—must be Canadian to qualify for Canadian content (CanCon) status. Without this designation, a recording may not receive favored playing status on Canadian radio, which directly impacts a song's position on the charts. In 1994, Brokop's single "Give Me A Ring Sometime" lost its CanCon status and position on the Canadian charts because of a commission ruling. Her 1996 album, which was recorded in Nashville with American musicians and songwriters, also failed to meet Canadian content standards.

Brokop maintained a positive outlook in spite of the difficulties she encountered while making music for both Canadian and American listeners. Brokop told Rod Campbell of the *Edmonton Sun* that the songs on her 1996 album were chosen because "we ... went for the best songs I could find. We hoped people in radio would play them because they love them, and not because they were CanCon."

More than one music critic has commented on Brokop's impressive and powerful voice. One reviewer at *Stereo Review* praised Brokop's work on her self-titled 1996 album, noting her "distinctive huskily searching voice and ... quasi-spiritual song selection that burrows beneath the obvious." A *Billboard* reviewer noted that although her 1996 single "Before He Kissed Me" might not be her ticket to greater fame, she had an exceptional voice, one "possessing a strength and clarity that should make her a star."

One of Brokop's more popular tunes has been "She Can't Save Him," a song about a wife who's trying to save her alcohol-addicted husband. Although Brokop hasn't personally had this sort of experience, she felt presenting the theme might help others. She told *Calgary Sun* reporter Anika Van Wyk that fans have told her, "Because of that song I got out of a situation." Brokop finds having this sort of impact on fans gratifying and said, "It makes me realize there's a reason I'm doing this."

Signed with New Label

During 1996 Brokop toured throughout North America with artists such as Alan Jackson, George Strait, Marty Stuart, John Michael Montgomery, and Clay Walker. Some of her singles, including "Take That" and "Give Me A Ring Sometime," were now earning her international acclaim. She left Capitol Records by the end of 1996. Around the same time, she hooked up with a new management company and, in August 1997, Brokop signed a seven-record deal with Sony Music. By September of that year, she was in the studio working on her next release.

Aiming for Gold

Although she spent the bulk of her time during the fall of 1997 in Nashville—writing songs and working on her album—she made several brief "mini-tours." One included a handful of stops in British Columbia and Vancouver Island. In September 1997, she gained recognition for the song, "Two Names On An Overpass," which earned her a Canadian Country Music Award for Vocal Collaboration of the Year. Sung with Duane Steele, the cut was highly successful in Canada, where it made the Top Ten hit list.

The vocal tracks on Brokop's next CD were completed in January 1998. At that time, the album was to be called *When You Get To Be You,* and included eight songs co-written by Brokop. While awaiting the album's release, Brokop enjoyed some time out for her family and hobbies. Despite having average every day needs, Lisa Brokup's ambitions are anything but ordinary. She spoke about her goals with Les Wiseman in *British Columbia's Businessman:* "I want to have gold records, platinum records, double-platinum records. I'm a very competitive person, a perfectionist."

Selected discography

My Love, Libre Music, 1991.
Every Little Girl's Dream (includes "Give Me A Ring Sometime" and "Take That"), Capitol, 1994.
Lisa Brokop (includes "Before He Kissed Me" and "She Can't Save Him"), Capitol, 1996.
(With Duane Steele) "Two Names On An Overpass," from *P.O. Box 432; 1997.*

Sources

Periodicals

Billboard, July 15, 1995; March 9, 1996.
British Columbia's Businessman, December 1997, pp. 67-70.
Calgary Sun, July 11, 1996.
Edmonton Sun, March 22, 1996.
MacLean's, October 14, 1994, p. 42.
Stereo Review, May 1996.

Online

paddle4.canoe.ca
www.cdnow.com
www.cduniverse.com
www.lisabrokop.org
www.young-country.com

Additional materials provided by fan club coordinator Ann Brokop.

—*Debra Reilly*

Jeff Buckley

Singer, songwriter

With nothing more than a live EP, one full-length studio recording, and contributions to several other artists' records to his credit, singer-songwriter Jeff Buckley distinguishes himself as the rare artist who makes a lasting impression on both critics and fans. Thus, when the promising, alternative rocker died in a drowning accident in the Mississippi river on May 29, 1997, a stunned music industry mourned the loss of one whom *Entertainment Weekly* described as a "virtuoso" guitarist, an exceptionally promising songwriter of "soul-searching hymns," and a singer "capable of angelic delicacy and demonic fire." From the time he emerged on the music scene in the early 1990s to the time of his death, Buckley worked to establish himself as an artist to be reckoned with. Ultimately, he became one who—like Tim Buckley, the musician father he scarcely knew—would leave a legend and a legacy in his wake.

Buckley was born on November 17, 1966, in Orange County, California, during the brief marriage between his mother, Panamanian-born classical pianist Mary Guibert, and his father, 1960s and 1970s eccentric singer-songwriter Tim Buckley. Despite that lineage, Buckley endured an often difficult and rootless childhood that was marked by poverty. Along with his mother, he moved repeatedly, packing his possessions in paper bags because he didn't have any luggage. As friend and New York performance artist Penny Arcade recounted to Fred Schruers in *Rolling Stone,* "Jeff has been going through turbulence ever since he was born."

When he began to perform, the younger Buckley seemed in danger of falling under the long shadow cast by his father, in spite of the elder's notable absence in his son's life. Tim Buckley was revered by many for his musical daring, as he restlessly shifted from folk to jazz to rock and seemed indifferent to the mixed commercial fortunes that resulted. But while Tim Buckley enjoyed professional success, his parenting skills apparently left something to be desired. Jeff reportedly met his father only once, when he spent a week with him at age eight. In 1975, an almost penniless Tim Buckley died of an accidental heroin overdose, just a few months after that encounter. It was Jeff's stepfather, auto mechanic Ron Moorhead, whom he came to consider as his father. Between 1971 and 1973, Buckley and his mother lived with Moorhead, whose surname Buckley adopted for several years before returning to his given name, Jeffrey Scott Buckley. Moreover, Buckley kept in touch with Moorhead even after the relationship with his mother had ended.

Perhaps not surprisingly, given the fact that both of his biological parents were musicians, Buckley connected with music at a young age. Inspired by a copy of Led Zeppelin's *Physical Graffiti* given to him by his stepfather, Buckley decided, at the age of 12, to become a musician. But even before then, Buckley was immersed in music. He told reporter Ray Rogers of *Interview,* "I just always sang. My mom and I would always listen to the radio while driving to school. 'Summer Breeze' would come on, and she would sing the second harmony, and I would sing the third harmony. Music was like my first real toy."

The teenage Buckley was something of a misfit and loner at Loara High School in Anaheim, California, a place he would later say was populated by "'Disneyland Nazi youth,'" in *Rolling Stone.* After high school, he played in a few fledgling Los Angeles bands while he studied guitar at the Los Angeles Musicians Institute and got a job in a hotel.

Move Promoted Music Career

It wasn't until he relocated to New York in the early 1990s that Buckley "blossomed," as he told *Interview* reporter Ray Rogers. Soon thereafter, a reluctant Buckley agreed to perform at a tribute concert for his father in April of 1991 at St. Ann's Church in Brooklyn. As he recalled in a 1994 *Rolling Stone* interview, "'It wasn't my work, it wasn't my life. But it bothered me that I hadn't been to his funeral, that I'd never been able to tell him anything. I used that show to pay my last

For the Record . . .

Born Jeffrey Scott Buckley November 17, 1966 in Orange County, CA; died by accidental drowning May 29, 1997, Memphis, TN; son of Tim Buckley (a singer-songwriter) and Mary Guibert (a classical pianist).

Performed at a tribute concert for his late musician father in New York in April of 1991; became regular performer at New York clubs and coffeehouses in early 1990s; signed with Columbia; released debut EP, *Live at Sin-é,* in 1993; released full-length album *Grace* in 1994; collaborated with artists such as Patti Smith, Jazz Passengers, and John Zorn; died shortly before he was to start work on second album in a Memphis studio.

Awards: Academie Charles CROS, Gran Prix International Du Disque, 1995, for *Grace.*

Address: *Record company*—Columbia Records2100 Colorado Ave., Santa Monica, CA 90404.

respects." While he may have been uneasy about the gig, Buckley's performance caught the attention of many notable individuals in the music industry, including show organizer and producer Hal Willner. Performers and audience members alike were astonished by Buckley's remarkable vocal prowess. As Willner sums up in *New York,* the younger Buckley "just absolutely had it. It's definitely a voice from Heaven."

It was at the tribute concert that Buckley met guitarist and former Captain Beefheart member Gary Lucas, who invited Buckley to join his band, Gods and Monsters. Although creative differences eventually drove Buckley to split from the band, Lucas and Buckley were able to mend those differences long enough to collaborate on two songs that appeared on Buckley's first full-length solo record.

In the artistic mecca of New York, Buckley found the ideal spot in which to nurture his burgeoning songwriting and musical skills. He took up residence in an East Village apartment and began performing a mix of covers and original material at New York coffeehouses and clubs, most notably Sin-é. It was there that Buckley said he learned to perform. "I learned how to use everything in the room as music," he was quoted in *Interview.* "A tune has to resonate with whatever is happening around it. So if people are talking, I let them talk. That just means they're part of the music." Buckley's Sin-é performances resulted in his first record, the 1993 EP *Live at Sin-é.* With its two original tracks and covers of Edith Piaf's "Je N'en Connais Pas La Fin" and Van Morrison's "The Way Young Lovers Do," the album concisely demonstrated Buckley's eclectic musical influences, including jazz legend Billy Holiday, Led Zeppelin's Robert Plant, and Pakistani devotional singer Nusrat Fateh Ali Khan. As producer Andy Wallace, who later worked with Buckley on his full-length debut, recalled in *Rolling Stone,* "[Buckley] had the audio equivalent of a photographic memory.... Not only everything from [Charles] Mingus to Sonic Youth, but every verse of 'Yummy, Yummy, Yummy.'"

Buckley spent early 1994 on a solo tour of clubs and coffeehouses throughout North America and Europe. Shortly before the release of *Live at Sin-é,* Buckley, guitarist Matt Johnson, and bass player Mick Grohdahl started working in the studio with Wallace on tracks that would eventually appear on the 1994 LP *Grace.* The album was released in the United States to generally positive and, in some cases, positively glowing reviews. *Entertainment Weekly*'s Dimitri Ehrlich called it a "dreamy and stunningly original set of songs," while *Gentlemen's Quarterly*'s Rob Tannenbaum applauded Buckley's "spectacularly sensitive tenor" and "imagistic lyrics." The heartbreaking single "Last Goodbye," which chronicled the end of a relationship, hit number 19 on the *Billboard* modern rock chart, while the album itself went on to sell roughly 250,000 copies.

Buckley spent much of the next couple of years on the road in the United States and abroad in support of the album. In 1995, he was awarded France's Gran Prix International Du Disque for *Grace.* Recipients of the honor—who include Edith Piaf, Yves Montand, Bob Dylan, and Bruce Springsteen—are selected by music industry professionals, journalists, producers, and the president of French Culture.

Solo Work and Collaborations

Besides his work as a solo artist, Buckley collaborated on a number of other recordings. He sang "Jolly Street" on 1994's *In Love,* the sixth album from the progressive New York jazz outfit the Jazz Passengers, and he added vocals or instrumentation to albums by Brenda Kahn, Rebecca Moore, Patti Smith, and John Zorn, among others. Known to occasionally read his own poetry, Buckley read Edgar Allan Poe's poem "Ulalume—A Ballad" on *Closed on Account of Rabies (Poems & Tales by Edgar Allan Poe),* and added instrumentation to a track with Nymph's vocalist Inger Lorre on *kicks joy darkness,* a compilation tribute to poet Jack Kerouac. And it was Buckley who penned the liner notes for Nusrat Fateh Ali Kahn's *The Supreme Collection.*

Remembered His Roots

Despite his increasing fame, Buckley never forgot the tiny venues where he began making a name for himself. Returning several times to Sin-é and playing a series of surprise solo shows in late 1996, he appeared under various pseudonyms, including the Crackrobats and A Puppet Show Named Julio. Even after he and his bandmates headed to Memphis in February of 1997 to prepare for June recording sessions at Easley Studios, the small gigs continued. He started a series of weekly shows at a local club called Barrister's in late March of that year. Determined not to place himself in "an ivory tower," as he told Rogers, Buckley was modest about his songwriting skills and vowed that he would continue to play intimate venues. He said, 'I'm not the greatest songwriter yet; I daydream thinking about great songwriters. I was brought up with all these different influences—Nina Simone, Nusrat Fateh Ali Khan, Patti Smith—people who showed me music should be free, should be penetrating, should carry you."

On the night he drowned, Buckley was traveling to a rehearsal with friend and roadie Keith Foti. En route, they stopped at a Memphis marina, where Buckley waded into the river fully-clothed to cool off. Waves tossed ashore by a passing boat forced Foti to briefly turn his attention away from Buckley as he protected the musician's radio and guitar. By the time he looked back to the river, Buckley had vanished. Six days after his disappearance, a massive search was ended when police discovered Buckley's body near Memphis's famous Beale Street. As of late 1997, there were plans to honor Buckley with a bench and a plaque at the city zoo, a spot he reportedly frequented. Buckley was survived by his mother and half-brother Corey.

Final Album Prepared by Others

A posthumous two-CD set, *SKETCHES (for my sweetheart, the drunk)* was slated for release. Compiled under the direction of his mother and friends such as Chris Cornell and Michael Clouse, the set consisted of home recordings and Buckley's final studio work. At the time of his death, he was believed to have penned more than 100 songs since the release of *Grace.* Although Buckley had not yet officially begun recording his second album, he and his bandmates had recorded from time to time during 1996-97 with producer Tom Verlaine (formerly of Television). During his time in Memphis, Buckley had also made recordings of cover songs and new material on a four-track machine at his rented cottage. In a Columbia Records press release, Guibert reflected on the process of assembling her son's album: "Listening to the recordings was both painful and fulfilling.... It was heartrending to listen to the sound of Jeff's voice, but the songs were stunningly beautiful! Even the rough four-tracks had their own particular charm because they showed so vividly Jeff's musical genius."

Those who knew him were often struck by what they say was Buckley's genuineness and pure artistic gift. As friend and Shudder to Think guitarist Nathan Larson commented in *People,* "Jeff was music. He was the real thing, undiluted, ferocious. He was in direct communication with a spiritual place that a lot of artists can only theorize about. No one came away from him unmoved."

Selected discography

Live at Sin-é, Columbia, 1993.
Grace, 1994.
SKETCHES (for my sweetheart, the drunk), 1998.

Sources

Books

Buckley, Jonathan, and Mark Ellingham, editors, *Rock: The Rough Guide,* Rough Guides, 1996.
Erlewine, Michael, executive editor, *All Music Guide to Rock,* second edition, Miller Freeman Books, 1997.
Larkin, Colin, editor, *Guiness Encyclopedia of Popular Music,* Stockton Press, 1995.
Romanowski, Patricia, and Holly George-Warren, editors, *New Rolling Stone Encyclopedia of Rock & Roll,* Fireside, 1995.
Weisband, Eric, and Craig Marks, editors, *Spin Alternative Record Guide,* Vintage, 1995.

Periodicals

Billboard, June 14, 1997.
Chicago Tribune, June 6, 1997.
Detroit Free Press, March 1, 1994; September 15, 1995; June 4, 1997.
Entertainment Weekly, August 26, 1994; June 13, 1997; November 21, 1997; December 26, 1997.
Gentlemen's Quarterly, September 1994.
Interview, February 1994; January 1996; August 1997.
Knight-Ridder/Tribune News Service, June 16, 1997.
Los Angeles Times, June 5, 1997; June 6, 1997.

Newsweek, June 16, 1997.
New York, November 14, 1994.
People, September 5, 1994; May 8, 1995; June 16, 1997; December 29, 1997.
Rolling Stone, April 16, 1992; February 24, 1994; March 10, 1994; October 20, 1994; August 7, 1997.
Time, June 16, 1997.

Additional information was provided by Columbia Records publicity materials, 1998.

—*K. Michelle Moran*

Don Byron

Clarinetist, composer

Clarinetist and composer Don Byron can most often be heard playing jazz, but he is also capable of playing in classical settings and has recorded an album of Jewish klezmer standards. Byron plays the music he enjoys and as an African American musician, avoids the stereotypes that ensnare black musicians.

Don Byron was born on November 8, 1958, to parents who both appreciated and played music. His father, a bassist in a calypso band, and his mother, who played piano, exposed him to classical, salsa, and jazz music as a child. This eclectic background helped him forge an individualistic streak in his music, but was initially a social hurdle. In school bands, he recalled to the *New York Times Magazine,* "Nobody wanted to believe I was capable of doing the classical stuff. I'd show up and they'd say, 'You want to play jazz.' In the classical pedagogy, I had teachers telling me my lips were too big."

By the time Byron graduated from the New England Conservatory of Music in 1984, he was the leader of The Klezmer Conservatory Band, which played high-energy Eastern European Jewish music. He left that band in 1987 to be a sideman for some of the most cutting-edge jazz musicians of the time, including bassist Reggie Workman, baritone saxophonist Hamiet Bluiett, and guitarist Bill Frisell.

Don Byron's 1991 debut album, *Tuskegee Experiments,* takes its title from a series of ethically questionable medical and psychological experiments the U.S. Public Health Service performed on African-American men in 1932. Featuring both Frisell and Workman, the album features versions of Robert Schumann's "Auf Einer Burg" and Duke Ellington's "Mainstem" among brooding originals and poetry. The *Penguin Guide to Jazz* praised the album, considering it "masterful, one of the most exciting debuts in more than a decade."

Klezmer Album Attracted Attention

His next album, *Plays the Music of Mickey Katz,* was a surprise to those who were unaware of Byron's previous klezmer affiliations. He was making a statement about American popular culture by taking the music of a famous Yiddish performer of the 1950s from which the Jewish community distanced itself. He explains in the *New York Times Magazine,* "People today think that Jewish musicians of the 20's, the generation that could have been klezmers, had the greatest attitude about their own music. But really, those cats didn't want to know ... klezmer. They wanted to play jazz or symphony —anything to avoid being stereotyped by klezmer." *Plays the Music of Mickey Katz* had the unfortunate effect of stereotyping Byron. "I run into people all the time who don't know I made anything after the Mickey Katz record," he lamented to *Down Beat,* "No matter how much I've done before and after, it always seems to be that stuff they want to talk about and hear. Sometimes I'm sorry I did it."

Prior to the release of his 1995 album *Music for Six Musicians*, Don Byron discussed with *New York Times Magazine* the stylistic divide in jazz music between the mainstream and more avant-garde elements: "Me and most of the cats I hang with, we're too left-wing to be around [mainstream jazz institution Jazz At] Lincoln Center. They should be presenting the freshest, baddest stuff. I don't even exist in jazz the way these people perceive it to be.... I've gotten to the point where I can't care what other jazz cats think."

Music for Six Musicians celebrates the Afro-Cuban music of Byron's childhood neighborhood in the Bronx. The Latin jazz elements are another aspect of his musical personality, and he is able to infuse them into his music without sounding trite or dilettantish. Byron continued to infuse his music with his radical politics; the album opens with poet Sadiq's "White History Month," which contains lines like "You think it fair if there was a white history month? ... I picture a kind of under-

For the Record . . .

Born Donald Byron, November 8, 1958, in New York, NY; son of Donald Byron (a postal worker) and Daisy (White) Byron (a phone company employee); *Education:* attended New York University, Manhattan School of Music c. 80s;, New England Conservatory of Music, 1984, graduated with Bachelor of Music Degree.

Began playing clarinet and composing professionally, c. 1985; released debut *Tuskegee Experiments,* 1992; on Elektra/Nonesuch, *Plays the Music of Mickey Katz,* 1993; *Music for Six Musicians,* 1995; *No Vibe Zone,* on Knitting Factory Works label, 1996; *Bug Music,* on Elektra/Nonesuch, 1997; appeared in film *Kansas City*, 1996; conducted Semaphore, modern classical music quintet, c. 1990s.

Awards: *Down Beat* Jazz Artist of the Year, 1992; *Down Beat* Critics Poll, Best Clarinetist, 1992, 1993, 1994, 1995, 1996, 1997.

Address: *Record company*—Elektra/Nonesuch Records, 75 Rockefeller Plaza, New York, NY 10019.

ground railroad, Delivering us in the dead of night from the inner city to the suburbs, Yea, like right into the hands of the Klan?"

In 1996 Don Byron was part of the cast of Robert Altman's film *Kansas City,* along with many other leading artists on the cutting edge of jazz. The soundtrack to the film, set in the early-to-mid 1930s was not trying to recreate the classic jazz of the period, but capture and convey it's essence in a contemporary manner. According to music director Hal Willner, "If you listen to records like 'Lafayette' [by Count Basie] or 'Prince of Wails', there was as much energy as any punk-rock I've ever heard." Byron's featured solo is Eddie Durham's "Pagin' the Blues,"

Reinterpreted Lost Classics

Don Byron's latest album *Bug Music* mixes compositions of Cotton Club-era Duke Ellington, an unquestionable classic period of an undisputed jazz master, with compositions by composers John Kirby and Raymond Scott, who were discredited by music critics in their time despite the fact that both men's music was technically complex and commercially popular. Byron explained in *Music and The Arts,* "Even in Gunther Schuller's *The Swing Era,* [he says] it's not really good music.... When you look at the era those cats came up in, that was the stuff that was turning everybody out."

The title "Bug Music" was inspired by an episode of *The Flintstones* which featured a parody of The Beatles before their music became acceptable by the standards of mainstream music critics. In the hands of Don Byron's ensemble, the music of Kirby, Scott, and Ellington commingle seamlessly, despite the subjective boundaries placed upon it at the time of its release.

By following his own inspiration and avoiding the subjective traps of music critics, Don Byron has become one of the most interesting voices in music of the nineties. In a *New York Times Magazine* profile, Byron illustrated the folly of stereotyping musicians, "Nobody calls up Eric Clapton and says, 'Yo, Clapton, you're the white guy that plays all that black [expletive], right? Why don't you come play at a rally?' What makes them think they can do that to me?"

Selected discography

Tuskegee Experiments, Elektra/Nonesuch, 1992.
Plays the Music of Mickey Katz, Elektra/Nonesuch, 1993.
Music for Six Musicians, Elektra/Nonesuch, 1995.
No Vibe Zone, Knitting Factory Works, 1996.
Bug Music, Elektra/Nonesuch, 1997.

Sources

Books

Cook, Richard and Brian Morton, *The Penguin Guide to Jazz,* Penguin, 1994.

Periodicals

Down Beat, April, 1994; January, 1995; June, 1995; November, 1996; January, 1997; December, 1997.
Entertainment Weekly, July 30, 1993.
New York Times Magazine, Januray 16, 1994.

Additional information was obtained from Nonesuch press material.

—*Jim Powers*

Joi Cardwell

Singer, songwriter

In 1997, R& B and dance music vocalist and songwriter/producer Joi Cardwell garnered attention with her hit singles "Run to You " and "Found Love" in her self titled release in 1997. The *Advocate*'s pop music critic, Barry Walters, wrote, "Neither glamour queen nor earth mamma, Cardwell focuses on her music, which she writes and often produces herself.... Cardwell's definitive approach is to sing meditative ballads set to extroverted, thump-intensive arrangements. "Entertainment Weekly's William Stevenson described Cardwell's music as "infectious dance music, "ebullient, and "propulsive," and described her voice as "R&B-ready".

In the 1980s, before the advent of house music, Cardwell was closely connected to the urban R&B sound. Born in New York City in the mid-1960s and raised in various areas of Queens; her early influences included Billie Holiday, Barbra Streisand, and Minnie Riperton. Cardwell appeared on stage at Carnegie Hall at the age of five in a dance recital, and was used to being on a stage by the time she was a teen-ager. She worked as a back-up session vocalist for Melba Moore, Jermaine Jackson, rap icon LL Cool J, and the Pointer Sisters. After graduating from New York University with degrees in English and Music in the mid-1980s, she studied voice for a year primarily in order to master control, as she had already developed and retained her own personal style. After her studies, she wrote and published songs for major R&B acts such as Kashif, LA Posse, and Malika Thomas.

Her close affiliation with Kashif led to an album deal with Arista Records in 1988 for her pop R&B girl-group, The Promise. Since the market in the 1980s was already saturated with sweet-sounding, bubbly R&B groups, it was difficult for The Promise to stand. As a result, Cardwell decided to answer an ad in the *Village Voice* that read, "Epic recording artist looking for a background singer for a live tour. "The recording artist turned out to be house-music innovator Li'l Louis of Li'L Louis and The World, whose 1992 hits "Club Lonely" and "Saved My Life" from the album Journey with the Lonely featured Cardwell on vocals.

Cardwell's experience as a vocalist and songwriter turned out to be exactly what Li'l Louis had been searching for in a singer. He proved to be an early influence for Cardwell's sound, which melds a new dance beat with a thoughtful lyrical twist. Cardwell creates material that sounds as though she's musing quietly about life while a dancing throng gyrates with joy nearby, and her lyrics are soulful, romantic, and thought-provoking. Shortly after meeting Li'l Louis, Cardwell conceived the single "Dancing in My Sleep, "and within a week of penning it, she was in Chicago cutting demos and well on her way to a career as a dance-hall diva and R&B songstress. When "Club Lonely "reached the number one mark, Cardwell distanced herself from the Li'l Louis project and, in 1993, toured Japan for eight months as a background singer for Japanese soul singer Toshinobu Kabot. Cardwell gleaned experience from the large overseas tour returned to the U.S. significantly more focused and ready to tackle a solo singing career. In 1995 Cardwell contributed the single "The Creator Has A Master Plan" to the Brooklyn Funkessentials' album Cool & Steady & Easy, and the single "Luv Connection " to the Towa Tei (of Dee-Lite) album Future Listening.

Walters wrote, "Cardwell focuses on her music, which she writes and often produces herself. Like her peers Kristine W and Billy Ray Martin, this upstart...possesses the kind of depth that demands control over her art. "She instills introspection and authenticity in dance floor music, and retains almost complete control over her material, favoring producers who will give her wide berth. Although Cardwell can belt out roof-rasing, gospel-influenced anthems, her trademark approach is to craft meditative ballads and well-tempered, controlled classics such as "Love and Devotion," "Run to You," "Trouble," and "Soul to Bare ". Cardwell released the single "Trouble" in 1994 on EightBall Records, which was a double-pack single including remixes from Junior Vasquez, Sotoshi Tomiie, and Deep Dish.

For the Record . . .

Born on October 8th, 1967 in New York City. *Education:* Degree in English and music from New York University.

Worked as a back-up session vocalist for Melba Moore, Jermaine Jackson, LL Cool J, and the Pointer Sisters; wrote and published songs for major R&B acts Kashif, LA Posse, and Malika Thomas; formed R&B girl-group The Promise; was featured on Li'l Louis' hit singles "Club Lonely" and "Saved My Life" in 1992; toured Japan as a background singer for Japanese soul singer Toshinobu Kabota for eight months in 1993; released the single "Trouble" in 1994; contributed the single "The Creator Has A Master Plan" to the Brooklyn Funkessentials album *Cool & Steady & Easy* in 1995; contriuted the single "Luv Connection" to Towa Tei of Dee-Lite's *Future Listening* album in 1995; released the single "Love and Devotion" in 1995; released the single "Jump for Joi" in 1995; released *The World is Full of Trouble* in 1995; released *Joi Cardwell* in 1997.

Address:*Record company*—EightBall Records, 175 Fifth Avenue, New York, NY 10010, (212) 253-6700. *Website*—www.eightballnyc.com

Cardwell released an album of house anthems titled *The World is Full of Trouble* in 1995, followed by *Joi Cardwell* in 1997. Walters wrote, "On her sophomore solo album, Cardwell refines the rawness of her debut while maintaining its emotional honesty. Whereas her first album sometimes suffered from skeletal arrangements and static sonics, Joi Cardwell is much more lush and club-ready, the songs fully fleshed out, not crying out for further remixing." Stevenson wrote, "Cardwell reemerges as a leading dance diva on her second album. It's hard not to get up and move.... Joy is exactly what Joi brings..." Cardwell's second album combined three of her most successful singles, "You Got to Pray," "Soul to Bare," and "Run to You," with nine original tracks, and it received favorable reviews; What sets Cardwell apart from other dance music vocalists is her offbeat style of fusing classics with house music, intertwining soft vocals with thumping beats, introducing unexpected gospel-like forays in her material, and blurring the line between R&B, house music, and introspective ballads. Her songs reflect a hopeful urgency that embraces the urban community. She tackles the topics of homeless and unemployment with as much ease as discovering a new love or a spiritual quest, and can make traditionally morose topics sound uplifting and joyful. As the underlying message in many of her songs is: "we will survive.:" She champions strength during adversity.

Cardwell's single "Holdin On" was created by producer Kyle "Small" Smith, and Smith let her have free reign with the song. It was originally sung by the teen music sensation Kim Moore and her male counterpart Jay, and Jay sang with Cardwell on the single as well. The single was remixed into jazz versions, and even though Cardwell didn't change it much, it was still impossible not to notice her unique stamp. Along with Cardwell's musical ability and creative approach to house music, the secret to her success was discipline, strength, fortitude, and above all else, a genuine love of music. Cardwell told Kristopher Flowers of Underground News, "All the divas from opera to the disco queens ... to the dance queens of today of whatever genre ... really love music and work hard to put out the best music they can. I want to make my mark. I want to be inspiring to someone like those who inspired me." In an interview with *Contemporary Musicians,* she was asked what advice she would give to those who want to emulate her success. She said, "Work hard and don't ever give up. "

Selected discography

Singles

"Trouble," EightBall Records, 1994.
"Love and Devotion," EightBall Records, 1995.
"Jump for Joi," EightBall Records, 1995.

Albums

The World is Full of Trouble, EightBall Records, 1995.
Joi Cardwell, EightBall Records, 1997.

Sources

Periodicals

The Advocate, December 13, 1997.
Entertainment Weekly, December 19, 1997.
Underground News, Issue #17, 1995.

Additional information was provided by Joi Cardwell in an interview with *Contemporary Musicians,* and from publicity material provided by EightBall Records.

—*B. Kimberly Taylor*

Bob Carlisle

Singer, songwriter

Carlisle jokes about *Butterfly Kisses,* his 1997 album with the hit song of the same name, making him an overnight sensation. The album was first released in 1996 as *Shades of Grace* for the Christian Contemporary market and only later garnered Grammy and Country Music Association Award nominations. "This overnight sensation," Carlisle told *TV Guide,* "was about 23 years in the making."

A singer, songwriter, and guitarist, Bob Carlisle began performing in clubs during the 1970s. He gained a reputation as a session musician in the early 1980s, doing background vocals for other recording artists and groups, including Barry Manilow, REO Speedwagon, Juice Newton, Motley Crue, and Poison. In 1984, he formed The Allies with Randy Thomas and Sam Scott. The group performed together for nine years and released six albums. He released two solo albums with Sparrow Records, *Bob Carlisle* in 1993 and *The Hope Of A Man* in 1994. He finally won national attention in 1997 with *Butterfly Kisses (Shades of Grace),* an album on Jive Records that went double platinum (two million

AP/Wide World Photos

For the Record . . .

Born in Santa Ana, CA; married late 1970s; wife's name, Jacque; children Brooke, and Evan.

Worked as a session musician during the early 1980's doing background vocals for Barry Manilow, REO Speedwagon, Juice Newton, Motley Crue, Poison, and others; formed the Christian rock band, The Allies with Randy Thomas and Sam Scot, 1984; co-wrote songs recorded by other country artists, including "Why'd You Come In Here Lookin' Like That," by Dolly Parton; released his first solo album, *Bob Carlisle,* on Sparrow Records, 1993;*The Hope of a Man*, 1994; he signed with Diadem, released *Shades of Grace,* 1996; *Shades of Grace* was repackaged and reissued as *Butterfly Kisses* on Jive Records, 1997.

Awards: "Butterfly Kisses" won the Gospel Music Association (GMA) Dove Award for Inspirational Song of the Year and Song of the Year, 1997; *Butterfly Kisses/Shades of Grace* certified double platinum, 1997; "Butterfly Kisses" named Song of the Year, 1998.

Addresses: *Record Company*—Jive, 137-139 West 25th St., New York, NY 10001. *Manager*— Ray Ware Management, 251 Second Ave. South, Suite 5, Franklin, TN 37064. *Website*— www.bobcarlisle.com.

units sold). Ironically "Butterfly Kisses" had been written as a gift for his daughter Brooke's sixteenth birthday and was a song Carlisle had never intended to record.

A strong family man, Carlisle's family origins were influential on his music. He tells a story about his seventh birthday when his dad took him to Montgomery Ward's and allowed the birthday boy to pick out anything he wanted. After giving the matter some thought, Carlisle selected a guitar. Afterwards his father let him take guitar lessons as well. This was the beginning of Carlisle's lifelong passion for music. He learned how to play guitar and read music; eventually he even learned arranging and orchestration.

Carlisle has a variety of musical roots. R & B was one early influence, with Otis Redding, Wilson Pickett, and James Brown among his favorites. He grew up around bluegrass and down-home country music. His father, a dealer in acoustic musical instruments, often allowed Carlisle to jam with his buddies; musical greats like guitarist Doc Watson and dobro player Tut Taylor.

Disillusion with Christian Music Scene

As a teen, Carlisle became interested in the music of the Jesus movement in Southern California. He joined his first band, Good News, when he was sixteen. His next group was Psalm 150 where he first met Randy Thomas, with whom he would later collaborate on many songs. Psalm 150 made one album. Eventually, however, Carlisle became disillusioned with the opportunities of the Christian music scene to make a living.

After high school, Carlisle was offered a college music scholarship but turned it down to keep performing. In the late 1970s he married his wife, Jacque. They had two children together, a daughter Brooke and a son Evan. It was then that Carlisle established himself as a well paidsession musician, doing background vocals for many artists and groups. At the same time, he was learning the ropes of record production and he also had a regular gig at Rosie's, a club in Los Angeles.

In 1984, Carlisle once again found himself unhappy with his work. The Christian singer hated the clubs and bars he was playing. One night, in the middle of a show, he walked offstage in disgust and prayed for guidance. Within a week, Sam Scott and his old friend Randy Thomas, who had been singing with the Sweet Comfort Band, a Christian group, invited Carlisle to become a vocalist for a new band called The Allies. This was the answer to Carlisle's prayers. The Allies soon signed with Light Records. They stayed together nine years and recorded six albums together.

Became Solo Artist

The Allies were based in Colton, California, but played most of their gigs in venues east of the Rocky Mountains. They soon realized that a move to Nashville made sense. After the group broke up, Carlisle stayed in Nashville, Tennessee, to pursue his career as a Contemporary Christian artist and songwriter. "Why'd You Come In Here Lookin' Like That," a song Carlisle and Randy Thomas co-wrote, was a hit for Dolly Parton and its success bolstered Carlisle's confidence in his songwriting talents.

His first solo album, *Bob Carlisle,* was released on the Sparrow label in 1993 and not much later his second Sparrow album, *The Hope of a Man,* came out. Carlisle was released from his Sparrow contract in 1994 and when Diadem President George King offered him a contract, Carlisle figured he had nothing to lose. At that point he changed his entire attitude toward music. "I decided to just write music out of my heart and soul," he told Audrey T. Hingley of *Christian Reader,* "and quit chasing musical success." That decision resulted in the successful *Shades of Grace,* released on Diadem in 1996. The album featured the Christian hit single, "Mighty Love," and the surprise hit, "Butterfly Kisses."

"Butterfly Kisses" was Carlisle's first big success as an artist. It was also the song that enabled him to cross over from Christian contemporary to pop music. Jive Records repackaged *Shades of Grace* for a mainstream audience in 1997 and in July of that year, *Butterfly Kisses (Shades of Grace)* went double platinum. After having been number one on the contemporary Christian charts almost one year, "Butterfly Kisses" was a surprise hit on the *Billboard* charts during 1997. It remained in the number one spot on *Billboard*'s Top 200 Album Chart for seven weeks and made its mark on pop and country charts as well.

Family Values

Carlisle's songs characteristically contain simple messages and are delivered with his expressive vocals. His lyrics and heartfelt emotion often express his strong connection to family values. Many songs on *Butterfly Kisses* also express Carlisle's feelings towards other members of his family. "You Must Have Been An Angel," for example, is a love song to his wife, Jacque. In "Man Of His Word," Carlisle sings about his parents. "Butterfly Kisses" is a highly personal song of his love and appreciation for his daughter, Brooke. Carlisle wrote the song after looking through some photos of his daughter that had been taken over the years. At the time she was almost sixteen and Carlisle realized that Brooke would be leaving home before long. He chronicled his wistful nostalgia in his song that contains vignettes of her life from early childhood to the time she would become a bride. Carlisle's wife later persuaded him to play "Butterfly Kisses," which he never meant to record, for George King, who in turn convinced Carlisle to include it on his *Shades of Grace* album.

"Butterfly Kisses" radio play elicited an incredible response. Two veteran radio programmers, Roger Christian of WMJQ of Buffalo, New York and Joe Hann of WRCH of Hartford, Connecticut, each with over 20 years radio experience, noted that the demand for the song was unlike anything they had ever known. Carlisle produced a remixed country version of "Butterfly Kisses," and two additional country versions were released soon after the original, one by the Raybon Brothers and another by Jeff Carson. For a while it was the battle of "Butterfly Kisses" as the three versions simultaneously competed on the country radio hit charts. Carlisle's album sales were fueled by his appearance on the Oprah Winfrey show and her endorsement of *Butterfly Kisses.*

Panned By Many Critics

Critics were almost universally puzzled by the song's popularity. *Time*'s reviewer called it "syrupy enough to serve with waffles." Heather Bird of the *Toronto Sun* called it "silly, vapid, saccharin." While Kieran Grant, also of the *Toronto Sun,* noted Carlisle's "sincerity," but thought the tune "insipid and instantly forgettable...." On a positive note, *Wall Street Journal* reviewer, Andrew Peyton Thomas, observed that "Butterfly Kisses" was so immensely popular because it was "genuine ... a rare song ... destined to become a classic."

In spite of the mixed reviews, Carlisle's fans seemed to have no reservations about "Butterfly Kisses." Carlisle delivered a song that touched the hearts of many with his candid expression of love for his daughter. The song inspired countless reconciliations between estranged parents and children, and the song soon became a standard at weddings. Carlisle himself sang the tune at Brooke's high school graduation at Page High School in Franklin, Tennessee.

Song for Son

Carlisle defined a butterfly kiss for Ann Oldenburg of *USA Today* as "the fluttering of one's eyelashes on the cheek of another person." Carlisle has repeatedly been asked if he plans a song about his son Evan. "Yeah," he told Oldenburg, "it's called, 'Get Down Off Of That!'" But he and Randy Thomas actually did write a tune for both of their sons called "A Father's Love." Regarding his future plans Carlisle commented to *R & R,* "I'm going to do what I've always done, and that is to write and sing songs out of my own need and my own passion."

Carlisle is enjoying his present success although demands on his time have been fierce. The success of *Butterfly Kisses* spawned several book tie-ins, some of them written by Carlisle. He turns down TV specials and other lucrative offers in order to honor previous commitments, like small shows at churches and county fairs and to be with his family, which he considers his top priority. The success of *Butterfly Kisses* will undoubtedly open doors to other mainstream music opportunities for Carlisle.

Selected Discography

Bob Carlisle, Sparrow, 1993.
The Hope of A Man, Sparrow, 1994.
Shades of Grace, (includes "Mighty Love" and "Butterfly Kisses"), Diadem, 1996.
Butterfly Kisses (Shades of Grace), (includes "You Must Have Been An Angel," "Man Of His Word," and "Butterfly Kisses"), Jive, 1997.

with The Allies

Allies, Light, 1985.
Virtues, Light, 1986.
Shoulder to Shoulder, DaySpring, 1988.
Long Way From Paradise, DaySpring, 1989.
The River, DaySpring, 1990.
Man With A Mission, DaySpring, 1991.

Selected writings

(With Randy Thomas) "Why'd You Come In Here Lookin' Like That" (song), Dolly Parton, 1984.
Butterfly Kisses (children's book), Tommy Nelson Publishing, 1997.
Butterfly Kisses (children's book, available as audio read by Carlisle and daughter, Brooke), Golden Books, 1997.
Butterfly Kisses (letters between fathers and daughters), Jack Countryman/Word Publishing, 1997.
A Journal of Butterfly Kisses (journal for fathers and daughters), Word Publishing, 1997.
Butterfly Kisses and Bittersweet Tears (stories told to and by Carlisle), Word Publishing, 1998.
"Louisiana Moon," (song), Mel McDaniels.
"Red-Neck Son," (song), Ty England.

Sources

Periodicals

Billboard, May 31, 1997; June 28, 1997; July 5, 1997.
Chicago Tribune, July 10, 1997.
Christian Reader, September/October 1997, p. 21-24.
R & R, May 30, 1997.
Time, June 30, 1997.
Toronto Son, August 19, 1997; July 17, 1997.
TV Guide, September 20, 1997, p. 34-35.
USA Today, May 12, 1997.
Wall Street Journal, July 22, 1997.

Online

www.allmusic.com
www.bobcarlisle.com
www.canoe.ca/JamAlbumsC/Carlisle_b_butterfly.html
www.young-country.com/BobCarlisle.html

Additional information supplied by publicist, Melissa Hambrick, of Spin Cycle.

—Debra Reilly

Regina Carter

Jazz violinist

Courtesy of NIA Entertainment

Jazz violinist Regina Carter began playing at the age of four in a class that used the Suzuki method. This method of instruction does not require a child to read music; they learn by hearing a song and trying to mimic the notes with a tiny violin. In an issue of *Downbeat,* Carter joked, "They had just started to use the Suzuki method at the school where I was studying. And I don't think they got it quite right. You see, they didn't check my playing against the real song for accuracy, like they're supposed to. If they had, I don't think I'd be playing violin today!" She just released her second jazz solo album called *Something for Grace.*

Carter was exposed to a variety of music growing up in Detroit where she started playing the piano at the age of two and switched to violin at four. Her early influences were mainly classical music. She performed with the Detroit Civic Symphony. "People are only used to hearing violin in European classical music or country music," Carter once said. She proved to audiences that the violin is capable of playing many types of music—from Latin to Rhythm & Blues.

When she attended the prestigious Cass Technical High School in Detroit, she listened to Motown, Latin, Middle Eastern, and R & B styles of music. She told *Downbeat,* "There's a big Latin community—Mexican Village—and we used to go down to Clark Park where you can hear all kinds of music all the time." During high school, she also developed a love for jazz after she heard Jean-Luc Ponty. She recalled, "I just immediately fell in love with it and started studying jazz a little bit in high school." After high school, Carter attended the New England Conservatory in Boston, Massachusetts and Oakland University in Michigan. During that time, she belonged to a multi-cultural band that played all types of music—including lyrics in Arabic.

Straight Ahead to Jazz

In 1987 Carter joined an all-female jazz band based in Detroit. The band, called Straight Ahead, performed often in Detroit and gained enough of a following to grab the attention of Atlantic Records. Carter recorded two albums with Straight Ahead and then decided to move to New York to pursue other interests. In New York, Carter worked with Oliver Lake, Max Roach, and the Uptown String Quartet. In 1993 she became a regular violinist for the well-known String Trio of New York, a jazz band that formed in 1979. The group performs avant-garde and post-bop styles of jazz, with plenty of improvisation—Regina Carter's passion. Her first album with the String Trio, *Octagon,* received rave reviews. Jon Andrews of *Downbeat* wrote, "Regina

For the Record . . .

Born Regina Carter. *Education*: attended New England Conservatory and Oakland University.

Started playing violin at age four—learned by Suzuki method; exposed to variety of music in Detroit including Latin, R & B, and jazz; joined jazz band Straight Ahead, 1987; recorded two albums with Straight Ahead and performed in concert often; left Straight Ahead and moved to New York, 1992; played with Oliver Lake, Max Roach, and Uptown String Quartet; joined String Trio of New York, 1993; recorded two albums with String Trio of New York: *Octagon* and *Blues...?*; worked with bassist Mark Helias on *Loopin' the Cool*, 1995; recorded first jazz solo album for Atlantic Jazz titled *Regina Carter*, 1995; toured with Wynton Marsalis and the Lincoln Center Jazz Orchestra for *Blood on the Fields* epic, 1996; recorded second solo album for Atlantic Jazz titled *Something for Grace*, 1997.

Address: *Record company*—Atlantic Records, 1290 Avenue of the Americas, New York, NY 10104.

Carter's arrival as a violinist, along with new material, changes the formula significantly. Throughout *Octagon,* Carter plays with a clear, pure tone...." In 1996 the String Trio released *Blues...?*. Jon Andrews again approved of Carter's effort. He wrote, "She maintains a beautiful tone while strutting and gliding through these tracks, including her own reggae-based 'Hurry Up and Wait." *Blues...?* covers tunes from Charlie Parker, Miles Davis, and Lee Morgan as well as originals from bassist John Lindberg.

In 1995 Carter also worked with bassist Mark Helias on his album *Loopin' the Cool.* Ellery Eskelin played tenor saxophone on the record. Mark Corbett of *Downbeat* commented, "With the Carter/Eskelin frontline, Helias has created a provocative combination—the tenor/violin mix is startling, especially on the many unison sections that feature the two in tandem." He also remarked, "Carter exercises complete control, avoiding the high-harmonic flurries to which other violinists often gravitate; check her feature 'El Baz'." Other artists have benefited from Carter's unique jazz/R & B violin including: Antonio Hart, Faith Evans, Vanessa Rubin, Daniel Johnston, Mary J. Blige, and Patti Labelle.

Making a Name for Herself

In 1995 Carter recorded her first solo effort for Atlantic Records, simply titled *Regina Carter.* Her producer, Victor Bailey focused on the "smooth jazz" radio audiences and tried to make the record easy listening. Carter explained, "There's a certain formula for how a tune has to be put together. It might be that you need to state the melody a second time or a little bit more so people really remember that melody. And alot of times I find, on records that are more for ... commercial radio, the solos should be very limited because people aren't really listening for that." Carter is aware that if her solo records don't sell, the record company may dump her. She manages to keep her perspective. She said, "The record isn't my goal. My goal is to continue to write and play music that's true to me, and if I remember that always, no one can take that away from me."

Carter dedicated her second solo effort *Something for Grace* to her mother, whom Carter praises for her encouragement and support. This album was also targeted for the smooth-jazz radio format. Ben Ratliff of the *New York Times* calls the format "jazz's blander shadow-world." However, Frank-John Hadley of *Downbeat* was impressed. He wrote, "Carter is her own woman and she records the kind of music that she deems suitable for honest expression...." Arif Mardin produced three of the tracks on the album. Carter admitted to being a little tense about working with him. "We were all uptight," she recalled. "But then Arif walked in, ordered lunch, and instantly broke the tension. He knows exactly how to bring the best out of people." Hadley wrote, "[Mardin] frames Carter's adoration of melody and modest flair for improvisation...."

Carter built her reputation as a great jazz violinist with years of solid live performances that left critics dazzled. One of her greatest achievements was performing with Wynton Marsalis and the Lincoln Center Jazz Orchestra on their international tour of *Blood on the Fields.* In January 1998, Carter appeared at New York's Sweet Basil for a series of concerts. Ben Ratliff of the *New York Times* wrote, "she proved something that perhaps didn't need proving except for the fact that there's so little evidence of it: that the violin's role in deeply swinging jazz is perfectly natural...." He described her music as "rapid, hornlike chromatic improvising, whinnying, double-stopped fragments of the blues and ... glassy harmonics that sounded like pan pipes."

Carter gives all the credit for her talent to God. She said, "What I'm doing and I'm playing is not really mine. I'm being used as a vessel, and I have to thank God." Her liner notes read, "Praise GOD from whom all blessings flow." No doubt she considers Suzuki one of those many blessings from God.

Selected discography

with Straight Ahead

Look Straight Ahead, Atlantic Records, 1992.
Body and Soul, Atlantic Records1993.

with String Trio of New York

Intermobility, 1993.
Octagon, Black Saint, 1994.
Blues...? (includes "Hurry Up and Wait"), Black Saint, 1996.

Solo

Regina Carter, Atlantic Records,1995.
Something for Grace, Atlantic Records1997.

With others

(Mary J. Blige) *My Life,* 1994.
(Daniel Johnston) *Fun,* 1994.
(Vanessa Rubin) *I'm Glad There Is You-A Tribute to Carmen McRae,* 1994.
(Faith Evans) *Faith Evans,* 1995.
(Antonio Hart) *It's All Good,* 1995.
(Mark Helias) *Loopin' the Cool* (includes "El Baz"), 1996.
(Hollywood Bowl Orchestra) *Prelude to a Kiss,* 1996.
(Madeline Peyroux) *Dreamland,* 1996.
(Rachel Z) *Room of One's Own,* 1996.
(Johnny Almendra) *Reconfirmando,* 1997.
(Patti Labelle) *Flame,* 1997.
(Billy Lawrence) *Come On,* 1997.
(Quartette Indigo) *Afrika Afrika,* 1997.
(Gary Smulyan) *Gary Smulyan with Strings,* 1997.

Sources

Periodicals

Downbeat, June, 1996; September, 1994; November, 1997; December, 1997.
New York Times, January 8, 1998.
Time, February 9, 1998.

Additional information provided by the Atlantic Records website and Atlantic press materials; liner notes from *Something for Grace;* the Music Boulevard website on America Online; All-Music Guide, A Complete Online Database of Recorded Music, provided by Matrix Software.

—Christine Morrison

Congo Norvell

Pop duo

Congo Norvell, comprised of singer Sally Norvell and guitarist Kid Congo Powers, blends melodramatic melodies with dark lyrics about outcasts and loners to achieve a uniquely gothic, mysterious sound. A reviewer noted in the *Village Voice* , "In their demonic torch songs, [Kid Congo] Powers' playing is wily and wise, like he knows who did it and isn't telling. [Norvell] belts and moans like she knows who did it, and it was her." Powers was formerly with Nick Cave and the Bad Seeds, the Cramps, and the Gun Club, and Congo Norvell's murky, dirge-like tempo reflects his past musical experience: the lyrics and presentation are reminiscent of Nick Cave, the offbeat campiness recalls the Cramps, and the hard-edged rock element recalls the Gun Club. Norvell, formerly with The Norvells, released an album with that group called *Prohibition* in 1980, which featured members of Glass Eye, Jesus Lizard, and Scratch Acid covering songs from the 1920s in an avant-garde manner.

When the duo wants to fill out their sound they enlist keyboardist Kristian Hoffman of the Mumps and Swinging Madisons, drummer Jim Sclavunos of the Lydia Lunch band, and bassist Mary Mullen of the Europe-based The Hesitations. Sandi Salina Messana of the *Los Angeles Village View* described the band's music as, "Campy and witty ... an impeccably sweet vocalist backed by spare, atmospheric playing ... mood-evoking music ... sensuous timbres...."

Powers didn't know how to play a guitar before the age of 18, but when his friend Jeffery Lee Pierce from the Gun Club, formally called the Creeping Ritual, asked him if he wanted to join a band, he said yes, and has since mastered the guitar. Powers started there as a guitarist and eventually moved on to join the Cramps within a year. He then moved on to Nick Cave and the Bad Seeds, and contributed to the German instrumental band Die Haut.

Norvell and Powers formed their band in 1990 after meeting at a hospital where both were paying their last respects to the wife of a mutual friend, who was dying of AIDS. Each had been cast in a Wim Wenders film: Norvell in *Paris, Texas,* and Powers in *Wings of Desire.* Both also shared a similar musical background; Norvell founded The Norvells in Austin, Texas in 1979 and Powers had been in numerous punk rock bands dating as far back as 1979. In 1994, Powers told *Option* magazine's Holly George-Warren, "The idea I had was to gather a bunch of true eccentrics and see how eccentric this music might turn out.... Sally and I wanted to do something that would affect people on an emotional level. Extreme melodrama seemed like a good start—we're learning to be a bit more subtle now."

Jetsetted to New York

Films influence the music of Congo Norvell, perhaps because Norvell had experience as an independent film maker, and both turn to movies for musical inspiration. Norvell and Powers like to imagine that their music would be the soundtrack for an imaginary film when composing it. Douglas Sirk, Roman Polanski, Wim Wenders, and John Cassavetes are their favorite directors. In addition to recording and performing original compositions, the band sometimes includes material by Louis Armstrong, Nancy Sinatra, and an eclectic array of other traditional musical icons.

Norvell finds inspiration in the music of Maria Callas, Sarah Vaughan, Ella Fitzgerald, Latin singer Mercedes Souza, Marion Anderson, and music of the 1920s; Mullen listens to Native American chant music; Powers to offbeat 1960s music; Sclavunos listens to Tav Falco; and Hoffman likes pop rock bands like Abba. Their wide range of musical influences contributes to their unique sound. Powers told George-Warren, "You put it all [the diverse musical influences] in a blender and it comes out like this—it's not a sound any of us could have pulled off individually."

The band released *Lullabies,* a four-song EP, on Fiasco with Kristian Hoffman, Mary Mullen, and Jim Sclavunos

For the Record . . .

Members include **Sally Norvell,** vocals; **Kid Congo Powers,** guitar. Occasional members include **Kristian Hoffman** (of the Mumps), keyboards; **Mary Mullen** (of the Hesitations), bass; **Jim Sclavunos** (of the Lydia Lunch band), drums.

Powers was formerly with Nick Cave and the Bad Seeds, the Cramps, and the Gun Club; he appeared in the Wim Wenders film *Wings of Desire.* Norvell was formerly with the Norvells and released *Prohibition* with them in 1980; she appeared in the Wim Wenders film *Paris, Texas.* Formed Congo Norvell in 1990; released their first EP *Lullabies* on Fiasco label in 1993; signed with Basura!-Priority Records and released *Music to Remember Him By* in 1994; recorded the unreleased *The Dope, The Lies, The Vaseline* in 1996; released *Abnormals Anonymous* for Jetset Records in 1997.

Address: *Record company*—Jetset Records, 67 Vestry Street, Suite 5C, New York, NY 10013; (212) 625-0202; Internet—www.sinner.com/jetset.

in 1993. A staff writer for *San Francisco Weekly* wrote of *Lullabies,* "The songs, ghoulishly and dramatically orchestrated, make the idea of a terrifying love seem mighty appealing. The sound is half troubled torch song, half tortured atmospherics, with ominous, dirge like drumbeats and great crashing piano chords urging on Novell's vocals." Mick Harvey, of the Australian goth-thrash band Crime & the City Solution and the Bad Seeds, produced Congo Norvell's debut album. The Congo Norvell single "Angel" was written by Crime & the City Solution's singer/songwriter Simon Bonney.

Congo Norvell released *Music to Remember Him By* in 1994 on Basura!-Priority Records, and recorded *The Dope, The Lies, The Vaseline* for the same label in 1996. Priority decided to fold its Basura! rock label—which included Congo Norvell on its roster. Their album *The Dope, The Lies, The Vaseline* was never released, so the band decided to move to New York City and to switch over to the New York-based Jetset Records as a result.

Congo Norvell released *Abnormals Anonymous* for Jetset in 1997, with Mark Eitzel contributing vocals on five tracks. After the release of *Abnormals Anonymous,* Powers told *CMJ*'s Cella Holms, "I do think that we're creating music that is more daring than what a lot of people are doing. We're not using hip-hop beats. First and foremost I like things pretty classical, music-wise, sound-wise, and I'm always striving for beauty." *Abnormals Anonymous* is about outcasts and loners. The single "Brother Jack" is about a musician who returned home after the death of his father, only to be rejected by his family members. Powers told *Interview* magazine's Marc Weingarten, "People always need a place to put their grief and anger, and they usually pick people who've chosen a path different from their own. I've had similar things happen to me."

No Formal Training

Neither Powers nor Norvell had formal music training before joining bands. Norvell's mother encouraged her and her sisters to do whatever made them happy, and Norvell felt drawn to film and music. Powers played music by instinct. He told *Entertainment*'s Steven Mirkin, "My roots are in very traditional kinds of music. Old blues, John Lee Hooker, Sunhouse, Howlin' Wolf, it's just instinctual playing.... I think that's why Jefferey Lee Pierce, or Nick Cave, or ourselves, tend to go for that. It has a lot more to do with the emotional impact of playing than it does with any kind of technical proficiency." Powers produced an album for a Texas-cum-New York City band called The Factory Press in 1998, and planned on playing drums and guitar with the band Bottleneck Drag.

Norvell had a son in the mid-1990s, and Powers became publicly outspoken about the fact that he was gay, granting interviews to the *Advocate* and *Out* magazines. He had always been frank with his band members about his sexuality—and they viewed his freedom as an asset—but it wasn't until he and Norvell lost a friend to the AIDS epidemic that he decided to be outspoken about it. When speaking with Barry Walters of the *Advocate*, Powers said, "I've got the big blond woman singing. I think we're also quite dramatic. In the same way that a lot of gay people relate to someone like Billie Holiday, I would hope that people could relate to what we're doing."

Selected discography

Lullabies (EP), Fiasco, 1993.
Music to Remember Him By, Basura!-Priority, 1994.
The Dope, The Lies, The Vaseline (Unreleased), Basura!-Priority, 1996.
Abnormals Anonymous, Jetset, 1997.

Sources

Advocate, February 1998.
Alternative Press, March 1998.
CMJ, October 27, 1997; November 14, 1997.
Entertainment Weekly, November 14, 1997.
Eye Deal, December 1997.
Guitar Magazine, March 1998.
Instant Magazine, November 1997.
Interview, December 1997.
Lollipop, December 1997.
Los Angeles Village View, April 5, 1997.
Magnet, January/February 1998.
Musician, February 1998.
New Music, November 1997.
New York Times, November 14, 1997.
Option, January/February 1994.
Out, May 1998.
Philadelphia City Paper, January 30-February 5, 1998.
San Francisco Weekly, November 20, 1997.
Time out, December 4-11, 1997.
Village Voice, January, 1998.

—B. Kimberly Taylor

Celia Cruz

Singer

The Queen of Salsa, the Queen of Mambo, the Queen of Latin Music—Celia Cruz reigns as supreme diva. During her illustrious career, Cruz has performed across the globe with other top Latin musicians, recorded more than 50 albums—20 of which went gold, and earned over 100 awards from various countries. The legendary singer with the rich, powerful, contralto voice covering several octaves is known for her incredible ability at improvisation, flamboyant costumes and for sprinkling audiences with sugar during live performances. She has opened doors for other women performers during her career spanning almost fifty years, in a formerly male dominated Latin music world. Although some try to compare her style to jazz greats like Ella Fitzgerald and Sara Vaughan because of her quick staccato interjections of jazz-like scat, Cruz has a unique style, unrivaled by another; she has created her own musical niche.

Salsa sound has been described as Cuban music combined with Puerto Rican and other influences, and behind it all, African religious music. Salsa has a wide range of colorful associations, with an up beat tempo,

Courtesy of RMM Records

For the Record . . .

Born on October 21, 1924; raisedp in the Barrio Santo Suarez, Cuba; came to the United States in 1960, and became a citizen in 1961; married Pedro Knight, trumpeter, 1962; *Education:* Studied at Havana, Cuba's National Conservatory of Music, 1947-50.

Began singing on Cuban radio in the late 1940's; in 1950, became the lead singer of Cuban big band, La Sonora Matancera, recording and touring with them until 1965; joined Tito Puente Orchestra in 1966; recorded eight albums with him; sang the role of Gracia Divina at Carnagie Hall in Larry Harlow's *Hommy-A Latin* opera, 1973; during the 1980's and 1990's performed with such artists as pop singer David Byrne, Emilio Estefan, and Willie Chirino; cameo roles in *The Mambo Kings* and *The Perez Family;* has recorded over 50 albums, 20 of which became gold; performed worldwide.

Awards: Grammy Award for Best Tropical Latin Album, 1989, awarded medal by President Clinton from the National Endowment of the Arts, 1994.

Addresses: *Record Company*—Omar Pardillo-Cid, RMM Records, 568 Broadway, Suite 806, New York, NY 10012; *Agent*—Bookings Online Talent Agency, Ltd., 236 West 26th St., Ste. 701, New York, NY 10001. *Websites*—www.rmmrecords.com.

and includes a wide range of Latin styles and rhythms. Cruz described salsa for *World Music: The Rough Guide,* "Salsa is Cuban music with another name. It's mambo, chachacha, rumba, son.... All the Cuban rhythms under one name." Myth claims that the term "salsa" was created by a Venezuelan radio disc jockey.

Salsa's roots hail back to the 18th century with the Cuban "son," a rhythm created by Theodora Ginez. It evolved with the influx of Haitians and French to Cuba, and for a while the government officially forbade its playing, saying its lyrics, which protested slavery, encouraged riots. "Son" combined both the African and Spanish roots of Cuban music, with the African percussion and rhythm, the flavor of Spanish guitar, and the style of call and response between one or two male singers. The unifying theme behind it all are the references to a conglomeration of various religions, including Afro-Catholic, incorporating the inconsistencies among them. Through song, the singers hail deities and invoke various goddesses. Although links to deities, goddesses, and saints may be unspoken, many in the audiences understand the connections through the singer's actions on stage.

Celia Cruz was born on October 21, 1924, and grew up in the Barrio, Santo Suarez, near Havana, Cuba. She was one of four children. As a child she often sang for her family, many times singing her siblings to sleep at night. Later as a teen, she sang in school programs, and soon began entering and winning local radio talent shows. By 1947 she had won her first prize on a radio program, and enrolled in Havana's National Conservatory of Music, which she attended until 1950. Encouraged by her father, she first dreamt of becoming a teacher. Then a professor at the Conservatory persuaded her she was destined to be a professional singer, and soon Cruz's first big opportunity would present itself.

Cruz said one of her first influences was a singer, Paulina Alvarez, who was the first singer she ever saw performing in front of an orchestra. Cruz dreamt of performing as Alvarez did, in spite of her different singing style. It was a dream destined to come true. Her big break came when she was chosen to replace the lead singer for the popular Cuban big band, La Sonora Matancera. Beginning in1950, Cruz recorded and toured extensively with the band throughout Latin America and Mexico for the next fifteen years. She and La Sonora came to be known as "Cafe con Leche" ("coffee with milk").

Cruz left Cuba with La Sonora Matancera after the revolution when Fidel Castro came to power, arriving in the United States in 1960. The following year, in 1961, Cruz became a U.S. citizen. Also during 1961, she met Pedro Knight, a trumpet player with the orchestra she was contracted to perform with at Hollywood, California's Palladium. In 1962 she married Knight, who in 1965 put his own career aside to manage his wife's career. During the 1920s and 1930s the salsa style had regained popularity with various bands continuing innovations to el son. Perez Prado's 1949 hit, "Mambo #5," officially kicked off the mambo era.

Performed with Many Salsa Innovators

Tito Puente was among those who adapted Prado's sound for audiences and the dance crowds of New York during the 1950s. In 1966 Cruz joined Tito Puente's Orchestra and recorded eight albums with him on Tico Records. Cruz maintained her alliance with Puente into the 1990s, performing in Europe with him. Puente is known as the King of Latin Music.

In 1973 Cruz sang at Carnagie Hall in the role of Gracia Divina in Larry Harlow's *Hommy-A Latin* opera, an adaption of the rock opera, *Tommy,* by the Who. It was during this time that salsa music was revitalized in the United States. Throughout the 1970's Cruz performed with many others including Johnny Pacheco, Willie Colon, and the Fania All-Stars. The All-Stars included other salsa notables such as Bobby Cruz, Ricardo Ray, Ismael Quintana, Larry Harlow, Ray Barretto, and many more. During this time as a featured singer with the Fania All-Stars she toured worldwide with the group including spots in London, England, Cannes, France, and Zaire, Africa.

Willie Colon, singer and trombonist, was responsible for much innovation in salsa in New York, as was Johnny Pacheco, musician and producer who directed Fania Records. Cruz and Pacheco made the album, *Celia and Johnny,* which went gold. She and Pacheco would team up and produce two more hit albums. Soon this style was copied in Latin America, and the Caribbean, but New York maintained its position as the creative and evolutionary center of the Latin music world.

Gained Worldwide Recognition

During the 1980s and 1990s Cruz performed with a wide range of talent, including David Byrne, Emilio Estefan, and Willie Chirino. She has appeared in cameo roles in *The Perez Family* and *The Mambo Kings;* exposure in both films gained her the attention of a greater non-Latin audience. Although Cruz is one of the few Latin singers with an extensive audience in the U.S., language barriers interfere with breakthrough onto pop charts in the United States. Unlike many European countries where people speak several languages, and American music is played alongside the music of that country, salsa may get limited air time in the United States because it isn't in English.

Cruz has been recognized in countries worldwide by various institutions, newspapers, and magazines. Some of her awards include an honorary doctorate degree from Yale University, a star on Hollywood Boulevard in California, a Grammy Award in 1989 for Best Tropical Latin Album, plus many Grammy nominations over the years. She received a medal from President Clinton in 1994 from the National Endowment of the Arts. Cruz is included in Walks of Fame in Costa Rica, Venezuela, and Mexico . She has earned many other awards during her career, over 100 total.

She continues recording and performing live, showing no signs of slowing down. Cruz tours about ten months out of each year. "Azucar" is her calling card, and she is known for her ability at improvisation as well as her talent to bring a sense of euphoria through her music to her audience. Peter Watrous of the *New York Times,* described her voice during a 1995 performance: "Her voice sounded, as if it were made of cast iron, durable and pure." In a later review, of a performance in November 1996 at the Blue Note, Greenwich Village, New York, which Watrous also covered for the *New York Times,* he noted Cruz's use of "rich, metaphorical language." He added, "This was virtuosity that is rarely heard, where a combination of languages, cultures, and epoches all added up to a deep intelligence, a Creole vision of the New World's promise."

In spite of her monumental success, reigning as supreme diva over Latin music for over 40 years, one of Cruz's fondest desires has nothing to do with music. She told *Beat* interviewer, Derek Rath, she would welcome the opportunity to return to Cuba, to visit her mother's grave. Cruz's greatest rewards come from her ability to bring others happiness through her music. She told Rath, "When I sing I put everything I have inside me into it, a lot of love. Music is the only gift I have that was given to me by God.... [it] is my purpose in life.... I want people to feel their hearts sing and their spirits soar."

Selected discography

The Winners, Vaya, 1987.
Best, Sony/Globo, 1992, originally issued on Fania Records.
Best Vol. 2, Sony Discos/Globo, 1994.
Canciones Premiadas, Palladium, 1994.
Irrepetible, UNI/RMM, 1994.
La Tierna Conmovedora Bambolea, Palladium, 1994.
Homenaje a Los Santos, Polydor, 1994.
Cuba's Queen of Rhythm, Palladium, 1995.
Canta Celia Cruz, Palladium, 1995.
Irresistible, Sony Discos/Orfeon, 1995.
Azucar Negra, UNI/RMM, 1998.
Su Favorita Celia Cruz, Secco.
Reflexiones De Celia Cruz, Secco.
Bravo Celia Cruz, Tico.

With Tito Puente

Cuba Y Puerto Rico Son, Tico.
El Quimbo Quimbumbia, Tico.
Alma Con Alma, Tico.
Algo Especial Para Recordar, Tico.
Homenaje A Beny More, Vaya.

With La Sonora Matancera

100% Azucar: The Best of Celia, Rhino Records, 1997.
Cuba's Foremost Rhythm Singer with Sonora Matancera, Secco.
Con Amor: Celia Cruz with La Sonora Matancera, Secco.
La Incomparable Celia and Sonora Matancera, Secco.
Feliz Encuentro, Barbaro.
Nostalgia Tropical, Orfeon.

With Others

Duets, UNI/RMM, 1997.
Fania All-Stars, Sony Discos, 1997.
Celia and Johnny, Vaya.
Celia and Willie Colon, Vaya.

Sources

Books

Broughton, Simon, Mark Ellingham, David Muddyman, and Richard Trillo, editors, *World Music: The Rough Guide,* Rough Guides, 1994.
Erlewine, Michael, Chris Woodstra, and Vladimir Bogdanov, editors, *All-Music Guide,* Miller Freeman Books, 1994.
Slonimsky, Nicolas, editor, *Baker's Biographical Dictionary of Musicians,* Schirmer Books, 1992.

Periodicals

Beat, #6, 1995, p. 42-45.
Interview, November 1996.
Metro Times (Detroit, MI), November 5-11, 1997, p. 50.
Mirabella, June 1994.
New York Times, July 4, 1995, p. 26; November 23, 1996, p. 14; (magazine) November 1, 1992.
Stereo Review, January 1995, p. 8.

Online

www.cduniverse.com/
www.rmmrecords.com/

Additional information was provided by publicist, Omar Pardillo-Cid of RMM Records.

—Debra Reilly

The Dandy Warhols

Rock band

The Dandy Warhols have been slyly dubbed "the best British band to come out of America," but the quartet of Oregonians with the self-imposed, somewhat moronic name put forth an intense and complexly psychedelic sound. Critics have compared them—favorably—to a pantheon of trip-rocksters ranging from the Velvet Underground and T. Rex to Galaxie 500 and the Jesus and Mary Chain. The Dandys themselves cite early, Syd Barrett-era Pink Floyd as a profound influence on their music, a creation described by *Rolling Stone* as "an aggressive mix of psychedelic guitar, lush dissonance and stoner vocals."

Singer/songwriter Courtney Taylor serves as the photogenic poster boy for the Dandy Warhols, a band whose genesis occurred in the laundry room of his apartment building. Taylor had been a drummer for a number of Portland bands, but wished to sing and play guitar. Keyboardist and bass player Zia McCabe grew up on the Portland River in a log cabin her father had built, a home she once described as a sort of commune and erstwhile shelter for drug-warrant fugitives. Guitarist Peter Holmstrom was a refugee from art studies at New York University. Later, the three were joined by a drummer Eric Hedford. Since they had begun the Dandys when sitting on the floor of the laundry room, Taylor later told *Spin* magazine that afterward, he basically had to learn to play the guitar all over again—standing up.

The band soon built up a local cult following because of their memorable live shows. The Dandys' freeform, trippy-psychedelic rock sound was marked by lots of guitar, lots of fuzz pedal, lots of reverb, and lots of cheek; they once played their set sitting on big cushions onstage. Writing in the *Oregonian,* Curt Schulz called McCabe a modern-day, real-life version of the early 1970s cartoon classic *Josie and the Pussycats* for her one-handed keyboard playing and tambourine jangling in the other. He described their sonic vibe "highly polished modern pop, liquid and smooth." Fans also came to see the band get comfortable onstage, since they had a reputation for disrobing.

By the 1994, the Dandys were signed to the same label as Everclear, the Portland-based Tim/Kerr Records. Their first single was "The Little Drummer Boy," released that same year. A full album followed with 1995's *Dandy's Rule OK.* This and their 1995 single "TV Theme Song" were well-received and created the usual indie buzz about the band. As the band recalled in a 1997 press release, back then—with the excellent reception of *Dandy's Rule OK*—"we had every major label A + R person and their mom following us around." Furthermore, after the early 1990s Seattle scene, record labels were sniffing around for the next hot Northwest city that would spawn a slew of credible, yet revenue-producing bands, and the Dandys helped intensify the talk about Portland's being passed the torch.

At a North by Northwest Music and Media Conference in the fall of 1995, there was insider gossip over the major-label bidding war that the Dandys' talents had incited. It was announced then that they had signed with Capitol, supposedly for a large sum of money. They played live on closing night of the conference—"and the Dandy Warhols killed," declared Patrick MacDonald in the *Seattle Times* in a review of the show. "The band has it all.... The music was modern, with all the intensity of Bush, Everclear, Filter, Silverchair and the other bands that are defining the future. But the Dandy Warhols stood out enough in showmanship, originality and talent to challenge those other contenders."

Problems with the Record Company

In full rock-star mode, the Dandys promptly began squandering their large cash advances while preparing to record their major-label debut. There were some personality conflicts within the band, however, and they were also unhappy with the studio and new producer. In turn, Capitol executives were less than enthused about the songs that resulted, and rumors again flew, this time to the effect that it was a very big, expensive contractual

For the Record . . .

Members include **Eric Hedford**, drums; **Peter Holmstrom**, guitar; **Zia McCabe** keyboards, bass; and **Courtney Taylor**, guitar.

Band formed, c. 1993, in Portland, OR; signed with Tim/Kerr Records, c. 1994; released the single "The Little Drummer Boy," 1994; signed with Capitol Records, 1995; released ... *The Dandy Warhols Come Down,* 1997.

Addresses: *Record company*—Capitol Records, 1750 N. Vine, Hollywood, CA 90028-5274.

mess in which the Dandys were now involved. "We didn't have the stamina to stay in there," Taylor said of this time in an interview with Jim Sullivan of the *Boston Globe,* "... to maintain focus on the aesthetic sensibilities. It became too confusing, and it became too depressing." Eventually they gave up and went back to the basement in Portland where they used to practice. Taylor wrote new songs, and they recruited the co-producer on first record, Tony Lash, to help them out again.

In the spring of 1996 the Dandy Warhols opened for Love and Rockets, and had seemingly returned to their normal, iconoclastic selves. At one venue, they played only two songs—one a sixteen-minute-long groove entitled "It's a Fast Driving Rave-Up with the Dandy Warhols' Sixteen Minutes." The long-awaited album with the self-chastening tag, *...The Dandy Warhols Come Down,* was finally released in the summer of 1997, and the media response was laudatory. *Rolling Stone* reviewer Barney Hoskyns called it "the most exhilarating '60s-into-'90s excursion yet attempted by an American band," and described the Dandys as "masters of the hypnotically droning riff delivered in waves of fuzz guitar and garage-band keyboards." *Paper*'s Richard Baimbridge used similar terminology, describing it as "a wonderfully minimalistic, droning album," and in an assessment in the *Boston Globe,* Sullivan declared the Dandys have created "a brilliant disc that merges their experimental nature and their keen pop sensibility."

Dandy's Down on Drugs

...The Dandy Warhols Come Down also attracted media attention for its anti-drug paean, "Not If You Were the Last Junkie on Earth," which happened to dovetail perfectly with the widespread backlash against "heroin chic" that same summer. Taylor said that the words he wrote—"I never thought you'd be a junkie because heroin is so passé"—hardly reflected any teetotalling image of himself or the band, but explained that "when people from stupid frat-boy bands start OD-ing on heroin, it's just not cool anymore," he told Sullivan in the *Boston Globe.* "People should not be addicted to anything except sex. You can't like sex too much." Capitol put a lot of money behind the song, however, and renowned photographer David LaChapelle was recruited to direct it. It depicts noir game show with cheesy imagery from the 1980s, and the Dandys as hapless contestants where the "prizes" includea toilet bowl for vomiting and a tombstone.

The Dandys profess to enjoying all the perks of the rock 'n' roll train. In their next video, the band was filmed pulling an unbelievable stunt that involved changing the sign on the famed Capitol Records building in Hollywood to read "DANDY" Records—a costly endeavor whose financing was somehow approved by executives inside. Indulgences seemed a part of the whole Dandy Warhol mystique. "Music is all about addressing feelings," Taylor told Schulz in the *Oregonian* interview. "I think it's a cop-out if the only feeling you care to express is angst, like a lot of groups seem to limit themselves to. I'm not as much into anger as I am into sensory pleasures, like red wine and chocolate."

Selected discography

"The Little Drummer Boy," T/K Records, 1994.
Dandy's Rule OK, T/K Records, 1995.
"TV Theme Song," T/K Records, 1995.
"Ride," T/K Records, 1996.
"Nothing to Do," T/K Records, 1996.
...The Dandy Warhols Come Down, T/K Records/Capitol, 1997.

Sources

Periodicals

Billboard, July 12, 1997, p. 86.
Boston Globe, August 22, 1997.
Oregonian, March 3, 1995; June 7, 1996, p. 38; April 18, 1997;
Paper, October 1997.
Rolling Stone, November 16, 1995; July 2, 1997; September 4, 1997, p. 22.
Seattle Times, October 8, 1995.
Spin, October 1997; December 1997.

Online

http://www.dandywarhols.com.

—Carol Brennan

Dead Milkmen

Rock and roll band

The Dead Milkmen were part of same loose but lucid, satirical early-eighties American punk scene that also spawned Camper Van Beethoven, but were usually ignored or vilified by critics. They had an intensely loyal cult following, however, and reaped great success from college radio in that medium's freeform heyday. The band's best-loved songs—"Bitchin' Camaro," "Instant Club Hit (You'll Dance to Anything)," and "Punk Rock Girl"—showcased their ability to viciously lampoon targets ranging from dumb suburban teenagers to overdressed club kids. A *Trouser Press Record Guide* assessment used terms such as "only spottily amusing," "dementedly parodic cultural concepts," and "disappointingly lame" to describe some of the Dead Milkmen's recorded efforts.

The Dead Milkmen grew out of some exploits to remedy teenage boredom in Wagontown, Pennsylvania. This small town in the heart of Amish country was home to core Dead Milkmen members Rodney Anonymous and Joe Jack Talcum, who had teamed with a third friend in high school to make comedy tapes. They created a fictional band called Dead Milkmen, fronted by the equally fictional Jack Talcum. The mock band's bizarre exploits and rock-star failures provided endless fodder for the proto-musical tapes and then the *Dead Milkmen Newzletter,* which chronicled the fake band and its "music" in even greater detail. The newsletter idea was a not-very-flattering homage to similar communiqués put out by Paul McCartney's seventies band, Wings.

Joe left Wagontown to study communications at Philadelphia's Temple University around 1980. There he met David Reckner, who would later become the Dead Milkmen's manager. Reckner, in turn, introduced Joe to Dean Clean and Mike, who played in a band called Narthex. When Joe brought his friend from Wagontown, Rod, to see the band, their raw punk incompetence inspired them to take their Dead Milkmen idea to another level. As the band would later write in their *official* history, they thought, "if these guys can get away with it, so can we!"

Around this same time, in early 1982, Joe became acquainted with two brothers, one of whom had a bass guitar. Thus, with Rod singing lead, Joe playing guitar, Dean on drums, bass player Dave Blood, and Dave's brother Joe S. writing songs, the Dead Milkmen was formed.

The band played their first show in the summer of 1983 in Harleyvsille, Pennsylvania. Their primitive punk sound, combined with an abandoned, no-holds-barred comic sensibility, soon attracted a rabid Philly fan base. "The wheels of the milk truck began to roll," the band wrote in its web site. The band started making their own tapes and selling them at shows, and one of them included the song "Bitchin' Camaro," a paean to an out-of-control hot rod. It became an underground hit, and in May of 1984 helped land the DeadMilkmen an on-air gig at an influential radio station. The disc jockey there put them in touch with a local business school professor who also happened to own a record label, Fever.

For less than a thousand dollars, the band recorded their debut album for Fever, *Big Lizard in My Backyard.* Released in 1985, its 21 tracks included "Bitchin' Camaro," which became a huge hit on college and fledgling alternative radio. The band's popularity was further boosted when a baseball player for the Detroit Tigers named Jim Walewander trumpeted the band. Other tracks on *Big Lizard* included "Right Wing Pigeons," "Rastabilly," and "Laundromat Song." More speed-punk satire occurred with *Eat Your Paisley,* issued in 1986 and buoyed by such tracks as "Air Crash Museum," "The Thing That Only Eats Hippies," and "Where the Tarantula Lives."

After "Bitchin' Camaro," perhaps the most recognizable Dead Milkmen track emerged with "Instant Club Hit (You'll Dance to Anything)," a derisive, drum-machine-abusing track that appeared on the 1987 Dead Milkmen LP *Bucky Fellini.* Spewing venom against eighties dance-club culture, Rodney sang the song's ever-changing, anthemic verse: "You'll dance to anything ... by Depeche Mode/You'll dance to anything ... by Public Image...." Its success helped the band win a deal with Enigma Records, and for their new label they recorded

For the Record . . .

Members are known as **Rodney Anonymous** (also known as Rodney Amadeus, Rodney Mellencamp; married October 15, 1994, to Vienna), vocals; **Dave Blood** (attended Indiana University, mid-1990s), bass; **Dean Clean,** drums; and **Joe Jack Talcum** (attended Temple University), guitar.

Band formed in Philadelphia, PA, c. 1983.

Addresses: P.O. Box 58152, Philadelphia, PA 19102-8152.

Beelzebubba. That effort's first single, "Punk Rock Girl," found success with a video that received airplay on MTV, but when their next LP, *Metaphysical Graffiti,* failed to yield a similar moneymaker, Enigma lost interest. The label went under not long afterward, and the Dead Milkmen were dropped.

The band found a new home on Hollywood Records, part of the Disney entertainment empire, and recorded *Soul Rotation.* This 1992 release offered a less punk, far poppier sound, but failed to gain them anything more than the cult following they had long enjoyed. They put out the EP *If I Had a Gun* on Hollywood that same year, and then *Not Richard, But Dick* the following year. The label, however, would later gain notoriety in the music industry for its inept management, and the Dead Milkmen soon found themselves adrift once more in late 1993.

The year 1993 also marked a return for the Milkmen to their original DIY (do it yourself) formula in 1993 with *Now We Are Ten,* a limited edition self-release that included four live tracks recorded in a Pennsylvania barn in 1983. They also found a new corporate home on Restless Records, which had been distributing their early Fever releases. On Restless they released *Chaos Rules—Live at the Trocadero* in 1994, and their last studio effort, *Stoney's Extra Stout (Pig),* issued the following year. In late 1994 the band officially called it quits after a final tour, "to regroup only for funerals and rare TV appearances," as they wrote in the *Dead Milkmen Newzletter,* which was still going strong at Issue #58.

Restless released the Dead Milkmen compilation, *Death Rides a Pale Cow—The UltimateCollection,* in 1997, but no tracks from its two 1992 and 1993 releases on Hollywood Records were included, since the label refused to give permission. Though they still exist in name and on their cyberspace home, at http://www.deadmilkmen.com, the band members indicated they had no plans to ever record again or tour. Most have gone on to other musical projects, except for former bassist Dave, whose interest in Balkan history was piqued during a 1991 Dead Milkmen tour of the onetime Yugoslavia. He went on to attend graduate school at Indiana University. Rod formed a Celtic-influenced band called Burn Witch Burn with his wife, and Joe went on to play in a band called the Town Managers. Dean, involved in a burlesque ensemble called the Big Mess Cabaret Players in Philadelphia, found work with an advertising agency.

Selected discography

Released several cassettes on the Jerrock label, 1982-84.
Big Lizard in My Backyard, Restless, 1985.
Eat Your Paisley, Restless, 1986.
Bucky Fellini, Enigma, 1987.
Beelzebubba, Enigma, 1988.
Smokin' Banana Peels (EP), Enigma, 1988.
Metaphysical Graffiti, Enigma, 1990.
Soul Rotation, Hollywood, 1992.
If I Had a Gun (EP), Hollywood, 1992.
Now We Are Ten, self-released, 1993.
Not Richard, But Dick, Hollywood, 1993.
Chaos Rules—Live at the Trocadero, Restless, 1994.
Stoney's Extra Stout (Pig), Restless, 1995.
Death Rides a Pale Cow—The Ultimate Collection, Restless, 1997.

Sources

Periodicals

Billboard, February 11, 1989, p. 31.
Entertainment Weekly, December 9, 1994, p. 76.
People, September 24, 1990, p. 17.
Sports Illustrated, May 16, 1988, p. 85.

Online

http://www.cclabs.missouri.edu/~c510292/dead.milkmen.newsletter.58.html
http://www.deadmilkmen.com
http://www.imusic.com
http://www.sonicnet.com
http://www.trouserpress.com

—Carol Brennan

Chris de Burgh

Singer, songwriter

Irish singer and songwriter Chris de Burgh was a classic example of an artist who was massively popular throughout the world but remained relatively unknown in two of the largest musical markets in the world, the United States and England. While this scenario would be an extremely daunting and vexing situation for many other artists, de Burgh actually relished it and actively sought to follow his musical muse far from the pop paparazzi of England and America's all encompassing entertainment monolith. His global chart smash hit, "Lady in Red," was de Burgh's only entrant into the higher echelons of the British and American pop charts. This was fine by de Burgh as he explained to *Billboard*'s Ken Stewart, "you have to go in for the big picture. I've always been one to jump over England as an important record market. I think it's been overrated as a source of talent, certainly new talent. And it's difficult to break into England unless you're prepared to play the game English bands play."

De Burgh was born October 15, 1948, in Argentina. His parents were British citizens who traveled around quite

AP/Wide World Photos

For the Record . . .

Born October 15, 1948, in Argentina; married; wife's name, Diane; childern: Rosanna, Michael, and Hubie (son). *Education:* Degree in English and French from Trinity Collige, Dublin, Ireland.

Signed with A&M Records in 1974; released *Beyond These Castle Walls,* 1975; *Spanish Train and other Stories,* 1975; *At the Ende of a Perfect Day,* 1977; *Crusader,* 1979, *Live in South Africa,* 1979; *Eastern Wind,* 1980; *Best Moves,* 1981; *Get Away,* c. 1982, *Man on the Line,* c. 1983; licensed to Telstar and released *Very Best of Chris de Burgh,* 1984; *Into the Light* (includes "Lady in Red"), 1986; *Flying Colours,* 1988; *Spark to a Flame,* c. 1989; *High on Emotion,* c. 1991; *Power of Ten,* 1992; *This Way Up,* 1994; *Beautiful Dreams,* 1995; *Love Songs,* 1997

Awards: Canadian platinum certification for *Spanish Train and Other Stories,* 1975; Canadian gold certification for *Beautiful Derams,* 1995.

Address: *Record company*—A&M, 595 Madison Ave., New York, NY 10022.

a bit when de Burgh was growing up. Their frequent moves were due to the nature of de Burgh's father's work. After Argentina, the family's rich and colorful travel itinerary included moves to Malta, Nigeria, Zaire, and finally to Ireland around 1961. When the family moved to the Emerald Isle, de Burgh's parents purchased a decrepit castle that they decided to turn into a bed and breakfast. De Burgh related to Lyn Cockburn of the *Calgary Sun* that "the family was broke but there was something stupidly romantic about buying a tumbled down 12th century Irish castle." From the age of 14 and continuing on for the next seven years, de Burgh entertained the guests who stayed at the castle by singing and playing the guitar. He remarked to Cockburn that, "[the early 1960s] was the time of the Beatles and Dylan and everybody banged away at a guitar, so it was natural for me to start singing. Great way to meet girls."

Despite the more than ample practice he received entertaining guests at his parents' bed and breakfast, de Burgh did not initially intend to become a musician. Instead, he chose to attend college and enrolled at Trinity College in Dublin, where he pursued studies in both English and French. It was only after he graduated with his degree from Trinity, that he began to contemplate a career in music in order to pay the bills. De Burgh then set off for London where there was a greater possibility to obtain a recording contract and attempted to pursue a successful musical career.

In the autumn of 1972, de Burgh was invited to a party in London, where an influential recording publisher was also invited to attend. De Burgh had the opportunity to meet and perform for Doug Flett. Flett, along with his partner Guy Fletcher, was the owner of Egg Productions. Flett was impressed with what he saw and heard and scheduled de Burgh to meet with his partner, Fletcher. Fletcher was also impressed with de Burgh and offered him a publishing contract with Egg. Hungry for success, de Burgh signed on to Egg. From then on, Egg owned all of de Burgh's songs and he was forced to take on numerous odd jobs in order to try to make ends meet. De Burgh's deal with Egg was not that lucrative and the stress and strain from his outside jobs took a toll on him. He was not able to write much and when he did, his songs were disjointed at best.

A sabbatical at his family's castle in Ireland provided de Burgh with relaxation and renewed his song writing process. De Burgh began to write for himself in the spring of 1974, after moving back to Ireland. After his self imposed hiatus, de Burgh returned to London and showed Egg the demo tapes he had been working on in Ireland. Egg Productions liked the material and were impressed enough that they called up the head of A&M's Artists & Repertoire (A&R) department to sing the praises of de Burgh's work. The head of the A&R department at A&M decided to check out de Burgh, and he, too, was impressed with de Burgh's work. A&M offered Egg a contract so they could have de Burgh on their roster.

When the contract between Egg and A&M was signed, de Burgh began work on his debut album. *Beyond These Castle Walls* was released by A&M in early 1975 and was a smash hit in Brazil where it stayed at number one for 30 weeks. De Burgh's follow up album, *Spanish Trains and Other Stories* was released later that year. *Spanish Trains and Other Stories* was even more successful than its predecessor, as it gave de Burgh his first platinum record in Canada. Commenting on his Canadian success, de Burgh told Cockburn, "I view myself as a storyteller and Canada was one of the key places where I realized I did have a style and it was the storytelling thing."

At the End of a Perfect Day was released in 1977 and was followed two years later by *Crusader*. De Burgh also released *Live in South Africa* that same year. The album chronicled his successful tour of the country. *Eastern Wind* was released the next year and de Burgh's first greatest hits package, *Best Moves,* followed in 1981.The early 1980s saw numerous de Burgh albums released in relatively short succession. *Get Away* followed 1981's *Best Moves. Get Away* was the first whole album of new material from de Burgh since the 1980 release, *Eastern Wind. Man on the Line* was de Burgh's next release. In 1984, Telstar released the *Very Best of Chris de Burgh.*

Arguably, the most famous and familiar album of de Burgh's career to date, *Into the Light,* was released in 1986. *Into the Light* brought both de Burgh and his music into the collective pop musical consciousness of both England and the United States, which were probably the only two nations on the globe that had not yet fallen in love with de Burgh's charms. *Into the Light* contained the worldwide smash hit ballad, "Lady in Red." "Lady in Red" eventually climbed up to number one in the United Kingdom and number two in the United States. According to Dave Doohan of the Surfshak web site, the song "Lady in Red" was inspired by a fleeting glance de Burgh had of his wife in a crowded club. At first he failed to recognize her as his wife and, "as a result, he realized that often people never quite appreciate that the most important person in their lives is taken for granted, and, how after a while, you fail to notice the things that brought you together." In commenting to Cockburn about the success of "Lady in Red" de Burgh stated that "it has opened a lot of doors for me . . . the only stigma is that I wish the biggest song I'd done was a rock-oriented song rather than a ballad."

The follow up to the highly successful *Into the Light* was 1988's *Flying Colours.* Another greatest hits album was released not long after this and was entitled *Spark to a Flame. High on Emotion* was released in the early 1990s and it showcased material from de Burgh's most recent Irish concerts. *Power of Ten* was released in 1992. In two years time, deBurgh released *This Way Up,* which was the first de Burgh album released in America since 1988's *Flying Colours.* When asked about his lack of success in America by the *Edmonton Sun*'s Mike Ross, de Burgh noted, "America wasn't a country I wanted to pursue, because it meant doing three years there, being away from the family—and I'm not that mad about making money."

In 1995, de Burgh released *Beautiful Dreams,* which went gold in Canada. Two years later saw the release of *Love Songs* which was a compilation of de Burgh's best known romantic tunes and a few new ones. It was also the first album to be released in the United States since 1994's *This Way Up.*

De Burgh was very committed to giving his very best to his fans. According to the Surfshak web site, de Burgh was driven by the twin forces of pleasing both himself and his fans. He remarked, "I'm glad that people appear to take my music to their hearts and the knowledge of that makes it very interesting for me when I come to write my songs. I know that I can't let myself down and, apart from that—I can't let anybody else down."

Selected discography

Beyond These Castle Walls, A&M, 1975.
Spanish Train and Other Stories, A&M, 1975.
At the End of a Perfect Day, A&M, 1977.
Crusader, A&M, 1979.
Live in South Africa, A&M, 1979.
Eastern Wind, A&M, 1980.
Best Moves, A&M, 1981.
Get Away, A&M, c. 1982.
Man on the Line, A&M, c. 1983.
Very Best of Chris de Burgh, Telstar, 1984.
Into the Light (includes "Lady in Red"), A&M, 1986.
Flying Colours, A&M, 1988.
Spark to a Flame, A&M, c.1989.
High on Emotion, A&M, c.1991.
Power of Ten, A&M, 1992.
This Way Up, A&M, 1994.
Beautiful Dreams, A&M, 1995.
Love Songs, A&M, 1997.

Sources

Periodicals

Billboard, October 5, 1991.
Calgary Sun, September 13, 1996.
Edmonton Sun, September 12, 1996.
Ottawa Sun, September 27, 1996.

Online

"Chris de Burgh," http://www.crl.com/jderouen/cdeb/html (February 24, 1998).
"Chris de Burgh," http://www.surfshak.co.uk/cdeb/cdebbio.html (January 22, 1998).

—*Mary Alice Adams*

Deftones

Alternative rock band

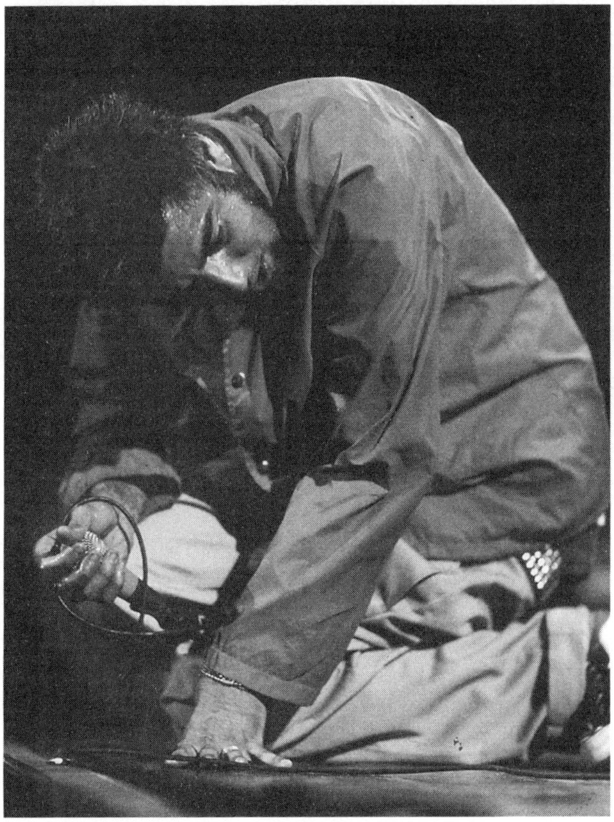

Courtesy of Ken Settle

The Deftones' 1997 release, *Around the Fur,* on Maverick Records, clearly sets them apart from other heavy metal, grunge, and punk bands to which they have been compared in the past. Unlike some of the bands that have evoked comparisons, their main focus is projecting excitement through their intense energy and creativity. The band likes to be known for what it called its "abstract sonics and lyrics." After touring the United States almost non-stop for the past three years, the group has developed an intensely loyal following of metalheads, punkers, and skaters. The band is a multi-ethnic favorite among the mosh pit crowd; their fans love the combination of loud, metallic grunge. Frontman Chino Moreno's wide range of vocals exhibit bipolar emotions; one moment his voice projects hushed, barely heard whispers, the next moment he's uttering screams that sound, according to Tom Wictor of *Bass Player,* "as if he's being boiled alive."

The band first formed around 1988 in Sacramento, California. Guitarist Stephen Carpenter began playing while recovering from a near fatal accident; he'd been hit by a drunk driver while skateboarding. Carpenter was 15 years old at the time. With the money he received from the legal settlement after his accident, Carpenter purchased equipment for a band. Soon he and drummer, Abe Cunningham, were jamming and needed a singer. Although Moreno claimed he did not know how to sing, he told Sean O'Neill of *BAM* that his response was, "OK, I'll do it. It sounds like fun." With that the trio was formed and began jamming in Carpenter's garage. From the very beginning, the group played not with visions of becoming a big name group, but to have fun. Realizing they needed a bassist, they discovered Chi Cheng, who would complete the group. Although Cheng initially couldn't play the bass, he reminded guitarist Carpenter of a member of the band, Death Angel, and that was good enough for him.

During jam sessions in Carpenter's garage, the Deftones began writing original material and progressed to playing for parties. After about two years, they got a gig at a local club in the Sacramento, California, area. With the help of local promoter, Jerry Perry, they began playing at various clubs throughout the Bay Area and they toured with the band Psychefunkepus. After developing a following in the Sacramento area and throughout Northern California, they expanded their range to include Reno, Nevada, and Southern California. Closing for bigger name bands in Los Angeles would prove to be the forum where they got their big break.

After an associate of a Maverick Record executive appeared at one performance, a demo found its way to

For the Record . . .

Members include **Stephen Carpenter**, guitar; **Chi Cheng**, bass; **Abe Cunningham**, drums; and **Chino Moreno**, vocals.

Began with trio Moreno, Carpenter, and Cunningham in Sacramento, CA, late 1980s; added bassist, Chi Cheng, and began writing original material and playing gigs together in 1989; began touring, playing in such cities as Reno, NV, and Los Angeles, CA; signed to Maverick Records, 1994; released *Adrenaline*, 1995; performed "Can't Even Breathe," on *Escape From L.A.* (soundtrack), Atlantic, 1996, and "Teething," on the *The Crow: City of Angels* (soundtrack), PGD/ Hollywood, 1996; released *Around the Fur*, 1997; toured Europe and the U.S., fall 1997.

Addresses: *Record company*—Maverick Records, 9348 Civic Center Drive, Beverly Hills, CA 90210. *Publicist*—Mitch Schneider Organization, 14724 Ventura Blvd., Suite 410, Sherman Oaks, CA 91403. *Fan Club*—Maverick Records, attn: Deftones friends and family, 8000 Beverly Blvd., Los Angeles, CA 90048. *Website*—www.deftones.com.

Maverick. The group was then contacted and a showcase performance was scheduled with Freddy DeMann and Guy Oseary. After hearing the group play three songs the record execs wanted the Deftones on their label. Although they received other offers, the group decided to sign with Maverick in 1994 because they thought Maverick was a label that really cared about their bands.

Shortly after signing, the group hit the tour circuit, stopping only long enough in 1995 to record their debut album, *Adrenaline,* which would sell over 220,000 copies by the end of 1997. Most of the cuts on *Adrenaline* were recorded live. Producer Terry Date used this approach to capture the incredible energy projected by the Deftones.

Moreno's Vocals Exploded Into Extremes

The throbbing heavy metal instrumentation behind Moreno's extreme vocals, including his shrieking and howling, deliver high intensity feelings of passion, frustration, and persistence. *Adrenaline* was described by Bob Hernandez of *PLOW* as "an explosive mix of extremes, musically showcasing a savage and abrasive blend of harmony and chaos." Hernandez noted that Moreno's vocalizations "enhanced the music," especially on the cuts "Minus Blindfold" and "Seven Words." Kim Kenneally of *Guitar School,* called the debut album, "a 40-minute primal scream, built on Carpenter's percussive riffing, judiciously applied bursts of dissonance, and delicate, if creepy, open chord patterns." Another reviewer, Katherine Turman, of *Car Audio,* noted: "If this is what heavy metal is evolving into, it's a ... good thing."

Following the production of their first album, the Deftones performed at the 1996 Warped Tour and continued touring with many bands across the United States including Korn, Ozzy Osbourne, Bad Brains, Pantera, White Zombie, L7, Quicksand, Kiss, and others. Also during 1996, the group was featured on the soundtracks *Escape From L.A.,* with their cut "Can't Even Breath," and *The Crow: City of Angels,* with "Teething."

Musically Influenced by Variety

The individual band members claim a wide range of musical influences. This may partially explain the extremes they exhibit through their collective music. Vocalist Moreno claims that he was initially influenced by Bad Brains but lyrically inspired by Depeche Mode.

Guitarist Carpenter listens to a wide range of pop and heavy metal music, some of which include Pantera, Sepultura, Down, and Helmet. He also enjoys Morrissey, the Cure, and Depeche Mode, and told Jen Wiederhorn of *Guitar World* that the Deftones were working on cuts to be included on forthcoming Depeche Mode and Duran Duran tribute albums.

Bass player Cheng talked about his approach to playing with Thomas Wictor of *BASS Player* in May 1997. Cheng has a taste for reggae, soul, blues, and jazz, and felt his heavy use of 16th-notes "comes from listening to Tower of Power. I'm such a fan of Rocco Prestia." Cheng plays the bass with his fingers rather than a pick and feels that this "more organic" technique allows him to be closer to the instrument.

Drummer Cunningham discussed his personal favorites in an interview with Randy Sanders of *Drummer Dude,* and said "I was raised on so much different music." A few artists and bands he mentioned include Queen, Neil Young, Prince, and Miles Davis. Other bands cited as influenceson the band's style include Smashing Pumpkins and Jane's Addiction.

The Deftones second release, *Around the Fur,* hit the music scene in October 1997, debuting at number 29 and overall receiving very good reviews. Many critics felt that this second effort was an improvement. Stephen Thomas Erlewine noted in an online interview that "they're about to come into their own." *Around the Fur* also features Max Cavalera on vocals and guitar on the cut, "Headup," and Annalyn Cunningham, wife of drummer, Abe Cunningham, also on vocals, in "MX." *Around the Fur* continues the band's tradition of extremes with both ends of Moreno's vocal styles, which when combined with the intense, heavy metal guitar, drums and bass, create a "firestorm" of music that explodes into hostility and aggression.

The consensus of reviews online is that the Deftones' second album is more powerful and fans of this genre would consider this album a "must-have." Sean Eric McGill of *Consumable Online* felt that Moreno's range of vocal extremes set the Deftones apart from other bands that they have previously been compared to. McGill stated that "they have created the best harder rock album of the year." Buzz Morison of *Guitar* complied, stating that "the quartet packs disturbingly heavy but fluidly thrashing riffs into dense, intense songs that Chino Moreno bellows with the feral force of a caged mongoose."

The band members discussed the album in an online interview with Aaron Parker. Carpenter called *Around the Fur* a "progression" in the band's musical evolution. Band members agreed that extensive touring and live performing have given them additional maturity and helped clarify communication among band members. Moreno explained that he has been influenced lately by female singers, like Polly Jean Harvey, who stress the passionate side of vocals. Moreno also discussed the theme of the newest release and called it his fascination with the darker, more seamy aspects of the fashion and glamour world and of prostitution.

Took Over Internet

As of early 1998, the Deftones have received limited exposure through radio and television; the only real media attention they received came after a concert in Tempe, Arizona, when a riot broke out while they were performing. Security had cut the band's power after four songs, and their fans went nuts. Reports of the riot were shown on *Hard Copy, American Journal,* and *Real TV.*

The band is continuing its tradition of live performances and simultaneously discovering that the Internet is a great avenue for promotion. After the band previewed their new album before a group of 300 fans with a concert at a rehearsal studio in Los Angeles, their performance was also broadcast live over the Internet through the LiveConcerts' website. That broadcast captured enough viewers to become the number five most watched broadcast of the 300 that LiveConcerts had hosted up until then. The preview concert was subsequently archived at the Deftones' own official website.

The end of 1997 found the band on the road again, on the "World Annihilation" tour, including performances across the United States. Although extensive touring has been the group's primary key to success, it can be a difficult life to maintain. They note redeeming moments like when they discovered they had fans in Copenhagen, Denmark while performing at the Roskilde Festival. Moreno enjoys knowing that the Deftones' style brings together all sorts of different kids including punk rockers and skateboarders. Hernandez of *PLOW* asked the group if they were still having fun. Moreno responded in the affirmative, "Hell, yeah, ... if I wasn't having fun anymore ... I would get me a job."

Selected discography

Adrenaline (includes "Minus Blindfold," and "Seven Words"), Maverick Records, 1995.
Around the Fur (includes "Headup," and "MX"), Maverick Records, 1997.

With Others

"Can't Even Breathe," *Escape From L.A.* (soundtrack), WEA/Atlantic, 1996.
"Teething," *The Crow: City of Angels* (soundtrack), PGD/Hollywood, 1996.

Sources

Periodicals

BAM, November 16, 1995.
BASS Player, May 1997.
Car Audio, January 1996.
Drummer Dude, Issue #6.
Guitar, December 1997.
Guitar School, April 1996.
Guitar World, October 1997.
LiveWire, June/July 1996.
PLOW: Snowboarding Magazine, March 1997.

Online

www.allmusic.com
www.buzzine.com

www.cduniverse.com
www.jamtv.com
www.maverickrc.com/roster
www.music.warnerbros.com

Additional information was provided by the Mitch Schneider Organization, publicist for the Deftones.

—Debra Reilly

John Denver

Singer, songwriter

Archive Photos

An internationally-loved singer and songwriter, John Denver was also a some-time actor and an active humanitarian. In 1976, a *Newsweek* writer did not hesitate to describe him as "the most popular pop singer in America." His music career spanned nearly three decades and he touched the hearts of millions with his wholesome uplifting lyrics and country-style folk songs that celebrate the natural beauty of the environment and the joy of simply being alive. At the age 53, Denver's life and career came to an end when his experimental Long-EZ model plane suddenly nose-dived into the Pacific Ocean at Monterey Bay, California, killing him instantly in the crash.

Throughout his career, Denver wrote and sang songs exuding the joy that he felt for life, love, and nature. His clear tenor vocals and folksy-country pop style brimmed with sincerity and optimism. A poet at heart, he was influenced by folk greats Joan Baez and Bob Dylan. He took much inspiration for his music from his love of the outdoors. He particularly loved the mountains and enjoyed camping, hiking, backpacking, and fishing. He was also an avid golfer, photographer, pilot, and was known to be a daredevil. Denver told Rick Overall of the *Ottawa Sun,* "When I was growing up, my first and best friend was the outdoors and when I began to express myself, I used images from nature." This love coupled with his desire to serve humanity would become the inspiration for much of Denver's environmental conservation and humanitarian work, in which his music found many outlets.

Denver was born Henry John Deutschendorf Jr. on December 31, 1943, in Roswell, New Mexico. He moved frequently while growing up with his parents, U.S. Air Force Colonel and pilot Henry John and Erma Deutschendorf, and younger brother Ronald. He lived in Arizona, Alabama, Oklahoma, Texas, and Japan. When he was eight years old, one of his grandmothers gave him a vintage Gibson guitar. Some of his fondest memories from childhood were times spent on his other grandmother's farm in Corn, Oklahoma. There he would listen to country music, play with the animals, and sleep under the stars.

Heart Longs for Mountains

A member of a rock band in high school, Denver continued performing while attending Texas Tech University in Lubbock, Texas during the early 1960s. However, after more than two years studying architecture, the pull of music prevailed. He left school in 1964, adopted the stage name of John Denver and headed to Los Angeles, California. He told *Newsweek* he chose

For the Record . . .

Born Henry John Deutschendorf Jr., December 31, 1943, in Roswell, NM; died October 12, 1997; son of Henry John and Erma Deutschendorf; married Ann Martell, June 1967 (divorced 1983); children: Zachary and Anna Kate (both adopted); married Cassandra Delaney (divorced 1991); children: Jessie Belle. *Education:* Attended Texas Tech University in Lubbock, TX, 1961-64.

Began music career while in college, but left school for Los Angeles, CA, in 1964; adopted stage name, c. 1964; replaced Chad Mitchell of the Chad Mitchell Trio, 1965; wrote number one hit song, "Leaving On A Jet Plane," recorded by Peter, Paul, and Mary, 1967; signed with RCA, 1969; started his own label, Windsong, 1975; appeared in the film, *Oh, God!,* 1977; wrote "The Gold And Beyond" for the Winter Olympics in Sarajevo; became first Western artist to tour China, 1992; appeared in the film *Walking Thunder,* 1993; published autobiography, *Take Me Home,* 1994.

Awards: Poet laureate of Colorado, 1974; Country Music Association, Entertainer of the Year, 1975; American Music Awards, Favorite Male Artist, Pop/Rock, 1975 and 1976; American Music Awards, Favorite Male Artist, Country, and Favorite Album, Country, 1976; Emmy Award, Best Musical Variety Special, 1976, for *Rocky Mountain Christmas*; Presidential World Without Hunger Award, 1987; Albert Schweitzer Music Award, 1993.

Addresses: *Record Company*—Sony Music, 550 Madison Ave., Suite 1775, New York, NY 10022-3211. *Website*—www.music.sony.com/Music/ArtistInfo/JohnDenver/index.html.

"Denver" because "my heart longed to live in the mountains." In Los Angeles, he played the acoustic guitar, sang folk songs, and performed at a club called Ledbetter's. He also became a member of the Back Porch Majority. Denver's first big break was in New York City, when he replaced Chad Mitchell of the Chad Mitchell Trio. He sang with the group, played guitar and banjo, and recorded pop and folk songs with them from 1965-68. He met his first wife, Ann Martell, while performing with the trio at her college; the couple were married in 1967.

In 1969, after the song Denver wrote for Peter, Paul, and Mary, "Leaving On A Jet Plane," became a number one hit, he signed with RCA Records. Denver would go on to release many singles and albums which would become worldwide hits. The first of his million-selling singles was "Take Me Home, Country Roads," written with Bill and Taffy Danoff in 1971. This triumph was followed by a string of hits, including "Rocky Mountain High," "Annie's Song," "Thank God I'm A Country Boy," "Sunshine On My Shoulders," and many more. His 1973 album, *John Denver's Greatest Hits,* remains one of the biggest selling albums in the history of RCA Records, surviving on *Billboard's* Top 200 for over three years, with sales topping 10 million copies.

In 1975, Denver founded his own label, Windsong Records, and released Starland's Vocal Band's song, "Afternoon Delight," which became a number one single. By the 1990s he had 14 gold and eight platinum albums to his credit.

During the 1970s and 1980s, Denver was a popular and frequent television performer. He performed with various artists, including Itzhak Perlman, Placido Domingo, Beverly Sills, Julie Andrews, and the Muppets. He won many music awards, and garnered an Emmy Award in 1976 for his television special, *Rocky Mountain Christmas.*

In 1977 he appeared in the film *Oh, God!,* also starring George Burns, and later he acted in the 1993 film *Walking Thunder.* When such incredible popular success did not translate into critical acceptance, Denver remained cheerful. He told Chet Flippo of *Rolling Stone,* "I don't mind if [critics] call me the Mickey Mouse of rock."

Music Promotes Goodwill Causes

During the 1980s the popularity of Denver's music waned in the United States, with the rise of new wave music and disco; but he continued touring internationally. He also donated his time to various charitable and political causes. In 1984, he toured the Soviet Union and recorded a duet with Russian pop singer Alexandre Gradsky, called "Let Us Begin (What Are We Making Weapons For?)." Also that year, he wrote and performed a song for the Winter Olympics in Sarajevo, "The Gold And Beyond."

In 1987 he received the Presidential World Without Hunger Award from Ronald Reagan, his documentary about endangered species, *Rocky Mountain Reunion,* won six awards, and he performed a benefit concert for the survivors of the Chernobyl nuclear reactor disaster. In 1992 Denver became the first western artist to tour China.

In 1993, Denver became the first nonclassical musician to receive the Albert Schweitzer Music Award for his humanitarian efforts. Nearly two decades earlier, the musician had expressed his views on social activism in the *Saturday Evening Post:* "People on an individual basis will make changes—not protesters or lobbyists. People who do what they really know to be right or true. Little things. In traffic, in grocery stores, you let somebody else in front of you. That's peace." And yet, he proceeded to make so many contributions that could not be called "little."

He co-founded the Windstar Foundation in 1975 and, later, the Hunger Project. He was a member of a United Nations Children's Fund (UNICEF) delegation that toured drought-suffering African nations. He was a board member of the National Space Institute and the Cousteau Society, and Wildlife Conservation Society (WCS). He performed a live concert in 1995 celebrating the 100th anniversary of WCS. The concert was recorded and later released on a double CD and on video. One of his favorite charities was a camp for deaf children in Aspen, Colorado.

Final Album and "Take Me-Home"

His final album of all original material, *Different Directions,* was released in 1991 under his Windstar label. One of his later albums, a compilation of tunes following a theme of trains and railroads was called *All Aboard.* Reviewer and fan Doug Speedie of *Jam! Showbiz* felt it was "John Denver at his best." Another reviewer for *Publishers Weekly* rated the album an "A" and noted Denver's range of musical styles including swing, bluegrass, mournful a capella, and even yodeling. However, his 1994 autobiography, *Take Me Home,* was given low marks by a reviewer for *Publishers Weekly,* who called it "self-indulgent."

The last five or six years of Denver's personal life had been rocky. In 1991 he and his second wife, Cassandra Delaney, divorced. In 1993 and 1994 he was arrested on drunk driving charges. Through these difficulties, friends and family said Denver never lost his enthusiasm for life. Longtime producer and friend Milt Okun claimed that Denver had cleaned up his behavior and that during a phone call the Friday preceding his death, Denver had talked excitedly about plans he had for the future, including picking up his new experimental plane. Denver flew his plane in spite of a 1996 suspension of his aviation license, reportedly connected to his drunk driving charges. However, alcohol was not suspected to be involved in his crash, according to Monterey County Sheriff, Norman Hicks.

Memorial services followed Denver's private funeral. On October 17, 1997, some 2,000 people mourned his death at the Faith Presbyterian Church in Aurora, Colorado. A second service, at the Aspen Music Tent Amphitheater the next day, attracted about 1,500 people. During a tribute, Paul Winter played "Icarus," a song based on the mythological story about a boy who flew too close to the sun and perished. Denver's ashes were to be scattered over the Rockies. He is survived by three children.

Selected discography

(With the Mitchell Trio) *The Mitchell Trio: That's the Way It's Gonna Be,* Mercury, 1965.
Rhymes and Reasons, RCA, 1969.
Take Me To Tomorrow, RCA, 1970.
Whose Garden Was This, RCA, 1970.
Poems, Prayers, and Promises, RCA, 1971.
Aerie, RCA, 1972.
Farewell Andromeda, RCA, 1973.
John Denver's Greatest Hits (includes "Take Me Home Country Road," "Rocky Mountain High," "Sunshine on My Shoulders," "Leaving On A Jet Plane"), RCA, 1973, reissued, 1988.
Back Home Again (includes "Annie's Song" and "Thank God I'm a Country Boy"), RCA, 1974.
Rocky Mountain Christmas, RCA, 1975.
An Evening With John Denver, RCA, 1975.
Windsong, RCA, 1975.
Live in London, RCA, 1976.
Spirit, RCA, 1976.
I Want To Live, RCA, 1977.
The Best of John Denver, Volume 2, RCA, 1977.
John Denver, RCA, 1979.
A Christmas Together With the Muppets, RCA, 1979.
Autograph, RCA, 1980.
Some Days Are Diamonds, RCA, 1981.
Perhaps Love, CBS, 1981.
Seasons of the Heart, RCA, 1982.
Its About Time, RCA, 1983.
Collection, Telstar, 1984.
Dreamland Express, RCA, 1985.
One World (includes "Let Us Begin [What Are We Making Weapons For?]"), RCA, 1986.
Different Directions, Windstar, 1991.
Wildlife Concert, Sony Legacy, 1995.
The Rocky Mountain Collection, RCA, 1996.
All Aboard, Columbia/Sony, 1997.
The Best of John Denver Live, Legacy, 1997.

Selected writings

(With Arthur Tobier) *Take Me Home: An Autobiography,* Harmony, 1994.

Sources

Books

Rees, Dafydd and Luke Crampton, editors, *Encyclopedia of Rock and Roll,* Dorling Kindersly, 1996.
Romanowski, Patricia and Holly George-Warren, editors, *The New Rolling Stone Encyclopedia of Rock and Roll,* Fireside, 1995.

Periodicals

Detroit News, October 18, 1997.
Entertainment Weekly, October 24, 1997.
Jam! Showbiz, October 15, 1997.
Newsweek, December 20, 1976, pp. 60-62, 65.
New York Times, October 14, 1997, p. B11.
Ottawa Sun, October 14, 1997.
People, November 3, 1997, p. 30.
Publishers Weekly, October 17, 1994, p. 69; September 8, 1997, p. 33.
Rolling Stone, November 27, 1997, p. 24.
Saturday Evening Post, January 1974, p. 57-58, 85.
U.S. News & World Report, October 27, 1997, p. 18.
USA Today, October 14,1997. p. 1-2D.

Online

www.cdnow.com/
www.cduniverse.com/
www.sky.net/~emily/articles/biograph.jd

Additional information was provided by Sony Music.

—*Debra Reilly*

Dire Straits

Rock band

Combining country, blues, and R&B influences, Dire Straits made their mark on the late-1970s and 1980s music scene with a rock-n-roll sound that stood out among the punk, new wave, and heavy metal trends. Getting back to the roots of rock, Dire Straits featured a simple sound that filled a stylistic gap. Led by singer Mark Knopfler, the group launched into stardom in the mid-1980s with their album *Brothers in Arms* and the mega-hit single "Money for Nothing."

Dire Straits began in London with the collaboration of bassist John Illsley and Mark Knopfler. Knopfler had graduated with a degree in English and was writing for the *Yorkshire Evening Post.* He left this job to pursue a career in music and took a part-time job as a teacher at Loughton College to stay financially solvent. Knopfler performed with pub bands around town, including Brewer's Droop and Cafe Racers. After a divorce and financial difficulties, he ended up sleeping on the floor of his brother David's flat, where Illsley also lived. David Knopfler also played guitar and, in 1977, the three men decided to form a band. After recruiting drummer Pick

AP/Wide World Photos

For the Record . . .

Members include **Alan Clark** (born March 5, 1952, in Durham, England), keyboards; **Danny Cummings**, percussion; **Guy Fletcher**, keyboards; **John Illsley** (founding member, born June 24, 1949, in Leicester, England), bass; **David Knopfler** (founding member, born December 27, 1952, in Glasgow, Scotland), guitar; **Mark Knopfler** (founding member, born August 12, 1949, in Glasgow, Scotland), guitar, vocals; **Hal Lindes** (born June 30, 1953, in Monterey, California), guitar; **Phil Palmer**, guitar; **Jack Sonni**, guitar; **Chris White**, saxophone; **Chris Whitten**, drums; **Pick Withers** (founding member, born April 4, 1948), drums; and **Terry Williams**, drums.

Band formed in London, England, 1977; signed U.K. recording contract with Phonogram Records, 1977; signed North American recording contract with Warner Bros., 1978; released self-titled debut, 1978; released four albums, 1979-1984; released *Brothers in Arms,* 1985; band called it quits, 1988; reformed and released *On Every Street,* 1991; final band break-up, 1993.

Awards: BRIT Award for Best British Group, 1983, 1986; Grammy Awards for Best Rock Performance by a Duo or Group with Vocal and Best Engineered Recording (Non-Classical), 1986; MTV Video Music Award for Best Group video and Best Video, 1986; BRIT Award for Best British Album, 1987; Grammy Award for Best Music Video, Long Form, 1987.

Withers, they began rehearsing. A friend of Mark Knopfler's helped them decide on their name, a reference to their financial situation. "We never said anything about this to each other," David Knopfler told Diasann McLane in *Rolling Stone,* "but I had a feeling something was going to start happening, for real."

Soon after the band members borrowed some money to record a five-song demo tape, which included their future single "Sultans of Swing." They took the tape to a deejay named Charlie Gillett, who had a radio show called "Honky Tonk" on BBC Radio London. Originally, they just wanted some feedback from Gillett, but the announcer liked the music so much, he played "Sultans of Swing" on the radio. Two months later, Dire Straits signed a recording contract with Phonogram Records.

In 1978, Dire Straits began touring Great Britain as the opening band for Talking Heads. After their debut single "Sultans of Swing" started to climb the U.K. charts, the group went on their own headlining tour. Their new-found notoriety led to a U.S. recording contract with Warner Bros. Records, and before the end of the year, Dire Straits had released their self-titled debut worldwide. They received more and more attention in the United States and landed at the top of the charts in Australia and New Zealand.

The following year, Dire Straits performed in their first North American tour. They played 51 sold-out concerts over a 38-day period. "Sultans of Swing" scaled the charts to number four in the United States and number eight in Great Britain, while *Dire Straits* reached number two and number five on the respective album charts. Bob Dylan, who saw the band play in Los Angeles, was so impressed that he invited Mark Knopfler and Pick Withers to play on his next album, *Slow Train Coming.*

By the end of 1979, Dire Straits had released their sophomore effort, *Communique,* which included the single "Lady Writer." Again, the album flew up the charts, reaching number eleven in the United States and number five in Great Britain. Mark Knopfler began to establish himself as a sought-after guitarist and put into motion what would become a long string of side work. In 1980, he played as a guest guitarist on Phil Lynott's album *Solo in Soho* and Steely Dan's *Gaucho.*

In July of 1980, David Knopfler officially quit Dire Straits to pursue a solo career. "David was under a lot of strain," John Illsley explained to Ken Tucker and David Fricke in *Rolling Stone.* "Mark felt very responsible for David and didn't quite know what to do. Once [the next release] *Making Movies* was out and David had left, it seemed to lift a tremendous strain. Mark felt very freed."

Music Progressed to Another Level

Shortly after David Knopfler left the group, Dire Straits added former Darlings guitarist Hal Lindes and keyboardist Alan Clark to their ranks. They immediately headed into the studio to record their next LP, *Making Movies,* which included the singles "Skateaway," "Romeo and Juliet," and "Tunnel of Love." The differences in the band and in Mark Knopfler didn't go unnoticed. David Fricke commented in *Rolling Stone,* "*Making Movies* is the record on which Mark Knopfler comes out from behind his influences, and Dire Straits come out from behind Mark Knopfler."

The band embarked on an extensive tour, but took some time off before releasing *Love Over Gold* in 1982, which included the single "Industrial Disease." Knopfler's songwriting sessions were so prolific that the song "Private Dancer" didn't make it on the album, but it became a huge hit for Tina Turner. After the album's release, drummer Pick Withers left the band and was later replaced by Terry Williams. The following year, Dire Straits performed another world tour. Knopfler had also moved into producing albums for other artists and composing film scores. At the end of the year, he took some time off from work to marry his second wife, Lourdes Salomone. In 1984, Dire Straits released a live album from their previous tour called *Alchemy—Dire Straits Live.* John Illsley also released a solo album on Vertigo/Phonogram called *Never Told a Soul.*

Broke Sound (& Video) Barrier

In 1985, Hal Lindes left the band and was replaced by guitarist Jack Sonni. The new ensemble released the most successful Dire Straits album in the band's history, *Brothers in Arms.* The album debuted at number one in Great Britain and quickly soared to the top of the charts in the United States as well. It went on to become a number one album in 25 countries and sold 20 million copies worldwide. The chart-topping hit single "Money for Nothing" featured guest vocalist Sting on the unforgettable "I want my MTV" refrain. Dire Straits produced an animated video for the song, directed by Steve Barron, which quickly jumped to heavy rotation on MTV (Music Television). In fact, Sting's phrase became the tag line for the cable station. Other singles on *Brothers in Arms* included "Walk of Life" and "So Far Away."

Following the release of *Brothers in Arms,* Dire Straits went on a 12-month tour across the world. In 1986, they were nominated for eight Grammy Awards and received two: Best Rock Performance by a Duo or Group with Vocal and Best Engineered Recording (Non-Classical). They garnered two more awards for "Money for Nothing" at the third annual MTV Video Music Awards, for Best Group Video and Best Video. They also secured honors for Best British Group and Best British Album at the BRIT Awards. The following year, they were awarded yet another Grammy in the category of Best Music Video, Long-Form, for *Dire Straits Brothers in Arms.*

With the enormous success of *Brothers in Arms,* the members of Dire Straits were under a significant amount of stress. In September 1988, Mark Knopfler officially announced the break-up of the band. "A lot of press reports were saying we were the biggest band in the world," Knopfler told Rob Tannenbaum in *Rolling Stone.* "There's not an accent then on the music, there's an accent on popularity. I needed a rest." The dissolution of the band was followed up with a greatest hits compilation called *Money for Nothing.*

Brief Resurrection

In addition to his guest appearances, production, and film work, Knopfler formed another band called the Notting Hillbillies. In 1990 the group released the album *Missing ... Presumed Having a Good Time.* After the recording's release, Knopfler, Illsley, and manager Ed Bicknell decided to resurrect Dire Straits. In August of 1991, the reformed band began a two-year, 300-show tour and played in front of some 7.1 million ticket-buying fans. This time, Dire Straits included original members Knopfler and Illsley, along with keyboardists Guy Fletcher and Alan Clark, saxophonist Chris White, drummer Chris Whitten, and percussionist Danny Cummings. The following month, the group released the album *On Every Street,* which included the singles "Calling Elvis," "Heavy Fuel," and "My Parties." As the first Dire Straits album in six years, it moved up the charts to number one in Great Britain and number 12 in the United States.

The extensive tour proved to be too much for Dire Straits members and led to the band's second demise. Bill Flanagan described the sequence of events in *Gentleman's Quarterly:* "The subsequent world tour lasted nearly two years, made mountains of money and drove Dire Straits into the ground. When the tour was over, both Knopfler's marriage and his band were gone."

Following the tour, Knopfler took some time off from the music business. In 1993, he received an honorary music doctorate from the University of Newcastle-upon-Tyne. Two more Dire Straits albums were released: the live album *On the Night* in 1993 and *Live at the BBC,* featuring the band's early live recordings, in 1995. Knopfler returned to the limelight in 1996 with his solo album *Golden Heart,* which included the single "Darling Pretty." This song also appeared on the soundtrack for the film *Twister.* Knopfler discussed his career's resolution with Flanagan in *Gentleman's Quarterly:* "I am in show business," Knopfler explained. "It's the most embarrassing game in the world. It would be much better if you could just send your paintings to the dealer and disappear.... I am also in love with music ... so you have to find a way." Despite the end of Dire Straits, Knopfler has carried on the band's signature guitar and vocal styles.

Selected discography

Dire Straits, Warner Bros., 1978.
Communique, Warner Bros., 1979.
Making Movies, Warner Bros., 1980.
Love Over Gold, Warner Bros., 1982.
Alchemy — Dire Straits Live, Warner Bros., 1984.

Brothers in Arms, Warner Bros., 1985.
Money for Nothing, Warner Bros., 1988.
On Every Street, Warner Bros., 1991.
On the Night, Warner Bros., 1993.
Live at the BBC, Windsong Records, 1995.

Sources

Books

Rees, Dafydd and Luke Crampton, editors, *Encyclopedia of Rock Stars,* DK Publishing, 1996.

Periodicals

Billboard, March 17, 1979; June 2, 1984; June 14, 1986; September 20, 1986; October 29, 1988.
Gentleman's Quarterly, June 1996.
Guitar Player, June 1992.
Newsweek, November 4, 1985.
People Weekly, September 2, 1985.
Rolling Stone, April 5, 1979; February 5, 1981; February 18, 1982; January 20, 1983; November 21, 1985; April 24, 1986; April 5, 1990; April 30, 1992.
Teen, July 1986.

—Sonya Shelton

Dubstar

Pop band

With a string of successful singles and their debut album *Disgraceful,* released in 1995, England's Dubstar immediately proved to be the rare bird within the often banal menagerie of pop groups: a trio that combined infectious hooks and melodies and witty, understated lyrics. Their following output, including the 1997 album *Goodbye,* was just as strong, again meshing the best elements of electronic pop music from the 1980s into a fresh, often elegant composition rich in emotional resonance. However, despite launching their career during a resurgence of British pop bands such as Oasis and Spice Girls, it seemed unclear whether Dubstar would find an audience in the U.S. to equal their share of commercial and critical success in their native U.K.

Dubstar formed in 1993 around Gateshead, a city in the northeast of England, after its three young members-to-be discovered a shared musical appreciation. The band's key songwriter, London-born Steve Hillier, had spent several years as a deejay in local nightclubs, as well as working at music mega-stores such as Our Price

Corbis

For the Record . . .

Band members include **Sarah Blackwood,** vocals and lyrics; **Steve Hillier**, keyboards and lyrics; **Chris Wilkie**, guitar.

Band formed by Hillier and Wilkie in 1993 in Gateshead, England, under the name The Joans; joined by vocalist Blackwood the following year; released their debut single "Stars" on Food Records, 1995; released *Disgraceful* in the U.K., October 1995; support Erasure on their European tour; released *Goodbye,* 1997; contribute their version of the Pet Shop Boys "Jealousy" on the benefit album of cover versions *Come Again,* 1997.

Addresses: *Record company*—Dubstar Exclusive Worldwide Management, c/o Stevo, 124 New Bond St., London W1Y9AE, England. *Fan club*—Dubstar, P.O. Box 460, High Wycombe, Buckinghamshire, HP1245R, England.

and HMV, when he met guitarist Chris Wilkie. Both had been influenced by a number of seminal British pop bands of the 1980s, including the ethereal Cocteau Twins, the minimalist guitar-based outfit The Durutti Column, and the sampling pioneers Colourbox. In particular, Wilkie found inspiration in Johnny Marr, who had defined a generation of pop guitar playing through his work with The Smiths. Before long, the duo launched themselves under the moniker The Joans, which referred to Hillier's aunt.

With Wilkie on guitar and Hillier playing keyboards, as well as supplying sparse vocal tracks, The Joans began their unsatisfactory first dabblings. When Hillier found a practice tape of amateur singer Sarah Blackwood at a friend's house, he and Wilkie soon tracked her down. Blackwood, at the time a student of design at a university in nearby Halifax, promised to be the much needed missing element in the fledgling outfit. "We messed around a lot because we lacked a decent vocalist," Hillier recalled in an online interview. "But Sarah put a focus on the more experimental things of before." With a voice that exuded at the same time warmth, clarity, and a decidedly British cynicism, Blackwood proved to be the ideal front for the band, which then opted to change their name from The Joans to Dubstar.

The band tinkered with their sound for a year before making their work public, but once Dubstar's first demo tapes began to circulate, word of mouth spread among record companies. After the band played their debut live show, the band was accosted by an agent from the semi-independent label Food Records, which had released popular British acts such as Blur and Jesus Jones. With little ado, a deal was cut and the band released its first single, "Stars," in June of 1995. While its performance on sales charts was modest, "Stars" garnered the favor of British critics and established Dubstar's style of melancholic pop. Additionally, the single pricked the ears of the high-profile producer Stephen Hague, who had worked extensively with legends of electronic pop New Order and Pet Shop Boys and agreed to team up with Dubstar.

While Dubstar amassed material for what would be their first album, they also took to the road to perform at smaller venues under trying conditions, sometimes traveling in a cramped Yugo in lieu of a tour bus. "The first proper show we did was at a ball at St. Mary's College in London," recalled Hillier in an online interview. "It was an absolute disaster; they had this trip switch on the P.A. which went off every time the music got too loud." Despite such misfires, Dubstar's career was on the upswing.

After releasing a second single, "Anywhere," in the fall of 1995, the band released the album *Disgraceful,* produced with the smooth craftsmanship of Stephen Hague—a fact that incited comparisons with both New Order and Pet Shop Boys, in addition to contemporary synth act Saint Etienne. Comparisons aside, the album was widely acclaimed by the press, and occasioned pop superstars Erasure to invite Dubstar on their European tour as an opening act. By the time their third single, "Not So Manic Now," a cover version of a song by the obscure West Yorkshire, England, outfit Brick Supply, hit record shops, Dubstar had gained enough momentum with the public for the single to enter the Top 20 charts.

Disgraceful was an impressive showcase of eleven songs ranging in scope from the euphoric "Anywhere" to the icily bitter "The Day I See You Again," all of them a testament to Dubstar's mastery of the electronic pop genre. Like New Order before them, what set Dubstar apart from lesser synth-oriented groups was their fusion of electronic innovation and understated emotional richness. As Hillier responded in an interview via e-mail, "electronic instruments are only good when you know what you want them to do.... Dubstar [is] about soul songs (I don't mean R&B or Motown, but music that hits you in the heart) and we use modern technology to communicate our emotions." Such pathos was not lost on most reviewers of the album, such as reviewer Liz

Schwartz, who in particular praised the album's "Just A Girl She Said." "[The song] will echo for quite a while in the male ego," wrote Schwartz. "The lyrics are a far cry from riot girl (a genre of vitriolic female-fronted guitar rock), but more the wit and cynicism of a pop diva. They show Sarah as a touchable, personable singer."

Continuing on their tour of Europe with the newly gained momentum of an acclaimed album, the band had obtained a modest degree of fame — as well as infamy. The original cover of *Disgraceful* featured artwork which depicted female genitalia, and was quickly withdrawn in favor of a less controversial cover for subsequent pressings, which included the release of the album in the United States. In the face of this legal to-do, the band remained unshaken, and perhaps press coverage from the fiasco ultimately lent a success of scandal to Dubstar's advantage. At any rate, the band was soon back in the studio, ready to release their new single, "No More Talk," in July of 1997, which charted at Number 20 on the British sales charts.

While "No More Talk" received mixed reviews, it marked no serious departure from the band's established style. Perhaps its flipside, "Unchained Monologue," was a better representation of Dubstar's strength. "It's bitterly cynical stuff," commented *New Musical Express,* "a fine list song of dishonesty and paranoia delivered in a perfectly dull Yorkshire girl brogue that pretty much translates every tired lie about dying relationships into mundane tragic truth."

In the fall of 1997, Dubstar released their second full-length recording, again with the production expertise of Steven Hague, and again with provocative artwork, this time involving plastic baby dolls, among other things. Entitled *Goodbye,* the album was on par with *Disgraceful* and offered a similarly rewarding blend of bubblegum pop and scathing irony and hit home with British fans and critics. This time, the roster of musicians was expanded to include brass and string instruments alongside the band's electronic arsenal. Unfortunately, the album was released in a mutilated form in the U.S. which incorporated a large part of *Disgraceful* while eschewing half of the new album's fresh material.

A marketing strategy designed to win over American audiences deemed unreceptive to the characteristically "British" sensibilities of Dubstar's material, this editing move disrupted the integrity of the album and may not have helped boost U.S. sales after all. Still, Dubstar has remained hopeful in regards to breaking the crucial American market and, at the same time, has shown no signs of surrendering the band's personal songwriting approach in order to sell records and cater to the whims of label executives. "When bands start writing about hotels, they have lost it," Hillier remarked in a *Billboard* interview. "If we start writing about hotels or record companies, then that's it. It's nothing that people can identify with."

Selected discography

Singles

"Stars," Food, 1995.
"Not So Manic Now," Food, 1995.
"Elevator Song," Food, 1996.
"I Will Be Your Girlfriend," Food, 1997.

Albums

Disgraceful, Food, 1995.
Goodbye, Food, 1997.

Sources

Periodicals

Billboard, August 16, 1997.
Music Week, February 22, 1997.
New Musical Express, July 7, 1997.

Online

http://www.gre.ac.uk/~mr.10
http://www.homepages.enterprise.net/jbromley/dubstar

—*Shaun Frentner*

The Faces

Rock band

The Faces helped introduce flashy showmanship and a festive atmosphere to rock music performances in the early 1970s. The group was a consolidation of former members of the Small Faces and the Jeff Beck group. Throughout their history, the Faces dealt with a great deal of confusion between their work as a unit and as a back up to singer Rod Stewart's solo career. Because of this mix-up, the band was also referred to as Rod Stewart & the Faces—for Stewart's solo recordings—and as Rod Stewart/Faces. After the group's demise, Stewart and guitarist Ron Wood, who joined the Rolling Stones, went on to widely successful careers in music.

The Faces was a progression of the British band Small Faces, which began with bass player Ronnie Lane, drummer Kenny Jones, singer and guitarist Steve Marriot, and organist John Winstone. Not long after their formation, they replaced Winstone with Ian McLagan. Within the band's first six weeks together, the Small Faces had a manager and a single on the U.K. charts, called "Watcha Gonna Do 'Bout It."

Archive Photos

For the Record . . .

Members included **Kenny Jones** (born September 16, 1948, in London, England), drums; **Ronnie Lane** (born Ronald Frederick Lane, April 1, 1946, in London, England), bass; **Ian McLagan** (born May 12, 1945, in Hounslow, Middlesex, England), keyboards; **Rod Stewart** (born Roderick Stewart, January 10, 1945, in London, England), vocals; **Ron Wood** (born June 1, 1947, in Hillingdon, Middlesex, England), guitar; Lane was replaced by **Tetsu Yamauchi** (born October 21, 1947, in Fukuoka, Japan), bass.

Band formed with members of the Small Faces and the Jeff Beck group, 1969; released debut album *First Step,* 1970; released three more albums as a band, 1971-1973; dissolved band, 1975; Stewart continued solo career; Wood joined the Rolling Stones.

By 1969, Steve Marriot had decided to leave the Small Faces, but the remaining members wanted to continue the band. First, they recruited guitarist Ron Wood, who had just left the Jeff Beck group. Wood invited a former Jeff Beck bandmate, Rod Stewart, to check out a rehearsal. Stewart had already signed a recording contract as a solo artist with Mercury Records. However, when asked to join the Faces, he agreed. Stewart believed the ensemble hadn't quite jelled, but got along with the group so well that he had to join. "I was more impressed with them as people," Stewart told Robert Green in *Rolling Stone.* "I said, 'What a nice bunch of guys—I'll join that band!' Literally, that's what I said, and that's exactly what I did."

In June of 1969, the new formation of the Faces was complete, and the band signed a recording contract with Warner Bros. Records. They released their debut album, *First Step,* along with the single "Flying" the following year. In the United States, the album was still released under the name Small Faces.

Stewart Became Most-Recognized Face

The year 1971 became an important milestone for all the members of the band. They released the album *Long Player* and the single "Had Me A Real Good Time" reached number 29 on the U.S. charts. In October, Rod Stewart's solo career also took off with the hit single "Maggie May" and the album *Every Picture Tells A Story.* The other members of the Faces performed with Stewart on his television publicity and concert tour. This combination began the reference to Rod Stewart & the Faces, which created some difficulties in the band.

The group followed up their recording debut with the release *A Nod's As Good As A Wink ... To A Blind Horse,* which reached number two in Great Britain and number six in the United States. Bassist Ronnie Lane took over on vocals for some of the tracks on the album, including "You're So Rude," "Last Orders Please," and "Debris." Comparisons between the Faces albums and Rod Stewart's solo work started to surface, especially since the same musicians played on both recordings. Jon Landau wrote in *Rolling Stone,* "The gap in achievement between Stewart's albums and the Faces is too great for it to go on."

Critics weren't the only ones who recognized such differences. Ronnie Lane explained to Andrew Bailey in *Rolling Stone,* "I think Rod's records have been better than the band's.... When we do it as the band as a whole, there are five opinions to take into account. When we play on Rod's album, everyone just strolls in, [does it], and it comes out great."

Struggled for Unification

The lack of distinction between a solo Stewart and the Faces extended into their live performances. The band would combine all their material in concert, making billing even more complicated. Stewart recognized the predicament and often attempted to submerge his solo identity with the ensemble's. "We're a band, and I want people to realize it's a band up there," Stewart told Green in *Rolling Stone.* "The other guys in the band are strong, too, in what they do. I wouldn't be in this band if I didn't think they were equally strong."

The Faces spent most of 1972 on the road. They released the single "Stay With Me," which climbed to number six in Great Britain and number 17 in the United States. They performed in the Great Western Express Festival, along with the Beach Boys and Monty Python. In 1973, they released their next album, *Ooh La La,* which soared to the top of the charts in Great Britain and hit number 21 in the United States. This time, four of the songs on the album were sung by other members of the band.

In May of 1973, bassist Ronnie Lane decided to leave the band. "It's time for me to move on," Lane said in a press statement. "I feel the need for a change." He went on to form a group called Slim Chance and later moved with his family to a 100-acre farm in the hills between England and Wales. Lane worked as a sheepherder on his farm and continued to play music in a small studio on his property. In 1978, however, he was diagnosed with multiple sclerosis, making it impossible for him to play professionally again.

After Lane's departure, the Faces enlisted Tetsu Yamauchi, a former bassist for Free. Soon thereafter, the band decided to take some time off. During this interval, Stewart released *Smiler*. Ron Wood also released a solo album, and Kenny Jones made a guest performance on a Jackson Browne record. The following year, Rod Stewart moved to the United States because of tax issues in England, and the Faces began touring again. According to Barbara Charone's review in *Rolling Stone,* the break did them some good. "Kenny Jones, Tetsu, Ian McLagan, and Wood ceased being Stewart's straightmen for the singer's more flamboyant antics," she wrote, noting that "sloppy, good-time atmospheres were replaced by tighter musicianship." But in June of 1975, Wood toured the United States as a temporary member of the Rolling Stones and rumors began to fly about the band's possible breakup.

When the Faces returned to Great Britain to perform, the British Musicians Union denied Yamauchi's work permit. Sensing the band was beginning to crumble, Stewart contemplated giving up his solo career to pursue work with the Faces 100 percent of the time. "Everybody should face up to the fact that we haven't made good albums as a band," Stewart told Cameron Crowe in *Rolling Stone.* "Everybody knows." Then, Wood commented, "He just means we didn't accomplish what we set out to do—capture the spirit of our live shows."

Dissolved into Separate Careers

"I don't think the Faces have been given a chance yet, as far as recording a good album," Kenny Jones told Tom Nolan in *Rolling Stone.* "The ones we've made in the past were mostly leftover ideas, from Rod's albums and later from Woody's. You've got to go in with concrete ideas. We've never done that." With the members drifting off into different directions, the Faces never got that chance. On October 12, 1975, they played what would be their last concert together. The split became official at a London press conference on December 18, 1975. Stewart began working on his next solo album immediately. "The thing is, now I can have a band that's exactly what I want it to be," Stewart told *Rolling Stone.* "It doesn't have to be a set load of musicians onstage, like the Faces. Now I can have who I want."

After the breakup, Rod Stewart continued a successful solo career; Ron Wood officially joined the Rolling Stones. And Kenny Jones and Ian McLagan made a futile attempt to reform the Small Faces. In 1979, Jones replaced Keith Moon as the drummer for the Who. McLagan released a few solo albums, then toured as a backup band member for the Rolling Stones. In 1993 the original members of the Faces, with the exception of Ronnie Lane, reunited for one more show. They performed with bassist Bill Wyman in recognition of Rod Stewart's Lifetime Achievement Award at the twelfth annual BRIT Awards.

Despite all of the obstacles that arose during the band's tenure, the Faces became well known as the launch pad for Rod Stewart and Ron Wood's careers. The members agreed with much of their negative press; namely, that the group worked better on stage and on Stewart's albums than they did on their own records. The live performances, polished off with lots of glitter and flashy satin, were where the Faces made their mark in music history.

Selected discography

First Step, Warner Bros., 1970.
Long Player, Warner Bros., 1971.
A Nod's As Good As A Wink ... To A Blind Horse, Warner Bros., 1971.
Ooh La La, Warner Bros., 1973.
Coast to Coast Overture and Beginners, Mercury, 1974.
The Best of the Faces, Warner Bros., 1977.

Sources

Books

Rees, Dafydd and Luke Crampton, editors, *Encyclopedia of Rock Stars,* DK Publishing, 1996.

Periodicals

Billboard, September 6, 1971; January 8, 1972; September 30, 1972; March 15, 1975.
People, December 19, 1983.
Rolling Stone, March 18, 1971; November 25, 1971; January 6, 1972; June 8, 1972; June 7, 1973; June 21, 1973; September 27, 1973; February 27, 1975; April 24, 1975; October 9, 1975; January 29, 1976; April 22, 1976.
Stereo Review, August 1972.
Texas Monthly, August 1986.

—Sonya Shelton

Fairport Convention

Folk rock band

After virtually creating the British folk rock form in the late 1960s, Fairport Convention proceeded to establish itself as an institution in the genre. During an era when many British bands were exploring blues sounds, Fairport Convention looked to the folk scene in England and North America for inspiration. In 1989, founding member Simon Nicol was quoted by Greg Kot in the *Chicago Tribune* as reflecting, "We weren't into the 'mop-top' or Mersey-beat sound; we wanted something with more meat on it. We also wanted to get away from the 12-bar [blues] format and into something more melodic."

The result was a fusion of rock instrumentation and traditionally-influenced songwriting that made the group stand apart. Having passed the 30-year mark—after suffering a frequently changing lineup, but only one official breakup—the band released the album *Who Knows Where the Time Goes* in 1997, and continued to headline an annual folk festival in Cropredy, England.

The band was formed in 1966 by Nicol on guitar, Ashley Hutchings on bass, Richard Thompson on guitar, Martin

Archive Photos

For the Record . . .

Members include **Martin Allcock** (born January 5, 1957, Manchester, England), guitar, electric bouzouki; **Sandy Denny** (born January 6, 1947, London, replaced Dyble), vocals; **Jerry Donahue** (born September 24, 1946, New York City, replaced Thompson, 1972), guitar; **Judy Dyble** (born February 13, 1949), vocals; **Shaun Frater,** drums; **Ashley Hutchings** (born January 26, 1945, London, England), bass; **Martin Lamble** (born August 28, 1949, London, replaced Frater, 1966), drums; **Chris Leslie** (replaced Allcock, 1997), violin, mandolin, and bouzouki; **Trevor Lucas** (born December 25, 1943, Bungaree, Australia, replaced Thompson, 1972), guitar; **Dave Mattacks** (born March of 1948, Edgware, Middlesex, England, replaced Lamble, 1969), drums; **Ian Matthews** (born 1946, Lincolnshire, England), vocals; **Simon Nicol** (born October 13, 1950, London), guitar; **Dave Pegg** (replaced Hutchings), bass; **Bruce Rowlands,** drums; **Ric Sanders,** violin; **Dave Swarbrick** (born April 5, 1947, London), violin; and **Richard Thompson** (born April 3, 1949, London), guitar.

Group formed in London, 1966; released its first single "If I Had a Ribbon Bow," 1967; debut album *Fairport Convention,* released 1968; other albums include *History of Fairport Convention,* 1972; *A Bonny Bunch of Roses,* 1977; *Moat on the Ledge,* (live album), 1982; *Red and Gold,* 1989; *Jewel in the Crown,* 1995; and *The Cropredy Box,* 1998; officially disbanded, 1979; held a successful reunion concert, sparking new fan interest and led to the founding of the annual Cropredy Folk Festival in England, which they have played at each year, 1980; released first new album since disbanding seven years earlier, 1986.

Addresses: *Record company*—Woodworm Records, P.O. Box 37, Banbury, Oxfordshire OX16 8YN, England.

Lamble on drums, and Judy Dyble and Ian Matthews, vocals. They named themselves after Nicol's parent's home, "Fairport," where they rehearsed. The fledgling group's musical influences included Bob Dylan and Joni Mitchell. Fairport Convention's first single, "If I Had a Ribbon Bow," was released in 1967; it had been recorded previously by Maxine Sullivan in 1936. After performing on the "underground" circuit in London, the group was more prominently showcased at London's Saville Theatre in 1968, performing with Procol Harum. Several months later, the group released its first album, *Fairport Convention.* The recording included original material and several Joni Mitchell covers.

Traditional Folk

Shortly after the album's release, Dyble left the band, to be replaced by Sandy Denny, a singer with a folk background. The switch coincided with the group's increased use of English folk elements, which were heard on their second album, *What We Did On Our Holidays.* The new direction displeased Matthews, who quit the band after having only worked on one of the album's tracks. Amid a growing contemporary-versus-traditional debate, the band lost drummer Lamble in a traffic accident. In May of 1969, the band's van crashed, killing Lamble and Thompson's girlfriend. After canceling a proposed U.S. performance at the Newport Folk Festival that summer, the band completed *Unhalfbricking,* their first recording to appear on the British "hit" charts. Featuring covers of Bob Dylan tunes, the album also included the work of fiddler Dave Swarbrick, who subsequently became a full-fledged member.

Drummer Dave Mattacks joined Fairport Convention on the album *Liege & Lief,* on which six of eight tracks were traditional folk tunes. Both Hutchings and Denny were unhappy with the band's artistic focus, with Hutchings leaning to the traditional side and Denny preferring more contemporary music. Both left the band in 1970. Denny was not replaced, but bassist Dave Peggjoined the group. When Thompson left the band in 1971 to pursue a solo career, it left Nicol as the last remaining founding member. In later years, a number of former members would rejoin or make reunion appearances; and after some 20 years, 20 different members had belonged to the band. Denny and Thompson left perhaps the most important legacies behind them—Denny for leading the band further into folk music and Thompson for his jazz-inspired style of guitar playing. Kot remarked that Thompson was viewed as "the Coltrane of rock guitar."

Cropredy Tradition

In 1979, Fairport Convention officially disbanded, but only a year later gave its first "reunion" concert. Nicol told Kot, "More people showed up for [the first reunion show] than the farewell gig." The program became an annual tradition, and grew into the largest folk festival in Europe. Called the Cropredy Folk Festival, the show is held in Cropredy, England, a village known for being the site of a 1644 civil war battle. It hosts as many as 15,000

Fairport Convention fans each summer. The program is unusual because it is shaped by the whims of Fairport Convention members. Nicol described the show to Kot as "an orgy of self-indulgence" where the band plays as long as it wants and invites whomever it likes to perform.

The reunion concerts led to a more permanent recreation of Fairport Convention in 1986, when Mattacks, Pegg, and Nicol decided they wanted to create some new music together. They recorded the album *Gladys' Leap* and toured with Jethro Tull as "Fairport Friends" with new members Martin (a.k.a. Maartin) Allcock on keyboards and Ric Sanders on violin. In 1989, the quartet recorded *Red & Gold,* a collection of story songs that frequently shared political themes. The title track was Ralph McTell's imagined account of the previously mentioned battle at Cropredy. In a review for *Rolling Stone,* David Fricke praised *Red and Gold,* saying "the astute choice of tunes, full-bodied arrangements and delicious [guitar] picking ... sound like the work of a Fairport half—nay a *fifth*—its age." He further noted that it was the first Fairport Convention album that didn't "beg comparisons" with work from the Thompson-Denny era, but rather stood on its own merits.

Where the Time Goes

In 1989, the video *It All Comes 'Round Again* provided a documentary look at the first 22 years of the band's existence. The title repeated a line from the band's 1968 song, "Meet on the Ledge." The production included interviews with band members, clips from television performances and concerts, and the only known footage of Denny performing. Writing for *Video,* John Walker deemed the film "both a fan's dream and a stellar example of musical documentary," with its greatest asset being its uncut and rarely seen archival material.

For the 1995 release of *Jewel in the Crown,* the Fairport Convention roster repeated that of *Red and Gold:* Simon Nicol, Dave Pegg, Dave Mattacks, Ric Sanders, and Martin Allcock. Because none of the members considered themselves songwriters, this quartet looked outside the band for songs and did so quite successfully. Like the band's previous recording, their selections for *Jewel in the Crown* often addressed political issues. Mike Joyce commented in the *Washington Post* that *Jewel in the Crown* showed "an impressive level of songcraft that never flags." He also found that "true to form, the band's melding of folk and rock styles often seems as natural as its wit, charm and bite."

By the end of the decade, the band had adopted an almost exclusively acoustic performance format, and in early 1998 Mattacks decided to leave in order to pursue other projects. Chris Leslie had replaced Allcock the prior year, playing a variety of instruments including violin, mandolin, and bouzouki. With the 1997 release of *Who Knows Where the Time Goes,* Fairport Convention marked 30 years since its first recording. The band's longevity—in one form or another—is certainly remarkable, as is its lasting contribution to rock music. As Fricke noted, "Having plugged into one tradition, Fairport unwittingly created another, siring a nation of electric folk bands." Fricke went on to characterize the band's impact on contemporary music as "the small but significant way that Fairport Convention changed rock & roll."

Selected discography

"If I Had a Ribbon Bow" (single), Track Records, 1967.
Fairport Convention, Polydor, 1968.
What We Did On Our Holidays, Island, 1969.
Unhalfbricking, Island, 1969.
Liege & Lief, Island, 1969.
Full House, Island, 1970.
Angel Delight, Island, 1971.
Babbacombe Lee, Island, 1972.
History of Fairport Convention (double compilation set), Island, 1972.
Rosie, Island, 1973.
Nine, Island, 1973.
Live Convention, Island, 1974.
Rising for the Moon, Island, 1975.
Gottle 'O Geer, Island, 1976.
Live At The L.A. Troubador, Island, 1977.
A Bonny Bunch of Roses, Vertigo, 1977.
Tippler's Tales, Vertigo, 1978.
Farewell, Farewell, Vertigo, reissued on Simons, 1979.
Moat On the Ledge (live album), 1982.
Gladys' Leap, Varrick, 1986.
Expletive Delighted, Varrick, 1987.
Full House, Hannibal/Carthage, 1987.
Heydey, Hannibal, 1987.
In Real Time, Island, 1988.
The Best of Fairport Convention, Island, 1988.
Red and Gold, Rough Trade, 1989.
Fairport Convention, Polydor, 1990.
The Five Seasons, Polydor, 1990.
Jewel in the Crown, Green Linnet, 1995.
Old, New, Borrowed, Blue, Green Linnet, 1996.
Encore, Encore, Resurgence, 1997.
Who Knows Where the Time Goes, Green Linnet, 1997.
The Cropredy Box, Woodworm, 1998.

Sources

Periodicals

Chicago Tribune, May 5, 1989.
Rolling Stone, March 9, 1989; June 15, 1989, p. 145.
Video, September 1988, p. 131.
Washington Post, June 2, 1995, p. 14:5.

Online

Additional information was gathered from the Fairport Convention Home Page: www.novpapyrus.com/fairport/.

—Paula Pyzik Scott

Fatboy Slim

Techno artist

Recording under the name Fatboy Slim, Norman Cook is an English disc jockey, musician, and record producer who achieved mainstream alternative success in America in the latter half of 1997 with his release *Better Living Through Chemistry*. The title was a nod to his friends, fellow "big beat" subgenre remixers the Chemical Brothers. *Better Living* gained ground with American listeners—not an easy market for the Brit techno pack to crack—with the success of its loopy, near-vocal-less track "Going Out of My Head." Writing in the *Village Voice*, Simon Reynolds noted the rock-meets-rave feel of Fatboy Slim's music and likened it to the equivalent of "pub rock—the laddish, unsophisticated but necessary prequel to an imminent (here's hoping!) punk-style reformulation/intensification of rave's unruly essence."

Cook is a Brighton native who came of age during the late 1970s in the midst of the disco era. At the age of 15, he was DJing in local clubs. A career on the turntables and a love of music led him to the Housemartins, a pleasant pop act that hit it big around 1987 with their hit "Caravan of Love." He spent time as the bass player for the group, riding on the major label gravy train. "It was too nice of an opportunity to turn down, but it was never me," Cook later told *Billboard* magazine. He eventually returned to DJing and began some attempts at making music himself. "I was a white bloke who liked dance music—or 'black music,' as it was called back then," he explained to *Rolling Stone*'s Matt Hendrickson. "I wanted to make black music without sounding like Simply Red."

Technology finally caught up with his dreams when affordable synthesizers and samplers began coming on the market, and Cook relaunched himself at the helm of an ensemble called Beats International. Success arrived immediately with the single "Dub Be Good to Me" in 1989. The song, which reached No. 1 on the U.K. charts, was built around a sample from a 1970s disco classic.

The Beats project would be just one of many musical sub-categories and aliases through which Cook found success. Next came his Pizzaman tag, which recorded several singles and a full-length album that *Mixmag*'s Kim Taylor called "an incendiary concoction of pumping house and heady club beats." Subsequent projects included Norman Cook Presents Wildski and Fried Funk Food; Cook also remixed dance singles for other artists, including A Certain Ratio, the Bassbin Twins, and the Stereo MCs.

Cook's second actual "band" experience came when he formed Freakpower with Ashley Slater. Their 1993 single, "Turn On, Tune In, Cop Out," achieved some notoriety when it was used in a European television ad that featured a transvestite. With Slater, Cook recorded an entire album, *Drive-Thru Booty,* which didn't do very well, but they did tour with the Red Hot Chili Peppers. The gigs proved lucrative, but the pressures of being on the road eventually exhausted Cook, and he went back to recording solo efforts under various monikers. Again, he hit upon a winning mix of beats and samples with the Mighty Dub Katz, whose biggest success was the Latin-hooked dub-dance hit "Magic Carpet Ride."

Cook's Fatboy Slim incarnation grew out of the "Sunday Social" night at a popular London club. Tom Rowlands and Ed Simons, who would go on to huge fame in the U.S. as the Chemical Brothers in late 1996 with their "Setting Sun" single, were the DJs, and Cook loved what they played—huge, heavy beats built around catchy samples, all crafted into a fantastically crescendo-laden mix.

Indeed, a whole social set of like-minded studio whizzes arose around the Sunday night gigs, an insiders' club that included Rowlands and Simons, Richard Fearless from Death in Vegas, and Monkey Mafia's John Carter. Cook began to DJ there as well: "I had such a laugh that I started playing again, but I didn't have enough records to play the set that I wanted to play," he told Justin Hampton in *Sonic Soul's Retina*. "I was

For the Record . . .

Born Norman Cook, c. 1963, in England.

Cook was once the bass player for the British pop band the Housemartins, late 1980s; formed Beats International, c. 1989; later released records as a solo artist under the names Pizzaman, Norman Cook Presents Wildski, Fried Funk Food, and Mighty Dub Katz, among others; formed Freakpower with Ashley Slater, c. 1993; Fatboy Slim incarnated, c. 1994.

Addresses: *Record company*—Astralwerks, 104 W. 29th St., 4th Floor, New York, NY 10001.

playing trip-hop records at 45," along with early Chemical Brothers tracks. Cook then went into his home studio and made "Santa Cruz"—a winding, acid-guitar brain soaker," as Taylor described it.

Signed with Skint

The club success of "Santa Cruz" led to more, and in time, Cook found that "I was actually making all of these records that I wish somebody else had made, but they hadn't," as he told Hampton. His talents came to the attention of a Brighton scenester, Damian Harris, who had just started up a label called Skint Records. Harris, as well as Rowlands and Simons—then achieving success in Europe with their Chemical Brothers singles—loved Cook's work and encouraged him to do more. Most of the Fatboy Slim tracks began around one memorable sample—like the opening guitar riff from The Who's "I Can't Explain" that was reformulated into "Going Out of My Head." The song would eventually become the first single from an entire album, a work that Cook had finished by early 1996. *Better Living Through Chemistry* was released on Harris's Skint label and did so well in the U.K. that it was picked up by Astralwerks/Caroline.

Released the following year onto the U.S. alternative market, the album found an audience early and steady radio airplay for "Going Out of My Head." Stacy Osbaum, reviewing *Better Living* for *Request,* wrote that Cook's wizardry "sculpts bludgeoning behemoths of beats, unleashing gargantuan, head-swelling breaks." A *Raygun* review by Kevin Raub compared the overall effort to the Housemartins—"simple formulas riding on the edge of greatness." *Spin* put Fatboy Slim on its "Love" list for October of 1997, calling Cook "the drinking man's DJ." Though *Rolling Stone* writer Nathan Brackett felt that its lead single "strays into novelty" and deemed it far from *Better Living*'s best track, he described the Fatboy Slim debut as "one of the most fun, shamelessly genre-hopping dance albums of the year."

Reynolds, writing in the *Village Voice,* echoed the sentiment. "I can't think of a more entertaining dance album released this year," he declared. Cook himself told *Sonic Soul's Retina* that *Better Living Through Chemistry* is "a party record.... It's not one to sit and listen to and tryto digest. It's all pretty stupid isn't it? It's not very intellectual." His most biting sentiment was probably reserved for the track "Michael Jackson," the genesis of which he explained to Taylor of *Mixmag*—"because he's my least favorite person in the music industry," Cook said. "He was blessed with one of the greatest soul voices ever yet he chooses to shout all over his records. He could have been a great spokesperson for black culture yet wants to be white.... Oh, and he's claiming to be Jesus. To me, he personifies everything that's wrong with the music business."

Living Large and Loving It

Cook's success as Fatboy Slim brought him additional work. He was asked to produce a record for Bootsy Collins, toe bass player for George Clinton's stellar P-Funk outfit. Collins was so excited by one big-beat track that Cook for played him that he actually stomped a hole through the floor of Cook's bedroom studio. Such damages bother Cook not; he is known as one of Brighton's best party-throwers, with a living room decorated with yellow smiley faces and an easy-to-clean carpet. After the clubs let out, a wide network of friends frequently wind up at what many call "the house of love"; one soiree lasted a record 38 hours. He continues to make his own dance singles under a variety of tags, and the market in his native U.K. seems boundless for such records. There, the club scene is far more pervasive than in the United States—even the smallest towns boast a legit rave/techno warehouse with a massive sound system. "Most people spend two nights a week in a nightclub and you're making the soundtrack to that," Cook told Hampton.

Still, Cook remains unfazed by his mainstream success and describes himself as "a happy, drunken idiot," as he told Hendrickson. He and his Sunday-Social set are also thrilled that their sound, the big-beat or chemical-beat subgenre, has caught on. "Now everyone's doing really well and we're all just laughing and saying, 'Oh my God, everybody else gets it,'" Cook told Taylor.

Selected discography

Better Living Through Chemistry, Astralwerks/Caroline, 1997.

Sources

Billboard, August 9, 1997.
Mixmag, October 1997.
Ray Gun, October 1997.
Request, October 1997.
Rolling Stone, September 18, 1997, p. 102; October 2, 1997, p. 26.
Sonic Soul's Retina, September/October 1997.
Spin, September 1997; October 1997.
Village Voice, October 7, 1997, p. 66.

Additional information for this profile was provided by Astralwerks/Caroline Records publicity materials, 1997.

—*Carol Brennan*

Fine Young Cannibals

Pop group

With only two albums to their name—not counting a later greatest hits collection and a remix—Fine Young Cannibals made a big splash on the pop music scene during the late 1980s. The trio of vocalist Roland Gift, guitarist Andy Cox, and keyboard/bass player David Steele, initially had a hard time selling their blend of soul and pop music, but a London television appearance playing "Johnny Come Home" had record producers and music consumers clamoring for more. Their debut album, self-titled *Fine Young Cannibals,* subsequently sold over two million copies and tracks "She Drives Me Crazy" and "Good Thing" from *The Raw and the Cooked* enjoyed weeks at the top of the U.S. singles chart. The second album cemented the band's fame as well as Gift's near eclipse of his band mates in press coverage. With significant critical and fan support to sustain a healthy touring and recording schedule, the band's members have nonetheless chosen to pursue other career paths amid calls for their return.

In 1984, Cox and Steele were looking for a singer to front a new band. Having split with the English Beat,

Corbis

For the Record . . .

Members include **Andy Cox** (born January 25, 1960, in Birmingham, England), guitars; **Roland Gift** (born May 28, 1962, in Birmingham), vocalist; and **David Steele** (born September 8, 1960, on the Isle of Wight) keyboards and bass.

Cox and Steele sought to form band and, in 1984, invited Gift to join them as lead singer; released *Fine Young Cannibals,* 1986; *The Raw And the Cooked,* released 1989; later issued remix, *The Raw & The Remix,* 1990; released greatest hits album, *Finest,* 1996; their music was used in films *Tin Men,* in which they did a cameo, and *Something Wild;* Gift's acting projects and Cox and Steele's producing/recording jobs have kept the band members busy during the 1990s.

Addresses: *Record company*— MCA Records Inc., 70 Universal City Plaza, North Hollywood, CA 91608-1011.

the ska-inspired English band that produced the 1979 hit cover of "Tears of a Clown," they had established themselves as skilled pop-rock writers. However, they did not share the recognizability of English Beat lead singers Dave Wakeling and Ranking Roger. Cox and Steele's talent search was extensive; they listened to hundreds of demos, only to pick a former saxophone player who had been in a English Beat opening act, Roland Gift. Cox said in the *Chicago Tribune,* "We'd been looking for just the right voice for months, going to see people all over the world, in fact, before we discovered Roland singing round the corner from us.... The moment we heard him, we knew we'd found the right guy." Their offer elevated the singer from a temporary job as a used-fur coat salesman at a London flea market.

The trio named themselves after the 1960 Natalie Wood and Robert Wagner film *All the Fine Young Cannibals,* liking the name but never having seen the movie. The group's slow start continued to drag on, as I.R.S. Records—with whom Cox and Gift still had a contract—balked at their new name and lineup. What finally jump-started Fine Young Cannibals was a 1985 appearance on the London television program *The Tube,* which was followed by a recording deal with London Records. Released in 1985, the album *Fine Young Cannibals* spawned multiple U.S. and U.K. hit singles and led to a 1986 U.S. tour. By comparison, however, *The Raw and the Cooked* was even more successful with its two number one hits. Released after a three year hiatus, the second album was described by Daisann McLane in the *Village Voice* as "more rocking, more mainstream than the dance pop of their eponymous debut album." Sounding a rare note of discord, critic Jon Pareles was unmoved by a 1989 performance, and he commented in the *New York Times,* "[they] have returned to ordinary pop topics and clichés, retaining only the mildest of ironies by setting morosely lovelorn lyrics to uptempo tunes." Pareles did allow, however, that "The Fine Young Cannibals have a sure sense of what makes a pop song tick, along with the chutzpah to borrow from the best."

The diverse musical influences of Gift, Cox, and Steele created a sound that was hard to pigeonhole. As *Rolling Stone* writer Steve Pond explained, the band "thought that their music—soul-based pop written by musicians reared on punk and ska and as fond of De la Soul as they were of Otis Redding—crossed enough barriers that either no radio station would play it or every station would." Steele and Cox entered the music business with an interest in punk music, a form that Steele later came to see as outmoded. He commented in *Rolling Stone,* "For me, people who are still obsessed with the Clash, the Sex Pistols and the Buzzcocks, that are not into De la Soul or whoever ... they're mixed up. They don't understand how punk can connect with hip-hop. To me it seems like there's a direct line: punk, 2-tone, whatever, then hip-hop." The Steele-Cox partnership can be credited for giving Fine Young Cannibals its "balance [of] retro grooves and high tech hip," according to McLane who further noted, "[their] smart pop craft is the major reason the Cannibals have conquered the big-buck U.S. market that unlike Britian's, is ruled by radio airplay, not image."

Roland Gift, on the other hand, stands out as the voice and face of Fine Young Cannibals. Pond described Gift as "strikingly handsome" with a "fluttery, almost freakish voice." Gift is very stylish—he clearly loves clothes—and his visibility as lead singer turned him into a sex symbol, particularly in Britain. McLane explained that Gift's multi-racial good looks—his mother is white, his father is black—were the height of fashion, saying, "Ethnic crossover is to the current pop scene what androgyny was to the '70s." Gift's dramatic on-camera presence in Fine Young Cannibals videos recommended him to several filmmakers. The singer landed a sexy part in the 1987 British film *Sammy and Rosie Get Laid,* in which he has a nude scene. Two years later, he appeared as a Jamaican gangster in *Scandal,* a film about a 1960s British government sex scandal. Reportedly, Gift turned down an offer to play Che Guvara in the movie version of *Evita* for two million dollars. Acting promises to be more than a passing fancy for Gift, who is pursuing roles on stage and screen.

Gift's work as an actor is often targeted as the primary reason for the on again-off again status of Fine Young Cannibals. Many other factors, however, are at play. The group does not like to tour and was more often engaged in projects such as providing songs and incidental music for director Barry Levinson's *Tin Men,* in which the trio had a cameo as a bar band. Steele and Cox show a reluctance to cooperate in promoting the band, leaving a more enthusiastic Gift to talk to the media about the band—and himself. The pair of musicians have been involved in a wide range of projects when not performing as Fine Young Cannibals. They record as "Two Men A Drum Machine And A Trumpet," produce tracks for British acts, and did music for the John Hughes film *Planes, Trains and Automobiles.*

Although there has been speculation about hard feelings between the band members because of Gift's acting jobs, little is communicated in print. Gift gave his own take on the situation in the *Chicago Tribune:* "The whole idea of what a group can be is very different today.... The old image is a bunch of musicians living together inseparably. The reality is that it's a springboard to doing all kinds of projects." In 1996 the band released a greatest hits album, *Finest.* It included three previously unreleased songs and prompted *Billboard*'s Larry Flick to reflect, "Makes ya wish for the return of the band." At that time, however, it had already been seven years since Cox, Steele, and Gift had recorded together.

Selected discography

Fine Young Cannibals, I.R.S./MCA, 1986.
The Raw And The Cooked, I.R.S./MCA, 1989.
The Raw & The Remix, MCA, 1990.
Finest, London/MCA, 1996.

Sources

Billboard, November 16, 1996, p. 78.
Chicago Tribune, April 16, 1989, sec. 13, p. 22-23.
New York Times, September 17, 1989, p. sec. 1, p. 79.
Rolling Stone, October 5, 1989, p. 47-52.
Village Voice, September 19, 1989, p. 33-35.

—Paula Pyzik Scott

Flaming Lips

Alternative rock band

Corbis

The odd band known as the Flaming Lips languished on the edges of alternative rock obscurity for more than a decade, known only to fellow fringe-music aficionados who appreciated the band's unique, distorted sound. Music writer Jim DeRogatis has called them "one of the most ambitious, imaginative, twisted, and for the most part sadly unheralded bands in rock and roll today."

The Flaming Lips have been fixtures around the Oklahoma City, Oklahomamusic scene since the mid-1980s. Their music, and the panache with which they deliver it, springs from frontman Wayne Coyne. "If I was to talk about my own life, it would probably seem like a stupid Bob Seger song about some dumb guy being in a rock band," Coyne told *Addicted to Noise* contributor Jaan Uhelzski. Coyne learned to play guitar from his older brother Mark's friends, and as a young adult living in the college town of Norman, Oklahoma, during the early 1980s, he kept running into Michael Ivins at punk-rock concerts. The two became friends and teamed up with Mark Coyne to start their own band around 1983.

Adding drummer Richard English, the Flaming Lips began playing live shows and built up a virtual cult following in the area. Their first full-length release came on Restless Records in 1986, *Hear It Is.* By this point, however, Mark Coyne had left the band and Wayne now sang and wrote the odd lyrics that would become part of the band's appeal. In 1987 they released *Oh My Gawd!!! The Flaming Lips,* which was reviewed, rather improbably, in *People* magazine. Journalist Michael Small noted the band's similarities with early Pink Floyd, and found that "though nearly every song on the album includes some degree of chaos.... each note still sounds precise."

Prank Phone Calls

Coyne's voice has been described as "weepy Neil Young-ish," but it is the eccentric nature of his lyrics that have won the band a cult following. This was showcased with their 1989 release *Telepathic Surgery,* with its tracks about odd pop-culture waste backed by psychedelic guitar. Yet internal and external problems also plagued the band during this era. English quit, and their Restless label went under shortly after the release of 1990's *In a Priest-Driven Ambulance.* Bored and nearly broke, Coyne and Ivins began making almost crank phone calls to A&R people at Warner Brothers, looking for a record deal. A short time later, an A&R person who had not heard of their stunts around the office called them out of the blue, then came to Oklahoma City to see a live show. "She didn't know anything about it. We still

For the Record . . .

Members include **Mark Coyne,** vocals (left band, c. 1985); **Wayne Coyne** (born c. 1961), guitar, vocals; **Jonathan Donahue** (c. 1989-93), guitar; **Stephen Drozd,** drums, guitar, vocals (joined band, 1993); **Richard English,** drums (left band, c. 1989); **Michael Ivins,** bass, guitar, vocals; **Ronald Jones,** guitar (joined band, 1993-96); and **Nathan Roberts** (c. 1989-93), drums.

Band formed, 1983, in Norman, OK; signed to Restless Records and released four albums with Restless including *Hear It Is,* 1986; signed to Warner Brothers, 1991 and released four albums with them including *Hit to Death in the Future Head,* 1992.

Addresses: *Record company*—Warner Brothers, 3300 Warner Blvd., Burbank, CA 91505-4694.

thought it was a joke when she called up," Coyne explained to *Addicted to Noise.*

The Flaming Lips' major-label debut was *Hit to Death in the Future Head,* but its 1992 release was delayed by legal problems resulting from their use of a sample from the movie *Brazil.* More line-up changes followed—they lost another drummer and a second guitarist as well—but by this point had thoroughly perfected the Flaming Lips' vinyl personality. Coyne's band, wrote DeRogatis in *New Times,* "had forged a thoroughly distinctive sound that merged the psychedelic shenanigans of bands like My Bloody Valentine and the Butthole Surfers with the twisted-pop sensibilities of Syd Barrett and Brian Eno."

Transmissions from the Satellite Heart would prove to be the breakthrough album for the Flaming Lips. Released in 1993, it contained a peculiar track called "She Don't Use Jelly," with lyrics recounting one tale, among others, of a girl who dyes her hair with tangerines. The song began receiving airplay on modern-rock stations and was a slow but sure hit—not to mention a huge surprise for the band. They did a video for the song that became an MTV favorite and were then invited to play dates on the second stage of summerfest Lollapalooza in 1994. Sales of the LP were healthy, and Mike Metterl of *Guitar Player,* described *Transmissions* as "a relief map of clashing textures ranging from scratchy surface noise over delicate pedal steel lines... to faint acoustic fills backing the squeal-o-rama." They appeared on the *Late Night with David Letterman* show, and even more improbably, were called to guest-star as a live band at a bar frequented by the cast in one episode of *Beverly Hills 90210.* Admittedly, Coyne and the rest of the band were somewhat unfamiliar with the Fox-TV teen drama, but gladly seized the opportunity when it knocked.

By the mid-1990s, after over ten years of togetherness, the Flaming Lips were earning widespread critical acclaim as well as opening slots for huge acts such as the Stone Temple Pilots and Porno for Pyros. With their 1995 release, *Clouds Taste Metallic,* however, the unexpected success of "She Don't Use Jelly" worked against them. Warner, perhaps hoping the album would yield another surprise hit with so little effort, put little marketing muscle behind it. A press release tried to sum it up by describing it as "full of stories about birds, brains, giraffes, sub-atomic molecules, travels to other worlds and other scientific oddities." Sales were less than stratospheric.

Parking Garage Symphonies

The band was slated to tour with the Red Hot Chili Peppers in late 1995, but bad luck struck when the other band's drummer broke his wrist and the tour was postponed— Stephen Drozd pounds the drums so hard during recording sessions that his headset must be attached to his head with duct tape. Good fortune, however, does seem to smile upon the Flaming Lips occasionally—or perhaps just the fruits of Coyne's committed cheek. In the mid-1990s, he began experimenting with odd performance-art concerts in parking lots. His concept was inspired by waiting in line for concert tickets for hours as a teenager—he loved how his fellow rock fans brought portable stereos to kill the time and show their devotion to their favorite rock gods and was struck by an idea: "Wouldn't it be crazy if you could organize it so everybody's tapes played together?" he explained to *Rolling Stone* writer Jason Cohen. Coyne began making dissimilar assemblages of sonic experiments on tape but designed them to be played all at once. He began by convincing friends in Oklahoma City, where he shares a house with his bandmates, to contribute their car stereos to the project, then did it with a hundred boomboxes, and lastly managed to get permission and participants at alternative-music industry conventions.

Selling a bottom-line conscious major-label on the idea, however, was no easy task, even for Coyne. First, it was demonstrated to Warner what the live experience was like with a parking-lot concert at their Burbank headquarters, and then Coyne and the band, who have some loyal devotees of their music inside the Warner offices, managed to convince them on 1997's limited-edition *Zaireeka* by promising to also record a more accessible, radio friendly album slated for spring of 1998. *Zaireeka,* however, was a first in the industry: a four-CD release that required four separate CD players to play them simultaneously to hear the entire effect. It was, in essence, the first octaphonic CD and was not expected to be a huge seller at its $20-plus retail price. The aural result, however, "is enthrallingly huge," opined Ethan Smith in *Entertainment Weekly.*

Zaireeka was just another day at the recording studio for Coyne, however, ever the visionary—and a musician certainly astonished that he has managed to actually make a career from his extraordinary inner inspirations. "I still feel like we're getting away with a major scam here, that someday someone is going to call up and go, OK we've discovered that you guys are just a bunch of jokers, major impostors, and the whole thing is over," Coyne told *Addicted to Noise's* Uhelzski. "Every day we wake up and it's like, they still haven't found out."

Selected discography

Flaming Lips (EP), 1985.
Hear It Is, Restless, 1986
Oh My Gawd!!! The Flaming Lips, Restless, 1987.
Telepathic Surgery, Restless, 1989.
In a Priest-Driven Ambulance, Restless, 1990.
Hit to Death in the Future Head, Warner, 1992.
Transmissions from the Satellite Heart, Warner, 1993
Clouds Taste Metallic, Warner, 1995.
Zaireeka, Warner, 1997.

Sources

Periodicals

Austin-American Statesman, November 13, 1997, p. 18.
Entertainment Weekly, November 14, 1997.
Guitar Player, September 1993, p. 129; November 1993, p. 16.
New Times (Los Angeles), October 23, 1997.
People, February 8, 1988.
Rolling Stone, March 9, 1995, p. 26; November 2, 1995, p. 68; July 10, 1997, p. 46; December 11, 1997.

Online

http://www.geocities.com/SoHo/Lofts/4533/flips (1/24/98)

Additional information for this profile was obtained from Warner Brothers publicity materials.

—Carol Brennan

Kirk Franklin

Gospel singer

AP/Wide World Photos

Gospel singer Kirk Franklin combines hip hop rhythms with overtly religious messages and has found massive crossover success in both Christian and pop music in America. Franklin and his back-up group the Family scored a hit in 1993 with "Song We Sing"—a rare crossover success. This rather impressive feat was overshadowed four years later by the song "Stomp," a song recorded with the group God's Property and featuring a sample from "One Nation Under a Groove." "Stomp" stormed up the charts and became the first gospel video to air in heavy rotation on MTV (Music Television). Franklin's appeal lay in the fact that he rather adeptly blends urban rhythms with his religious rhetoric, producing a savvy contemporary Christian mix aimed at members of the hip hop nation. John Morthland of *Texas Monthly* said that "the lean goateed Franklin is able to score with hard gospel largely because he has the qualities other gospel stars lack: charisma, sex appeal, stage presence, ambition, business savvy, and street credibility."

It was not always this easy for Franklin. Born out of wedlock to teenage parents who never married nor lived together, he had sporadic contact with his parents while he was growing up. When he was three, Franklin's mother put him up for adoption at a Fort Worth church. His great-aunt Gertrude Franklin, who was then in her mid 60s, took him in and eventually adopted him, insisting that he get involved in her church and in its youth activities, especially the choir. Growing up in the church under his great-aunt's watchful eye gave Franklin the drive to excel in the choir. By the age of seven, his innate talent had earned him the opportunity to pursue a gospel music recording contract. His great-aunt expressly forbade this, citing Franklin's extremely young age. A mere four years later, Franklin had attained the rank of minister of music at the Mt. Rose Baptist Church. In this position, he was responsible for all of the music for all of the choral groups at the church.

While was growing up, the choir and its attendant lifestyle were still more of a sideline to Franklin than his life's vocation. Commenting on this to Morthland, Franklin said; "I was always a moody child. In the house, it was just me and an older woman. When I got around my peers, I just went buck wild, because I wanted to be a kid, you know?" Hedonism filled Franklin's days when he was not in church. His rebellious antics included fighting, hanging around with gang members, hanging out at pool halls, causing trouble at school, fighting, and smoking marijuana.

When he was 16, Franklin's friend, 17-year-old Eric Pounds, was killed when his parents' gun fell from the top of the closet and accidentally discharged. Devastated, Franklin

For the Record . . .

Born c. 1970, in Fort Worth, TX; married c. 1996; children: Kerrion, son.

Began career performing with the Dallas-Fort Worth Mass Choir; performed on *Look How Far We've Come* on Savoy, 1991; performed on *Another Chance* on Savoy, 1993; left to pursue a solo career; signed with Gospo-Centric and released *Kirk Franklin and the Family*, 1993; released *Kirk Franklin and the Family Christmas*, 1995; released *What'cha Lookin' 4,* 1996; contributed to *Don't Be a Menace* film soundtrack, 1996; contributed to *Special Gift*, 1996; contributed to *Soul Train Christmas Starfest*, 1997; contributed to *Get on the Bus* film soundtrack, 1997; *God's Property from Kirk Franklin's Nu Nation*, 1997.

Awards: Gospel Music Award for Song of the Year, 1993; Gospel Music Award for Best New Artist, 1993; Platinum certification for *Kirk Franklin and the Family*, 1993.

Addresses: *Record company*—B-rite Music, 417 East Regent St., Englewood, CA, 90301.

sought solace from the church, reading the Bible, and getting more involved in music. The following year, Franklin's faith was tested again when he got his girlfriend pregnant. Franklin told Allison Samuels of *Newsweek*: "those two things changed my life and got me in touch with the Lord and the Lord's music." He added to Morthland that "what I had done [getting his girlfriend pregnant out of wedlock] was wrong, but God forgave me, so I was able to forgive myself." Franklin's girlfriend gave birth to a son named Kerrion. She raised him by herself until early 1996. It was then that Franklin decided to do for his son what was never done for him. "I didn't want my son raised like I was. I wanted him to know his father," he explained to Morthland.

Joins Gospel-Centric

At 19, Franklin met Milton Biggham, executive director of Savoy Records, the leading label in gospel music. Biggham persuaded him to join his newly established Dallas-Fort Worth Mass Choir. The Dallas-Fort Worth Mass Choir released two albums on Savoy with Franklin, 1991's *Look How Far We've Come* and *Another Chance* in 1993. Biggham, who was Franklin's mentor in the industry, offered him a solo recording contract with Savoy. After much thought, Franklin politely declined feeling that on the Savoy label he would only be a small fish in a big pond. Not long after this, Franklin was contacted by Vicky Latallaide who had recently established the Los Angeles based Gospo-Centric label. After days of prayerful deliberation, he signed up with Gospo-Centric.

The breakthrough success of *Kirk Franklin and the Family* in 1993 exceeded the expectations of both Gospo-Centric and Franklin. The album, which teamed Franklin up with his back-up group, the Family, contained the hit inspirational track, "Why We Sing," which not only topped the gospel music charts but managed to break out of the gospel ghetto and attract serious attention and air play on rhythm and blues (R&B) stations as well. Latallaide told *Billboard*'s Phyllis Stark that " we didn't know if they [R&B stations] would pick it up; we just wanted to make them aware of it because it was doing so well in gospel ... [the record's mainstream success] kind of caught us off guard . . . [adding nonetheless that the success of "Why We Sing"] was something we had quietly prayed for." Gina Deeming, Gospo-Centric's business affairs manager, further elaborated on the matter to Stark adding that "we basically called it an act of God. It's anointed and it's God's record, and we just try to take care of it."

Numerous program directors from R&B and urban music stations across America mentioned that the positive uplifting message of "Why We Sing" hit a nerve with R&B and urban music listeners. It was such a contrast to the graphically profane and sexually explicit lyrical content of a lot of the current urban music. Franklin explained his appeal to Samuels saying, "Black youth are looking for spirituality and a better way to live. I'm doing what it takes to get the attention of my generation. Kids are killing their parents. They're lost. Someone has to bring them back."

Franklin's hard work paid off as "Why We Sing" won the Gospel Music Song of the Year Award in 1993 and he and his band took home the award for the year's Best New Artist as well. Accolades and recognition did not stop there. The album, *Kirk Franklin and the Family*, became the first gospel album to go platinum in America. The sales were fueled, in no small part, by the success of "Why We Sing" on the Contemporary Christian, gospel, R&B, and pop charts.

The 1995 Christmas release, *Kirk Franklin and the Family Christmas,* was also popular and the release of

Whatcha' Looking 4, debuted at number 23 on the pop albums chart in 1996. Also that year, Franklin contributed tracks to the *Special Gift* Christmas compilation, the *Soul Train Christmas Starfest,* and to the soundtrack for the film *Don't be a Menace.*

Holy Dope Dealer

Franklin's previous work served as a prelude to the phenomenally unprecedented success of his 1997 album, *God's Property from Kirk Franklin's Nu Nation* as the album went gold, selling half a million copies in its first month of release. It topped not only the gospel charts but the R&B charts as well and even managed to make it to number three on the pop charts. The albums success was driven by the smash hit "Stomp," which sampled George Clinton's funky "One Nation Under a Groove" and featured a rap from Cheryl James, also known as Salt, from Salt n' Pepa. Franklin first met God's Property at a gospel concert where the Dallas-Fort Worth Mass Choir and the Family were performing on the same bill. Franklin invited God's Property to sing on *Whatcha Lookin' 4* and he then get a song on the soundtrack for Spike Lee's 1997 film *Get on the Bus.*

Although never released as a single, "Stomp" became the first gospel song to make it into heavy rotation on MTV. "Stomp" also managed to seduce young people who had strayed from the church with its propulsive beats, rhythmic clapping and intoxicating chorus. Defending his use of hip hop to promote the word of God, Franklin told *U.S. News & World Report* writer, Thom Geier, "there's nothing sinful about the beat. When I've got their attention, I hit them with the holy dope. I'm a holy dope dealer." Linda Searight, the music teacher who formed God's Property in Dallas in 1992 concurred with Franklin and told Morthland, "going into nightclubs, that's just God comin' through, where ever He wants to come through. The nature of what we're doing is outreach. And that means you have to reach out to bring in."

Selected discography

(With Dallas-Fort Worth Mass Choir) *Look How Far We've Come*, Savoy, 1991.
(With Dallas-Fort Worth Mass Choir) *Another Chance*, Savoy, 1993.
Kirk Franklin and the Family (includes "Why We Sing"), B-rite, 1993.
Kirk Franklin and the Family Christmas, B-rite, 1995.
Whatcha Lookin' 4, B-rite, 1996.
(Contributor) *Don't be a Menace*, Island, 1996.
(Contributor) *Special Gift*, Island, 1996.
(Contributor) *Soul Train Christmas Starfest*, Epic, 1997.
(Contributor) *Get on the Bus*, Interscope, 1997.
God's Property from Kirk Franklin's Nu Nation (includes "Stomp"), B-rite, 1997.

Sources

Billboard, December 11, 1993; December 3, 1994.
Jet, December 25, 1995.
Newsweek, September 1, 1997.
Texas Monthly, September, 1996; September, 1997.
U.S. News & World Report, July 7, 1997.

—*Mary Alice Adams*

Fu Manchu

Rock band

The Santa Monica, California, based rock band Fu Manchu draws inspiration from Ozzy Osborne, early punk rock before it had an official name, drag races, bongs, wild guitar riffs, and the 1970s counter-culture. Comfortable with the labels heavy rock and stoner rock, drummer Brant Bjork summed up the band's philosophy for *BAM* magazine's Dan Epstein by saying, "It either rocks or it doesn't, man!" *Entertainment Weekly's* Tom Sinclair described Fu Manchu as, "Invoking the legendary thunder of Blue Cheer as well as the clanging cowbell boogie of Mountain ... (Fu Manchu) creates a near-perfect facsimile of circa-'71 hard rock." The band is comprised of drummer Brant Bjork, guitarist Bob Balch, vocalist/guitarist Scott Hill, and bass player Brad Davis.

Fu Manchu released four 7-inch discs before a debut CD, *No One Rides for Free,* in 1994. In 1990, the band released the singles "Kept Behind the Trees," "Bouillabaisse," and "Jr. High School Ring" on Slap-A-Ham Records. Two years later they released "Senioritis," "Pinbuster," and "El Don" on Germany's Zuma Records,

Corbis

For the Record . . .

Members include **Bob Balch**, guitar; **Brant Bjork** , drums; **Brad Davis**, bass; **Eddie Glass,** guitar; **Scott Hill** vocals and guitar (left 1996); **Ruben Romano,** drums (left 1996).

Released "Kept Behind the Trees," "Bouillabaisse," and "Jr. High School Ring" in 1990. Released "Senioritis," "Pinbuster," and "El Don" in 1992 on Germany's Zuma Records. Released 7-inch compilation including "Pick-Up Summer" and "Vankhana" and 7-inch compilation including "Don't Bother Knockin" and "Space Sucker" in 1992 for Elastic. Released *No One Rides for Free* in 1994, *Daredevil* in 1995, and *In Search Of* ... in 1996. Re-released the 7-inch compilation including "Asphalt Risin'" and "Chevy Van" in 1996. Released a 10-inch compilation including "Godzilla," "Module Overload," and "Living Legend" in 1996. Released *The Action is Go* in 1997.

Addresses: *Record company*—Mammoth Records, 500 S. Buena Vista, Burbank, CA 91521-3790. Website—http://www.mammoth.com.

as well as a 7-inch compilation including "Pick-Up Summer" and "Vankhana" for Elastic Records, and another 7-inch compilation including "Don't Bother Knockin" and "Space Sucker," also for Elastic. By 1994 the band was primed for *No One Rides for Free,* released on Bongload Custom Records. A year later, Fu Manchu released *Daredevil* on Bongload, followed by *In Search Of* ... in 1996 on Mammoth. A 7-inch compilation including "Asphalt Risin'" and "Chevy Van" was also released in 1996, and in 1997 they released a 10-inch compilation which included "Godzilla," "Module Overload," and "Living Legend."

Fu Manchu released *The Action is Go* in 1997, and *BAM*'s Epstein wrote, "Be advised that you also can't go wrong with *The Action is Go* ... [it] features 13 bowel-blistering originals—as well as a cover of "Nothing Done" by Boston hardcore legends SSD—which filter the single-minded riffage of Black Sabbath and AC/DC through a thick Indica haze." *The Action is Go* was produced by White Zombie's J. Yuenger, and it differed from the band's other releases in that it was more focused, with a heavier rock sound and more unabashed experimentation. Guitarist Scott Hill told Epstein, "J. helped us arrange stuff better .... He knew the sound we wanted—the big, fuzzy, heavy thing." The band chose the title U from an old motorcycle film called *On Any Sunday.* Hill watched the movie repeatedly during the 1970s when he was young, since he used to ride motocross, and the title typifies the offbeat, irreverent wit of the band's members. The release's single "Evil Eye" was inspired by Hill's experience at a figure eight demolition derby, where a brakeless driver had an evil eye painted on his car. Davis told Epstein, "It's our first album where I'm happy with all the songs on it. When I listen to it at home, I don't skip over any of the tracks."

Shared Perspective

Original band members guitarist Eddie Glass and drummer Ruben Romano were replaced withdrummer Bjork of Kyuss and guitarist Balch before the release of *The Action is Go* in 1997. Glass and Romano wanted to give Fu Manchu more of a 1960s-era sound and Hill and Davis favored the heavy rock sound of the 1970s. Bjork and Balch were more in keeping with the vision Hill and Davis shared, and Bjork was a longstanding fan of Fu Manchu, harking back to when he was with Palm Desert's Kyuss. Bjork joined Fu Manchu during the middle of their 1996 tour with Clutch. Balch joined the band a few months after Bjork and, like Hill and Davis, he was from the El Toro/Mission Viejo area. Hill writes all the lyrics, but the band's songs develop organically from jam sessions. Hill told Epstein, "Someone will bring a riff to practice, and we'll work on it from there. Once it's pretty much arranged, I'll take it back and do the lyrics. I don't see how people can write lyrics first and then make the song around it." Hill favors a stream-of-consciousness approach to lyrics, which results in an impressionistic account of unusual things like Bigfoot sightings, demolition derbies, skateboarding, surfing, and kitschy television programs.

Fu Manchu members view their material and popularity as particular enough to appeal to a limited but appreciative audience, much like Ozzy Osborne's fan base. The band toured successfully with Osborne in 1997. Artists such as Black Crowes, Wool, Kyuss, Monster Magnet, Masters of Reality, White Zombie, The Melvins, and The Obsessed have either shared the stage with Fu Manchu or have gone to their shows regularly in search of a good time. Band members aren't on a quest for fame so much as a quest for fun, kinship, and the opportunity to create their unique, "heavy as an anvil" rock. They have never failed to see the humor often found in popular culture. When discussing the single "Grendel, Snowman" with *BAM*'s Epstein, lyricist Hill said, "Usually the first line of a song makes sense to me; after that, it's like, there it goes." Many of Hill's lyrics have been inspired by his favorite films, as exemplified by "Over The Edge," "Viva Knievel!," and "The Van." *The Van,* a 1970s teen film featuring Danny DeVito, inspired most of the lyrics for Fu Manchu's songs.

Tapped into Underground Youth Culture

The Fu Manchu single "Redline" was included on the soundtrack of Roger Corman's B-movie *Caged Heat 3000,* and the Fu Manchu singles "Push Button Magic" and "Trapeze Freak" were featured in the film *Citizen Ruth* starring Laura Dern. Fu Manchu's music also appears in the surf video *Players.* Channel One Skateboards in Huntington Beach, California, designed special edition Fu Manchu skateboard decks and other skateboard stores followed suit. The band's memorable and kitschy devil-over-two-demolition-cars logo inspired devil horn salutations from enthusiastic crowd members when the band performed live, and the band also has favored vintage car and van logos. *Entertainment Weekly's* Sinclair wrote, "Lyrically, Fu Manchu's songs [about strolling astronomers, burning roads, abominable snowmen] mean next to nothing, but the music's sheer goon density should strike a chord in the hearts of ... America." Fu Manchu has been savoring a good time, and the band's listeners have been going along for the joyride ... in a van, of course.

Selected discography

Singles

"Kept Between Trees," Slap-A-Ham Records, 1990.
"Bouillabaisse," Slap-A-Ham Records, 1990.
"Jr. High School Ring," Slap-A-Ham Records, 1990.
"Senioritis,"Zuma Records, Germany, 1992.
"Pinbuster," Zuma Records, Germany, 1992.
"El Don," Zuma Records, Germany, 1992.
"Pick-Up Summer," Elastic Records, 1992.
"Vankhana," Elastic Records, 1992.
"Don't Bother Knockin," Elastic Records, 1992.
"Space Sucker," Elastic Records, 1992.
"Asphalt Risin'," Mammoth Records, 1996.
"Chevy Van," Mammoth Records, 1996.
"Ojo Rojo," Mammoth Records U.K., 1996.
"Missing Link," Mammoth Records U.K., 1996.
"Godzilla," Man's Ruin Records, 1997.
"Module Overload," Man's Ruin Records, 1997.
"Living Legend," Man's Ruin Records, 1997.

Albums

No One Rides For Free, Bongload Custom Records, 1994.
Daredevil, Bongload Records, 1995.
The Action Is Go, Mammoth Records, 1997.

Sources

Periodicals

BAM Magazine, November 6, 1997.
Entertainment Weekly, November 7, 1997.
Rocket, November 1997.

Online

AMG (All-Music Guide), http://205.186.189.2/cg/amg.exe
http://www.geocities.com/SunsetStrip/Alley/9338/fumanchu.html
http://www.themusiczone.com/fu.html

—B. Kimberly Taylor

Julie Gold

Songwriter, singer

Courtesy of Julie Gold Music

Aspiring songwriters would be wise to listen to advice from songwriter Julie Gold. "I tell people to stick to their dreams," she said in a *Ladies' Home Journal* interview, just a few months after her song, "From A Distance," captured a Grammy for Song of the Year. Gold toiled in near anonymity for a decade before hitting the big time with Bette Midler's cover of her song. Since then, Gold's songs have been performed by the likes of Kathy Mattea, Donna Summer, Andrea Marcovicci, Cliff Richard, and Judy Collins. "From A Distance," her best-known composition, remains one of the most memorable hits of the early 1990s.

Julie Gold was born in Philadelphia on February 3, 1956. One of two children of a Russian-born mother, who worked as a school secretary, and an American-born father, who worked in the Philadelphia police department's personnel office, Gold seems to have been born to write songs. She made up her first songs when she was four years old and began writing them down when she was 13. It was during her college years at Temple University in Philadelphia that she began performing them at local clubs. Gold graduated from Temple in 1978, then immediately moved to New York to be at the epicenter of the music industry. She landed a job as a barroom piano player after less than a year, but lost it when the management decided to discontinue live music. Over the next few years, Gold moved through a progression of menial day jobs—including stints as a department store vacuum cleaner demonstrator and as a secretary at HBO—to support her nighttime career as a struggling musician.

Composed Hit on Childhood Piano

Throughout these hard times, Gold never gave up her dream of making the big time as a songwriter. She actively sent out demo tapes of her songs to publishers and record companies. Usually there was no response. In spite of the rejections, Gold continued to work at her craft, developing her songwriting skills even in the absence of encouragement from the industry. According to Gold, the turning point in her career came on her 30th birthday, in February of 1986. As she explained to Shana Aborn of *Ladies' Home Journal,* "Until then, I had been writing on a junky electric keyboard. For my birthday, my parents shipped me the upright piano I had grown up with. The very next day, I wrote 'From A Distance' on it."

Writing the music and lyrics to "From A Distance," the song that changed the course of her life, took all of one hour. The record companies and music publishers still failed to take notice. It was through the intervention of

For the Record . . .

Born February 3, 1956, in Philadelphia, PA; daughter of Ann (a school secretary) and Aaron Gold (a police department employee); *Education:* Temple University, BA.

Wrote first song in third grade; began performing in folk clubs, c. 1975; moved to New York to launch professional songwriting career, 1978; "From A Distance" recorded by Nanci Griffith, 1987; hit version of "From A Distance" recorded by Bette Midler, 1990; performed and toured with Four Bitchin' Babes, c. 1992; publishing agreement with Cherry Lane Music, 1993- ; released solo CD *Dreaming Loud,* 1997, rereleased by Gadfly Records, 1998.

Awards: Grammy Award for Song of the Year for "From A Distance," 1991; New York Music Awards, Rising Star Award; BMI Million-Airs Award, for "From A Distance;" Seven Seals Award, U.S. Department of Defense.

Addresses: *Office*—Julie Gold Music, 332 Bleecker St., Suite D39, New York, NY 10014; *Publishing company*—Cherry Lane Music, 10 Midland Ave., Port Chester, NY 10573; *Record company*—Gadfly Records, P.O. Box 5231, Burlington, VT, 05402.

Gold's close friend, folk singer Christine Lavin, that "From A Distance" finally saw the light of day. Lavin played a tape of the song for another folk singer friend, Nanci Griffith. Griffith liked it so much that she decided to use it on her album, *Lone Star State of Mind,* which was released in 1987.

Griffith's version of "From A Distance" became a hit in Europe, where she enjoyed a strong following. Griffith then invited Gold to tag along on part of her U.S. tour and provide piano accompaniment on the song, including a performance at Carnegie Hall. In spite of these successes, Gold was still not able to support herself through songwriting—receiving royalties from Europe is a slow and grueling process—and by 1989 she was still toiling at her day job as a secretary at HBO. Nearly discouraged, Gold asked her parents to pay her rent for six months so that she could quit HBO and concentrate on music full time. Just as her six month reprieve was about to expire in January of 1990, two events changed the course of her career. First, the foreign royalty checks from Griffith's version began to arrive. The second was a call from Bette Midler's musical director saying that Midler wanted to record "From A Distance."

Earned Grammy for "From A Distance"

Midler's version of "From A Distance" was released in September of 1990, and by mid-December it had risen to number two on the pop charts. The single went platinum—one million copies sold—a few weeks later. On February 20, 1991, Gold found herself on the stage of the Grammy Awards ceremony accepting the honor for "Song of the Year." Since then, the song has been redone by scores of performers, including James Galway, Jack Jones, and Patti LaBelle. There have even been marching band arrangements of it. Tens of thousands of copies of the sheet music were purchased, and it was translated into and recorded in, among other languages, German, Spanish, French, Hebrew, and Cantonese. It also became something of an anthem among armed forces personnel serving in the Gulf War.

With the success of "From A Distance," Gold was finally able to devote herself to music full-time. Griffith recorded another Gold composition, "Heaven," on her 1991 album *Late Night Grande Hotel.* In addition, another song of Gold's, "The Journey"—originally written for, then cut from, the feature film *For the Boys*—was recorded by singer Lea Salonga and Gold's "Try Love" was chosen by her former employer, HBO, as between-movie music.

Gold also began to cultivate a performing career of her own, touring the East Coast and Midwest. She also appeared on television, often with Griffith, including spots on the Nashville Network's "American Music Shop" and PBS's "Austin City Limits." She became a member of the Lavin-led group Four Bitchin' Babes, which toured extensively and recorded on the Philo label. In 1993 Gold signed a publishing deal with Cherry Lane Music. The deal made Cherry Lane the international administrator of "From A Distance," and called for Gold to continue churning out songs on a steady basis. The following year, Gold's song "Thanks to You" was featured in the Paramount motion picture *Andre.*

Gave Up Most Touring

Eventually, Gold came to the realization that the life of a touring musician was not for her. She much preferred to spend her time at the keyboard crafting songs. "I'm not made of the right stuff to go on the road and instantly tour, and I became very comfortable with my role as a songwriter," she was quoted as saying in *Billboard.* "That is what I am, and that is what I love."Gold was not prepared to give up performing altogether, however. She has maintained a steady presence on the Greenwich Village cabaret scene, and received glowing notices for her one-woman show "From A Distance & Other Songs of Hope."

As the 1990s continued, Gold began to feel the urge to put out an album of her own. In spite of her success as a songwriter, however, she received no encouragement from record companies, which shied away mainly because of her stated distaste for touring. Undaunted, as usual, Gold decided to go it alone. She made her own CD, *Dreaming Loud,* a collection of 12 songs originally recorded as demos to be sent to record companies and music publishers. The sincerity of Gold's own versions of her songs captured the attention of Mitch Cantor, president of the Vermont-based indie label Gadfly Records. "Lots of people have had the opportunity to hear Julie's songs as recorded by others," Cantor was quoted as saying in *Billboard.* "But the truth is that she delivers them with an impact that is more powerful than any of the covers I've heard." Gadfly made plans to reissue *Dreaming Loud* in the spring of 1998, in hopes that the strength of the songs themselves would lead to radio airplay, even without the benefit of a supporting concert tour.

Meanwhile, Gold chooses not to let the ups and downs of a career in the music industry change her. Her success as a songwriter has meant that she could move into a bigger apartment and stop working at other jobs. Aside from that, she continues to do what she had always done; namely, hang out with friends, perform when she feels like it, and, above all, indulge in her main passion: writing songs. "I'm a simple songwriter putting out a simple product," she told *Billboard's* Jim Bessman, "and hoping that some of the public gets it." Obviously, millions of members of the record-buying public get it.

Selected compositions

"From A Distance"
"Try Love"
"Heaven"
"Thanks to You"
"The Journey"
"Good Night, New York"

Selected discography

Dream Loud, Julie Gold, 1997 (reissued by Gadfly Records, 1998).

Sources

Billboard, December 1, 1990, p. 30; October 5, 1991, p. 43; November 20, 1993, p. 23; August 27, 1994, p. 18; January 24, 1998.
Fast Forward, Winter 1998, p. 1.
Ladies' Home Journal, May 1991, p. 20.
New York Times, February 20, 1991, p. C14.

Additional material was provided by Julie Gold and by Gadfly Records.

—Robert R. Jacobson

Teddy Harris

Jazz musician, composer, arranger

Courtesy of Dr. Harris

A longtime figure of Detroit's jazz scene, Theodore "Teddy" Harris Jr. has found international acclaim as a pianist, soprano saxophonist, composer, and arranger. In his travels around the world, he has played command performances for the Emperor of Japan and Jordan's King Hussein. Affectionately known as the "Good Doctor," Harris has worked with numerous jazz greats, stage personalities, and famed Motown artists, including the Supremes for whom he served as music director for sixteen years. Though a noted musician and bandleader, Harris earns his livelihood from composing and arranging music for ensemble instrumentation, stage performances, and motion picture soundtracks: "That's how I make my living," he stated in *The Detroit News,* "with that pencil." Through his New Breed Bebop Society Orchestra, and as an artist in residence in the Highland Park school system, Harris instructs and inspires young musicians to find their own creative voices within Detroit's great jazz tradition.

Born in Detroit, Michigan, on August 27, 1934, Theodore Harris Jr., hailed from a musical family. Harris' grandfather played trombone, and his mother the keyboard. A pianist and organist, his father performed in the pit orchestra of Detroit's Paradise Theatre, backing such famed jazzmen as Cab Calloway and Oran "Hot Lips" Page. At age seven, Harris first heard Duke Ellington at the Paradise Theatre, an event which, as he stated in a 1993 promotional program, "had the biggest affect on my musical life. I liked everything about Ellington.... I knew exactly what I wanted to do after that." By age fourteen Harris was allowed to sit-in at the Paradise with Lionel Hampton's big band.

Harris attended Eastern and Northern High School, where he served as student band director at both institutions. While at Northern he formed a student band with trumpeter Donald Byrd and bassist Paul Chambers. Known for its wealth of talented jazz pianists, Detroit provided Harris with musical mentors such as Tommy Flanagan and Barry Harris. Five years his senior, Barry Harris was, as Teddy Harris recounted in a private interview, "a natural teacher. We all met at his house. Barry did all the playing and I learned from him informally by observing his technique." Also a student of reed instruments, Harris played his first professional music job on tenor saxophone, while accompanying his father in a organ trio at the Club Gay 90s.

In mid 1950s Harris recorded for Jack Brown's Fortune label, cutting sides with such local groups as the Diablos and Andre Williams. "Fortune was a small label—a nickel and dime operation—but it put out a lot of music," recalled Harris in a private interview. "Fortune's owner, Jack Brown, would give you twenty dollars

For the Record . . .

Born Teddy Harris Junior, August 27, 1934, in Detroit, Michigan; son of Theodore Harris Sr. (pianist and organist) and Ruth Harris; married Matha Harris (production company owner and booking agent); children Tanya, Karla, Margo; education: New England Conservatory of Music, 1955-1957; studied with Nadia Boulanger 1959-1961.

At age 14 performed on saxophone with father at local club; early 1950s recorded for Detroit-based Fortune label; 1957 recorded on Jackie Wilson's hit "Reet Petite"; performed in Paris with saxophonist Eli "Lucky" Thompson in 1959-1961; performed in local Detroit clubs 1961 and in 1962 joined Motown Record's Motortown Revue; worked with bassist Ernie Farrow 1963; mid 1960s served as musical director for Aretha Franklin; member of the Paul Butterfield Blues Band 1969-1970; served as musical director for the Supremes 1970-1986; 1973 scored tile number for motion picture *Jonathan Livingston Seagull;* early 1980s formed the New Breed Bebop Society Orchestra; embarked on world tour with the Michigan Jazz Masters.

Awards: Outstanding Contributions (United Negro College Fund) 1986; Distinguished Recognition Medal (City of Detroit) 1990; State of Michigan Special Tribute 1992; Legends of Jazz International Hall of Fame; Michiganian of the Year 1993; Jazz Masters Award 1993; 1993 Key to the City of Detroit; Spirit of Detroit Award 1994, Governor's Michigan Artist Award 1995.

Address: 12950 John R., Detroit, Michigan, 48203

to play some music, and later I'd hear myself playing on records as an unknown member on a Diablo or Andre Williams' band."

Drafted into the Army

In 1955 Harris attended the New England Conservatory of Music in Boston, where he studied with Dr. Russ Morganstern. In 1957 he recorded with several other local Detroiters on Jackie Wilson's first hit "Reet Petite (The Finest Girl You Ever Want to Meet)." During the same year, while studying at the conservatory, Harris was drafted into the army, and eventually became a member of the Fourth Armored Division. He performed as guest saxophonist with the 7th Army Symphony Orchestra and Soldier's Show Company, a ensemble featuring Eddie Harris, Don Ellis, Cedar Walton, Albert "Tootie" Heath, and Leo Wright. As Harris related in a private interview, "Eddie Harris showed me things on the piano and I would show him things on the saxophone. Later, he would become an international talent as a tenor horn player." Around 1958 Harris wrote his first composition "Soul Sister," which he sent to Yusef Lateef who later recorded it on the Impulse! label.

In 1959 Harris received an overseas discharge from the army in Germany and traveled to Paris, where he encountered his friend, saxophonist Eli "Lucky" Thompson, performing at the Blue Note. Hired by Thompson at the Blue Note, he spent a year at the club playing piano behind the famous saxophonist. In Paris, Harris studied musical composition and orchestration with Nadia Boulanger, whom Tyler Stovall called, in his work *Paris Noir, African Americans in the City of Light*, "the world's leading teacher of music theory whose former pupils included many of the great names in the twentieth-century classical tradition."

Back in Motown

In 1961, after arriving back in Detroit, Harris performed with a drummer in the Swamp Room of Sunnie Wilson's Mark Twain Hotel, and eventually expanded his group into a formidable unit. Harris' job at he Swamp Room also allowed him to meet many of the hotel's famous jazz guests who often sat in with the band. Around 1962, while performing at Odum's Cave, Harris was hired by Flint bandleader Choker Campbell to play in the orchestra for the Motortown Revue. During his years with the revue Harris traveled with such stellar acts as Marvin Gaye, the Temptations, Stevie Wonder, and Smokey Robinson. Always balancing his work in popular music with jazz, Harris worked with bassist Ernie Farrow in 1963. As he stated in the *Detroit News*, "... Bebop—that is what I love; that is all I want to do."

During his career Harris has sought, through his skills as an arranger, to imbue popular and soul songs with a sophisticated harmonic sensibility. During the 1960s, Harris spent five and-a-half years as musical director for Aretha Franklin. Caught in performance on Aretha Franklin's 1965 album *Yeah! In Person With Her Quartet,* Harris—in the company of bassist James "Beans Richardson", drummer Hindel Butts, and special guest guitarist Kenny Burrell—provides fine support behind

Franklin whose voice, set within a jazz musical backdrop, covers a range of standards and blues numbers. Jazz writer and scholar Dan Morganstern noted, in the album's liner notes, the quality of the assembled accompanists, including Harris, "who," as he noted, "always seems to know where Aretha is going."

By the late 1960s Harris performed with fellow Motown Revue artist Thomas "Beans" Bowles in the Dashki band. During this time, harmonica/bandleader Paul Butterfield contacted Harris. Following Buttterfield's attempt to hire Gil Evans as arranger, he, upon the recommendation of the band's bassist Rod Hicks, hired Harris as pianist and arranger for his progressive blues ensemble. With Butterfield's ten piece band, Harris appeared on the 1969 Elektra album *Keep On Moving,* a work which featured "Love March." Collectively written by Harris and other band members, "Love March" served as the theme for the Woodstock Music and Arts Festival when the band appeared at the legendary concert in 1969. A year later, Harris' appeared on the album *The Paul Butterfield Blues Band Live,* a recording which included his composition "Number Nine." The Butterfield Blues Band was one of the best bands I've ever played with," recounted Harris in a private interview. "We had a number of fine musicians like saxophonists David Sanborn and George Dinwiddie, and when I discovered that Butterfield could play flute I eventually arranged music for four flutes."

Musical Director for the Supremes

In 1970, after his stint with the Butterfield Blues Band, Harris became musical director and arranger for the Supremes—a job which would span sixteen years, and would include shows in Europe, the Middle East, and South America. The group's rhythm section played live performances within an orchestral setting, and often opened the show with Harris' original jazz compositions. Throughout the decade Harris also played jazz musicians such as Thad Jones, Kenny Burrell, and Lionel Hampton.

In 1973 Harris scored music for the title song of the motion picture *Jonathan Livngston Seagull,* "I Must Learn to Fly." While taking part in such projects, Harris remained a stalwart figure in the local Detroit jazz scene. On January 2 and April 2, 1976, he attended sessions for the album *The Hastings Street Jazz Experience,* where he played soprano saxophone, piccolo, piano, and contributed the original composition "Yes Lord." In 1978 Harris led a large ensemble for a concert series, Composers Concepts Concert. Billed with Yusef Lateef, Harris showcased such original compositions, "Yes Lord" and "Passion Dance." Attending the performance a local music writer noted, in *Extra,* "Passion Dance' was an exotic Harris composition in which he made excellent use of all the music forces present. Strings and voices were perfectly blended and the piece featured fiery solos by Herbie Williams on trumpet, Ron English on guitar, and Dr. Beans Bowles on baritone sax."

In the early 1980s Harris formed the New Breed Bebop Society Orchestra while heading a summer arts workshop for economically disadvantaged youngsters—a program founded by Motown singer Kim Weston. In her memoir, *Dancing in the Streets,* Motown singer Martha Reeves expressed, "Kim's project was created to allow underprivileged teenagers a chance to learn music firsthand from some of the best teachers available, like Teddy Harris, Earl Van Dyke, Ernie Rogers, and Arnold Clarrington. It was ingenious and kept a lot of music students out of trouble during their summer vacation from school." Harris also reaches people of the community by holding workshops in high schools, libraries, and the basement of his home, which too has served as a rehearsal space for local and nationally famous artists.

During the mid 1980s, Harris led the house band at Dummy George's, and led a big band often accompanied with The Detroit Voices. He too served as musical director for Martha Reeves & The Vandellas for several of the group's 1980s European appearances. Recipient of the 1993 Arts Midwest Jazz Award, Harris embarked on a 1995 world tour with The Michigan Jazz Masters, comprised of Arts Midwest Jazz award-winners drummer Roy Brooks, trumpeter Marcus Belgrave, pianist Harold McKinney, and clarinetist Wendell Harrison. On their tour the Jazz Masters played a command performance for Jordan's King Hussein at the Royal Cultural Center in Amman. That same year, the Michigan Jazz Masters recorded the album *Urban Griots,'* which features Harris original bebop-styled composition "That's Cool."

"Detroit's Godfather of Jazz"

Harris continues to balance his career as a musician and educator—a role which prompted a writer in the *Detroit News,* to honor him as "Detroit's godfather of jazz." Over the last seventeen years his position as artist in residence with the Highland Park School system has allowed Harris to instruct young musicians in the art of jazz. In the *Detroit News* Harris discussed his role as educator: "Some of these kids have talent, but not the social skills to go along with it. I was the same way coming up. If it hadn't been for the older guys wrapping their arms around me, showing me things....So I'm just giving back." In a private interview, Harris asserted, "I am honored to be associated with the city. When I'm overseas, and people find out I'm from Detroit, I'm automatically accorded a great deal of respect as a musician." Whether performing in small groups or conducting for large ensembles, Harris makes Detroit his home and the continents of the world his stage.

Selected discography

Passion Dance, Teddy Harris Jr. Quartet, Platinum Disc Records.
I Won't Say Goodbye, Teddy Harris Jr. Quartet, Platinum Disc Records.
Dr. Tee's Blues, Teddy Harris Jr. Quartet, Platinum Disc Records.
M.T.K.M., Teddy Harris Jr. Quintet, Platinum Disc Records.
Yes Lord, Teddy Harris Sextet, Platinum Disc Records.
Here's To Beans, Teddy Harris Quartet, Platinum Disc Records.
Teddy Harris & The Bebop Society Plays Bebop, Disc LTD Records.
Teddy Harris & The New Breed Bebop Society Play Motown, Masterpiece Records.

With Others

Aretha Franklin, Yeah! In Person With Her Quartet, Columbia, 1965.
The Detroit Jazz Composers Ltd., Hastings Jazz Experience, Midnite Records, 1976.
The Supremes Live In Japan, Tamala/Motown.
Jackie Wilson, Mr. Excitement! Rhino, 1992.
The Paul Butterfield Blues Band, Keep On Moving, Elecktra, 1969.
Paul Butterfield Blues Band Live, 1970.
The Paul Butterfield Blues Band, Golden Butter, Elektra, 1972.
Michigan Jazz Masters, Urban Griots,' 1995.
The Elektra Anthology Years, The Paul Butterfield Blues Band, Elektra, 1997.

Sources

Books

Reeves, Martha, with Mark Bego, *Dancing in the Streets, Confessions of a Motown Diva,* Hyperion, 1994, p. 229.
Stovall, Tyler, *Paris Noir: African Americans in the City of Light,* Houghton Mifflin Co., 1996.

Periodicals

Detroit Free Press, May 2, 1995.
Detroit News, June 15, 1975; December 19, 1980; April 3, 1994.
Extra (Detroit), April 1978.
Michigan Chronicle, June 20, 1981; May 7, 1988.

Additional information for this profile obtained from liner notes by Dan Morganstern to *Aretha Franklin Yeah! In Person With HerQuartet,* Columbia, 1965; promotional bill from the Key to the City Celebration, Detroit 1993; and from a private interview, Detroit, Michigan, February 25, 1998.

—Christine Morrison

Insane Clown Posse

Rap duo

AP/Wide World Photos

The Insane Clown Posse, two Detroit rappers with a devoted Midwestern following, garnered substantial national media attention during the summer of 1997 when their label, Hollywood Records, shipped *The Great Milenko* to record stores and then six hours later recalled it. Apparently, label executives—Hollywood is a subsidiary of the Walt Disney Corporation—learned a bit late of the obscenity-laden and, in some cases, violence-advocating songs and became nervous. The Insane Clown Posse controversy was an unusual one on several fronts, but most interestingly because many record stores simply ignored the recall order. Also, the anti-Disney backlash served to elevate two rappers known for their crude lyrics into unlikely First-Amendment heroes. Though critics lambasted *Milenko* artistically, the Insane Clown Posse, known to fans as ICP, has attracted a massive cult fan base, comprised primarily of suburban youth. *Detroit Free Press* writer Brian McCollum termed them "Halloween hip-hop," but also reflected that they remain "just possibly the wildest show to come out of the Motor City since Iggy Pop contorted himself and frolicked in busted glass two decades ago."

The Insane Clown Posse, whose records have also earned comparisons to those of the early Beastie Boys, is the creation of two Detroiters, Joseph Bruce ("Violent J") and Joseph Utsler ("Shaggy 2 Dope"). Both grew up in poor, single-parent households in a rough section of Detroit, that by the late 1980s was attracting a mix of residents. Whites of Southern origin, Hispanics, and African-Americans shared shaky ground in Detroit's notorious Southwest corner, and the evident tension could be charted by the plethora of teen gangs that sprang up. Allegedly, Violent J and Shaggy 2 Dope formed a gang known as the "Inner City Posse," which soon evolved from a social fraternity into a rap act. Using the same name, they began making homemade tapes of rap songs they penned themselves that reflected their violent and tense surroundings.

In time Violent J and Shaggy 2 Dope were performing live; but in a subterfuge against retribution from other gangs, they wore heavy black and white clown paint, which was also a nod to the appeal of their rap genre across color lines. "We put on the makeup because people in the suburbs view gang kids in the city as clowns," Violent J told *Detroit Free Press* reporter Carol Teegardin in 1994. From basement-made tapes Violent J and Shaggy 2 Dope progressed to self-released records on their own Psychopathic label. These included 1992's *Carnival of Carnage,* the 1993 EP *Beverly Kills 50187,* and the 1994 EP *Terror Wheel.* The lyrics were disturbing and gory, and attracted many teen male listeners. Tracks like "Crime Pays, "Guts on the Ceiling,"

For the Record . . .

Members are **Shaggy 2 Dope** (born Joseph Utsler, c. 1974) and **Violent J** (born Joseph Frank Bruce, c. 1972).

Band formed as Inner City Posse in Detroit, MI, c.1989; signed with Jive Records, 1995; released *The Riddlebox* on Jive/Battery, 1995; negotiated out of Jive contract, signed with Hollywood Records, c. 1996; released *The Great Milenko*, June 1997; record pulled from stores the same day; negotiated release from Hollywood Records and signed with Island Records, July 1997; re-released *The Great Milenko* on Island, August 1997.

Addresses: *Record company*—Island Records, 400 Lafayette St., 5th Floor, New York, NY 10003. *Website*—www.insaneclownposse.com.

"Ghetto Freak Show," and "For the Maggots" reflected their preoccupation with carnage, mass murder, and other typically scream-flick fare. "The music we do is horror rap," Violent J told Teegardin. "It's extremely violent. We use four-letter words, and we get hate mail. But some people like us because we rap about the anger you feel in your everyday life. It's not a pretty thing."

Yet it was also partly because of their outrageous live shows that ICP gained local renown. Playing all-ages shows, Violent J and Shaggy 2 Dope offered a form of adolescent performance art, tossing rubber chickens into the audience—made up of devoted fans who showed up for concerts dressed as their favorite ICP rapper simply to wait in line hours beforehand—and spraying them with bottles of Faygo-brand carbonated soft drink, a Detroit-made product. The Faygo became a focal point of the entire ICP act, and soon the promotion-savvy company was trucking up to 150 two-liter bottles to the stage doors, free of cost. Other ICP crowd-pleasers include jumping from a trampoline into the audience, but when the act was signed to Jive Records in 1995 and was sent on a national tour, the red-soda-pop-and-clown look did not translate. "In some cities, we still get booed off," Violent J told the *Detroit Free Press*'s McCollum in 1995. On that tour, they opened for Onyx and Das EFX.

ICP's Jive/Battery release, 1995's *The Riddlebox,* did well both locally and nationally, selling over 80,000 copies. But Violent J and Shaggy 2 Dope were dissatisfied with the label's marketing efforts, and managed to terminate their contract in 1996. They were then signed by Hollywood Records, a former suitor before the Jive/Battery deal. When they questioned the Disney-owned label's policies on lyrics and content prior to inking the deal, ICP and their management were assured complete artistic freedom. After studio sessions with renowned Detroit producer Mike Clark, ICP submitted the completed *The Great Milenko* to the label. Hollywood Records executives then requested that some lyrics be revised. Violent J told *Billboard* writer Chris Morris that at that point, he informed executives "'I'm not gonna change it,' and they said 'Then the record's gonna be shelved until you do.'"

But he and Shaggy 2 Dope held out until "the pressure got to us," Violent J admitted to *Billboard.* They capitulated and changed the lyrics, and in June of 1997 *Milenko,* after a large promotional effort, was shipped. Six hours later, after Violent J and Shaggy 2 Dope came home from autographing copies of it at a local record store, they received a call that Hollywood had recalled the album because Disney had deemed its contents "inappropriate for a product released under any label of our company," according to a press release. ICP had been assured that Disney played no role in its music division's decisions, but supposedly Disney chair Michael Eisner personally gave the word to recall the record.

Baptists Boycott Disney

Interestingly, many record stores did not comply with the unprecedented recall, and *The Great Milenko* became a top seller in Detroit. The story was even more complex and at times slightly baffling: supposedly one Hollywood Records executive, Joe Roth, had been shown a video for one of *The Great Milenko*'s tracks—a song in which ICP urges brutal retribution for men who abuse their wives. In essence, the two rappers, both raised by single moms, were speaking out against domestic assault. Yet Roth spoke to Eisner and voiced concern about the entire LP, and the flap grew from there. Other events also conspired against ICP—just the day before, thepowerful Southern Baptist Convention, convening nationally in Florida, condemned Disney for its "anti-family value" stance, sparked in part by the television sitcom *Ellen* (ABC is also part of the Disney entertainment empire). Coincidentally, there was a song on *The Great Milenko* mocking preachers who ask for money from their flocks.

There was more on *The Great Milenko* than just controversial lyrics, however. Violent J, Shaggy 2 Dope, and Clark, their producer, had invited some outstanding musicians to help out, including the original shock-rock star, Alice Cooper, along with one-time Sex Pistol Steve Jones, and Slash of Guns 'N' Roses. It was soon at No. 63 on the *Billboard* Top 200 album chart, and became one of the best successes for the Hollywood label—which had become infamous in the music industry for its notorious string of failures. (The back catalogue of British pop-rock act Queen is its only moneymaker.) Yet executives remained determined to wash their hands of ICP, and canceled all scheduled tour dates and the band's contract as well, which incited a huge bidding war. Hollywood Records then tried to block ICP from negotiation talks, and eventually forced them to pay $1 million of the act's $2.5 million deal with Island Records, ostensibly to recoup production and marketing outlays.

Critics have never been kind to ICP. In the *Detroit Free Press,* McCollum noted that "while purporting to rail against the evils of racists, rednecks and suburban gang poseurs, the group rolls around in heavy-duty death, misogyny and scatological, um, humor." A December, 1997 *Spin* magazine piece, drawn by Detroit artist Mark Dancey and written by *Spin* contributor and onetime Detroiter Mike Rubin, lambasted the group and its devoted fan base. More trouble plagued Violent J and Shaggy 2 Dope as a rough year came to a close. Around Thanksgiving, an overzealous Albuquerque, New Mexico, fan came onstage and grabbed Violent J's hair and reportedly would not let go; the singer then hit him with a microphone and afterward was arrested on aggravated battery charges, but was later released on bail. And in early 1998 the ICP tour bus slid down an embankment near the Indiana/Ohio border, although no one was seriously injured.

Selected discography

"Dog Beats" (maxi-single), Psychopathic Records, 1991.
Carnival of Carnage, Psychopathic Records, 1992.
Beverly Kills 50187 (EP), Psychopathic Records, 1993.
The Ringmaster, Psychopathic Records, 1994.
Terror Wheel (EP), Psychopathic Records, 1994.
"Dead Pumpkins" (limited-edition cassette single), Psychopathic Records, 1994.
Carnival X-mas (EP), Psychopathic Records, 1994.
"Chicken Hunting Slaughterhouse" (CD single), Jive/Battery, 1995.
Forgotten Freshness, Jive/Battery, 1995.
The Riddlebox, Jive/Battery, 1995.
"Mr. Rotten Treats" (limited-edition cassette single), Psychopathic Records, 1995.
Tunnel of Love (EP), Jive/Battery, 1996.
"Witches and Warlocks" (limited-edition cassette single), Psychopathic Records, 1996.
The Great Milenko, Hollywood Records, June 1997, re-released on Island Records, August 1997.

Sources

Detroit Free Press, October 28, 1994, p. 10D; December 22, 1995, p. 1D; May 5, 1996, p. 2H; June 22, 1997, p. 4G; June 27, 1997, p. 1A; December 14, 1997.
Detroit News, June 27, 1997, p. E1; September 11, 1997, p. F3; November 21, 1997, p. C7.
Rolling Stone, November 2, 1995, p. 40.

—Carol Brennan

Joe Jackson

Musician

Archive Photos

Self-styled, eclectic artist Joe Jackson has been a prominent name in modern rock since his seminal new wave albums *Look Sharp!* and *I'm The Man* were released in 1979. Since then,the chameleon-like Jackson has experimented with styles of music and production, which has included instrumental albums and eight soundtracks. After roaming the terrain of pop music for two decades, Jackson released *Heaven and Hell,* which placed him on the Sony Classical label and returned the artist to his roots at the Royal Academy of Music, where he studied as a teenager. Jackson had finally decided that the pop world had never really acknowledged the scope of his records and is a place whose boundaries are often too restrictive and imposing. Undeniably, there has always been a strong rock influence in his work, but Jackson has progressively continued to mix a stew of assorted genres into each album. "All I can say is, it just doesn't feel natural or honest to me to work within the limits of one clearly defined genre," Jackson claimed in a press release for the album *Night Music.*

While going to primary school in Portsmouth, England, Jackson took up violin lessons at the age of 11 as a way to avoid taking school sports. He soon developed an interest in creating his own compositions, and talked his parents into buying him a piano to create his own music. Joe gained a love for Beethoven along with rock and jazz -- from the beginning his musical appetite was marked in its diversity. When he was 16, Jackson began taking formal lessons and began to play in public. Within two years, he entered the prestigious Royal Academy of Music in London on a piano scholarship. During his sojourn at the Academy, he focused on composition, piano, percussion, and orchestration by day, and played in a string of fleeting Top 40 cover bands in the evenings.

One of these bands, Arms & Legs, was signed in 1976 by the MAM U.K. label and quickly released three singles which Jackson now calls "disastrous." After spending only one year together, Arms & Legs went their separate ways, and Joe headed home to Portsmouth to perform at the Playboy Club, where he began to assemble a collection of demo tapes. After inviting back the previous bass-guitarist from Arms & Legs, Graham Maby, and collecting Gary Sanford for guitar and Dave Houghton for drums, Jackson had composed enough material to confidently craft his solo debut. Jackson was signed to A&M records and began recording in August of 1978 to produce what would be the album he would be forever known for, *Look Sharp!* Packed with catchy singles, the album captured the energy of punk and new wave, and showed clear signs of an ironic, subtle songwriter.

For the Record . . .

Born Joe Jackson August 11, 1954 at Burton-on-Trent, Staffordshire, England; studied at Royal Academy of Music, London from September 1971-74.

Played in pub band Edward Bear; signed recording deal with MAM UK for three singles before break-up in 1976; Joe Jackson band formed, 1978; released debut album *Look Sharp,* containing his first hit single "Is She Really Going Out With Him?", 1979; *Night and Day* released in 1982 with single "Steppin' Out" charting; played in live TV concert "Rockpalast" in West Germany, 1983; "You Can't Get What You Want" from *Body and Soul,* 1984; played piano for Suzanne Vega's single "Left of Center" from the movie *Pretty In Pink,* 1986; Jackson band signed onto Virgin America for two albums, 1991; switched to Sony Classical for *Heaven & Hell,* 1997.

Awards: band received the prestigious Edison Award in Holland for the second album *I'm The Man,* 1979

Addresses: *Internet*— majordomo@lists.primenet.com

Fresh from the studio, the Joe Jackson Band toured the London area in the fall of 1978, supporting a local band named the Pleasers. Meanwhile, Jackson's band recorded the single "Is She Really Going Out With Him?" and released it on Halloween 1978. The single was aired for the Tony Blackburn show on November 3, and while it would later become a new wave staple and one of Jackson's signature tunes, it failed to make the U.K. charts it's first time around.

Looked Sharp

In January of 1979, the album *Look Sharp!* was finally released, resulting in invitations for the band to create more BBC sessions for the John Peel and Kid Jensen radio shows, both crucial showcases for new talent in the U.K. From April until June, the Joe Jackson Band continuously toured the United States and Europe. After some delay, the exposure from these many gigs and radio airings pushed "Is She Really Going Out With Him" to *Billboard*'s Top 40, reaching number 21. The single was subsequently re-released in the U.K. due to public demand and this time peaked at the Number 13. All the while, Jackson had gained appreciation from critics, who gave kudos to the performer for the freshness of his songwriting, as well as for the energy of his live performances.

Working industriously, Jackson and his outfit went on to make two more albums in as many years. The first, *I'm The Man,* scored a Number five hit in the U.K. with "It's Different For Girls" and the album itself snared Jackson the prestigious Edison Award for music, awarded from Holland. As a *New Musical Express* writer saw it, "an excellent debut album has been chased back home by a sequel which refines, expands, extends, and finally surpasses its creators opening gambit." *Beat Crazy* was the follow-up, as well as the last album to feature the original Joe Jackson Band line up. Eschewing the new wave style of Jackson's earliest efforts in favor of a blend of influences including ska and reggae, *Beat Crazy* failed to chart heavily with its singles, and by 1980 the group had split up.

Never an artist to become crestfallen after commercial letdowns, Jackson forged ahead in his intake of a world of musical styles. In between *I'm The Man* and *Beat Crazy,* Jackson had produced three tracks for reggae artist Lincoln Thompson, as well as an album for the reggae group The Rasses, entitled *Natural Wild,* and these interactions only bolstered Jackson's growing interest in music other than contemporary pop. In addition, while he was recuperating from an long illness in 1981, Jackson began listening to 1940s jump and swing music at his home. He decided that it would be fun to make a cover album ofthat era's music and took a holiday from his own writing and recorded the album *Jumpin' Jive* with longtime associate Graham Maby and a group of professional jazz musicians. As *Hi-Fi News & Record Reviews* commented, Jackson "obviously loves and understands the music with which he is dealing and is not merely content to employ it as this year's gimmick."And yet as with much of Jackson's output, it received well-favored reviews, but fell flat commercially.

Jackson returned to his own writing for the next album, 1982's *Night and Day,* which was conceived and recorded in New York City. Perhaps the melancholic urban romance of that city was a key influence of the flavor of *Night and Day,* which was an instant success in the U.S. While hinting at the somber coolness of intimate club jazz, the album stayed for the most part within the parameters of the pop music format, perhaps one reason for its strong commercial reception. In the words of a critic writing for Italian magazine *Mucchio Selvaggio,* "thanks to this album Joe Jackson can be called a 'great musician;' he shows us his eclecticism, intelligence, and respect for the New York musical history. A real sound poet." Its first single, "Steppin' Out," rode up the charts to Number six, and Jackson was asked to play on the NBC television show *Saturday Night Live* in October of that year. The Joe Jackson band, with a new roster of members, supported the album with an 11 month tour, and the re-release of "Steppin' Out" in the U.K. and the popularity of the moody ballad "Breaking Us In Two" raised *Night and Day* to number three on the charts.

During the *Night and Day* tour, Jackson accepted the invitation to score the film *Mike's Murder,* a fairly forgettable thriller starring Debra Winger. Some of the songs were leftovers from the *Night and Day* sessions along with a number of original instrumental tracks. While some of the soundtrack's material got a decent amount of radio play, the film was cut so harshly that most of Jackson's score did not make the final product. Nevertheless, the album's material was strong and became the first in a number of successful film collaborations for Jackson.

The next album from Jackson was released in March of 1984, called *Body and Soul,* and featured the Number 15 single "You Can't Get What You Want."The single as well as the album demonstrated mastery in the kind of cosmopolitan pop he had been known to invent. As a critic for *Ciao 2001* magazine assessed, "*Body and Soul* is a masterpiece of a thirty year old boy who doesn't know how to be a rock star and doesn't want to; an out of time musician able to charm with a few piano notes." The album's almost unanimous critical acclaim bolstered his reputation as a composer breaking ground between pop and "serious" music. Consequently, after the album's promotional tour, Jackson was again invited to compose a film score, this time for a Japanese IMAX film called *Shijin No Ie* or *House of the Poet.* Comprised of a twenty minute piece with a full orchestra, the score was reworked and released later on the album *Will Power* as "Symphony in One Movement".

In January of 1996, the album *Big World* was recorded live at the Roundabout Theatre in New York City, which generated a video of the performances alongside the three-sided LP. The expansiveness of the record allowed for Jackson to include the same songs twice, but in radically re-orchestrated versions that showed Jackson's imagination in arrangements as well as songwriting. Stretching the limits of pop to its limits, *Big World* was perhaps a preparation for Jackson's next album to come out, which was a decisive deviation from the pop world.

Jackson's studio band was mostly kept intact, but was buttressed by a full piece orchestra. The album, called *Will Power*, contained all instrumental material and was perhaps a slap in the face for those expecting standard popular radio fare. Taking yet another step in this direction, Jackson swung back to another soundtrack project when film maverick Francis Ford Coppola gave him the opportunity to use some well-known British jazz performers in creating a score for the film *Tucker: The Man and His Dream,* which was released by A&M.

Following the 1988 album *Blaze of Glory,* which essentially went unpromoted,Jackson took a break to recoup, even though this album still is one of the artist's own favorites, and ranks "right up there with *Night and Day,"* as critic Jim Bessman agreed. While laying low, Jackson spent his time at small clubs trying out material for what took shape in his next album *Laughter & Lust,* which was released on the Virgin records label. Between recording and touring, Jackson again wrote the score for the movie *Queens Logic,* after which he took a well-deserved break.

A Comeback to the Beginning

The album *Night Music* was welcomed in 1994 to rave reviews by the critics, but the air time it received was as weak as *Blaze of Glory.* A review from *Harburger Nachrichten* in Germany explained the predicament: "I really like it, but I can't review it unless it starts getting a lot of airplay or gets into the charts." The press volleyed the album back and forth saying it was too old for their audiences, or chided Jackson for his refusal to create another pop single. His mature blends of music just didn't fit in anywhere. Even if it was worth listening to, there seemed no way to promote it properly. Along with these troubles, some commentators thought he was taking himself too seriously. An article in the *Stereo Review* stated that Jackson had "abandoned regulation pop music instrumentation...as if conventional pop structures would unfairly rein in a prodigious, sweeping talent such as his ... the only thing missing was a sign on the stage reading 'Quiet! Artist at Work!'"

Jackson has taken it all in stride, as he sees no viable alternative. "I'm totally aware that what I do doesn't fit very neatly, and that makes life difficult at times," he told journalist Gary Graff in his own defense. He fears that the critics still see him as the angry young man from his early rock and roll years and *Look Sharp!* Now that he has matured out of single-making pop structures he explains that"... to me, it feels a bit like I'm the ugly sister of Cinderella, and they keep trying to force the glass slipper onto my foot; but I don't WANT it. I mean, I'm PROUD to be ugly!"

Heaven & Hell brought Joe Jackson home to where his compositional roots lie. It was released in September of

1997 on the Sony Classical Label, denoting the final severance from the milieu of commercial popular music. A concept album whose music embodies the seven deadly sins, *Heaven and Hell* featured introspective pop singer Suzanne Vega, classical soprano Dawn Upshaw, and Crash Test Dummies' lead singer Brad Roberts, and may stand as the ultimate testament to Jackson's vibrant eclecticism.

Selected discography

Look Sharp! A&M, 1979.
I'm The Man, A&M, 1979.
Beat Crazy, A&M, 1980.
Night And Day, A&M, 1982.
Body And Soul, A&M, 1984.
Big World, A&M, 1986.
Will Power, (Instrumental), A&M, 1986.
Jumpin Jive, A&M, 1987
Laughter & Lust, Virgin America, 1991.
Night Music, Virgin America, 1994.
Heaven & Hell, Sony Classical, 1997.

Sources

Periodicals

Billboard, August 2, 1997.
Ciao 2001, April 1984.
Harburger Nachrichten, 1994.
Hi-Fi News & Record Reviews, September, 1981.
Interview, May 1994.
Mucchio Selvaggio, September 1982.
Musician, November 1997.
New Musical Express, October 6, 1979.
Rolling Stone, December 13, 1979; October 14, 1982.
Stereo Review, 1994.
Vancouver Sun, April 27, 1995.
Variety, August 29, 1997.

Online

http://www.cryst.bbk.ac.uk/~ubcg5ab/JJ/bio.html
http://www.joejackson.com

—Shaun Frentner

Wyclef Jean

Guitarist

AP/wide World Photos

Multi-talented hip-hop guitarist Nel Wyclef Jean, one third of the renowned band The Fugees, released a platinum-selling solo debut album titled *The Carnival* in 1998 to positive—and often gushing—reviews. Jean drew upon Creole folk music, Afro-Cuban, reggae, rhythm and blues, funk, and rap music to forge the refreshing brand of hip-hop found on his solo debut release, a variety of musical styles, also evident in the music of The Fugees. In addition to artfully fusing a myriad of musical styles, Jean is one of the few hip-hop artists to play the guitar and still be accepted as a rapper by hardcore hip-hop fans. In this respect, he melded together an appreciative alternative music fan base with his hip-hop and rap fans and achieved a rare feat. *People* magazine's Amy Linden wrote, 'Filled with humor, smarts and a true sense of playfulness, *The Carnival* is what hip hop should be all about.' *Time* magazine's Christopher John Farley wrote, "*The Carnival* puts Wyclef up there with Billy Corgan, Trent Reznor and Tricky as one of the most creative people working in pop music."

Jean was born in Haiti in 1971 and moved to Brooklyn near Coney Island in New York City with his parents at the age of nine, before eventually moving to Newark, New Jersey in high school. His father, Gesner Jean, was pastor of Newark's Good Shepherd Church of the Nazarene and fought to keep his four sons and a daughter off the streets through prayer. Jean studied at Newark's Vailsburg High School, learning as much as he could about music and the music business. Prakazrel 'Pras' Michel of the Fugees, his cousin, lived in South Orange, NJ, and Jean began experimenting with hip-hop along with Michel and Lauryn Hill of The Fugees while still in high school. Michel and Jean both have fathers who are deeply involved in their religious communities; Jean told Rolling Stone's David Sprague, "When I'd come back from the studio, I'd get a whipping from my dad, 'cause I was playing devil's music." When Jean was still underage, a recording contract fell through because his father refused to condone it.

In 1988 the Vailsburg High School Swing choir included Jean on bass and his cousin Pras on vocals; they sang for the Young Americans National Invitational Performance Choir Festival in Hollywood, CA. The choir won an award for costumes and Jean was honored for an original composition. Jean would write songs on the choir's bus from one event to another. Back in Newark, they formed a rap group called Exact Change, which was distinguished by the fact that they wore tuxedoes, rapped in six languages, and had a positive message. Then the two Haitian cousins and Lauryn Hill began rapping together under the name Tranzlator Crew, and by 1993 they were signed to Ruff House/Columbia Records and working on their first full- length release.

For the Record . . .

Born Nel Wyclef Jean in Haiti in 1971; one of four sons and daughter born to Gesner Jean a pastor at Newark's Good Shepherd Church of the Nazarene and his wife; moved to Brooklyn near Coney Island in New York City with his parents at the age of nine.

Formed high school bands with Fuggees member Lauryn Hill and Prakazrel "Pras" Michel; the trio began rapping together as Tranzlator Crew and signed with Ruff House/Columbia Records, 1993; released *Blunted on Reality* as The Fugees, 1993; released *The Score,* 1996; released solo debut *The Carnival,* 1997.

Address: *Record company*—Ruff House/Columbia Records, 51 West 52nd Street, New York, NY 10019; (212) 833-4321

Star-Studded Debut Solo

The group changed their name due to a legal objection by a new-wave group named Translator, and chose The Fugees as a shortened version of refugees—since they sought refuge in their music. Their first release, *Blunted on Reality,* was released to positive review, in late 1993. After producing their second release, *The Score,* in their own studio in East Orange, New Jersey, free of the constricting terms of their original production contract, the group saw their sophomore effort attain instant success. *The Score* was more focused and strident, and drew from the band's myriad musical influences—everything from Caribbean music to Roberta Flack and early '80s new wave music like Tears for Fears and the Pet Shop Boys. The Score topped the chart for weeks, sold more than 15 million copies worldwide, and was followed by an extensive tour that ended in Port-au-Prince, Haiti. *The Score*'s 'Killing Me Softly,' a remake of Roberta Flack's early 1970s single, graced the R&B singles chart for seven months and the pop chart for six months. When the Fugees returned to the group's native homeland for a concert at the Bicentenaire in Port-au-Prince, an estimated 80,000 jubilant fans greeted them.

While The Fugees were touring, Jean continued recording; he initially intended to release a solo album of songs in Creole, but he expanded his reach. He also did remixes for Cypress Hill, Sublime, Simply Red, Whitney Houston, TLC, Michael Jackson, and Bounty Killer while the band was on the road. The prolific Jean was the primary writer, producer, and performer on *The Carnival,* but he enlisted an impressive array of international talent for his debut solo release. Lauryn Hill and Prakazrel assisted his effort, as did the Latin supernova salsa singer Celia Cruz on "Guantanamera," the New Orleans-based Neville Brothers on "Mona Lisa," members of the New York Philharmonic Orchestra, conducted by Jean on "Gone 'Til November," and reggae's I Threes on "Gunpowder." Pablo Diablo was featured on 'Crazy Sam and "Talent." "Yele" features the Creole folk music of Jean's homeland, Haiti, as does "Sang Fezi," "Jaspora," and the calypso-infused "Carnival." The French-Creole songs on *The Carnival* topped the charts in Haiti. Jean is also slated to star as Jimmy Cliff's son in a sequel to the film "The Harder They Come."

Jean told Now magazine's Matt Galloway, "I represent the Caribbean to the fullest on this record ... I've always had a Caribbean vibe to my music ... (but) the foundation is still hip-hop. *Carnival*'s a big charade where anything can happen. That basically translates into the streets of New York City and what goes on every day....It's not everyday rap music." Jean pointed out in an interview with Michael Roberts of the *Phoenix Newtimes* that older groups like Earth, Wind, & Fire and Kool and the Gang were comprised of musicians who could really sing and play music, and it's this adherence to genuine talent and depth that sets Jean and the Fugees apart from the rap and hip-hop fray. Roberts wrote, "Unlike a lot of their contemporaries, The Fugees aren't a gimmick. There's substance in their grooves." Jersey Online interviewed Wayne Slappy, Jean's high school music teacher; now a screenwriter, said of Jean,"Whatever planet he stopped at, he would just take over. That's part of his genius. I guess in his own way, he's the Michael Jordan of rap."

Selected discography

Blunted on Reality (with the Fugees), Ruff House/Columbia Records, 1993.
The Score (with the Fugees), Ruff House/Columbia Records, 1996.
The Carnival, Ruff House/Columbia Records, 1997.

Sources

Periodicals

Billboard, June 14, 1997.
Ebony, November 1996.
Entertainment Weekly, December 26, 1997.

Guitar Player, January 1998.
Harper's Bazaar, June 1996.
Interview, May 1996.
Newsweek, October 6, 1997.
People, July 7, 1997.
Rolling Stone, September 5, 1996.
Time, July 28, 1997.
Us, August 1996.

Online

http://www.nj.com/spotlight/wyclef/
http://www.now.com/issues/16/48/Ent/feature.html
http://www.ubl.com/cards/017/0/88.html

—B. Kimberly Taylor

Ingrid Jensen

Jazz trumpeter

Courtesy of Ingrid Jensen

A jazz trumpet player is often judged by how fast, high, and loud he can play. Typically, there is a certain swagger to the sound. When the "he" is a "she," however, we are forced to rethink the criteria by which we evaluate trumpet prowess. Although she is capable of wailing with the best of them, Ingrid Jensen stands out because she brings a softer, more feminine sensibility to this most masculine of instruments. In addition to her own sound, which has been compared to the likes of Miles Davis, Chet Baker, and Woody Shaw, Jensen's strength lies in her willingness to shun to egotistic mentality of the stereotypical jazz soloist. Driven primarily by the search for beautiful blends of sound, she manages to resist an urge that most players with as much talent find irresistible—namely, the urge to show off.

Jensen was born in 1967 in Cedar, outside of Vancouver, British Columbia. Her mother was a working musician, and Jensen grew up listening to her play ragtime and other styles at home. After high school, Jensen majored in music at Canada's Malaspina College. She then enrolled in the esteemed Berklee School of Music in Boston. After receiving her master's degree from Berklee in 1989, Jensen moved to New York, the epicenter of jazz in the United States. The New York jazz scene was a bit too cutthroat for her liking, however, and she found it difficult to launch a career in that competitive atmosphere.

Left U.S. With VAO

The opportunity to escape the Big Apple came in 1990, when she landed a job with the Vienna Art Orchestra production *Fe & Males,* a project that involved seven men and seven women playing the same instruments: trumpet, trombone, tuba, saxophone, bass, drums, and piano. Jensen embarked on a European tour with the Vienna group, and when the tour ended she opted to linger in Austria. She applied for a position as jazz trumpet professor on the faculty of Austria's Bruckner Conservatory. Jensen won the job, becoming, at the age of 25, the youngest teacher at the school.

Europe proved to be a much more fruitful setting than New York for the development of both Jensen's career and her musicianship. In addition to teaching, she found the time to jam with top European musicians, as well as with many of the prominent U.S. jazz figures who happened to be making their ways across the continent. She collaborated on projects with French bassist Helene LaBarriere, leader of an experimental free-jazz collective called Machination. She also sat in with, among others, vibes legend Lionel Hampton. Her performance

For the Record . . .

Born Jan.12, 1966 in Cedar, British Columbia, Canada; daughter of Karen Cormons (a pianist) and Helge Jensen (an electrician and company president). *Education:* Malaspina College, Nanaimo, BA; Berklee College of Music, MA; studied with Laurie Frink, Freddie Hubbard, and George Garzone.

Toured Europe with Vienna Art Orchestra, 1990; Bruckner Conservatory, jazz trumpet instructor, 1991-94; signed with Enja records, 1994; joined all-woman big band Diva, 1994; released first CD as leader, *Vernal Fields,* 1995; International Association of Jazz Educators conference, guest artist, 1995-97; performs with a variety of other groups and artists, including Helene Labarriere, Maria Schneider Orchestra, Guillermo Klein, and Magali Souriau, 1995- .

Awards: Juno Award, "Best Mainstream Artist of the Year," 1995; Boston Globe, number two in Critic's Choice "Best New Artist of the Year category, 1995; Carmine Caruso International Jazz Trumpet Solo Competition, first place, 1995.

Addresses: *Record company*—Enja, Matthias Winckelmann GmbH, Postfach 19 03 33, 80603 München, Germany; *office*—364 W. 23rd St., Apt. 2F, New York, NY 10011.

with Hampton's Golden Men of Jazz, and the resulting support from Hampton and bandmate Clark Terry—a renowned trumpet player and bandleader in his own right—eventually led to a record deal for Jensen with the German label Enja.

Returned Triumphantly to New York

Although things were going fairly smoothly in Europe, by 1994 Jensen was ready to give North America another try. While attending a workshop in Banff in the summer of 1994, she heard about an opening in a New York-based, all-woman big band called Diva. She auditioned for and won the spot. Jensen has lived in New York ever since. The Big Apple has been kinder to her the second time around. Touring worldwide with Diva, she quickly became one of the group's most visible soloists. Jensen also began working with another big band, the Maria Schneider Jazz Orchestra. She also became active on the New York freelance circuit, both as a sideperson and as leader of her own groups. Other bands with which she began performing regularly included those led by Guillermo Klein and Magali Souriau.

1995 was a big year for Jensen. Her debut album, *Vernal Fields,* was released that year. It earned her a Juno Award—Canada's equivalent of a Grammy—for "Best Mainstream Artist of the Year." *Down Beat* magazine's Thomas Conrad wrote that "*Vernal Fields* has the fresh energy and affirmation of a young artist in the act of discovering the outer reaches of her talent." Trumpet legend Art Farmer, one of the players whom many listeners detect a trace of in Jensen's sound, noted that "her playing contains all of the elements in rich detail that make this music so loved, such as feeling, swing, drive, taste, grace, and lyricism." Jensen received several other honors as well. She was named "Best Newcomer" at the Cork (Ireland) Jazz Festival, and a few weeks later she took the top prize at the 1995 Carmine Caruso International Jazz Trumpet Solo Competition held at Western Michigan University in Kalamazoo. This wave of recognition led to an invitation to perform and conduct clinics at the International Association of Jazz Educators annual conference.

Maintained Pace With Second CD

Jensen's star continued to rise during 1996. She continued to tour internationally with Diva, the Schneider band, and her own quartet, including stops in Japan, Chile, and various parts of Europe and North America. Back home in Canada, Jensen led her group across the Great White North as part of the 1996 du Maurier Jazz Festival circuit. She also headlined at Toronto's Beaches Jazz Festival. When she wasn't performing in some corner of the world, Jensen was in the recording studio, both working on her own project and contributing to those of other musicians. She recorded with Diva and with saxophonist Virginia Mayhew. In September of 1996, Jensen began work on her second Enja CD. That recording, *Here On Earth,* was released in the spring of 1997. The CD features Jensen's trumpet and flugelhorn in tandem with Gary Bartz on saxophone, George Colligan on Fender Rhodes, and on two tracks, vocalist Jill Seifers.

Fueled by her second well-received album, Jensen's career has continued to surge. A committed jazz educator, she conducts clinics frequently. At the same time, she continues to develop her own artistry. For Jensen, maintaining a certain harmony between her life and her music is key. She summarizes this approach elegantly in her publicity material: "I try to keep my life and music on a parallel course and my goal is to be growing in both realms. There are so many elements in music that can be discovered and expressed when we are honest about the directionthat our lives are taking us. That's all I'm trying to do—follow the spirit of the muse and play."

Selected discography

Vernal Fields, Enja, 1995.
Here On Earth, Enja, 1997.

With Diva

Something's Coming, Perfect Sound, 1996.

With Vienna Art Orchestra

FE & Males, Polygram, 1994.

With Helen Labarrierre

Machination, Deux Z.

With Virginia Mayhew

Virginia Mayhew, Chiaroscuro, 1996.

Sources

Down Beat, November 1995, p. 52; October 1997, p. 45; December 1997, p. 104.
Jazz Player, December/January 1997, p. 10.
Jazz Times, October 1995, p. 23.
The Times (London), October 3, 1997.

Additional material for this profile was provided by Enja Records.

—*Robert R. Jacobson*

Jimmie's Chicken Shack

Alternative rock band

The music produced by the high energy four piece band, Jimmie's Chicken Shack (JCS), is anything but tame. They combine the heavy metal, post-grunge, funk, jazz fusion, alternative rock sound of guitars, vocals, bass, and drums with humorous lyrics and serious subjects like AIDS and drug use. Vocalist, Jimi HaHa described JCS's sound in an A&M press release, "It's funky without being funk, punky without being punk, hard without being hardcore, metallic without being metal, bluesy without being blues, and poppy without being pop." Their rocking, rolling, explosive sound has also been called "mutt rock," according to John Ferguson of the *Intelligencer Journal,* because of the wide variety of musical styles it incorporates.

Since the band formed in 1992, Jimmie's Chicken Shack has performed frequently in the Mid-Atlantic area of the United States. And despite signing with a major record company in 1996, the group vowed to continue it's commitment to the local Baltimore, Maryland/Washington, D.C. music scene. Jimmie's Chicken Shack founded the independent label, Fowl Records, and released

Burgess World Co.

For the Record . . .

Members include **Jimmy Chaney,** drums; **Dave Dowling,** guitar; **Jimi HaHa** (born James Davies), guitar, vocals; **Che Colovita Lemon,** bass; **Jimmy McD,** guitar.

Group formed in 1992 in Annapolis, MD; performed at local clubs and festivals; founded independent label, Fowl Records; released two live albums, *Chicken Scratch,* 1994, and *Spit Burger Lottery,* 1995 which were later combined and released on one CJ, *Two for One Special* (Fowl); recorded final Fowl release, *Giving Something Back;* signed with Rocket Records/A&M in 1996 and released *Pushing the Salmanilla Envelope,* 1997.

Addresses: *Record company*—Rocket Records/A&M/ PolyGram, Worldwide Plaza, 825 Eighth Ave., New York, NY 10019; Fowl Records, P.O. Box 3901, Crofton, MD 21114. *Home*—Jimmie's Chicken Shack, Jimi HaHa, P.O Box 3617, Annapolis, MD 21403. *Fan club*—Chicken Nation, P.O. Box 6827, Arlington, VA 22206; *Manager*—Richard Burgess, Burgess World Co., 3925 Rhode Harbor Rd., Mayo, MD 21037; *E-mail*—shaknation@aol.com. *Website*—www.fowl.com/jimmies.

three well-received albums. Among their many performances, the band played at the HFS festival in 1996 and 1997. Soon after performing at the 1996 HFSfestival at Washington, D.C.'s RFK Stadium, the group signed a two-album contract with Elton John's Rocket Records. In 1997, Rocket Records released the band's debut album, *Pushing the Salmanilla Envelope.*

Ironically, Jimmie's Chicken Shack began as an acoustic guitar duo featuring HaHa and Jimmy McD. The original four member group got together in 1992 in Annapolis, Maryland, playing music that was anything but acoustic. The group, with HaHa on guitar and vocals, Jimmy Chaney on drums, Jimmy McD on guitar, and Che Colovita Lemon (pronounced lay-MOHN) on bass, has performed hundreds of shows throughout the East Coast area of the United States. Both HaHa and Chaney were formerly with the group Ten X Big. Lemon was in many other bands, including Fluid Union. Jimmy McD was a member of Ghost in the Graveyard. Guitarist Dave Dowling, also known as Double D, joined the band in January 1998.

Popularity Grew in Baltimore Area

One reviewer called Jimmie's Chicken Shack the biggest thing to hit the Annapolis, Maryland music scene since Frank Zappa, and claimed that the band is bringing new life to the area as well as creating a stir nationwide. Their music combines hard rock, funk, punk, blues and jazz fusion interspersed with messages of social concerns. Jimmie's Chicken Shack has enjoyed considerable popularity in the Mid-Atlantic area for several years. They attract rowdy crowds, and are a favorite among slam dancers. They have performed on a monthly basis at Baltimore, Maryland's Eight by Ten Club and the Bayou in Washington, D.C.

Jimmie's Chicken Shack takes its name from a blues restaurant in New York's Harlem section where jazz legend Charlie Parker was said to have once been a dishwasher. On the subject of names, Jimi Haha's real name is James Davies. Growing up in Bowie, Maryland, HaHa said hechanged the spelling of his first name after rock guitar hero Jimi Hendrix. He acquired his current last name of "HaHa" after laughing at an opponent during a pool game. The man was said to have later asked Davies' friend, "Where's your friend Jimmie HaHa?" Davies thought it was funny and the name stuck.

Band Founded Fowl Records

In 1994, Jimmie's Chicken Shack started it's own record label, Fowl Records. Between 1994-95 they released two live albums, *Chicken Scratch* and *Spit Burger Lottery,* which were later released on a single CD as *Two for One Special.* That CD and a later release, *Giving Something Back,* sold well for the band. Jimi HaHa told an interviewer at *Musician,* "The main ingredient in doing it yourself is ass busting." Besides using Fowl Records as a vehicle for their own promotion, the band has also signed other area bands to the label. Dozens of other promising bands from Baltimore/Washington area, including the Almighty Senators and Godpocket have released albums on Fowl Records. JCS hopes to bring national attention and success to other bands from the area.

In 1996, they performed on the side stage at the HFSfestival, sponsored by area alternative radio station, WHFS. The annual festival is one of the largest radio sponsored music events in the country, and draws approximately 60,000 fans every year. The forum allows popular and newer bands to showcase their talents. Since it's inception in 1990, it has been held annually at Washington, D.C.'s RFK Stadium, and has included such bands as No Doubt, Everclear, Presidents of the

U.S.A., Foo Fighters, and Soul Coughing, among others. During the 1996 show, Jimmie's Chicken Shack played on the second stage, and received positive reviews. The band performed at the 1997 HFSfestival, as well, this time on the main stage, and used the event to kick off their 1997 tour. Kelly Connelly of *Music Monthly* gave JCS' performance rave reviews.

Richard Burgess, the band's manager, "discovered" the group while in Annapolis, Maryland. He sparked a bidding war among various record companies. Shortly after the 1996 HFSfestival concert, Jimmie's Chicken Shack signed with Rocket Records, a subsidiary of A&M Records. Their 1997 Rocket Record's debut, *Pushing the Salmanilla Envelope* was recorded at OZ Studios in Baltimore. Produced by Steven Haigler, the group has remained true to its rock roots on *Pushing Salmanilla Envelope,* with the loud, hard driving, heavy metal sound of guitars, bass, and drums with a hint of reggae and funk. The album includes six old songs—"properly recorded this time" according to the band—and six new ones with lyrics by HaHa.

Their style on *Pushing the Salmanilla Envelope* has been compared to that of Red Hot Chile Peppers, Bad Brains, Living Colour, and Soundgarden. The lyrics of the album's first single, "High," contain some confusing and contradictory messages about drug use. Confusing because the band has played concerts that support the legalization of marijuana while the lyrics from "High" seem to be anti-drugs. Some of the other songs—"Dropping Anchor," "Spiderweb," and "Hole"—have themes about persistence and determination. The song "Blood" mixes rhythmic rock sound with lyrics that clearly speak of AIDS. "Will you share your blood with me? I'll share mine with you ... Let's risk it. Here we go. It's in my blood."

Lyrics also Exhibited Humor

An online review of *Pushing the Salmanilla Envelope* gave the new release thumbs up overall. Although reviewer Ben Reed admitted Jimmie's Chicken Shack is not exactly breaking any musical ground, he said the group "plays some catchy tunes," and he appreciates the sense of humor the band exhibits through its lyrics. Reed described Jimmie's Chicken Shack as a good band that "serves up some good, heavy fun nuggets."

At least one of the band members has a reputation for accidentally breaking other musicians' equipment on stage. According to HaHa, Lemon never had his own equipment, so he'd borrow it from other bands. Then Lemon would get so into playing that he would forget he was trying to stand up at the same time. He would fall onto the equipment, break it, and continue to play. That same focused energy has transmitted into some wild behavior by the audience at times, including fans diving into the slam-dancers' "mosh" pits.

Although some might think Jimmie's Chicken Shack spends a lot of time practicing to perfect their explosive sound, Jimi HaHa admitted the band is pretty lazy when it comes to practicing: "A lot of times we even work things out live ... Sometimes it's messy but it keeps things exciting.: The band performs throughout the entire East Coast, and plans to tour nationally. As McD said in an online article, "The only place Jimmie's Chicken Shack has to go is up!"

Selected discography

Chicken Scratch, Fowl Records, 1994.
Spit Burger Lottery, Fowl Records, 1995
Two for One Special, Fowl Records.
Giving Something Back, Fowl Records.
Pushing the Salmanilla Envelope, (includes "High," "Dropping Anchor," and "Spiderweb"), Rocket Records, 1997.

Sources

Books

Billboard International Buyers Guide, BPI Communications, 1997.
Clynes, Tom, ed., *Music Festivals from Bach to Blues: A Traveler's Guide,*, Visible Ink Press, Detroit, 1996.

Periodicals

City Paper (Baltimore), April 23, 1997
Guitar World, August 1997.
HITS, June 23, 1997, p. 58.
Intelligencer Journal, March 21, 1997.
Mean Street, August 1997.
Music Connection, July 7, 1997.
Musician, February 1998, p. 14.
MusicMonthly, June 1997; July 1997, p. 26.
Pro Sound News, July 1997.
Thrasher, August 1997.

Online

http://dc.musicwwweb.com/Archives/Reviews/aug97rev.html#jcs
http://watt.seas.virginia.edu/~jah6t/hfs.htm
http://www.allmusic.com/

http://www.amrecords.com/
http://www.comcastpc.com/baltmedia/bullpen/jimmies.htm
http://www.fowl.com/
http://www.spinalcolumn.com/reviews/1097/jimmies.html
http://www.themusiczone.com/jcs.html
http://www4.nando.net/links/nandonext/volume5/hfstival.html

Additional information was provided by Laura Morgan of A&M Record's press department, and Richard Burgess of Burgess World Co.

—Debra Reilly

Carol Kaye

Bass player, guitarist, studio musician

Courtesy of Carol Kaye

The title, *First Lady On Bass,* Carol Kaye's 1996 release as primary artist hints at her legendary career as an electric bass player. Beginning in 1957 as a guitarist, and spanning over 35 years, Kaye's successful career as a studio musician includes performances on soundtracks recorded for television, film, and advertising, as well as several hit records. As of early 1998, she continued to hold the record for the most recorded performances on electric bass in the world—male or female, with over 10,000 studio recording performances to her credit. In addition to all her studio work, she has played live at festivals, tradeshows, clinics, and seminars, and is considered a leader in instruction on the Electric Bass. Beginning in 1969, Kaye wrote and published many tutorial books, audio cassettes, and video tapes instructing others how to play the bass. Kaye has also taught many now well-known bass players and has given workshops throughout the United States.

Carol Kaye was born on March 24, 1935 in Everett, Washington, to professional musician parents, Clyde and Dot Smith. Six years later, in 1941, the family moved to California, and lived in a housing project in Wilmington, California. At age 13, Kaye took guitar lessons for three months with Horace Hatchett and within one year, in 1949, she was teaching others on the guitar. Shortly after that, she began playing semi-jazz jobs and by the age of 20 was playing on the road with big bands.

Kaye was strongly influenced musically by both of her musician parents, Clyde and Dot Smith. Other notable influences include Ray Charles, Charlie Christian, Duke Ellington, Miles Davis, Hampton Hawes, Ralph Pena, Howard Roberts, Artie Shaw, Horace Silver, and Sonny Stitt.

From 1956-63 Kaye played behop with some of the most popular jazz groups from Los Angeles, mostly in black clubs, which were known to be the hot spots. Her earliest work as a studio performer had serendipitous beginnings; during 1957 she "accidentally" fell into studio work doing recordings with Sam Cooke. Bumps Blackwell heard Kaye play at the Beverly Caverns when she was performing with the Teddy Edwards jazz group, which also included Curtis Counce on bass and Billy Higgins on drums. For the first five years of her studio recording career, from 1957-62, she played guitar on many big recordings including almost all of Phil Spector's 1960's sessions. She, along with others who worked with Spector, were known as "The Wrecking Crew."

Her next lucky break occurred in 1963 when a bassist failed to show up for a recording date at Capitol

For the Record . . .

Born March 24, 1935 in Everett, WA, to musician parents Clyde and Dot Smith.

Began playing professionally with big bands and top jazz groups, 1949; began studio work playing guitar, 1957; began playing Fender or Electric Bass, 1963; First Call on bass by studios recording music for records, movies, television and commercials, c. 1964-69; performed with many popular recording artists including The Beach Boys, Barbra Streisand, Sonny and Cher, The Monkees, Joe Cocker, Ike and Tina Turner, Johnny Mathis, Nancy Sinatra, Ray Charles, Glen Campbell, Frank Zappa, and Herb Albert; studio credits for performances on television show themes include *MASH, Mission Impossible, Hawaii Five-0, The Brady Bunch, Room 222, Cannon,* and *Wonder Woman;* began writing bass tutoring books, 1969; collaborations with other artists include *Some People Can Do What They Like,* with Robert Palmer (Island Records, 1989); *Shades,* with J.J. Cale (Mercury Records, 1991); *Talkin' Verve: Roots of Acid Jazz,* with Jimmy Smith (Verve, 1996); and *Out of Limits,* with The Marketts (Sundazed Music, Inc., 1996).

Addresses: Carol Kaye, P.O. Box 2122, Canyon Country, CA 91386. *E-mail*—carolkaye@earthlink.net.

Records. Kaye stepped in and that initiated her career as a bass player. She created an entirely new sound on the bass by using her guitar pick. After her accidental initiation on the electric bass in 1963, she quickly became the mospopular player on the electric bass, a position she held throughout the 1960s. Kaye was the first person called to play bass at recording studiosbecause of her ability to create good lines. She worked for record, film and television companies, and played in commercial advertising pieces. She worked under the direction of such notables as Quincy Jones, Elmer Bernstein, Ernie Freeman, John Williams, and David Rose.

Performed with Many Recording Artists

Just a tiny selection of the hit songs on which she performed include "Help Me Rhonda" (The Beach Boys), "These Boots Are Made For Walking" (Nancy Sinatra), "Wichita Lineman" (Glen Campbell), "I Got You Babe" (Sonny and Cher), and "Feeling Alright" (Joe Cocker). Some of the other recording artists she has worked with include Barbra Streisand, Ray Charles, Frank Zappa, Ike and Tina Turner, Johnny Mathis, Simon and Garfunkel, The Righteous Brothers, The Marketts, Herb Alpert and The Tijuana Brass, Andy Williams, The Buckinghams, Paul Revere and The Raiders, Gary Lewis and The Playboys, and The Doors.

Television themes on which she has performed include *Mission Impossible, M.A.S.H., Kojak, Get Smart, FBI, Hogan's Heroes, The Love Boat, McCloud, Mannix, It Takes a Thief, The Streets of San Francisco,* and *Peyton Place.* Kaye, who has recorded at the most prestigious studios including Universal, Fox, Warner Bros., and Paramount, recalled how Bill Cosby picked up a tambourine to play with the others during recording for the soundtrack of the first *Cosby Show.*

Gave How-to Advice

Life as a studio recording performer was anything but glamorous. The pace was frantic and many times Kaye remembered eating on the run, getting food from vending machines, and sleeping on the floor when the performers had a five minute break. She said that getting eight hours sleep at night was unknown, four or five hours was more likely. When outsiders would ask how to break into studio recording, Kaye responded in an online interview that one had to "learn how to grab a parking place, don't be late, and carry a pencil, don't be egotistical, oh and yes, know how to create, read music, and play your ass off."

Although there was much comradery between musicians, the competition was fierce. Kaye said that "you NEVER turned down a record date, or a movie/TV film call ... and you rarely announced an 'out-of-town' vacation." She recalled one time when she got away with her family for a vacation on a houseboat in the Bay area, and they made their way to a lake in the Northern California area only to be tracked down by a movie contractor who demanded she return right away to do a movie score. Kaye felt that if she didn't obey such a directive from a contractor that another performer would gladly have stepped into her place.

Music Added Sparkle to Life

During the time Kaye worked as a studio recording artist in the 1960s and early 1970s, there were about 17,000 other musicians doing similar work. They were called "studio musicians," and were all independent artists belonging to the Local 47 Musician's Union in the Los Angeles, California, area. Membership in the Union included a listing in the Union book, which is still printed today, and each "independent" would place bookings via an "answering service."

Although the competition between them could be intense, the musicians also created a sort of community among themselves and would encourage new talent whenever possible. Kaye and a core group of some 300 fellow musicians performed together regularly from 1958-81. From her earliest memories, Kaye had always found that music added a certain "sparkle" to her life whenever she heard it. During an online interview at her official website, she discussed the comradery between fellow musicians and the enjoyment she still gets upon hearing fellow performers years later on the radio: "The sparkle is still there years later after all the recording we did.... I grew fond of so many, we were all in it together." When asked if she missed the frantic pace of studio recording, she responded, "You bet I do, nothing like it, and we all miss each other too, they were the best!"

Selected discography

First Lady On Bass, EFA Records, 1996.

With Others

More of the Monkees, with The Monkees, 1967, reissued Rhino Records, 1994.
Sugar, with Nancy Sinatra as primary artist, 1967, reissued Sundazed Music, Inc., 1995.
Smackwater Jack, with Quincy Jones as primary artist, 1971, reissued Mobile Fidelity Sound Lab, 1991.
Some People Can Do What They Like, Island Records, 1976.
Shades, with J.J. Cale, Mercury Records, 1981.
Out Of Limits, with The Marketts, Sundazed Music, Inc., 1996.
Talkin' Verve: Roots Of Acid Jazz, with Jimmy Smith, Verve, 1996.
California Creamin', Carol Kaye and The Hitmen, EFA Records, 1997.

Selected Writings

How To Play The Electric Bass, (book and tape), Alfred Publishing Co., Inc.
Jazz Bass, cassette and guide book, Alfred Publishing Co., Inc.
Pro's Jazz Phrases - bass clef, Alfred Publishing Co., Inc.
Pro's Jazz Phrases - treble clef, Alfred Publishing Co., Inc.
Rock-Funk Bass, cassette and guide book, Alfred Publishing Co., Inc.

Sources

Periodicals

Musician, February 1998, p. 12.

Online

www.best.com/~abbeyrd/carolkay.htm
www.cdnow.com

Additional information provided by Carol Kaye.

—Debra Reilly

Kenny Wayne Shepherd

Guitarist, songwriter

In an era when rap and alternative music ruled the airwaves of America, a young guitarist from Louisiana stormed the stage with a blazing blusey style reminiscent of the masters of the Mississippi Delta and a technical virtuosity seldom witnessed before. Kenny Wayne Shepherd has been described as a blues prodigy, much like Stevie Ray Vaughn who was one of Shepherd's mentors and earliest influences. Chris Layton, the drummer for Vaughn's band Double Trouble remarked to *Guitar Player*'s Rusty Russell that, "Kenny can nail the style of about any great blues artist you can name, but he's very much his own guy. A young artist takes pieces from all his influences, puts them together, and develops his own thing. I saw Stevie go through it, and I can see the same thing happening with Kenny." On his record label website, Shepherd remarked that "I'm a purist myself. I've been listening to blues since I was very young. I've researched it. But what I bring to it is a young person's approach to the blues. It's free flowing and wide open." He further commented to Russell that "if you're a kid and you're playing the blues, it's hard to prove yourself to those guys [the blues masters and

Courtesy of Ken Settle

For the Record . . .

Born c. 1977, in Shreveport, LA.

Signed to Giant Records, 1993; contributed to *Jewel Spotlights the Blues, Volume I*, 1994; contributed to *Jewel Spotlights the Blues, Volume II*, 1994; released *Ledbetter Heights*, 1995; contributed to *Michael* film soundtrack, 1996; released *Trouble Is,* 1997.

Awards: Gold certification for *Ledbetter Heights,* 1995.

Addresses: *Record company*—Revolution, 729 Seventh Avenue, 12th Floor, New York, NY 10019. *Internet*—www.revolution-online.com/shepherd/bio_frame.html.

legends]. They want to know you're not just messing around with it before they take you seriously."

Shepherd, the Shreveport, Louisiana native, was born in the late 1970s, and at a very young age, developed an avid interest in blues music which has influenced him ever since. He recalled being taken by his father, who was affiliated with the radio industry, to a music festival when he was only seven years old. The guitar virtuoso Vaughn was there performing with his band at the festival as well. Thanks to his father's intervention, Shepherd was able to meet Vaughn. Vaughn allowed the young Shepherd to sit on the side of the stage and watch the show from there.

Taught Himself the Guitar

Around the same time, his father had noted that Shepherd was nosing through his father's blues records and trying to teach himself the riffs from a Muddy Waters song. Shepherd was hooked on the blues from then on. He then begged his parents to buy him a guitar so that he could learn the playing styles and techniques of Vaughn, BB King, Howlin' Wolf, Muddy Waters, Albert Collins, and Albert King. Shepherd then proceeded to teach himself how to play guitar by copying what he heard off the records. The younger Shepherd continued to practice the guitar in his bedroom until he was 13. By that time, he had become something of a local phenomenon.

Not long after this, Shepherd went with his family on a vacation to New Orleans. While there, he met the blind blues player Brian Lee. After much coaxing and persuading, Lee allowed Shepherd to play with him on stage one night. His debut public performance blew away not only Lee but much of the crowd as well. The impromptu gig with Lee not only cemented the relationship between him and Shepherd but it signaled the start of an inspired friendship between the two musicians. The show with Lee also proved to Shepherd that his plans for the future should include performing his beloved blues music.

Shepherd he next few years spent honing and refining his craft through performances with other musicians and gigs at various radio conventions. He eventually formed his own blues band. In 1993, Shepherd was signed by Irving Azoff to Giant Records, which became RevolutionRecords. The following year saw the release of *Jewel Spotlights the Blues Volume I* and its companion *Jewel Spotlights the Blues Volume II.* Both of the albums featured tracks by Willie Dixon featuring some guitar over-dub work performed by Shepherd.

Ledbetter Caused Stir

With his backing band, Shepherd began to work on the sessions and songs that were to comprise his debut album, *Ledbetter Heights. Ledbetter Heights* was released in 1995 and almost immediately caused a quite a stir. Shortly after the sessions for the album were completed, Shepherd and his band were asked to open for the Eagles at their Austin, Texas concert. Requests for their services as an opening act also came from Bob Dylan as well. Azoff remarked on one of the Shepherd websites that, "he is truly a phenomenon. He plays like someone who's lived a lot longer than he has. You don't learn what he has, it's given to you." What was also given to Shepherd was additional accolades from the likes of blues legend BB King who was quoted on one of Shepherd's websites as saying that, "if he continues to grow, he'll be fantastic."

Ledbetter Heights garnered Shepherd a number of prestigious honors. It spawned three top ten singles on the rock charts including the smash hit "Deja Voodoo." *Ledbetter Heights* also received gold certification. The album had a lock on the number one spot on the *Billboard* Top Blues Albums chart for an amazing period of five months straight.

More Mature Style

The following year, Shepherd contributed a track for the motion picture soundtrack for *Michael.* He also began work on his sophomore album, *Trouble Is*. *Trouble Is* was released in 1997 and according to Shepherd it highlighted a more mature and greatly improved style of playing and writing than was evident on its highly acclaimed predecessor. In commenting on *Trouble Is*, Shepherd told James Rotondi of *Guitar Player* that "the real challenge on the fast tempo stuff is to avoid the temptation to play fast myself. The goal is to make just a few notes sound right and fit in.... My chops have gotten so much better from playing nearly every night, not to mention from the maturity that comes from playing for two years on a professional level. If I were to do *Ledbetter Heights* today, it would sound a lot better. I know I've progressed, that I've stepped up a level or two. I don't think I'm guilty of overplaying much any more, and I can hear that my rhythm work has gotten a lot tastier."

After the release of *Trouble Is,* Shepherd took to the road to promote the new album. A support slot on Dylan's 1998 tour further helped to bring Shepherd's new bluesy revival to the masses and was yet another way Shepherd sought to educate, enlighten, and inform the newest members of the blues community. He related on one of his websites that, "I don't want people to just listen to my music. I want them to hear it. Having people appreciate what I do is the ultimate satisfaction for me. I think there's a big explosion in blues-based music and it's very exciting. I'm glad to be a part of it. I want to turn my generation on to it. I want to help keep it alive for them."

Selected discography

(Contributor) *Jewel Spotlights the Blues, Volume I,* Jewel, 1994 .

(Contributor) *Jewel Spotlights the Blues, Volume II,* Jewel, 1994.

Ledbetter Heights (includes "Deja Voodoo"), Giant, 1995.

(Contributor) *Michael* (soundtrack), Revolution, 1996.

Trouble Is, Revolution, 1997.

Sources

Periodicals

Billboard, August 30, 1997.

Guitar Player, October, 1995; January, 1998.

Musician, October, 1997.

On-line

"Kenny Wayne Shepherd," http://fly.hiwaay.net/jcarnell/kwsbio.htm (February 12, 1998).

"Kenny Wayne Shepherd," http://ugalumni.uogleph.ca/bswitzer/kws/index.html (February 12, 1998).

"Kenny Wayne Shepherd," http://www.kwsband.com/bios (February 12, 1998).

"Kenny Wayne Shepherd," http://www.revolution-online.com/shepherd/bio_frame.html (January 22, 1998).

—Mary Alice Adams

King Missile

Rock band

King Missile, the alternative rock darlings of the collegiate circuit seemed to have not only actively pursued and courted fans of college music and the alternative scene but they managed to build and sustain their entire career on left of center lyricism and quirky odd ball pop tunes. The band formed in 1986 when wacky lyricist John S. Hall met and befriended Dogbowl, who had formerly been a member of the Schizocrats. After his father died in 1986, Hall received a $10,000 inheritance that he was determined to squander on recording some of his and Dogbowl's musical forays and the equipment associated with it.

Hall and Dogbowl hooked up with drummer Steve Danziger and decided to call themselves King Missile (Dog Fly Religion). The latter part of the band's name was an invention of Dogbowl. King Missile then proceeded to work out a production and recording deal with the venerated alternative independent music producer Kramer. Kramer had just set up his new label Shimmy Disc and King Missile (Dog Fly Religion) were one of the first bands to record for his new label.

King Missile's debut album, *Fluting on the Hump,* was released in 1987. *Fluting on the Hump* was followed the next year by King Missile's second album, *They.* Dogbowl left left the band to pursue a solo career and to concentrate on other projects, after the release of *They.* After he left, Hall decided to drop the (Dog Fly Religion) part of the name since it was an invention of Dogbowl. By 1989, Danziger too had left, leaving Hall all by himself and forced with the unenviable task of searching for new members to fill out the line up for the second version of King Missile.

Hall's new band was simply called King Missile. Hall recruited drummer Roger Murdock, keyboard and multi-instrumentalist Chris Xefos, and former Bongwater guitarist Dave Rick. The new permutation of King Missile released its first album, and the third in the collective cannon of King Missile releases, in 1990. The album was entitled *Mystical Shit. Mystical Shit* was also packaged as a two in one album package deal with *Fluting on the Hump* released in 1990.

Mystical Shit contained the biggest college underground hit single of King Missile's career up to that point, "Jesus Was Way Cool." Hall's humorously absurd lyrics were brought to a wider audience than ever before and the success of "Jesus Was Way Cool" served to hint at the madcap mayhem that lay ahead for King Missile. Hall ommented on his song writing to *Rolling Stone*'s Carl Arrington, "I wrote to protect my sanity. Or to regain my insanity. Just to make sure that I could straighten things out at night or in the morning when I woke up. I guess it started from emotional traumas. I found that if I wrote about it for long enough, it made me feel better."

King Missile nearly broke up for the second time in its brief career after the release of *Mystical Shit.* Hall remarked on one of the web sites devoted to King Missile that, "Dave and Chris said they wouldn't do another record for Shimmy. So if we hadn't gotten signed [to Atlantic], we wouldn't have survived." Atlantic signed the group and King Missile survived afterall. King Missile's first release for Atlantic was *Way to Salvation,* released in 1991. Commenting on the musical stylings of King Missile, Rick told Chuck Crisafulli of *Guitar Player* that, "since we're supporting John's different word pieces, it's kind of hard not to do a genre-hopping thing. We just try to satisfy ourselves as players and have some fun on stage."

The following year saw King Missile break out of the alternative college rock ghetto with the release of their second Atlantic album, *Happy Hour. Happy Hour* more than lived up to its name as it spawned the surprise cult-novelty hit "Detachable Penis." As Hall related to Arrington, "Detachable Penis" was a long time in the making. Hall stated that "the idea started one night in a club in 1989, when I announced that our next single would be called 'Detachable Penis.' All I had was the title, but it got this big reaction from the

For the Record . . .

Members include **Dogbowl** (left group, c. 1989, rejoined, 1995); **John S. Hall**, vocals; **Roger Murdock** (1989-94), drums; **Dave Rick** (1989-94), guitar; **Chris Xefos** (1989-94), keyboards.

Group formed in New York, in 1986; signed to Shimmy Disc and released *Fluting on the Hump*, 1987;*They*, 1988; *Mystical Shit/Fluting on the Hump*, 1990; *Mystical Shit*, 1990; signed to Atlantic and released *Way to Salvation*, 1991, *Happy Hour,* 1992; *King Missile*, 1994; disbanded c. 1995.

Addresses: *Record company*—Atlantic, 75 Rockefeller Plaza, New York, NY 10019. *Internet*—JOHNSHALL @aol.com.

crowd." After musing and mulling over the concept for the song, Hall created the story behind the song and with musical collaborations from Xefos, Murdock, and Rick, "Detachable Penis" was born. Commenting further, Hall explained, "what I think is great about 'Detachable' is that it works on the lowest common denominator of writing. You can look at the words and see how they work. There are some stupid puns in it, but also all these undercurrents of uncertainties regarding masculinity and castration anxiety. That's a constant theme in my work. Self castration, actually. Arms, legs, heads. It's like this masochistic Christian martyr thing."

The song "Detachable Penis" sold albums and lit up the radio airwaves. This was due, in no small part, to the somewhat obscenely taboo subject matter of the song. The second single from the album, "Martin Scorsese" was an oddly bizarre homage to the famous film director. It failed to ignite the charts as "Detachable Penis" had done. Despite this, *Happy Hour* became the most successful album of King Missile's career.

An interlude of two years had passed before King Missile released their follow up to *Happy Hour.* During this interlude, the band toured for *Happy Hour* and worked on the songs that were to become their final album. The self titled *King Missile* was released in 1994 and by then, the band was starting to disintegrate. Tempers, tensions, and inter-band strife and stress were starting to flare up around the time of the making and release of *King Missile.* The album did not sell as well as its predecessor and subsequently Atlantic dropped King Missile. The band decided to disband after they were dropped. Elaborating on this in one of the King Missile web sites , Hall stated that, "we broke up after Atlantic dropped us because there was no reason for us to stay together. Nobody really liked being in the band, with the possible exception of Chris, who I think was the most reasonable and fairest member of the band. I know I certainly wasn't." Adding in another King Missile website interview, Hall said that, "the people in King Missile didn't ever get along with me very well. The only reason King Missile stayed together as long as it did was that people kept buying the records and coming to the shows. As soon as they stopped, we did."

After the demise of King Missile, Hall went back to his spoken word monologues and readings. He was accompanied by some musicians on these readings and he released a solo album called *The Body Has a Head* in 1995. Also around this same time, Hall reunited with Dogbowl andthey conducted a 1995 King Missile (Dog Fly Religion) reunion tour and after that, laid the band to rest. On the legacy of King Missile, Hall told Arrington that, "my goal is to write in such a way that the songs can be followed on different levels. Like Dr. Seuss."

Selected discography

Fluting on the Hump, Shimmy Disc, 1987.
They, Shimmy Disc, 1988.
Mystical Shit/Fluting on the Hump, Shimmy Disc, 1990.
Mystical Shit (includes "Jesus is Way Cool"), Shimmy Disc, 1990.
Way to Salvation, Atlantic, 1991.
Happy Hour (includes "Detachable Penis" and "Martin Scorsese"), Atlantic, 1992.
King Missile, Atlantic, 1994.

Sources

Periodicals

Guitar Player, October, 1994.
Rolling Stone, April 15, 1993.

On-line

"John S. Hall," http://www.geocities.com/SunsetStrip/Towers/2441/interview.html (February 11, 1998).
"King Missile," http://www.indiana.edu/wius/kingmisvu.html (February 11, 1998).
"John S. Hall," http://www.jmu.edu/wxjm/oc1/johnshal.html (February 11, 1998).

—Mary Alice Adams

Less Than Jake

Rock band

Corbis

Arguably the biggest band to break out of the college town of Gainesville, Florida, Less Than Jake melded punk with power pop, added a healthy dose of horns, mixed it all together and covered it with silly string for the ska-starved youth of America. "They were completely left of center," Craig Aaronson, the Capitol Records Artists and Repertoire (A&R) executive who signed them, told *Moon Magazine*'s Michael Rennie. "It was the first thing I'd heard with horns in a long time, but horns with an edge. You get so much pop-punk coming in, but these guys had something original. And, more importantly, they had good old-fashioned song writing."

According to *Caffeine Nation,* Less Than Jake got their name—which means something like "not quite up to snuff"—from drummer Vinnie Balzano. Balzano claimed he was fed only TV dinners while growing up; Jake, the family dog, however, was given meals from Red Lobster. If one believes the story, Balzano has been "less than Jake" for most of his life.

In the summer of 1992, Balzano joined up with singer and guitarist Chris Neil and a long-forgotten bass player and formed the pop-punk trio Less Than Jake. By early 1993, the original bassist had left and been replaced with Roger Sixx. They also incorporated a horn section comprised of Jessica Horner on saxophone and Buddy Lee on trombone. Baritone saxophone player, Derron Mars, joined a short while later. With the line up intact, Less Than Jake started playing the Gainesville club circuit.

Balzano described their sound to *Jam Magazine.* "It's three chords that has punk, that has ska, that has pop sensibilities, that has a bunch of horns. There's no real ground-breaking—it's just the songs we play. It's Less Than Jake." Neil concurred. "The whole reason for adding the horns," he told Rennie, "was just to do something different. Three-chord pop-punk—there's only so much you can do with it."

At first, Less Than Jake was embraced by the Gainesville musical community. But, as Balzano told Brian Jarmon of *This is the Sound,* things soon began to change. "After we started adding ska elements into it, we were shunned from the Gainesville music scene. As we stuck it out and kept doing it, we were brought back into the fold of the music scene in general, not necessarily the punk scene but the Gainesville music scene. So, yeah, we were supported and we're supported now. But there was a time when we weren't supported by anybody. We were pretty much on our own, doing what we had to do."

Less Than Jake released a five-song seven inch, *Smoke Spot,* on No Idea Records in January, 1993. This was

For the Record . . .

Members include **Vinnie Balzano**, drums; **Jessica Horner** (joined group, 1993), tenor saxophone; **Buddy Lee** (joined group, 1993), trombone; **Derron Mars**, baritone saxophone; **Chris Neil**, vocals and guitar; **Roger Sixx** (joined group, 1993), bass and vocals.

Formed in Gainesville, Florida in 1992; released *Smoke Spot* on No Idea Records, 1993; contributed to *3-way Split* on No Idea Records, 1993; released *Better Class of Losers* on Fueled by Ramen Records, 1994; contributed to *No Idea Fanzine II* on No Idea Records, 1994; contributed to *Six Pack to Go* on Stiff Pole Records, 1995; contributed to *Songs About Drinking* on Too Many Records, 1995; contributed to *Attaining the Supreme* on Whirled Records, 1995; contributed to *Misfits of Ska* on Dill Records, 1995; contributed to *Punk TV* on Red Dawg, 1995; contributed to *Genetic Skaca* on Stiff Dog, 1995; released *Unglued* on No Idea Records, 1995; released *Pez Kings* on Toybox Records, 1995; released *10 Song Sampler* on Dill Records, 1995; released *Pezcore* on Dill Records, 1995; signed to Capitol and released Losing Streak, 1996.

Addresses: *Record company*—Capitol, 750 Vine St., Hollywood, CA, 90028.

followed by a track on the seven inch compilation, *3-way Split,* released on Toybox Records six months later. Less Than Jake was committed to the do-it-yourself work ethic of punk and they recorded incessantly, as Sixx told *Jam Magazine.* "No matter what, the first thing a band should do, immediately upon writing songs, is attempt to release a record. It doesn't matter if a label does it for you, just go through the process of recording and sticking together through all that—that's the most important thing you can do as a band." That was the band's philosophy throughout 1994 and 1995 when they released a multitude of records and contributed to numerous compilations, including a six song cassette, *Better Class of Losers* on their own Fueled by Ramen label, and a track on the *No Idea Fanzine II* compilation.

1995 turned out to be an extremely busy year for Less Than Jake. From January through August, the band was either in the recording studio churning out albums and seven-inch records, recording tracks for various compilation records, or touring. Their own recordings from this time include the *Unglued* seven inch on No Idea Records, *Pez Kings* on Toybox Records, *10 Song Sampler* on Dill Records, and the *Pezcore* album, also on Dill Records. Less Than Jake also contributed songs to a number of compilations: *Six Pack to Go, Songs About Drinking, Attaining the Supreme, Misfits of Ska, Punk TV,* and *Generic Skaca.*

In the interview with Jarmon, Balzano explained how Less Than Jake came to be so prolific. "It's just that people who like us make compilation tapes for friends. There was a time when we would be on everything. If someone said, 'I want you to be on our tape compilation. Do you want to do it?' Sure, take a song. And we just did it and did it and did it. I think that's one of the reasons It's because the people who like us, like us a lot and they spread the word."

A copy of their demo tape eventually found its way to Capitol Records. After listening to it, Aaronson decided to check out Less Than Jake on tour. He liked what he heard and followed the band around America for the next six months before signing them to Capitol. Ironically, Less Than Jake was not even courting any major label deals when Capitol became interested in them. "Less Than Jake doesn't rely on the record company to break them—they're going to break themselves," Aaronson told *Jam Magazine.* "They're like a well oiled machine that's been doing this for a long time. They know how to tap into their audience much better than we do. What we're going to try to do is, spring off from the base that they've laid and try to take it to the next level. The hardest fans to get are the first 25,000 and they've already got them on their own from 3-4 years of hard work."

Less Than Jake's recording contract with Capitol gives them a great deal of freedom. They are allowed to release a specific number of compilation tracks and seven inch records on their own, provided that those do not interfere with any albums Capitol is marketing. "The reason we did this is because they felt it was important for them to stay true to what they've been doing for so long, so well, and continue to sell to their base audience," Aaronson told *Jam Magazine,* "and we think that's the right thing to do."

The year 1996 saw the release of Less Than Jake's Capitol Records debut album, *Losing Streak,* yet another rousing blend of ska, pop and punk. They were well aware that they were perceived as part and parcel of the American ska/punk revival of the late 1990s. Neil summed it up for *Jam Magazine.* "When [the ska/punk revival] gets overblown, it'll be as cheesy as Poison and everyone will know it, and we'll get kicked off the label, and we'll be sitting here with our thumb in our ass collecting unemployment. If you over saturate anything, it's just gonna die."

Selected discography

Smoke Spot, No Idea Records, 1993.
3-way Split, (Compilation), Toybox Records, 1993.
Better Class of Losers, Fueled by Ramen Records, 1994.
No Idea Fanzine II, (Compilation), No Idea Records, 1994.
Six Pack to Go, (Compilation), Stiff Pole Records, 1995.
Songs About Drinking, (Compilation), Too Many Records, 1995.
Attaining the Supreme, (Compilation), Whirled Records, 1995.
Misfits of Ska, (Compilation), Dill Records, 1995.
Punk TV, (Compilation), Red Dawg, 1995.
Generic Skaca, (Compilation), Stiff Dog, 1995.
Unglued, No Idea Records, 1995.
Pez Kings, Toybox Records, 1995.
10 Song Sampler, Dill Records, 1995.
Pezcore, Dill Records, 1995.
Losing Streak, Capitol, 1996.

Sources

"Less Than Jake," http://www.afn.org/ltj/text/jam96.html (January 22, 1998).
"Less Than Jake," http://www.afn.org/ltj/text/moon1.html (January 22, 1998).
"Less Than Jake," http://www.caffeinenation.com/ltj.htm (January 22, 1998).
"Less Than Jake," http://qstart.com/the sound/star/jake (September 25, 1997).

—*Mary Alice Adams*

Letters to Cleo

Alternative rock band

With the release of their third album, *Go!,* under a newly reorganized Revolution Records, in October 1997, Letters to Cleo seem poised to expand beyond their Boston, Massachusetts based roots and become a nationwide phenomenon. After a six month hiatus from the grueling tour schedule of the past few years, the reorganization of former Giant label to its new incarnation—Revolution Records, and with the infusion of energy by newest band member, drummer, Tom Polce, Letters to Cleo seem to be bursting with new found vitality and zest. The alternative rock quintet with the punk edge, known primarily for its lofty melodies, intense guitar, and emotional vocalizations of lead singer, Kay Hanley, hope to move forward in their musical evolution with their latest release. Hopefully, *Go!* will allow them to minimize the past connection to the hit television series, *Melrose Place,* where they first gained national attention for their hit single and video, "Here and Now."

The original five members of LTC got together in Boston, Massachusetts in 1989. The group included Kay Hanley,

Courtesy of Creamer Management/Revolution

For the Record . . .

Members include frontwoman, **Kay Hanley,** vocals; **Michael Eisenstein,** guitar; **Stacy Jones,** drums (left band 1997); **Greg McKenna,** guitar; **Tom Polce,** drums (joined band 1997); **Scott Riebling,** bass.

Career: Original five member band formed in Boston, MA in 1989; performed locally in clubs; debut release *Aurora Gory Alice,* 1993; signed a six-album deal with Giant, October 1994; later re-released *Aurora Gory Alice* under Giant, 1994; cut from *Aurora Gory Alice,* "Here and Now" gained them national recognition after video aired on *MTV* and also played through the credit's of the hit television show, *Melrose Place;* second album, *Wholesale Meats and Fish,* released in 1995; band toured extensively after it's release including doing benefit performances with other alternative bands; the benefits were held after the murders of two female employees at two Brookline, MA abortion clinics, and the funds were donated to women's health programs and battered women's shelters; performed with various artists on *Spirit of '73- Rock For Choice,* Sony Music, 1995; *Safe and Sound: A Benefit in Response to the Brookline Clinic,* was released in 1996 with proceeds benefitting women's shelters and the National Clinic Access Project; newest album, *Go!,* was released in October 1997.

Addresses: Record Company—Revolution Records, 8900 Wilshire Blvd., Beverly Hills, CA 90211. E-mail: cleo@world.std.com. *Band*—Letters to Cleo, 32 Oak Square Ave., Brighton, MA 02135-2517. *Fan Club*—Cleophiles/LTC Fan Club, 149 Kirby St., Portsmouth, VA 23702. *Internet*—Official: http://letterstocleo .com/, or www.revolution-online.com.

vocals; Michael Eisenstein, guitar; Stacy Jones, drums; Greg McKenna, guitar; and Scott Riebling, bass. They performed in many clubs in the Boston area. The newest member, Tom Polce, on drums, joined the band in 1997, replacing veteran Stacy Jones who left during the band's 1997 hiatus to join Veruca Salt.

Frontwoman, Hanley, vocalist and main lyricist for the band, has been performing since her teens. She was a member of the new wave band, Rebecca Lula. Although she has since changed her appearance, currently sporting a short-cropped more punk-like do, reviewer Daina Darzin of *Rolling Stone* noted in a September 1994 review of Letters to Cleo's performance at the Mercury Lounge in July 1997, in New York City, that Hanley's somewhat "Gidget"-like, "wholesome and cute appearance" seemed to clash with her vocal style that was called "quirky and flawless, with a pissed-off edge."

TV Show Gained LTC Recognition

Letters to Cleo's debut album, *Aurora Gory Alice,* released initially on independent label, Cherry Disc, in 1993, and later re-released jointly by Cherry Disc and Giant, in 1994, was well received. One reviewer from *Seventeen* said that *Aurora Gory Alice* was "...one of those rare CD's where every song is good enough to be a single." The band received mainstream recognition after the video of single "Here and Now" was aired during the credits of the hit television series, *Melrose Place,* in 1994. The video also aired on television's *MTV.* Another reviewer, from *Q Magazine,* gave the album four stars — an "excellent" rating and said, "...Hanley, with her honey'n'blowtorch vocal, is clearly destined for stardom." The band signed a six-record deal with Giant in 1994 that allowed Cherry Disc to remain involved in the band's marketing efforts.

The band toured extensively from 1995 to early 1997, performing some gigs beyond their Boston based roots, but staying primarily in the area, performing in local clubs. It was during 1995 thatthe band also got heavily involved in doing benefit performances, lead by Hanley, after the December 1994 murders of two local women, Shannon Lowney and Leann Nichols during two separate attacks on abortion clinics in the Boston area. One benefit concert which kicked off Letters to Cleo's summer tour in 1995, drew over 50,000 fans to hear LTC perform, along with other bands, on the banks of the Charles River in Boston. That show was partially to benefit the pro-choice organization that had been formed after the murders and is named after one of the young women, called "Friends of Shannon," after Shannon Lowney. Lowney had been connected to the local music scene.

Performed Benefit Concerts

Letters to Cleo was among many other local bands who performed at benefits. Compilation albums were released including the 1995 release, *Spirit of '73-Rock For Choice,* by Sony Music, which received good reviews. *Rolling Stone* gave it three stars, and stated that while the album was clearly meant to be a benefit, "...its ... playful tone prove that ... benefit albums do not have to be dry and preachy...." Part of the proceeds from *Spirit of '73* were donated to Rock For Choice.

Additionally, Hanley was the strongest force behind a series of winter concerts in 1995 called "Safe and Sound," the proceeds of which benefitted "Friends of Shannon." Along with LTC, many other top bands from the Boston area performed during the series, including Morphine, Gigolo Aunts, Throwing Muses, and The Mighty Bosstones. The pro-choice movement became the inspiration for the concerts as well as the compilation released, *Safe and Sound: A Benefit in Response to the Brookline Clinic Violence,* under Mercury Records, in 1996.

Also during 1995, their second album, *Wholesale Meats and Fish,* was released by Giant; it received mixed reviews and unfortunately wasn't considered a very strong commercial success, in spite of the music generally being considered more upbeat than their debut album. One reviewer from *Musician,* commented that LTC had created "...glorious turbo-charged pop with near perfect accuracy," but continued that "repeated listening ... is like washing down blueberry pie with a whisky chaser...." Another reviewer from *New Musical Express* stated that although LTC's latest release sounded similar to many other pop bands, the redeeming factor for the effort was their ability to project a sense of fun through the music.

Although Hanley admits that *Wholesale Meats and Fish* was a "commercial failure," she and the other band members were happy with the album. They felt it was their best effort up to that time. Shortly after its release, the Giant label underwent a name change and the upheaval that goes along with significant changes of staff. Letters to Cleo's main supporter, who originally signed the group to the Giant label, A & R executive, Jeff Aldrich, remained with the newly formed Revolution Records and helped the group members during the transition from the Giant label to the new Revolution.

Band took Hiatus

The group decided to take a break from the grueling tour schedule they had maintained during the approximately two and one-half year period between 1995 and early 1997. They found themselves exhausted and in need of rejuvenation. The decision to take time off cost them the loss of veteran drummer, Stacy Jones, who left the group during their hiatus. In addition to spending lots of time doing nothing and writing songs. During the break, Hanley expanded her own musical dimensions by co-starring in the Boston Rock Opera production of *Jesus Christ Superstar playing* Mary Magdalene. She told an interviewer for *Billboard* that the experience "...was just a blast!"

Letters to Cleo's third release, *Go!,* represents a departure in style for LTC in regard to their recording style. With their earlier two releases, much of the material were cuts they had performed many times before live audiences. The music on *Go!* was primarily unplayed before audiences. In an interview with *Billboard,* Hanley explained the making of *Go!,* "It was just a very fly-by-the-seat-of-your-pants kind of thing...." Because the album was recorded in a relatively short time, only about five weeks including recording and mixing, the result is an album that has a more spontaneous and less rehearsed sound. More like a live production.

Poised to *Go!* National

The music on their latest release was described by *Billboard* as including tastes of everything from the pop sound reminiscent of the 1960's in the cut, "Co-Pilot," to "bittersweet acoustic ballads" like "Alouette & Me," to the "candy-coated rock of "Anchor."" "Anchor" is the album's first single release. *Go!* also features the former-Cars, keyboardist, Greg Hawkes.

Revolution Records' Head of U.S. Marketing, Mindy Espy, said that the label's intention was "to move away from the *Melrose Place* tie-in," and hoped to re-establish the band's "credibility," as what she termed Letters to Cleo's image as "a real rock band with great songs." As of October or November 1997, the band was scheduled to begin a new tour including spots throughout the United States and some performances in Canada.

Go! has received mixed reviews, and although reviewer Wook Kim of *Entertainment Weekly* rated it a "C," she also admitted "there were a few retro gems here." Basically, according to Kim, *Go!* is just more of the same. Marisa Sandora of *People* gave *Go!* a "B," and seemed to enjoy the group's ability to produce what she called "pleasing pop melodies." Sandora also noted the "high-energy" delivery, "catchy power-pop tracks" of lead singer, Hanley, that seemed to be "floating above the fuzzy-guitar work...."

It may be premature after only a few months to determine the commercial success or failure of Letters to Cleo's latest effort. Natalie Walaeik, Vice President and Director of Purchasing for Boston based music sellers, Newbury Comics, told *Billboard* that while she realized LTC has a strong following throughout the local area, in that same interview she talked about the potential impact of *Go!* saying, "If they get support from radio, this could be the one [*Go!*] that propels them from local to national stars."

Selected discography

Aurora Gory Alice, (Includes "Here and Now"), Cherry Disc, 1993, reissued, Cherry Disc/Giant, 1994.
Wholesale Meats and Fish, Cherry Disc/Giant Records, 1995.
Go!, (Includes "Co-Pilot," "Alouette & Me," and "Anchor"), Revolution Records, 1997.

With others

Spirit of '73-Rock For Choice, Sony Music, 1995.
(Contributor) *The Craft* (soundtrack), Sony Music, 1996.
Safe and Sound: A Benefit in Response to the Brookline Clinic Violence, Big Rig/Mercury, 1996.

Sources

Periodicals

Billboard, September 24, 1994, p. 10; September 6, 1997, p. 13.
Entertainment Weekly, August 11, 1995, p. 52; October 17, 1997, p. 77.
Mademoiselle, September 1995, p. 162.
Musician, October 1995, p. 81-82, 86; February 1997, p. 127.
New Musical Express, August 26, 1995, p. 47; January 20, 1996, p. 44.
Option, January/February 1996, p. 118-119.
People, December 16, 1996, p. 32; November 24, 1997, p. 28.
Q Magazine, June 1995, p. 124.
Rolling Stone, September 8, 1994, p. 42; June 15, 1995, p. 39; October 5, 1995, p. 73.
Seventeen, June 1995, p. 107.

Online

http://letterstocleo.com/
http://paddle4.canoe.ca/en/sbin/iar
www.cdnow.com/
www.cduniverse.com/
www.revolution-online.com/ltc/

Additional information was provided by Revolution Records.

—Debra Reilly

Charles Lloyd

Saxophonost, composer

AP/Wide World Photos

Composer/tenor saxophonist Charles Lloyd was one of the first jazz musicians to sell a million copies of a recording ("Forest Flower"), to predate the World Music movement by decades by infusing his music with sounds of distant shores, and to funnel the psychedelic sound of the 1960s into avant-garde jazz improvisation. Lloyd worked with some of jazz and blues music's legends—Ornette Coleman, Don Cherry, Eric Dolphy, Charlie Haden, Howlin' Wolf, Cannonball Adderley, B.B. King, Babatunde Olatunji, and Chico Hamilton—and counted among his friends and peers musicians such as Miles Davis, John Coltrane, and Coleman Hawkins. Lloyd was voted "Jazz Artist of the Year" by *Down Beat* magazine in 1967 and was part of the first American jazz group to play in the Soviet Union by invitation of the Soviet people. He paved the entranceway for jazz to enter the realm of rock, and has thrived for four decades. *Wired* magazine's James Rozzi wrote, "Nary a review is written about saxophonist Charles Lloyd without mentioning his kinship to John Coltrane, both sonic and spiritual. But while Coltrane's sound became more strident with time, Lloyd's has grown lush and haunting."

Charles Lloyd was born in 1938 in Memphis, TN, approximately 400 miles north of New Orleans on the Mississippi river. Memphis boasted a rich musical heritage, encompassing blues, gospel, and jazz, and Lloyd soaked it all in: he was given his first saxophone at the age of nine. Radio broadcasts of Charlie Parker, Coleman Hawkins, Lester Young, Billie Holiday and Duke Ellington riveted Lloyd in the 1940s, and his childhood friend, Booker Little, turned out to be a lauded trumpet player. Lloyd's teachers in Memphis were luminaries such as pianist Phineas Newborn and saxophonist George Coleman. While still a teenager, Lloyd played sideman for blues greats B.B. King, Howlin' Wolf, Johnny Ace, and Bobby Blue Bland.

At the age of eighteen Lloyd left Memphis to study for his Master's in Music at the University of Southern California in Los Angeles. Lloyd studied classical music under Halsey Stevens, who was considered the foremost authority on Bartok. Although he spent his days in an atmosphere of academia, his evenings were spent playing in jazz clubs with Ornette Coleman, Charlie Haden, Eric Dolphy, Billy Higgins, Scott LaFaro, and other west coast jazz titans in local clubs. In 1960, at the age of twenty-two, Lloyd became the music director of drummer Chico Hamilton's group after Eric Dolphy left to join Charles Mingus. Hungarian guitarist Gabor Szabo and Albert "Sparky" Stinson joined Lloyd in the band, and it was during this period of prolific composing that Lloyd found his unique sound as a saxophonist. The two most memorable recordings with

For the Record . . .

Born March 15, 1938, in Memphis, TN; *Education:* Received a Master's in Music from U.S.C. in Los Angeles; studied classical music under Halsey Stevens

Began playing saxophone at age 9; played in jazz clubs in Los Angeles with Ornette Coleman, Charlie Haden, Eric Dolphy, Billy Higgins, Scott LaFaro; became the music director of drummer Chico Hamilton's group , 1960; moved to New York City in the early 1960s and played at noted jazz clubs; befriended Miles Davis, John Coltrane, Thelonius Monk, Charles Mingus, and Coleman Hawkins; collaborated with Babatunde Olatunji; joined the Cannonball Adderley sextet, 1964; released *Discovery* , 1964; *Of Course, Of Course* in 1965; formed his own quartet, 1965; debut release *Dream Weaver*, 1966, other releases *Forest Flower: Live at Moneterey* in 1966; *Forest Flower* was one of the first jazz recordings to sell a million copies; the quartet was the first jazz group to play at the Fillmore Auditorium in San Francisco and other rock venues; quartet made headlines in the *New York Times*, *Life*, and *Time* magazine when they were the first American jazz group invited to play in the Soviet Union; dropped from public sight to pursue an inner quest in Big Sur, CA in 1971; broke his public silence in 1981 after meeting a gifted seventeen-year-old pianist from France at big Sur named Michel Petrucciani; produced two live records: *Montreux '82* and *A Night in Copenhagen* in 1982; formed a new quartet in 1988; released *Fish Out of Water* in 1989, released *Notes from Big Sur* in 1991; released *The Call* in 1993, *All My Relations* in 1994, and *Canto* in 1997.

Awards: *Down Beat* magazine's "Best New Artist" award in 1965; voted "Jazz Artist of the Year" by *Down Beat* magazine in 1967.

Address: *Record company*—ECM Records/BMG Classics, 1540 Broadway, New York, NY 10036-4098. Telephone: (212) 930-4958. Fax: (212) 930-4278. *Website*—http://www.ecmrecords.com

Hamilton, *Passin' Through* and *Man from Two Worlds*, were his own compositions. Lloyd moved to New York City in the early 1960s and played at noted jazz clubs like Birdland, the Village Vanguard, the Half-Note, Jazz Gallery, and the Five-Spot. Along the way he befriended Miles Davis, John Coltrane, Thelonius Monk, Charles Mingus, and Coleman Hawkins; he also collaborated with Babatunde Olatunji when he wasn't on the road with Hamilton.

Catapulted to Fame with Cannonball Adderley

In 1964, at the age of twenty-six, Lloyd joined the Cannonball Adderley sextet, playing alongside Nat Adderley, Joe Zawinul, Sam Jones, and Louis Hayes. He also signed a contract with CBS Records to record as a leader, and released *Discovery* in 1964 and *Of Course, Of Course* in 1965, with Roy Haynes and Tony Williams on drums, Richard Davis and Ron Carter on bass, Gabor Szabo on guitar, and Don Friedman on piano. That same year Lloyd won *Down Beat* magazine's "Best New Artist" award. Lloyd left the Cannonball Adderley sextet in 1965 to form his own quartet, which included Keith Jarrett on piano, Jack DeJohnette on drums, and Cecil McBee on bass. Their debut release was *Dream Weaver*, followed by *Forest Flower: Live at Moneterey* in 1966. *Forest Flower* earned a place in history as as one of the first jazz recordings to sell a million copies.

Lloyd's acoustic quartet made a smooth crossover to the popular mass market due to heavy FM radio airplay. The quartet was the first jazz group to play at the Fillmore Auditorium in San Francisco and other rock venues, sharing stages with Jimi Hendrix, Janis Joplin, Cream, the Grateful Dead, and Jefferson Airplane. The quartet also made the traditional jazz festival rounds: Montreux, Antibes, Molde, the Newport Jazz Festival, and the Monterey Jazz Festival. The group melded masterful jazz improvisation with elements of ethnic music, impressionistic harmony, and sporadic rock rhythms. Their open-ended, acoustic musical flights of fancy mirrored the freewheeling spirit of the 1960s, and Lloyd was free to experiment with a constantly changing combination of musical tropes. Electric jazz and rock fused together at the time, and Lloyd was one of the first jazz artists to reach younger fans in the psychedelic era, paving the way for musicians like Miles Davis to further push the envelope.

In 1967, at the age of twenty-nine, Lloyd was voted "Jazz Artist of the Year" by Down Beat magazine, and the quartet toured throughout the world, playing in China, the Soviet Union, and Eastern Bloc countries that had never been exposed to live American jazz performances. At the height of the Cold War, Lloyd's quartet made headlines in the *New York Times*, *Life*, and *Time* magazine when they were the first American jazz group invited to play in the Soviet Union. The quartet played in Tallinn in Estonia, Leningrad, and Moscow. When audience members in Tallinn heard the KGB might not let the group play, they began screaming, "Lloyd jazz! Lloyd jazz!" When Lloyd returned to Estonia in 1997, Marju Kuut—who saw his group's original performance—told *Down Beat* magazine's Thomas Conrad, "Europeans played in jazz, but something was missing. Lloyd was real, real American jazz. They didn't play for ... show. They played for themselves."

Had It All, Then Dropped Out of Sight

At the peak of his career momentum in 1971, Lloyd dropped from public sight to pursue an inner quest in Big Sur, CA, the unorthodox haven that had attracted artists and musicians such as Robinson Jeffers, Langston Hughes, Henry Miller, Lawrence Ferlingetti, and Jack Kerouac. He spent a decade in solitude from the media, then broke his public silence after meeting a gifted seventeen-year-old pianist from France at big Sur named Michel Petrucciani. Lloyd's collaboration with Petrucciani led to European and Japanese tours in 1982 and 1983. Along with Petrucciani on piano and Lloyd on saxophone, Son Ship Theus played drums, and Palle Danielsson played bass; the group produced two live records: *Montreux '82* and *A Night in Copenhagen*—which featured Bobby McFerrin. Lloyd formed a new quartet in 1988 with the Swedish pianist Bobo Stenson, and Lloyd referred to the group as "the full-service orchestra of love". In 1989 Lloyd released *Fish Out of Water*. In 1991, he released *Notes from Big Sur*, followed by *The Call* in 1993, *All My Relations* in 1994, and *Canto* in 1997 (Lloyd played the Tibetan oboe for *Canto*). Linton Chiswick of *Gramophone* wrote, "*Canto* has the most exquisite opening of any jazz record made in a very long time.... Canto is a masterpiece. Resonant with the fragile, ethereal concentration that forms the life-force of Lloyd's music, it is the sound of a group that has actually managed to create its own language."

Selected discography

Discovery, CBS Records, 1964.
Of Course, Of Course, CBS, 1965.
Forest Flower: Live at the Monterey Jazz Festival, CBS, 1967.
Montreux '82, Blue Note Records, 1982.
A Night in Copenhagen, Blue Note, 1982.
Fish Out of Water, ECM Records, 1989.
Notes From Big Sur, ECM, 1991.
The Call, ECM, 1993.
All My Relations, ECM, 1994.
Canto, ECM, 1997.

With Chico Hamilton

Passin' Through, Impulse Records, 1961.
Man From Two Worlds, Impulse, 1962.

Sources

Christian Science Monitor, August 27, 1997.
CMJ, June 30, 1997.
Down Beat, July 1997.
Gavin, July 4, 1997.
Gramophone, October 1997.
Jazz News, July/August 1997.
L.A. Jazz Scene, July 1997.
Option, September/October 1997.
San Francisco, June 1997.
San Francisco Bay Guardian, June 25, 1997.
Stereophile, July 1997.
Wired, November 1997.

Additional source material was found at the website ecm-info@ecmrecords.com and was provided by the publicity department at ECM Records/BMG Classics.

—*B. Kimberly Taylor*

Aimee Mann

Singer, songwriter, bassist

For every action there was an equal and opposite reaction. This was not only the essence of the great physicist Sir Isaac Newton's third law of motion, it also seemed to be the governing principle of Aimee Mann's life. Her breakthrough success with 'Til Tuesday in 1985 eventually became a struggle against a label that wanted to mold her into the new flavor of the month. When she finally went solo, her debut album was critically received but she soon became enmeshed in rather torturous negotiations to extricate herself from her now defunct label. She was signed to a new label and finally got the chance to release her sophomore effort and faced the rather dubious task of re-establishing herself in the minds of her fans. What kept Mann going was her song writing drive, as she commented on in her DGC web site, "at one point before *Whatever* [her debut solo album] came out, things were looking pretty grim and I was getting really depressed. I was talking to a friend and I said, 'I don't know how to get out of this hole.' He said, 'your job is to write songs. So you just keep doing your job.' You do it because there are people who will get it. You do it for them. And you do it just to say

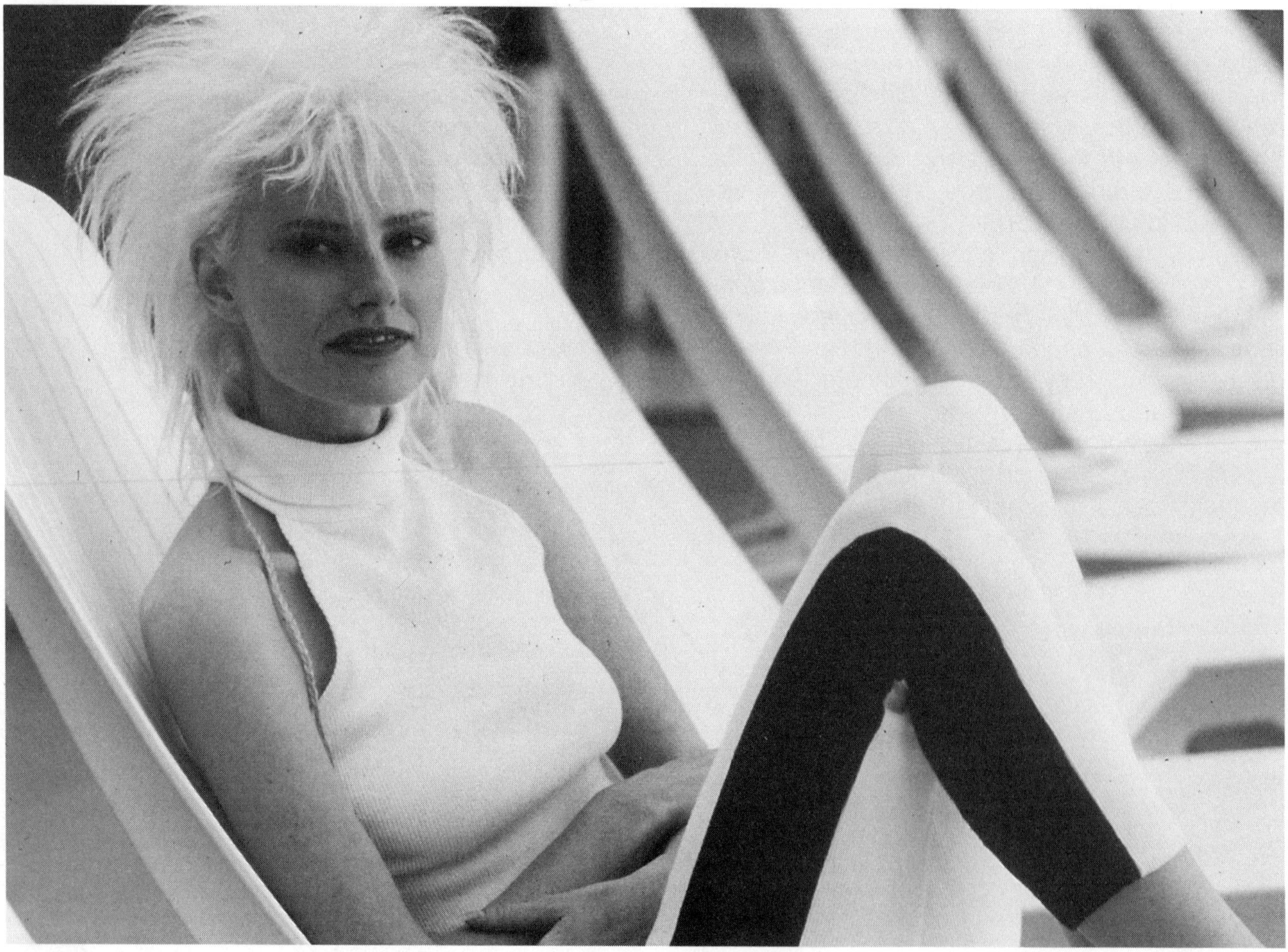

Michael Ochs Archives

For the Record . . .

Born August 9, 1960, in Richmond, VA. *Education:* attended Berklee School of Music.

Joined the Boston based Young Snakes c. 1980; left and formed 'Til Tuesday, 1982; signed with Epic and released *Voices Carry,* 1985; *Welcome Home,* 1986; released *Everything's Different Now*, 1988; disbanded 'Til Tuesday and pursued a solo career; signed with Imago and released *Whatever*, 1993; contributed to *Melrose Place* soundtrack, 1994; released *Coming Up Close,* 1996; signed with DGC and released *I'm With Stupid*, 1996.

Awards: Gold certification for *Voices Carry,* 1985; Music Television (MTV) Award for Best New Artist in a Video, 1985.

Addresses: *Record company*—DGC, 75 Rockefeller Plaza, New York, NY 10019. *Internet*—www.geffin.com/aimeemann/bio/html.

it. Just telling the truth has power and value. Whether or not anyone understands, just tell it. Just say it."

Mann was born August 9, 1960 in Richmond, Virginia. Her parents divorced when she was about three years old. She continued to live with her father after the divorce. When she was four, her mother absconded with her as Mann related to *Billboard*'s Timothy White, "my mother and her new man concocted this plan to kidnap my brother and I and go off to Europe, with his kids from a previous marriage. They couldn't get my brother, but I went with them. My father, an advertising executive, was searching for me with private detectives for a year!" She was eventually reunited with her father after the ordeal and remained with him while she was growing up.

About with mononucleosis when she was about 12 turned young Mann's attention to music. She began to learn how to play her brother's guitar and while she was recovering, she struggled to master the songbooks of Neil Young and Elton John. Mann then practiced the guitar through out high school. After graduating from high school, Mann was undecided about what to do with her life. Her father suggested that a summer course at the Berklee School of Music in Boston might help her to sort out her vocational choices. The move to Boston and life in the big city changed Mann's life. She grew confident in her playing as she progressed from only knowing four Neil Young chords to identifying the structural compositions of songs.

Her newly acquired technical expertise enabled her to be accepted at Berklee as a vocal major. Mann swiftly changed her major to bass and related, on the DGC web site, her rational for changing her major, "no one could teach me how to sing, so I switched to bass. I didn't want to become a bass player necessarily—I wanted to learn how to read music. But guitar and piano didn't really interest me because it seemed that everybody else was just supposed to support those instruments. And I always liked the idea of how all the elements fit in with each other. Playing as one fourth of a band was much more interesting to me."

After a few years at Berklee, Mann left the school and joined up with a Boston area post punk outfit called the Young Snakes. Discord as opposed to harmony was the rule of the day for the Young Snakes. The band managed to garner attention in and around the local area before Mann decided to call it quits, citing her love of melody and music as opposed to chaotic noise.

Mann formed 'Til Tuesday in 1982 and by the following year they were signed to Epic Records. In 1985, 'Til Tuesday released their debut album, *Voices Carry.* The album, which went gold in America, catapulted 'Til Tuesday from Boston area favorites to new pop sensations and media darlings of the moment in a few short months. This was due to the break through success of their top ten single "Voices Carry." "Voices Carry" seemed to strike a nerve with 'Til Tuesday's audience as it detailed a relationship gone wrong and how the woman came to grips with it. The video for the song earned kudos as well earning the band MTV's Best New Artist in a Video Award in 1985.

1986 saw the release of *Welcome Home,* which the follow up to *Voices Carry.* Although popular, *Welcome Home* failed to ignite the charts as its predecessor had done. By this time, Mann's savvy at writing pop songs had been noticed and remarked on by numerous critics, fans, and fellow musicians alike. She was developing a propensity to write somewhat scathing indictments on bad relationships and the pitfalls of life all under the guise of pure pop songs. As her critical acclaim grew her popularity among the populous waned so that by the time of 'Til Tuesday's third and final release, *Everything's Different Now,* they were critical darlings with an ever decreasing fan base. 'Til Tuesday had, in effect, disbanded by 1988 and the tour in support of *Everything's Different Now* became more of a solo outing for Mann than a full band venture.

Wrangled with Epic

For three years, Mann wrangled with Epic to either release her from her contract or to release her new solo work. The label finally relented and released her from her contract in 1992. Mann's manager helped to finance her debut solo album, *Whatever. Whatever* was finally released on Imago in 1993. It generated rave reviews and she started to win back some of her estranged fan base who, not knowing of the impasse between Mann and her old label, had thought that she had called it a day.

Much of 1994 was spent in London working on the sessions for her sophomore effort *I'm With Stupid.* The only real diversion from this task was when Mann was asked to contribute a song to the soundtrack for the television program *Melrose Place.* The resulting single "That's Just What You Are" grazed the Top 100 and became Mann's first semi-hit in quite some time.

After her London sojourn, Mann returned to Boston to record *I'm With Stupid.* During the recording, Mann's label Imago lost its distribution deal and was forced to file for bankruptcy. Imago's president, who owned Mann's contract, decided to pitch Mann's now completed album to the various major labels. As a personal favor to the president of Imago, Warner offered to release the album. Mann insisted that she would not promote the album if it was released on Warner because the label lacked a commitment to her and her album. Mann eventually extricated herself from this predicament and was able to sign with Geffen Records, who eventually released *I'm With Stupid* in early 1996. Despite the fact that *I'm With Stupid* was more guitar driven than her previous album, Mann still managed to release an album full of melodious pop. Also in 1996, Epic released the 'Til Tuesday retrospective *Coming Up Close.*

Honesty and openness, Mann told White, were the gifts she hoped to share with her audience. "Telling what you feel, trying to talk about what's important to you, does not make you weaker. That's the big secret nobody seems to get. I think the role of artists and song writers is to say 'maybe you can't do this, but I'll do it for you.' In other words, I'll try to sing, out loud, the truth of what you and I both feel. I have nothing but disdain for people who spend a lot of energy trying to protect their emotions."

Selected discography

Whatever, Imago, 1993.
(Contributor) *Melrose Place* (soundtrack, includes "That's Just the Way you Are"), Giant, 1994.
I'm With Stupid, DGC, 1996.

With 'Til Tuesday

Voices Carry (includes "Voices Carry"), Epic, 1985.
Welcome Home, Epic, 1986.
Everything's Different Now, Epic, 1988.
Coming Up Close, Epic, 1996.

Sources

Periodicals

Billboard, March 20, 1993; January 6, 1996; July 6, 1996.
New York, July 15, 1985.
People, November 11, 1985.
Rolling Stone, September 26, 1985.

Online

"Aimee Mann,"http://www.bostonphoenix.com/alt1/archive/music/reviews/01-18-96/AIMEE_MANN.html (February 16, 1998).
"Aimee Mann," http://www.geffen.com/aimeemann/bio.html (February 16, 1998).

—*Mary Alice Adams*

Master P

Producer, rap artist

Percy Miller, known as Master P, chartered a remarkably successful career as founder and CEO of the independent record company No Limit Records. In addition to overseeing his record label, he is a rap artist, film and videodirector, actor, and business entrepreneur. In less than ten years Miller rose from record store retailer to owner of one of the country's most successful independent record companies, enjoying forays into film and video as well. When he forged a distribution deal with Priority Records, Miller retained financial control of his company, No Limit Records, and also insisted on complete creative control. This financial and creative freedom allowed Miller and the artists on his label to branch out into film and video and to work with whomever they please—attracting more high-profile artists to the label. In less than ten years, No Limit Records grew into a multimillion-dollar operation with offices in Baton Rouge and Los Angeles; in September of 1997, No Limit Records had five of the top 150 albums in the country.

The 6'2", 180-pound Miller was born in 1970 in the uptown portion of New Orleans, LA, near the French Quarter, and was raised in the city's third ward 1,800-unit Calliope housing projects. His parents separated when he was three years old and his mother moved to Richmond, CA. Miller and his younger brother Kevin were raised by their paternal grandmother. Miller slept on a bare wood floor in the hallway of his grandmother's three-bedroom apartment, as there were eleven other children in his grandmother's care. He visited his mother in Richmond frequently, and told the *Washington Post*'s Jay W. Babcock, "You would hope that my mom was livin in a big old fancy house, but she was in the 'hood' too."

Miller's high school basketball coach, Moon Jones, took him under his wing and provided him with encouragement throughout his teen years. The University of Houston gave Miller a scholarship as a point guard, and he spent two years at the college before suffering a leg injury and conceding that the scholarship wasn't sufficient to cover his expenses. He returned to New Orleans, where—as was his experience in high school—he had to hustle jobs on the street to make ends meet. He told Babcock, "I wasn't hustlin' to buy a car or nothin' like that, I was hustlin' to survive. I was hustlin' to keep the bills paid, I was hustlin' so my brothers didn't have to hustle."

A $10,000 medical malpractice payment related to the death of his grandfather funded a trip to Richmond, CA, for Miller. He opened a rap music store there in 1990 and learned about the record industry from the bottom up. Miller was an aspiring rapper and fan of rap music even before he opened his music store, called No Limit, in the Oakland satellite of Richmond. By 1992, he was ready to start his own label. He told Carlito Rodriguez of *The Source,* "I seen a lot of good rappers and a lot of people in the business, but they wasn't owning it. They was taking their business to somebody for a percentage and settling for less.... if I could just sell half of what they selling ... and own my stuff, I could make some changes."

Miller's business strategy and acumen was honed by his experience managing his own store. He also received valuable tutelage from one of the Bay Area's music distributors—a man named Saint Charles, who owned the Solar Music Group. Charles also mentored the musician E-40 and most of the independent-minded musicians from the area. Miller asked as many questions as possible from local distributors like Charles in order to piece together an accurate overview of the industry, and then released his first album, *The Ghetto's Tryin' to Kill Me.* Miller told Rodriguez, "Hands on, I think, is the most successful way you can learn something.... If you get out there and make a few mistakes, you'll know how to do it."

After releasing *The Ghetto's Tryin' to Kill Me* in 1993, Miller planned on selling just enough albums to see a return on his investment. Without any help from video, radio, or wide-scale distribution, the record sold more

For the Record . . .

Born Percy Miller in 1970 in New Orleans, LA; parents separated when he was three and a half years old. *Education:* received basketball scholarship as a point guard to University of Houston in Texas, attended college for two years.

Opened the No Limits record/cd store in Richmond, CA in 1990; founded No Limit Records in 1992; released *The Ghetto's Tryin' to Kill Me,* 1993; *99 Ways to Die,* 1995; which led to a distribution deal with Priority Records; released *The Ice Cream Man,* 1996; *Ghetto D,* 1997; released soundtrack to the video *I'm 'Bout It* in 1997.

Address: *Record company*—No Limit Records, P.O. Box 2590, Los Angeles, CA 90078 (213) 436-0250, fax (213) 436-0019

than 120,000 copies. Miller was then certain there was a market for his music and he knew he could compete with rap music's business leaders by eliminating the middlemen involved in creating, marketing, and promoting his music. His second release, *99 Ways to Die,* sold almost 300,000 copies and led to his lucrative distribution deal with Priority Records in 1995. His third release, *The Ice Cream Man,* ushered in an array of successful albums for No Limit Records. His fourth release was *Ghetto D,* which featured a moving tribute to his deceased brother, Kevin. It debuted on the top of the *Billboard* chart . Miller also signed Mia X, Mr. Serv-On, TRU (composed of Master P and his younger brothers Corey 'C-Murder' and Zyshonne 'Silkk the Shocker'), Mystikal, Kane & Abel, Mercedes, Sons of Funk, Mo B. Dick, West Coast Bad Boyz, the Down South Hustlers, and Steady Mobb'n to No Limit, and released the soundtrack to the movie he co-wrote, directed with Moon Jones and also starred in, *I'm 'Bout It.* The film was released as a video, in 1997, instead of as a feature due to a lack of interested distributors. More than 200,000 copies of the video were shipped in five weeks.

Part of the key to No Limit's success has been it's variety of artists from differing parts of the country who bring their distinctive regional sounds to the label. Miller drew his entrepreneurial inspiration from the success of rap music's Death Row Records and other black-owned, independent music labels. He told Rodriguez, 'It inspired me. When I seen Lil' Jay and Tony Draper (owners and CEOs of Rap-A-Lot and Suave House, respectively), it let me know it can be done."

Marketing Genius

Miller shuns radio and television when marketing new releases, and places ads in specific consumer magazines such as *Vibe, The Source,* and *XXL.* He also displays the album covers of forthcoming releases in the jackets of current cassettes and compact discs. He told Soren Baker of the *Chicago Tribune,* "If we have a Master P record sell a million copies, why not advertise the newer groups that are coming out" B.J. Kerr. president of Atlanta's PatchWerk Recordings, told Baker, "Everything (Miller) does is promotion for the next thing, whether it's a movie or his T-shirts. He's a marketing genius." Miller also packs more songs per album on his label's releases than other labels, figuring consumers appreciate more for their money.

Miller hired family members, high school friends, and people he knew in the projects to work with him at No Limits, and the general feeling at the label is that the group is one big family, striving together for success. Miller also hopes to serve as a role model for children in the ghetto, offering hope and a blueprint for economic independence. After creating an R& B department at No Limit, Miller has branched out beyond music, video and film into the realm of real estate and business franchising for Foot Locker in Baton Rouge. He told Rodriguez, "The ghetto wasn't nothing but a place for me....that ain't where my mind stopped at.... My mind was thinking, 'I'm gon' take my mamma up out of here. I'm gon' take my sisters and brothers up out of here'.... that's what this No Limit thing is all about: we 'bout holding on to something and surviving."

Selected discography

The Ghetto's Tryin' to Kill Me, No Limit Records, 1993.
99 Ways to Die, No Limit Records, 1995.
The Ice Cream Man, No Limit Records, 1996.
Ghetto D, No Limit Records, 1997.
I'm 'Bout It, (Soundtrack), No Limit Records, 1997.

Sources

Chicago Tribune, September 4, 1997.
Los Angeles Times, September 14, 1997.
The Source, October 1997.
Washington Post, September 25, 1997.

—*B. Kimberly Taylor*

Eric Matthews

Musician, songwriter

Alternative pop artist Eric Matthews wears an array of musical hats by composing, arranging, conducting, singing, producing, and playing the guitar, trumpet, piano, harpsichord, and flugelhorn on his albums. A consummate songwriter with an ear for perfect orchestration, *Rolling Stone*'s Rob O'Connor described Matthews' 1995 solo debut release, *It's Heavy in Here,* as "filled with natural textures: trumpet, harpsichord, piano, violin, viola and tenor sax.... Guitar, bass, and drums are still used—they're just harder to find.... *It's Heavy in Here* remains singular in the current alternative-rock sweepstakes. Although the tendency is to call this music 'pop' ... most of the musical references are much more obscure." Chris Nickson of the *Rocket* declared *It's Heavy in Here* "the Northwest album of the year, a glowing, intimate record." Placing Matthews into any particular musical niche proves difficult; O'Connor wrote, "*It's Heavy in Here* doesn't sound like anyone else's record." Still, Matthews has been compared to Nick Drake, the Beatles, Burt Bacharach, the Bee Gees, and the Beach Boys. Matthews layers his pop music with stately orchestration and well-crafted melodies, which renders his style memorably atmospheric. His lyrics are sung in a smoky tone, and are generally dark and low-key.

Matthews was raised in Gresham, Oregon, where he was exposed to an array of music. He told *CMJ*'s Dawn Sutter, "My parents ... were Miles Davis fans and they had a lot of orchestral music and a lot of Russian composers, so I was listening to a lot of trumpet sections ... and then *Star Wars* came out. John Williams was writing so specifically and predominantly for trumpet. I fell in love with it." He took up the trumpet at the age of ten and decided he wanted to make a career of it. However, he refused to play in his high school's marching band because he felt it was more an athletic exercise than a musical one.

He applied to a musical conservatory rather than a conventional college, and trained as a classical trumpet player at the San Francisco Conservatory of Music, but the choice was short-lived. Matthews found work at clubs in San Francisco while studying and was able to support himself as a trumpet player, but his academic pursuits were largely unsuccessful. After two years at the conservatory, he moved to the Boston area and attempted to pick up where he left off by studying with Thomas Morrison, a principal in the Boston Symphony Orchestra. Once again, Matthews didn't feel the choice was right for him. Just as he was wrestling with his career options, his father and brother sent him a tape of original material they had recorded at home with new recording equipment. Matthews told Sutter that his reaction was, "This is so much more interesting than me trying to play Mozart like every other trumpet player has tried to do for the last 300 years. I basically got off the train on my way to my first lesson."

Propelled into Indie Rock Realm

Matthews met Australian singer/songwriter Richard Davies of the Moles through friend and Sebadoh member Bob Fay. Davies and Matthews decided almost immediately to collaborate on material. They released the album *Cardinal* in 1994, and Matthews found himself pitched into the unfamiliar indie rock world. *Cardinal* had been primarily a showcase for Davies and his songs, and Matthews acted as producer, arranger, and co-singer. Neil Strauss, in an article for the *New York Times,* described it as, "an excellent album of soft, pristine pop."

Matthews struck out on his own in 1995 with his debut release *It's Heavy in Here,* which met with rave reviews. *Interview* magazine's Jennie Ryan wrote, "Matthews songs have a pristine, musicianly quality—as if sprung whole from a time capsule, circa early experimental Beatles." *Musician* magazine's Ken Micallef wrote, "Matthews' music recalls Andy Partridge and Prokofiev ('Angels for Crime'), Brian Wilson and Bach ('Fried Out Broken Girl')." Kurt B. Reighley, in a review for *Paper* magazine, wrote, "From the opening brass of 'Fanfare,'

For the Record . . .

Born Eric Matthews; raised in Gresham, OR.

Took up the trumpet at age ten; trained as a classical trumpet player at the San Francisco Conservatory of Music for two years; studied with Thomas Morrison, a principal in the Boston Symphony Orchestra; collaborated with Richard Davies of the Moles to create the album *Cardinal,* 1994; released solo debut album *It's Heavy in Here,* 1995; released *The Lateness of the Hour,* 1997.

Address: *Record company*—Sub-Pop Records, P.O. Box 20645, Seattle, WA 98102 (206) 441-8441; fax (206) 441-8245. *Website*—Official Eric Matthews World Wide Web Site: http://www.subpop.com/bands/eric-matthews/matthews.html.

through 12 cuts of wide-eyed, Donovan-esque vocals, string arrangements and psychedelic titles ... Eric Matthews pulls off the impressive feat of refashioning almost every style of 60's pop into something fresh on his Sub-Pop debut."

Matthews followed *It's Heavy in Here* with his second release, *The Lateness of the Hour.* Like his previous release, this album featured lush orchestral arrangements and a "swirling" guitar sound. Along with Matthews' 451 Philharmonic orchestra, Jason Faulkner and Tony Lash were featured players on the album. *Rolling Stone*'s David Greenburger wrote of *The Lateness of the Hour,* "Standard guitar-bass-drums trappings are but foot soldiers amid platoons of horns and harpsichords, all of which must answer to that higher power: the carefully crafted song.... this is pop music for the rain and fire rather than the beach."

Anti-Grunge on a Grunge Label

Matthews is an unlikely musician for the Sub-Pop label, as he has little reverence for rock, grunge, punk, or metal music—yet he is signed to a label particularly equated with alternative rock: Mudhoney, Nirvana, and Soundgarden are part of the Sub-Pop roster. Matthews told James Hunter of *Details,* "We did have this big movement of orchestral pop music, but now we've gotten away from that, and I'm stuck in this indie-rock category, talking to people who enjoy really bad rock records." Some of Matthews' favorite artists include the Moody Blues, Herb Albert & the Tijuana Brass, Scott Walker, Talk Talk, ABC, Burt Bacharach, and Art of Noise, and he doesn't hesitate to admit he knows little about rock music. He told Sutter, "It [rock music] all simply sounds loud ... I couldn't be any less in love with the aesthetic of guitars and guitar records." Ironically, Matthews is alternative on an alternative label, offering something refreshingly original and paving the way for more anti-alternative, orchestrated pop music. Chris Nickson of *Alternative Press* wrote of Matthews' material, "You won't be tapping your toes, but you will be nodding your head, and sometimes you'll even want to cry."

Selected discography

Cardinal, Flydaddy, 1994.
It's Heavy in Here, Sub-Pop, 1995.
The Lateness of the Hour, Sub-Pop, 1997.

Sources

Periodicals

Alternative Press, November 1995; August 1997; October 1997.
Billboard, August 23, 1997.
CMJ New Music Report, September 11, 1995; August 11, 1997.
CMJ New Music Monthly, November 1995; August 1997; October 1997.
Details, September 1997.
Interview, November 1995.
Magnet, September/October 1997.
Musician, November, 1995.
New York Times, September 18, 1995.
Our Town, August 18, 1997.
Paper, November 1995.
Ray Gun, November 1995; October 1997.
Request, September 1997.
Rolling Stone, November 16, 1995; September 4, 1997.
Spin, November 1995.

Online

http://www.subpop.com/bands/ericmatthews/matthews.html
http//www.allstarmag.com
http://musiccentral.msn.com

—B. Kimberly Taylor

Maxwell

Singer, songwriter

Heralded as the savior of soul music in the 1990s, Maxwell, the self professed former nerd, rocketed from relative obscurity to infamy with his romantic concept album, *Urban Hang Suite.* Maxwell's debut album not only earned him a Grammy, three Soul Train Music Awards, and three National Association for the Advancement of Colored People (NAACP) Awards but it also earned him countless comparisons to the great soul singers of the 1960s and 1970s.

The depressed and dangerous section of Brooklyn known as East New York was where Maxwell was born on May 23, 1973. His father, who died when Maxwell was three, was from the West Indies, while Maxwell's mother was of Puerto Rican decent. His mother did not allow him to play outside very often after his father died. He was a loner, who stayed inside the apartment reading the Bible and watching television, rather than play and socialize with the other children in the neighborhood.

Raised as a devout Baptist, Maxwell often attended church as much as five times a week while growing up.

Reuters/Archive Photos

For the Record . . .

Born May 23, 1973, in Brooklyn, NY.

Signed to Columbia and released *Urban Hang Suite*, 1996; released *Unplugged*, 1997.

Awards: Grammy award, 1996; three National Association for the Advancement of Colored People (NAACP) Image Awards, 1996; three Soul Train Music Awards, 1996; Platinum certification for *Urban Hang Suite*, 1997.

Addresses: *Record company*—Columbia, 550 Madison Ave., New York, NY 10022. *Internet*—www.maxwell.appreciators.com.

Despite his later successful endeavors in the field of music, Maxwell did not participate in the church choir when he was little. It was only when joined in with the congregation when they were singing hymns that people took notice of his voice. As he explained to Michael George in *American Visions,* "people heard me humming and said 'Boy, you better go do something.' But I never wanted to be in front. One of my biggest fears was ... maybe I should just put what's inside of me someplace deep. I'm madly private. I'm a very private individual."

High school was not very easy for the shy, sheltered Maxwell, as he related to Chris Dickinson of the *St. Louis Post-Dispatch*, "being into books, having the glasses, being in the back of the class. Knowing the answers but being afraid to answer. I'm not Einstein or anything, but I definitely went through a period of trying to be who I'm not." He was nicknamed "Maxwell House Coffee" by his classmates who taunted and teased him. The soon-to-be ladies man had an extremely difficult time with women as well. Maxwell only had two girlfriends throughout high school and did not even attend his senior prom.

Things slowly started to change for Maxwell, once he discovered music. When he was about 17, a friend loaned him a beat up Casio keyboard and Maxwell began to immerse himself in the popular music of the secular world. Patriae Rushen, the SOS Band, and other Rhythm and Blues (R&B) artists served as musical mentors for the teenage Maxwell. Soul Fuze's Warren Mason reported that in his Columbia Records biography, Maxwell stated that his influences were derived from the early 1980s because, "the early 80s had the perfect combination of computerized instrumentation with a live feel. Later the music got all into hip-hop and some of the dynamics were lost."

Maxwell would barricade himself in his room for hours listening to music and practicing on the keyboard. He eventually taught himself how to play not only the keyboard but the guitar and some other instruments he had acquired by then as well. Also around this same time, Maxwell started to move away from the church as his interest in secular music grew and blossomed. He did not give up on religion, rather he delved into the spiritual side of life. Maxwell elaborated on this to George saying, "it's like something bigger came into the situation. Loving God and loving higher things became rules: what you have to do and how you have to do it, and a particular method in how you reach God. For me, it became less about that and more about the universal message that he or she lives inside you and you are a part of it—that everyone is part of everyone. That whole thing came to play around the music."

At 19, Maxwell started to play shows throughout the New York club circuit. He supported himself by waiting tables by day and performing his music at nights in his off hours from work. Through a friend of a friend, he was able to gain access to a 24 track recording studio and started to record songs for a demo tape that he began passing out to his friends. The demo caused enough interest in him that his first proper concert at Nell's in New York City had a good turnout for the relatively unknown singer.

Signed with Columbia

Between 1992-94, he continued to play shows and demoed some 300 or so songs. Interest in Maxwell was starting to develop as more and more people came to check out his soulful alternative gigs, including a writer from *Vibe* who proclaimed him the "next Prince." Shortly thereafter, Maxwell signed a recording contract with Columbia Records.

Columbia reluctantly allowed Maxwell to have creative freedom in his contract. The label was even more hesitant to let Maxwell produce the album by himself, so they brought in a producer from Chicago, who only managed to last for the first few tracks. Despite this, Maxwell soldiered on writing and producing the various songs on the album. He had some high profile help from veteran session musicians who had worked with Marvin Gaye, Motown, and Sade. The sessions for *Urban Hang Suite*, as the album was called, lasted for much of early 1995, finally finishing in March of that year.

Although *Urban Hang Suite* was completed in 1995, it would not see the light of day for another year or so due to the fact that Columbia's Urban Music Department was in the midst of a personnel overhaul. Maxwell decided it was best to wait out the change in staff. He began involve himself with writing and demoing songs for his next album, along with embarking on an African American college tour with Groove Theory and the Fugees.

After Columbia's Urban Music Department had completed their personnel overhaul, both the label and Maxwell were reluctant to release *Urban Hang Suite.* Columbia feared that the listeners would fail to comprehend Maxwell's romantic concept album and image. Maxwell himself did not help the matter any by refusing to allow his picture to be placed on the album's front cover, preferring to have the track listing and pertinent information about the album to take the place of a photo of him. The label reached a compromise and placed a shot of him on the back cover.

Columbia reluctantly came to an agreement with Maxwell to allow the music, not his image speak for the album. *Urban Hang Suite* was finally released in America in the spring of 1996. The album's sales were slow at first but began to grow through word of mouth. Maxwell rationalized his appeal to *Vibe*'s Quohnos Mitchell as "it's about being real and true to your flow. My flow is about music. People identify with honesty and risk. Some artists use their lives as a gimmick or gift to get them to the next level. I'm not about that. People enjoy music that opens them up to and takes them on a journey."

Romantic at Heart

To his fans, Maxwell's *Urban Hang Suite* lures them into the heart of a romantic encounter that ends with a marriage proposal. The honest, sincere sexuality has struck a collective nerve with many in his audience who have built, renewed, or refined relationships based on the many messages found in the songs from *Urban Hang Suite*. Maxwell explained his romantic notions to George as "yeah, I'm a big sucker for the cheesy, mushy stuff. But I've always been. I think that comes from my grandmother and the other West Indian women I know. And most of them are the foundation of society in the islands. There is such a respect for commitment and sacrifice. I think that women represent the ultimate sacrifice in their daily lives, and I go crazy when I see them."

Maxwell's main muse was women as he told *Interview*'s Dimitri Erhlich, "I think creativity is innately feminine. Obviously women at 12 or 13 get either cursed or blessed with the fact that they're vessels for human life to come through. And that's what music—what creativity—is to me. I guess being a man is a truly physical state and mentally it's a little bit limiting. But what I'm talking about is not a person's 'female side' or 'male side'. The only way I can pay homage to that feminine thing—not necessarily women but to what they represent as creative forces—is by getting artistic and making music."

Maxwell's emotive power seduced not only significant numbers of both the urban and pop audiences but critics as well. *Urban Hang Suite* achieved platinum certification in America in March of 1997. Later that year, he released the *Unplugged* album. In commenting on the new soul revival in music, Maxwell told *Entertainment Weekly*'s Larry Blumefeld that "everything out there musically was inspired or influenced by something from the past. It's not about creating some superfresh new thing. If it doesn't lend itself to your history, how is it going to extend to your future? That's what's really brilliant about looking into children's eyes—you can see their parents in them."

Selected discography

Urban Hang Suite, Columbia, 1996.
Unplugged, Columbia, 1997.

Sources

Periodicals

American Visions, April-May, 1997.
Billboard, January 13, 1996.
Entertainment Weekly, January 24, 1997.
Interview, May, 1997.
People, April 21, 1997.

Online

"Maxwell," http://members.aol.com/soul4luv/soulfuze/maxwell/sfmaxw11.html (January 22, 1998).
"Maxwell," http://www.vibe.com/archive/nov96/docs/maxwell.html (January 22, 1998).

—Mary Alice Adams

Mindy McCready

Country singer

AP/Wide World Photos

Mindy McCready's striking appearance and musical delivery has caught the attention of many young country music fans, particularly young women who see her as someone to emulate. Part of a new breed of country music performers, she is unafraid to address issues through her music that had previously been avoided. Her fresh, direct, open style and relative youth allow her to empathize with young people beginning romantic relationships. McCready released albums in 1996 and 1997 and seems poised to become one of country music's next superstars.

The singer was born Malinda Gayle McCready in Ft. Myers, Florida on November 30, 1975 to parents Tim and Gayle. She has two younger brothers, Tim Jr. and Josh, and a half-brother, Kolton Skyler. Her first public performance was at the tender age of three when she performed a solo in church, following the examples set by her mother and grandfather, who sang in the choir. At ten she reluctantly began vocal lessons but ultimately found the experience very helpful as she increased her vocal range and learned proper breathing techniques.

McCready's strongest influence during her adolescence, outside of her immediate family, was singer Amy Grant. She emulated Grant and paid careful attention to her videos and music. McCready's voice teacher suggested she also study the singing style of gospel singer Sandi Patty. The young vocalist was also influenced by Twilla Paris, the group Alabama, and the song "Elvira" by the Oak Ridge Boys. A highly motivated young woman, McCready took extra classes while in high school so that she could graduate at age 16.

Although McCready's mother had hopes of her daughter going to law school, the younger McCready had other ideas for herself. At age 18, McCready packed up, gathered her arsenal of karioke tapes, and headed north to Nashville, Tennessee. She and her mother had a deal: she would have one calendar year to pursue and establish a career in music; after that, if she was not successful, she would go to college.

McCready readily admits that she knew little about getting into the music business. She remembers how people laughed at her because of it. Shortly after arriving in Nashville, she met producer Norro Wilson. Taking a liking to McCready, Wilson decided to help the naive singer. He listened to her karioke tapes and soon introduced McCready to another producer, David Malloy. Both men felt McCready was a natural talent. Malloy spoke about his initial reaction to McCready's voice in an online interview for www.flash.net: "She has such a purity of voice, such a charismatic tone to her vocals—

For the Record . . .

Born Malinda Gayle McCready on November 30, 1975, Fort Myers, FL; daughter of Tim and Gayle McCready.

Signed with BNA, part of BMG Entertainment/RCA Nashville, 1994; debut album, *Ten Thousand Angels,* BNA, 1996; *If I Don't Stay The Night,* BNA, 1997; appeared on the 32nd annual Academy of Music Awards, *Tonight Show with Jay Leno* on February 25, both in 1997; toured throughout the United States and Canada during 1997.

Awards: Country Music Radio Awards, Best New Artist, 1997.

Addresses: *Record Company*—RCA Records/Nashville, One Music Circle North, Nashville, TN 37203-4310. *Fan Club*—Mindy McCready Fan Club, P.O. Box 23411, Nashville, TN 37202; email McCready at mmcready@twangthis.com. *Management*—Moress Nanas Entertainment, 1209 16th Ave. South, Nashville, TN 37212. *Websites*—Official McCready web site: www.twangthis.com.

and on top of that she has this great open, uninhibited personality." Malloy and McCready subsequently worked together helping McCready develop and perfect her own style, and to produce a suitable demo tape to present to record companies. As the deadline imposed by her mother neared, the demo was finished and evaluated by record executive Thom Schyler of RLG, a subsidiary of BMG.

Addressed Real Life Issues

Schyler subsequently scheduled a live audition for McCready with Joe Galante, head of RLG. After 51 weeks in Nashville, McCready had her record contract in sight. By 1994 she was signed with RLG's sister label BNA. Two years later, McCready's debut album, *Ten Thousand Angels* was released and went on to gain platinum status. Produced by Norro Wilson and David Malloy, the album introduces McCready's slick and sassy style of vocals. The album's songs directly tackle some tough real-life issues that men and women are often faced with, but may be reluctant to talk about. A reviewer from *Entertainment Weekly* described McCready's style aptly: "[she] serve[s] up a thoughtful program of postfeminist attitudes toward gender equality, love, and, lust. That, combined with a fetching voice and winning melodies, makes McCready a welcome—and unusual—Nashville newcomer."

The cut "Guys Do It All The Time" may cause some men distress as McCready addresses the double-standard is sometimes found in relationships between men and women. In this cut, a favorite of her female audience, McCready pulls a role reversal on the guys who stay out all night partying with their friends, neglecting other responsibilities. Both "Guys Do It All The Time" and title cut "Ten Thousand Angels" were released as singles and were number one country hits. In 1997, McCready released a second album, *If I Don't Stay The Night.* An enhanced CD, it contains multimedia computer files as well as audio recordings.

Rejected "Bimbo " Image

McCready talked about the inspiration for much of the material on *If I Don't Stay The Night* in an online interview at www.country.com. She said that much of the album content was inspired by conversations with her younger brothers, Tim and Josh. Both brothers live with her in Nashville, and she knows that she is a role model for them, as well as for thousands of fans. This includes young women who write the singer for advice on relationships and who express their desire to look like her. After realizing that some people had initially pegged her as a "bimbo," McCready took pains to change that image. In an online interview at www.country.com she remarked that the photos used on her first album, *Ten Thousand Angels,* were "fake-looking glamour" poses. She feels it is bad to project an image like this to young impressionable girls who regret that they will never look this way. She said anyone, given "$50,000 worth of photography" could look glamourous. To this end, McCready has scaled down her own use of cosmetics and dresses simply, buying clothes that can be found at local malls. For the photos on *If I Don't Stay The Night,* McCready intentionally went for a more natural look.

Took a New Approach

McCready reaches her young fans in part because she is so near them in age. Just barely out of her teens herself, she has been able to empathize with their concerns. Her refreshingly honest and direct approach to subjects that are rather new to country music has endeared her to many young listeners. The primary theme throughout *If I Don't Stay The Night* is a spin on the issues of sex and romance, because it comes from a young woman's perspective.

McCready won the Country Music Radio Award for Best New Artist in 1997. By this time, she had done considerable touring across the United States and Canada, opening for acts including George Strait, Alan Jackson, and Tim McGraw. She performed at the 1997 Jamboree In The Hills, which is known by country music fans as the "Super Bowl of Country Music." The annual country music festival is held outdoors in St. Clairsville, Ohio; it lasts four days and attracts some 90,000 fans each year. McCready appeared and performed on television for the 32nd annual Academy of Country Music Awards and on *The Tonight Show with Jay Leno*. She has also performed with other artists on recordings including *Country Cares For Kids: A Holiday Album,* which directed its proceeds to the St. Jude's Children's Research Hospital.

Unfortunately, McCready was sidelined in late 1997 with tonsillitis. The condition required surgery and rest for her voice, but the singer hoped to return to work by the middle of 1998. Also planned for 1998 was McCready's marriage to actor Dean Cain, who is best known as Superman on the television series *Lois and Clark.*

Selected discography

Ten Thousand Angels, (includes "Ten Thousand Angels" and "Guys Do It All The Time"), BNA, 1996.
If I Don't Stay The Night, BNA, 1997.
(With others) *Various Artists: Going West Across America,* RCA Records, 1997.
(With others) *Country Cares For Kids: A Holiday Album,* BMG/BNA Entertainment, 1997.

Sources

Periodicals

Country Weekly, May 14, 1996, p. 24.
Entertainment Weekly, May 3, 1996, p. 79.
Nashville Record Review, June 1-2, 1996.

Online

http://cgi.canoe.ca/JamMusicArtistsL2Q/mccready_mindy.html
http://musiccentral.msn.com/
www.1200.ckxm.com/1997countrymusicradioawards.html
www.cdnow.com/
www.cduniverse.com/
www.country.com/article/mus-countryam/mindy-feature.html
www.countrystars.com/artists/mccready.html
www.flash.net/~jtpayne/mindy/
www.jamboreeusa.com/
www.nbc.com/entertainment/specials/acmawards/frpv_mccready.html
www.twangthis.com
www.young-country.com/MindyMcCready.html

—*Debra Reilly*

Brian McKnight

R&B singer, songwriter, producer

Corbis

Brian McKnight 's professional accomplishments as a musician have been many and varied during the past nine years, after signing with Mercury Records at the tender age of 19 in 1989. A gifted singer known primarily as a romantic balladeer based on his first two releases, he departed from this style on his 1997 album, *Anytime,* which includes the single, "You Should Be Mine," with rapper, Mase. This departure from the romantic crooning heard on his first two albums challenged him and forced him to stretch musically. The results of this collaboration first came to the attention of the mainstream after his 1993 duet with Vanessa Williams, "Love Is," from the "Beverly Hills 90210" soundtrack, which hit number three on the Hot 100. McKnight has proven that although he sped up the music ladder to stardom, he has what it takes to maintain his place.

McKnight is also a prolific songwriter. He writes much of his own material as well as writing songs for other artists. Known as a brilliant producer, this versatile artist plays a number of instruments as well, including the piano, trumpet, and bass. In addition to being lead vocalist, songwriter, and/or producer of three of his own albums during the past five years, he has also performed and recorded with Take 6, Boyz II Men, Vanessa Williams, Quincy Jones, the Boys Choir of Harlem, and others. Additionally, McKnight has produced and co-produced many other releases for various artists.

Coming from a highly musical family, McKnight always thought singing and playing music were as natural as "walking and talking" according to an online interview. He was born in Buffalo, New York, on June 5, 1969, the youngest of four boys. His success was obviously strongly influenced by his family and his earliest experiences. McKnight learned to sing at the age of four, seated on his mother's lap while she sang in the alto section of the church choir. McKnight's grandfather was the minister of music at the church, and had been a big band leader. Here in the Emanuel Temple in Buffalo, New York, McKnight absorbed the joyous spiritual melodies that are a trademark of the African-American church. That grounding in gospel harmonies remain a foundation in his work today.

Influenced by Gospel Music

While still a young boy, McKnight and his three older brothers formed a gospel quartet, called the McKnight Brothers. The boys modeled themselves after the great gospel groups, the Swan Silvertones and Mighty Clouds of Joy. McKnight looked up to his three older brothers, Claude, Freddie, and Michael, who were role models to

For the Record . . .

Born June 5, 1969 in Buffalo, NY; Known to friends as "B"; children: Brian Jr. and Niko. *Education*: Attended Oakwood College, Huntsville, AL, 1987-89.

Signed contract with Mercury Records, 1989; released debut album, *Brian McKnight*, 1992, *I Remember You*, 1995, and *Anytime*, 1997; performed on and produced many other albums with a wide variety of artists including Take 6, a duet with Vanessa Williams, "You Got To Go," from her album *Comfort Zone* (Wing, 1991); "Love Is," top five hit single from the *Beverly Hills 90210* soundtrack; *Christmas Interpretations*, Boyz II Men (Motown Records, 1993); *Q's Jook Joint*, Quincy Jones, (Qwest, 1995).

Addresses: *Record company*—Mercury Records/Polygram, World Wide Plaza, 825 8th Ave., New York, NY 10019. *Website*—www.mercuryrecords.com/artists/brian_mcknight/brian_mcknight.html.

him. Following their lead of listening to jazz outside of church, the youngest McKnight told David Ritz, in a online interview that "Church music thrilled me, but jazz stimulated my mind." His childhood was filled with a wide variety of music including The Platters, Nat King Cole, Woody Herman, and Gino Vannelli. Inspired by the Four Freshman and HiLos albums brought home by his older brothers, McKnight taught himself how to play piano by ear.

His other passion was and continues to be sports. He idolized the Philadelphia 76'ers and Dr. J, as well as the Dallas Cowboys and Tony Dorset. As a youngster he had two dreams—to be a professional ball player and a professional musician. When he was eight years old, his family moved from the snowy region of Buffalo, New York, to sunny Florida. Even before he was a teenager, he played jazz piano. He studied the masters, Oscar Peterson and Art Tatum, whom he considered "geniuses." Still the playing field of sports beckoned. During junior high he ran on the track team and was a starter on both the football and basketball teams. His passion for sports and music continued to compete, until he was won over by the music of Stevie Wonder. He felt that Wonder's singing is "almost athletic." Wonder's Original Musicquarium had a major impact on the direction of his life.

During high school, McKnight was into the trumpet and followed the work of Wynton Marsalis, who became another role model for the young artist. By age 17, he had formed a group called Spontaneous Inventions, named after Bobby McFerrin's album. Unbeknownst to his mother, he would paint a mustache on his face to play in clubs.

Soon afterwards in 1987, McKnight followed his older brother Claude to the Christian college, Oakwood, in Huntsville, Alabama. Huntsville was also Brian McKnight's first opportunity to work in a professional recording studio. It was at Sound Cell that he met Brandon Barnes, another gifted writer and musician who would later become Knight's partner and mentor. Barnes showed him the ropes, taught him how to make demo's, and how to cut tracks. Barnes co-wrote three songs on *Anytime,* including the title track. Two years later, in 1989, McKnight's college career came to a sudden end when he was expelled for having a woman in his room; the incident proved to be the catalyst which would jump start his music career.

Remaining in Huntsville, McKnight began working at the Sound Cell and would soon record an amazing 65 songs. Determined to succeed as a musician, he began sending demo tapes to record companies and in 1989 Mercury Records signed 19 year old McKnight to a recording contract.

Established As Romantic Balladeer

In 1992, McKnight's self-titled debut album was released on the Mercury label. Well received and a commercial success, the album included the hit single, "One Last Cry." *Entertainment Weekly* called it "black pop suitable for framing," with McKnight's lush tenor voice adding a heartfelt quality to the poetic love songs. During this time he also received accolades for his production work on Vanessa Williams' album, *Comfort Zone,* and duet with Williams,"You Got To Go." Another duet with Vanessa Williams, "Love Is," from the *Beverly Hills 90210* soundtrack helped establish McKnight as a serious balladeer.

With 1995's *I Remember You,* McKnight was further established in the pop/R&B arena. He continued crooning about love and desire, and showed he was unafraid to reveal the sensitiveside of the contemporary man. "McKnight revels in being a hopeless romantic who fervently believes in the healing power of love," stated *Rolling Stone.* But *People*'s Jeremy Helligar opined that "most of *I Remember You* is all too easy to forget." Whatever the opinion of this album, the jazz influence showed through the soulful sound as McKnight began melding jazz and pop sounds with his own heartfelt vocals. McKnight told Ritz that the feelings he writes about must move him first: "The sentiments must be real, the melodies must be magic."

Crooned Into Rap World

In addition to his many other projects, McKnight released his third album with Mercury, 1997's *Anytime*. The single, "You Should Be Mine (Don't Waste Your Time)," featured rapper Mase, while the album attempts to reach a younger audience with the rap beat. Giving up some of the control on the production end, he sought out producer Sean "Puffy" Combs for the single, "You Should Be Mine." Mary J. Bilge wrote the lyrics for "Hold Me," and both Diane Warren and Trackmasterz's songwriting talents were also enlisted for *Anytime*.

McKnight was determined to break new musical ground for himself and feels that *Anytime* presents a broader picture of his musical talents and avoids limiting him to being known as only a singer of romantic ballads. McKnight told Teddy D. in an online interview that part of the inspiration for the album came from his desire to do something "a little more dangerous. I wanted to show every side of my personality." But Helligar, writing for *Entertainment Weekly,* disagreed with McKnight's new approach, saying "hip-hopping onto the Sean 'Puffy' Combs bandwagon is not the way to go about it."

When asked by interviewer Teddy D. what he feels is the most significant accomplishment of his life, McKnight stated, "My kids without a doubt.... It's just amazing to see there is nothing else that I could do in life that would be as important or mean as much to me as them." During that same interview McKnight said between performing, producing, and songwriting he enjoys songwriting the best. The advice he gives to aspiring artists is to "never enter into anything half hearted." And just to show that he hasn't totally given up on his other dream to become a professional ball player, when asked what his long term goals are he replied, laughing, "To play in the NBA," then in a more serious tone added, "Maintain and continue to perfect my craft."

Selected discography

Brian McKnight, (Includes "One Last Cry"), Mercury Records, 1992.
I Remember You, Mercury Records, 1995.
Anytime, (Includes "You Should Be Mine" and "Hold Me"), Mercury Records, 1997.

With Others

(With Vanessa Williams) *Comfort Zone,* Wing, 1991.
Always Be Around, Capitol/EMI Records, 1991.
Beverly Hills 90210 (soundtrack) Giant/Warner Brothers, 1992.
(With Boyz II Men)*Christmas Interpretations,*, Motown Records, 1993.
(With The Boys Choir of Harlem) *Sound of Hope,* EastWest America, 1994.

Sources

Periodicals

Billboard, April 29, 1995, p. 44; June 10, 1995, p. 20-22; August 2, 1997, p. 27.
Entertainment Weekly, August 14, 1992, p. 62; October 10, 1997, p. 40.
Jet, September 16, 1991, p. 59.
People, August 21, 1995, p. 25.
Rolling Stone, September 21, 1995, p. 82.
The Source, November 1997, p. 174.
Vibe, September 1995, p. 168.

Online

www.cdnow.com/
www.cduniverse.com/
www.geocities.com/BourbonStreet/8764/bio.htm
www.mercuryrecords.com/artists/brian_mcknight/brian_mcknight.html
www.polygram-us.com/mondo/brian_mcknight/story.html
www.rbpage.com/backissue23.html

—Debra Reilly

Ron Miles

Trumpeter, bandleader, composer

Trumpeter, composer, and band leader Ron Miles is an accomplished master of improvisational and classical jazz. The structure of his musical pieces develops from intuitive, artful ensemble playing with solos imbedded into the composition. He combines the rhythms of hip-hop and the textures of alternative music with New Orleans polyphony and the techniques of jazz collage. Miles is a member of guitarist Bill Frisell's Quartet, an Assistant Professor of Music at Denver's Metropolitan State College, and the leader of his own group of Denver-based musicians, the Ron Miles Trio Plus. After the release of his fourth album *Woman's Day* in 1997, *Down Beat's* Dan Ouellette wrote, "(Miles) makes an art out of avoiding the pitfalls of modern jazz.... As a composer, Miles also scores top grades with his twelve originals." Miles told Michael Roberts of *Denver Westword,* "I think what I have to say hasn't really been done by other folks," and the compositions on his four releases verify the truthfulness of his statement.

Miles was raised in Indianapolis, IN, and moved with his family to Denver, CO, at the age of eleven because his family hoped the climate would soothe his asthma. His mother taught summer school in Denver and wanted to occupy Ron and his sister while she was in school. A summer band program had an opening, so Miles was taken to the band room and told to choose an instrument. "The trumpet looked nice and shiny," Miles told Roberts, "I didn't even know what it sounded like.... I was the last chair trumpet, but my folks would never let me quit. And I was sad—very, very sad—as a player."

His love of music and of the trumpet in particular wasn't sparked until he was in high school; before then, his perception of music stemmed from the cartoon versions of The Jackson Five and The Archies. He laughingly told Roberts, "If I didn't see it on stage with them, I didn't know what it was." Miles developed musical role models in high school; his earliest influences were Maynard Ferguson and Chuck Mangione. He searched for and read old *Down Beat* magazines from the 1950s and read about legends like Miles Davis and Clifford Brown. After listening to their music, he turned to Ornette Coleman, Lester Bowie, and musicians who would push the jazz envelope a little further. He taped all of his trumpet playing while in junior high, high school, and college—even when he was practicing. He would replay the tapes of his trumpet playing regularly, often noting what seemed to work in his music and what didn't work. He was constantly editing his own music, using the material that sounded right in future projects, and discarding the material that was less than ideal. Miles taped his first solo in junior high school, knowing he would want it for posterity.

Limits to Music Education

After high school Miles attended the University of Colorado in Boulder and the Manhattan School of Music in New York City. He felt his instructors at both schools didn't promote individuality and striving to create a uniquely personal sound. He told Roberts, "The teachers I had the hardest time with were the ones who said it has to be done a certain way, because it was a given that I would fight tooth and nail to do the exact opposite." When Miles became a music instructor at Metro State and the University of Colorado, his approach was to give his students an anchor in the basic elements of music, present them with an array of options, and then to stand back and watch what they develop on their own. Miles told *Down Beat's* Linda Gruno, "You don't need school, but the advantage of it is having a community of your peers and hopefully some instructors who can provide some clues.... Schools can help, but they won't make a great player." Miles pointed out to Gruno that musicians have varied talents and leanings, and that some teachers can only teach one way—so if the student differs from the teachers in significant respects, then the student can't learn much from the teacher.

As a teacher, Miles places an emphasis on the contributions that black Americans made to jazz music as well

For the Record . . .

Born in 1964; raised in Indianapolis, IN; married to flutist Kari Miles of the Colorado Evergreen Chamber Orchestra; moved to Denver, CO, in 1975 and took up the trumpet that year; *Education:* University of Colorado in Boulder 1982-84, Manhattan School of Music in New York City in 1985;

Became a music instructor at Metropolitan State College and the University of Colorado; released *Distance For Safety* on Prolific Records in 1986; released *Witness* on Capri Records in 1990; joined the Bill Frisell Quartet in 1995; leader of his own group of Denver-based musicians, the Ron Miles Trio Plus; released *My Cruel Heart* on Gramavision in 1996; released *Woman's Day* in 1997, featuring bassist Artie Moore, drummer Rudy Royston, guitarist Bill Frisell, guitarist Todd Ayers, bass clarinetist Mark Harris, pianist Eric Gunnison, and bassist Kent McLagen.

Address: *Record company*—Gramavision Records/ Rykodisc, Shetland Park, 27 Congress Street, Salem, MA 01970; phone (508) 744-7678, fax (508) 741-4506.

as their starring role in creating, presenting, and developing jazz. He told David Kirby of the Colorado Daily, "Jazz education has really become Stan Kenton.... Guys like Duke Ellington and Fletcher Henderson become fringe elements. I think part of it is pure racism." Although Miles appreciates and draws from the jazz of the early 1960s, his heart and soul is with improvisational jazz, especially with artists like Charlie Parker, John Coltrane, and Albert Ayler. On his second release, *Witness,* Miles included the Charles Mingus classic "Pithecanthropus Erectus" and Billy Strayhorn's "A Flower is a Lovesome Thing," and Thelonius Monk's "Ugly Beauty." Other musical influences on the pop end of the spectrum include Kurt Cobain from the alternative/ grunge band Nirvana, Prince, Public Enemy, James Brown, U2, and Living Colour. Olu Dara, Sonny Rollins, John Lennon and Paul McCartney were also listed by Miles as musical influences, underscoring his broad range of interest. Kirby wrote, "This is Miles' game, the turf he's staked out for himself: his own pieces, stretching between major key folk balladry and cerebral compositional exercise, and some overlooked covers by masters gone by."

Miles released *Distance For Safety* on Prolific Records in 1986, followed by *Witness* on Capri Records in 1990. He joined the Bill Frisell Quartet in 1995, and released *My Cruel Heart* on Gramavision in 1996. All of the compositions on *My Cruel Heart* were original, and Miles featured the music of his wife on the release, flutist Kari Miles of the Colorado Evergreen Chamber Orchestra. Miles doesn't hesitate to infuse his music with political themes or current events; "Howard Beach" on *My Cruel Heart* was a personal comment on the attack of three black men by a group of white teenagers in the Howard Beach area of Queens, NY, "Erase Yourself" was a song of empathy for the wife of mayor Marion Barry after his infamous crime in Washington D.C., and "Say It Loud" pays homage to funk and soul music's James Brown.

Woman's Day was released in 1997, featuring all original compositions and bassist Artie Moore, drummer Rudy Royston, guitarist Bill Frisell, guitarist Todd Ayers, bass clarinetist Mark Harris, pianist Eric Gunnison, and bassist Kent McLagen. The tone of *Woman's Day* ranges from chamber music contours to funk and churning thrash music. *Down Beat*'s Ouellette wrote of *Woman's Day,* "[Miles has] obviously been picking up pointers on how to stretch the jazz boundaries," which is exactly what Miles set out to do when he reluctantly chose the trumpet as his instrument for summer band practice back in 1975.

Selected discography

Distance For Safety, Prolific Records, 1986.
Witness, Capri Records, 1990.
My Cruel Heart, Gramavision, 1996.
Woman's Day, Gramavision, 1997.

Sources

Colorado Daily, July 1990.
Denver Post, December 1990,
Denver Westword, January 1991.
Down Beat, June 1991; July 1997.

—*B. Kim Taylor*

Ronnie Montrose

Guitarist

Ronnie Montrose never considered himself a very apt businessman. From the moment he started playing guitar at the age of 17, he always put his music first and the business somewhere at the end. As a result, his career ranged from guitar contributions for other artists to bandleader of a heavy metal band to experimental instrumental albums and a soundtrack for a video game. He became recognized for his talent and style by a sort of underground following, yet remained virtually unknown in the mainstream commercial realm.

Ronnie Montrose was born in San Francisco, California, in 1947. His family moved to Denver, Colorado, when Ronnie was just two years old. Although his father played drums for jazz bands in college, Ronnie Montrose didn't play more than his stereo until he was 17 years old. From the first moment he held a guitar in his hands, his fate was sealed. He fell in love with the feel and sound of the instrument. He taught himself to play on a guitar he had borrowed from a friend. Then, when he felt ready, he joined his first band: the Grim Reapers.

In the early years of playing, Montrose was influenced by other guitarists, such as Eric Clapton, Johnny Smith, Jeff Beck, Jimmy Page, and Jimmy Hendrix. Spurred by the "San Francisco sound" that was gaining popularity all over the country, Montrose decided to return to the city of his birth in 1968. He took jobs doing minor repair and carpentry work during the day and played his guitar at night.

In 1970, Montrose joined the San Francisco band Sawbuck. On an office remodeling job, he met promoter Bill Graham, who introduced him to his partner, producer David Rubinson. Graham and Rubinson owned a small record label called Fillmore Records, and signed a recording contract with Sawbuck. Rubinson was especially impressed by Montrose_s talent and ambition. He set the guitarist up for session work with the Pointer Sisters and keyboardist Herbie Hancock before he arranged for Montrose's big break.

In 1971, Van Morrison had moved to San Francisco. Rubinson heard that he was putting together a new band and arranged for Montrose to audition. He landed the job and played mostly acoustic guitar on Van Morrison's two subsequent albums, *Tupelo Honey* and *St. Dominic's Preview.* When Van Morrison moved on to another band after the second record, Montrose played a three-month tour as the guitarist for Boz Scaggs.

Montrose's career took a major turn in 1972 when he joined the Edgar Winter Group. He played on the album *They Only Come Out at Night*, released on Epic Records, and the tour that followed. "Playing with Edgar was an extreme learning experience because he truly lives and breathes music," Montrose told Jon Sievert in *Guitar Player.*

Launched His Own Band

Montrose's work with Edgar Winter gave him the freedom to express himself both musically and on stage. Soon, Montrose had gained some notoriety for being a wild rock guitarist. In the summer of 1973, he decided it was time for him to move on to his own career as a bandleader and left Edgar Winter. He recruited a young, unknown singer named Sammy Hagar, along with drummer Denny Carmassi and bassist Bill Church. The foursome formed the band Montrose and signed a record deal with Warner Bros.

Before the end of the year, the band released *Montrose*, which would become Ronnie Montrose's most successful record. The album included long-lasting tracks, such as "Rock Candy" and "Bad Motor Scooter," which would still receive sporadic airplay on radio stations decades later.

In 1974, Montrose released *Paper Money*, which boosted the band's popularity even higher. Barry Taylor wrote in *Billboard*, "As a high-energy quartet, Montrose

For the Record . . .

Born in San Francisco, CA, c. 1947; married Michele Graybeal, November 8, 1997.

Began playing guitar in the San Francisco band Sawbuck, 1970; recorded with Van Morrison, 1971-72; member, Edgar Winter Group, 1972-73; formed band, Montrose, and released self-titled debut album on Warner Bros., 1973; recorded debut solo record, *Open Fire*, 1978; formed Gamma, 1979; released solo LP *Territory* on Enigma, 1986; with Montrose band, released *Mean* on Enigma, 1987; released three solo albums on various labels, 1988-94; released first video game soundtrack, *Mr. Bones*, Sega Music Group, 1996.

succeeded where others have failed due to the accessibility of their material and their razor-sharp arrangements." A few months after their second release, Ronnie Montrose fired singer Sammy Hagar, saying he was "too limited." Hagar went on to his own successful solo career, and sang with the rock band Van Halen for 11 years. "We have a long-standing joke now, because I did fire him from the Montrose band for some of the same reasons that I left the Edgar Winter Group," Montrose told John "Wedge" Wardlaw. "He was on to his own thing."

Vocalist Bob James replaced Hagar, and Montrose released two more albums—*Warner Bros. Presents Montrose* and *Jump On It.* The band had also added keyboardist Jim Alcivar to the line-up. However, the latter two albums never matched the success of the first two. *Rolling Stone* reviewer Andy McKaie described *Warner Bros. Presents Montrose* as "slick and spiritless" and "utterly pedestrian." He wrote, "For a band that started with so much promise, this is a sad situation."

Attempted Second Hard-Rock Project

Ronnie Montrose dissolved the Montrose band in 1976 and began experimenting with his own music. In 1978, he emerged with his first solo album, *Open Fire*, produced by Edgar Winter. The album included a reworking of Gene Pitney's "Town Without Pity," which would later change the guitarist's direction once again. According to Jon Sievert in *Guitar Player*, "The all-instrumental album disappointed, even angered, hardcore Montrose metal fans."

In response to criticism about *Open Fire*'s lack of marketability, Montrose formed another hard rock band called Gamma in the fall of 1979. This time, he recruited singer Davey Pattison, bassist Alan Fitzgerald, drummer Skip Gillette, and keyboardist Jim Alcivar. The group signed a record contract with Elektra records. They released three albums—*Gamma 1, Gamma 2,* and *Gamma 3*—over the next three years.

By 1981, Gamma had replaced Jim Alcivar with Mitchell Froom on keyboards. At the Bay Area Music Awards, Montrose and Froom played a critically acclaimed version of "Town Without Pity." The performance laid the groundwork for Montrose's next project as a duo with Froom. Gamma disbanded the following year, when Montrose felt the group was falling into the same rut as the Montrose band had.

Experimented with New Genres

In 1983, Montrose and Froom played a club tour showcasing their new music, an all-instrumental hard rock style combined with jazz and progressive rock. He also performed a piece written for electric guitar and orchestra with the Berkeley Symphony. The orchestra had previously performed one of Ronnie Montrose's own songs called "My Little Mystery." During the same year, he contributed to Paul Kantner's solo album *Planet Earth Rock & Roll Orchestra.* Montrose continued to combine different styles of music on his next solo album *Territory*, released in 1986. One reviewer wrote in *Down Beat*, "Ronnie Montrose offers a varied menu on *Territory.* From pop to disco to grinding rock and fusion to New Age, it's an ambitious undertaking."

A year later, Ronnie Montrose resurrected the Montrose band name with singer Johnny Edwards, bassist Glenn Letsch, and drummer James Kottak. The new group only released one album on Enigma Records called *Mean.* By 1988, Ronnie Montrose had returned to his solo career with the album *The Speed of Sound.* "This all-instrumental effort tends to focus more on his crunching, power side coupled with ethereal lyricism," wrote Jon Sievert in *Guitar Player.*

Two years later, Montrose rejoined with singer Davey Pattison for a few songs on his *The Diva Station* album. Then after another two-year break, Montrose released *Mutatis Mutandis* on I.R.S. Records. "Ronnie Montrose is back as the thinking blue-collar man's guitar hero," Robin Tolleson wrote in his *Down Beat* review, "playing with authority and—on tracks like "Heavy Agenda" and "Velox"—with a lot of soul." During the same year, Montrose contributed to guitarist Marc Bonilla's album *EE Ticket.*

In 1994, Montrose released *Music From Here* on Fearless Urge Records. The album featured his future wife, Michele Graybeal, on drums and percussion. He also continued to play on recordings for other artists. In 1995, he performed on four songs for Anti-M's *Positively Negative* album.

Grooved to High-Tech Gaming

The following year, Montrose entered another world of music endeavors with a soundtrack for the Sega Genesis video game *Mr. Bones*. The game featured a wandering blues guitarist, and Montrose contributed all of the background music for the game. "It's the first time a soundtrack CD is selling one-for-one with the game itself," Montrose told Gregory Isola in *Guitar Player*. "Last summer was the first in years that I didn_t have to spend pounding the pavement and playing clubs to pay the rent."

After recording *Mr. Bones*, Montrose moved to Southern California. His fiancee, Michele Graybeal (whom he married in November of 1997), had a job working for Warner Bros. Animation, and Montrose decided it was time for a change of location. In early 1997, Montrose regrouped with the original members of the Montrose band—Sammy Hagar, Denny Carmassi, and Bill Church—for the song "Leaving the Warmth of the Womb" on Hagar's *Marching to Mars* album.

Montrose recalled his experience with his former bandmates in an interview with John "Wedge" Wardlaw. "It was only after getting together with the four of us in the studio, hanging out and jamming with each other for the first time in about 20 years, that I rediscovered and realized how awesome a trio that was," said Montrose.

"Obviously, if I had cared about making a tremendous amount of money, I would have stuck with the first Montrose album," Montrose told Jon Sievert in *Guitar Player*. After decades of staying true to his musical muse, Montrose planned to spend the rest of his career pursuing work on soundtracks, contributing to the work of other artists, and following his own solo style of music in whatever direction it would take him.

Selected discography

Open Fire, Warner Bros., 1978.
Territory, Enigma, 1986.
The Speed of Sound, Enigma, 1988.
The Diva Station, Enigma, 1990.
Mutatis Mutandis, I.R.S., 1992.
Music From Here, Fearless Urge, 1994.
Mr. Bones, Sega Music Group, 1996.

With Van Morrison

Tupelo Honey, Warner Bros., 1971.
St. Dominic's Preview, Warner Bros., 1972.

With the Edgar Winter Group

They Only Come Out at Night (includes "Free Ride"), Epic, 1972.

With Montrose

Montrose (includes "Rock Candy" and "Bad Motor Scooter"), Warner Bros., 1973.
Paper Money, Warner Bros., 1974.
Warner Bros. Presents Montrose, Warner Bros., 1975.
Jump on It, Warner Bros., 1976.
Mean, Engima, 1987.

With Gamma

Gamma 1, Elektra, 1980.
Gamma 2, Elektra, 1981.
Gamma 3, Elektra, 1982.

Sources

Periodicals

Billboard, March 23, 1974; June 29, 1974; November 15, 1975; January 15, 1977.
Down Beat, October 1986, February 1992, April 1992.
Guitar Player, July 1982, October 1983, June 1988, April 1997.
High Fidelity, September 1987, October 1988.
People, May 14, 1990.
Rolling Stone, December 18, 1975; March 11, 1976; December 16,
Variety, June 19, 1974; October 14, 1975; November 24, 1976;March 22, 1978; December 19, 1979.

Online

http://www.west.net/~wedge/rminterview.html, (1997)

—Sonya Shelton

Peter Murphy

Singer, song writer

Credited with spearheading and personifying the gothic rock movement, the godfather of the genre, Peter Murphy, was responsible for popularizing the "goth" look with his sharp and angular features, reminiscent of a dark and brooding vampire. His twisted lyrical musings on misanthropy, mythology, and the underworld were to inspire and influence generations of black clad mascara wearers to come. Murphy's presence was such a powerful and all consuming force that he immediately became identified as the archetype of the goth movement. This misguided typecasting of his image and music has haunted Murphy from his earliest days in the genre defining band Bauhaus and throughout his solo career.

Murphy was born outside of the English midlands city of Northampton on July 11, 1957. He was the youngest of nine children born to working class and staunchly Catholic parents. His father was a chef and a furnace worker, while his mother was a homemaker. Murphy was exposed to music at a very early age as he told *Rolling Stone*'s Moira Mc Cormick. His mother sang to him quite a bit as a small child. "They [his mother's songs] were great gigs. She hummed melodies to me which sounded quite morose and lullaby-like. I tend to make my own music with mood and atmosphere; I can see a connection." Although Murphy was an artistically inclined teenager, he turned down the opportunity to go to art college because he claimed he was anti-social. Instead, he opted to work as a printer's assistant and chose to pursue singing, writing and painting in his free time.

Around 1979, an old school friend of Murphy's, guitarist and fellow artist Daniel Ash, got in touch with him and asked him if he would like to join his new band, Bauhaus. The band, whose name was taken from the famous early 20th century German art school, was comprised of Murphy on vocals, Ash on guitar, David J. on bass, and his brother Kevin Haskins on drums. Their first release, the classic "Bela Lugosi's Dead," was released in 1979 on the independent Small Wonder label. With a hypnotically driving bass line and Murphy's seductively sombre vocalization, the single instantly won them a rabidly loyal cult following, particularly enhanced when the single became a surprise dance club hit. The success of the single highlighted the schism in popular opinion between the band's loyal fans and the popular press in Britain, which dogged the band and its many spin-offs from then on. Fans across the globe loved Bauhaus, while critics, most notably the ever fickle British press, loathed them.

Undeterred, Bauhaus pressed on and released their first album, *In the Flat Field,* on 4AD in 1980. With *In the Flat Field,* Bauhaus launched a rather lucrative career of putting the undead and its associated imagery to music. Part glam rock and part punk, Bauhaus was wholly its own creation and one that spawned legions of imitators and even some innovators. Promotional clips and live concert dates showcased Murphy's love of theatrics.

Bauhaus signed to Beggars Banquet after the release of *In the Flat Field.* By then, they had amassed a hardcore following that delighted in dressing as dark and stately as their idols. 1981 marked the release of *Mask,* the first Bauhaus album for their new record company. *Mask,* like its predecessor, also featured oddly compelling and hypnotic rhythms courtesy of J. and Haskins. Murphy's now signature morosely misanthropic and melancholy word play was present as well. A live album, *Press the Eject and Give Me the Tape* was released the following year as well as Bauhaus' third studio album, *Sky's Gone Out.*

By the time Bauhaus was ready to commence work on their fourth studio album, tensions, and inter-band stress were both on the rise. Neither Ash nor Jay was too thrilled with the idea that, increasingly, the image of the band was becoming rather inextricably tied to that of Murphy and vice versa. Also, since both Jay and Ash either wrote or co-wrote all of the band's songs, they felt that they should get their share of the limelight for their efforts. The feelings of Jay and Ash combined with

For the Record . . .

Born July 11, 1957, in Northamptonshire, England; married Beyhan Foulkes, c.1987; children: one son, one daughter.

Joined Bauhaus c. 1978; signed to Small Wonder and released "Bela Lugosi's Dead," 1979; signed to 4AD and released *In the Flat Field*, 1980; signed to Beggars Banquet and released *Mask*, 1981; *Sky's Gone Out*, 1982; *Press the Eject and Give Me the Tape*, 1982; *Burning From the Inside*, 1983; *The Singles 1981-1983*, 1983; formed Dali's Car and released *Waking Hour*, 1984; *1979-1983*, 1985; disbanded Dali's Car and pursued a solo career; released *Should the World Fail to Fall Apart*, 1986; *Love Hysteria*, 1988; *Swing the Heartache*, 1989; *Deep*, 1990; *Holy Smoke*, 1992; *Rest in Peace*, 1992; *Cascade*, 1995.

Addresses: *Record company*—Beggars Banquet, 274 Madison Avenue, Ste. 804, New York, NY 10016.

Murphy's rather sudden illness at the start of the sessions for their last studio album, lead to the early demise of Bauhaus.

Bauhaus Disbanded

When Murphy was well enough to return to the studio he was shocked and a bit hurt to find out that the band had proceeded to record most of the tracks for the album without him. Ash, Jay and Haskins had laid down the music for Bauhaus' 1983 release *Burning From the Inside* and had left just a few songs for Murphy to sing. There were a number of tracks on *Burning From the Inside* that either Ash or Jay sang lead vocals on for the first time. These collaborations between Ash, Haskins, and Jay would eventually lead to the formation of Love and Rockets a few years later.

In 1983 after touring in support of *Burning From the Inside*, Bauhaus disbanded just as they were on the brink of national success in their native England. Also in 1983, Bauhaus released *The Singles 1981-1983*. Posthumously in 1985, Beggars Banquet released the Bauhaus retrospective *1979-1983* and in 1989 released *Swing the Heartache, the BBC Sessions*. Three years after this, Nemo released a recording of the last Bauhaus concert entitled *Rest in Peace*.

Dali's Car

After the demise of Bauhaus, Murphy began collaborations with Mick Karn, who had previously worked as a multi-instrumentalist for the band Japan. Together they formed Dali's Car. The duo released one album in 1984 entitled *Waking Hour* before they disbanded. After Dali's Car broke up, Murphy began to seriously study the fundamentals of dance with his soon to be wife, Beyhan Foulkes, who was a professional choreographer.

Murphy was forced, out of the need to survive, to form another band. He was very reluctant to do this because of the ever looming shadow of Bauhaus. Eventually, in 1986, he hooked up with a number of studio musicians who were later to be known as the Hundred Men and recorded his debut solo record *Should the World Fail to Fall Apart*. Hardcore Murphy and Bauhaus fans snatched the new album up but it failed to storm up the charts or to excite the general public. He released his second solo album two years later. *Love Hysteria* faired a little better than its predecessor in terms of sales due in part to its release in America.

Breakthrough Album

Deep, Murphy's third solo release came out in 1990. It was the breakthrough album he had been hoping. *Deep* sold 350,000 copies in America alone and contained the number one modern rock song of 1990, "Cuts You Up." The surprising success of "Cuts You Up" propelled the sales of the nearly gold album to the number 41 spot on *Billboard*'s Top 100 Albums chart. Buoyed by the success of *Deep*, Murphy sought to concentrate his efforts on making it big in America, by touring extensively there.

Two years later saw the release of *Holy Smoke*, which failed to storm the charts as *Deep* had done. A move to Turkey and time spent in his new home with his wife and children occupied most of Murphy's time for the next three years. In 1995, he released *Cascade*. The complacency of the album helped it to avoid charting in either the United Kingdom or America.

Murphy continued to focus on his live performances as he informed *B-Side*'s Sandra Garcia, "you don't really get that much contact with the fans...but I keep myself in complete focus on the creativity end, of making the show happen and being as vital each night as I was last night. It's the idea of keeping that alive. I think it's a celebration thing. If I'm transported, then I want them to be a part of what's happening on stage, and that's me."

Selected discography

Should the World Fail to Fall Apart, Beggars Banquet, 1986.
Love Hysteria, Beggars Banquet, 1988.
Deep (includes "Cuts You Up"), Beggars Banquet, 1990.
Holy Smoke, Beggars Banquet, 1992.
Cascade, Beggars Banquet, 1995.

With Bauhaus

"Bela Lugosi's Dead," Small Wonder, 1979.
In the Flat Field, 4AD, 1980.
Mask, Beggars Banquet, 1981.
Sky's Gone Out, Beggars Banquet, 1982.
Press the Eject and Give Me the Tape, Beggars Banquet, 1982.
Burning From the Inside, Beggars Banquet, 1983.
The Singles 1981-1983, Beggars Banquet, 1983.
1979-1983, Beggars Banquet, 1985.
Swing the Heartache, Beggars Banquet, 1989.
Rest in Peace, Nemo, 1992.

With Dali's Car

Waking Hour, Beggars Banquet, 1984.

Sources

Books

Shirley, Ian, *Dark Entries: Bauhaus and Beyond*, SAF, 1994.

Periodicals

Rolling Stone, May 3, 1990.

On-line

"Peter Murphy," http://itis.com/murphy/interviews/bside.html (February 11, 1998).
"Peter Murphy," http://members.aol.com/burning ski/peter1.htm (March 3, 1998).

—Mary Alice Adams

Our Lady Peace

Alternative band

Courtesy of Ken Settle

Toronto based quartet Our Lady Peace has estab lished itself as one of Canada's most successful alternative rock bands. Indeed, the band's heavy, melodic sound coupled with singer Raine Maida's emotional lyrics have earned Our Lady Peace something very foreign to most Canadian artists-a sizeable American audience. Although touring with rock super stars Jimmy Page and Robert Plant, Van Halen, and the Rolling Stones ensured the band massive U.S. exposure, the key to their state-side success, says Maida, is what the did with that exposure. "They [fans] don't care that we're from Canada," remarked Maida in *Jam! Music.* "They just care that they're connecting with the music and lyrics.

Our Lady Peace had humble beginnings. The first two members, Maida and guitarist Mike Turner, met while studying at the University of Toronto in 1992, and soon recruited Chris Eacrett on bass, and drummer Jeremy Taggart. Duncan Coutts joined band in October 1995, replacing Eacrett on bass. The quartet took its name from Mark Van Doren's poem called "Our Lady Peace." The band sent unsolicited demos to a number of large labels, and were shocked and amazed when Sony Music Canada gave them not only a contract, but complete creative control. They signed with Sony Music Canada after only 14 months together, seven shows under their belts, only four songs produced, and no touring experience. Maida told Mike Ross of *Express Writer,* "We were a bunch of naïve kids."

Debut Bearer of Good News

In March of 1994, Our Lady Peace released its debut album, *Naveed,* on Sony Canada; it debuted in the United States on Relativity Records one year later. According to *Billboard* the album means "bearer of good news," and reflects a title of Middle Eastern influence. In its review of *Naveed, Entertainment Weekly* noted the "anguished vocals a la Pearl Jam, and churning guitars by way of Stone Temple Pilots ," and called it an album that definitely would attract "grunge addicts." A *New York Times* critic called Our Lady Peace's music "passionate, hones, empathetic."

The single, "Starseed," brought the band it's first taste of major success, reaching th Top Ten in Canada as well as the Top 40 in the United States. Although the single initially received limited radio play in Canada, the video received extensive exposure on Canada's *MuchMusic* video channel. "Starseed" also caught the attention of rock god Robert Plant's ear during radio play in New York during 1995. Plant contacted Our Lady Peace's management and before they knew it, the band was

For the Record . . .

Members include **Duncan Coutts,** bass/keyboards (joined band October 1995)/ **Chris Eacrett,** bass (left band October 1995); **Raine Maida,** vocals; **Jeremy Taggart,** drums; **Mike Turner,** (born in England), guitar.

Toronto based band began in 1993 with vocalist, Maida, and guitarist Turner; recruited bassist, Chris Eacrett and drummer, Jeremy Taggart; within one year had three songs recorded on demo; signed with Sony Canada, 1994; released debut album *Naveed,* in Canada, 1994 under Sony Canada; on Relativity label March 1995 in U.S.; ; toured extensively in the U.S. and Canada with Robert Plant and Jimmy Page, Van Halen, and Blind Melon; released *Clumsy,* 1997 on Columbia label; debuted at number one on the Canadian SoundScan chart; within three weeks hit platinum in Canada and double-platinum soon after.

Awards: Favorite Group, 1997 Canadian *MuchMusic* video awards.

Addresses: *Record company*—Columbia Records, 550 Madison Ave., New York, NY 10022-3211. Sony Music Canada, 1121 Leslie St., North York, Ontario M3C 2J9, Canada. *Website*—www.ourladypeace.com.

opening for Jimmy Page and Robert Plant in Chicago. Plant told the band how much he "loved" the record, and he felt they emitted the most "conviction" he had noticed in a band in a number of years. In addition to opening for Page and Plant, the band has toured extensively in the United States and Canada with other major acts. In 1995 and 1996 they opened for Van Halen and Alanis Morissette in Edmonton, and, in November of 1997, they opened for the Rolling Stones in Quebec City. Since their beginning, the band has performed over 400 live shows, for over a half million people.

Clumsy's Sales Hardly Ungainly

In early 1997, Our Lady Peace signed to Columbia Records and released their second album, *Clumsy.* Although one reviewer, Jan Stevenson of the *Toronto Sun,* found *Clumsy* a bit lacking in "passion and originality, making this sophomore effort less powerful than their winning debut," the band's fans apparently felt differently. The album debuted at number one on the Canadian pop chart, and within three weeks of release sold over 100,000 units. *Clumsy* was recorded at Arnyard Studios in Toronto by Arnold Lanni, who produced their debut album, as well. The album's first single, "Superman's Dead," gained the band exposure on MTV. Maida provided some insight into the lyrics of "Superman's Dead" in an interview with Karen Bliss of *Jam! Music.* He discussed the difficulties kids have growing up in today's world, and about how strong the messages are from the media. He compared the old *Superman* shows and to today's *Beavis and Butt-Head.* "
He [Superman] was a real hero but I think Beavis and Butt-Head wins today."

One of Maida's biggest heroes in singer, Sinead O'Connor. Maida admires her ability to pour herself out to audiences, and told Kerry Gold of the *Vancouver Sun* that, "she [O'Connor], for me, is the ultimate." Other inspirations for Maida include Otis Redding, U2, Janis Joplin, and Stevie Wonder. In an interview with *Alternative Rock World* online, the other members claimed to be "music junkies," naming Radiohead, Portishead, U2, the Beatles, and Elton John as some of their musical influences.

Change of Venue Required Adaptation

After several years of touring as a support band for better known bands, Our Lady Peace began its first headlining tour in 1998. This tour took them out of the small intimate clubs and on to the stages of large arenas. While the increased size of the venues they were now playing called for many technical adjustments, it also created certain emotional problems, such as the band's ability to remain connect with the audience. In an attempt to compensate for the size and lack of intimacy of large arenas, Our Lady Peace shot a series of short films to accompany their live concerts, hoping to reach each member of their audiences, emotionally, regardless of one's proximity to the stage.

With two hit albums and over 400 live performances in the United States and Canada, it looks like Our Lady Peace has two countries conquered, with thousands of fans on both sides of the border. The band hopes to have staying power, too, using their arena tours as an opportunity to secure their relationship with fans. It appears their fears of being just another "disposable" band or being a one-hit wonder are groundless. As Lisa Wilton of the *Calgary Sun* said, "it was only a matter of time before Our Lady Peace attempts to take on the world." To which Maida replied, "Absolutely."

Selected discography

Naveed, (included "Starseed"), Sony Canada, 1994; Relativity, 1995
Clumsy, (includes "Superman's Dead"), Columbia, 1997.

Sources

Periodical

Billboard, February 25, 1995, p. 18.
.*Calgary Sun,* August 26, 1997; January 8, 1998.
CNN Interactive, November 19, 1997.
Entertainment Weekly, March 312, 1995, p. 62.
Express Writer, January 21, 1997; August 29, 1997; January 18, 1998.
Free Press (Detroit), February 9, 1998.
Jam! Music, November 20, 1997.
Ottawa Sun, January 17, 1998.
Pollstar, October 13, 1997.
Scrawl Magazine, Spring 1998.
Sound Check, November/December 1997.
Toronto Sun, May 20, 1995; January, 19, 1997; January 21, 1997; January 8, 1998.
Vancouver Sun, January 22, 1998.

Online

www.allmusic.com/
www.altrockworld.com/
www.ourladypeace.com/

Additional information was provided by Columbia Records' publicity, Fran DeFeo, New York, NY.

—*Debra Reilly*

Portishead

Trip-hop band

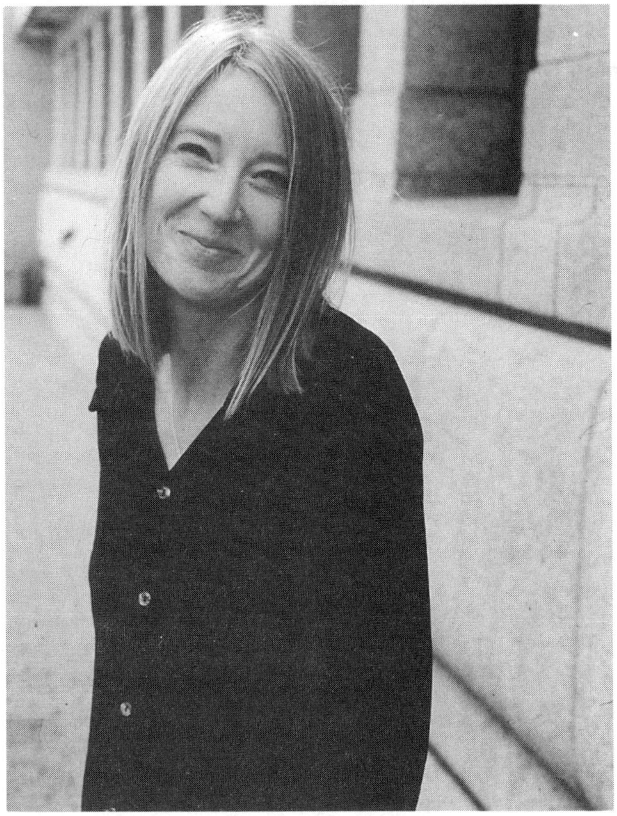
Corbis

The Bristol band Portishead has been credited with launching an entirely new genre in alternative music—"trip-hop," a dense, narcotic sound that combines hip-hop, reggae-esque dub, and acid jazz with, in Portishead's case, a swank, James Bond-style cinematic mood. With their stellar 1994 debut, *Dummy,* the reclusive sound engineer and depths-of-gloom-summoning vocalist that make up the nucleus of Portishead, Geoff Barrow and Beth Gibbons, produced "an atmosphere of voodoo noir," wrote the *Village Voice*'s Erik Davis. A British disc jockey told *Billboard* that Portishead is best categorized as "present-day urban blues." The band has usually inspired laudatory press of the superlative nature. Jason Fine, summing up the Portishead vibe for *Guitar Player,* declared that the duo, with the help of some outstanding additional studio talent, "combines densely layered acoustic and electric instrumentation, soulful crooning, and the studio techniques of hip hop into one of the most richly inventive sounds in modern pop."

Portishead was a band that came together under rather unusual circumstances. Beth Gibbons and Geoff Barrow met in a program sponsored by the local unemployment office in Bristol. The program offered re-training for those between jobs or careers, and Gibbons and Barrow wound up in the "musician" classes. Gibbons was from the English town of Devon, where she had once worked at a clock-making company before moving to London.

There she sang in a number of bands over the years, including one in which she performed Janis Joplin songs, and wound up in Bristol in the early 1990s. Despite the uprootings, Gibbons's life still was a relatively uneventful one, but one from which some rather bleak and stirring lyrics would later arise. She admits to being baffled about the source of such misery, but did concede that there was a bit of family dissonance in her youth—"I have divorced parents, which didn't help, but I don't like it when I blame things on my parents," Gibbons told *Rolling Stone*'s Al Weisel.

Barrow was a native of a town not far from Bristol called Portishead. "It looks really pretty and twee, but it's actually quite horrible," Barrow told Weisel. He was a studio whiz at an early age, and worked on Neneh Cherry's *Homebrew* LP while still a teenager. Soul music, hip-hop, and James Bond movie soundtracks were his favorites. When he and Gibbons met, they shared little except their enrollment in the training program. They did find, however, that they both had a strange love for disquieting, under-the-skin strains of music. "I like emotionally disturbing songs," Barrow told Weisel in *Rolling Stone,* and loved one song Gibbons made him listen to that was "nasty and weird."

For the Record . . .

Members include **Geoff Barrow** (born c. 1972), keyboards; and **Beth Gibbons** (born c. 1965), vocals; **Adrian Utley** (born c. 1958), guitar.

Band formed, c. 1991, in Bristol, England; released its first album *Dummy*, on London Record's Go! Beat label, 1994; *Portishead,* 1997.

Awards: Mercury Music Prize, 1995, for *Dummy*.

Addresses: *Record company*—London Records, 825 Eighth Ave., 26th Floor, New York, NY 10019.

Barrow, who found work as a tape operator at a Bristol recording studio, eventually came into contact with two others who would become supporting, yet elemental, members of Portishead; sound engineer Dave McDonald, and a guitarist named Adrian Utley. The veteran musician had played in a number of blues bands as well as with famed electronic virtuoso Jeff Beck. When the quartet began working in the Coach House studio where Barrow was employed, it was a collaborative effort that sometimes utilized odd production techniques. For instance, Barrow would record outtakes from old films and Seventies classics from groups like War and Weather Report, and sample them into a new song. Utley's Fender Rhodes was sometimes recorded onto vinyl, or recorded into a dictaphone, then also sampled into a final mix. They also made heavy use of the Theremin, the world's first electronic instrument, which produces a sound best known for its use in the Beach Boys hit "Good Vibrations"; it was also used in many sci-fi and horror movies of the 1950s and `60s.

The result of all this electronic experimentation and production-stage tweaking was *Dummy,* released in England in August of 1994 to critical acclaim. Though its songs were anything but radio-friendly, word-of-mouth about the band and its fresh, unusual sound soon spread to Europe, then North America. *Dummy* debuted in American record stores two months later in October. Reviews were laudatory, despite the rather depressing vibe of the whole album best exemplified by its American single, "Sour Times (Nobody Loves Me)," which charted well and received much alternative radio air play. *Rolling Stone* described *Dummy* as "Gothic hip-hop," a sound that "come across both sad and sexy." The *Village Voice*'s Davis likened it to "an invitation to a seance," and noted that Gibbons and her eerie vocal style—almost always the focal point of any review—"seems to teeter at the edge of some narcoleptic void." A later *Village Voice* assessment of Portishead's sonic allure, written by Sarah Powell, remarked, "there's ... something old and English and fairytale-like about Gibbons's voice."

Soon Portishead were being asked to translate their unique sound into the work of other musical acts through studio remixes. During 1995 and 1996 they revamped singles for bands that included Primal Scream and Depeche Mode. They also used the windfall from *Dummy* to fund the construction of their own studio, and went to work to record a follow-up. The process was more arduous than expected, and the band admitted to being intimidated by their unexpected success from *Dummy.* "We kind of got lost for about a year," Utley told Nina Pearlman for *Rocket.* "A lot of the sounds that we made on *Dummy,* we [later] heard from other bands and on adverts on television," Utley said. "It kind of made us unhappy with our own sound for awhile." Tensions ran so high that at one point they almost broke up after it became impossible to actually finish a track at all, a process of creative chaos that went on for almost a year.

In the end, Portishead's second effort, *Portishead,* took two years from start to finish, and was released in late 1997. It offered more desolate songs, and again, Gibbons's trademark bleak and detached vocals—but once more Barrow, Gibbons, Utley, and the other Portishead collaborators had attempted to force studio technology into bending to their creative will. This time, they discarded the use of bits and pieces from film soundtracks and soul classics, and instead created their own samples by using archaic recording equipment. For *Portishead*'s long-anticipated debut, the group teamed with a thirty-piece orchestra in New York City for their first live show in over two years.

Reviews this time around were mixed. A *Rolling Stone* assessment from Elisabeth Vincentelli pointed out that the album lacks a certain diversity of style, noting that after a time, its mood of "morbid fascination turns into ennui." In the end, Vincentelli called it "an exercise in barren claustrophobia," but deemed Barrow "an amazing sonic architect." Powell, writing in the *Village Voice,* observed a progression in Gibbons's trademark sound. On this second LP, Powell declared, "... there's a brattier catch in her singing that wasn't there before. And sighing less is always a good idea." Powell also remarked upon the strain of Portishead's relentlessly bleaksonic architecture spread over an entire album—but conceded that Portishead "do the same song over and over and they do it really, really well."

Selected discography

Dummy, Go! Beat/London Records, 1994.
Portishead, Go! Beat/London Records, 1997.

Sources

Billboard, October 8, 1994, p. 1.
Guitar Player, May 1995, p. 22.
People, October 20, 1997, pp. 29-30.
Rocket, December 3, 1997.
Rolling Stone, February 23, 1995, p. 38; March 9, 1995, p. 66; October 15, 1997.
Time, October 20, 1997, p. 117.
Village Voice, December 6, 1994.

—*Carol Brennan*

Prodigy

Electronica band

With the release of their beat-driven, high-energy single "Firestarter" in 1996, U.K. dance act Prodigy grabbed American audiences with both their aggressive sound and the intentionally freakish style of vocalist/dancer Keith Flint. However, like many "overnight sensations," Prodigy had spent years gaining a steady popularity among British listeners. Whatever the band's credentials may have been, within less than a year many American critics predicted that Prodigy would spearhead an invasion of electronic dance music in the United States. Ironically, songwriter Liam Howlett has viewed Prodigy's role as ambassador of techno with a grain of salt. "I don't know. America's a funny place," Howlett quipped to *Rolling Stone*. "The [music] industry seems to be hyping the electronic scene up, saying it's the new thing. I don't agree. I don't think kids in America should be told to forget about rock music, because all this is, is another form of rock music."

Although Prodigy is comprised of numerous members and is often most identified with the multiple body pierced, rainbow haired Keith Flint, the band's backbone—and

AP/Wide World Photos

For the Record . . .

Members include **Keith Flint**, dancing, vocals; **Liam Howlett**, songwriting, programming, synthesizers, mixing; **Keeti Palmer** (Maxim Reality), vocals; **Leeroy Thornhill**, dancing.

Band formed by Howlett alone as a DJ in the late 1980s in London, England; Thornhill and Flint enlisted in the outfit, followed by Reality, 1991; released debut single "What Evil Lurks" in a pressing of 7000 copies, 1991; released debut album *The Prodigy Experience*, 1992; *Music For the Jilted Generation,* 1994; broke U.S. market with the single "Firestarter," 1996; released *Fat of the Land*, 1997.

Addresses: *Record company*—Maverick Recording Company, 9348 Civic Center Drive, Beverly Hills, CA 90210; 75 Rockefeller Plaza, New York, NY 10019.

only contracted member is songwriter and synthesizer player Liam Howlett, a native of Essex, England. Even as a pre-adolescent, Howlett had been attracted to dance-based music, namely the ska artists on the seminal Two Tone label. By the time he was in high school, Howlett was immersed in the world of hip-hop, a style that emerged primarily from urban, African American roots, exemplified by such artists as Grandmaster Flash and the many performers showcased in the 1985 film *Beat Street*, which Howlett viewed almost obsessively. "It was the first DIY [do-it-yourself] music after punk, I guess," Howlett told *Rolling Stone.* "Music I felt I almost could make."

Rave Music

Following such impulses, Howlett soon purchased a set of turntables and signed on as a DJ in a newly formed dance band called Cut to Kill, and in the meantime completed coursework for his graphic design degree. The outfit practiced intensely, played live occasionally, and were soon offered a nominal amount to cut a studio album. The naïve band of hip-hoppers grossly mismanaged their budget, and to compound matters, all of the members of Cut to Kill, excluding Howlett, signed a secret contract which effectively barred him from all rights to material he had collaborated on. Howlett's relationship with hip hop was strained by this time, and this fiasco only served as a final death knell.

By the summer of 1988, the rapidly-paced, technologically oriented dance music known as Acid House had made its way from clubs in Detroit and Chicago to London youth culture where it was rechristened "rave music", and Howlett was quick to succumb to its influence. "I really loved the music and the whole vibe," Howlett told a website interviewer. "I had never been into dancing that much, but it didn't matter, because you could enjoy it, you didn't have to dance properly." Howlett quickly became a figure within rave clubs, spinning records and introducing his own material, for the first time under the moniker Prodigy. Whether this title referred to the then 18 year old Howlett's precocious abilities or the brand of Moog synthesizer he used—both accounts have circulated—Howlett/Prodigy began turning heads among dance floor denizens of the Barn, Howlett's main venue. Most importantly, his innovative approach to acid house attracted Leeroy Thornhill, a nearly seven foot tall newfound raver, and Keith Flint, his globe-trotting friend who would later become the public face of Prodigy. The two fans offered to perform as stage dancers during Howlett's live sets, giving his DJ efforts the status of a bona fide group. Howlett accepted, and the group Prodigy was born.

Creating an Identity

After performing an inauspicious first gig at the Labyrinth, a club in East London, Prodigy decided that something was needed to spice up their persona, and quickly sought out reggae vocalist Maxim Reality—Keeti Palmer to MC for their outfit. While originally solicited as a temporary fixture, Palmer/Reality fit into the chemistry of Prodigy so well during their first performances that he was adopted as a permanent member. Prodigy had finally rounded out their full lineup, and by early 1991 took the next leap: releasing singles. In February of that year, Prodigy put out its maiden single, the ominous "Where Evil Lurks," in a limited pressing of 7000 copies. The song generated a modicum of buzz among club-goers, which grew even more with "Charly," another 1991 single which featured the gimmicky sample of a meowing cat from a television ad well-known in the U.K.

Prodigy continued to pump out singles that continued to allure dance fans with their violent, rapidly changing beats, and soon amassed enough output to release a debut album, *The Prodigy Experience.* The album featured many of the band's club hits, as well as the memorable "Weather Experience." While it sold well for an independent dance album, critically *The Prodigy Experience* was besieged by the kind of jeers that many acid house inspired have received – that it was musically superficial and unimaginatively repetitive. As writer Chris Heath commented in *Rolling Stone,* "[w]hat had begun as fresh was becoming stale ritual." Howlett and his cohorts realized this as well, and while their characteristic use of hyper break beats would continue, Prodigy's recorded material soon became more diverse.

After continuing to tour and occasionally cutting a single, Prodigy returned to the studio to generate what became *Music For The Jilted Generation.* Released in the summer of 1994, the album begins with a spoken preamble that sums up their new attitude: "So I've decided to take my work back underground—to stop it falling into the wrong hands." However much the band went "underground" with *Music For The Jilted Generation,* its success with British record buyers was mainstream: it entered the sales charts at Number One, and within two months had sold more than their debut had in two years. A sprawling 79 minute effort, Prodigy's second album evidenced Howlett's roots in hip-hop and hard dance, but more importantly showed an influx of rock riffs, ambient techno, and hints of jazz. Violently energetic and brimming with wide-eyed end of the millennium paranoia, *Jilted Generation*'s 13 tracks, highlighted by "Poison" and "Voodoo People," managed to charm critics as well with the band's new scope, and the album was instantly pegged as a potential Album of the Year by numerous reviewers. And yet, Prodigy's biggest success was still to come.

The Fire Is Started

While electronica music had more or less always had a wide acceptance in Europe, Americans traditionally have shown a greater degree of resistance to genres outside of established rock and pop. Until 1996, this had been the case with Prodigy as well, but before long the band became heralded as a driving force of electronic dance music within the United States. With the release of the single "Firestarter" in March of that year, Prodigy found the perfect weapon to break through America's stubborn armor: a dance track with an undeniable rock edge, bearing an aggressiveness nearing that of heavy metal. In addition, the song's video made maximum use of dancer —and now vocalist Keith Flint's eye catching presence. His epileptic movements and wild accouterment—an array of body piercings and a colorfully dyed inverted-Mohawk hairstyle—captured the attention of "alternative"-crazed America.

Prodigy's third album, *Fat of the Land,* was not released until a year after "Firestarter," but in the meantime the band, especially Flint, stayed in the limelight of MTV and other influential media in addition to touring. After such a hiatus, it became questionable whether a new album would benefit from "Firestarter's" momentum, or whether in fact that single's American success had been a fluke. When *Fat of the Land* made its debut in *Billboard* magazine's sales chart at the number one position, such questions were quickly stanched. Although the album had its moodier moments, notably "Minefields," the hard, relentless quality of "Firestarter" prevailed—in fact, "Fuel My Fire" is a cover of a song by the thrash-rock band L7. As *Fat of the Land's* sales remained steady, the band had gained enough notoriety to attract heavyweights such as U2, David Bowie, and Madonna, all of who approached Howlett in hopes of using his mixing expertise—and were refused. "I was, well, I'm quite flattered, to be honest, but I'm not going to do it," Howlett remarked on the subject to *Rolling Stone.* "That's possibly the worst move we could do right now—give Madonna our sound. I don't want to be spreading our sound around. I'm just not prepared to take that risk."

Critical reception of the album (and the band in general) ranged from praise to scorn, the latter party often attacking the band's "shock-value" aesthetics. With the release of the single "Smack My Bitch Up" in late 1997, this attack reached its peak. Despite the band's contrary claims that the song's title is ironic, some critics and listeners found the song to be offensively misogynist. "It's so offensive," Howlett countered, "that it can't actually mean that. That's where the irony is." Moreover, the video for the song, which contained images of nude anorexic bodies and vomit, among other things, was instantly pulled from many television channels around the world, and was banned in the U.K. Joss Ackerlund, the video's director pointed out to *New Musical Express* that he "didn't do it to shock the world with disgusting imagery—I had an idea, the Prodigy liked it, and we did it. If this had been in the art world, this is nothing." Such defenses did little to deter censors, and the powerful Wal-Mart chain used its clout to have the song's title bleeped on further pressings to be sold in their stores. In the long run, Prodigy seem to be a band who only benefit from controversy, and the censorship debacle seems to have done no damage to the band's increasing popularity.

Selected discography

Prodigy Experience, 1992.
Music For The Jilted Generation, Maverick/Sire, 1994.
Fat of the Land, Maverick/Sire, 1997.

Sources

Periodicals

Melody Maker, May 1997.
New Musical Express, February 1997; January 31,1998.
Rolling Stone, August 21, 1997.

Online

http://www.cs.may.ie/adowling/prodigy/band

—Shaun Frentner

Ma Rainey

Singer

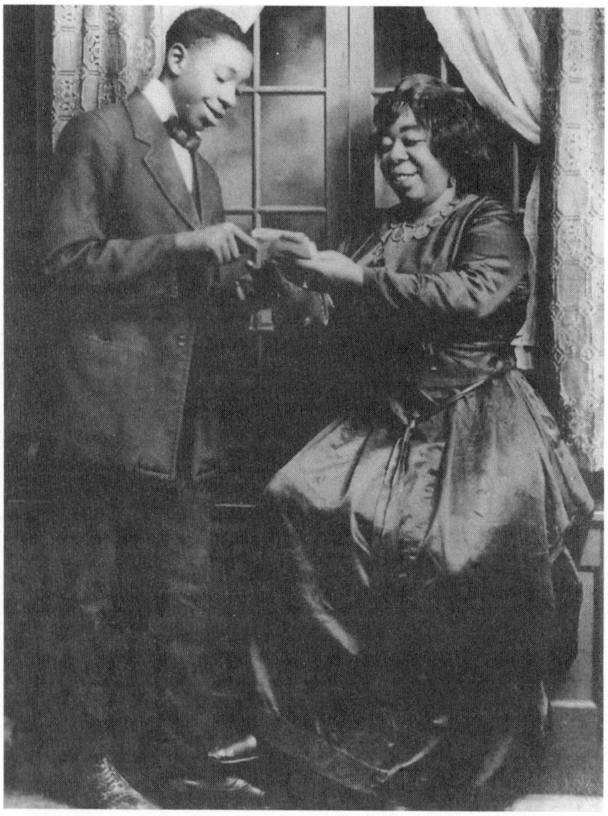

AP/Wide World Photos

The first popular stage performer to incorporate authentic blues in her song repertoire, "Ma" Gertrude Rainey emerged, during the first two decades of the twentieth century. Known as the "Mother of the Blues" Rainey enjoyed mass popularity during the women blues singer craze of the 1920s. Described by African American poet Sterling Brown in *Black Culture and Black Consciousness,* as "a person of the folk," Rainey recorded in various musical settings, and made a number of sides which exhibited the influence of authentic rural blues.

Ma Rainey was born Gertrude Pridgett in Columbus Georgia on April 26, 1886 to minstrel troupers—Thomas Pridgett Sr. and Ella Allen—Pridgett. She worked at the Springer Opera House in 1900, performing as a singer and dancer in the local talent show, "A Bunch of Blackberries." On February 2, 1904, Pridgett married comedy songster William "Pa" Rainey. Billed as "Ma" and "Pa" Rainey the couple toured Southern tent shows and cabarets. Though she did not hear blues in Columbus, Rainey's extensive travels had, by 1905, brought her into contact with authentic country blues, which she worked into her song repertoire. "Her ability to capture the mood and essence of black rural southern life," noted Daphane Harrison in *Black Pearls: Blues Queens of the 1920s*, "quickly endeared her to throngs of followers throughout the South."

While performing with The Moses Stokes troupe in 1912, the Raineys were introduced to the show's newly recruited dancer, Bessie Smith. Eight years Smith's senior, Rainey quickly befriended the young performer. Despite earlier historical accounts crediting Rainey as Smith's vocal coach, it has been generally agreed by modern scholars that Rainey played less of a role in the shaping of Smith's singing style. "Ma Rainey probably did pass some of her singing experience on to Bessie," explained Chris Albertson in the liner notes to *Giants Of Jazz, Bessie Smith,* "but the instruction must have been rudimentary. Though they shared an extraordinary command of the idiom, the two women delivered their messages in styles and voices that were dissimilar and manifestly personal."

Around 1915 the Rainey's toured with Fat Chappelle's Rabbit Foot Minstrels. Afterward, they were billed as the "Assassinators of the Blues" with Tolliver's Circus and Musical Extravaganza. Separated from her husband in 1916, Rainey subsequently toured with her own band, Madam Gertrude Ma Rainey and Her Georgia Smart Sets, featuring a chorus line and a five piece band. She also performed with other such entertainment organizations as Florida Cotton Blossoms Show, and Donald McGregor's Carnival Show.

For the Record . . .

Born: Gertrude Pridgett, April 26, 1886, in Columbus, Georgia; died December 22, 1939 in rome, Georgia; daughter of Thomas Priggett and Ella Allen (minstrel troupers); married William "Pa" Rainey (comedy performer) February 2, 1904.

Performed in local stage show 1900; toured South with husband William "Pa" Rainey 1904; member of Fat Chappelle's Rabbit Foot Minstrels; from the 1910s to the 1920s performed at various venues and concert halls in the south and midwest with shows that included Tolliver's Circus and Silas Green from New Orleans minstrel show; made recording debut for Paramount label in 1923; toured with own group Georgia Wild Cats Jazz Band 1924-1926; recorded with various sideman for Paramount until 1928; worked with revue show, Bandanna Babies, 1930; worked with Al Gaines Carnival Show 1933-1935. retired from music in 1935 and became theater owner.

Discovered by Paramount Records

Through the intercession of Mayo "Ink" Williams, Rainey first recorded for the Paramount label in 1923 (three years following the first blues side recorded by Mamie Smith). Already a popular singer in the Southern theater circuit, Rainey entered the recording industry as an experienced and stylistically mature talent. Her first session, cut with Austin and Her Blue Serenaders, featured the traditional number "Bo-Weevil Blues". Fellow blues singer, Victoria Spivey, later said of the recording, as quoted in *The Devil's Music,* "Ain't nobody in the world been able to holler 'Hey Boweevil' like her. Not like Ma. Nobody." 1923 also saw the release of Rainey's side "Moonshine Blues," with Lovie Austin, and "Yonder Comes the Blues" with Louis Armstrong. That same year, Rainey recorded "See See Rider," a number that, as Arnold Shaw observed in *Black Popular Music in America,* emerged as "one of the famous and recorded of all blues songs. [Rainey's] was the first recording of that song, giving her a hold on the copyright, and one of the best of the more than 100 versions."

In August 1924 Rainey—along with the twelve string guitar of Miles Pruitt (and unknown second guitar accompanist)—recorded the eight bar blues number "Shave 'Em Dry." In the liner notes to *The Blues,* folklorist W.K. McNeil observed that the number "is typical of Rainey's output, a driving, unornamated vocal propelled along by an accompanist who plays the number straight. Her artistry brings life to what in lesser hands would be a dull, elementary piece."

"Madam Rainey," A Reigning Blues Queen

Unlike many other blues musicians, Rainey earned a reputation as a professional on stage and in business. According to Mayo Williams, as quoted in the liner notes to *Ma Rainey's Black Bottom,* "Ma Rainey was a shrewd business woman. We never tried to put any swindles on her. During Rainey's five-year recording career at Paramount she cut nearly ninety sides, most of which dealt with the subjects of love and sexuality—bawdy themes that often earned her the billing of "Madam Rainey." As William Barlow explained, in *Looking Up at Down,* her songs were also "diverse, yet deeply rooted in day-today experiences of black people from the South. Ma Rainey's blues were simple, straightforward stories about heart break, promiscuity, drinking binges, the odyssey of travel, the workplace and the prison road gang, magic and superstition—in short, the southern landscape of African Americans in the Post-Reconstruction era."

The Wild Cats Jazz Band

With the success of her early recordings, Rainey took part in a Paramount promotional tour which featured a newly assembled back-up band. In 1924 pianist and arranger Thomas A. Dorsey (one of later founders of gospel music) recruited members for Rainey's touring band, The Wild Cats Jazz Band. Serving as both director and manager, Dorsey assembled able musicians who could read arrangements as well play in a down "home blues" style. Rainey's tour debut at Chicago's Grand Theater on State Street marked the first appearance of a "down home" blues artist at the famous southside venue. Draped in long gowns and covered in diamonds and a necklace of gold pieces, Rainey had a powerful command over her audiences. She often opened her stage show singing "Moonshine Blues" inside the cabinet of an over-sized victrola, from which she emerged to a greet a near-frantic audience. As Dorsey recalled, in *The Rise of Gospel Blues,* "When she started singing, the gold in her teeth would sparkle. She was in the spotlight. She possessed listeners; they swayed, they rocked, they moaned and groaned, as they felt the blues with her."

Until 1926, Rainey performed with her Wild Jazz Cats on the Theater Owner's Booking Association circuit (TOBA).

That year, after Dorsey left the band, she recorded with various musicians on the Paramount label—often under the name of Ma Rainey and her Georgia Jazz Band which, on various occasions, included musicians such as pianists Fletcher Henderson, Claude Hopkins, and Willie the Lion Smith, reed players Don Redman, Buster Bailey and Coleman Hawkins, and trumpeters Louis Armstrong and Tommy Ladnier. In 1927 Rainey cut sides such as "Black Cat, Hoot Owl Blues" with the Tub Jug Washboard Band. During her last sessions, held in 1928, she sang in the company of her former pianist Thomas "Georgia Tom" Dorsey and guitarist Hudson "Tampa Red" Whittaker, producing such numbers as "Black Eye Blues," "Runaway Blues" and "Sleep Talking Blues." As Bruce Cook noted in *Listen to the Blues,* these numbers "are as good as anything she ever recorded. Her voice is rich and full; she really sounds like the 'Mother of the Blues."

Retired from the Music Business

Though the TOBA and vaudeville circuits had gone into decline by the early 1930s, Rainey still performed, often resorting to playing tent shows. Following the death of her mother and sister, Rainey retired from the music business in 1935 and settled in Columbus. For the next several years, she devoted her time as the owner of two entertainment venues—the Lyric Theater and the Air-dome—as well as activities in the Friendship Baptist Church. Rainey died in Rome, Georgia—some sources cite Columbus—on December 22, 1939.

A great contributor to America's rich blues tradition, Rainey's music has served as inspiration for African American poets such as Langston Hughes and Sterling Brown, the latter of whom paid tribute to the majestic singer in the poem "Ma Rainey," which appeared in his 1932 collection *Southern Road.* More recently, Alice Walker looked to Ma Rainey's music as a cultural model of African American womanhood when she wrote the Pulitzer Prize-winning novel, *The Color Purple.* In *Black Pearls,* Daphane Harrison praised Rainey as the first great blues stage singer: "The good-humored, rollicking Rainey loved life, loved love, and most of all loved her people. Her voice bursts forth with a hearty declaration of courage and determination—a reaffirmation of black life."

Selected discography

Gertrude "Ma" Rainey—Complete Master Takes Vol. I: 1923-24, King Jazz.
Gertrude "Ma" Rainey—Complete Master Takes Vol. 2: 1924-1926, King Jazz.
Gertrude "Ma" Rainey—Complete Master Takes Vol. 3: 1926-1927, King Jazz.
Gertrude "Ma" Rainey—Complete Master Takes Vol. 4: 1927-1928, King Jazz.
The Immortal Ma Rainey, Roman Record Company.
Ma Rainey's Black Bottom, Yazoo, 1991.

Sources

Barlow, William, *Looking Up at Down: The Emergence of Blues Culture,* Temple University Press, pp. 155-164.
Cook, Bruce, *Listen to the Blues,* Da Capo, p. 189.
Harris, Michael W., *The Rise of Gospel Blues: The Music of Thomas Dorsey in the Urban Church,* p.86-95. .
Harrison, Daphane Duval. *Black Pearls: Blues Queens of the 1920s.* New Brunswick: Rutgers University Press, p. 34-41.
Levine, Lawrence W., *Black Culture and Black Consciousness: Afro-American Thought From Slavery to Freedom,* Oxford University Press, p. 232.
Oakley, Giles, *The Devil's Music: A History of the Blues,* Tappinger.
Shaw, Arnold, *Black Popular Music in America,* Schirmer Books, p. 100-101.

Additional information for this profile was also obtained from the liner notes to *Jazz Giants, Bessie Smith,* Time Life (1982), written by Chris Albertson, *Ma Raineys Black Bottom,* Yazoo(1992), written by Steve Calt.

—John Cohassey

Oumou Sangare

Malian singer, songwriter

Oumou Sangare is the voice of feminism in West Africa. In a region where polygamy is the norm, and women are often viewed as the property of their husbands, Sangare's music has come to symbolize the struggle against gender imbalance. In addition to their social content, Sangare's songs are full of the joy and spirit that the traditional rhythms of Mali have been communicating for generations. During the mid-1990s, Sangare has become one of Africa's biggest pop stars, as well as a major force in the European and American world music scenes.

Sangare was born in Bamako, the capital of Mali, in 1968. Her parents had migrated to the city from the rural Wassoulou region south of the Niger River. Her mother, Aminata Diakhite, was also a talented singer and encouraged her daughter to follow in her footsteps. Sangare made her public performing debut at the age of six, singing for a huge crowd at Bamako's main sports arena, the Stade des Omnisports. Before the show began, her mother counseled her, according to her Nonesuch Records bio, to "sing like you're at home in the kitchen."

Her mother's advice apparently paid off, for Sangare's talent soon earned her membership in The National Ensemble of Mali, which serves as a training ground for the best musicians in that country. In 1986 Sangare was invited by Bamba Dambele, known for his work with the African pop ensemble Super Djata Band, to tour Europe with his traditional percussion troupe Djobila. The European tour opened Sangare's eyes to the possibility of an international career of her own. Upon her return to Mali, she immediately went to work forming her own band and developing a songwriting style and sound that effectively blended Wassoulou tradition with a modern pop sensibility.

Since Mali gained its independence in the early 1960s, the Wassoulou region has produced a steady flow of wonderful female vocalists. These singers—a group that has included Coumba Sidibe, Sali Sidibe, and Flan Saran—collectively influenced the creation of a musical style based on the region's traditional dances and rhythms. Those rhythms, combined with local instruments such as the djembe drum and the kamalengoni—a harp-like instrument invented by local youths during this period—eventually gave rise to a new popular musical style called Wassoulou, named after the region in which it originated. The Wassoulou style communicates a sense of youthful rebellion and freedom.

Debut Album Created Sensation

Working with well-known arranger Amadou Ba Guindo, Sangare put together a band that included Boubacar Diallo on guitar and Aliou Traore on violin. The band's goal was to further update the sound of Wassoulou in order to keep it fresh. For example, they used a modern violin in place of the *soku,* the traditional horse-hair fiddle previously used in Wassoulou. After two years of experimentation, the band traveled to the Ivory Coast to make its first studio recording. The resulting cassette, *Moussolou*—meaning "Women"—consisted of six original songs by Sangare. Released in 1989, *Moussolou* eventually sold more than 200,000 copies, and made Sangare a sensation in her native country.

Over the next couple of years, Sangare became one of West Africa's biggest musical stars, and *Moussolou* has become a classic of African pop. It took until 1991, when the British label World Circuit picked up the rights for the album outside of Africa, for Sangare to gain a significant international following. With a growing reputation in Europe, Sangare went to work writing songs for her follow-up album. *Ko Sira* (Marriage Today) was recorded in Berlin and released on World Circuit in 1993. On *Ko Sira,* Sangare used a bigger band than on her previous album. Its songs included a tribute to Amadou Ba Guindo, who had died in an automobile crash, and several tunes dealing with the plight of women in Africa, forced to play the role of servants to their polygamous husbands. Well received all over the globe, *Ko Sira* was

For the Record . . .

Born in 1968 in Bamako, Mali; daughter of Aminata Diakhite (a singer); married, with one child (a son).

First public performance, at Stade des Omnisports, Bamako, 1974; member National Ensemble of Mali, mid-1980s; toured Europe with Bamba Dambele and Djoliba, 1986; formed own band, 1987; made first recording, *Moussolou,* 1989; *Moussolou* released internationally, 1991; released *Ko Sira,* 1993; released *Worotan,* 1996; toured throughout Europe and Africa, 1993; performed across U.S. as part of "Africa Fête" package tour, 1994-95; toured U.S. again in 1997.

Awards: European World Music Album of the Year, for *Ko Sira,* 1993.

Addresses: *Record labels*—World Circuit Ltd., Cleveland St., London W1P 5DP, U.K.; Nonesuch Records, 75 Rockefeller Plaza, New York, NY 10019. *Manager and booking agent*—Chazz! Wim Westerveld, P.O. Box 292, 6500 AG Nijmegen, Holland.

voted "European World Music Album of the Year" for 1993. Milo Miles of the *New York Times* attributed to the album "a rare grace ... that makes any future Sangare recordings and her promised live appearances ... as enticing as any in world pop."

Became a World Music Superstar

By this time Sangare had achieved idol status back home in Mali. Not slowed by the birth of her first child, she toured across Africa and Europe in 1993. The following year, she made her second trip to the United States, as part of the Africa Fête package tour. The highlight of her triumphant U.S. tour was a captivating appearance at Summer Stage in New York's Central Park. Sangare released her third album, *Worotan,* in the U.K. in 1996, and it remained atop the European world music charts for months. The album was released in the U.S. the following summer. On *Worotan*—which means "ten kola nuts," the traditional price for a wife in Mali—Sangare added a few new elements to her music, including the contribution of Pee Wee Ellis, a horn player who had made his mark as a sideman with soul giant James Brown. The album also featured a hot young guitarist by the name of Baba Salah. *Newsweek* magazine gushed that "*Worotan* brings seemingly distant issues like polygamy into uncanny poetic focus," and compared Sangare to a young Aretha Franklin.

In live performances, Sangare is by all accounts a striking presence. Standing well over six feet tall in heels and a towering headwrap, she projects as much power with her appearance as she does with her voice. She generally performs in stunningly colorful flowing robes and other traditional African garb. It is the music and its message rather than the apparel, however, that are making Sangare an international sensation. "When you do music, you do it for everyone ...," she was quoted as saying by the Africa News Service. "I welcome all ideas, all instruments. I want to mix everything, because I want everyone to participate."

Participation is easy for Westerners, who appreciate Sangare's music primarily for its danceable rhythms. For the African women whom she champions, participation is something that must befought for on a daily basis. "I speak of the women of Africa and of the whole world," Sangare's press kit quotes her as saying. "I fight for the improvement of women's situation, because African Women do not have as many rights as men .... But if that woman wants to speak in the society, she is not listened to. So I sing her cause."

Selected discography

Moussolou, World Circuit, 1991.
Ko Sira, World Circuit, 1993.
Worotan, World Circuit/Nonesuch, 1996.

Sources

Africa News, September 12, 1997.
ANS News Service, May 7, 1997.
Austin (Texas) American-Statesman, November 8, 1997, p. E8.
The Independent (London), July 26, 1996, p. 8.
Metro Times (Detroit), November 5, 1997, p. 51.
New York Times, February 20, 1994; November 20, 1997, p. E10.
Vibe, March 1997.

Additional material for this profile was provided by Nonesuch Records.

—Robert R. Jacobson

The Shadows

Instrumental group

The Shadows achieved renown as the best-selling British instrumental group of all time, and their career as a musical act is one of the longest—though perhaps also most cataclysmic in line-up—in British pop annals as well. Led by guitarist Hank Marvin, a well-known personality in British rock circles, the Shadows hit the charts in the summer of 1960 with a catchy instrumental called "Apache," and recorded numerous other singles and albums over the next three decades—some successful, others less so. Still, Marvin is considered one of the most distinguished of guitarists of the pre-rock era, and is credited with being the first musician in England to popularize the Fender Stratocaster electric guitar. Virtuosos such as Eric Clapton, Mark Knopfler, Pete Townsend—each of whom arrived later onto the rock scene—usually cite Marvin and his Stratocaster as a profound influence. In 1996 several noted contemporary rock guitarists appeared on *Twang! A Tribute to Hank Marvin and the Shadows.*

Almost all of the members of the Shadows, like those of other influential rock bands in the British wave, were

AP/Wide World Photos

For the Record . . .

Original members included **Jet Harris** (born Terence Hawkins, July 6, 1939, Kingsbury, Middlesex, England; left group, April 1962), bass; **Hank B. Marvin** (born Brian Robson Rankin, October 28, 1941, Newcastle-Upon-Tyne, England), lead guitar; **Tony Meehan** (born Daniel Meehan, March 2, 1943, Hampstead, England; left group, October 1961), drums; **Bruce Welch** (born Bruce Cripps, November 2, 1941, Bognor Regis, Sussex, England), rhythm guitar. Later members included **Brian Bennett** (born February 9, 1940, London; joined band, October 1961; left band, c. 1990), drums; **John Farrar** (born November 8, 1945, Australia), bass, guitar, and vocals; **Brian Locking** (born December 22, 1940, Bedworth, Coventry, England), bass, harmonica; **John Rostill** (born Kings Norton, Birmingham, England, June 16, 1942; died, November 26, 1973), bass.

Band formed as the Five Chesternuts, c. 1958; became the backing band for successful British pop singer Cliff Richard under the name the Drifters, c. 1958-68; Signed to EMI Columbia as the Drifters, c. 1959; renamed themselves the Shadows, 1959; released "Apache," which stayed at the U. K. pop charts for six weeks at No. 1, 1960; released debut album *The Shadows,* 1961; *The Shadows Greatest Hits,* 1963; disbanded, 1968; reformed by Marvin, 1969; bassist John Rostill was electrocuted to death by his guitar, 1973; hit the top 20 for the first time in ten years with "Let Me Be the One," 1975; disbanded, 1990.

Awards: Ivor Novello Award, British Academy of Songwriters, Composers and Authors, 1983.

Addresses: *Record company*—EMD Music Distribution, 21700 Oxnard St., Suite #700, Woodland Hills, CA 91367.

born during the World War II era. Marvin was grew up in Newcastle-upon-Tyne, and played the banjo as a teenager. In 1957, he joined the Railroaders, a skiffle group formed by fellow Newcastle teen Bruce Welch, and the following year the band journeyed to London to enter a talent contest. They took third place, and Marvin and Welch decided to stay in the capital. The pair lived in London's Soho area, both nearly destitute. For a time, they formed a band called the Five Chesternuts with some other musicians they had met in the contest, but the group had little success.

Marvin and Welch were discovered by the manager for Cliff Richard, then an up-and-coming British pop singer, in a Soho coffee bar. He asked them to join a band then forming to back Richard in a tour, and to record with him as well. The band would be called the Drifters; within a few months its line-up was fixed with the addition of bassist Jet Harris and drummer Tony Meehan. It was Harris who came up with the name "The Shadows" when a change was deemed necessary because of an American band called the Drifters. At first, the Shadows were simply a standard pop-rock act of the era, similar in style and vocals to the Everly Brothers. Instrumental tunes were tried out only during Richard's performance breaks. Meanwhile, Marvin was finessing the guitar style for which he would gain renown. It was a sound crafted with the legendary American-made Fender Stratocaster guitar, and it wasn't until he finally obtained one in 1959—they were difficult to come by in England, and Richard had to bring him one back directly—that his playing began to take a new turn.

Marvin's sound was epitomized in the Shadows' 1960 single, "Apache," an instrumental piece with an irresistible hook and otherworldly vibe. It spent twenty-one weeks on the British pop charts, six of those at number one—a success the result of "a stirring combination of Welch's acoustic strumming and Marvin's economical, echo-drenched picking," wrote Dan Epstein years later in *Guitar Player.* Marvin had bought an Italian-made echo-box device for his guitar and used it on the song that would become a trademark of the Shadow sound. Unfortunately, the success on the U.K. charts was not replicated in the United States; their label at the time, EMI of England, failed to promote it favorably overseas, and a cover version of "Apache" by a Danish guitarist soon made the U. S. charts.

Success in the Sixties

For the next several years the Shadows continued to maintain dual careers as Richard's backing band as well as their own efforts as a separate act. The latter forays were increasingly successful, though Richard himself was an extremely popular pop idol at the time—at times he and the Shadows even competed for chart space. Under Marvin's guidance, the band would enjoy several other Top-20 hits with the instrumentals that put his guitar virtuosity at the forefront of the mix. These hits included "Kon-tiki," "Atlantis," and "Shindig," among others. The group remained intact during this era, but Jet Harris suffered from alcoholism, and in 1962 he and

Meehan left the Shadows to embark upon a joint solo career that achieved modest success. They were replaced by Brian Bennett and Brian Locking.

As the decade progressed, however, immense changes took place in the British music scene. The light, pleasing virtuosity of the Shadows, anchored by Marvin's guitar abilities, gave way to a more "rock" sound typified by the Beatles and then the Rolling Stones. Teenagers allied themselves with the new groups to a frenzied degree, and the more pop side of British music began to be cornered by groups like Gerry and the Pacemakers, who typified the "Mersey" sound. Soon, the Shadows and Richard were not performing as well on the charts. They attempted to change along with times—adding vocals in 1965 to some songs, such as "Don't Make My Baby Blue," another Top-20 success. They also branched out into film, appearing in a number of comic films with Richard, such as *Expresso Bongo* and *Summer Holiday,* for which they also recorded songs.

A New Era

The Shadows continued as a solo act and Richard's backing band until 1968, when they officially parted ways. The breakup of the band itself came soon after, when Welch left. Yet the split was far from final—though Marvin and Welch's friendship suffered many ups and downs over the years—and after Marvin took Bennett and two other new members to Japan as the Shadows in 1969 for a tour, Welch rejoined Marvin to form a Crosby, Stills & Nash-inspired group they named Marvin, Welch & Farrar. It was less than successful. In the early 1970s, Marvin converted to the Jehovah's Witness faith, while Welch and John Rostill—the bassist on the Japan tour—began working with an up-and-coming Australian singer named Olivia Newton-John. Welch wrote and produced her hit "Please Mr. Please," while Rostill, who had played with Tom Jones, wrote another hugely successful single for her, "Let Me Be There." Tragically, in one of the strangest deaths in rock history, Rostill was electrocuted by his own guitar in his home studio in 1973.

The Marvin, Welch and Farrar lineup continued until 1973, and then Marvin and Welch officially revived the Shadows in 1973. Their sound evolved once more with the addition of keyboards, and some successful tour dates led to an invitation to represent Britain for the annual Eurovision song contest. Their entry, "Let Me Be the One," was only the runner-up, but it was their first Top 20 hit in a decade. When the Shadows compilation *20 Golden Greats* was released in 1977, it effectively revived their career and launched a retro resurgence on the part of both old and new fans. Though they continued to record, they achieved only minor successes and officially played together for the last time in 1990. Marvin moved to Australia in 1986 and owns a recording studio in Perth. His legendary talents with his trademark Stratocaster was honored in the late 1990s when Fender brought him in as a consultant for a special 40th anniversary issue of the guitar. Welch continues to work with Cliff Richard and wrote an autobiography in 1989, *Rock 'n' Roll: I Gave you the Best Years of My Life.* The Shadows' history is also chronicled in *The Story of the Shadows,* penned by Mike Read. Their U.S. compilation arrived with *Shadows Are Go!* on the Scamp label, its title a homage to a movie they once appeared in. *Thunderbirds Are Go. Twang! A Tribute to Hank Marvin and the Shadows,* released in 1996, honored Marvin and his cohorts with cover versions of their most well-known hits by Peter Frampton, Mark Knopfler, Neil Young, and Andy Summers, among others. Marvin sometimes tours with his son Ben, a guitarist.

Selected discography

The Shadows, 1961.
Out of the Shadows, 1962.
The Shadows Greatest Hits, 1963.
Dance with the Shadows, 1964.
The Sound of the Shadows, 1965.
More Hits, 1965.
Shadow Music, 1966.
Jigsaw, 1967.
From Hank, Bruce, Brian, and John, 1967.
Established 1958, 1968.
Somethin' Else, 1969.
Shades of Rock, 1970.
Rockin' with Curly Leads, 1974.
Specs Appeal, 1975.
Live at the Paris Olympia, 1975.
Tasty, 1977.
20 Golden Greats, 1977.
Thank You Very Much, 1978.
Change of Address, 1980.
String of Hits, 1980.
Another String of Hot Hits, 1980.
Hits Right Up Your Street, 1981.
Life in the Jungle/Live at Abbey Road, 1982.
XXV, 1983.
Guardian Angel, 1984.
Moonlight Shadows, 1986.
Simply Shadows, 1987.
Stepping to the Shadows, 1989.
At Their Very Best, 1989.
Reflections, 1991.
Themes and Dreams, 1991.

Sources

Books

The Guinness Encyclopedia of Popular Music, edited by Colin Larkin, Guinness Publishing, 1995.

The Rolling Stone Encyclopedia of Rock & Roll, edited by Patricia Romanowksi and Holly George-Warren, Fireside, 1995.

Periodicals

Guitar Player, September 1997, pp. 53-56.

Online

http://scofa.muse.com.au

http://www.stockportmbc.gov.uk/daved/shadows

—Carol Brennan

Carly Simon

Singer, songwriter

Courtesy of Arista Records

Establishing herself during the early 1970s, Carly Simon's latest release stretches her range and completes the trilogy of her standards. *Film Noir,* released in 1997 by Arista, features her sultry voice against an orchestra. Recorded mostly live, the album celebrates films of the 1940s, although not all cuts actually were in films. Reminiscent of another era, the mysterious and sometimes seductive music creates a romantic mood and evokes a sense of drama. The music conjures scenes set in a smoke filled bar, featuring the likes of Humphry Bogart and Lauren Bacall playing scenes to such music. Simon proves once again that she is no lightweight in the style department, and she continually seems able to delight an audience with the variety of resources she pulls from her creative well. Her latest album adds to the long list of classics by this classy singer and songwriter.

Simon was born in New York City on June 25, 1945 to Richard Simon, a co-founder of the Simon and Schuster publishing company, and Andrea Simon. She has two sisters, Lucy and Joanna, and a brother, Peter, all artists, musical or otherwise. Both of her parents were musically inclined. Simon grew up listening to the music of George and Ira Gershwin and Richard Wagner. She was exposed to folk music as a school girl, and after dropping out of Sarah Lawrence College after a few years, she and her sister, Lucy, formed a folk duo called the Simon Sisters. The pair performed at small clubs along the east coast, eventually performing on the television show *Hootenanny*. Soon afterwards they recorded an album with Kapp Records and their most popular single, "Winkin', Blinkin', and Nod," reached number 78 on music charts. The Simon Sisters stopped performing together in 1965 after Lucy married.

For a short time in 1969, Simon was the lead singer for a rock band called Elephant's Memory. She also sang jingles during this period. Soon a demo was favorably considered by Elektra Records, and in 1970 she signed with them. Her 1971 debut, *Carly Simon,* received much positive attention. Timothy Crouse of *Rolling Stone,* noted Simon's impressive vocals and described her voice as, "superbly controlled." Crouse also noticed a literary connection in Simon's music; he said, "some of the songs on *[Carly Simon]* sound like [John] Updike or [J.D.] Salinger short stories set to music." Simon earned a Grammy in 1971 for best new artist.

Nobody Did It Better

Simon followed her debut with a string of successful singles and gold albums during the 1970s. Her *No Secrets* album released in 1972 would become the first

For the Record . . .

Born on June 25, 1945, in New York City; daughter of Richard (publisher) and Andrea Simon; married James Taylor (singer/songwriter) on November 3, 1972 (divorced 1981); children: Sally, Ben; married James Hart (writer/businessman) December 23, 1987; *Education:* attended Sarah Lawrence College.

During the early 1960's, Simon and sister Lucy performed as a folk duo called the Simon Sisters; performed as lead singer for the rock group, Elephant's Memory, 1969; after singing jingles and making demos for two years, signed with Elektra label in 1970; released debut album, *Carly Simon,* 1971;*No Secrets,* 1972; during the early 1980s suffered severe stage fright; rebounded in 1987 with *Coming Around Again;* wrote scores for several motion pictures including co-writing hit "Nobody Does It Better" with Marvin Hamlisch and Carole Bayer Sager for the James Bond movie *The Spy Who Loved Me;* has published five children's books; wrote children's opera *Romulus Hunt,* which premiered in 1993; appeared on several television programs during the 1990s; reunited on stage with ex-husband James Taylor for a concert benefiting the Martha's Vineyard Agricultural Society, 1995.

Awards: Grammy for Best New Artist, 1971; Academy Award and Golden Globe for "Let The Rivers Run" from *Working Girl,* 1989; platinum cerification for *Coming Around Again,* 1988; inducted into Songwriters Hall of Fame, 1994; nominated for Grammy, Best Traditional Pop Vocal Performance for *Film Noir,* 1998.

Addresses: *Home*—Martha's Vineyard, MA. *Record Company*—Arista Records, Inc., Arista Building, 6 West 57th St., New York, NY 10019. *Fan Club*—The Carly Simon Fan Club, The Fan Emporium, P.O. Box 679, Branford, CT 06405. Websites—www.aristarec .com.

of many gold albums, and included the hit,"You're So Vain." This was followed by *Hotcakes* in 1974, which was called the year's top album in the pop category by *Cue* magazine; that release included hit single, "Haven't Got Time For The Pain," and a duet with husband of two years, James Taylor, "Mockingbird." These would be followed by others. Simon's style of fashioning songs from autobiographical material caused much speculation about who her songs were written about.

In 1974 Simon took a break from live performing after the birth of her first child, although she continued recording and released several additional albums from the mid 1970s to the early 1980s. In 1977, she had a hit with the theme "Nobody Does It Better," from the James Bond movie, *The Spy Who Loved Me.* Her 1978 album, *Boys In The Trees,* would go platinum.

The first half of the 1980s were difficult for Simon personally and professionally. She was in the process of a divorce from Taylor, and her young son, Ben, had undergone a serious kidney operation. After being pushed by Elektra executives to tour in 1981, she eventually collapsed from exhaustion and stage fright during a concert. This was followed by her 1985 album, *Spoiled Girl,* which even she admitted to *People* interviewer, Jane Hall, "just bombed."

Came Around Again

Simon rebounded in 1987 after penning the theme, "Coming Around Again," for Mike Nichols's film *Heartburn.* The hit was also released on an album of the same name, and included other hits, "Give Me All Night," and "As Time Goes By." *Rolling Stone* reviewer Rob Hoerburger said *Coming Around Again,* "... is a strong reminder of how refreshing a diversion Carly Simon can be." *Coming Around Again* was released on her new label, Arista Records, in 1987.

This was followed up with another hit single "Let The Rivers Run," from the film, *Working Girl,* which she wrote and performed. This theme earned her an Academy Award, an Oscar, and a Golden Globe Award. Also in 1987, she married writer and businessman James Hart on December 23; she recovered adequately from stage fright and performed a concert close to home in Martha's Vineyard, Massachusetts. The concert was filmed for an HBO special. In 1988, she released her gold album, *Greatest Hits Live.*

Simon's popularity and success as a singer and songwriter continued into the 1990s. She wrote the score for the film, *Postcards From The Edge,* and released *Have You Seen Me Lately?,* in 1990 which included eleven new songs by Simon and guest performances by sister, Lucy, and Judy Collins. Also in 1990 she released the second of her set of jazz/standards, *My Romance.* In 1992 she composed and recorded the soundtrack for the movie, *This Is My Life,* which spawned one of Simon's best love songs, "You're The Love Of My Life." She also performed on the hugely popular Frank Sinatra

Duets album, and wrote five children's books and the children's opera *Romulus Hunt* for the Metropolitan Opera Guild and the John F. Kennedy Center.

In November 1994, Simon released what she called "... the most personal album, in a sea of personal albums that I have ever made." Simon discussed her sources for the majority of her material at her online fan club site at www.fanemporium.com. With the exception of two songs, all the cuts from *Letters Never Sent* were written or co-written by Simon inspired by a real box of letters that Simon had written and never sent. "Like A River," was written soon after her mother's death and stemmed from Simon's strong desire to communicate with her mother. Reviewers agreed that this effort was a great success. *Entertainment Weekly* gave *Letters* a "B+" rating, and called Simon's action, "a daring move that pays off ." The *Pittsburgh Post-Gazette* called it the "best collection since the '70s."

The following year, in December of 1995, Arista released a boxed set, *Clouds In My Coffee,* which was a retrospective on a prolific career spanning from 1965 to 1995. It includes many of her previous hit songs, some new, some live, and some previously unrecorded cuts. Marjorie Rosen of *People* called the collection, "... some kinda wonderful." A *Billboard* reviewer called the collection, "... a must have for the Carly Simon fan and a long deserved tribute to an artist who has made immeasurable contributions to American pop, folk, and rock."

Some of the cuts include remixes of her timeless classics as well as two songs from her duet album with sister Lucy. Simon's first demo, recorded in 1965, "Play With Me" is included. In conjunction with the upcoming release of the retrospective, Simon kicked off her first concert tour in 14 years with performances in 16 cities. She received glowing reviews including one from Steve Morse of the *Boston Globe,* who commented on the high level of confidence that Simon displayed in a March 1995 performance at the Boston's Avalon. She was joined by daughter, Sally, singing Wilson Pickett's "Mustang Sally." Simon "stopped commuters in their tracks" according to *People,* during a live performance in New York's Grand Central Terminal on April 2, 1995. The performance was filmed and later released by PolyGram, called *Live At Grand Central;* it also aired on Lifetime TV.

Completed Trilogy of Standards

Simon's latest release, *Film Noir,* on Arista in 1997, completes her trilogy of standards. The first, *Torch,* 1981, and second, *My Romance,* 1990 were quite successful. The majority of songs included on this album hail from movies of the 1940s. The seductive, mysterious music sets a romantic mood, reminds one of another era, and evokes a sense of the drama reminiscent of the silver screen. Simon's sultry, smoky voice against the orchestra increases the lush, sensual sound of this production. The cuts were mainly taped live, giving the album a fresh, unrehearsed feeling. She and co-producer, Jimmy Webb, harmonize together on the Frank Loesser song, "Spring Will Be A Little Late This Year." Simon sang another duet, "Two Sleepy People," a sweet, light love song, with longtime friend, John Travolta.

The CD is an enhanced cassette disk (ECD) which contains multimedia files that can be used to interface with the Simon World Wide Web site and offers free time on America Online. Simon's son, Ben Taylor, joins in on several cuts. The reception of *Film Noir* has been deservedly positive; *New York Post* reviewer Liz Smith called the latest release, "... the sexiest CD of the year." Howard Cohen of the *Miami Herald* said, "... the first-take vocal aspect lends spontaneity and warmth."

Cohen also noted how Simon "... constantly shifts stylistic gears," on the newest album. Perhaps this is a factor which has aided Simon in maintaining the longevity of her professional success. Constantly looking for new ways to utilize her wealth of creativity, whether it be literary, insinging style, or the range of material from which she pulls themes, Simon continues to delight fans. She told *People* in November 1997, that continuing her tradition of always doing the opposite of her last, her next work will be "a stripped-down set of originals called *Stark.*" Her fans will wait in anticipation.

Selected discography

(With sister Lucy) *The Simon Sisters* (includes "Winkin', Blinkin', and Nod"), Kapp, 1964.
Carly Simon, Elektra, 1971.
Anticipation, Elektra, 1971.
No Secrets, (includes "You're So Vain"), Elektra, 1972.
Hotcakes, (includes "Haven't Got Time For The Pain" and "Mockingbird"), Elektra, 1974.
Playing Possum, Elektra, 1975.
Another Passenger, Elektra, 1976.
(Contributor) *The Spy Who Loved Me* (soundtrack, includes "Nobody Does It Better"), 1977, reissued Alliance, 1996.
Boys In The Trees, Elektra, 1978.
Spy, Elektra, 1979.
Come Upstairs, Warner Bros., 1980.
Torch, Warner Bros., 1981.
Spoiled Girl, Epic, 1985.

Coming Around Again, (includes "Coming Around Again," "Give Me All Night," and "As Time Goes By"), Arista, 1987.
Greatest Hits Live, Arista, 1988.
(Contributor) *Working Girl* (soundtrack, includes "Let The Rivers Run"), Arista, 1989.
My Romance, Arista, 1990.
Have You Seen Me Lately?, Arista, 1990.
(Contributor) *This Is My Life* (soundtrack, includes "You're The Love Of My Life"), Warner Bros., 1992.
Frank Sinatra's *Duets,* Capitol, 1993.
Letters Never Sent, (includes "Like A River"), Arista, 1994.
Clouds In My Coffee, (includes "Play With Me"), Arista, 1995.
Film Noir (includes "Spring Will Be A Little Late" and "Two Sleepy People"), Arista, 1997.

Selected writings

Amy And The Dancing Bear (juvenile), Doubleday, 1989.
Postcards From The Edge, score, 1990.
The Boy of The Bells (children's book), Doubleday, 1990.
The Fisherman's Song (children's book), Doubleday, 1992.
Romulus Hunt (an opera for children), 1992.
Midnight Farm (children's book), Simon and Schuster, 1997.
The Nighttime Chauffeur (children's book), Doubleday.

Sources

Books

Rees, Dafydd, and Luke Crampton, *Encyclopedia of Rock and Roll,* Dorling Kindersly, 1996.
Romanowski, Patricia, and Holly George-Warren, editors, *The New Rolling Stone Encyclopedia of Rock and Roll,* Fireside, 1995.

Periodicals

Billboard, December 2, 1995; December 16, 1995; January 27, 1996, p. 107; September 6, 1997; October 4, 1997.
Boston Globe, November 13, 1994; March 14, 1995.
Cue, December 9, 1974.
Entertainment Weekly, November 11, 1994, p. 77.
InStyle, July 1995, pp. 62-68.
Miami Herald, September 12, 1997.
New York Post, October 8, 1997.
MOJO, November 1997.
People, August 17,1987, pp. 38, 40; April 17, 1995; December 18, 1995, p. 23; November 3, 1997.
Rolling Stone, April 29, 1971; June 18, 1987, p. 85.
Toronto Sun, October 25, 1997.
TV Guide, May 13, 1995, p. 46.
USA Today, March 8, 1995; December 19,1995.

Online

www.arista.rec.com/aristaweb/CarlySimon/main.html
www.cdnow.com
www.cduniverse.com
www.fanemporium.com/carlysimon/history.htm
www.ziva.com/carly/clouds_pr.html

Additional information was provided by Arista Records.

—Debra Reilly

Spice Girls

Rock group

Credited with spearheading the pop music revival of the mid 1990s, England's oft derided Spice Girls took not only the United Kingdom by a blinding blitz-krieg-like storm but the world as well with their infectious bouncy bubblegum pop, which not only fired up their rabid fans but critics and album sales as well.

According to the *All Music Guide*'s Stephen Erlewine, the vast appeal of the Spice Girls was due to the fact that they "used dance-pop as a musical base, but they infused the music with a fiercely independent, feminist stance that was equal parts Madonna, post riot grrrl alternative rock feminism, and a co-opting of the good-times-all-the-time stance of England's new lad culture. Their proud all-girl image and catchy dance-pop appealed to younger listeners, while their colorful, sexy personalities and sense of humor appealed to older music fans, making the Spice Girls a cross generational success."

The feisty party of five known as the Spice Girls came into being in early 1994, when the various members

Archive Photos

For the Record . . .

Members include **Victoria Aadams** (Posh Spice); **Melanie Brown** (Scary Spice); **Emma Bunton** (Baby Spice); **Melanie Chisholm** (Sporty Spice); **Geri Halliwell** (Ginger Spice, left group May 31, 1998).

Group formed in London in 1994; signed to Virgin and released *Spice,* 1996; released *Spiceworld,* 1997; released *Spiceworld*, the movie, 1997.

Awards: Platinum status for *Spice,* 1997; platinum status for *Spiceworld*, 1998.

Addresses: *Record company*—Virgin, 338 North Foothills Rd., Beverly Hills, CA 90210.

responded to an advertisement in the *Stage* magazine. The advertisement was looking for "streetwise, ambitious, and dedicated" young women. The successful applicants were being assembled by their would be manager Chris Herbert, who was hoping to create a female version of the popular British boy pop band Take That.

In June of that year, five of the applicants, who had known each other from showing up at the same auditions in the greater London area, were selected to form the band Touch. The women who were chosen included: Victoria Aadams, Melanie Brown, Melanie Chisholm, Geri Halliwell, and Michelle Stephenson. Stephenson ended up leaving the group the following month because of an illness in her family and because she desired to go to college. In September, Emma Bunton was picked as the replacement for Stephenson.

Touch changed its name to the Spice Girls, in the autumn of 1994. Throughout the rest of the year and into early 1995, the Spice Girls lived in a rented house in the Maidenhead area of west London. While they lived there, they rehearsed and collaborated with numerous songwriters. During this time, the Spice Girls were becoming increasingly disenchanted with their manager. Their primary complaint was that Herbert and his father, who helped him co-manage the group, would not listen to what they had to say. By March of 1995, the Spice Girls had dismissed the Herberts as their managers.

The Spice Girls subsequently signed with Simon Fuller's 19 Management company. Fuller then put his new charges in touch with some of the songwriters who were associated with his company and they began collaborations with the Spice Girls, which would lead to their debut album. Throughout the summer of 1995, Fuller contacted various media outlets, record labels, and music publishers extolling the virtues of the Spice Girls.

Nicknames added Spice

It was at one such meeting with the British teen magazine, *Top of the Pops,* that each of the individual Spice Girls acquired her distinctive nickname. *Top of the Pops* editor Peter Loraine explained to Chris Heath of *Rolling Stone*, that "we [*Top of the Pops*' editorial staff] decided that they were the kind of group we could have a lot of fun with. We thought we could make up some stupid names." Thus, each member of the Spice Girls was ascribed with a nickname and identity based on her appearance and personality. Aadams, who was raised in a wealthy household, became "Posh Spice." Brown, who loved rap and hip hop music and had a pierced tongue was dubbed "Scary Spice." Bunton, the newest member of the bunch was "Baby Spice," while Chisholm's love of athletics earned her the name "Sporty Spice." Halliwell, who was known for her provocative outfits and an earlier stint as a nude model, was originally called "Sexy Spice," although it was later changed to "Ginger Spice," due to the color of her hair.

By August of 1995, an intense bidding war had erupted over who would hold the rights to the Spice Girls' publishing contract. A small not well known collective called Windswept Pacific eventually won the war for the rights to the Spice Girls' publishing contract. Also around this time, Fuller signed the Spice Girls up with Brilliant!, who were responsible for plugging and promoting the group, especially on television. In September, Virgin Records beat out a number of the major labels to the right to sign the Spice Girls up for a recording contract. On their signing with Virgin, Halliwell told Paul Gorman from *dotmusic* that "we decided on Virgin because they offered us the chance to go our own way. We feel as though we're breaking down a lot of barriers as women going up against the boy groups and against people's expectations. There's more to us than a lot of those other acts."

In early 1996, the Spice Girls began making personal appearances at a number of music industry events and awards showcases, all the while increasing their carefully calculated exposure in the media. The video for their first single, "Wannabe," was filmed in London in April. The following month saw the Spice Girls conduct their first print press interviews in both *dotmusic* and *Music Week*. Also in May, they made their first televised appearance on the English program *Surprise, Surprise.* They made their first public appearance at the "Clothes Show" roadshow in Glasgow, Scotland, around this time as well.

"Wannabe" Number One

The Spice Girls first single "Wannabe" was released in Britain in July of 1996. It debuted at number one on the British pop singles chart, where it remained for the next two months. Subsequent singles, "Say You'll Be There" and "2 Become 1" also debuted at number one on the pop singles chart in Britain. Their debut album, *Spice*, was released later that year. *Spice* debuted at number one on the British pop albums chart. With the number one pop album position and number one pop singles position firmly in their grasp, the Spice Girls became one of only three artists, in the history of pop, to hold both the number one single and album positionsin Britain over the coveted year end Christmas week period.

Chart domination by the Spice Girls was not a phenomenon solely confined to the British Isles. As the album was released in other nations across the globe, pop charts throughout the world became increasingly infatuated and inundated with all things spicy. Even the usually jaded isolationist America was not immune to the charms of the Spice Girls, when *Spice* was finally released there in early 1997. "Wannabe" eventually topped the Billboard top singles chart in the spring of 1997, while the follow up singles "Say You'll Be There" and "2 Become 1" were top ten dwellers. Fuller proclaimed to Gorman that "the girls helped British acts abroad. Other countries look to the source and see an English act, management, song writers, record company, and publisher." *Gavin's* managing editor, Ben Fong-Torres, concurred, adding that, "they have helped swing the pendulum toward pop. It has moved away from rap, metal, alternative, and other negative sounds."

A Day in Spiceworld

As 1997 progressed, sales of *Spice* continued to climb to nearly 20 million copies worldwide. Combined sales of the Spice Girls' singles were also on the upswing as they reached nearly ten million copies across the globe. The extremely lucrative marketing franchise known as the Spice Girls showed no signs of slowing the rather frenetic pace of goods and services bearing the "spice seal of approval" including Pepsi, Sony Playstation, Polaroid, Walker potato crisps, candy, and even the hallowed British Telecom. Dismissing the notion of mass media saturation and overkill, the Spice Girls launched into their next project, *Spiceworld*, the movie that was based loosely on a day in the whirlwind known as the life of a Spice Girl. The Spice Girls divided their time between work on their cinematic debut and their follow up to their smash debut album.

Spice Up Your Life" was the first single from the soon to be released *Spiceworld* album. The single was released in the autumn. While popular, catchy, and possessing a good dance beat, "Spice Up Your Life" failed to light up the charts as "Wannabe" had done. Critics viewed this as the inevitable media backlash but the Spice Girls remained undeterred. In early November of 1997, *Spiceworld* was released. Their sophomore album served as a soundtrack for the movie of the same name. Although selling a healthy 150,000 or so copies in its first week or so of release, *Spiceworld* was viewed as a disappointment in light of its predecessor's phenomenal sales record.

Less than two weeks after the release of *Spiceworld*, the Spice Girls had fired their manager Fuller, who was also known as "Svengali Spice," for his dealings behind the scenes. There were conflicting stories over why Fuller was fired. One account claimed that it was due to a nasty affair between him and Bunton, while another account said it was due to his 20 percent cut of all Spice Girls merchandise and goods. Halliwell took over as de facto manager until a suitable replacement was found.

The Spice Girls movie, *Spiceworld*, was released in Britain over the Christmas holidays. It made its American debut about a month later over the Super Bowl weekend in late January of 1998. The biggest impact of the movie was that it managed to somewhat bolster the rather lacklustersales of *Spiceworld*, the album, which helped to keep the group firmly in the eye of the media and the public.

Explaining "girl power" manifest of the Spice Girls, Halliwell told Gorman that, "we want to bring some of the glamour back to pop, like Madonna had when we were growing up. Pop is about fantasy and escapism, but there's so much bull. . .around at the moment. We want to be relevant to girls our age."

On May 31, 1998, Halliwell left the group claiming irreconcilable differences. Determined to forge ahead with their "girl power," the rest of the group is still committed to keep the band going. The remaining four do not feel the need to replace Halliwell. David Wigg of the British *Express* was quoted in *People* as saying, "they really don't need one."

Selected discography

Spice (includes "Wannabe," "Say You'll Be There," and "2 Become 1"), Virgin, 1996.
Spiceworld (includes "Spice Up Your Life"), Virgin, 1997.

Sources

Periodicals

Entertainment Weekly, November 7, 1997; December 12, 1997.
Newsweek, November 10, 1997.
Rolling Stone, April 10-24, 1997.

Online

"Spice Girls," http://www.allmusic.com/cgi-win/AMG.exe?sql=2P_IDP (February 23, 1998).
"Spice Girls," http://www.dotmusic.com/MWtalentspice.html (February 23, 1998).

—Mary Alice Adams

Spirit

Rock band

Beginning in one of the most fertile periods of American rock music, Spirit created some of the most memorable music of the past three decades, outlasting many pop music trends along the way. With its eclectic musical mix of rock, jazz, blues, and folk influences, Spirit was one of the premier West Coast rock bands to emerge during the late 60s. Although the band never reached superstar status, it has maintained a dedicated following. Spirit's musical activities came to a premature and tragic end with the accidental death of leader and guitarist Randy California in 1997.

The story of Spirit began at the folk club, The Ash Grove, in the early 60s. The Ash Grove hosted traditional artists such as Doc Watson, Brownie McGhee and Sonny Terry, Lightnin' Hopkins, and The Carter Family. The owner of the Ash Grove frequently brought artists to the home of his teenaged nephew, Randy Wolfe, an aspiring guitarist. In 1965, Wolfe's stepfather Ed Cassidy was the drummer in another of the Ash Grove's regular artists, the blues band The Rising Sons, which featured Taj Mahal and Ry Cooder.

Michael Ochs Archives

For the Record . . .

Members include **Mark Andes,** (b. February 19, 1948, member c. 1967-71, 1975), bass; **Matt Andes** (member c. 1976-1996), guitar; **Rachel Andes** (member 1996), vocals; **Randy California,** (b. Randy Craig Wolfe, February 20, 1951, Los Angeles, d. January 2, 1997, drowned, Molokai, Hawaii), guitar, vocals; **Ed Cassidy** (b. May 4, 1923), drums; **Jay Ferguson,** (b. John Arden Ferguson, February 5, 1947, member c. 1967-71), vocals; **Barry Keene** (member c. 1975), bass; **Larry Knight** (member c. 1973-78), bass; **John Locke,** (b. September 23, 1943, member c. 1967-72, 1975, 1996), keyboards; **Steve Loria** (member c. 1970s-96), bass; **Al Staehely** (member c. 1972), bass, vocals; **J. Christian Staehely** (member c. 1972), guitar.

Formed c. 1967, in Los Angeles; released debut album Spirit on Ode, 1967; appeared in and scored film *The Model Shop,* 1969; disbanded c. 1971; reformed c. 1973; formed Potato Records, 1978; formed W.E.R.C.C.R.E.W. Records, c. 1990s; disbanded c. 1997.

Awards - R.I.A.A. Gold Album Certification, *Twelve Dreams of Dr. Sardonicus,* c. 1976.

Address: *Record Company*—Spirit/W.E.R.C.C.R.E.W., P. O. Box 655, Ojai, CA, 93024.

By the end of the year, Cassidy had left the Rising Sons, and began sitting in with Wolfe's new folk-rock band The Red Roosters, with guitarist Jay Ferguson, bassist Mark Andes, and vocalist Mike Fondiler. The Roosters disbanded in 1966 when Wolfe's family moved to New York City. Wolfe later described losing his guitar during the move as "a stroke of luck", as he met Jimi Hendrix at Manny's Music Store. Hendrix dubbed Wolfe "Randy California" and invited him to join his band Jimmy James and the Blue Flames.

Soon Hendrix went to England to form the Experience, and Randy back to California. At a love-in in Hollywood, Randy and Ed Cassidy ran into former Red Roosters Ferguson and Andes. They reformed, adding pianist John Locke and called the band Spirits Rebellious after the book by Khalil Gibran. They soon shortened the name to Spirit. The band, its musical mentor Barry Hansen [radio DJ Dr. Demento] and families moved into a big yellow house in Topanga Canyon, California to rehearse.

Spirit played clubs around Los Angeles and auditioned for record companies early in 1967. Producer Lou Adler signed Spirit to his new label Ode Records. Spirit's self titled debut album begins with a series of enthusiastic shouts by the band members before launching into the insistent ensemble playing of "Fresh Garbage"; Spirit's sound reflected the many influences of each band member and their abilities to fuse them into a cohesive sound.

Spirit Gets A Line On A Classic Song

While *Spirit* reached the Top 40 of *Billboard*'s Album Chart, the band needed a hit single. California was up to the task with "I Got A Line On You", the leadoff track to 1968's *The Family That Plays Together.* An insistent guitar riff propelled the single to number 25 on the *Billboard*Charts. The album found the band further refining its sound and reflecting its concern for the spiritual well-being of humankind in its lyrics.

Spirit appeared in and scored parts of Jacques Demy's film *The Model Shop* in 1969. This activity caused the band to lose focus during recording sessions for *Clear.* Randy California recalls in the *Time Circle (1968-1972)* liner notes, "The album itself was an afterthought in that we were working on the soundtrack to the movie. ...So of all the albums, that was the least concentrated effort of the group..." Despite that humble summation by California, *Clear*boasted many strong tracks, including "Dark Eyed Woman". The band's fortunes were damaged by a radio tip sheet report that its single "1984" was "too political" for AM radio play, halting its progress in the charts.

Woodstock A Missed Opportunity

Most damaging for Spirit's career in 1969 was a management decision to send the band on a radio promotion tour instead of appearing at Woodstock, right before Randy California's old friend Jimi Hendrix. California recalled in *Clear*'s liner notes, "You can imagine how we all felt watching Woodstock on the 5 o'clock news knowing we should have been there."

Recording sessions for Spirit's fourth album were delayed when California fell from a horse and fractured his skull. After much delay, *Twelve Dreams of Dr. Sardonicus* was released late in 1970. The album featured Spirit's most structured material to date, put together to form a cohesive statement. Disheartened by the lukewarm reception it received, Spirit disbanded in 1971, with Ferguson and Andes forming the group Jo Jo Gunne. After an unsuccessful solo album, California quit the music business and relocated to Hawaii.

Ed Cassidy and John Locke attempted to revamp the group for 1973's unsuccessful *Feedback.* Eventually California returned to the fold, and Spirit recorded an album, *Journey Through Potatoland,* that remained unreleased until 1981. Touring enabled the band to finance further recording sessions which led to a contract with Mercury Records in 1975 and the albums *Spirit of '76* and *Son of Spirit.* 1976's *Farther Along* featured John Locke and Mark Andes for the first time since *Twelve Dreams of Dr. Sardonicus,* while *Future Games* was a bizarre, science fiction inspired solo album.

A Spirited Revival Cut Short

Spirit continued to record and tour throughout the 1980s. The 90s have seen a renewal of interest in Spirit's early work, culminating in Randy California's assistance with deluxe reissues of the first four Spirit albums. Yet Spirit would not remain a name from the past. The band contributed a new track, alongside the most innovative rock artists, to a benefit CD for the English magazine *Ptolemaic Terrascope* when it was in financial trouble. *California Blues,* the most recent Spirit album was released on the band's W.E.R.C.C.R.E.W. label. The lineup features California and Cassidy with guitarist Matt Andes, brother of former bassist Mark, and his daughter Rachel on vocals.

Spirit's career came to a tragic end on January 2, 1997, when Randy California was body surfing in Hawaii with his 12 year old son Quinn. Caught in a rip tide, Randy was able to push his son to safety but was dragged away by the waves. His body was never recovered.

Selected discography

Spirit, Ode, 1967, reissued Legacy, 1996.
The Family That Plays Together, Ode, 1968, reissued Legacy, 1996
Clear, Ode, 1969, reissued Legacy, 1996.
Twelve Dreams of Dr. Sardonicus, Epic, 1970, reissued Mobile Fidelity, 1992, reissued Legacy, 1996.
Feedback, Epic, 1972.
Best of Spirit (rec. 1967-73), Epic, 1973.
Spirit of '76, Mercury, 1975.
Son of Spirit, Mercury, 1975.
Farther Along, Mercury, 1976.
Future Games (A Magical Kahuna Dream), Mercury, 1977.
Live, Potato, 1979.
The Adventures of Kaptain Kopter and Commander Cassidy in Potatoland (rec. 1974), Rhino, 1981.
Spirit of '84, Mercury, 1984.
Rapture In The Chambers, I.R.S., 1989.
Tent of Miracles, Dolphin, 1990.
Time Circle (1968-1972), Epic, 1991.
Chronicles, W.E.R.C.C.R.E.W., 1992.
Potatoland, W.E.R.C.C.R.E.W., 1992.
Live At LaPaloma, W.E.R.C.C.R.E.W., 1992.
California Blues, W.E.R.C.C.R.E.W., 1996.
The Mercury Years (rec. 1975-1977), Mercury, 1997.
"Cages", from *Succour, A Terrascope Benefit Album,* Flydaddy, 1996.

Solo project

(by Randy California), *Kapt. Kopter and the (Fabulous) Twirly Birds,* Epic, 1973.
(By Randy California), "American Society", POT 6 EP accompanying *Ptolemaic Terrascope* Issue 6.

Sources

Books

Joynson, Vernon, *Fuzz, Acid, and Flowers,* Borderline, 1995.

Periodicals

Billboard, February 3, 1968; September 27, 1969; February 13, 1971; April 29, 1972; July 19, 1975; September 15, 1984.
Crawdaddy, March 19, 1972; May 14, 1972.
Creem, November, 1976.
Jazz & Pop, March, 1971.
Melody Maker, February 7, 1970; June 10, 1972; March 31, 1973; April 23, 1973; July 12, 1975; September 18, 1976; March 18, 1978; September 9, 1978; May 9, 1981.
Ptolemaic Terrascope, Issue 3; Issue 4; Issue 23.
Rolling Stone, March 4, 1971, August 14, 1975; January 1, 1976.
Variety, February 7, 1968; October 22, 1969; April 19, 1972; September 8, 1976; September 15, 1976.

Online

http://kspace.com/spirit
http://www.terrascope.org

Additional information was provided by W.E.R.C.C.R.E.W. Records.

—Jim Powers

Sugar Ray

Alternative pop band

Corbis

Sugar Ray grew out of the irreverent Southern California, Orange County-centered music scene that spawned such alternative successes as No Doubt and Sublime—bands who, like Sugar Ray, have helped infuse a spirited reworking of both the neo-punk and reggae genres into modern rock. Fronted by vocalist Mark McGrath, Sugar Ray hit it huge with their 1997 release *Floored* and its extremely successful single, "Fly." The reggae-esque song, wrote Michael Saunders of the *Boston Globe,* featured "pillowy bass lines and summer-camp-sloppy harmonies " Saunders deemed it "a track as simple as a virus and every bit as infectious." McGrath summed up "Fly"'s widespread success by pointing out to *USA Today*'s Cathy Hainer that the song has a basic appeal—"my grandma loves it, and my hard-core punk friends love it."

All members of Sugar Ray, with the exception of latecomer Craig "DJ Homicide" Bullock, grew up in the affluent Orange County enclave of Newport Beach. McGrath, a graduate of the University of Southern California, confessed to acquiring a love of punk rock music at an early age, while bandmate Rodney Sheppard admitted to learning to play guitar by copying Cheap Trick riffs. Sugar Ray's rhythm section is made up of Murphy Karges on bass and drummer Stan Frazier. Originally, they began as a cover band called the Shrinky Dinks that played rap and heavy-metal tunes at parties. "We were bad enough players that it all sounded like one wall of noise," McGrath told *Rolling Stone*'s David Wild, "but people were so amused by our antics, no one picked up on it." Later they were forced to find a new name when the toy company who manufactured a product called Shrinky Dinks objected and threatened to sue. The "Sugar Ray" tag came out of McGrath's love of sports and pays homage to boxer Sugar Ray Robinson.

Eventually Sugar Ray began writing their own material—from metal to punk to hip-hop. They also attracted a devoted fan base in their Orange County area with raucous live shows centered on McGrath's showmanship and penchant for near nudity at times. The labels soon came calling, and in 1994, when "anyone who played electric guitar was the next Nirvana," as McGrath told Wild in *Rolling Stone,* they were offered a deal with Lava Records. Success simply offered more opportunity for pranks. Their 1995 debut album, *Lemonade and Brownies* was delivered, true to irreverent Sugar Ray form, to the label offices by the band themselves clad only in jockstraps. Furthermore, it received far more attention for the provocative pose of Baywatch actress Nicole Eggert on the cover than the music. Inside, wrote Jerry Lee Williams of *Seconds*, it offered "a compendium of basic suburban AlternMetal Funk Hop movers."

For the Record . . .

Members include **Craig "DJ Homicide" Bullock,** turntables (joined band, c. 1996); **Stan Frazier,** drums; **Murphy Karges,** bass; **Mark McGrath,** vocals; and **Rodney Sheppard,** guitar. *Education:* McGrath graduated from the University of Southern California

Band formed as the Shrinky Dinks; signed to Atlantic Records, 1994; released first LP, *Lemonade and Brownies,* 1995; *Floored,* 1997.

Addresses: *Home*—Los Angeles, CA. *Record company*—Atlantic Records, 1290 Avenue of the Americas, New York, NY

Tracks on *Lemonade and Brownies* like "Danzig Needs a Hug" displayed the band's smart aleck side even further. Its first single, "Mean Machine," received some airplay, but it was a career-making appearance on Howard Stern's syndicated radio show that would fuel sales. Stern had once written a painfully bad, though somewhat precocious batch of songs as a teenager in the1960s, and once played them on his show. Sugar Ray learned to play one, "Psychedelic Bee," and included it on *Lemonade and Brownies.* Stern was so touched that he invited them on his show, and the subsequent televised version of the session, which aired on the cable-television channel E!, helped earn the band greater exposure and new fans.

Added DJ, New Grooves

Even on *Lemonade and Brownies,* Sugar Ray was displaying a talent for being able to cross over into a myriad of musical genres, from punk to ska to alterna-pop. "There are five guys in this band, and when we collaborate everyone contributes their different styles," drummer Stan Frazier explained to Doug Reece in *Billboard.* Their sound took on an added and fresh dimension when they added Craig "DJ Homicide" Bullock to spin turntables and give their songs a whole new live, quasi-Beastie Boys kind of mood with scratching, sampling, and heavy remixing of their own instruments. "Homicide is like a second guitar," bassist Murphy Karges told *Guitar World.*

Before their 1995 debut, Sugar Ray had never actually toured, though they were certainly veterans of performing live. They paid their dues over the next two years, however, playing extensively through 1996 and even opening for the revived Sex Pistols that summer of 1996. The band then headed into the studio to record their second album with renowned producer Dave Kahne. It was not an easy time for the band personally, but out of the tension came *Floored.* Within one week of its release in mid-1997, *Floored's* sales eclipsed that of *Lemonade and Brownies.*

"Fly" Soared

It was the extremely catchy second first single called "Fly" that launched Sugar Ray into alternative chart history. The non-radio version of the song featured a Jamaican dance-hall-reggae singer named Super Cat. Just a few days after the idea of adding a live "toaster" to the reggae-influenced track, Super Cat was in New York with them. Sugar Ray was, appropriately, floored "to see this guy put down a track with four white guys from Newport Beach—it was just a lucky act of fate," McGrath told *Spin*'s Jonathan Gold.

"What came out of those sessions with Super Cat," wrote *Details*' Pat Blashill, was "a sweet, slightly drunken song, wobbly with reggae flavor and a ridiculously sunny vibe." "Fly" stayed at the number one spot on *Billboard*'s Modern Rock charts through the summer and fall of 1997, and it made Sugar Ray one of the top alternative acts of the year. Ironically, the blithe song was actually borne out of some band friction during the New York recording sessions: McGrath didn't like the new songs that they wrote, was thinking about quitting, and disappeared for a few days. Meanwhile, Frazier was also depressed, but came up with "Fly"'s melody and the line "I just wanna fly!" Six months later, they received a gold record for the song.

Warped Focused

Floored also contained more teen-angst nostalgia with a cover of the Adam & the Ants classic "Stand and Deliver," as well as several original tracks that again ran the gamut from punk to hip-hop. Sugar Ray were now full-fledged rock stars, having appeared in the 1997 Ivan Reitman film *Father's Day,* starring Robin Williams and Billy Crystal,. The band spent most of the summer of 1997 on the Warped tour, the nexus for the skate-punk, surf-punk, Southern California area punk bands, before achieving more mainstream success. Afterward, they played some dates in Europe and then headlined an American tour, where they found that being rock stars had some unexpected drawbacks—they were startled to realize they needed aliases when checking into.

Even with a number one hit and a movie credit under their belts, Sugar Ray was not fazed by success. As McGrath explained to Gold in *Spin.* A video on MTV or a gold record do not necessarily equal wealth. Instead, "you see that you owe the bank of Atlantic records lots of dough." McGrath said he had to borrow money from his father just to pay his pager bill.

Neither touring nor the constant barrage of media encounters seem to bother them, and they profess that they had slogged so long as relative unknowns that they are thrilled with the idea of being rock stars. "In music, you work within a framework," McGrath told Blashill in *Details.* "You have to get in there, rob as much as you can, then get out."

Selected discography

Lemonade and Brownies, Lava/Atlantic, 1995.
Floored, Lava/Atlantic, 1997.

Sources

Alternative Press, October 1997, p. 33.
BAM, June 27, 1997.
Billboard, September 20, 1997, pp. 11, 81.
Boston Globe, July 11, 1997.
Details, September 1997; October 1997, p. 56.
Guitar World, October 1997.
Los Angeles Times, July 10, 1997, p. 38.
Maximum Guitar, November 1997, p. 49.
New York Daily News, July 21, 1997, p. 30.
Rolling Stone, November 21, 1997; February 5, 1998.
Seconds, August 1997.
Spin, November 1997.
USA Today, August 8, 1997.

Additional information was provided by Atlantic Records,.

—Carol Brennan

Bernie Taupin

Lyricist, vocalist

Bernie Taupin is best known for his 30-year collaboration with pop star Elton John, although he has released several solo albums and has written lyrics for others. Taupin's association with John has made him one of the most prolific lyricists of the 20th century. Although Taupin continues writing lyrics for John, he has also formed his own acoustic rock band. In 1996, he and four other musicians became the Farm Dogs, fulfilling a lifelong dream to have his own band. The group has released two albums, *Last Stand In Open Country* (1996) and *Immigrant Sons* (1998).

Born in Sleaford, Lincolnshire, England on May 22, 1950, Taupin was raised in a rural community where men had limited employment opportunities. One either became a farmer, as his father had temporarily, or went to work in a factory in a neighboring town. Taupin left school at age 16 and held various jobs as a young man. He worked as a farm laborer, in a factory, and as an apprentice printer. Taupin admitted to *Billboard* that he was "insubordinate" and got himself fired from the printing job, partially because it seemed like an eternity before he would be a full-fledged printer.

Taupin's songwriting style was influenced by literary and musical factors. He was an avid reader and enjoyed narrative poetry, including works by Alfred Lord Tennyson and Thomas Babington Macaulay. As a teen, he would listen to music in bed at night on a transistor radio. He could pick up the American Forces Network, which was broadcast to the American military in England. He also listed to American music on Radio Luxembourg, a kind of "pirate" radio station. Taupin's cousins lived in London, and when he visited them he discovered lots of interesting music by sorting through their piles of old 78 r.p.m. records. Some of his early musical influences included Leadbelly, Woodie Guthrie, Sonny Terry, Brownie McGhee, and Lightnin' Hopkins. Later, he was inspired by Johnny Horton, Johnny Cash, and Marty Robbins. Taupin appreciated the stories told through their music. Taupin credits Marty Robbins' song "El Paso" as the tune that actually inspired him to write his own songs. Other influences, that were acknowledged during his acceptance of a 1997 ASCAP Golden Word Award, included John Lennon and Joni Mitchell.

As a young man, Taupin enjoyed writing and was encouraged in this effort by his mother. In 1967, after working at various jobs unsuccessfully, he went to London to respond to an ad in the *New Musical Express*. Placed by the new independent label Liberty Records, it sought artists and composers. Taupin has saved these first lyrics, penned in response to the ad, and may include them in a future compilation project. Taupin told *Billboard* that those first few songs had names like "Coffee Colored Lady," "Year Of The Teddy Bear," and "Did Lightnin' Strike A Man," which he called, "all really horribly pretentious stuff."

Taupin began working with Elton John at age 17. His first lyric written in this joint effort was called "Scarecrow," a demo that was never recorded. John had been making demos at Dick James' studio and used some of Taupin's lyrics before they met in person. Finally, they were introduced at the studio; afterwards, they went to the nearby Lancaster Grill on Tottenham Court Road, where they agreed to do some songs together. Taupin never imagined that this would be the beginning of a long-term partnership. For the next year, he wrote lyrics and sent them to John from his home north of London. Eventually, Taupin moved to London and for a while lived at John's parents' home.

Developed Musical Rapport

It wasn't long before the pair developed a musical rapport that would serve them for 30 years. Taupin talked with Paul Gambaccini in *A Conversation with Elton John and Bernie Taupin* during the early 1970s, and told him why he felt they had lasted as a team and would continue to for "a good long time ... is because [we] can turn our ideas into anything, any sort of music." Taupin felt confident in John's ability to interpret his

For the Record . . .

Born May 22, 1950, Sleaford, Lincolnshire, England; has lived in the United States for 20 years and is now a U.S. citizen; married wife Stephanie; has two step-daughters.

A 30-year song-writing collaboration with Elton John began in 1967; produced hit songs and albums including "Goodbye Yellow Brick Road," "Daniel," "The One," "Candle In The Wind," and "Rocket Man;" albums include *Captain Fantastic and The Brown Dirt Cowboy, Tumbleweed, Honky Chateau, Goodbye Yellow Brick Road, Don't Shoot Me I'm Only The Piano Player;* in 1997 the pair reworked "Candle In The Wind," as a tribute to the late Princess Diana; Taupin also released three solo albums including *He Who Rides The Tiger,* 1980, and *Tribe,* 1987; formed quintet, the Farm Dogs; the group has released two albums, *Last Stand In Open Country,* 1996, and *Immigrant Sons,* 1998.

Awards: Songwriters Hall of Fame, inductee, 1992; Rock and Roll Hall of Fame, inductee, 1994; American Academy of Achievement, 1994; ASCAP, Songwriter of the Year, 1994; won six Ivor Novello Awards; INA International Achievement of Excellence; ASCAP, Golden Word Award, 1997.

Addresses: *Record Company and publicist*—Sire Records, Debra Brennan, 2034 Broadway, Santa Monica, CA 90404. Management Lippman Entertainment, Gilles Robitaille, 8900 Wilshire Blvd., Suite 340, Beverly Hills, CA 90211. *Websites*—www.farmdogs and www.discoveryrec.com.

lyrics appropriately, although he would rarely give John input or suggest a particular mood or tempo. Taupin told Gambaccini, "The songs that I write give the idea of how they should be anyway, so it's pretty easy to pick up the mood that should suit them."

By the time they worked together on the *Tumbleweed* album, which was released in 1970, Taupin and John had developed a style of collaboration in which Taupin worked alone, giving the lyrics to John who then developed the melodies. Taupin's writing habits have since changed; where once he simply sat down and wrote unaccompanied, he now finds using a guitar helpful in the creative process. He plays chords on the guitar as he writes the lyrics. It was a real first for Taupin after forming the Farm Dogs when the members sat around in a circle equipped with guitars, and worked out the music as a group.

Taupin has written lyrics for hundreds of songs, many of which Elton John has created melodies for and recorded. Some of their hit songs include "Your Song," "Daniel," "Rocket Man," "Goodbye Yellow Brick Road," and "Candle In The Wind." Their 1975 album, *Captain Fantastic and The Brown Dirt Cowboy* was autobiographical in nature: John was Captain Fantastic and Taupin was The Brown Dirt Cowboy. Taupin also released three solo albums during the 1970s and 1980s. He wrote lyrics for other artists too, including co-writing all ten songs on Alice Cooper's 1978 album *From The Inside.* Taupin wrote the lyrics for "We Built This City," recorded by Starship in 1985 and "These Dreams," recorded by Heart in 1986. He has also penned lyrics for Melissa Manchester, Rod Stewart, John Waite, and others.

Taupin's favorite songs with Elton John include "Sacrifice," 1989, and "The One," 1992. He also favors the original version of "Candle In The Wind," which was written as a tribute to Marilyn Monroe in 1973. Little did he know—as he told Gambaccini in the early 1970s, "I think [its] the best song we've ever written.... I think ... its going to be the best thing we've ever done"—the full magnitude of his words would carry some 20 years hence. Taupin reworked the lyrics at John'srequest in 1997. The new version of "Candle In The Wind" was performed as a tribute by John at Princess Diana's funeral and would go on to become the largest selling single ever, with sales of 35 million copies. John donated his proceeds to Princess Diana's Memorial Fund, which supports her favorite charities and is expected to raise over 160 million dollars.

Taupin had a fascination with the American West as a child. He was interested in the history and, particularly, the people who lived during the time of the gunslingers. He read books about Billy The Kid and Wyatt Earp. This interest eventually led him to move to the United States, where he has lived for over 20 years. He settled in California, became a United States citizen, and now raises cutting horses on a ranch in Santa Ynez Valley, California. With his new lifestyle, Taupin has become the image of the Brown Dirt Cowboy.

In 1996, Taupin fulfilled another lifelong dream and formed his own band, the Farm Dogs. Now he is raising horses, strumming on a git-fiddle, writing lyrics, and crooning with his new rock band rooted in Americana and blues. He told Rick de Yampert of the *Tennessean,*

"I've come full circle." He has certainly come a long way from his rural roots in northern England. Although Taupin regrets not having started his own band earlier, he's philosophical about his life. He told de Yampert, "I'm a great believer in things happening for a reason." Taupin continued, explaining that like every teenage kid, he had dreamed of being in a band. He speculated that perhaps he didn't have the confidence in his musical ability at that age, something he later gained during his "apprenticeship" with John.

Debuted with Farm Dogs

Taupin's Farm Dogs band mates include guitarists Jim Cregan and Robin LeMesurier, drummer Tony Brock and bassist, Tad Wadhams. Their 1996 debut album reflected Taupin's interest in gunfighters and cowboy ballads, entitled *Last Stand In Open Country.* The themes explore the analogy between the Western gunfighter and the man with a guitar. Taupin described the album at Discovery Records online as, "rootsy and authentic" and "blues, folk, country." The *Los Angeles Times* said *Last Stand* displayed "an earthiness of the acoustic settings and the unrefined lead vocals by Taupin."

The band's second album was released in February 1998, called *Immigrant Sons.* A *Hollywood Reporter* review by John Lappen described a February 1998 performance by the Farm Dogs as "a pastoral, calming experience." Lappen also noted that "Taupin sounded great; his raspy voice is perfect for this sort of material." He called the Farm Dogs "as cuddly as an old cur on a stormy night."

Taupin continues to write lyrics for John and he finds no difficulty in stretching his style to accommodate his long-time partner as well as the Farm Dogs. As he has done for 30 years, he writes his lyrics and sends them off to John. He told de Yampert that in order to write lyrics forJohn, "I just have to put myself in a different space and a different place and think about different things and subject matter." His latest effort with John was *The Big Picture,* a collection of standards dedicated to another of John's deceased friends, Gianni Versace. The album was released almost simultaneously with the "Candle In The Wind" single, in 1997.

Selected discography

With Elton John

Elton John (includes "Your Song"), 1970, reissued, Rocket Records, 1996.
Tumbleweed 1970, reissued, Rocket Records, 1996.
Honky Chateau (includes "Rocket Man"), 1972, reissued, Rocket Records, 1996.
Don't Shoot Me I'm Only The Piano Player (includes "Daniel," and "Crocodile Rock"), 1973, reissued, Rocket Records, 1996.
Goodbye Yellow Brick Road (includes "Candle In The Wind," "Goodbye Yellow Brick Road," and "Bennie and The Jets"), 1973, reissue, PGD/Polygram, 1996.
Caribou (includes "Don't Let The Sun Go Down on Me"), 1974, reissued, PGD/Polygram, 1996.
Captain Fantastic and The Brown Dirt Cowboy, 1975, reissued, Rocket Records, 1996.
Blue Moves, 1976, reissued, MCA Records, 1988.
Two Low For Zero, 1983, reissued, MCA Records, 1992.
Breaking Hearts, MCA Records, 1984.
Sleeping With The Past (includes "Sacrifice"), MCA Records, 1989.
The One (includes "The One"), MCA, 1992.
Big Picture, PGD/Polygram, 1997.

Solo

He Who Rides The Tiger, 1980.
Tribe, 1987.

With the Farm Dogs

Last Stand In Open Country, Discovery Records, 1996.
Immigrant Sons, Sire Records, 1998.

Singles

"Candle In The Wind 1997," A & M, 1997.

Sources

Books

Billboard International Buyers Guide, BPI Communications, 1997.
Gambaccini, Paul, *A Conversation With Elton John and Bernie Taupin,* Flash Books, 1975.
Rees, Dafydd and Luke Crampton, *Encyclopedia of Rock Stars,* Dorling Kindersly, 1996.

Periodicals

Associated Press (London), December 11, 1997.
Associated Press (Los Angeles), July 10, 1996.
Billboard, May 31, 1997; September 27, 1997; October 4, 1997.
Hollywood Reporter, February 12, 1998.
Los Angeles Times, February 13, 1998.
New Yorker, August 26-September 2, 1996, p. 108-9.

Tennessean (Nashville, TN), January 23, 1998.
Toronto Sun, September 18, 1997.

Online

pathfinder.com/people/sp/intrigue97/25most/john.html
www.ascap.com
www.billboard.com
www.cdnow.com
www.cduniverse.com
www.discoveryrec.com
www.farmdogs.com

Additional material was provided by publicist Debra Brennan of Sire Records.

—*Debra Reilly*

Ralph Towner

Guitarist, composer

Archive Photos

Classically oriented guitarist and composer Ralph Towner is known primarily for his work with the group Oregon as well as his releases with musicians John Abercrombie and Gary Burton. Towner's compositions, performed on classical and 12-string guitars, range from Baroque-sounding and serene to edgily contemporary and tonally textured. Towner's releases are marked by both brightly rhythmic and thoughtful, ruminative pieces. Don Heckman of the *L.A. Times,* in discussing Towner's 1997 release, *Solo Guitar,* added, "Towner is also a talented melodist ... On the seven works devised for the 12-string instrument, he exploits its myriad potential for unusual combinations of sound and texture."

Towner was born into a musical family in 1940 in Chehalis, Washington. He was able to improvise on the piano at the age of three, and he started trumpet lessons at the age of five. He spent his childhood mastering piano and trumpet but didn't take up guitar until he studied composition and music theory at the University of Oregon. After teaching himself the fundamentals of guitar, he began to compose for the instrument and eventually studied guitar under Karl Scheit in Vienna. He intended to use the piano as his vehicle for improvisational compositions and use the acoustic guitar for classical recitals, but a brief foray into Brazilian music shifted his priorities over to the guitar. Towner first played jazz in New York City in the late 1960s as a pianist and he was strongly influenced by legendary jazz pianist Bill Evans. By the early 1970s he was improvising on classical and 12-string guitars.

Exploring the Guitar

Towner didn't have guitar players as role models for his unique style of guitar improvisation. The influence of Bill Evans was channeled through the medium of guitar instead of piano, and Towner played the guitar in a "pianistic" manner, almost transcending the instrument in a way that makes it sound like a small orchestra. Towner formed alliances with musicians who worked with Bill Evans over the years, including flautist Jeremy Steig, bassists Eddie Gomez, Marc Johnson, and Gary Peacock, and lauded drummer Jack DeJohnette. Towner felt there was an orchestral way of expressing himself musically on a small instrument and the classical guitar seemed the ideal instrument for implying a lot by using very little. Towner's approach to his acoustic instruments has served as an influential model for a generation of guitarists, yet he retains his distinctly original style and sound. *DownBeat*'s Dan Ouellette wrote of Towner, "...The master guitarist displays impeccable technique, compositional brilliance and evocative

For the Record . . .

Born in 1940 in Chehalis, Washington. *Education:* Studied composition and music theory at the University of Oregon; studied guitar under Karl Scheit in Vienna, Austria.

Learned to improvise on the piano at the age of three; started trumpet lessons at the age of five; didn't take up guitar until attending the University of Oregon; first played jazz in New York City in the late 1960s as a pianist and was strongly influenced by Bill Evans; began improvising on classical and 12-string guitars in the late 1960s/early 1970s; formed alliances with musicians who worked with Bill Evans, including flautist Jeremy Steig, bassists Eddie Gomez, Marc Johnson, and Gary Peacock, and drummer Jack DeJohnette; released *Trios/Solos* in 1973 with Glen Moore, *Diary* in 1974; formed Solstice in the mid-1970s; formed Oregon in 1983; released *Ana* and *Selected Signs 1* in 1997; released *A Closer View* in 1998.

Address: *Record company*—ECM records/BMG Classics, 1540 Broadway, 40th floor, New York, NY 10036. Website—www.ecmrecords.com/ecm/artists/20.html.

improvisation...whether Towner is being thoughtful or passionate,he consistently surprises."

Long, Prolific Recording Career

Towner recorded his first album, *Trios/Solos*, on ECM Records in 1973 with Glen Moore, followed by *Diary* in 1974. He released *Matchbook* with Gary Burton in 1975, and *Sargasso Sea* with John Abercrombie in 1976. After forming the popular group Solstice in the mid-1970s, he released *Solstice* and *Sound and Shadows* in 1977. He was also featured with Jan Garbarek on *Dis* in 1977. Towner put out three albums the following year: *Batik*, *Sol Do Meio Dia* with Egberto Gismonti, and *Deer Wan* with Kenny Wheeler. In 1979, he released *Old Friends, New Friends*, and *Works* and in 1980 he released *Solo Concert*.

Towner continued to record, experiment, and grow throughout the 1980s and 1990s. In 1983 he released the album *Blue Sun* and, with the newly formed band Oregon. In 1985 Oregon released *Crossing*. A year later, Towner recorded *Slide Show* with Gary Burton, followed by *Ecotopia* with Oregon in 1987. He released *City of Eyes* in 1989 and *Open Letter* in 1992. With Arild Anderson, he recorded *If You Look Far Enough* in 1993, followed by two releases the following year: *Azimuth/The Touchstone/Depart* with Azimuth, and *Oracle* with Gary Peacock. Towner released *Lost and Found* in 1996, followed by *Ana* and *Selected Signs 1* in 1997, and *A Closer View* in 1998.

Lost and Found featured an acoustic guitar, saxophone, bass, and drums assembly reminiscent of Towner's work with Solstice in the 1970s, and marked the first time Towner recorded with drummer Jon Christensen since that era. They were joined with double-bass player Marc Johnson of the Abercrombie Trio, and multi-reeds player Denney Goodhew of First Avenue. Towner shared composer credits with Johnson and Goodhew on the release and revisited his 1973 composition "Mon Enfant" from *Diary*. *Lost and Found* was an important release because it juxtaposed solo and duet performances with ensemble pieces—as well as improvisations with structured tunes—and summarized many of Towner's primary aims as a guitarist. Towner alluded to much of his previous musical history in *Lost and Found*, a history spanning 24 years.

Neither Jazz nor Classical

Following the release of *Ana*, Ouelette wrote, "The first six tracks find Towner successfully blurring the distinctions between classical and jazz.... Towner sounds like he's playing the thumbpiano one moment, then fingerpicks with percussive glee and slaps at the slacked bass strings to create a gritty blues effect.... *Ana* is a highly recommended guitar delight." Towner is difficult to pigeonhole, as are most original artists, because his compositions are given wide berth. Some of his pieces are simple and ethereal, others are stark and impressionistic, some are flavored with salsa and rollicking guitar riffs, some are serene and reminiscent of the harpsichord, and others are gaily spirited and exclamatory. Neither classical in approach nor traditionally jazz, Towner's compositions are atmospheric, experimental, and uniquely from his own dignified language.

Towner uses unusual tunings: with 12-string guitars, it is possible to tune to many different pitches beside the octaves and unisons. When playing with a classical technique, Towner is able to utilize explosive unison chords that sound larger than life without being rolled or strummed. He then achieves percussive sounds as well as a keyboard sound. This keyboard-like component of the 12-string guitar melds well with Towner's masterful knowledge of piano and sometimes renders his sound harpsichordal in nature; the effect is serene and thoughtful and far more flexible than a traditional guitar approach. Towner achieved his personal goal of fusing piano with guitar and made a distinctive mark on the musical landscape with his original compositions.

Selected discography

On ECM records

(With Glen Moore) *Trios/Solos*, 1973.
Diary, 1974.
(With Gary Burton)*Matchbook*, 1975.
(With John Abercrombie)*Sargasso Sea*, 1976.
Solstice, 1977.
Sound and Shadows, 1977.
(With Jan Garbarek) *Dis*, 1977.
Batik, 1978.
(With Egberto Gismonti) *Sol Do Meio Dia*, 1978.
(With Kenny Wheeler) *Deer Wan*, 1978.
Old Friends, New Friends, 1979.
Works, 1979.
Solo Concert, 1980.
Blue Sun, 1983.
(With Oregon) *Oregon*, 1983.
Crossing, 1985.
Slide Show, 1986.
(With Oregon) *Ecotopia*, 1987.
City of Eyes, 1989.
Open Letter, 1992.
(With Arild Anderson) *If You Look Far Enough*, 1993.
(With Azimuth) *Azimuth/The Touchstone/Depart*, 1994.
(With Gary Peacock) *Oracle*, 1994.
Lost and Found, 1996.
Ana, 1997.
Selected Signs 1, 1997.
Solo Guitar, 1997.
A Closer View, 1998.

Sources

Periodicals

Crusader News, July 10, 1997.
Down Beat, July 1997.
Los Angeles Times, July 6, 1997.

Online

Additional information for this profile was obtained from ECM Records and online at http://www.ecmrecords.com/ecm/artists/20.html.

—B. Kimberly Taylor

Steve Turre

Trombonist

Courtesy of Herbert Barrett Management/Verve

Masterful trombonist Steve Turre distinguished himself first by playing with some of the jazz world's most lauded musicians, including Art Blakey, Woody Shaw, Rahsaan Roland Kirk, Cedar Walton, McCoy Tyner, and Dizzy Gillespie. He emerged as an artist in his own right by fusing his artistry on the trombone with shell-blowing, jazz samba/bossa nova, and Afro-Cuban rhythms with brass undertones and Brazilian-style vocals in his fourth release in 1997, the self-titled *Steve Turre* on Verve. His previous three accomplished releases hinted at where Turre was heading musically, and his bold, experimental sound reached full fruition with *Steve Turre. Down Beat*'s Dan Ouellette wrote, "(*Steve Turre*) not only represents Turre's finest hour to date, but also reaffirms the trombone/shell maestro's promising future."

Turre was born and raised in the San Francisco Bay area to parents who loved jazz and met at a Count Basie dance. Turre's childhood was infused with the strains of big band music along with the salsa and mariachi sounds of his Latin heritage. Whenever Duke Ellington and Count Basie performed in San Francisco, Turre's parents would take him and his younger brother to their shows, and this early exposure to jazz influenced the course of Turre's career. He studied the trombone in grade school, and became enrapt with the music of J.J. Johnson in high school. As an eighteen year old in 1970, Rahsaan Roland Kirk invited Turre to sit in with him during a concert at San Francisco's Jazz Workshop, and Turre was asked to return each time Kirk had a local appearance. Kirk was noted for fashioning instruments out of unorthodox objects like garden hoses and dented, antique instruments. Turre first heard the sound of a shell being played when Kirk banged an enormous gong and then blew a shell. Turre told *Down Beat*'s Jonathon Eig, "The sound of it touched me.... When you hear it live, it kind of goes through you in a way. It's simplicity. The shell is about rhythm and melody. That's it." Turre created a Sanctified Shells choir, but he has been careful not to let the shell-playing become a gimmick that overshadows the rest of his music.

Turre also worked with Van Morrison, Charles Moffet, and the Escovedo Brothers, but his musical break came when he was asked to tour with Ray Charles during his 1972 world tour. Turre spent the remainder of the 1970s working with many of the decade's greatest jazz artists: Cedar Walton, Art Blakey, Woody Shaw, Elvin Jones, Rahsaan Roland Kirk, and Thad Jones and the Mel Lewis Orchestra.

Between 1980-87 Turre worked with Woody Shaw; the association proved beneficial, as Turre and Shaw released twelve recordings and Turre gained credibility as a composer in his own right. Turre had a watershed

For the Record . . .

Born in 1952 in San Francisco Bay area; parents were avid jazz fans who met at a Count Basie concert; studied trombone in grade school; married to cellist Akua Dixon.

First played with Rahsaan Roland Kirk in 1970; spent the 1970s working with Cedar Walton, Art Blakey, Woody Shaw, Elvin Jones, Rahsaan Roland Kirk, and Thad Jones, the Mel Lewis Orchestra, Van Morrison, Charles Moffet, and the Escovedo Brothers; musical break came when he was asked to tour with Ray Charles on his 1972 world tour; Turre worked with Woody Shaw between 1980-87; released *Fire and Ice* in 1987; *Viewpoints & Vibrations* in 1989; *Right Here* in 1991; *Sanctified Shells* in 1993, and *Rhythm Within* in 1995; debut release for Verve Records was *Steve Turre* in 1997; worked with various bands and band leaders such as Lester Bowie, Manny O?Quendo, Dizzy Gillespie, and McCoy Tyner; created the ten-member Sanctified Shell Choir (shell players, trombonists, keyboard players, and percussionists); created various quintets, quartets, and sextets, and performed at jazz festivals and clubs across the country; composed music for television commercials and films, and performed as a trombonist regularly in the *Saturday Night Live* band.

Address: *Record company*— Verve Records, World-wide Plaza, 825 Eighth Avenue, New York, NY 10019 (212) 333-8000, fax (212) 333-8194. E-mail address: http:\\www.verveinteractive.com

moment while on a stopover in Mexico City during a Shaw tour: while visiting relatives, his uncle told him that his Aztec ancestors also had played shells as instruments. Turre visited some Aztec ruins in the area and found inspiration in the stone reliefs of ancient shell players, as he realized being a musicians and playing the shells was his birthright. He knew he was following his heart as well as his rich historical legacy.

Turre released *Fire and Ice* in 1987 and *Viewpoints & Vibrations* in 1989, both for Stash Records. For Antilles Records, he released *Right Here* in 1991, *Sanctified Shells* in 1993, and *RhythmWithin* in 1995. His debut for Verve Records was Steve Turre in 1997. He experimented with and refined his musical direction by working with various bands and band leaders such as Lester Bowie, Manny O'Quendo, Dizzy Gillespie, and McCoy Tyner. He created the ten-member Shell Choir—which consists of shell players, trombonists, keyboard players, and percussionists—as well as various quintets, quartets, and sextets, and performed at jazz festivals and clubs across the country. He also composed music for television commercials and films, and performed as a trombonist regularly in the *Saturday Night Live* band. Turre pointed out to *Down Beat*'s Eig at the end of 1997 that he and J.J. Johnson were the only trombonists with major-label recording deals at the time, and added, "I can't understand why Slide Hampton isn't recording, or why Curtis Fuller, Robin Eubanks, Frank Lacey, and Conrad Herwig don't have major record deals ... I've certainly paid my dues, but I thought the music business was about talent." Unlike days of yore when Glen Miller and Tommy Dorsey were noted for their trombone music, current musical promoters favor saxophone players and trumpeters. Turre told Eig, "If you play something that communicates with people ... they don't care what instrument you're playing."

Turre's shell instruments serve to set him apart from the fray and create a "hook" for the public. He utilizes the shells to broaden and enrich his sound and to create musical contradictions, which is also why he uses a plunger and Harmon mute. He told Eig, "Historically speaking, the shell is the root of the trombone.... It takes a little more endurance to play the shells. It takes more volume of air." Turre aspires to record material with a large orchestra and his Santified Shells shell choir in the future, and plans to record the Steve Turre Sextet With Strings in 1998, featuring Regina Carter on violin, Buster Williams on bass, Mulgrew Miller on piano, Lewis Nash on drums, and his wife Akua Dixon on cello.

Balance of Brass and Strings

Turre balances the sound of brass in his music with two strings, violin and cello, and feels this arrangement creates flawless equilibrium. He writes for strings the same way he writes for horns, and told Eig, "... we hit just as hard as if it had been a trumpet and saxophone.... as a trombone player ... I want the sound to rally around the trombone; that's got to be the center. A lot of times I voice the violin on top and the cello below. That's a beautiful sound." After the release of Turre's eponymous Verve debut in 1997, Oulette wrote, "Turre takes his recording career to the next level with a sumptuous collection of eight tunes that reflect his multifaceted jazz passions.... (He) weaves the plentitude of solos into the fabric of his compositions and steers his supporting cast into enticing rhythmic arrangements."

Billboard featured *Steve Turre* in its "Reviews & Previews" column shortly after it was released, and claimed, "The innovative jazz trombonist who introduced the conch shell to the genre makesan outstanding label debut ... excellent original themes." While performing outside in Chicago on a rainy Saturday afternoon in late 1997, Turre and his band members were greeted with theenthusiasm and excitement usually reserved for rock bands—in spite of the fact that the group is comprised of a violin, cello, trombone, and standard jazz rhythm section. Turre has invoked remarkable enthusiasm—and created an ardent base of fans—for his undeniably original style of jazz.

Selected discography

Fire and Ice, Stash 7 Records, 1987.
Viewpoints & Vibrations, Stash 2 Records, 1989.
Right Here, Antilles Records, 1991.
Sanctified Shells, Antilles Records, 1993.
Rhythm Within, Antilles Records, 1995.
Steve Turre, Verve Records, 1997.

Sources

Periodicals

Billboard, May 17, 1997.
Down Beat, July 1997; December 1997.
The Portland Skanner, May 21, 1997.
The San Francisco Bay Guardian, May 7, 1997.

Online

www.verveinteractive.com

Additional material was provided by the publicity department at Verve Records.

—*B. Kimberly Taylor*

Mike Watt

Bassist, vocalist, songwriter, producer

Courtesy of Martin Lyon

During the early 1980s, Mike Watt became an important influence on the development of the independent music scene in the United States. Beginning in 1980, Watt served as bassist, vocalist, and producer for the Minutemen. Five years later, after the accidental death of fellow Minuteman and longtime friend, D. Boon, the group disbanded. Shortly thereafter, a new trio would emerge containing Watt and Minutemen drummer George Hurley, along with singer and guitarist, Ed Crawford. The new band christened themselves fIREHOSE and released six albums before going their seperate ways in 1993. The flannel shirt-clad Watt is highly esteemed in alternative music circles and his work with the Minutemen and fIREHOSE helped open doors to newer bands like Nirvana and Pearl Jam, and helped make "indie" rock popular on *MTV.* Since the break up of fIREHOSE, Watt has released two solo albums, *Ball-Hog or Tugboat?,* in 1995, and 1997's *Contemplating The Engine Room.* Although very different in style, both were well received, with the latter validating Watt's decision to take an ambitious artistic risk.

Michael Watt was born in San Pedro, California on December 20, 1957, to James Richard, a 20-year Navy chief, and Jean V. Watt. At the age of 12, Watt began playing the bass when he and Boon started their first band. Watt considered Boon a major influence on his style of bass playing, telling Mark Rowland of *Musician,* "I didn't think I was supposed to play backup at all, and neither did D. Boon. He played really trebly and let me have all the midrange and low end. When people ask me what kind of a bass player I am, I say I'm D. Boon's bass player, because he had such an impact on me."

Influenced Independent Music Scene

The Minutemen was an avant-punk trio whose politics were libertarian flavored, spiced with heavy disdain for the music industry's methods of creating pop icons. In their five years together, the Minutemen released over ten albums, many on the SST record label. *Double Nickels On The Dime,* originally released in 1984 and reissued in 1989, is considered their "signature album." The trio took their name from an early decision by the group to play songs that were of 60-second duration. Tragedy struck the band in 1985, however, when guitarist D. Boon was killed in a car crash, and the group subsequently disbanded.

Soon after Boon's unfortunate and untimely death, a new incarnation of the Minutemen evolved. The two remaining Minutemen, Watt and Hurley, joined forces with singer and guitarist Ed Crawford to form a new trio called

For the Record . . .

Born December 20, 1957 and raised in San Pedro, California; parents are James Richard (a Navy officer) and Jean V. Watt; married to Kira Roessler from 1987-94.

Watt was an important influence in the development of independent music in the United States during the 1980's; former bassist and vocalist for the Minutemen, 1980-85; created new trio, fIREHOSE, with Minutemen drummer George Hurley and singer/guitarist Ed Crawford, 1985-93; first solo release, *Ball-Hog or Tugboat?,* released 1995, featured over 40 other artists including Pearl Jam's Eddie Vedder, Bikini Kill's Kathleen Hanna, and a long list of others; released *Contemplating the Engine Room,* 1997.

Addresses: *Home*—San Pedro, California. *Record companies*—Columbia Records, 550 Madison Ave., New York, NY 10022-3211; SST Records, (Minutemen/fIREHOSE), P.O. Box One, Lawndale, CA 90260.*Fan club*—Mike Watt Hoot Line, P.O. Box 1821, San Pedro, CA 90733. *Website*—www.wattage.com, www.columbiarecords.com.

fIREHOSE. From 1985 to 1993, Watt remained with fIREHOSE, as bassist, vocalist, and producer. The new punk group recorded six which were mostly well received and reviewed. *Spin* recommended *Flyin' The Flannel,* released in 1991, although noted "Crawford's voice tends toward chirpy ... [but] he can now hold his own and even push his bandmates a little." fIREHOSE's 1993 release, *Mr. Machinery Operator,* was given a "very good" rating by *New Musical Express,* as well as positive comments by other critics.

Went Solo

In 1995, Watt released his first solo album, *Ball-Hog or Tugboat?,* which featured over forty other musicians. Watt deliberately kept a low profile, playing bass throughout, but using his vocals only on the first cut, "Big Train." Among the featured musicians were Eddie Vedder of Pearl Jam, Nirvana's Dave Grohl and Krist Novoselic, Adam Horovitz and Mike D. from the Beastie Boys, Dave Pirner from Soul Asylum, Flea from the Red Hot Chili Peppers, J. Mascis from Dinosaur Jr., Thurston Moore from Sonic Youth, and a wealth of additional talent. The album was recorded in various studios in New York, Seattle, and Los Angeles over a four month period. Watt's bass became the glue as he rotated the combinations of musicians from song to song.

The featured musicians on his solo debut all hail from the "alternative" music world, and are those who have been inspired or affected by Watt with the Minutemen and fIREHOSE. The album's title, *Ball-Hog Or Tugboat?* ties the basketball scene to the nautical, and begged the question about the appropriate function of the bass guitar. Is it best used in a supporting role, more behind the scenes like a tugboat, or should it be showcased, commanding a more obvious presence a la Michael Jordan? The album received high marks by critics including a review by *Musician* noting one of the highlights of the album "is hearing other singers attempt to duplicate the Watt rumble." *Option* gave it a "B+," and said the album was, "consistently superb."

Connected Literary and Musical Influences

Watt attributes a wide range of influences to his style. His taste in music runs the gamut, from opera to John Coltrane. He started out as a big fan of T. Rex, the Who, and Creedence Clearwater Revival. His signature garb of flannel shirts actually began as a tribute to Creedence's John Fogerty. Many of his influences are literary, as well, and his 1997 release, *Contemplating The Engine Room,* was influenced by James Joyce's *Ulysses,* Dante's *Inferno,* and Richard McKenna's *The Sand Pebbles,* among others. Inspiration for *Contemplating The Engine Room* came while Watt was the guest bassist with Porno For Pyros in 1996. Watt told Neva Chonin of the *San Francisco Bay Guardian,* "I thought, why not make a valentine for them [the Minutemen] and D. Boon and my father?"

In addition to literary inspiration, Watt also found ideas by watching Italian opera on television and credited his Navy father for planting the seed of the idea. He explained how he would send his dad postcards from the different towns he performed in. He told Kieran Grant of the *Toronto Sun* at one point his dying father told him, "Y'know, you're like a sailor," referring to the musician's life of frequent stops in various towns. The album's cover features the elder Watt in his Navy uniform.

With *Contemplating The Engine Room,* Watt created a reflective, loosely autobiographical work which he calls a "punk-rock opera." Watt employs metaphorical language to create the 15 songs which borrows James Joyce's device from *Ulysses,* by having each cut document a 24 hour period in the lives of three men—based on the Minutemen—toiling in the engine room aboard a Navy ship. He parallels life at sea, which his father experienced while on his tour of duty with the Navy during the 1950s, to his life on the road with the Minutemen and likens the sailors's ship to the Minutemen's van. In addition to being a tribute, it is also a vehicle for Watt to examine his own life, using the metaphor of life at sea to parallel his own navigation upon the oceans of life.

Watt for the first time does all the vocals and according to Matt Diehl of *Rolling Stone,* "[Watt's] warm rasp serves these abstract confessionals well." With drummer Steve Hodges and Geraldine Fibbers's guitarist Nels Cline to lend support, Watt describes the CD in the liner notes as "one whole piece that celebrates three people playing together. The CD itself is an enhanced version which includes multimedia computer files and an Intenet browser allowing connection to Watt's web site. The files include excerpts of a film showing Watt riding his bike and driving through his hometown of San Pedro and talking about points of interest along the way. Diehl of *Rolling Stone* declared the album, "[Watt's] most personal, affecting work yet.... [it] weds two unlikely ideas; the rock-opera concept album and punk irreverence."

Forever the "Econoclast"

In spite of currently recording under the auspices of a large record company, Watt still considers himself an "econoclast." He explained the term to Matthew Lewis of *Reuters/Variety,* describing "econo" as "a commendably no-frills style," as compared to "arena rock" which he called "bloated commercialism and self-importance." Although recording with a major company, Watt continued extensive touring by driving his own Econoline van.

As he continues to take risks with his music, Watt admitted to Lewis there are times he can't believe he's on a major record label like Columbia. "I'm a very econo act for them, I'd say." With *Contemplating The Engine Room,* the final cut "Shore Duty," seems to point to Watt's recognition that he's discovered his creative place in life and is content with himself. He told Rowland of *Musician,* "Hey, I am what I am—like Popeye."

Selected discography

Ball-Hog Or Tugboat?, Columbia/Sony, 1995.
Contemplating The Engine Room, Columbia/Sony, 1997.

With the Minutemen

Double Nickels On The Dime, 1984, reissued, SST, 1989.
Politics Of Time, 1984, Alliance, reissued, SST, 1991.
Ballot Result, 1987, SST.

With fIREHOSE

If'n, SST, 1988.
Fromohio, SST, 1989.
Flyin' The Flannel, Sony, 1991.
Mr. Machinery Operator, Sony, 1993.

Sources

Periodicals

Billboard, September 6, 1997.
Boston Phoenix, October 24, 1997.
Entertainment Weekly, October 17, 1997, p. 77.
Guitar World Online, January 1998.
Musician, May 1995, p. 87; December 1997, p. 12.
New Musical Express, March 13, 1993, p. 32.
Option, May/June 1995, p. 146.
Philadelphia Inquirer, October 19, 1997.
Reuters/Variety, November 1997.
Rolling Stone, March 23, 1995, p. 119-121; October 30, 1997, p. 67; November 27, 1997.
San Francisco Bay Guardian, October 8, 1997.
San Francisco Examiner-Chronicle, October 5, 1997.
Spin, June 1991, p. 74-76.
Time Out (New York), October 30-November 6, 1997.
Toronto Sun, February 28, 1995; October 24, 1997.

Online

www.canoe.ca/JamAlbumsW/watt_m.html
www.music.sony.com/
www.wattage.com

Additional information obtained from Columbia Records.

—Debra Reilly

Tomica Woods-Wright

Producer, record company executive

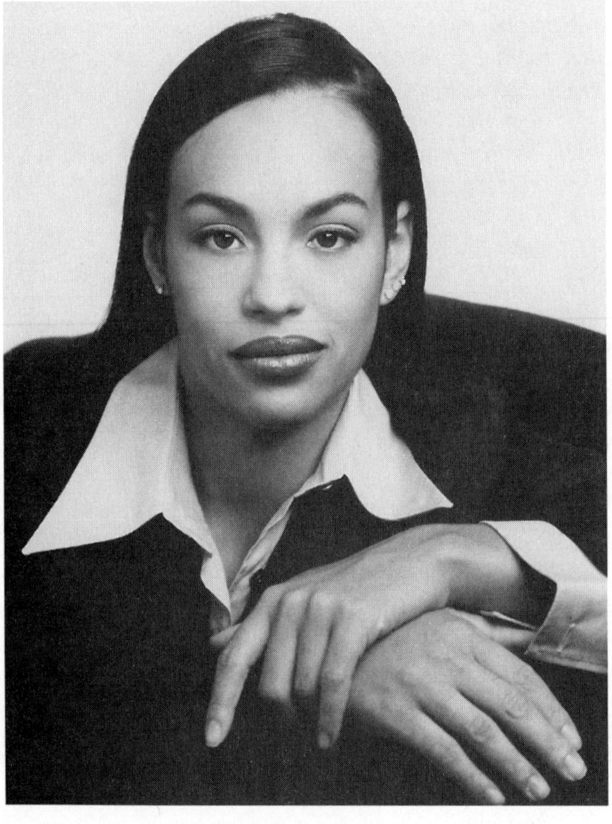

Courtesy of Tomica Woods-Wright

Tomica Woods-Wright, the owner and CEO of Ruthless Records, inherited the record company in 1995 from her husband, rap legend Eric Wright—a.k.a. Eazy-E.—after his untimely death due to A.I.D.S.-related pneumonia. The company was founded in March of 1987 and was one of the most successful independent labels in rap and hip-hop history, ushering in Cali-style Gangsta rap with artists such as N.W.A. (which included Ice Cube, Dr. Dre, Eazy-E., and M.C. Ren), Bone, Thugs 'n' Harmony, Above the Law, Yomo & Maulkie, D.O.C., J.J. Fad, Michel'le, Kid Frost, Atban Klann (now known as the Black Eyed Peas), Jimmie Z., and solo releases by Wright's own persona, Eazy-E. Ruthless Records was estimated to be worth $15 million at the time of Eric Wright's death.

As a largely unknown entity, Tomica Woods-Wright faced the challenge of keeping the label on top, staving off lawsuits from others who wanted a piece of the company, and convincing artists and industry executives that she possessed the necessary business acumen to oversee the successful label. Her inheritance proved to be a baptism-by-fire, but within two years of running Ruthless Records, she restructured the label, sought a better distribution deal, expanded the label's artist roster, and introduced new talent that would broaden the type of music the label embraced.

Woods-Wright was born in 1969 in Los Angeles, and at times lived with her mother in one town, then with her father in another, and in a foster home for a while as well. She went to high school in the San Fernando Valley, then attended Santa Monica and West L.A. Community College before procuring a position as a secretary to Tabu Records founder Clarence Avant; Tabu handled the S.O.S. Band, Cherelle, and Alexander O'Neal. When Avant accepted a position as chairman at Motown Records in 1993, he took Woods-Wright with him. Avant told *Vibe* magazine's A.J. Smith, "... She's bright.... Her family life has not been a-plus, B- or C-plus. She's from the street, with a lot of street knowledge. But if she went to Howard or Harvard, it wouldn't make any difference....Tomica can see a long ways in front of her. She's learned a lot of things that I did, and she's put them into practice."

Woods-Wright had a child at an early age, and worked as a single mother before inheriting Ruthless. She met Eric Wright at a Los Angeles nightclub in 1991 and was not immediately taken with him; in fact, she didn't know who he was. Their paths continued to cross, and she told Smith, "He was very down- to-earth, sweet. We'd laugh together when I got to know him a little better. And from then on, it was just ... history." They spent four years in a relationship and had two children, a son named

For the Record . . .

Born Tomica Woods, in 1969, in Los Angeles, California; attended Santa Monica and West L.A. Community College; procured a position as secretary to Tabu Records founder Clarence Avant; Avant accepted a position as chairman at Motown Records in 1993 and took Woods-Wright with him; mother of three children, two fathered by Ruthless Records founder Eric Wright, a.k.a. the rapper Eazy-E.; lived with Wright for four years before marrying him in 1995; inherited Ruthless Records in 1995 from her husband after his untimely death.

Signed a distribution deal with Epic/Sony in 1997; released a 10th anniversary Ruthless compilation album, *A Decade of Game,* in 1998; signed new artists comedian/actor Chris Tucker, Big Chan, N.X., Big Rocc, and soul trio Blulight.

Awards: *Billboard*'s number one Indie Label of the Year 1996;

Address: *Record company*—Ruthless Records, 8201 W. 3rd Street, Los Angeles, CA 90048; (213) 782-1888, Fax: (213) 782-0705.

Dominick and a daughter named Daijah, before marrying twelve days before Wright died. After Wright's death, his will was contested by six former girlfriends and two former business partners. In regard to one particular ex-partner, she told Smith, "He basically underestimated my relationship with Eric and underestimated me.... I did have business knowledge." Woods-Wright's response tothose who accused her seeking an easy fortune was to tell Smith, "(Before becoming president of the label) there was a lot less stress, a lot less responsibility, a lot less burden than there was before."

Broadening the Ruthless Roster

Woods-Wright viewed Avant as a mentor and teacher and learned much about the business of music from him but she learned the intricacies of operating an innovative corporation from her husband. While Avant represented corporate savvy, Wright represented street smarts and the art of the gamble—he achieved his early multi-platinum sales with virtually no radio or video exposure whatsoever. The court-appointed executive Ernie Singleton officially ran the company for a year while it was decided whether or not Woods-Wright would retain sole ownership. Woods-Wright told *BRE Magazine*'s Steven Ivory, "I was indirectly doing things for Eric at the company. In fact, I had already given Clarence (Avant) notice that I was leaving to join Ruthless as general manager when Eric went into the hospital. But until the court made it's ruling.... I had to move in slowly, first hired by Ernie as vice-president of Artist & Repretoire—A&R—and then ultimately, once everything was decided, as President."

Ruthless Records was in the precarious position of redefining itself two years after Woods-Wright stepped up to the helm; with the exception of the Cleveland-based Bone Thugs 'n' Harmony, the label didn't have a gold or platinum record between 1993 and early 1998, and the gangsta rap that defined its success was waning in popularity. Woods-Wright built a staff of about 20 employees that included three A&R people, and when she felt she had finally solidified the label's foundation in the post-Wright era, she began to aggressively seek out new talent. She signed comedian/actor Chris Tucker, Big Chan, N.X., Big Rocc, and soul trio Blulight. Woods-Wright also released a 10th anniversary Ruthless commemorative compilation record in 1998, titled *Decade of Game,* which featured two unreleased Eazy-E tracks, and singles by N.W.A., Above the Law, D.O.C., Michel'le, and JJ Fad. Woods-Wright negotiated a distribution deal with Epic/Sony in 1997, which gave the label more corporate leverage. Woods-Wright told Ivory, "The way the deal with Sony is structured serves Ruthless well—it's one thing to just put something out, but every record needs set-up."

In Her Own Fashion

Woods-Wright is optimistic about the future of Ruthless Records, and told Ivory the best is yet to come. She said, "I want the company to be known as more than just a rap label; this is a home for ground-breaking new and established artists catering to the urban community. Bones success was unexpected. I don't think even my husband expected that kind of success. But that's what Ruthless is about, catching a fire." She told Ann Brown of The Source, "I'm not my husband but I'm adding to his vision." Woods-Wright confided to Ivory that when people meet her for the first time, they expect to see a "home-girl" or hip-hop parody, but when they sit down to do business with her they get a much clearer picture of who she is and what she wants.

Selected discography

Ruthless Records

Boyz-N-the-Hood by Eazy E., 1987.
N.W.A. and the Posse by N.W.A., 1987 (rereleased in 1989)
Supersonic by JJ Fad, 1988.
Way Out by JJ Fad, 1988.
We Want Eazy by Eazy-E., 1988.
Straight Outta Compton by N.W.A., 1988.
Express Yourself by N.W.A., 1989.
Eazy Duz It by Eazy-E., 1988.
No One Can Do It Better by D.O.C., 1989.
It's Funky Enough by D.O.C., 1989.
Michel'le by Michel'le, 1990.
100 Miles and Runnin' by N.W.A., 1990.
EFIL4ZAGGIN by N.W.A., 1991.
Something in My Heart by Michel'le, 1991.
Are You Experienced? by Yomo & Maulkie, 1991.
5150 Home 4 Tha Sick by Eazy-E., 1992.
Kizz My Black Azz by M.C. Ren, 1992.
It's On (Dr. Dre) 187um Killa by Eazy-E., 1993.
Creepin' On Ah Come Up by Bone Thugs 'n' Harmony, 1994.
Thuggish, Ruggish Bone by Bone Thugs 'n' Harmony, 1994.
Smile Now, Die Later by Frost, 1994.
E. 1999 Eternal by Bone Thugs 'n' Harmony, 1996.
The Art of War by Bone Thugs 'n' Harmony, 1997.
Look into My eyes by Bone Thugs 'n' Harmony, 1997.
Decade of Game, Ruthless 10th Anniversary Compilation,: 1998.

Sources

BRE Magazine, March 13, 1998.
The Source, March 1998.
Vibe, June/July 1998,

Additional source material was provided by the publicity department at Ruthless Records.

—B. Kimberly Taylor

Maury Yeston

Composer, lyricist, educator

AP/wide World Photos

Composer/lyricist Maury Yeston's Broadway track record is so far perfect. Two of his works have come to Broadway—*Nine* in 1982, and *Titanic* in 1997—and both have won the Tony Award for best musical and best score. Yeston also made significant contributions to the Tony-nominated musical *Grand Hotel* in 1989. Yeston's musical version of the novel *The Phantom of the Opera*—not to be confused with Andrew Lloyd Webber's version—called *Phantom* has yet to reach Broadway but has been presented at hundreds of theatres around the world. "[Yeston] has written some of the most formally structured music in recent musical theatre. But he also has the gift for creating ravishing melody—once you've heard 'Love Can't Happen' from *Grand Hotel,* or 'An Unusual Way' from *Nine,* or 'Home' from *Phantom,* or any number of other Yeston songs, you'll be hooked," wrote Paula Vitaris in *Show Music* magazine.

Maury Yeston was born in Jersey City, New Jersey in 1945. His English-born father, David, founded the Dial Import Corporation, an international importing and exporting firm. Yeston's mother, Frances, helped run the family business. Both of Yeston's parents enjoyed music. His father sang English music hall songs around the house and his mother was an accomplished pianist. "My mother was trained in classical piano, and her father was a cantor in a synagogue. A lot of musical-theatre writers have something in common. Irving Berlin, George Gershwin, Kurt Weill—each one had a cantor in the family. When you take a young, impressionable child and put him at age three in the middle of a synagogue, and that child sees a man in a costume, dramatically raised up on a kind of stage, singing his heart out at the top of his lungs to a rapt congregation, it makes a lasting impression. Something gets in your blood," Yeston told *Playbill.*

At age five Yeston began taking piano lessons from his mother and by age seven had won an award for composition at a local community center. Attending the Yeshiva of Hudson County from kindergarten through grade eight, Yeston was further exposed to Jewish religious music. Yeston's interest in the musical theatre began at age ten when he was taken to see *My Fair Lady,* then the biggest hit on Broadway. During his high school years at Jersey Academy, a small private school in Jersey City, Yeston broadened his musical horizons beyond classical and religious music and Broadway show tunes to include jazz, folk, rock and roll, and early music. He took up folk guitar, played vibraphone with a jazz group, and participated in madrigal singing.

Music was not Yeston's only interest. As an undergraduate at Yale University he majored in music theory and composition and minored in literature, particularly French,

For the Record . . .

Born October 23, 1945, in Jersey City, NJ; son of David Yeston (an international importer and exporter) and Frances Haar (a business administrator). Married to Julianne Waldhelm; children: Jake and Max. *Education:* Yale University, New Haven, CT, B.A. 1967, Ph.D. 1974; Clare College, Cambridge University, Cambridge, England, M.A. 1972.

Composer and lyricist of Broadway musicals *Titanic,* 1997, and *Nine,* 1982. Contributed music and lyrics to the Broadway musical *Grand Hotel,* 1989. Other musicals include *Alice in Wonderland,* 1971; *One-Two-Three-Four-Five,* 1987; *Phantom,* 1991. Also wrote *Goya: A Life in Song,* a concept recording, 1989 ; *December Songs,* a cabaret song cycle, 1991. Publications include *The Stratification of Musical Rhythm,* 1976, and *Readings in Schenker Analysis* (editor), 1977. Recordings of his work include *Nine,* 1982; *Goya: A Life in Song,* 1989; *December Songs,* 1992; *Grand Hotel,* 1992; *Phantom,* 1993; and *Titanic,* 1997.

Awards: Antoinette Perry Awards for Best Score and Best Musical for *Titanic,* 1997, and *Nine,* 1982; Drama Desk Award for *Nine,* 1982.

Addresses: *Agent*—Flora Roberts Agency, 157 W.57th St., New York, NY 10019-2210. *Publicist*—Susan Senk, 18 E.16th St., 4th floor, New York, NY 10003.

German, and Japanese. Yeston's love of language is one reason why he writes for the musical theatre. "I am as much a lyricist as a composer, and the musical theatre is the only genre I know in which the lyrics are as important as the music. I write my own lyrics for the same reason I write my own music. They are equal avenues of self-expression," Yeston told Mary Kalfatovic of *Contemporary Musicians.*

Graduating from Yale in 1967, Yeston won a Mellon Fellowship to attend Clare College at England's Cambridge University. While at Cambridge he earned a master's degree, belonged to Footlights, a well-known dramatics organization, wrote several classical pieces and a musical version of *Alice in Wonderland.* The latter was eventually produced at the Long Wharf Theatre in Connecticut in 1971. He also did some serious thinking at Cambridge about what course his life should take. Yeston told *Show Music,* "I was given the time and the luxury to make a life decision at Cambridge, and the decision was this: That is, it is just as noble a life pursuit to try to write one perfect solo melody that lives a thousand years, as it is to try to write a composition for 85 instruments that last an hour and a half. You don't have to be Gustav Mahler to realize your artistic goals as a composer."

Enjoyed Academia

After Cambridge, Yeston returned to the United States to accept a Woodrow Wilson Fellowship which included a teaching position at Lincoln University in Pennsylvania, the country's oldest traditionally black college. At Lincoln, Yeston taught music, art, philosophy, religion, and western civilization, and started a course in the history of black music. Yeston enjoyed academia and the formal study of music but he also wanted to write musicals. In order to keep a foot in both camps, he enrolled in the doctorate program at Yale and joined the BMI musical theatre workshop in New York City. While studying music theory and working on his dissertation at Yale, Yeston travelled to New York City once a week to study musical theatre, including how lyrics function and how songs are integrated into a plot.

In 1974, Yeston completed a doctoral dissertation on the stratification of musical rhythm. His work was so impressive it was published as a book by the Yale University Press and Yeston was asked to join the Yale music faculty. He eventually became an associate professor, director of undergraduate studies in music, and was twice elected by the student body as one of Yale's ten best professors. Meanwhile, Yeston continued to attend the BMI workshop where his major project was a musical inspired by Italian director Federico Fellini's film *8 1/2.* As a teenager Yeston had seen the 1963 film, about a film director suffering a midlife crisis and a creativity drought, and was completely taken up by its themes. "I looked at the screen and said 'That's me.' I still believed in all the dreams and ideals of what is was to be an artist, and here was a movie about an artist—an artist in trouble. It became an obsession," Yeston told Carol Lawson of the *New York Times* in 1982. Yeston called the musical *Nine.* "When Fellini made *8 1/2* he already had done seven films and a documentary, so he called his next movie *8 1/2.* I thought, if you add music, it's like half a number more," Yeston explained to Lawson.

Directed and choreographed by Tommy Tune, with a book by playwright Arthur Kopit, *Nine* opened on Broadway's

46th Street Theatre in May 1982. "*Nine* has more than a few sequences that are at once hallucinatory and entertaining—dreams that play like showstoppers.... There's so much rich icing on *Nine* that anyone who cares about the progress of the Broadway musical will have to see it," wrote Frank Rich in the *New York Times*.

Wrote Musicals Full-time

Nine, which starred Raul Julia, won Tony Awards for best musical, score, director, and costumes, and ran for 732 performances. It has since been produced in England, France, Japan, Sweden, and other countries. The success of *Nine* allowed Yeston to give up his position as associate professor at Yale, though he continued as an adjunct professor for seven years, teaching a course every other semester on songwriting. "*Nine* absolutely changed my life, both financially and substantively. It made it possible to teach less and write more. Of course there was pressure to follow up on its success but, though future projects took a long time to get produced, the flow and quality of my work and level of writing output remained uninterrupted," Yeston remarked in his *Contemporary Musicians* interview.

After *Nine*, Yeston turned much of his attention to writing a musical version of Gaston Leroux's novel, *The Phantom of the Opera.* He was approached with the idea by actor/director Geoffrey Holder, who held the American rights to the novel. Initially, Yeston did not have much interest in such a project. "I laughed and laughed. 'What are you thinking?' That's the worst idea in the world! Why would you want to write a musical based on a horror story? I mean, what are you going to do next, *The Werewolf*? *The Invisible Man, The Musical*?'.... And then it occurred to me that the story could be somewhat changed ... [The Phantom] would be a Quasimodo character, an Elephant Man. Don't all of us feel, despite outward imperfections, that deep inside we're good? And that is a character you cry for," Yeston told *Show Music.*

Phantom Never Made Broadway

Yeston had completed much of *Phantom* and was in the process of raising money for a Broadway production when Andrew Lloyd Webber, composer of the blockbusters *Cats, Evita,* and *Jesus Christ Superstar,* announced plans for his own version of *The Phantom of the Opera.* After the Lloyd Webber show, which opened in London in the fall of 1986, proved a boxoffice smash, funding for Yeston's version dried up. Though Yeston's *Phantom* has never reached Broadway, it was given a full-scale, top quality production at Houston's Theatre Under the Stars in 1991 and has since been produced at over three hundred theatres around the world. The Houston production was recorded as an original cast album by RCA records. Yeston told *Contemporary Musicians* that his *Phantom* "differs radically from the English show in that it cleaves to the American model of a highly integrated book-and-score musical theatre piece, Operetta-like in tone (to reflect the 1890s period) and deeply French in style (for its Parisian setting) it tells the life story of the Phantom—a character of deep pathos who, misshapen from birth—radiates the beauty of music from within, despite his outward imperfections."

Collaborated with Placido Domingo

Among Yeston's numerous projects is the recording *Goya—A Life in Song,* featuring famed tenor Placido Domingo. Domingo was interested in starring in a stage musical about Spanish painter Francisco de Goya and suggested to producer Alan Carr that Yeston would be the right person for the job of coming up with such a vehicle. Domingo had greatly admired Yeston's work on *Nine.* "I met Placido and of course the professor in me went immediately to the library and read everything there was to read in English, Spanish, French, German, and Italian on Goya. I loved it as a project. It was going to be a show, but we decided to do a record, because of Placido's time commitments," Yeston told *Show Music.*

In 1989, Yeston was asked by his *Nine* colleague, director Tommy Tune, to help out with *Grand Hotel,* a musical that was foundering during tryouts in Boston. The show was based on the 1932 movie of the same name, and on an unsuccessful 1958 musical version called *At the Grand,* with a score by Robert Wright and George Forrest. Yeston provided six new songs for *Grand Hotel* and rewrote approximately half the lyrics in the entire show. *Grand Hotel* arrived on Broadway in November 1989 and won five Tony Awards. Yeston, along with Wright andForrest, was nominated for the Tony for best score. *Grand Hotel* ran for 1,077 performances. Other Yeston works include *1-2-3-4-5,* a musical based on the first five books of the Bible, presented at the Manhattan Theatre Club in 1987 and 1988, and *December Songs,* a song cycle adapted from Schubert's *Die Winterreise.* Originally written as a commissioned piece for the 1991 centennial celebration of New York's Carnegie Hall, *December Songs* evolved into special material for popular cabaret singer Andrea Marcovicci. "It's a classical song cycle, but it's written from a popular Broadway point of view and the world of cabaret. It's precisely the line between those worlds," Yeston told *Show Music.*

Fascinated by Titanic

The location of the wreckage of the Titanic in 1985 sparked Yeston's interest in writing a musical about the doomed oceanliner. "What drew me to the project was the positive aspects of what the ship represented — 1) humankind's striving after great artistic works and similar technological feats, despite the possibility of tragic failure, and 2) the dreams of the passengers on board: 3rd Class, to immigrate to America for a better life; 2nd Class, to live a leisured lifestyle in imitation of the upper classes; 1st Class, to maintain their privileged positions forever. The collision with the iceberg dashed all of these dreams simultaneously, and the subsequent transformation of character of the passengers and crew had, it seemed to me, the potential for great emotional and musical expression onstage," Yeston told *Contemporary Musicians.*

As it turned out, librettist Peter Stone, who collaborated with Yeston on *Grand Hotel,* was also intrigued by the Titanic. The two men began to throw around ideas for a musical about the ship, knowing that the idea would sound unpromising to most people. "I think if you don't have that kind of daring damn-the-torpedos, you shouldn't be in this business. It's the safe sounding shows that often don't do well. You have to dare greatly, and I really want to stretch the bounds of the kind of expression in musical theatre," Yeston explained in *BMI Music World.*

Yeston saw the greatness and tragedy of the Titanic as something peculiar to turn-of-the-century British culture, with its rigid social class system and its grand notions of progress through technology. "In order to depict that on the stage, because this is really a very English show, I knew I would have to have a color similar to the one found in the music of the great composers at that time, like Elgar or Vaughan Williams; this was for me an opportunity to bring in the musical theatre an element of the symphonic tradition that I think we really haven't had before. That was very exciting," Yeston told *BMI Music World.*

The high cost of *Titanic*'s set made it impossible for the $9 million show to have traditional out of town tryouts. *Titanic* opened at Broadway's Lunt-Fontanne Theatre in April 1997, after a month of preview performances at the same theatre. Reviews ran the gamut from rave to pan. "It seemed a foregone conclusion that the show would be a failure; a musical about history's most tragic maiden voyage, in which fifteen hundred people lost their lives, was obviously preposterous.... Astonishingly, *Titanic* manages to be grave and entertaining, somber and joyful; little by little you realize that you are in the presence of a genuine addition to American musical theatre," wrote Nancy Franklin in *The New Yorker.*

On the less positive side, Ben Brantley of the *New York Times* called *Titanic* "a perversely cool work, cerebral without being particularly imaginative or insightful.... Mr. Yeston, who did the appealing score for *Nine,* seems less confident here. There is evidence of intelligence and variety in the music (which often has a *Sweeney Todd* meets *Jaws* ominousness), but very little emotional pull, barring some full-throated anthemic chorales."

Titanic was one of four musicals to open on Broadway in same week and emerged as the audience favorite, if only by a narrow margin. *Titanic*'s strong showing at the Tony Awards in June enabled it to speed ahead of the competition. *Titanic* picked up Tonys for orchestration, book, score, scenic design, and best musical. A number from the show performed on the Tony Awards television broadcast, the stirring "Godspeed Titanic," gave audiences an idea of what *Titanic,* which had run an austere, cryptic advertizing campaign, was like.

An affable man who enjoys swimming, kayaking, cooking, art, and travel when not occupied with music and literature, Yeston lives in New York City with his wife Julianne Waldhelm. He has two sons from a previous marriage. Commenting on his relative obscurity among Broadway composers, Yeston told *Show Music,* "I don't think I'm in the world to be famous. I'm in the world to try and make wonderful music."

Sources

BMI Music World, Fall 1997, p. 24-29.
New Yorker, May 12, 1997, p. 102-103.
New York Times, May 9, 1982, sect.2, p. 1, 24; May 10, 1982, p. C13; May 23, 1982; p. D3, 23; May 23, 1997, sect.2, p. 6; April 24, 1997, p.C, p. 13; June 1, 1997, sect.2, p. 1; June 2, 1997, p. B1, July 20, 1997, sect.2., p. 5.
Newsweek, May 5, 1997, p. 70-73;
Playbill, May 31, 1997, p. 18-20.
Show Music, Spring 1997, p. 17-23.

Information also obtained directly from Maury Yeston via telephone and fax.

—Mary Kalfatovic

Zhane

R&B duo

The singing, songwriting, and piano-playing duo of Jean Norris and Renee Neufville have proven they are not just another one-hit wonder. The pair who make up Zhane, pronounced Jah-Nay—"Jah" for the beginning of Jean and "Nay" for the end of Renee—released their second album, 1997's *Saturday Night,* to generally positive reviews, following their platinum-selling debut album of 1994, *Zhane: Pronounced Jah-Nay.* Their hit from that album, "Hey Mr. DJ," became a hip-hop anthem but pigeonholed them in the dance/disco genre. Their second release finds Zhane trying to break out of that niche. "*Saturday Night* reflects many different styles," Norris explained in their record company bio. "We've got some jazz. We've got dance tracks, R&B, and a little pop." Neufville added, "[The album] demonstrates a lot of growth for us. It is a definite testament of where we are spiritually and musically, and where we are trying to go."

Neufville, born in Jamaica and raised in Brooklyn, New York, began playing piano as a five year old and began singing in high school. Meanwhile, Norris, who grew up

Michael Ochs Archives

For the Record . . .

Members includes **Renee Neufville** (born in Jamaica, grew up in Brooklyn, New York), vocals; **Jean Norris** (born in Rhode Island), vocals, piano, synthesized bass. *Education:* Both Neufville and Norris attended Temple University in Philadelphia.

Sang background vocals on "Ring My Bell," for Fresh Prince and Jazzy Jeff; recorded "Hey, Mr. DJ," for the various artist compilation *Roll Wit Tha Flava,* 1993; signed with Motown Records, 1994; released debut album, *Pronounced Jah-Nay,* 1994; *Saturday Night,* 1997' contributed to soundtrack *Higher Learning,* 1995, and the compilation *NBA At 50: A Musical Celebration,* 1996.

Addresses: *Record company*—Motown Records, 5750 Wilshire Blvd., Los Angeles, CA 90028. *Website*—www.motown.com, www.allmusic.com, http://musiccentral.msn.com.

in Moorestown, New Jersey also played piano at a young age, ultimately studying music at Temple University in Philadelphia. It was at Temple where Neufville and Norris initially began to sing together. To ease their individual heartaches when both ended relationships with boyfriends in the span of several days, the two put their emotions into their songs and their singing and soon felt they were good enough to begin performing in front of an audience.

"Hey Mr. DJ"

Their first professional venture was singing background vocals for Jazzy Jeff and the Fresh Prince on the single, "Ring My Bell," in 1992. The pair decided to strike out on their own when they were excluded from the video of "Ring My Bell." They started calling record labels and management companies and fell upon Queen Latifah's Flavor Unit Management where rap producer Kay Gee, of Naughty by Nature, had been searching for a female group to produce. As Norris recalled in their record company bio, "Kay Gee gave us our start. He brought this real hip-hop edge to us and we weren't sure what to expect because we were doing ballads. But the collaboration came together and worked!"

Zhane was showcased on the 1993 all-star compilation album, *Roll Wit Tha Flava,* with the song, "Hey Mr. DJ," the result of their collaboration with Kay Gee. The only R&B track on *Flava,* the song went to the top of the dance charts and won the attention of Motown Records, who signed the duo in 1994. Their debut album, *Zhane: Pronounced Jah-Nay,* was released by Motown in February of 1994 and went gold by year's end. The album would eventually obtain platinum status. Along with the hit "Hey Mr. DJ," the album included two Top 40 hits, "Sending My Love," and "Groove Thang." From 1994-6 Zhane performed with others on a number of recordings including *NBA At 50: A Musical Celebration, Hey Mr. DJ.: The 4th Compilation,* as well as on the soundtracks of *Higher Learning* and *A Low Down Dirty Shame.*

Stretching Out on *Saturday Night*

In 1997, Zhane released their second album, appropriately titled, *Saturday Night* since the topics and styles they present so often suggest a time and place of partying, relaxing, and dancing. In addition to writing all of the lyrics, and composing some of the sultry, satiny-smooth music, the pair became more involved in the production of their second album. "When you want your music to sound a certain way, you have to be involved in the production," Norris explained to Yvette Russell of *Essence.*

Not wanting to be confined or defined as a group that produces just party music or disco, the second release has a similar flavor to the debut, but adds a little more spice in stylistic expression. With *Saturday Night,* the duo illustrated their talents in creating soulful R&B with a rock and roll edge, touches of hip-hop, as well as traces of gospel, reggae, and jazz. In reviewing *Saturday Night* for *USA Today,* Nekesa Mumbi Moody declared that the duo, "actually grows artistically with thought-provoking lyrics and beautiful melodies, which match wonderfully with their powerful voices," adding, "Zhane has definitely broken the sophomore jinx." And while Laura Jamison of *Rolling Stone,* didn't share Moody's enthusiasm for the album's lyrics and vocals she said, "the duo's sexy, smooth sound will—at the very least—make you move."

"Not Just a One-Dimensional Group"

With their second album, Neufville and Norris decided to use a host of musicians to give the record a more live and spontaneous feel. To elicit the desired results from performers, the duo communicated their interpretations of the music to the musicians who through their individual instruments convey the expression of the songs. The cut "So Badd," features jazz guitarist, Norman

Brown, while on "Piece It Together," Najee is featured on the flute and R&B singer Will Downing performs his smooth vocal magic.

The album also features distinctive cover versions of Billy Joel's "The Longest Time," and Chic's "Good Times." The third single on the album, "Crush," formally presented the duo's jazz stylings. Norris explained to *Billboard*'s Shawnee Smith, the decisions that went into choosing the songs included in the release. "We did the ballads and the jazz-influenced songs because [those] are the songs that mean so much to us.... They show that we're not just a one-dimensional group."

Selected discography

Zhane: Pronounced Jah-Nay, Motown Records, 1994.
Saturday Night, Motown Records, 1997.

With others

Roll Wit Tha Flava, Sony Music, 1993.
Hey Mr. DJ. The 4th Compilation, Sony Music, 1993.
(Contributor) *Higher Learning* (soundtrack), Sony Music, 1995.
(Contributor) *NBA At 50: A Musical Celebration,* Polygram/PGD, 1996.
(Contributor) *Low Down Dirty Shame* (soundtrack)

Sources

Periodicals

Billboard, February 15, 1997, p. 24.
Brunswickan, June 16, 1997.
Essence, June 1997, p. 60.
Rolling Stone, June 12, 1997, p. 116.
USA Today, June 13, 1997.

Online

http://users.bart.nl/~hansvalk/zhane.html
http://musiccentral.msn.com/Album/Display/249039
www.allmusic.com/cg/amg.exe
www.cdnow.com
www.cduniverse.com
www.motown.com

—Debra Reilly

Cumulative Subject Index

Volume numbers appear in **bold**.

A cappella
Brightman, Sarah **20**
Bulgarian State Female Vocal Choir **10**
Nylons, The **6**
Take 6 **6**
Zap Mama **14**

Accordion
Buckwheat Zydeco **6**
Chenier, C. J. **15**
Chenier, Clifton **6**
Queen Ida **9**
Richard, Zachary **9**
Rockin' Dopsie **10**
Simien, Terrance **12**
Sonnier, Jo-El **10**
Yankovic, "Weird Al" **7**

Ambient/Rave/Techno
Aphex Twin **14**
Chemical Brothers **20**
Deep Forest **18**
Front Line Assembly **20**
KMFDM **18**
Kraftwerk **9**
Lords of Acid **20**
Man or Astroman? **21**
Orb, The **18**
2 Unlimited **18**
Shadow, DJ **19**

Bandoneon
Piazzolla, Astor **18**
Saluzzi, Dino **22**

Banjo
Bromberg, David **18**
Clark, Roy **1**
Crowe, J.D. **5**
Eldridge, Ben
See Seldom Scene, The
Fleck, Bela **8**
Also see New Grass Revival, The
Hartford, John **1**
Johnson, Courtney
See New Grass Revival, The
McCoury, Del **15**
Piazzolla, Astor **18**
Scruggs, Earl **3**
Seeger, Pete **4**
Also see Weavers, The
Skaggs, Ricky **5**
Stanley, Ralph **5**
Watson, Doc **2**

Bass
Brown, Ray **21**
Bruce, Jack
See Cream
Carter, Ron **14**
Chambers, Paul **18**
Clarke, Stanley **3**
Collins, Bootsy **8**
Dixon, Willie **10**
Entwistle, John
See Who, The
Fender, Leo **10**
Haden, Charlie **12**
Hill, Dusty
See ZZ Top
Hillman, Chris
See Byrds, The
Also see Desert Rose Band, The
Johnston, Bruce
See Beach Boys, The
Jones, John Paul
See Led Zeppelin
Kaye, Carol **22**
Lake, Greg
See Emerson, Lake & Palmer/Powell
Laswell, Bill **14**
Love, Laura **20**
Mann, Aimee **22**
McBride, Christian **17**
McCartney, Paul **4**
Also see Beatles, The
McVie, John
See Fleetwood Mac
Meisner, Randy
See Eagles, The
Mingus, Charles **9**
Ndegéocello, Me'Shell **18**
Porter, Tiran
See Doobie Brothers, The
Rutherford, Mike
See Genesis
Schmit, Timothy B.
See Eagles, The
Shakespeare, Robbie
See Sly and Robbie
Simmons, Gene
See Kiss
Sting **19**
Earlier sketch in CM **2**
Sweet, Matthew **9**
Vicious, Sid
See Sex Pistols, The
Also see Siouxsie and the Banshees
Was, Don **21**
Also see Was (Not Was)
Waters, Roger
See Pink Floyd
Watt, Mike **22**
Weymouth, Tina
See Talking Heads
Whitaker, Rodney **20**
Wyman, Bill
See Rolling Stones, The

Big Band/Swing
Andrews Sisters, The **9**
Arnaz, Desi **8**
Bailey, Pearl **5**
Basie, Count **2**
Beiderbecke, Bix **16**
Bennett, Tony **16**
Earlier sketch in CM **2**
Berrigan, Bunny **2**
Blakey, Art **11**
Calloway, Cab **6**
Carter, Benny **3**
Chenille Sisters, The **16**
Clooney, Rosemary **9**
Como, Perry **14**
Dorsey, Jimmy
See Dorsey Brothers, The
Dorsey, Tommy
See Dorsey Brothers, The
Dorsey Brothers, The **8**
Eckstine, Billy **1**
Eldridge, Roy **9**
Ellington, Duke **2**
Ferguson, Maynard **7**
Fitzgerald, Ella **1**
Fountain, Pete **7**
Getz, Stan **12**
Gillespie, Dizzy **6**
Goodman, Benny **4**
Henderson, Fletcher **16**
Herman, Woody **12**
Hines, Earl "Fatha" **12**
Jacquet, Illinois **17**
James, Harry **11**
Jones, Spike **5**
Jordan, Louis **11**
Krupa, Gene **13**
Lee, Peggy **8**
McKinney's Cotton Pickers **16**
Miller, Glenn **6**
Norvo, Red **12**
Parker, Charlie **5**
Prima, Louis **18**

Puente, Tito 14
Rich, Buddy 13
Rodney, Red 14
Roomful of Blues 7
Scott, Jimmy 14
Severinsen, Doc 1
Shaw, Artie 8
Sinatra, Frank 1
Squirrel Nut Zippers 20
Strayhorn, Billy 13
Teagarden, Jack 10
Torme, Mel 4
Vaughan, Sarah 2
Welk, Lawrence 13
Whiteman, Paul 17

Bluegrass
Auldridge, Mike 4
Bluegrass Patriots 22
Clements, Vassar 18
Country Gentlemen, The 7
Crowe, J.D. 5
Flatt, Lester 3
Fleck, Bela 8
Also see New Grass Revival, The
Gill, Vince 7
Grisman, David 17
Hartford, John 1
Krauss, Alison 10
Louvin Brothers, The 12
Martin, Jimmy 5
Also see Osborne Brothers, The
McCoury, Del 15
McReynolds, Jim and Jesse 12
Monroe, Bill 1
Nashville Bluegrass Band 14
New Grass Revival, The 4
Northern Lights 19
O'Connor, Mark 1
Osborne Brothers, The 8
Parsons, Gram 7
Also see Byrds, The
Reverend Horton Heat 19
Scruggs, Earl 3
Seldom Scene, The 4
Skaggs, Ricky 5
Stanley Brothers, The 17
Stanley, Ralph 5
Stuart, Marty 9
Watson, Doc 2
Wiseman, Mac 19

Blues
Allison, Luther 21
Ayler , Albert 19
Bailey, Pearl 5
Baker, Ginger 16
Also see Cream
Ball, Marcia 15
Berry, Chuck 1
Bland, Bobby "Blue" 12
Block, Rory 18
Blood, Sweat and Tears 7
Blues Brothers, The 3
Broonzy, Big Bill 13
Brown, Clarence "Gatemouth" 11
Brown, Ruth 13
Burdon, Eric 14
Also see War
Also see Animals, The
Cale, J. J. 16
Charles, Ray 1
Clapton, Eric 11
Earlier sketch in CM 1
Also see Cream
Also see Yardbirds, The
Collins, Albert 4
Cray, Robert 8
Davis, Reverend Gary 18
Diddley, Bo 3
Dixon, Willie 10
Dr. John 7
Dupree, Champion Jack 12
Earl, Ronnie 5
Also see Roomful of Blues
Fabulous Thunderbirds, The 1
Fuller, Blind Boy 20
Fulson, Lowell 20
Gatton, Danny 16
Guy, Buddy 4
Handy, W. C. 7
Hawkins, Screamin' Jay 8
Healey, Jeff 4
Holiday, Billie 6
Hooker, John Lee 1
Hopkins, Lightnin' 13
House, Son 11
Howlin' Wolf 6
James, Elmore 8
James, Etta 6
Jefferson, Blind Lemon 18
Johnson, Lonnie 17
Johnson, Robert 6
Jon Spencer Blues Explosion 18
Joplin, Janis 3
King, Albert 2
King, B. B. 1
King, Freddy 17
Leadbelly 6
Led Zeppelin 1
Little Feat 4
Little Walter 14
Lockwood, Robert, Jr. 10
Mayall, John 7
McClinton, Delbert 14
McDowell, Mississippi Fred 16
McTell, Blind Willie 17
Muldaur, Maria 18
Patton, Charley 11
Plant, Robert 2
Also see Led Zeppelin
Professor Longhair 6
Raitt, Bonnie 3
Redding, Otis 5
Reed, Jimmy 15
Rich, Charlie 3
Robertson, Robbie 2
Robillard, Duke 2
Roomful of Blues 7
Rush, Otis 12
Shaffer, Paul 13
Shines, Johnny 14
Smith, Bessie 3
Snow, Phoebe 4
Spann, Otis 18
Sunnyland Slim 16
Sykes, Roosevelt 20
Taj Mahal 6
Taylor, Koko 10
Thornton, Big Mama 18
Toure, Ali Farka 18
Turner, Big Joe 13
Ulmer, James Blood 13
Van Zandt, Townes 13
Vaughan, Stevie Ray 1
Waits, Tom 1
Walker, T-Bone 5
Wallace, Sippie 6
Washington, Dinah 5
Waters, Ethel 11
Waters, Muddy 4
Wells, Junior 17
Weston, Randy 15
Whitfield, Mark 18
Whitley, Chris 16
Whittaker, Hudson 20
Williams, Joe 11
Williamson, Sonny Boy 9
Wilson, Gerald 19
Winter, Johnny 5
Witherspoon, Jimmy 19
ZZ Top 2

Cajun/Zydeco
Ball, Marcia 15
Brown, Clarence "Gatemouth" 11
Buckwheat Zydeco 6
Chenier, C. J. 15
Chenier, Clifton 6
Doucet, Michael 8
Landreth, Sonny 16
Queen Ida 9
Richard, Zachary 9
Rockin' Dopsie 10
Simien, Terrance 12
Sonnier, Jo-El 10

Cello
Casals, Pablo 9
Gray, Walter
See Kronos Quartet
Harrell, Lynn 3
Jeanrenaud, Joan Dutcher
See Kronos Quartet
Ma, Yo-Yo 2
Rostropovich, Mstislav 17

Children's Music
Bartels, Joanie 13
Cappelli, Frank 14
Chapin, Tom 11

Chenille Sisters, The **16**
Harley, Bill **7**
Lehrer, Tom **7**
Nagler, Eric **8**
Penner, Fred **10**
Raffi **8**
Rosenshontz **9**
Sharon, Lois & Bram **6**

Christian Music
Anointed **21**
Ashton, Susan **17**
Audio Adrenaline **22**
Champion, Eric **21**
Chapman, Steven Curtis **15**
dc Talk **18**
Duncan, Bryan **19**
Eskelin, Ian **19**
Grant, Amy **7**
Jars of Clay **20**
King's X **7**
Paris, Twila **16**
Patti, Sandi **7**
Petra **3**
Point of Grace **21**
Smith, Michael W. **11**
Stryper **2**
Waters, Ethel **11**

Clarinet
Adams, John **8**
Bechet, Sidney **17**
Braxton, Anthony **12**
Byron, Don **22**
Dorsey, Jimmy
See Dorsey Brothers, The
Fountain, Pete **7**
Goodman, Benny **4**
Herman, Woody **12**
Shaw, Artie **8**

Classical
Anderson, Marian **8**
Arrau, Claudio **1**
Baker, Janet **14**
Bernstein, Leonard **2**
Boyd, Liona **7**
Bream, Julian **9**
Britten, Benjamin **15**
Bronfman, Yefim **6**
Canadian Brass, The **4**
Carter, Ron **14**
Casals, Pablo **9**
Chang, Sarah **7**
Clayderman, Richard **1**
Cliburn, Van **13**
Copland, Aaron **2**
Davis, Anthony **17**
Davis, Chip **4**
Fiedler, Arthur **6**
Galway, James **3**
Gingold, Josef **6**
Gould, Glenn **9**
Gould, Morton **16**
Hampson, Thomas **12**
Harrell, Lynn **3**
Hayes, Roland **13**
Hendricks, Barbara **10**
Herrmann, Bernard **14**
Hinderas, Natalie **12**
Horne, Marilyn **9**
Horowitz, Vladimir **1**
Jarrett, Keith **1**
Kennedy, Nigel **8**
Kissin, Evgeny **6**
Kronos Quartet **5**
Kunzel, Erich **17**
Lemper, Ute **14**
Levine, James **8**
Liberace **9**
Ma, Yo-Yo **2**
Marsalis, Wynton **6**
Masur, Kurt **11**
McNair, Sylvia **15**
McPartland, Marian **15**
Mehta, Zubin **11**
Menuhin, Yehudi **11**
Midori **7**
Nyman, Michael **15**
Ott, David **2**
Parkening, Christopher **7**
Perahia, Murray **10**
Perlman, Itzhak **2**
Phillips, Harvey **3**
Rampal, Jean-Pierre **6**
Rostropovich, Mstislav **17**
Rota, Nino **13**
Rubinstein, Arthur **11**
Salerno-Sonnenberg, Nadja **3**
Salonen, Esa-Pekka **16**
Schickele, Peter **5**
Schuman, William **10**
Segovia, Andres **6**
Shankar, Ravi **9**
Solti, Georg **13**
Stern, Isaac **7**
Sutherland, Joan **13**
Takemitsu, Toru **6**
Toscanini, Arturo **14**
Upshaw, Dawn **9**
von Karajan, Herbert **1**
Weill, Kurt **12**
Wilson, Ransom **5**
Yamashita, Kazuhito **4**
York, Andrew **15**
Zukerman, Pinchas **4**

Composers
Adams, John **8**
Allen, Geri **10**
Alpert, Herb **11**
Anka, Paul **2**
Atkins, Chet **5**
Bacharach, Burt **20**
Earlier sketch in CM **1**
Badalamenti, Angelo **17**
Beiderbecke, Bix **16**
Benson, George **9**
Berlin, Irving **8**
Bernstein, Leonard **2**
Blackman, Cindy **15**
Bley, Carla **8**
Bley, Paul **14**
Braxton, Anthony **12**
Brickman, Jim **22**
Britten, Benjamin **15**
Brubeck, Dave **8**
Burrell, Kenny **11**
Byrne, David **8**
Also see Talking Heads
Byron, Don **22**
Cage, John **8**
Cale, John **9**
Casals, Pablo **9**
Clarke, Stanley **3**
Coleman, Ornette **5**
Cooder, Ry **2**
Cooney, Rory **6**
Copeland, Stewart **14**
Also see Police, The **20**
Copland, Aaron **2**
Crouch, Andraé **9**
Curtis, King **17**
Davis, Anthony **17**
Davis, Chip **4**
Davis, Miles **1**
de Grassi, Alex **6**
Dorsey, Thomas A. **11**
Elfman, Danny **9**
Ellington, Duke **2**
Eno, Brian **8**
Enya **6**
Esquivel, Juan **17**
Evans, Bill **17**
Evans, Gil **17**
Fahey, John **17**
Foster, David **13**
Frisell, Bill **15**
Frith, Fred **19**
Galás, Diamanda **16**
Gillespie, Dizzy **6**
Glass, Philip **1**
Golson, Benny **21**
Gould, Glenn **9**
Gould, Morton **16**
Green, Benny **17**
Grusin, Dave **7**
Guaraldi, Vince **3**
Hamlisch, Marvin **1**
Hammer, Jan **21**
Hancock, Herbie **8**
Handy, W. C. **7**
Hargrove, Roy **15**
Harris, Eddie **15**
Hartke, Stephen **5**
Henderson, Fletcher **16**
Herrmann, Bernard **14**
Hunter, Alberta **7**
Isham, Mark **14**
Jacquet, Illinois **17**
Jarre, Jean-Michel **2**
Jarrett, Keith **1**
Johnson, James P. **16**
Jones, Hank **15**

Jones, Quincy **20**
Earlier sketch in CM **2**
Joplin, Scott **10**
Jordan, Stanley **1**
Kenny G **14**
Kenton, Stan **21**
Kern, Jerome **13**
Kitaro **1**
Kottke, Leo **13**
Lateef, Yusef **16**
Lee, Peggy **8**
Legg, Adrian **17**
Lewis, Ramsey **14**
Lincoln, Abbey **9**
Lloyd, Charles **22**
Lloyd Webber, Andrew **6**
Loesser, Frank **19**
Loewe, Frederick
See Lerner and Loewe
Mancini, Henry **20**
Earlier sketch in CM **1**
Marsalis, Branford **10**
Marsalis, Ellis **13**
Martino, Pat **17**
Masekela, Hugh **7**
McBride, Christian **17**
McPartland, Marian **15**
Menken, Alan **10**
Metheny, Pat **2**
Miles, Ron **22**
Mingus, Charles **9**
Moby **17**
Monk, Meredith **1**
Monk, Thelonious **6**
Montenegro, Hugo **18**
Morricone, Ennio **15**
Morton, Jelly Roll **7**
Mulligan, Gerry **16**
Nascimento, Milton **6**
Newman, Randy **4**
Nyman, Michael **15**
Oldfield, Mike **18**
Orff, Carl **21**
Osby, Greg **21**
Ott, David **2**
Palmieri, Eddie **15**
Parker, Charlie **5**
Parks, Van Dyke **17**
Peterson, Oscar **11**
Piazzolla, Astor **18**
Ponty, Jean-Luc **8**
Porter, Cole **10**
Post, Mike **21**
Previn, André **15**
Puente, Tito **14**
Pullen, Don **16**
Reich, Steve **8**
Reinhardt, Django **7**
Ritenour, Lee **7**
Roach, Max **12**
Rollins, Sonny **7**
Rota, Nino **13**
Sakamoto, Ryuichi **19**
Salonen, Esa-Pekka **16**
Sanders, Pharoah **16**
Satriani, Joe **4**
Schickele, Peter **5**
Schuman, William **10**
Shankar, Ravi **9**
Shaw, Artie **8**
Shorter, Wayne **5**
Silver, Horace **19**
Solal, Martial **4**
Sondheim, Stephen **8**
Sousa, John Philip **10**
Story, Liz **2**
Stravinsky, Igor **21**
Strayhorn, Billy **13**
Styne, Jule **21**
Summers, Andy **3**
Also see Police, The
Sun Ra **5**
Takemitsu, Toru **6**
Talbot, John Michael **6**
Tatum, Art **17**
Taylor, Billy **13**
Taylor, Cecil **9**
Tesh, John **20**
Thielemans, Toots **13**
Threadgill, Henry **9**
Towner, Ralph **22**
Tyner, McCoy **7**
Vangelis **21**
Was, Don **21**
Also see Was (Not Was)
Washington, Grover, Jr. **5**
Weill, Kurt **12**
Weston, Randy **15**
Whelan, Bill **20**
Whiteman, Paul **17**
Williams, John **9**
Wilson, Cassandra **12**
Winston, George
Winter, Paul **10**
Worrell, Bernie **11**
Yanni **11**
Yeston, Maury **22**
York, Andrew **15**
Young, La Monte **16**
Zimmerman, Udo **5**
Zorn, John **15**
Zappa, Frank **17**
Earlier sketch in CM **1**

Conductors

Bacharach, Burt **20**
Earlier sketch CM **1**
Bernstein, Leonard **2**
Britten, Benjamin **15**
Casals, Pablo **9**
Copland, Aaron **2**
Domingo, Placido **20**
Earlier sketch in CM **1**
Evans, Gil **17**
Fiedler, Arthur **6**
Gould, Morton **16**
Herrmann, Bernard **14**
Jarrett, Keith **1**
Jones, Hank **15**
Kunzel, Erich **17**
Levine, James **8**
Mancini, Henry **20**
Earlier sketch in CM **1**
Marriner, Neville **7**
Masur, Kurt **11**
Mehta, Zubin **11**
Menuhin, Yehudi **11**
Nero, Peter **19**
Previn, André **15**
Rampal, Jean-Pierre **6**
Rostropovich, Mstislav **17**
Salonen, Esa-Pekka **16**
Schickele, Peter **5**
Solti, Georg **13**
Toscanini, Arturo **14**
von Karajan, Herbert **1**
Welk, Lawrence **13**
Williams, John **9**
Zukerman, Pinchas **4**

Contemporary Dance Music

Abdul, Paula **3**
Aphex Twin **14**
Bee Gees, The **3**
B-52's, The **4**
Brown, Bobby **4**
Brown, James **2**
C + C Music Factory **16**
Cherry, Neneh **4**
Clinton, George **7**
Craig, Carl **19**
Deee-lite **9**
De La Soul **7**
Depeche Mode **5**
Earth, Wind and Fire **12**
English Beat, The **9**
En Vogue **10**
Erasure **11**
Eurythmics **6**
Exposé **4**
Fox, Samantha **3**
Fun Lovin' Criminals **20**
Gang of Four **8**
Hammer, M.C. **5**
Harry, Deborah **4**
Also see Blondie
Ice-T **7**
Idol, Billy **3**
Jackson, Janet **16**
Earlier sketch in CM **3**
Jackson, Michael **17**
Earlier sketch in CM **1**
Also see Jacksons, The
James, Rick **2**
Jones, Grace **9**
Madonna **16**
Earlier sketch in CM **4**
Massive Attack **17**
Moby **17**
M People **15**
New Order **11**
Orbital **20**
Peniston, CeCe **15**
Pet Shop Boys **5**
Pizzicato Five **18**

Portishead 22
Prince 14
Earlier sketch in CM 1
Queen Latifah 6
Rodgers, Nile 8
Salt-N-Pepa 6
Shadow, DJ 19
Simmons, Russell 7
Soul II Soul 17
Sugar Ray 22
Summer, Donna 12
Technotronic 5
TLC 15
Tricky 18
2 Unlimited 18
Vasquez, Junior 16
Village People, The 7
Was (Not Was) 6
Waters, Crystal 15
Young M.C. 4

Contemporary Instrumental/New Age

Ackerman, Will 3
Arkenstone, David 20
Clinton, George 7
Collins, Bootsy 8
Davis, Chip 4
de Grassi, Alex 6
Enigma 14
Enya 6
Esquivel, Juan 17
Hedges, Michael 3
Isham, Mark 14
Jarre, Jean-Michel 2
Kitaro 1
Kronos Quartet 5
Legg, Adrian 17
Story, Liz 2
Summers, Andy 3
Also see Police, The
Tangerine Dream 12
Tesh, John 20
Winston, George 9
Winter, Paul 10
Yanni 11

Cornet

Armstrong, Louis 4
Beiderbecke, Bix 16
Cherry, Don 10
Handy, W. C. 7
Oliver, King 15
Vaché, Jr., Warren 22

Country

Acuff, Roy 2
Akins, Rhett 22
Alabama 21
Earlier sketch in CM 1
Anderson, John 5
Arnold, Eddy 10
Asleep at the Wheel 5
Atkins, Chet 5
Auldridge, Mike 4
Autry, Gene 12
Bellamy Brothers, The 13
Berg, Matraca 16
Berry, John 17
Black, Clint 5
BlackHawk 21
Blue Rodeo 18
Bogguss, Suzy 11
Bonamy, James 21
Boone, Pat 13
Boy Howdy 21
Brandt, Paul 22
Brannon, Kippi 20
Brooks & Dunn 12
Brooks, Garth 8
Brown, Junior 15
Brown, Marty 14
Brown, Tony 14
Buffett, Jimmy 4
Byrds, The 8
Cale, J. J. 16
Campbell, Glen 2
Carpenter, Mary-Chapin 6
Carter, Carlene 8
Carter Family, The 3
Cash, Johnny 17
Earlier sketch in CM 1
Cash, June Carter 6
Cash, Rosanne 2
Chesney, Kenny 20
Chesnutt, Mark 13
Clark, Guy 17
Clark, Roy 1
Clark, Terri 19
Clements, Vassar 18
Cline, Patsy 5
Coe, David Allan 4
Collie, Mark 15
Cooder, Ry 2
Cowboy Junkies, The 4
Crowe, J. D. 5
Crowell, Rodney 8
Cyrus, Billy Ray 11
Daniels, Charlie 6
Davis, Linda 21
Davis, Skeeter 15
Dean, Billy 19
DeMent, Iris 13
Denver, John 22
Earlier sketch in CM 1
Desert Rose Band, The 4
Diamond Rio 11
Dickens, Little Jimmy 7
Diffie, Joe 10
Dylan, Bob 21
Earlier sketch in CM 3
Earle, Steve 16
Flatt, Lester 3
Flores, Rosie 16
Ford, Tennessee Ernie 3
Foster, Radney 16
Frizzell, Lefty 10
Gayle, Crystal 1
Germano, Lisa 18
Gill, Vince 7
Gilley, Mickey 7
Gilmore, Jimmie Dale 11
Gordy, Jr., Emory 17
Greenwood, Lee 12
Griffith, Nanci 3
Haggard, Merle 2
Hall, Tom T. 4
Harris, Emmylou 4
Hartford, John 1
Hay, George D. 3
Herndon, Ty 20
Hiatt, John 8
Highway 101 4
Hill, Faith 18
Hinojosa, Tish 13
Howard, Harlan 15
Jackson, Alan 7
Jennings, Waylon 4
Jones, George 4
Judd, Wynonna
See Wynonna
See Judds, The
Judds, The 2
Keith, Toby 17
Kentucky Headhunters, The 5
Kershaw, Sammy 15
Ketchum, Hal 14
Kristofferson, Kris 4
Lamb, Barbara 19
Lang, K. D. 4
Lawrence, Tracy 11
LeDoux, Chris 12
Lee, Brenda 5
Little Feat 4
Little Texas 14
Louvin Brothers, The 12
Loveless, Patty 21
Earlier sketch in CM 5
Lovett, Lyle 5
Lynn, Loretta 2
Lynne, Shelby 5
Mandrell, Barbara 4
Mattea, Kathy 5
Mavericks, The 15
McBride, Martina 14
McClinton, Delbert 14
McCoy, Neal 15
McCready, Mindy 22
McEntire, Reba 11
McGraw, Tim 17
Miller, Roger 4
Milsap, Ronnie 2
Moffatt, Katy 18
Monroe, Bill 1
Montgomery, John Michael 14
Morgan, Lorrie 10
Murphey, Michael Martin 9
Murray, Anne 4
Nelson, Willie 11
Earlier sketch in CM 1
Newton-John, Olivia 8
Nitty Gritty Dirt Band, The 6
Oak Ridge Boys, The 7

O'Connor, Mark **1**
Oslin, K. T. **3**
Owens, Buck **2**
Parnell, Lee Roy **15**
Parsons, Gram **7**
Also see Byrds, The
Parton, Dolly **2**
Pearl, Minnie **3**
Pierce, Webb **15**
Price, Ray **11**
Pride, Charley **4**
Rabbitt, Eddie **5**
Raitt, Bonnie **3**
Raye, Collin **16**
Reeves, Jim **10**
Restless Heart **12**
Rich, Charlie **3**
Richey, Kim **20**
Rimes, LeAnn **19**
Robbins, Marty **9**
Rodgers, Jimmie **3**
Rogers, Kenny **1**
Rogers, Roy **9**
Sawyer Brown **13**
Scruggs, Earl **3**
Scud Mountain Boys **21**
Seals, Dan **9**
Shenandoah **17**
Skaggs, Ricky **5**
Sonnier, Jo-El **10**
Statler Brothers, The **8**
Stevens, Ray **7**
Stone, Doug **10**
Strait, George **5**
Stuart, Marty **9**
Sweethearts of the Rodeo **12**
Texas Tornados, The **8**
Tillis, Mel **7**
Tillis, Pam **8**
Tippin, Aaron **12**
Travis, Merle **14**
Travis, Randy **9**
Tritt, Travis **7**
Tubb, Ernest **4**
Tucker, Tanya **3**
Twain, Shania **17**
Twitty, Conway **6**
Van Shelton, Ricky **5**
Van Zandt, Townes **13**
Wagoner, Porter **13**
Walker, Clay **20**
Walker, Jerry Jeff **13**
Wariner, Steve **18**
Watson, Doc **2**
Wells, Kitty **6**
West, Dottie **8**
White, Lari **15**
Whitley, Keith **7**
Williams, Don **4**
Williams, Hank, Jr. **1**
Williams, Hank, Sr. **4**
Willis, Kelly **12**
Wills, Bob **6**
Wynette, Tammy **2**
Wynonna **11**
Yearwood, Trisha **10**
Yoakam, Dwight **21**
Earlier sketch in CM **1**
Young, Faron **7**

Dobro
Auldridge, Mike **4**
Also see Country Gentlemen, The
Also see Seldom Scene, The
Burch, Curtis
See New Grass Revival, The
Knopfler, Mark **3**
Also see Dire Straits
Whitley, Chris **16**

Drums
Aronoff, Kenny **21**
See **Percussion**

Dulcimer
Ritchie, Jean **4**

Fiddle
MacIsaac, Ashley **21**
See **Violin**

Film Scores
Anka, Paul **2**
Bacharach, Burt **20**
Earlier sketch in CM **1**
Badalamenti, Angelo **17**
Berlin, Irving **8**
Bernstein, Leonard **2**
Blanchard, Terence **13**
Britten, Benjamin **15**
Byrne, David **8**
Also see Talking Heads
Cafferty, John
See Beaver Brown Band, The
Cahn, Sammy **11**
Cliff, Jimmy **8**
Copeland, Stewart **14**
Also see Police, The
Copland, Aaron **2**
Crouch, Andraé **9**
Dibango, Manu **14**
Dolby, Thomas **10**
Donovan **9**
Eddy, Duane **9**
Elfman, Danny **9**
Ellington, Duke **2**
Ferguson, Maynard **7**
Froom, Mitchell **15**
Gabriel, Peter **16**
Earlier sketch in CM **2**
Also see Genesis
Galás, Diamanda **16**
Gershwin, George and Ira **11**
Gould, Glenn **9**
Grusin, Dave **7**
Guaraldi, Vince **3**
Hamlisch, Marvin **1**
Hancock, Herbie **8**
Harrison, George **2**
Hayes, Isaac **10**
Hedges, Michael **3**
Herrmann, Bernard **14**
Isham, Mark **14**
Jones, Quincy **20**
Earlier sketch in CM **2**
Knopfler, Mark **3**
Also see Dire Straits
Lennon, John **9**
Also see Beatles, The
Lerner and Loewe **13**
Loesser, Frank **19**
Mancini, Henry **20**
Earlier sketch in CM **1**
Marsalis, Branford **10**
Mayfield, Curtis **8**
McCartney, Paul **4**
Also see Beatles, The
Menken, Alan **10**
Mercer, Johnny **13**
Metheny, Pat **2**
Montenegro, Hugo **18**
Morricone, Ennio **15**
Nascimento, Milton **6**
Nilsson **10**
Nyman, Michael **15**
Parks, Van Dyke **17**
Peterson, Oscar **11**
Porter, Cole **10**
Previn, André **15**
Reznor, Trent **13**
Richie, Lionel **2**
Robertson, Robbie **2**
Rollins, Sonny **7**
Rota, Nino **13**
Sager, Carole Bayer **5**
Sakamoto, Ryuichi **18**
Schickele, Peter **5**
Shankar, Ravi **9**
Taj Mahal **6**
Waits, Tom **12**
Earlier sketch in CM **1**
Weill, Kurt **12**
Williams, John **9**
Williams, Paul **5**
Willner, Hal **10**
Young, Neil **15**
Earlier sketch in CM **2**

Flugelhorn
Sandoval, Arturo **15**

Flute
Anderson, Ian
See Jethro Tull
Galway, James **3**
Lateef, Yusef **16**
Mann, Herbie **16**
Najee **21**
Rampal, Jean-Pierre **6**
Ulmer, James Blood **13**
Wilson, Ransom **5**

Folk/Traditional
Altan **18**
America **16**

Arnaz, Desi **8**
Baez, Joan **1**
Belafonte, Harry **8**
Black, Mary **15**
Blades, Ruben **2**
Bloom, Luka **14**
Blue Rodeo **18**
Brady, Paul **8**
Bragg, Billy **7**
Bromberg, David **18**
Buckley, Tim **14**
Bulgarian State Female Vocal Choir **10**
Byrds, The **8**
Carter Family, The **3**
Chandra, Sheila **16**
Chapin, Harry **6**
Chapman, Tracy **20**
Earlier sketch in CM **4**
Chenille Sisters, The **16**
Cherry, Don **10**
Chieftains, The **7**
Childs, Toni **2**
Clegg, Johnny **8**
Cockburn, Bruce **8**
Cohen, Leonard **3**
Collins, Judy **4**
Colvin, Shawn **11**
Cotten, Elizabeth **16**
Crosby, David **3**
Also see Byrds, The
Cruz, Celia **22**
Earlier entry in CM **10**
de Lucia, Paco **1**
DeMent, Iris **13**
Donovan **9**
Dr. John **7**
Drake, Nick **17**
Dylan, Bob **3**
Elliot, Cass **5**
Enya **6**
Estefan, Gloria **15**
Earlier sketch in CM **2**
Fahey, John **17**
Fairport Convention **22**
Feliciano, José **10**
Galway, James **3**
Germano, Lisa **18**
Gilmore, Jimmie Dale **11**
Gipsy Kings, The **8**
Gorka, John **18**
Griffith, Nanci **3**
Grisman, David **17**
Guthrie, Arlo **6**
Guthrie, Woody **2**
Hakmoun, Hassan **15**
Hardin, Tim **18**
Harding, John Wesley **6**
Hartford, John **1**
Havens, Richie **11**
Henry, Joe **18**
Hinojosa, Tish **13**
Ian and Sylvia **18**
Iglesias, Julio **20**
Earlier sketch in CM **2**
Indigo Girls **20**
Earlier sketch in CM **3**
Ives, Burl **12**
Khan, Nusrat Fateh Ali **13**
Kingston Trio, The **9**
Klezmatics, The **18**
Kottke, Leo **13**
Kuti, Fela **7**
Ladysmith Black Mambazo **1**
Larkin, Patty **9**
Lavin, Christine **6**
Leadbelly **6**
Lightfoot, Gordon **3**
Los Lobos **2**
Makeba, Miriam **8**
Mamas and the Papas **21**
Masekela, Hugh **7**
McLean, Don **7**
Melanie **12**
Mitchell, Joni **17**
Earlier sketch in CM **2**
Moffatt, Katy **18**
Morrison, Van **3**
Morrissey, Bill **12**
Nascimento, Milton **6**
N'Dour, Youssou **6**
Near, Holly **1**
Ochs, Phil **7**
O'Connor, Sinead **3**
Odetta **7**
Parsons, Gram **7**
Also see Byrds, The
Paxton, Tom **5**
Pentangle **18**
Peter, Paul & Mary **4**
Pogues, The **6**
Prine, John **7**
Proclaimers, The **13**
Redpath, Jean **1**
Ritchie, Jean, **4**
Roches, The **18**
Rodgers, Jimmie **3**
Sainte-Marie, Buffy **11**
Santana, Carlos **1**
Seeger, Pete **4**
Also see Weavers, The
Selena **16**
Shankar, Ravi **9**
Simon, Paul **16**
Earlier sketch in CM **1**
Snow, Pheobe **4**
Steeleye Span **19**
Story, The **13**
Sweet Honey in the Rock **1**
Taj Mahal **6**
Thompson, Richard **7**
Tikaram, Tanita **9**
Toure, Ali Farka **18**
Van Ronk, Dave **12**
Van Zandt, Townes **13**
Vega, Suzanne **3**
Wainwright III, Loudon **11**
Walker, Jerry Jeff **13**
Watson, Doc **2**
Weavers, The **8**
Whitman, Slim **19**

French Horn
Ohanian, David
See Canadian Brass, The

Funk
Bambaataa, Afrika **13**
Brand New Heavies, The **14**
Brown, James **2**
Burdon, Eric **14**
Also see War
Also see Animals
Clinton, George **7**
Collins, Bootsy **8**
Fishbone **7**
Gang of Four **8**
Jackson, Janet **16**
Earlier sketch in CM **3**
Khan, Chaka **19**
Earlier sketch in CM **9**
Mayfield, Curtis **8**
Meters, The **14**
Ohio Players **16**
Parker, Maceo **7**
Prince **14**
Earlier sketch in CM **1**
Red Hot Chili Peppers, The **7**
Stone, Sly **8**
Toussaint, Allen **11**
Worrell, Bernie **11**

Funky
Front 242 **19**
Jamiroquai **21**
Wu-Tang Clan **19**

Fusion
Anderson, Ray **7**
Beck, Jeff **4**
Also see Yardbirds, The
Clarke, Stanley **3**
Coleman, Ornette **5**
Corea, Chick **6**
Davis, Miles **1**
Fishbone **7**
Hancock, Herbie **8**
Harris, Eddie **15**
Johnson, Eric **19**
Lewis, Ramsey **14**
Mahavishnu Orchestra **19**
McLaughlin, John **12**
Metheny, Pat **2**
O'Connor, Mark **1**
Ponty, Jean-Luc **8**
Reid, Vernon **2**
Ritenour, Lee **7**
Shorter, Wayne **5**
Summers, Andy **3**
Also see Police, The
Washington, Grover, Jr. **5**

Gospel
Anderson, Marian **8**
Baylor, Helen **20**
Boone, Pat **13**
Brown, James **2**
Caesar, Shirley **17**
Carter Family, The **3**
Charles, Ray **1**
Cleveland, James **1**
Cooke, Sam **1**
Also see Soul Stirrers, The
Crouch, Andraé **9**
Dorsey, Thomas A. **11**
Five Blind Boys of Alabama **12**
Ford, Tennessee Ernie **3**
Franklin, Aretha **17**
Earlier sketch in CM **2**
Franklin, Kirk **22**
Green, Al **9**
Hawkins, Tramaine **17**
Houston, Cissy **6**
Jackson, Mahalia **8**
Kee, John P. **15**
Knight, Gladys **1**
Little Richard **1**
Louvin Brothers, The **12**
Mighty Clouds of Joy, The **17**
Oak Ridge Boys, The **7**
Paris, Twila **16**
Pickett, Wilson **10**
Presley, Elvis **1**
Redding, Otis **5**
Reese, Della **13**
Robbins, Marty **9**
Smith, Michael W. **11**
Soul Stirrers, The **11**
Sounds of Blackness **13**
Staples, Mavis **13**
Staples, Pops **11**
Take 6 **6**
Waters, Ethel **11**
Watson, Doc **2**
Williams, Deniece **1**
Williams, Marion **15**
Winans, The **12**
Womack, Bobby **5**

Guitar
Ackerman, Will **3**
Adé, King Sunny **18**
Allison, Luther **21**
Allman, Duane
See Allman Brothers, The
Alvin, Dave **17**
Atkins, Chet **5**
Autry, Gene **12**
Baxter, Jeff
See Doobie Brothers, The
Beck **18**
Beck, Jeff **4**
Also see Yardbirds, The
Belew, Adrian **5**
Benson, George **9**
Berry, Chuck **1**
Berry, John **17**
Bettencourt, Nuno
See Extreme
Betts, Dicky
See Allman Brothers, The
Block, Rory **18**
Bloom, Luka **14**
Boyd, Liona **7**
Bream, Julian **9**
Bromberg, David **18**
Brown, Junior **15**
Buck, Peter
See R.E.M.
Buckingham, Lindsey **8**
Also see Fleetwood Mac
Burrell, Kenny **11**
Campbell, Glen **2**
Chesney, Kenny **20**
Chesnutt, Mark **13**
Christian, Charlie **11**
Clapton, Eric **11**
Earlier sketch in CM **1**
Also see Cream
Also see Yardbirds, The
Clark, Roy **1**
Cockburn, Bruce **8**
Collie, Mark **15**
Collins, Albert **19**
Earlier entry in CM **4**
Cooder, Ry **2**
Cotten, Elizabeth **16**
Cray, Robert **8**
Cropper, Steve **12**
Dale, Dick **13**
Daniels, Charlie **6**
Davis, Reverend Gary **18**
de Grassi, Alex **6**
de Lucia, Paco **1**
Del Rubio Triplets **21**
Denver, John **22**
Earlier entry in CM **1**
Dickens, Little Jimmy **7**
Diddley, Bo **3**
DiFranco, Ani **17**
Di Meola, Al **12**
Drake, Nick **17**
Earl, Ronnie **5**
Also see Roomful of Blues
Eddy, Duane **9**
Edge, The
See U2
Ellis, Herb **18**
Emmanuel, Tommy **21**
Etheridge, Melissa **16**
Earlier sketch in CM **4**
Fahey, John **17**
Feliciano, José **10**
Fender, Leo **10**
Flatt, Lester **3**
Flores, Rosie **16**
Ford, Lita **9**
Frampton, Peter **3**
Frehley, Ace
See Kiss
Fripp, Robert **9**
Frisell, Bill **15**
Frith, Fred **19**
Fuller, Blind Boy **20**
Fulson, Lowell **20**
Garcia, Jerry **4**
Also see Grateful Dead, The
Gatton, Danny **16**
George, Lowell
See Little Feat
Gibbons, Billy
See ZZ Top
Gill, Vince **7**
Gilmour, David
See Pink Floyd
Gorka, John **18**
Green, Grant **14**
Green, Peter
See Fleetwood Mac
Guy, Buddy **4**
Hackett, Bobby **21**
Haley, Bill **6**
Hardin, Tim **18**
Harper, Ben **17**
Harrison, George **2**
Hatfield, Juliana **12**
Also see Lemonheads, The
Havens, Richie **11**
Healey, Jeff **4**
Hedges, Michael **3**
Hendrix, Jimi **2**
Hillman, Chris
See Byrds, The
Also see Desert Rose Band, The
Hitchcock, Robyn **9**
Holly, Buddy **1**
Hooker, John Lee **1**
Hopkins, Lightnin' **13**
Howlin' Wolf **6**
Iommi, Tony
See Black Sabbath
Ives, Burl **12**
James, Elmore **8**
Jardine, Al
See Beach Boys, The
Jean, Wyclef **22**
Jefferson, Blind Lemon **18**
Jobim, Antonio Carlos **19**
Johnson, Eric **19**
Johnson, Lonnie **17**
Johnson, Robert **6**
Jones, Brian
See Rolling Stones, The
Jordan, Stanley **1**
Kantner, Paul
See Jefferson Airplane
Keith, Toby **17**
Kenny Wayne Shepard **22**
King, Albert **2**
King, B. B. **1**
King, Freddy **17**
Klugh, Earl **10**
Knopfler, Mark **3**
Also see Dire Straits
Kottke, Leo **13**
Landreth, Sonny **16**

Larkin, Patty **9**
Leadbelly **6**
Legg, Adrian **17**
Lennon, John **9**
Also see Beatles, The
Lindley, David **2**
Lockwood, Robert, Jr. **10**
Loeb, Lisa **19**
Marr, Johnny
See Smiths, The
See The The
Martino, Pat **17**
Matthews, Eric **22**
May, Brian
See Queen
Mayfield, Curtis **8**
McClinton, Delbert **14**
McCoury, Del **15**
McDowell, Mississippi Fred **16**
McGuinn, Roger
See Byrds, The
McLachlan, Sarah **12**
McLaughlin, John **12**
McLennan, Grant **21**
McReynolds, Jim
See McReynolds, Jim and Jesse
McTell, Blind Willie **17**
Metheny, Pat **2**
Mitchell, Joni **17**
Earlier sketch in CM **2**
Montgomery, Wes **3**
Morrissey, Bill **12**
Mo', Keb' **21**
Muldaur, Maria **18**
Nugent, Ted **2**
Oldfield, Mike **18**
Owens, Buck **2**
Page, Jimmy **4**
Also see Led Zeppelin
Also see Yardbirds, The
Parkening, Christopher **7**
Parnell, Lee Roy **15**
Pass, Joe **15**
Patton, Charley **11**
Perkins, Carl **9**
Perry, Joe
See Aerosmith
Petty, Tom **9**
Phair, Liz **14**
Phillips, Sam **12**
Prince **14**
Earlier sketch in CM **1**
Raitt, Bonnie **3**
Ray, Amy
See Indigo Girls
Redbone, Leon **19**
Reed, Jimmy **15**
Reid, Vernon **2**
Also see Living Colour
Reinhardt, Django **7**
Richards, Keith **11**
Also see Rolling Stones, The
Richman, Jonathan **12**
Ritenour, Lee **7**
Robbins, Marty **9**
Robertson, Robbie **2**
Robillard, Duke **2**
Rodgers, Nile **8**
Rush, Otis **12**
Saliers, Emily
See Indigo Girls
Santana, Carlos **19**
Earlier sketch in CM **1**
Satriani, Joe **4**
Scofield, John **7**
Segovia, Andres **6**
Sharrock, Sonny **15**
Shines, Johnny **14**
Simon, Paul **16**
Earlier sketch in CM **1**
Skaggs, Ricky **5**
Slash
See Guns n' Roses
Springsteen, Bruce **6**
Stewart, Dave
See Eurythmics
Stills, Stephen **5**
Stuart, Marty **9**
Summers, Andy **3**
Also see Police, The
Taylor, Mick
See Rolling Stones, The
Thielemans, Toots **13**
Thompson, Richard **7**
Tippin, Aaron **12**
Toure, Ali Farka **18**
Towner, Ralph **22**
Townshend, Pete **1**
Travis, Merle **14**
Trynin, Jen **21**
Tubb, Ernest **4**
Ulmer, James Blood **13**
Vai, Steve **5**
Van Halen, Edward
See Van Halen
Van Ronk, Dave **12**
Vaughan, Jimmie
See Fabulous Thunderbirds, The
Vaughan, Stevie Ray **1**
Wagoner, Porter **13**
Waits, Tom **12**
Earlier sketch in CM **1**
Walker, Jerry Jeff **13**
Walker, T-Bone **5**
Walsh, Joe **5**
Also see Eagles, The
Wariner, Steve **18**
Watson, Doc **2**
Weir, Bob
See Grateful Dead, The
Weller, Paul **14**
White, Lari **15**
Whitfield, Mark **18**
Whitley, Chris **16**
Whittaker, Hudson **20**
Wilson, Nancy
See Heart
Winston, George **9**
Winter, Johnny **5**
Wiseman, Mac **19**
Wray, Link **17**
Yamashita, Kazuhito **4**
Yarrow, Peter
See Peter, Paul & Mary
Yoakam, Dwight **21**
Young, Angus
See AC/DC
Young, Malcolm
See AC/DC
York, Andrew **15**
Young, Neil **15**
Earlier sketch in CM **2**
Zappa, Frank **17**
Earlier sketch in CM **1**

Harmonica

Dylan, Bob **3**
Guthrie, Woody **2**
Horton, Walter **19**
Lewis, Huey **9**
Little Walter **14**
McClinton, Delbert **14**
Musselwhite, Charlie **13**
Reed, Jimmy **15**
Thielemans, Toots **13**
Waters, Muddy **4**
Wells, Junior **17**
Williamson, Sonny Boy **9**
Wilson, Kim
See Fabulous Thunderbirds, The
Wonder, Stevie **17**
Earlier sketch in CM **2**
Young, Neil **15**
Earlier sketch in CM **2**

Heavy Metal

AC/DC **4**
Aerosmith **22**
Earlier sketch in CM **1**
Alice in Chains **10**
Anthrax **11**
Black Sabbath **9**
Blue Oyster Cult **16**
Cinderella **16**
Circle Jerks **17**
Danzig **7**
Deep Purple **11**
Def Leppard **3**
Dokken **16**
Faith No More **7**
Fishbone **7**
Ford, Lita **9**
Guns n' Roses **2**
Iron Maiden **10**
Judas Priest **10**
King's X **7**
Led Zeppelin **1**
L7 **12**
Megadeth **9**
Melvins **21**
Metallica **7**
Mötley Crüe **1**

Motörhead **10**
Nugent, Ted **2**
Osbourne, Ozzy **3**
Pantera **13**
Petra **3**
Queensryche **8**
Reid, Vernon **2**
Also see Living Colour
Reznor, Trent **13**
Roth, David Lee **1**
Also see Van Halen
Sepultura **12**
Skinny Puppy **17**
Slayer **10**
Soundgarden **6**
Spinal Tap **8**
Stryper **2**
Suicidal Tendencies **15**
Tool **21**
Warrant **17**
Whitesnake **5**
White Zombie **17**

Humor
Borge, Victor **19**
Coasters, The **5**
Jones, Spike **5**
Lehrer, Tom **7**
Pearl, Minnie **3**
Russell, Mark **6**
Sandler, Adam **19**
Schickele, Peter **5**
Shaffer, Paul **13**
Spinal Tap **8**
Stevens, Ray **7**
Yankovic, "Weird Al" **7**

Inventors
Fender, Leo **10**
Harris, Eddie **15**
Paul, Les **2**
Scholz, Tom
See Boston
Teagarden, Jack **10**
Theremin, Leon **19**

Jazz
Adderly, Cannonball **15**
Allen, Geri **10**
Allison, Mose **17**
Anderson, Ray **7**
Armstrong, Louis **4**
Bailey, Mildred **13**
Bailey, Pearl **5**
Baker, Anita **9**
Baker, Chet **13**
Baker, Ginger **16**
Also see Cream
Barbieri, Gato **22**
Basie, Count **2**
Bechet, Sidney **17**
Beiderbecke, Bix **16**
Belle, Regina **6**
Bennett, Tony **16**
Earlier sketch in CM **2**
Benson, George **9**
Berigan, Bunny **2**
Blackman, Cindy **15**
Blakey, Art **11**
Blanchard, Terence **13**
Bley, Carla **8**
Bley, Paul **14**
Blood, Sweat and Tears **7**
Brand New Heavies, The **14**
Braxton, Anthony **12**
Bridgewater, Dee Dee **18**
Brown, Ray **21**
Brown, Ruth **13**
Brubeck, Dave **8**
Burrell, Kenny **11**
Burton, Gary **10**
Calloway, Cab **6**
Canadian Brass, The **4**
Carter, Benny **3**
Also see McKinney's Cotton Pickers
Carter, Betty **6**
Carter, James **18**
Carter, Regina **22**
Carter, Ron **14**
Chambers, Paul **18**
Charles, Ray **1**
Cherry, Don **10**
Christian, Charlie **11**
Clarke, Stanley **3**
Clements, Vassar **18**
Clooney, Rosemary **9**
Cole, Holly **18**
Cole, Nat King **3**
Coleman, Ornette **5**
Coltrane, John **4**
Connick, Harry, Jr. **4**
Corea, Chick **6**
Davis, Anthony **17**
Davis, Miles **1**
DeJohnette, Jack **7**
Di Meola, Al **12**
Eckstine, Billy **1**
Eldridge, Roy **9**
Also see McKinney's Cotton Pickers
Ellington, Duke **2**
Ellis, Herb **18**
Evans, Bill **17**
Evans, Gil **17**
Ferguson, Maynard **7**
Ferrell, Rachelle **17**
Fitzgerald, Ella **1**
Flanagan, Tommy **16**
Fleck, Bela **8**
Also see New Grass Revival, The
Fountain, Pete **7**
Frisell, Bill **15**
Galway, James **3**
Getz, Stan **12**
Gillespie, Dizzy **6**
Goodman, Benny **4**
Gordon, Dexter **10**
Grappelli, Stephane **10**
Green, Benny **17**
Green, Grant **14**
Guaraldi, Vince **3**
Hackett, Bobby **21**
Haden, Charlie **12**
Hampton, Lionel **6**
Hancock, Herbie **8**
Hardcastle, Paul **20**
Hargrove, Roy **15**
Harris, Eddie **15**
Harris, Teddy **22**
Hawkins, Coleman **11**
Hawkins, Erskine **19**
Hedges, Michael **3**
Henderson, Fletcher **16**
Henderson, Joe **14**
Herman, Woody **12**
Hines, Earl "Fatha" **12**
Hirt, Al **5**
Holiday, Billie **6**
Horn, Shirley **7**
Horne, Lena **11**
Humes, Helen **19**
Hunter, Alberta **7**
Incognito **16**
Isham, Mark **14**
Jackson, Milt **15**
Jacquet, Illinois **17**
James, Boney **21**
James, Harry **11**
Jarreau, Al **1**
Jarrett, Keith **1**
Jensen, Ingrid **22**
Jobim, Antonio Carlos **19**
Johnson, James P. **16**
Johnson, Lonnie **17**
Jones, Elvin **9**
Jones, Hank **15**
Jones, Philly Joe **16**
Jones, Quincy **20**
Earlier sketch in CM **2**
Jones, Thad **19**
Jordan, Stanley **1**
Kennedy, Nigel **8**
Kenny G **14**
Kenton, Stan **21**
Kirk, Rahsaan Roland **6**
Kitt, Eartha **9**
Klugh, Earl **10**
Kronos Quartet **5**
Krupa, Gene **13**
Laine, Cleo **10**
Lateef, Yusef **16**
Lee, Peggy **8**
Lewis, Ramsey **14**
Lincoln, Abbey **9**
Israel "Cachao" Lopez **14**
Lloyd, Charles **22**
Lovano, Joe **13**
Mahavishnu Orchestra **19**
Mancini, Henry **20**
Earlier sketch in CM **1**
Manhattan Transfer, The **8**
Mann, Herbie **16**
Marsalis, Branford **10**

Marsalis, Ellis **13**
Marsalis, Wynton **20**
Earlier sketch in CM **6**
Martino, Pat **17**
Masekela, Hugh **7**
McBride, Christian **17**
McFerrin, Bobby **3**
McKinney's Cotton Pickers **16**
McLaughlin, John **12**
McPartland, Marian **15**
McRae, Carmen **9**
Metheny, Pat **2**
Mingus, Charles **9**
Monk, Thelonious **6**
Montgomery, Wes **3**
Morgan, Frank **9**
Morton, Jelly Roll **7**
Mulligan, Gerry **16**
Najee **21**
Nascimento, Milton **6**
Norvo, Red **12**
O'Day, Anita **21**
Oliver, King **15**
Palmer, Jeff **20**
Palmieri, Eddie **15**
Parker, Charlie **5**
Parker, Maceo **7**
Pass, Joe **15**
Paul, Les **2**
Pepper, Art **18**
Peterson, Oscar **11**
Ponty, Jean-Luc **8**
Powell, Bud **15**
Previn, André **15**
Professor Longhair **6**
Puente, Tito **14**
Pullen, Don **16**
Rampal, Jean-Pierre **6**
Redman, Joshua **12**
Reeves, Dianne **16**
Reid, Vernon **2**
Also see Living Colour
Reinhardt, Django **7**
Rich, Buddy **13**
Roach, Max **12**
Roberts, Marcus **6**
Robillard, Duke **2**
Rodney, Red **14**
Rollins, Sonny **7**
Saluzzi, Dino
Sanborn, David **1**
Sanders, Pharoah **16**
Sandoval, Arturo **15**
Santana, Carlos **19**
Earlier entry in CM **1**
Schuur, Diane **6**
Scofield, John **7**
Scott, Jimmy **14**
Scott-Heron, Gil **13**
Severinsen, Doc **1**
Sharrock, Sonny **15**
Shaw, Artie **8**
Shorter, Wayne **5**
Silver, Horace **19**
Simone, Nina **11**
Solal, Martial **4**
Strayhorn, Billy **13**
Summers, Andy **3**
Also see Police, The
Sun Ra **5**
Take 6 **6**
Tatum, Art **17**
Taylor, Billy **13**
Taylor, Cecil **9**
Teagarden, Jack **10**
Thielemans, Toots **13**
Threadgill, Henry **9**
Torme, Mel **4**
Tucker, Sophie **12**
Turner, Big Joe **13**
Turtle Island String Quartet **9**
Tyner, McCoy **7**
Ulmer, James Blood **13**
US3 **18**
Vaughan, Sarah **2**
Walker, T-Bone **5**
Washington, Dinah **5**
Washington, Grover, Jr. **5**
Weather Report **19**
Webb, Chick **14**
Weston, Randy **15**
Whitaker, Rodney **20**
Whiteman, Paul **17**
Whitfield, Mark **18**
Whittaker, Rodney **19**
Williams, Joe **11**
Wilson, Cassandra **12**
Wilson, Nancy **14**
Winter, Paul **10**
Witherspoon, Jimmy **19**
Young, La Monte **16**
Young, Lester **14**
Zorn, John **15**

Juju
Adé, King Sunny **18**

Keyboards, Electric
Aphex Twin **14**
Bley, Paul **14**
Brown, Tony **14**
Chemical Brothers **20**
Corea, Chick **6**
Davis, Chip **4**
Dolby, Thomas **10**
Emerson, Keith
See Emerson, Lake & Palmer/Powell
Eno, Brian **8**
Foster, David **13**
Froom, Mitchell **15**
Hammer, Jan **21**
Hancock, Herbie **8**
Hardcastle, Paul **20**
Jackson, Joe **22**
Earlier entry in CM **4**
Jarre, Jean-Michel **2**
Jones, Booker T. **8**
Kitaro **1**
Man or Astroman? **21**
Manzarek, Ray
See Doors, The
McDonald, Michael
See Doobie Brothers, The
McVie, Christine
See Fleetwood Mac
Orbital **20**
Palmer, Jeff **20**
Pierson, Kate
See B-52's, The
Sakamoto, Ryuichi **19**
Shaffer, Paul **13**
Sun Ra **5**
Waller, Fats **7**
Wilson, Brian
See Beach Boys, The
Winwood, Steve **2**
Also see Spencer Davis Group
Also see Traffic
Wonder, Stevie **17**
Earlier sketch in CM **2**
Worrell, Bernie **11**
Yanni **11**

Liturgical Music
Cooney, Rory **6**
Talbot, John Michael **6**

Mandolin
Bromberg, David **18**
Bush, Sam
See New Grass Revival, The
Duffey, John
See Seldom Scene, The
Grisman, David **17**
Hartford, John **1**
Lindley, David **2**
McReynolds, Jesse
See McReynolds, Jim and Jesse
Monroe, Bill **1**
Rosas, Cesar
See Los Lobos
Skaggs, Ricky **5**
Stuart, Marty **9**

Musicals
Allen, Debbie **8**
Allen, Peter **11**
Andrews, Julie **4**
Andrews Sisters, The **9**
Bacharach, Burt **20**
Earlier sketch in CM **1**
Bailey, Pearl **5**
Baker, Josephine **10**
Berlin, Irving **8**
Brightman, Sarah **20**
Brown, Ruth **13**
Buckley, Betty **16**
Earlier sketch in CM **1**
Burnett, Carol **6**
Carter, Nell **7**
Channing, Carol **6**
Chevalier, Maurice **6**

Crawford, Michael **4**
Crosby, Bing **6**
Curry, Tim **3**
Davis, Sammy, Jr. **4**
Garland, Judy **6**
Gershwin, George and Ira **11**
Hamlisch, Marvin **1**
Horne, Lena **11**
Johnson, James P. **16**
Jolson, Al **10**
Kern, Jerome **13**
Laine, Cleo **10**
Lerner and Loewe **13**
Lloyd Webber, Andrew **6**
LuPone, Patti **8**
Masekela, Hugh **7**
Menken, Alan **10**
Mercer, Johnny **13**
Moore, Melba **7**
Patinkin, Mandy **20**
Earlier sketch in CM **3**
Peters, Bernadette **7**
Porter, Cole **10**
Robeson, Paul **8**
Rodgers, Richard **9**
Sager, Carole Bayer **5**
Shaffer, Paul **13**
Sondheim, Stephen **8**
Styne, Jule **21**
Waters, Ethel **11**
Weill, Kurt **12**
Yeston, Maury **22**

Oboe
Lateef, Yusef **16**

Opera
Adams, John **8**
Anderson, Marian **8**
Baker, Janet **14**
Bartoli, Cecilia **12**
Battle, Kathleen **6**
Bocelli, Andrea **22**
Bumbry, Grace **13**
Callas, Maria **11**
Carreras, José **8**
Caruso, Enrico **10**
Copeland, Stewart **14**
Also see Police, The
Cotrubas, Ileana **1**
Davis, Anthony **17**
Domingo, Placido **20**
Earlier sketch in CM **1**
Freni, Mirella **14**
Gershwin, George and Ira **11**
Graves, Denyce **16**
Hampson, Thomas **12**
Hendricks, Barbara **10**
Herrmann, Bernard **14**
Horne, Marilyn **9**
McNair, Sylvia **15**
Norman, Jessye **7**
Pavarotti, Luciano **20**
Earlier sketch in CM **1**
Price, Leontyne **6**
Sills, Beverly **5**
Solti, Georg **13**
Sutherland, Joan **13**
Te Kanawa, Kiri **2**
Toscanini, Arturo **14**
Upshaw, Dawn **9**
von Karajan, Herbert **1**
Weill, Kurt **12**
Zimmerman, Udo **5**

Percussion
Aronoff, Kenny **21**
Baker, Ginger **16**
Also see Cream
Blackman, Cindy **15**
Blakey, Art **11**
Bonham, John
See Led Zeppelin
Burton, Gary **10**
Collins, Phil **20**
Earlier sketch in CM **2**
Also see Genesis
Copeland, Stewart **14**
Also see Police, The
DeJohnette, Jack **7**
Densmore, John
See Doors, The
Dunbar, Aynsley
See Jefferson Starship
Also see Journey
Also see Whitesnake
Dunbar, Sly
See Sly and Robbie
Fleetwood, Mick
See Fleetwood Mac
Hampton, Lionel **6**
Hart, Mickey
See Grateful Dead, The
Henley, Don **3**
Jones, Elvin **9**
Jones, Kenny
See Who, The
Jones, Philly Joe **16**
Jones, Spike **5**
Kreutzman, Bill
See Grateful Dead, The
Krupa, Gene **13**
Mason, Nick
See Pink Floyd
Moon, Keith
See Who, The
Mo', Keb' **21**
N'Dour, Youssou **6**
Otis, Johnny **16**
Palmer, Carl
See Emerson, Lake & Palmer/Powell
Palmieri, Eddie **15**
Peart, Neil
See Rush
Powell, Cozy
See Emerson, Lake & Palmer/Powell
Puente, Tito **14**
Rich, Buddy **13**
Roach, Max **12**
Sheila E. **3**
Starr, Ringo **10**
Also see Beatles, The
Walden, Narada Michael **14**
Watts, Charlie
See Rolling Stones, The
Webb, Chick **14**

Piano
Allen, Geri **10**
Allison, Mose **17**
Amos, Tori **12**
Arrau, Claudio **1**
Bacharach, Burt **20**
Earlier sketch in CM **1**
Ball, Marcia **15**
Basie, Count **2**
Berlin, Irving **8**
Blake, Eubie **19**
Bley, Carla **8**
Bley, Paul **14**
Borge, Victor **19**
Brickman, Jim **22**
Britten, Benjamin **15**
Bronfman, Yefim **6**
Brubeck, Dave **8**
Bush, Kate **4**
Charles, Ray **1**
Clayderman, Richard **1**
Cleveland, James **1**
Cliburn, Van **13**
Cole, Nat King **3**
Collins, Judy **4**
Collins, Phil **20**
Earlier sketch in CM **2**
Also see Genesis
Connick, Harry, Jr. **4**
Crouch, Andraé **9**
DeJohnette, Jack **7**
Domino, Fats **2**
Dr. John **7**
Dupree, Champion Jack **12**
Ellington, Duke **2**
Esquivel, Juan **17**
Evans, Bill **17**
Evans, Gil **17**
Feinstein, Michael **6**
Ferrell, Rachelle **17**
Flack, Roberta **5**
Flanagan, Tommy **16**
Frey, Glenn **3**
Galás, Diamanda **16**
Glass, Philip **1**
Gould, Glenn **9**
Green, Benny **17**
Grusin, Dave **7**
Guaraldi, Vince **3**
Hamlisch, Marvin **1**
Hancock, Herbie **8**
Harris, Teddy **22**
Helfgott, David **19**
Henderson, Fletcher **16**
Hinderas, Natalie **12**

Hines, Earl "Fatha" **12**
Horn, Shirley **7**
Hornsby, Bruce **3**
Horowitz, Vladimir **1**
Jackson, Joe **22**
Earlier entry in CM **4**
Jarrett, Keith **1**
Joel, Billy **12**
Earlier sketch in CM **2**
John, Elton **20**
Earlier sketch in CM **3**
Johnson, James P. **16**
Jones, Hank **15**
Joplin, Scott **10**
Kenton, Stan **21**
Kissin, Evgeny **6**
Levine, James **8**
Lewis, Jerry Lee **2**
Lewis, Ramsey **14**
Liberace **9**
Little Richard **1**
Manilow, Barry **2**
Marsalis, Ellis **13**
Matthews, Eric **22**
McDonald, Michael
See Doobie Brothers, The
McPartland, Marian **15**
McRae, Carmen **9**
McVie, Christine
See Fleetwood Mac
Milsap, Ronnie **2**
Mingus, Charles **9**
Monk, Thelonious **6**
Morton, Jelly Roll **7**
Newman, Randy **4**
Nero, Peter **19**
Palmieri, Eddie **15**
Perahia, Murray **10**
Peterson, Oscar **11**
Post, Mike **21**
Powell, Bud **15**
Pratt, Awadagin **19**
Previn, André **15**
Professor Longhair **6**
Puente, Tito **14**
Pullen, Don **16**
Rich, Charlie **3**
Roberts, Marcus **6**
Rubinstein, Arthur **11**
Russell, Mark **6**
Schickele, Peter **5**
Sedaka, Neil **4**
Shaffer, Paul **13**
Solal, Martial **4**
Solti, Georg **13**
Spann, Otis **18**
Story, Liz **2**
Strayhorn, Billy **13**
Sunnyland Slim **16**
Sykes, Roosevelt **20**
Tatum, Art **17**
Taylor, Billy **13**
Taylor, Cecil **9**
Tyner, McCoy **7**
Vangelis **21**
Waits, Tom **12**
Earlier sketch in **1**
Waller, Fats **7**
Weston, Randy **15**
Wilson, Cassandra **12**
Winston, George **9**
Winwood, Steve **2**
Also see Spencer Davis Group
Also see Traffic
Wonder, Stevie **17**
Earlier sketch in CM **2**
Wright, Rick
See Pink Floyd
Young, La Monte **16**

Piccolo
Galway, James **3**

Pop
A-ha **22**
Abba **12**
Abdul, Paula **3**
Adam Ant **13**
Adams, Bryan **20**
Earlier sketch in CM **2**
Adams, Oleta **17**
Air Supply **22**
All-4-One **17**
Alpert, Herb **11**
America **16**
Amos, Tori **12**
Andrews Sisters, The **9**
Arden, Jann **21**
Arena, Tina **21**
Armatrading, Joan **4**
Arnold, Eddy **10**
Astley, Rick **5**
Atkins, Chet **5**
Avalon, Frankie **5**
Bacharach, Burt **20**
Earlier sketch in CM **1**
Backstreet Boys **21**
Bailey, Pearl **5**
Bananarama **22**
Bangles **22**
Basia **5**
Beach Boys, The **1**
Beatles, The **2**
Beaver Brown Band, The **3**
Bee Gees, The **3**
Belly **16**
Bennett, Tony **16**
Earlier sketch in CM **2**
Benson, George **9**
Benton, Brook **7**
B-52's, The **4**
Better Than Ezra **19**
Blige, Mary J. **15**
Blondie **14**
Blood, Sweat and Tears **7**
Blue Rodeo **18**
BoDeans, The **20**
Earlier sketch in CM **3**
Bolton, Michael **4**
Boo Radleys, The **21**
Boone, Pat **13**
Boston **11**
Bowie, David **1**
Boyz II Men **15**
Bragg, Billy **7**
Branigan, Laura **2**
Braxton, Toni **17**
Brickell, Edie **3**
Brooks, Garth **8**
Brown, Bobby **4**
Browne, Jackson **3**
Bryson, Peabo **11**
Buckingham, Lindsey **8**
Also see Fleetwood Mac
Buckley, Tim **14**
Buffett, Jimmy **4**
Burdon, Eric **14**
Also see War
Also see Animals
Cabaret Voltaire **18**
Campbell, Glen **2**
Campbell, Tevin **13**
Cardigans **19**
Carey, Mariah **20**
Earlier sketch in CM **6**
Carlisle, Belinda **8**
Carnes, Kim **4**
Carpenters, The **13**
Case, Peter **13**
Chandra, Sheila **16**
Chapin, Harry **6**
Chapman, Tracy **20**
Earlier sketch in CM **4**
Charlatans, The **13**
Charles, Ray **1**
Checker, Chubby **7**
Cher **1**
Cherry, Neneh **4**
Chicago **3**
Chilton, Alex **10**
Clapton, Eric **11**
Earlier sketch in CM **1**
Also see Cream
Also see Yardbirds, The
Clayderman, Richard **1**
Clooney, Rosemary **9**
Coasters, The **5**
Cocker, Joe **4**
Cocteau Twins, The **12**
Cole, Lloyd **9**
Cole, Natalie **21**
Earlier entry in CM **1**
Cole, Nat King **3**
Cole, Paula **20**
Collins, Judy **4**
Collins, Phil **20**
Earlier sketch in CM **2**
Also see Genesis
Colvin, Shawn **11**
Como, Perry **14**
Connick, Harry, Jr. **4**
Cooke, Sam **1**
Also see Soul Stirrers, The
Cope, Julian **16**

Costello, Elvis **12**
Earlier sketch in CM **2**
Cranberries, The **14**
Crash Test Dummies **14**
Crenshaw, Marshall **5**
Croce, Jim **3**
Crosby, David **3**
Also see Byrds, The
Crow, Sheryl **18**
Crowded House **12**
Cure, The **20**
Earlier sketch in CM **3**
Daltrey, Roger **3**
Also see Who, The
D'Arby, Terence Trent **3**
Darin, Bobby **4**
Dave Clark Five, The **12**
Davies, Ray **5**
Davis, Sammy, Jr. **4**
Davis, Skeeter **15**
Dayne, Taylor **4**
DeBarge, El **14**
Del Amitri **18**
Del Rubio Triplets **21**
Denver, John **1**
Depeche Mode **5**
Des'ree **15**
Devo **13**
Diamond, Neil **1**
Dion **4**
Dion, Céline **12**
Doc Pomus **14**
Donovan **9**
Doobie Brothers, The **3**
Doors, The **4**
Dubstar **22**
Duran Duran **4**
Dylan, Bob **21**
Earlier entry in CM **3**
Eagles, The **3**
Earth, Wind and Fire **12**
Easton, Sheena **2**
Edmonds, Kenneth "Babyface" **12**
Electric Light Orchestra **7**
Elfman, Danny **9**
Elliot, Cass **5**
Enigma **14**
En Vogue **10**
Estefan, Gloria **15**
Earlier sketch in CM **2**
Eurythmics **6**
Everly Brothers, The **2**
Everything But The Girl **15**
Exposé **4**
Fabian **5**
Fatboy Slim **22**
Feliciano, José **10**
Ferguson, Maynard **7**
Ferry, Bryan **1**
Fiedler, Arthur **6**
Fine Young Cannibals **22**
Fisher, Eddie **12**
Fitzgerald, Ella **1**
Flack, Roberta **5**
Fleetwood Mac **5**
Fogelberg, Dan **4**
Fordham, Julia **15**
Foster, David **13**
Four Tops, The **11**
Fox, Samantha **3**
Frampton, Peter **3**
Francis, Connie **10**
Franklin, Aretha **17**
Earlier sketch in CM **2**
Frey, Glenn **3**
Also see Eagles, The
Garfunkel, Art **4**
Gaye, Marvin **4**
Gayle, Crystal **1**
Geldof, Bob **9**
Genesis **4**
Gershwin, George and Ira **11**
Gibson, Debbie **1**
Gift, Roland **3**
Gin Blossoms **18**
Goodman, Benny **4**
Gordy, Berry, Jr. **6**
Grant, Amy **7**
Grebenshikov, Boris **3**
Green, Al **9**
Guthrie, Arlo **6**
Hall & Oates **6**
Hammer, M.C. **5**
Hancock, Herbie **8**
Hanson **20**
Harding, John Wesley **6**
Harrison, George **2**
Also see Beatles, The
Harry, Deborah **4**
Also see Blondie
Hawkins, Sophie B. **21**
Healey, Jeff **4**
Henley, Don **3**
Also see Eagles, The
Herman's Hermits **5**
Hitchcock, Robyn **9**
Holland-Dozier-Holland **5**
Hootie and the Blowfish **18**
Horne, Lena **11**
Hornsby, Bruce **3**
Houston, Whitney **8**
Human League, The **17**
Humperdinck, Engelbert **19**
Ian, Janis **5**
Idol, Billy **3**
Iglesias, Julio **20**
Earlier sketch in CM **2**
Indigo Girls **20**
Earlier sketch in CM **3**
Ingram, James **11**
Isaak, Chris **6**
Isley Brothers, The **8**
Jackson, Janet **16**
Earlier sketch in CM **3**
Jackson, Joe **22**
Earlier entry in CM 4
Jackson, Michael **17**
Earlier sketch in CM **1**
Also see Jacksons, The
Jacksons, The **7**
Jam, Jimmy, and Terry Lewis **11**
James **12**
James, Harry **11**
James, Rick **2**
Jarreau, Al **1**
Jayhawks, The **15**
Jefferson Airplane **5**
Jodeci **13**
Joel, Billy **12**
Earlier sketch in CM **2**
Johansen, David **7**
John, Elton **20**
Earlier sketch in CM **3**
Johnston, Freedy **20**
Jolson, Al **10**
Jones, Quincy **20**
Earlier sketch in CM **2**
Jones, Rickie Lee **4**
Jones, Tom **11**
Joplin, Janis **3**
Kaye, Carol **22**
Khan, Chaka **19**
Earlier sketch in CM **9**
King, Ben E. **7**
King, Carole **6**
Kiss **5**
Kitt, Eartha **9**
Knight, Gladys **1**
Knopfler, Mark **3**
Also see Dire Straits
Kool & the Gang **13**
Kraftwerk **9**
Kristofferson, Kris **4**
LaBelle, Patti **8**
Lauper, Cyndi **11**
Lee, Brenda **5**
Leiber and Stoller **14**
Lemper, Ute **14**
Lennon, John **9**
Also see Beatles, The
Lennon, Julian **2**
Lennox, Annie **18**
Lightning Seeds **21**
Also see Eurythmics, The
Lewis, Huey **9**
Liberace **9**
Lightfoot, Gordon **3**
Loeb, Lisa **19**
Loggins, Kenny **20**
Earlier sketch in CM **3**
Lovett, Lyle **5**
Lowe, Nick **6**
Lush **13**
Lynne, Jeff **5**
MacColl, Kirsty **12**
Madonna **16**
Earlier sketch in CM **4**
Mamas and the Papas **21**
Mancini, Henry **20**
Earlier sketch in CM **1**
Manhattan Transfer, The **8**
Manilow, Barry **2**
Marley, Bob **3**
Marley, Ziggy **3**
Marsalis, Branford **10**

Martin, Dean **1**
Martin, George **6**
Marx, Richard **21**
Earlier sketch in CM **3**
Mathis, Johnny **2**
Mazzy Star **17**
McCartney, Paul **4**
Also see Beatles, The
McFerrin, Bobby **3**
McLachlan, Sarah **12**
McLean, Don **7**
McLennan, Grant **21**
Medley, Bill **3**
Melanie **12**
Michael, George **9**
Midler, Bette **8**
Mighty Mighty Bosstones **20**
Mike & the Mechanics **17**
Miller, Mitch **11**
Miller, Roger **4**
Milli Vanilli **4**
Mills Brothers, The **14**
Minnelli, Liza **19**
Mitchell, Joni **17**
Earlier sketch in CM **2**
Money, Eddie **16**
Monkees, The **7**
Montand, Yves **12**
Moore, Chante **21**
Morrison, Jim **3**
Morrison, Van **3**
Morissette, Alanis **19**
Morrissey **10**
Mouskouri, Nana **12**
Moyet, Alison **12**
Murray, Anne **4**
Myles, Alannah **4**
Neville, Aaron **5**
Also see Neville Brothers, The
Neville Brothers, The **4**
New Kids on the Block **3**
Newman, Randy **4**
Newton, Wayne **2**
Newton-John, Olivia **8**
Nicks, Stevie **2**
Nilsson **10**
Nitty Gritty Dirt Band **6**
No Doubt **20**
Nyro, Laura **12**
Oak Ridge Boys, The **7**
Ocasek, Ric **5**
Ocean, Billy **4**
O'Connor, Sinead **3**
Odds **20**
Oldfield, Mike **18**
Orchestral Manoeuvres in the Dark **21**
Orlando, Tony **15**
Osborne, Joan **19**
Osmond, Donny **3**
Page, Jimmy **4**
Also see Led Zeppelin
Also see Yardbirds, The
Page, Patti **11**
Parks, Van Dyke **17**
Parsons, Alan **12**
Parton, Dolly **2**
Pendergrass, Teddy **3**
Peniston, CeCe **15**
Penn, Michael **4**
Pet Shop Boys **5**
Peter, Paul & Mary **4**
Phillips, Sam **12**
Piaf, Edith **8**
Pizzicato Five **18**
Plant, Robert **2**
Also see Led Zeppelin
Pointer Sisters, The **9**
Porter, Cole **10**
Prefab Sprout **15**
Presley, Elvis **1**
Priest, Maxi **20**
Prince **14**
Earlier sketch in CM **1**
Proclaimers, The **13**
Prodigy **22**
Pulp **18**
Queen **6**
Rabbitt, Eddie **5**
Raitt, Bonnie **3**
Rea, Chris **12**
Redding, Otis **5**
Reddy, Helen **9**
Reeves, Martha **4**
R.E.M. **5**
Republica **20**
Richard, Cliff **14**
Richie, Lionel **2**
Riley, Teddy **14**
Robbins, Marty **9**
Robinson, Smokey **1**
Rogers, Kenny **1**
Rolling Stones **3**
Ronstadt, Linda **2**
Ross, Diana **1**
Roth, David Lee **1**
Also see Van Halen
RuPaul **20**
Ruffin, David **6**
Sade **2**
Sager, Carole Bayer **5**
Sainte-Marie, Buffy **11**
Sanborn, David **1**
Seal **14**
Seals, Dan **9**
Seals & Crofts **3**
Secada, Jon **13**
Sedaka, Neil **4**
Selena **16**
Shaffer, Paul **13**
Sheila E. **3**
Shirelles, The **11**
Shonen Knife **13**
Siberry, Jane **6**
Simon, Carly **22**
Earlier entry in CM **4**
Simon, Paul **16**
Earlier sketch in CM **1**
Sinatra, Frank **1**
Smiths, The **3**
Snow, Pheobe **4**
Sobule, Jill **20**
Soul Coughing **21**
Sparks **18**
Spector, Phil **4**
Spice Girls **22**
Springfield, Dusty **20**
Springfield, Rick **9**
Springsteen, Bruce **6**
Squeeze **5**
Stansfield, Lisa **9**
Starr, Ringo **10**
Steely Dan **5**
Stereolab **18**
Stevens, Cat **3**
Stewart, Rod **20**
Earlier sketch in CM **2**
Also see Faces, The
Stills, Stephen **5**
Sting **19**
Earlier sketch in CM **2**
Also see Police, The
Story, The **13**
Straw, Syd **18**
Streisand, Barbra **2**
Suede **20**
Summer, Donna **12**
Sundays, The **20**
Supremes, The **6**
Sweat, Keith **13**
Sweet, Matthew **9**
SWV **14**
Talking Heads **1**
Talk Talk **19**
Taylor, James **2**
Tears for Fears **6**
Teenage Fanclub **13**
Temptations, The **3**
10,000 Maniacs **3**
The The **15**
They Might Be Giants **7**
Thomas, Irma **16**
Three Dog Night **5**
Tiffany **4**
Tikaram, Tanita **9**
Timbuk 3 **3**
TLC **15**
Toad the Wet Sprocket **13**
Tony! Toni! Toné! **12**
Torme, Mel **4**
Townshend, Pete **1**
Also see Who, The
Turner, Tina **1**
Valli, Frankie **10**
Vandross, Luther **2**
Vega, Suzanne **3**
Vinton, Bobby **12**
Walsh, Joe **5**
Warnes, Jennifer **3**
Warwick, Dionne **2**
Was (Not Was) **6**
Washington, Dinah **5**
Waters, Crystal **15**

Watley, Jody **9**
Webb, Jimmy **12**
"Weird Al" Yankovic **7**
Weller, Paul **14**
Who, The **3**
Williams, Andy **2**
Williams, Dar **21**
Williams, Deniece **1**
Williams, Joe **11**
Williams, Lucinda **10**
Williams, Paul **5**
Williams, Vanessa **10**
Williams, Victoria **17**
Wilson, Jackie **3**
Wilson Phillips **5**
Winwood, Steve **2**
Also see Spencer Davis Group
Also see Traffic
Womack, Bobby **5**
Wonder, Stevie **17**
Earlier sketch in CM **2**
XTC **10**
Young, Neil **15**
Earlier sketch in CM **2**
Young M.C. **4**

Producers
Ackerman, Will **3**
Albini, Steve **15**
Alpert, Herb **11**
Austin, Dallas **16**
Baker, Anita **9**
Benitez, Jellybean **15**
Bogaert, Jo
See Technotronic
Brown, Junior **15**
Brown, Tony **14**
Browne, Jackson **3**
Burnett, T Bone **13**
Cale, John **9**
Clarke, Stanley **3**
Clinton, George **7**
Collins, Phil **2**
Also see Genesis
Combs, Sean "Puffy" **16**
Costello, Elvis **2**
Cropper, Steve **12**
Crowell, Rodney **8**
Dixon, Willie **10**
DJ Premier
See Gang Starr
Dr. Dre **15**
Also see N.W.A.
Dolby, Thomas **10**
Dozier, Lamont
See Holland-Dozier-Holland
Edmonds, Kenneth "Babyface" **12**
Enigma **14**
Eno, Brian **8**
Ertegun, Ahmet **10**
Foster, David **13**
Fripp, Robert **9**
Froom, Mitchell **15**
Gordy, Jr., Emory **17**
Gray, F. Gary **19**
Grusin, Dave **7**
Hardcastle, Paul **20**
Holland, Brian
See Holland-Dozier-Holland
Holland, Eddie
See Holland-Dozier-Holland
Jackson, Millie **14**
Jam, Jimmy, and Terry Lewis **11**
Jones, Booker T. **8**
Jones, Quincy **20**
Earlier sketch in CM **2**
Jourgensen, Al
See Ministry
Krasnow, Bob **15**
Lanois, Daniel **8**
Laswell, Bill **14**
Leiber and Stoller **14**
Lillywhite, Steve **13**
Lynne, Jeff **5**
Marley, Rita **10**
Martin, George **6**
Master P **22**
Mayfield, Curtis **8**
McKnight, Brian **22**
Miller, Mitch **11**
Osby, Greg **21**
Parks, Van Dyke **17**
Parsons, Alan **12**
Post, Mike **21**
Prince **14**
Earlier sketch in CM **1**
Riley, Teddy **14**
Robertson, Robbie **2**
Rodgers, Nile **8**
Rubin, Rick **9**
Rundgren, Todd **11**
Shocklee, Hank **15**
Simmons, Russell **7**
Skaggs, Ricky **5**
Spector, Phil **4**
Sure!, Al B. **13**
Sweat, Keith **13**
Swing, DeVante
See Jodeci
Too $hort **16**
Toussaint, Allen **11**
Tricky **18**
Vandross, Luther **2**
Vasquez, Junior **16**
Vig, Butch **17**
Walden, Narada Michael **14**
Was, Don **21**
Watt, Mike **22**
Wexler, Jerry **15**
Whelan, Bill **20**
Willner, Hal **10**
Wilson, Brian
See Beach Boys, The
Winbush, Angela **15**
Woods-Wright, Tomica **22**

Promoters
Clark, Dick **2**
Geldof, Bob **9**
Graham, Bill **10**
Hay, George D. **3**
Simmons, Russell **7**

Ragtime
Johnson, James P. **16**
Joplin, Scott **10**

Rap
Anthony, Marc **19**
Arrested Development **14**
Austin, Dallas **16**
Bambaataa, Afrika **13**
Basehead **11**
Beastie Boys, The **8**
Biz Markie **10**
Black Sheep **15**
Bone Thugs-N-Harmony **18**
Busta Rhymes **18**
Campbell, Luther **10**
Cherry, Neneh **4**
Combs, Sean "Puffy" **16**
Coolio **19**
Cypress Hill **11**
Das EFX **14**
De La Soul **7**
Digable Planets **15**
Digital Underground **9**
DJ Jazzy Jeff and the Fresh Prince **5**
Dr. Dre **15**
Also see N.W.A.
Eazy-E **13**
Also see N.W.A.
EPMD **10**
Eric B. and Rakim **9**
Franti, Michael **16**
Fugees, The **17**
Gang Starr **13**
Geto Boys, The **11**
Grandmaster Flash **14**
Hammer, M.C. **5**
Heavy D **10**
House of Pain **14**
Ice Cube **10**
Ice-T **7**
Insane Clown Posse **22**
Jackson, Millie **14**
Kane, Big Daddy **7**
Kid 'n Play **5**
Knight, Suge **15**
Kool Moe Dee **9**
Kris Kross **11**
KRS-One **8**
L.L. Cool J. **5**
Last Poets **21**
MC Breed **17**
MC Lyte **8**
MC 900 Ft. Jesus **16**
MC Serch **10**
Master P **22**
Nas **19**
Naughty by Nature **11**
N.W.A. **6**
Notorious B.I.G. **20**
Pharcyde, The **17**
P.M. Dawn **11**

Public Enemy **4**
Queen Latifah **6**
Rage Against the Machine **18**
Riley, Teddy **14**
Rubin, Rick **9**
Run-D.M.C. **4**
Salt-N-Pepa **6**
Scott-Heron, Gil **13**
Shaggy **19**
Shanté **10**
Shocklee, Hank **15**
Simmons, Russell **7**
Sir Mix-A-Lot **14**
Snoop Doggy Dogg **17**
Spearhead **19**
Special Ed **16**
Sure!, Al B. **13**
TLC **15**
Tone-L c **3**
Too $hort **16**
Tribe Called Quest, A **8**
Tricky **18**
2Pac **17**
US3 **18**
Vanilla Ice **6**
Wu-Tang Clan **19**
Young M.C. **4**
Yo Yo **9**

Record Company Executives
Ackerman, Will **3**
Alpert, Herb **11**
Brown, Tony **14**
Busby, Jheryl **9**
Combs, Sean "Puffy" **16**
Davis, Chip **4**
Davis, Clive **14**
Ertegun, Ahmet **10**
Foster, David **13**
Gabriel, Peter **16**
Earlier sketch in CM **2**
Also see Genesis
Geffen, David **8**
Gordy, Berry, Jr. **6**
Hammond, John **6**
Harley, Bill **7**
Harrell, Andre **16**
Jam, Jimmy, and Terry Lewis **11**
Knight, Suge **15**
Koppelman, Charles **14**
Krasnow, Bob **15**
LiPuma, Tommy **18**
Madonna **16**
Earlier sketch in CM **4**
Marley, Rita **10**
Martin, George **6**
Mayfield, Curtis **8**
Mercer, Johnny **13**
Miller, Mitch **11**
Mingus, Charles **9**
Near, Holly **1**
Ostin, Mo **17**
Penner, Fred **10**
Phillips, Sam **5**
Reznor, Trent **13**
Rhone, Sylvia **13**
Robinson, Smokey **1**
Rubin, Rick **9**
Simmons, Russell **7**
Spector, Phil **4**
Teller, Al **15**
Too $hort **16**
Wexler, Jerry **15**
Woods-Wright, Tomica**22**

Reggae
Bad Brains **16**
Black Uhuru **12**
Burning Spear **15**
Cliff, Jimmy **8**
Dube, Lucky **17**
Inner Circle **15**
Israel Vibration **21**
Marley, Bob **3**
Marley, Rita **10**
Marley, Ziggy **3**
Mystic Revealers **16**
Skatalites, The **18**
Sly and Robbie **13**
Steel Pulse **14**
Third World **13**
Tosh, Peter **3**
UB40 **4**
Wailer, Bunny **11**

Rhythm and Blues/Soul
Aaliyah **21**
Abdul, Paula **3**
Adams, Oleta **17**
Alexander, Arthur **14**
All-4-One **17**
Austin, Dallas **16**
Ballard, Hank **17**
Baker, Anita **9**
Ball, Marcia **15**
Basehead **11**
Belle, Regina **6**
Berry, Chuck **1**
Bland, Bobby "Blue" **12**
Blessid Union of Souls **20**
Blige, Mary J. **15**
Blues Brothers, The **3**
Bolton, Michael **4**
Boyz II Men **15**
Brandy **19**
Braxton, Toni **17**
Brown, James **16**
Earlier sketch in CM **2**
Brown, Ruth **13**
Brownstone **21**
Bryson, Peabo **11**
Burdon, Eric **14**
Also see War
Also see Animals
Busby, Jheryl **9**
C + C Music Factory **16**
Campbell, Tevin **13**
Carey, Mariah **20**
Earlier sketch in CM **6**
Charles, Ray **1**
Cole, Natalie **21**
Earlier sketch in CM **1**
Cooke, Sam **1**
Also see Soul Stirrers, The
Cropper, Steve **12**
Curtis, King **17**
D'Angelo **20**
D'Arby, Terence Trent **3**
DeBarge, El **14**
Des'ree **15**
Dibango, Manu **14**
Diddley, Bo **3**
Domino, Fats **2**
Dr. John **7**
Earth, Wind and Fire **12**
Edmonds, Kenneth "Babyface" **12**
En Vogue **10**
Evora, Cesaria **19**
Fabulous Thunderbirds, The **1**
Four Tops, The **11**
Fox, Samantha **3**
Franklin, Aretha **17**
Earlier sketch in CM **2**
Gaye, Marvin **4**
Gill, Johnny **20**
Gordy, Berry, Jr. **6**
Green, Al **9**
Hall & Oates **6**
Hayes, Isaac **10**
Holland-Dozier-Holland **5**
Incognito **16**
Ingram, James **11**
Isley Brothers, The **8**
Jackson, Freddie **3**
Jackson, Janet **3**
Jackson, Michael **17**
Earlier sketch in CM **1**
Also see Jacksons, The
Jackson, Millie **14**
Jacksons, The **7**
Jam, Jimmy, and Terry Lewis **11**
James, Etta **6**
Jodeci **13**
Jones, Booker T. **8**
Jones, Grace **9**
Jones, Quincy **20**
Earlier sketch CM **2**
Jordan, Louis **11**
Kelly, R. **19**
Khan, Chaka **19**
Earlier sketch CM **9**
King, Ben E. **7**
Knight, Gladys **1**
Kool & the Gang **13**
LaBelle, Patti **8**
Los Lobos **2**
Maxwell **22**
Mayfield, Curtis **8**
McKnight, Brian **22**
Medley, Bill **3**
Meters, The **14**
Milli Vanilli **4**
Mills, Stephanie **21**
Mo', Keb' **21**
Moore, Chante **21**

Moore, Melba **7**
Morrison, Van **3**
Ndegéocello, Me'Shell **18**
Neville, Aaron **5**
Also see Neville Brothers, The
Neville Brothers, The **4**
Ocean, Billy **4**
Ohio Players **16**
O'Jays, The **13**
Otis, Johnny **16**
Pendergrass, Teddy **3**
Peniston, CeCe **15**
Pickett, Wilson **10**
Pointer Sisters, The **9**
Priest, Maxi **20**
Prince **14**
Earlier sketch in CM **1**
Rainey, Ma **22**
Rawls, Lou **19**
Redding, Otis **5**
Reese, Della **13**
Reeves, Martha **4**
Richie, Lionel **2**
Riley, Teddy **14**
Robinson, Smokey **1**
Ross, Diana **6**
Also see Supremes, The
Ruffin, David **6**
Also see Temptations, The
Sam and Dave **8**
Scaggs, Boz **12**
Secada, Jon **13**
Shanice **14**
Shirelles, The **11**
Shocklee, Hank **15**
Sledge, Percy **15**
Soul II Soul **17**
Spinners , The **21**
Stansfield, Lisa **9**
Staples, Mavis **13**
Staples, Pops **11**
Stewart, Rod **20**
Earlier sketch in CM **2**
Also see Faces, The
Stone, Sly **8**
Subdudes, The **18**
Supremes, The **6**
Also see Ross, Diana
Sure!, Al B. **13**
Sweat, Keith **13**
SWV **14**
Temptations, The **3**
Third World **13**
Thomas, Irma **16**
TLC **15**
Thornton, Big Mama **18**
Tony! Toni! Toné! **12**
Toussaint, Allen **11**
Turner, Tina **1**
Vandross, Luther **2**
Was (Not Was) **6**
Waters, Crystal **15**
Watley, Jody **9**
Wexler, Jerry **15**
White, Karyn **21**
Williams, Deniece **1**
Williams, Vanessa **10**
Wilson, Jackie **3**
Winans, The **12**
Winbush, Angela **15**
Womack, Bobby **5**
Wonder, Stevie **17**
Earlier sketch in CM **2**
Zhane **22**

Rock

311 **20**
AC/DC **4**
Adam Ant **13**
Adams, Bryan **20**
Earlier sketch in CM **2**
Aerosmith **22**
Earlier sketch in CM **3**
Afghan Whigs **17**
Alarm **2***
Albini, Steve **15**
Alexander, Arthur **14**
Alice in Chains **10**
Allman Brothers, The **6**
Alvin, Dave **17**
America **16**
American Music Club **15**
Animals **22**
Anthrax **11**
Aquabats **22**
Archers of Loaf **21**
Art of Noise **22**
Audio Adrenaline **22**
Aztec Camera **22**
Babes in Toyland **16**
Bad Brains **16**
Bad Company **22**
Baker, Ginger **16**
Also see Cream
Ballard, Hank **17**
Band, The **9**
Barenaked Ladies **18**
Barlow, Lou **20**
Basehead **11**
Beach Boys, The **1**
Beastie Boys, The **8**
Beatles, The **2**
Beaver Brown Band, The **3**
Beck, Jeff **4**
Also see Yardbirds, The
Beck **18**
Belew, Adrian **5**
Belly **16**
Ben Folds Five **20**
Benatar, Pat **8**
Berry, Chuck **1**
Bettie Serveert **17**
Biafra, Jello **18**
Big Audio Dynamite **18**
Big Head Todd and the Monsters **20**
Bjork **16**
Black Crowes, The **7**
Black, Frank **14**
Black Flag **22**
Black Sabbath **9**
Blackman, Cindy **15**
Blind Melon **21**
Blondie **14**
Blood, Sweat and Tears **7**
Blue Oyster Cult **16**
Blue Rodeo **18**
Blues Traveler **15**
Blur **17**
BoDeans, The **20**
Earlier sketch in CM **3**
Bon Jovi **10**
Boston **11**
Bowie, David **1**
Brad **21**
Bragg, Billy **7**
Breeders **19**
Brickell, Edie **3**
Browne, Jackson **3**
Buckingham, Lindsey **8**
Also see Fleetwood Mac
Buckley, Tim **14**
Buffalo Tom **18**
Burdon, Eric **14**
Also see War
Also see Animals
Burnett, T Bone **13**
Bush **18**
Butthole Surfers **16**
Buzzcocks, The **9**
Byrds, The **8**
Byrne, David **8**
Also see Talking Heads
Cale, J. J. **16**
Cale, John **9**
Camel **21**
Captain Beefheart **10**
Cardigans **19**
Cars, The **20**
Catherine Wheel **18**
Cave, Nick **10**
Charlatans, The **13**
Charm Farm **20**
Cheap Trick **12**
Cher **1**
Chicago **3**
Chumbawamba **21**
Church, The **14**
Cinderella **16**
Circle Jerks, The **17**
Clapton, Eric **11**
Earlier sketch in CM **1**
Also see Cream
Also see Yardbirds, The
Clash, The **4**
Clemons, Clarence **7**
Clinton, George **7**
Coasters, The **5**
Cochrane , Tom **22**
Cocker, Joe **4**
Collective Soul **16**
Collins, Phil **2**
Also see Genesis

Congo Norvell **22**
Cooder, Ry **2**
Cooke, Sam **1**
Also see Soul Stirrers, The
Cooper, Alice **8**
Cope, Julian **16**
Costello, Elvis **12**
Earlier sketch in CM **2**
Cougar, John(ny)
See Mellencamp, John
Counting Crows **18**
Cracker **12**
Cramps, The **16**
Cranberries, The **14**
Crash Test Dummies **14**
Cream **9**
Creedence Clearwater Revival **16**
Crenshaw, Marshall **5**
Crosby, David **3**
Also see Byrds, The
Crow, Sheryl **18**
Crowded House **12**
Cult, The **16**
Cure, The **20**
Earlier sketch in CM **3**
Curry, Tim **3**
Curve **13**
Dale, Dick **13**
Daltrey, Roger **3**
Also see Who, The
Dandy Warhols, The
Daniels, Charlie **6**
Danzig **7**
D'Arby, Terence Trent **3**
Dave Clark Five, The **12**
Dave Matthews Band **18**
Davies, Ray **5**
dc Talk **18**
de Burgh, Chris **22**
Dead Can Dance **16**
Dead Milkmen **22**
Deep Purple **11**
Def Leppard **3**
Deftones **22**
Del Amitri **18**
Depeche Mode **5**
Devo **13**
Diddley, Bo **3**
DiFranco, Ani **17**
Dinosaur Jr. **10**
Dire Straits **22**
Doc Pomus **14**
Dog's Eye View **21**
Dokken **16**
Doobie Brothers, The **3**
Doors, The **4**
Duran Duran **4**
Dylan, Bob **3**
Eagles, The **3**
Echobelly **21**
Eddy, Duane **9**
Einstürzende Neubauten **13**
Electric Light Orchestra **7**
Elliot, Cass **5**
Emerson, Lake & Palmer/Powell **5**
English Beat, The **9**
Eno, Brian **8**
Erickson, Roky **16**
Escovedo, Alejandro **18**
Etheridge, Melissa **16**
Earlier sketch in CM **4**
Eurythmics **6**
Everclear **18**
Extreme **10**
Faces, The **22**
Fairport Convention **22**
Faithfull, Marianne **14**
Faith No More **7**
Fall, The **12**
Ferry, Bryan **1**
fIREHOSE **11**
Fishbone **7**
Flaming Lips **22**
Fleetwood Mac **5**
Flores, Rosie **16**
Fogelberg, Dan **4**
Fogerty, John **2**
Also see Creedence Clearwater Revival
Foo Fighters **20**
Ford, Lita **9**
Foreigner **21**
Fox, Samantha **3**
Frampton, Peter **3**
Franti, Michael **16**
Frey, Glenn **3**
Also see Eagles, The
Front 242 **19**
Froom, Mitchell **15**
Fu Manchu **22**
Fugazi **13**
Gabriel, Peter **16**
Earlier sketch in CM **2**
Also see Genesis
Gang of Four **8**
Garcia, Jerry **4**
Also see Grateful Dead, The
Gatton, Danny **16**
Genesis **4**
Geraldine Fibbers **21**
Gift, Roland **3**
Gin Blossoms **18**
Glitter, Gary **19**
Goo Goo Dolls, The **16**
Graham, Bill **10**
Grant Lee Buffalo **16**
Grateful Dead **5**
Grebenshikov, Boris **3**
Green Day **16**
Guided By Voices **18**
Guns n' Roses **2**
Gwar **13**
Hagar, Sammy **21**
Hall & Oates **6**
Harper, Ben **17**
Harrison, George **2**
Also see Beatles, The
Harry, Deborah **4**
Also see Blondie
Harvey, Polly Jean **11**
Hatfield, Juliana **12**
Also see Lemonheads, The
Healey, Jeff **4**
Helmet **15**
Hendrix, Jimi **2**
Henley, Don **3**
Also see Eagles, The
Henry, Joe **18**
Hiatt, John **8**
Hole **14**
Holland-Dozier-Holland **5**
Hooters **20**
Hootie and the Blowfish **18**
Idol, Billy **3**
INXS **21**
Earlier sketch in CM **2**
Iron Maiden **10**
Isaak, Chris **6**
Jackson, Joe **22**
Earlier entry in CM **4**
Jagger, Mick **7**
Also see Rolling Stones, The
Jane's Addiction **6**
Jars of Clay **20**
Jayhawks, The **15**
Jefferson Airplane **5**
Jesus Lizard **19**
Jesus and Mary Chain, The **10**
Jethro Tull **8**
Jett, Joan **3**
Jimmie's Chicken Shack **22**
Joel, Billy **12**
Earlier sketch in CM **2**
Johansen, David **7**
John, Elton **20**
Earlier sketch in CM **3**
Jon Spencer Blues Explosion **18**
Joplin, Janis **3**
Journey **21**
Joy Division **19**
Judas Priest **10**
KMFDM **18**
Kennedy, Nigel **8**
Kidjo, Anjelique **17**
King Crimson **17**
King Missile **22**
Kinks, The **15**
Kiss **5**
Knopfler, Mark **3**
Also see Dire Straits
Korn **20**
Kravitz, Lenny **5**
Landreth, Sonny **16**
Led Zeppelin **1**
Leiber and Stoller **14**
Lemonheads, The **12**
Lennon, John **9**
Also see Beatles, The
Lennon, Julian **2**
Less Than Jake **22**
Letters to Cleo **22**
Lindley, David **2**
Little Feat **4**

Little Texas **14**
Live **14**
Living Colour **7**
Loggins, Kenny **20**
Earlier sketch in CM **3**
Los Lobos **2**
Love and Rockets **15**
Love Spit Love **21**
L7 **12**
Luna **18**
Luscious Jackson **19**
Lush **13**
Lydon, John **9**
Also see Sex Pistols, The
Lynne, Jeff **5**
Lynyrd Skynyrd **9**
MacIsaac, Ashley **21**
Madder Rose **17**
Marilyn Manson **18**
Martin, George **6**
Marx, Richard **3**
McCartney, Paul **4**
Also see Beatles, The
McClinton, Delbert **14**
MC5, The **9**
McKee, Maria **11**
McMurtry, James **10**
Meat Loaf **12**
Meat Puppets, The **13**
Megadeth **9**
Mekons, The **15**
Mellencamp, John **20**
Earlier sketch in CM **2**
Metallica **7**
Midnight Oil **11**
Mighty Mighty Bosstones **20**
Mike & the Mechanics **17**
Miller, Steve **2**
Ministry **10**
Moby Grape **12**
Money, Eddie **16**
Moody Blues, The **18**
Morphine **16**
Morrison, Jim **3**
Also see Doors, The
Morrison, Van **3**
Murphy, Peter **22**
Mötley Crüe **1**
Motörhead **10**
Mould, Bob **10**
Mudhoney **16**
Muldaur, Maria **18**
Myles, Alannah **4**
Nelson, Rick **2**
New York Dolls **20**
Newman, Randy **4**
Nicks, Stevie **2**
Also see Fleetwood Mac
Nirvana **8**
NRBQ **12**
Nugent, Ted **2**
Oasis **16**
Ocasek, Ric **5**
O'Connor, Sinead **3**
Offspring **19**
Ono, Yoko **11**
Orbison, Roy **2**
Osbourne, Ozzy **3**
Our Lady Peace **22**
Page, Jimmy **4**
Also see Led Zeppelin
Also see Yardbirds, The
Palmer, Robert **2**
Pantera **13**
Parker, Graham **10**
Parker, Maceo **7**
Parsons, Alan **12**
Parsons, Gram **7**
Also see Byrds, The
Pavement **14**
Pearl Jam **12**
Pere Ubu **17**
Perkins, Carl **9**
Petty, Tom **9**
Phillips, Sam **5**
Phish **13**
Pigface **19**
Pink Floyd **2**
Pixies, The **21**
Plant, Robert **2**
Also see Led Zeppelin
Pogues, The **6**
Poi Dog Pondering **17**
Poison **11**
Police, The **20**
Pop, Iggy **1**
Presley, Elvis **1**
Pretenders, The **8**
Primal Scream **14**
Primus **11**
Prince **14**
Earlier sketch in CM **1**
Prine, John **7**
Proclaimers, The **13**
Pulp **18**
Queen **6**
Queensryche **8**
Rage Against the Machine **18**
Raitt, Bonnie **3**
Ramones, The **9**
Red Hot Chili Peppers, The **7**
Redd Kross **20**
Reed, Lou **16**
Earlier sketch in CM **1**
Also see Velvet Underground, The
Reid, Vernon **2**
Also see Living Colour
R.E.M. **5**
Replacements, The **7**
Residents, The **14**
Reverend Horton Heat **19**
Reznor, Trent **13**
Richards, Keith **11**
Also see Rolling Stones, The
Richman, Jonathan **12**
Robertson, Robbie **2**
Rolling Stones, The **3**
Rollins, Henry **11**
Roth, David Lee **1**
Also see Van Halen
Rubin, Rick **9**
Rundgren, Todd **11**
Rush **8**
Ryder, Mitch **11**
Santana, Carlos **19**
Earlier entry in CM **1**
Satriani, Joe **4**
Scaggs, Boz **12**
Scorpions, The **12**
Screaming Trees **19**
Scud Mountain Boys **21**
Seal **14**
Seger, Bob **15**
Sepultura **12**
Sex Pistols, The **5**
Shadows, The **22**
Shaffer, Paul **13**
Shannon, Del **10**
Shocked, Michelle **4**
Shonen Knife **13**
Shudder to Think **20**
Silverchair **20**
Simon, Carly **22**
Earlier sketch in CM **4**
Simon, Paul **16**
Earlier sketch in CM **1**
Simple Minds **21**
Siouxsie and the Banshees **8**
Skinny Puppy **17**
Slayer **10**
Sleater-Kinney **20**
Smashing Pumpkins **13**
Smith, Patti **17**
Earlier sketch in CM **1**
Smithereens, The **14**
Smiths, The **3**
Social Distortion **19**
Son Volt **21**
Sonic Youth **9**
Soul Asylum **10**
Soundgarden **6**
Sparks **18**
Specials, The **21**
Spector, Phil **4**
Spencer Davis Group **19**
Spin Doctors **14**
Spinal Tap **8**
Spirit **22**
Sponge **18**
Springsteen, Bruce **6**
Squeeze **5**
Starr, Ringo **10**
Also see Beatles, The
Steeleye Span **19**
Steely Dan **5**
Steppenwolf **20**
Stevens, Cat **3**
Stewart, Rod **2**
Stills, Stephen **5**
Sting **19**
Earlier sketch in CM **2**
Stone Roses, The **16**
Stone, Sly **8**
Stone Temple Pilots **14**
Straw, Syd **18**
Stray Cats, The **11**

Stryper **2**
Sublime **19**
Sugarcubes, The **10**
Suicidal Tendencies **15**
Summers, Andy **3**
Also see Police, The
Tears for Fears **6**
Teenage Fanclub **13**
Television **17**
10,000 Maniacs **3**
Tesla **15**
Texas Tornados, The **8**
The The **15**
They Might Be Giants **7**
Thin Lizzy **13**
Thompson, Richard **7**
Three Dog Night **5**
Throwing Muses **15**
Timbuk 3 **3**
Toad the Wet Sprocket **13**
Tool **21**
Townshend, Pete **1**
Also see Who, The
Traffic **19**
Tragically Hip, The **18**
T. Rex **11**
Treadmill Trackstar **21**
Trynin, Jen **21**
Tsunami **21**
Turner, Tina **1**
Tuxedomoon **21**
U2 **12**
Earlier sketch in CM **2**
Ulmer, James Blood **13**
Urge Overkill **17**
Uriah Heep **19**
Vai, Steve **5**
Valli, Frankie **10**
Van Halen **8**
Vaughan, Stevie Ray **1**
Velvet Underground, The **7**
Ventures **19**
Veruca Salt **20**
Verve, The **18**
Verve Pipe, The **20**
Vincent, Gene **19**
Violent Femmes **12**
Waits, Tom **12**
Earlier sketch in CM **1**
Wallflowers, The **20**
Walsh, Joe **5**
Also see Eagles, The
War **14**
Warrant **17**
Weezer **20**
Weller, Paul **14**
Whitesnake **5**
White Zombie **17**
Whitley, Chris **16**
Who, The **3**
Winter, Johnny **5**
Winwood, Steve **2**
Also see Spencer Davis Group
Also see Traffic
Wray, Link **17**
X **11**
Yardbirds, The **10**
Yes **8**
Young, Neil **15**
Earlier sketch in CM **2**
Zappa, Frank **17**
Earlier sketch in CM **1**
Zevon, Warren **9**
ZZ Top **2**

Rock and Roll Pioneers

Ballard, Hank **17**
Berry, Chuck **1**
Clark, Dick **2**
Darin, Bobby **4**
Diddley, Bo **3**
Dion **4**
Domino, Fats **2**
Eddy, Duane **9**
Everly Brothers, The **2**
Francis, Connie **10**
Glitter, Gary **19**
Haley, Bill **6**
Hawkins, Screamin' Jay **8**
Holly, Buddy **1**
James, Etta **6**
Jordan, Louis **11**
Lewis, Jerry Lee **2**
Little Richard **1**
Nelson, Rick **2**
Orbison, Roy **2**
Otis, Johnny **16**
Paul, Les **2**
Perkins, Carl **9**
Phillips, Sam **5**
Presley, Elvis **1**
Professor Longhair **6**
Sedaka, Neil **4**
Shannon, Del **10**
Shirelles, The **11**
Spector, Phil **4**
Twitty, Conway **6**
Valli, Frankie **10**
Wilson, Jackie **3**
Wray, Link **17**

Saxophone

Adderly, Cannonball **15**
Ayler , Albert **19**
Barbieri, Gato **22**
Bechet, Sidney **17**
Braxton, Anthony **12**
Carter, Benny **3**
Also see McKinney's Cotton Pickers
Carter, James **18**
Chenier, C. J. **15**
Clemons, Clarence **7**
Coleman, Ornette **5**
Coltrane, John **4**
Curtis, King **17**
Dibango, Manu **14**
Dorsey, Jimmy
See Dorsey Brothers, The
Getz, Stan **12**
Golson, Benny **21**
Gordon, Dexter **10**
Harris, Eddie **15**
Hawkins, Coleman **11**
Henderson, Joe **14**
Herman, Woody **12**
Jacquet, Illinois **17**
James, Boney **21**
Kenny G **14**
Kirk, Rahsaan Roland **6**
Koz, Dave **19**
Lateef, Yusef **16**
Lloyd, Charles **22**
Lopez, Israel "Cachao" **14**
Lovano, Joe **13**
Marsalis, Branford **10**
Morgan, Frank **9**
Mulligan, Gerry **16**
Najee **21**
Osby, Greg **21**
Parker, Charlie **5**
Parker, Maceo **7**
Pepper, Art **18**
Redman, Joshua **12**
Rollins, Sonny **7**
Sanborn, David **1**
Sanders, Pharoah **16**
Shorter, Wayne **5**
Threadgill, Henry **9**
Washington, Grover, Jr. **5**
Winter, Paul **10**
Young, La Monte **16**
Young, Lester **14**
Zorn, John **15**

Sintir

Hakmoun, Hassan **15**

Songwriters

Acuff, Roy **2**
Adams, Bryan **20**
Earlier sketch in CM **2**
Aikens, Rhett **22**
Albini, Steve **15**
Alexander, Arthur **14**
Allen, Peter **11**
Allison, Mose **17**
Alpert, Herb **11**
Alvin, Dave **17**
Amos, Tori **12**
Anderson, Ian
See Jethro Tull
Anderson, John **5**
Anka, Paul **2**
Armatrading, Joan **4**
Astbury, Ian
See Cult, The
Atkins, Chet **5**
Autry, Gene **12**
Bacharach, Burt **20**
Earlier sketch in CM **1**
Baez, Joan **1**
Baker, Anita **9**

Balin, Marty
See Jefferson Airplane
Barlow, Lou **20**
Barrett, (Roger) Syd
See Pink Floyd
Basie, Count **2**
Becker, Walter
See Steely Dan
Beckley, Gerry
See America
Belew, Adrian **5**
Benton, Brook **7**
Berg, Matraca **16**
Berlin, Irving **8**
Berry, Chuck **1**
Bjork **16**
Also see Sugarcubes, The
Black, Clint **5**
Black, Frank **14**
Blades, Ruben **2**
Blige, Mary J. **15**
Bloom, Luka **14**
Bono
See U2
Brady, Paul **8**
Bragg, Billy **7**
Brandt, Paul **22**
Brickell, Edie **3**
Brokop, Lisa **22**
Brooke, Jonatha
See Story, The
Brooks, Garth **8**
Brown, Bobby **4**
Brown, James **16**
Earlier sketch in CM **2**
Brown, Junior **15**
Brown, Marty **14**
Browne, Jackson **3**
Buck, Peter
See R.E.M.
Buck, Robert
See 10,000 Maniacs
Buckingham, Lindsey **8**
Also see Fleetwood Mac
Buckley, Jeff **22**
Buckley, Tim **14**
Buffett, Jimmy **4**
Bunnell, Dewey
See America
Burdon, Eric **14**
Also see War
Also see Animals
Burnett, T Bone **13**
Burning Spear **15**
Bush, Kate **4**
Byrne, David **8**
Also see Talking Heads
Cahn, Sammy **11**
Cale, J. J. **16**
Cale, John **9**
Calloway, Cab **6**
Captain Beefheart **10**
Cardwell, Joi **22**
Carlisle, Bob **22**
Carpenter, Mary-Chapin **6**
Carter, Carlene **8**
Cash, Johnny **17**
Earlier sketch in CM **1**
Cash, Rosanne **2**
Cetera, Peter
See Chicago
Chandra, Sheila **16**
Chapin, Harry **6**
Chapman, Steven Curtis **15**
Chapman, Tracy **4**
Charles, Ray **1**
Chenier, C. J. **15**
Childs, Toni **2**
Chilton, Alex **10**
Clapton, Eric **11**
Earlier sketch in CM **1**
Also see Cream
Also see Yardbirds, The
Clark, Guy **17**
Clements, Vassar **18**
Cleveland, James **1**
Clinton, George **7**
Cockburn, Bruce **8**
Cohen, Leonard **3**
Cole, Lloyd **9**
Cole, Nat King **3**
Collins, Albert **4**
Collins, Judy **4**
Collins, Phil **2**
Also see Genesis
Cooder, Ry **2**
Cooke, Sam **1**
Also see Soul Stirrers, The
Collie, Mark **15**
Cooper, Alice **8**
Cope, Julian **16**
Corgan, Billy
See Smashing Pumpkins
Costello, Elvis **12**
Earlier sketch in CM **2**
Cotten, Elizabeth **16**
Crenshaw, Marshall **5**
Croce, Jim **3**
Crofts, Dash
See Seals & Crofts
Cropper, Steve **12**
Crosby, David **3**
Also see Byrds, The
Crow, Sheryl **18**
Crowe, J. D. **5**
Crowell, Rodney **8**
Daniels, Charlie **6**
Davies, Ray **5**
Also see Kinks, the
de Burgh, Chris **22**
DeBarge, El **14**
DeMent, Iris **13**
Denver, John **22**
Earlier entry in CM **1**
Des'ree **15**
Diamond, Neil **1**
Diddley, Bo **3**
Difford, Chris
See Squeeze
DiFranco, Ani **17**
Dion **4**
Dixon, Willie **10**
Doc Pomus **14**
Domino, Fats **2**
Donelly, Tanya
See Belly
Also see Throwing Muses
Donovan **9**
Dorsey, Thomas A. **11**
Doucet, Michael **8**
Dozier, Lamont
See Holland-Dozier-Holland
Drake, Nick **17**
Dube, Lucky **17**
Duffy, Billy
See Cult, The
Dulli, Greg **17**
See Afghan Whigs, The
Dylan, Bob **21**
Earlier entry in CM **3**
Earle, Steve **16**
Edge, The
See U2
Edmonds, Kenneth "Babyface" **12**
Eitzel, Mark
See American Music Club
Elfman, Danny **9**
Ellington, Duke **2**
Emerson, Keith
See Emerson, Lake & Palmer/Powell
Emmanuel, Tommy **21**
Enigma **14**
Erickson, Roky **16**
Ertegun, Ahmet **10**
Escovedo, Alejandro **18**
Estefan, Gloria **15**
Earlier sketch in CM **2**
Etheridge, Melissa **16**
Earlier entry in CM **4**
Everly, Don
See Everly Brothers, The
Everly, Phil
See Everly Brothers, The
Fagen, Don
See Steely Dan
Faithfull, Marianne **14**
Ferry, Bryan **1**
Flack, Roberta **5**
Flatt, Lester **3**
Fogelberg, Dan **4**
Fogerty, John **2**
Also see Creedence Clearwater Revival
Fordham, Julia **15**
Foster, David **13**
Frampton, Peter **3**
Franti, Michael **16**
Frey, Glenn **3**
Also see Eagles, The
Fripp, Robert **9**
Frizzell, Lefty **10**
Gabriel, Peter **16**
Earlier sketch in CM **2**
Also see Genesis
Garcia, Jerry **4**
Also see Grateful Dead, The

Gaye, Marvin **4**
Geldof, Bob **9**
George, Lowell
 See Little Feat
Gershwin, George and Ira **11**
Gibb, Barry
 See Bee Gees, The
Gibb, Maurice
 See Bee Gees, The
Gibb, Robin
 See Bee Gees, The
Gibbons, Billy
 See ZZ Top
Gibson, Debbie **1**
Gift, Roland **3**
Gill, Vince **7**
Gilley, Mickey **7**
Gilmour, David
 See Pink Floyd
Gold, Julie **22**
Goodman, Benny **4**
Gordy, Berry, Jr. **6**
Gorka, John **18**
Grant, Amy **7**
Green, Al **9**
Greenwood, Lee **12**
Griffith, Nanci **3**
Guthrie, Arlo **6**
Guthrie, Woodie **2**
Guy, Buddy **4**
Haggard, Merle **2**
Hall, Daryl
 See Hall & Oates
Hall, Tom T. **4**
Hamlisch, Marvin **1**
Hammer, M.C. **5**
Hammerstein, Oscar
 See Rodgers, Richard
Hardin, Tim **18**
Harding, John Wesley **6**
Harley, Bill **7**
Harper, Ben **17**
Harris, Emmylou **4**
Harrison, George **2**
 Also see Beatles, The
Harry, Deborah **4**
 Also see Blondie
Hart, Lorenz
 See Rodgers, Richard
Hartford, John **1**
Hatfield, Juliana **12**
 Also see Lemonheads, The
Hawkins, Screamin' Jay **8**
Hayes, Isaac **10**
Healey, Jeff **4**
Hedges, Michael **3**
Hendrix, Jimi **2**
Henley, Don **3**
 Also see Eagles, The
Henry, Joe **18**
Hersh, Kristin
 See Throwing Muses
Hiatt, John **8**
Hidalgo, David
 See Los Lobos
Hillman, Chris
 See Byrds, The
 Also see Desert Rose Band, The
Hinojosa, Tish **13**
Hitchcock, Robyn **9**
Holland, Brian
 See Holland-Dozier-Holland
Holland, Eddie
 See Holland-Dozier-Holland
Holly, Buddy **1**
Hornsby, Bruce **3**
Howard, Harlan **15**
Hutchence, Michael
 See INXS
Hynde, Chrissie
 See Pretenders, The
Ian, Janis **5**
Ice Cube **10**
Ice-T **7**
Idol, Billy **3**
Isaak, Chris **6**
Jackson, Alan **7**
Jackson, Janet **16**
 Earlier sketch in CM **3**
Jackson, Joe **22**
 Earlier entry in CM **4**
Jackson, Michael **17**
 Earlier sketch in CM **1**
 Also see Jacksons, The
Jackson, Millie **14**
Jagger, Mick **7**
 Also see Rolling Stones, The
Jam, Jimmy, and Terry Lewis **11**
James, Rick **2**
Jarreau, Al **1**
Jennings, Waylon **4**
Jett, Joan **3**
Joel, Billy **12**
 Earlier sketch in CM **2**
Johansen, David **7**
John, Elton **20**
 Earlier sketch in CM **3**
Johnson, Lonnie **17**
Johnson, Matt
 See The The
Jones, Brian
 See Rolling Stones, The
Jones, George **4**
Jones, Mick
 See Clash, The
Jones, Quincy **20**
 Earlier sketch in CM **2**
Jones, Rickie Lee **4**
Joplin, Janis **3**
Judd, Naomi
 See Judds, The
Kane, Big Daddy **7**
Kantner, Paul
 See Jefferson Airplane
Kee, John P. **15**
Keith, Toby **17**
Kelly, R. **19**
Ketchum, Hal **14**
Khan, Chaka **19**
 Earlier sketch in CM **9**
King, Albert **2**
King, B. B. **1**
King, Ben E. **7**
King, Carole **6**
King, Freddy **17**
Kirkwood, Curt
 See Meat Puppets, The
Knopfler, Mark **3**
 Also see Dire Straits
Kottke, Leo **13**
Kravitz, Lenny **5**
Kristofferson, Kris **4**
Lake, Greg
 See Emerson, Lake & Palmer/Powell
Landreth, Sonny **16**
Lang, K. D. **4**
Larkin, Patty **9**
Lavin, Christine **6**
LeDoux, Chris **12**
Lee, Peggy **8**
Lehrer, Tom **7**
Leiber and Stoller **14**
Lennon, John **9**
 Also see Beatles, The
Lennon, Julian **2**
Lewis, Huey **9**
Lightfoot, Gordon **3**
Little Richard **1**
Llanas, Sammy
 See BoDeans, The
L.L. Cool J **5**
Loggins, Kenny **20**
 Earlier sketch in CM **3**
Love, Courtney
 See Hole
Love, Laura **20**
Loveless, Patty **5**
Lovett, Lyle **5**
Lowe, Nick **6**
Lydon, John **9**
 Also see Sex Pistols, The
Lynn, Loretta **2**
Lynne, Jeff **5**
Lynne, Shelby **5**
Lynott, Phil
 See Thin Lizzy
MacColl, Kirsty **12**
MacDonald, Barbara
 See Timbuk 3
MacDonald, Pat
 See Timbuk 3
Madonna **16**
 Earlier sketch in CM **4**
Manilow, Barry **2**
Mann, Aimee **22**
Manzarek, Ray
 See Doors, The
Marley, Bob **3**
Marley, Ziggy **3**
Marx, Richard **3**
Mattea, Kathy **5**
May, Brian
 See Queen
Mayfield, Curtis **8**
MC Breed **17**

McCartney, Paul **4**
Also see Beatles, The
McClinton, Delbert **14**
McCoury, Del **15**
McDonald, Michael
See Doobie Brothers, The
McGuinn, Roger
See Byrds, The
McLachlan, Sarah **12**
McLean, Don **7**
McLennan, Grant **21**
McMurtry, James **10**
MC 900 Ft. Jesus **16**
McTell, Blind Willie **17**
McVie, Christine
See Fleetwood Mac
Medley, Bill **3**
Melanie **12**
Mellencamp, John **20**
Earlier sketch in CM **2**
Mercer, Johnny **13**
Merchant, Natalie
See 10,000 Maniacs
Mercury, Freddie
See Queen
Michael, George **9**
Miller, Roger **4**
Miller, Steve **2**
Milsap, Ronnie **2**
Mitchell, Joni **17**
Earlier sketch in CM **2**
Moffatt, Katy **18**
Morrison, Jim **3**
Morrison, Van **3**
Morrissey **10**
Morrissey, Bill **12**
Morton, Jelly Roll **7**
Mould, Bob **10**
Moyet, Alison **12**
Nascimento, Milton **6**
Ndegéocello, Me'Shell **18**
Near, Holly **1**
Nelson, Rick **2**
Nelson, Willie **11**
Earlier sketch in CM **1**
Nesmith, Mike
See Monkees, The
Neville, Art
See Neville Brothers, The
Newman, Randy **4**
Newmann, Kurt
See BoDeans, The
Nicks, Stevie **2**
Nilsson **10**
Nugent, Ted **2**
Nyro, Laura **12**
Oates, John
See Hall & Oates
Ocasek, Ric **5**
Ocean, Billy **4**
Ochs, Phil **7**
O'Connor, Sinead **3**
Odetta **7**
Orbison, Roy **2**
Osbourne, Ozzy **3**
Oslin, K. T. **3**
Owens, Buck **2**
Page, Jimmy **4**
See Led Zeppelin
Also see Yardbirds, The
Palmer, Robert **2**
Paris, Twila **16**
Parks, Van Dyke **17**
Parnell, Lee Roy **15**
Parker, Graham **10**
Parsons, Gram **7**
Also see Byrds, The
Parton, Dolly **2**
Paul, Les **2**
Paxton, Tom **5**
Peniston, CeCe **15**
Penn, Michael **4**
Perez, Louie
See Los Lobos
Perkins, Carl **9**
Perry, Joe
See Aerosmith
Petty, Tom **9**
Phair, Liz **14**
Phillips, Sam **12**
Pickett, Wilson **10**
Pierson, Kate
See B-52's, The
Plant, Robert **2**
Also see Led Zeppelin
Pop, Iggy **1**
Porter, Cole **10**
Prince **14**
Earlier sketch in CM **1**
Prine, John **7**
Professor Longhair **6**
Rabbitt, Eddie **5**
Raitt, Bonnie **3**
Ray, Amy
See Indigo Girls
Rea, Chris **12**
Redding, Otis **5**
Reddy, Helen **9**
Reed, Lou **16**
Earlier sketch in CM **1**
Also see Velvet Underground, The
Reid, Charlie
See Proclaimers, The
Reid, Craig
See Proclaimers, The
Reid, Vernon **2**
Also see Living Colour
Rich, Charlie **3**
Richards, Keith **11**
Also see Rolling Stones, The
Richey, Kim **20**
Richie, Lionel **2**
Richman, Jonathan **12**
Riley, Teddy **14**
Ritchie, Jean **4**
Robbins, Marty **9**
Roberts, Brad
See Crash Test Dummies
Robertson, Robbie **2**
Robillard, Duke **2**
Robinson, Smokey **1**
Rodgers, Jimmie **3**
Rodgers, Richard **9**
Roland, Ed
See Collective Soul
Roth, David Lee **1**
Also see Van Halen
Russell, Mark **6**
Rutherford, Mike
See Genesis
Sade **2**
Sager, Carole Bayer **5**
Saliers, Emily
See Indigo Girls
Sandman, Mark
See Morphine
Sangare, Oumou **22**
Satriani, Joe **4**
Scaggs, Boz **12**
Schneider, Fred III
See B-52's, The
Scott-Heron, Gil **13**
Scruggs, Earl **3**
Seal **14**
Seals, Dan **9**
Seals, Jim
See Seals & Crofts
Secada, Jon **13**
Sedaka, Neil **4**
Seeger, Pete **4**
Also see Weavers, The
Seger, Bob **15**
Shannon, Del **10**
Sheila E. **3**
Shepherd, Kenny Wayne **22**
Shocked, Michelle **4**
Siberry, Jane **6**
Simmons, Gene
See Kiss
Simmons, Patrick
See Doobie Brothers, The
Simon, Carly **22**
Earlier entry in CM **4**
Simon, Paul **16**
Earlier sketch in CM **1**
Skaggs, Ricky **5**
Sledge, Percy **15**
Slick, Grace
See Jefferson Airplane
Smith, Patti **17**
Earlier sketch in CM **1**
Smith, Robert
See Cure, The
Also see Siouxsie and the Banshees
Snoop Doggy Dogg **17**
Sondheim, Stephen **8**
Spector, Phil **4**
Springsteen, Bruce **6**
Stanley, Paul
See Kiss
Stanley, Ralph **5**
Starr, Ringo **10**
Also see Beatles, The
Stevens, Cat **3**
Stevens, Ray **7**

Stewart, Dave
See Eurythmics, The
Stewart, Rod **20**
Earlier sketch in CM **2**
Also see Faces, The
Stills, Stephen **5**
Sting **19**
Earlier sketch in CM **2**
Also see Police, The
Stipe, Michael
See R.E.M.
Strait, George **5**
Straw, Syd **18**
Streisand, Barbra **2**
Strickland, Keith
See B-52's, The
Strummer, Joe
See Clash, The
Stuart, Marty **9**
Styne, Jule **21**
Summer, Donna **12**
Summers, Andy **3**
Also see Police, The
Sure!, Al B. **13**
Sweat, Keith **13**
Sweet, Matthew **9**
Swing, DeVante
See Jodeci
Taj Mahal **6**
Taupin, Bernie **22**
Taylor, James **2**
Taylor, Koko **10**
Thompson, Richard **7**
Thornton, Big Mama **18**
Tikaram, Tanita **9**
Tilbrook, Glenn
See Squeeze
Tillis, Mel **7**
Tillis, Pam **8**
Timmins, Margo
See Cowboy Junkies, The
Timmins, Michael
See Cowboy Junkies, The
Tippin, Aaron **12**
Tone-L c **3**
Torme, Mel **4**
Tosh, Peter **3**
Toussaint, Allen **11**
Townshend, Pete **1**
Also see Who, The
Travis, Merle **14**
Travis, Randy **9**
Treadmill Trackstar **21**
Tricky **18**
Tritt, Travis **7**
Trynin, Jen **21**
Tubb, Ernest **4**
Twain, Shania **17**
Twitty, Conway **6**
2Pac **17**
Tyler, Steve
See Aerosmith
Vai, Steve **5**
Also see Whitesnake
Vandross, Luther **2**
Van Halen, Edward
See Van Halen
Van Ronk, Dave **12**
Van Shelton, Ricky **5**
Van Zandt, Townes **13**
Vedder, Eddie
See Pearl Jam
Vega, Suzanne **3**
Wagoner, Porter **13**
Waits, Tom **12**
Earlier sketch in CM **1**
Walden, Narada Michael **14**
Walker, Jerry Jeff **13**
Walker, T-Bone **5**
Waller, Fats **7**
Walsh, Joe **5**
Also see Eagles, The
Wariner, Steve **18**
Warren, Diane **21**
Waters, Crystal **15**
Waters, Muddy **4**
Waters, Roger
See Pink Floyd
Watt, Mike **22**
Webb, Jimmy **12**
Weill, Kurt **12**
Weir, Bob
See Grateful Dead, The
Welch, Bob
See Fleetwood Mac
Weller, Paul **14**
West, Dottie **8**
White, Karyn **21**
White, Lari **15**
Whitley, Chris **16**
Whitley, Keith **7**
Williams, Dar **21**
Williams, Deniece **1**
Williams, Don **4**
Williams, Hank, Jr. **1**
Williams, Hank, Sr. **4**
Williams, Lucinda **10**
Williams, Paul **5**
Williams, Victoria **17**
Wills, Bob **6**
Wilson, Brian
See Beach Boys, The
Wilson, Cindy
See B-52's, The
Wilson, Ricky
See B-52's, The
Winbush, Angela **15**
Winter, Johnny **5**
Winwood, Steve **2**
Also see Spencer Davis Group
Also see Traffic
Womack, Bobby **5**
Wonder, Stevie **17**
Earlier sketch in CM **2**
Wray, Link **17**
Wynette, Tammy **2**
Yoakam, Dwight **21**
Earlier entry in CM **1**
Young, Angus
See AC/DC
Young, Neil **15**
Earlier sketch in CM **2**
Zappa, Frank **17**
Earlier sketch in CM **1**
Zevon, Warren **9**

Trombone
Anderson, Ray **7**
Dorsey, Tommy
See Dorsey Brothers, The
Miller, Glenn **6**
Teagarden, Jack **10**
Turre, Steve **22**
Watts, Eugene
See Canadian Brass, The

Trumpet
Alpert, Herb **11**
Armstrong, Louis **4**
Baker, Chet **13**
Berigan, Bunny **2**
Blanchard, Terence **13**
Cherry, Don **10**
Coleman, Ornette **5**
Davis, Miles **1**
Eldridge, Roy **9**
Also see McKinney's Cotton Pickers
Ferguson, Maynard **7**
Gillespie, Dizzy **6**
Hargrove, Roy **15**
Hawkins, Erskine **19**
Hirt, Al **5**
Isham, Mark **14**
James, Harry **11**
Jensen, Ingrid **22**
Jones, Quincy **20**
Earlier sketch in CM **2**
Jones, Thad **19**
Loughnane, Lee **3**
Marsalis, Wynton **20**
Earlier sketch in CM **6**
Masekela, Hugh **7**
Matthews, Eric **22**
Mighty Mighty Bosstones **20**
Miles, Ron **22**
Mills, Fred
See Canadian Brass, The
Oliver, King **15**
Rodney, Red **14**
Romm, Ronald
See Canadian Brass, The
Sandoval, Arturo **15**
Severinsen, Doc **1**

Tuba
Daellenbach, Charles
See Canadian Brass, The
Phillips, Harvey **3**

Vibraphone
Burton, Gary **10**
Hampton, Lionel **6**

Jackson, Milt **15**
Norvo, Red **12**

Viola
Dutt, Hank
See Kronos Quartet
Jones, Michael
See Kronos Quartet
Killian, Tim
See Kronos Quartet
Menuhin, Yehudi **11**
Zukerman, Pinchas **4**

Violin
Acuff, Roy **2**
Anderson, Laurie **1**
Bell, Joshua **21**
Bromberg, David **18**
Bush, Sam
See New Grass Revival, The
Carter, Regina **22**
Chang, Sarah **7**
Clements, Vassar **18**
Coleman, Ornette **5**
Daniels, Charlie **6**
Doucet, Michael **8**
Germano, Lisa **18**
Gingold, Josef **6**
Grappelli, Stephane **10**
Gray, Ella
See Kronos Quartet
Harrington, David
See Kronos Quartet
Hartford, John **1**
Hidalgo, David
See Los Lobos
Kennedy, Nigel **8**
Krauss, Alison **10**
Lamb, Barbara **19**
Lewis, Roy
See Kronos Quartet
Marriner, Neville **7**
Menuhin, Yehudi **11**
Midori **7**
O'Connor, Mark **1**
Perlman, Itzhak **2**
Ponty, Jean-Luc **8**
Salerno-Sonnenberg, Nadja **3**
Shallenberger, James
See Kronos Quartet
Sherba, John
See Kronos Quartet
Skaggs, Ricky **5**
Stern, Isaac **7**
Whiteman, Paul **17**
Wills, Bob **6**
Zukerman, Pinchas **4**

Cumulative Musicians Index

Volume numbers appear in **bold**.

A-ha **22**
Aaliyah **21**
Abba **12**
Abbott, Jacqueline
See Beautiful South
Abbott, Jude
See Chumbawamba
Abbruzzese, Dave
Abdul, Paula **3**
Abong, Fred
See Belly
Abrahams, Mick
See Jethro Tull
Abrantes, Fernando
See Kraftwerk
AC/DC **4**
Ace of Base **22**
Ackerman, Will **3**
Acland, Christopher
See Lush
Acuff, Roy **2**
Acuna, Alejandro
See Weather Report
Adam Ant **13**
Adamendes, Elaine
See Throwing Muses
Adams, Bryan **20**
Earlier sketch in CM **2**
Adams, Clifford
See Kool & the Gang
Adams, Craig
See Cult, The
Adams, Donn
See NRBQ
Adams, John **8**
Adams, Mark
See Specials, The
Adams, Oleta **17**
Adams, Terry
See NRBQ
Adams, Victoria
See Spice Girls
Adcock, Eddie
See Country Gentleman, The
Adderly, Cannonball **15**
Adderly, Julian
See Adderly, Cannonball
Adé, King Sunny **18**
Adler, Steven
See Guns n' Roses
Aerosmith **22**
Earlier sketch in CM **3**
Afghan Whigs **17**
Afonso, Marie
See Zap Mama
AFX
See Aphex Twin
Air Supply **22**
Ajile
See Arrested Development
Akingbola, Sola
See Jamiroquai
Akins, Rhett **22**
Alabama **21**
Earlier sketch in CM **1**
Alarm **22**
Albarn, Damon
See Blur
Albert, Nate
See Mighty Mighty Bosstones
Alberti, Dorona
See KMFDM
Albini, Steve **15**
Albuquerque, Michael de
See Electric Light Orchestra
Alexakis, Art
See Everclear
Alexander, Arthur **14**
Alexander, Tim
See Asleep at the Wheel
Alexander, Tim "Herb"
See Primus
Ali
See Tribe Called Quest, A
Alice in Chains **10**
Allcock, Martin
See Fairport Convention
Also see Jethro Tull
Allen, April
See C + C Music Factory
Allen, Dave
See Gang of Four
Allen, Debbie **8**
Allen, Duane
See Oak Ridge Boys, The
Allen, Geri **10**
Allen, Johnny Ray
See Subdudes, The
Allen, Papa Dee
See War
Allen, Peter **11**
Allen, Red
See Osborne Brothers, The
Allen, Rick
See Def Leppard
Allen, Ross
See Mekons, The
All-4-One **17**
Allison, Luther **21**
Allison, Mose **17**
Allman, Duane
See Allman Brothers, The
Allman, Gregg
See Allman Brothers, The
Allman Brothers, The **6**
Allsup, Michael Rand
See Three Dog Night
Alpert, Herb **11**
Alphonso, Roland
See Skatalites, The
Alston, Andy
See Del Amitri
Alston, Shirley
See Shirelles, The
Altan **18**
Alvin, Dave **17**
Also see X
Am, Svet
See KMFDM
Amedee, Steve
See Subdudes, The
Ament, Jeff
See Pearl Jam
America **16**
American Music Club **15**
Amos, Tori **12**
Anastasio, Trey
See Phish
Anderson, Al
See NRBQ
Anderson, Andy
See Cure, The
Anderson, Brett
See Suede
Anderson, Cleave
See Blue Rodeo
Anderson, Emma
See Lush
Anderson, Gladstone
See Skatalites, The
Anderson, Ian
See Jethro Tull
Anderson, John **5**
Anderson, Jon
See Yes
Anderson, Laurie **1**
Anderson, Marian **8**
Anderson, Pamela
See Incognito
Anderson, Ray **7**

Anderson, Signe
See Jefferson Airplane
Andersson, Benny
See Abba
Andes, Mark
See Spirit
Andes, Matt
See Spirit
Andes, Rachel
See Spirit
Andrews, Barry
See XTC
Andrews, Julie **4**
Andrews, Laverne
See Andrews Sisters, The
Andrews, Maxene
See Andrews Sisters, The
Andrews, Patty
See Andrews Sisters, The
Andrews Sisters, The **9**
Andy, Horace
See Massive Attack
Anger, Darol
See Turtle Island String Quartet
Animals **22**
Anka, Paul **2**
Anointed **21**
Anonymous, Rodney
See Dead Milkmen
Anselmo, Philip
See Pantera
Ant, Adam
See Adam Ant
Anthony, Marc **19**
Anthony, Michael
See Massive Attack
Anthony, Michael
See Van Halen
Anthrax **11**
Anton, Alan
See Cowboy Junkies, The
Antoni, Mark De Gli
See Soul Coughing
Antunes, Michael
See Beaver Brown Band, The
Aphex Twin **14**
Appice, Vinnie
See Black Sabbath
Aquabats **22**
Araya, Tom
See Slayer
Archers of Loaf **21**
Arden, Jann **21**
Ardolino, Tom
See NRBQ
Arellano, Rod
See Aquabats
Arena, Tina **21**
Arkenstone, David **20**
Arm, Mark
See Mudhoney
Armatrading, Joan **4**
Armerding, Jake
See Northern Lights
Armerding, Taylor
See Northern Lights
Armstrong, Billie Joe
See Green Day
Armstrong, Louis **4**
Arnaz, Desi **8**
Arnold, Eddy **10**
Arnold, Kristine
See Sweethearts of the Rodeo
Aronoff, Kenny **21**
Arrau, Claudio **1**
Arrested Development **14**
Arthurs, Paul
See Oasis
Art of Noise **22**
Ash, Daniel
See Love and Rockets
Ashcroft, Richard
See Verve, The
Ashton, Susan **17**
Asleep at the Wheel **5**
Astbury, Ian
See Cult, The
Astley, Rick **5**
Astro
See UB40
Asuo, Kwesi
See Arrested Development
Atkins, Chet **5**
Atkinson, Sweet Pea
See Was (Not Was)
Audio Adrenaline **22**
Auf Der Maur, Melissa
See Hole
Augustyniak, Jerry
See 10,000 Maniacs
Auldridge, Mike **4**
Also see Country Gentlemen, The
Also see Seldom Scene, The
Austin, Cuba
See McKinney's Cotton Pickers
Austin, Dallas **16**
Autry, Gene **12**
Avalon, Frankie **5**
Avery, Eric
See Jane's Addiction
Avory, Mick
See Kinks, The
Aykroyd, Dan
See Blues Brothers, The
Ayler, Albert **19**
Aztec Camera **22**
B, Daniel
See Front 242
Baah, Reebop Kwaku
See Traffic
Babatunde, Don
See Last Poets
Babes in Toyland **16**
Babjak, James
Babyface
See Edmonds, Kenneth "Babyface"
Bacharach, Burt **20**
Earlier sketch in CM **1**
Bachman, Eric
See Archers of Loaf
Backstreet Boys **21**
Badalamenti, Angelo **17**
Bad Brains **16**
Bad Company **22**
Badger, Pat
See Extreme
Bad Livers, The **19**
Badrena, Manola
See Weather Report
Baez, Joan **1**
Bailey, Mildred **13**
Bailey, Pearl **5**
Bailey, Phil
See Earth, Wind and Fire
Bailey, Victor
See Weather Report
Baker, Anita **9**
Baker, Bobby
See Tragically Hip , The
Baker, Chet **13**
Baker, Ginger **16**
Also see Cream
Baker, Janet **14**
Baker, Jon
See Charlatans, The
Baker, Josephine **10**
Balakrishnan, David
See Turtle Island String Quartet
Balch, Bob
See Fu Manchu
Balch, Michael
See Front Line Assembly
Baldursson, Sigtryggur
See Sugarcubes, The
Baldwin, Donny
See Starship
Baliardo, Diego
See Gipsy Kings, The
Baliardo, Paco
See Gipsy Kings, The
Baliardo, Tonino
See Gipsy Kings, The
Balin, Marty
See Jefferson Airplane
Ball, Marcia **15**
Ballard, Florence
See Supremes, The
Ballard, Hank **17**
Balsley, Phil
See Statler Brothers, The
Baltes, Peter
See Dokken
Balzano, Vinnie
See Less Than Jake
Bambaataa, Afrika **13**
Bamonte, Perry
See Cure, The
Bananarama **22**
Band, The **9**
Bangles **22**
Banks, Nick
See Pulp

Banks, Peter
See Yes
Banks, Tony
See Genesis
Baptiste, David Russell
See Meters, The
Barbarossa, Dave
See Republica
Barbata, John
See Jefferson Starship
Barber, Keith
See Soul Stirrers, The
Barbero, Lori
See Babes in Toyland
Barbieri, Gato **22**
Bardens, Peter
See Camel
Barenaked Ladies **18**
Bargeld, Blixa
See Einstürzende Neubauten
Bargeron, Dave
See Blood, Sweat and Tears
Barham, Meriel
See Lush
Barile, Jo
See Ventures, The
Barker, Paul
See Ministry
Barker, Travis Landon
See Aquabats
Barlow, Barriemore
See Jethro Tull
Barlow, Lou **20**
Also see Dinosaur Jr.
Barlow, Tommy
See Aztec Camera
Barnes, Danny
See Bad Livers, The
Barnes, Micah
See Nylons, The
Barnwell, Duncan
See Simple Minds
Barnwell, Ysaye Maria
See Sweet Honey in the Rock
Barr, Ralph
See Nitty Gritty Dirt Band, The
Barre, Martin
See Jethro Tull
Barrere, Paul
See Little Feat
Barrett, Dicky
See Mighty Mighty Bosstones
Barrett, (Roger) Syd
See Pink Floyd
Barron, Christopher
See Spin Doctors
Barrow, Geoff
See Portishead
Bartels, Joanie **13**
Bartholomew, Simon
See Brand New Heavies, The
Bartoli, Cecilia **12**
Barton, Lou Ann
See Fabulous Thunderbirds, The
Bartos, Karl
See Kraftwerk
Basehead **11**
Basher, Mick
See X
Basia **5**
Basie, Count **2**
Bass, Colin
See Camel
Bass, Colin
See Chumbawamba
Batchelor, Kevin
See Steel Pulse
Batel, Beate
See Einstürzende Neubauten
Battin, Skip
See Byrds, The
Battle, Kathleen **6**
Bauer, Judah
See Jon Spencer Blues Explosion
Baumann, Peter
See Tangerine Dream
Bautista, Roland
See Earth, Wind and Fire
Baxter, Jeff
See Doobie Brothers, The
Bayer Sager, Carole
See Sager, Carole Bayer
Baylor, Helen **20**
Baynton-Power, David
See James
Bazilian, Eric
See Hooters
Beach Boys, The **1**
Beale, Michael
See Earth, Wind and Fire
Beard, Frank
See ZZ Top
Beasley, Paul
See Mighty Clouds of Joy, The
Beastie Boys, The **8**
Beatles, The **2**
Beauford, Carter
See Dave Matthews Band
Beautiful South **19**
Beaver Brown Band, The **3**
Bechet, Sidney **17**
Beck, Jeff **4**
Also see Yardbirds, The
Beck, William
See Ohio Players
Beck **18**
Becker, Walter
See Steely Dan
Beckford, Theophilus
See Skatalites, The
Beckley, Gerry
See America
Bee Gees, The **3**
Beers, Garry Gary
See INXS
Behler, Chuck
See Megadeth
Beiderbecke, Bix **16**
Belafonte, Harry **8**
Belew, Adrian **5**
Also see King Crimson
Belfield, Dennis
See Three Dog Night
Bell, Andy
See Erasure
Bell, Brian
See Weezer
Bell, Derek
See Chieftains, The
Bell, Eric
See Thin Lizzy
Bell, Jayn
See Sounds ofBlackness
Bell, Joshua **21**
Bell, Melissa
See Soul II Soul
Bell, Ronald
See Kool & the Gang
Bell, Taj
See Charm Farm
Belladonna, Joey
See Anthrax
Bellamy, David
See Bellamy Brothers, The
Bellamy, Howard
See Bellamy Brothers, The
Bellamy Brothers, The **13**
Belle, Regina **6**
Bello, Frank
See Anthrax
Belly **16**
Belushi, John
See Blues Brothers, The
Benante, Charlie
See Anthrax
Benatar, Pat **8**
Benedict, Scott
See Pere Ubu
Ben Folds Five **20**
Benitez, Jellybean **15**
Bennett, Brian
See Shadows, The
Bennett, Tony **16**
Earlier sketch in CM **2**
Bennett-Nesby, Ann
See Sounds of Blackness
Benson, George **9**
Benson, Ray
See Asleep at the Wheel
Benson, Renaldo "Obie"
See Four Tops, The
Bentley, John
See Squeeze
Benton, Brook **7**
Bentyne, Cheryl
See Manhattan Transfer, The
Berenyi, Miki
See Lush
Berg, Matraca **16**
Bergeson, Ben
See Aquabats
Berggren, Jenny
See Ace of Base

Berggren, Jonas
See Ace of Base
Berggren, Linn
See Ace of Base
Berigan, Bunny **2**
Berlin, Irving **8**
Berlin, Steve
See Los Lobos
Bernstein, Leonard **2**
Berry, Bill
See R.E.M.
Berry, Chuck **1**
Berry, John **17**
Berry, Robert
See Emerson, Lake & Palmer/Powell
Best, Nathaniel
See O'Jays, The
Best, Pete
See Beatles, The
Bettencourt, Nuno
See Extreme
Better Than Ezra **19**
Bettie Serveert **17**
Betts, Dicky
See Allman Brothers, The
Bevan, Bev
SeeBlack Sabbath
Also see Electric Light Orchestra
B-52's, The **4**
Bezozi, Alan
See Dog's Eye View
Biafra, Jello **18**
Big Audio Dynamite **18**
Big Head Todd and the Monsters **20**
Big Mike
See GetoBoys, The
Big Money Odis
See Digital Underground
Bin Hassan, Umar
See Last Poets
Bingham, John
See Fishbone
Binks, Les
See Judas Priest
Biondo, George
See Steppenwolf
Birchfield, Benny
See Osborne Brothers, The
Bird
See Parker, Charlie
Birdsong, Cindy
See Supremes, The
Birdstuff
See Man or Astroman?
Biscuits, Chuck
See Danzig
Also see Social Distortion
Bishop, Michael
See Gwar
Biz Markie **10**
BizzyBone
See Bone Thugs-N-Harmony
Bjelland, Kat
See Babes in Toyland
Björk **16**
Bjork, Brant
See Fu Manchu
Black, Clint **5**
Black Crowes, The **7**
Black Flag **22**
Black Francis
See Black, Frank
Black, Frank **14**
Black, Mary **15**
Black Sabbath **9**
Black Sheep **15**
Black Uhuru **12**
Black, Vic
See C + C Music Factory
BlackHawk **21**
Blackman, Cindy **15**
Blackmore, Ritchie
See Deep Purple
Blackwood, Sarah
See Dubstar
Blades, Ruben **2**
Blake, Eubie **19**
Blake, Norman
See Teenage Fanclub
Blakey, Art **11**
Blanchard, Terence **13**
Bland, Bobby "Blue" **12**
Blessid Union of Souls **20**
Bley, Carla **8**
Bley, Paul **14**
Blige, Mary J. **15**
Blind Melon **21**
Block, Rory **18**
Blondie **14**
Blood, Dave
See Dead Milkmen
Blood, Sweat and Tears **7**
Bloom, Eric
See Blue Oyster Cult
Bloom, Luka **14**
Bluegrass Patriots **22**
Blue Oyster Cult **16**
Blue Rodeo **18**
Blues, Elwood
See Blues Brothers, The
Blues, "Joliet" Jake
See Blues Brothers, The
Blues Brothers, The **3**
Blues Traveler 15
Blunt, Martin
See Charlatans, The
Blur **17**
BoDeans, The **20**
Earlier sketch in CM **3**
Bob, Tim
See Rage Against the Machine
Bocelli, Andrea **22**
Boff, Richard
See Chumbawamba
Bogaert, Jo
See Technotronic
Bogdan, Henry
See Helmet
Bogguss, Suzy **11**
Bogle, Bob
See Ventures, The
Bolade, Nitanju
See Sweet Honey in the Rock
Bolan, Marc
See T. Rex
Bolton, Michael **4**
Bon Jovi **10**
Bon Jovi, Jon
See Bon Jovi
Bonamy, James **21**
Bonebrake, D. J.
See X
Bone Thugs-N-Harmony **18**
Bonham, John
See Led Zeppelin
Bonnecaze, Cary
See Better Than Ezra
Bonner, Leroy "Sugarfoot"
See Ohio Players
Bono
See U2
Bonsall, Joe
See Oak Ridge Boys, The
Boo Radleys, The **21**
Books
See Das EFX
Boone, Pat **13**
Booth, Tim
See James
Boquist, Dave
See Son Volt
Boquist, Jim
See Son Volt
Bordin, Mike
See Faith No More
Borg, Bobby
See Warrant
Borge, Victor **19**
Borowiak, Tony
See All-4-One
Bostaph, Paul
See Slayer
Boston **11**
Bostrom, Derrick
See Meat Puppets, The
Bottum, Roddy
See Faith No More
Bouchard, Albert
See Blue Oyster Cult
Bouchard, Joe
See Blue Oyster Cult
Bouchikhi, Chico
See Gipsy Kings, The
Bowen, Jimmy
See Country Gentlemen, The
Bowens, Sir Harry
See Was (Not Was)
Bowie, David **1**
Bowman, Steve
See Counting Crows
Box, Mick
See Uriah Heep

Boy Howdy **21**
Boyd, Eadie
See Del Rubio Triplets
Boyd, Elena
See Del Rubio Triplets
Boyd, Liona **7**
Boyd, Milly
See Del Rubio Triplets
Boyz II Men **15**
Bozulich, Carla
See Geraldine Fibbers
Brad **21**
Bradbury, John
See Specials, The
Bradshaw, Tim
See Dog's Eye View
Bradstreet, Rick
See Bluegrass Patriots
Brady, Paul **8**
Bragg, Billy **7**
Bramah, Martin
See Fall, The
Brand New Heavies, The **14**
Brandt, Paul **22**
Brandy **19**
Branigan, Laura **2**
Brannon, Kippi **20**
Brantley, Junior
See Roomful of Blues
Braxton, Anthony **12**
Braxton, Toni **17**
B-Real
See Cypress Hill
Bream, Julian **9**
Breeders **19**
Brennan, Paul
See Odds
Brenner, Simon
See Talk Talk
Brevette, Lloyd
See Skatalites, The
Brickell, Edie **3**
Brickman, Jim **22**
Bridgewater, Dee Dee **18**
Briggs, James Randall
See Aquabats
Briggs, Vic
See Animals
Bright, Ronnie
See Coasters, The
Brightman, Sarah **20**
Briley, Alex
See Village People, The
Brindley, Paul
See Sundays, The
Britten, Benjamin **15**
Brittingham, Eric
See Cinderella
Brix
See Fall, The
Brockenborough, Dennis
See Mighty Mighty Bosstones
Brockie, Dave
See Gwar
Brokop, Lisa **22**
Bromberg, David **18**
Bronfman, Yefim **6**
Brooke, Jonatha
See Story, The
Brookes, Jon
See Charlatans, The
Brooks, Baba
See Skatalites, The
Brooks, Garth **8**
Brooks, Leon Eric "Kix"
See Brooks & Dunn
Brooks & Dunn **12**
Broonzy, Big Bill **13**
Brotherdale, Steve
See Joy Division
Also see Smithereens, The
Broudie, Ian
See Lightning Seeds
Brown, Bobby **4**
Brown, Clarence "Gatemouth" **11**
Brown, Donny
See Verve Pipe, The
Brown, Duncan
See Stereolab
Brown, George
See Kool & the Gang
Brown, Harold
See War
Brown, Heidi
See Treadmill Trackstar
Brown, Ian
See Stone Roses, The
Brown, James **16**
Earlier sketch in CM **2**
Brown, Jimmy
See UB40
Brown, Junior **15**
Brown, Marty **14**
Brown, Melanie
See Spice Girls
Brown, Mick
See Dokken
Brown, Norman
See Mills Brothers, The
Brown, Ray **21**
Brown, Ruth **13**
Brown, Selwyn "Bumbo"
See Steel Pulse
Brown, Steven
See Tuxedomoon
Brown, Tim
See Boo Radleys, The
Brown, Tony **14**
Browne, Jackson **3**
Also see Nitty Gritty Dirt Band, The
Brownstein, Carrie
See Sleater-Kinney
Brownstone **21**
Brubeck, Dave **8**
Bruce, Dustan
See Chumbawamba
Bruce, Jack
See Cream
Bruford, Bill
See King Crimson
Also see Yes
Bruster, Thomas
See Soul Stirrers, The
Bryan, David
See Bon Jovi
Bryan, Karl
See Skatalites, The
Bryan, Mark
See Hootie and the Blowfish
Bryant, Elbridge
See Temptations, The
Bryson, Bill
See Desert Rose Band, The
Bryson, David
See Counting Crows
Bryson, Peabo **11**
Buchanan, Wallis
See Jamiroquai
Buchholz, Francis
See Scorpions, The
Buchignani, Paul
See Afghan Whigs
Buck, Mike
See Fabulous Thunderbirds, The
Buck, Peter
See R.E.M.
Buck, Robert
See 10,000 Maniacs
Buckingham, Lindsey **8**
Also see Fleetwood Mac
Buckley, Betty **16**
Earlier sketch in CM **1**
Buckley, Jeff **22**
Buckley, Tim **14**
Buckwheat Zydeco **6**
Budgie
See Siouxsie and the Banshees
Buerstatte, Phil
See White Zombie
Buffalo Tom **18**
Buffett, Jimmy **4**
Bulgarian State Female Vocal Choir, The **10**
Bulgarian State Radio and Television Female Vocal Choir, The
See Bulgarian State Female Vocal Choir, The
Bulgin, Lascelle
See Israel Vibration
Bullock, Craig
See Sugar Ray
Bumbry, Grace **13**
Bumpus, Cornelius
See Doobie Brothers, The
Bunker, Clive
See Jethro Tull
Bunnell, Dewey
See America
Bunskoeke, Herman
See Bettie Serveert
Bunton, Emma
See Spice Girls

Burch, Curtis
See New Grass Revival, The
Burchill, Charlie
See Simple Minds
Burden, Ian
See Human League, The
Burdon, Eric
See Animals
Burdon, Eric **14**
Also see War
Burgess, Paul
See Camel
Burgess, Tim
See Charlatans, The
Burke, Clem
See Blondie
Burkum, Tyler
See Audio Adrenaline
Burnett, Carol **6**
Burnett, T Bone **13**
Burnette, Billy
See Fleetwood Mac
Burnham, Hugo
See Gang of Four
Burning Spear **15**
Burns, Bob
See Lynyrd Skynyrd
Burns, Karl
See Fall, The
Burr, Clive
See Iron Maiden
Burrell, Boz
See Bad Company
Burrell, Kenny **11**
Burrell
See King Crimson
Burton, Cliff
See Metallica
Burton, Gary **10**
Burton, Tim
See Mighty Mighty Bosstones
Busby, Jheryl **9**
Bush **18**
Bush, Dave
See Fall, The
Bush, John
See Anthrax
Bush, Kate **4**
Bush, Sam
See New Grass Revival, The
Bushwick, Bill
See Geto Boys, The
Busta Rhymes **18**
Butler, Bernard
See Suede
Butler, Richard
See Love Spit Love
Butler, Terry "Geezer"
See Black Sabbath
Butler, Tim
See Love Spit Love
Butterfly
See Digable Planets
Butthole Surfers **16**
Buzzcocks, The **9**
Byers, Roddy
See Specials, The
Byrds, The **8**
Byrne, David **8**
Also see Talking Heads
Byrne, Dermot
See Altan
Byrom, Larry
See Steppenwolf
Byron, David
See Uriah Heep
Byron, Don **22**
Byron, Lord T.
See Lords of Acid
C + C Music Factory **16**
Cabaret Voltaire **18**
Cachao
See Lopez, Israel "Cachao"
Caesar, Shirley **17**
Cafferty, John
See Beaver Brown Band, The
Cage, John **8**
Cahn, Sammy **11**
Cain, Jonathan
See Journey
Cale, J. J. **16**
Cale, John **9**
Also see Velvet Underground, The
Calhoun, Will
See Living Colour
California, Randy
See Spirit
Calire, Mario
See Wallflowers, The
Callahan, Ken
See Jayhawks, The
Callas, Maria **11**
Callis, Jo
See Human League, The
Calloway, Cab **6**
Camel **21**
Cameron, Duncan
See Sawyer Brown
Cameron, G. C.
See Spinners, The
Cameron, Matt
See Soundgarden
Campbell, Ali
See UB40
Campbell, Glen **2**
Campbell, Kerry
See War
Campbell, Luther **10**
Campbell, Martyn
See Lightning Seeds
Campbell, Phil
See Motörhead
Campbell, Robin
See UB40
Campbell, Tevin **13**
CanadianBrass, The **4**
Cantrell, Jerry
See Alice in Chains
Canty, Brendan
See Fugazi
Capaldi, Jim
See Traffic
Cappelli, Frank **14**
Captain Beefheart **10**
Cardigans **19**
Cardwell, Joi **22**
Carey, Danny
See Tool
Carey, Mariah **20**
Earlier sketch in CM **6**
Carlisle, Belinda **8**
Carlisle, Bob **22**
Carlos, Bun E.
See Cheap Trick
Carlos, Don
See Black Uhuru
Carlson, Paulette
See Highway 101
Carnes, Kim **4**
Carpenter, Bob
See Nitty Gritty Dirt Band, The
Carpenter, Karen
See Carpenters, The
Carpenter, Mary-Chapin **6**
Carpenter, Richard
See Carpenters, The
Carpenter, Stephen
See Deftones
Carpenters, The **13**
Carr, Ben
See Mighty Mighty Bosstones
Carr, Eric
See Kiss
Carr, Martin
See Boo Radleys, The
Carrack, Paul
See Mike & the Mechanics
Also see Squeeze
Carreras, José **8**
Carrigan, Andy
See Mekons, The
Carroll, Earl "Speedo"
See Coasters, The
Carruthers, John
See Siouxsie and the Banshees
Cars, The **20**
Carter, Anita
See Carter Family, The
Carter, A. P.
See Carter Family, The
Carter, Benny **3**
Also see McKinney's Cotton Pickers
Carter, Betty **6**
Carter, Carlene **8**
Carter, Helen
See Carter Family, The
Carter, James **18**
Carter, Janette
See Carter Family, The
Carter, Jimmy
See Five Blind Boys of Alabama
Carter, Joe
See Carter Family, The
Carter, June **6**
Also see Carter Family, The

Carter, Maybell
See Carter Family, The
Carter, Nell **7**
Carter, Nick
See Backstreet Boys
Carter, Regina **22**
Carter, Ron **14**
Carter, Sara
See Carter Family, The
Carter Family, The **3**
Carthy, Martin
See Steeleye Span
Caruso, Enrico **10**
Casady, Jack
See Jefferson Airplane
Casale, Bob
See Devo
Casale, Gerald V.
See Devo
Casals, Pablo **9**
Case, Peter **13**
Cash, Johnny **17**
Earlier sketch in CM **1**
Cash, Rosanne **2**
Cassidy, Ed
See Spirit
Cates, Ronny
See Petra
Catherall, Joanne
See Human League, The
Catherine Wheel **18**
Caustic Window
See Aphex Twin
Cauty, Jimmy
See Orb, The
Cavalera, Igor
See Sepultura
Cavalera, Max
See Sepultura
Cave, Nick **10**
Cavoukian, Raffi
See Raffi
Cease, Jeff
See Black Crowes, The
Cervenka, Exene
See X
Cetera, Peter
See Chicago
Chamberlin, Jimmy
See Smashing Pumpkins
Chambers, Martin
See Pretenders, The
Chambers, Paul **18**
Chambers, Terry
See XTC
Champion, Eric **21**
Chance, Slim
See Cramps, The
Chancellor, Justin
See Tool
Chandler, Chas
See Animals
Chandra, Sheila **16**
Chaney, Jimmy
See Jimmie's Chicken Shack
Chang, Sarah **7**
Channing, Carol **6**
Chapin, Harry **6**
Chapin, Tom **11**
Chapman, Steven Curtis **15**
Chapman, Tony
See Rolling Stones, The
Chapman, Tracy **20**
Earlier sketch in CM **4**
Chaquico, Craig
See Jefferson Starship
Charlatans, The **13**
Charles, Ray **1**
Charles, Yolanda
See Aztec Camera
Charm Farm **20**
Chea, Alvin "Vinnie"
See Take 6
Cheap Trick **12**
Checker, Chubby **7**
Che Colovita, Lemon
See Jimmie's Chicken Shack
Cheeks, Julius
See Soul Stirrers, The
Chemical Brothers **20**
Cheng, Chi
See Deftones
Chenier, C. J. **15**
Chenier, Clifton **6**
Chenille Sisters, The **16**
Cher **1**
Cherone, Gary
See Extreme
Cherry, Don **10**
Cherry, Neneh **4**
Chesney, Kenny **20**
Chesnutt, Mark **13**
Chevalier, Maurice **6**
Chevron, Phillip
See Pogues, The
Chicago **3**
Chieftains, The **7**
Childress, Ross
See Collective Soul
Childs, Toni **2**
Chilton, Alex **10**
Chimes, Terry
See Clash, The
Chisholm, Melanie
See Spice Girls
Chopmaster J
See Digital Underground
Christ, John
See Danzig
Christian, Charlie **11**
Christina, Fran
See Fabulous Thunderbirds, The
Also see Roomful of Blues
Chuck D
See Public Enemy
Chumbawamba **21**
Chung, Mark
See Einstürzende Neubauten
Church, Kevin
See Country Gentlemen, The
Church, The **14**
Cieka, Rob
See Boo Radleys, The
Cinderella **16**
Cinelu, Mino
See Weather Report
Circle Jerks, The **17**
Cissell, Ben
See Audio Adrenaline
Clapton, Eric **11**
Earlier sketch in CM **1**
Also see Cream
Also see Yardbirds, The
Clark, Alan
See Dire Straits
Clark, Dave
See Dave Clark Five, The
Clark, Dick **2**
Clark, Gene
See Byrds, The
Clark, Guy **17**
Clark, Keith
See Circle Jerks, The
Clark, Mike
See Suicidal Tendencies
Clark, Roy **1**
Clark, Steve
See Def Leppard
Clark, Terri **19**
Clark, Tony
See Blessid Union of Souls
Clarke, Bernie
See Aztec Camera
Clarke, "Fast" Eddie
See Motörhead
Clarke, Michael
See Byrds, The
Clarke, Stanley **3**
Clarke, Vince
See Depeche Mode
Also see Erasure
Clarke, William
See Third World
Clash, The **4**
Clayderman, Richard **1**
Claypool, Les
See Primus
Clayton, Adam
See U2
Clayton, Sam
See Little Feat
Clayton-Thomas, David
SeeBlood, Sweat and Tears
Clean, Dean
See Dead Milkmen
Cleaves, Jessica
See Earth, Wind and Fire
Clegg, Johnny **8**
Clements, Vassar **18**
Clemons, Clarence **7**
Cleveland, James **1**
Cliburn, Van **13**

Cliff, Jimmy **8**
Clifford, Douglas Ray
See Creedence Clearwater Revival
Cline, Nels
See Geraldine Fibbers
Cline, Patsy **5**
Clinton, George **7**
Clivilles, Robert
See C + C Music Factory
Clooney, Rosemary **9**
Coasters, The **5**
Cobain, Kurt
See Nirvana
Cobham, Billy
See Mahavishnu Orchestra
Cochran, Bobby
See Steppenwolf
Cochrane, Tom **22**
Cockburn, Bruce **8**
Cocker, Jarvis
See Pulp
Cocker, Joe **4**
Cocking, William "Willigan"
See Mystic Revealers
Coco the Electronic Monkey Wizard
See Man or Astroman?
Cocteau Twins, The **12**
Codenys, Patrick
See Front 242
Codling, Neil
See Suede
Coe, David Allan **4**
Coffey, Jeff
See Butthole Surfers
Coffie, Calton
See Inner Circle
Cohen, Jeremy
See Turtle Island String Quartet
Cohen, Leonard **3**
Cohen, Porky
See Roomful of Blues
Colbourn, Chris
See Buffalo Tom
Cole, David
See C + C Music Factory
Cole, Holly **18**
Cole, Lloyd **9**
Cole, Natalie **21**
Earlier sketch in CM **1**
Cole, Nat King **3**
Cole, Paula **20**
Cole, Ralph
See Nylons, The
Coleman, Ornette **5**
Collective Soul **16**
Colley, Dana
See Morphine
Collie, Mark **15**
Collin, Phil
See Def Leppard
Collins, Albert **19**
Earlier sketch in CM **4**
Collins, Allen
See Lynyrd Skynyrd
Collins, Bootsy **8**
Collins, Judy **4**
Collins, Mark
See Charlatans, The
Collins, Mel
See King Crimson
See Camel
Collins, Phil **20**
Earlier sketch in CM **2**
Also see Genesis
Collins, Rob
See Charlatans, The
Collins, William
See Collins, Bootsy
Colomby, Bobby
See Blood, Sweat and Tears
Colt, Johnny
See Black Crowes, The
Coltrane, John **4**
Colvin, Shawn **11**
Colwell, David
See Bad Company
Combs, Sean "Puffy" **16**
Comess, Aaron
See Spin Doctors
Como, Perry **14**
Congo Norvell **22**
Conneff, Kevin
See Chieftains, The
Connelly, Chris
See KMFDM
Connick, Harry, Jr. **4**
Connors, Marc
See Nylons, The
Conti, Neil
See Prefab Sprout
Conway, Billy
See Morphine
Conway, Gerry
See Pentangle
Cooder, Ry **2**
Cook, Jeffrey Alan
See Alabama
Cook, Paul
See Sex Pistols, The
Cook, Stuart
See Creedence Clearwater Revival
Cook, Wayne
See Steppenwolf
Cooke, Sam **1**
Also see Soul Stirrers, The
Cool, Tre
See Green Day
Coolio **19**
Cooney, Rory **6**
Cooper, Alice **8**
Cooper, Jason
See Cure, The
Cooper, Martin
See Orchestral Manoeuvres in the Dark
Cooper, Michael
See Third World
Cooper, Paul
See Nylons, The
Cooper, Ralph
See Air Supply
Coore, Stephen
See Third World
Cope, Julian **16**
Copeland, Stewart **14**
Also see Police, The
Copland, Aaron **2**
Copley, Al
See Roomful of Blues
Corea, Chick **6**
Corella, Doug
See Verve Pipe, The
Corgan, Billy
See Smashing Pumpkins
Corina, Sarah
See Mekons, The
Cornelius, Robert
See Poi Dog Pondering
Cornell, Chris
See Soundgarden
Cornick, Glenn
See Jethro Tull
Corrigan, Brianna
See Beautiful South
Cosper, Kina
See Brownstone
Costello, Elvis **12**
Earlier sketch in CM **2**
Coté, Billy
See Madder Rose
Cotoia, Robert
See Beaver Brown Band, The
Cotrubas, Ileana **1**
Cotten, Elizabeth **16**
Cotton, Caré
See Sounds of Blackness
Cougar, John(ny)
See Mellencamp, John
Counting Crows **18**
Country Gentlemen, The **7**
Coury, Fred
See Cinderella
Coutts, Duncan
See Our Lady Peace
Coverdale, David
See Whitesnake **5**
Cowan, John
See New Grass Revival, The
Cowboy Junkies, The **4**
Cox, Andy
See English Beat, The
Also see Fine Young Cannibals
Cox, Terry
See Pentangle
Coxon, Graham
See Blur
Coyne, Mark
See Flaming Lips
Coyne, Wayne
See Flaming Lips
Cracker **12**
Craig, Albert
See Israel Vibration
Craig, Carl **19**
Crain, S. R.
See Soul Stirrers, The

Cramps, The **16**
Cranberries, The **14**
Crash Test Dummies **14**
Crawford, Dave Max
See Poi Dog Pondering
Crawford, Da'dra
See Anointed
Crawford, Ed
See fIREHOSE
Crawford, Michael **4**
Crawford, Steve
See Anointed
Cray, Robert **8**
Creach, Papa John
See Jefferson Starship
Cream **9**
Creedence Clearwater Revival **16**
Creegan, Andrew
See Barenaked Ladies
Creegan, Jim
See Barenaked Ladies
Crenshaw, Marshall **5**
Cretu, Michael
See Enigma
Criss, Peter
See Kiss
Croce, Jim **3**
Crofts, Dash
See Seals & Crofts
Cropper, Steve **12**
Crosby, Bing **6**
Crosby, David **3**
Also see Byrds, The
Cross, David
See King Crimson
Cross, Mike
See Sponge
Cross, Tim
See Sponge
Crouch, Andraé **9**
Crover, Dale
See Melvins
Crow, Sheryl **18**
Crowded House **12**
Crowe, J. D. **5**
Crowell, Rodney **8**
Cruikshank, Gregory
See Tuxedomoon
Cruz, Celia **22**
Earlier sketch in CM **10**
Cuddy, Jim
See Blue Rodeo
Cult, The **16**
Cummings, Danny
See Dire Straits
Cummings, David
See Del Amitri
Cunningham, Abe
See Deftones
Cuomo, Rivers
See Weezer
Cure, The **20**
Earlier sketch in CM **3**
Curless, Ann
See Exposé
Curley, John
See Afghan Whigs
Curran, Ciaran
See Altan
Currie, Justin
See Del Amitri
Currie, Steve
See T. Rex
Curry, Tim **3**
Curtis, Ian
See Joy Division
Curtis, King **17**
Curve **13**
Custance, Mickey
See Big Audio Dynamite
Cuthbert, Scott
See Everclear
Cutler, Chris
See Pere Ubu
Cypress Hill **11**
Cyrus, Billy Ray **11**
D'Angelo **20**
Dacus, Donnie
See Chicago
Dacus, Johnny
See Osborne Brothers, The
Daddy G
See Massive Attack
Daddy Mack
See Kris Kross
Daellenbach, Charles
See Canadian Brass, The
Dahlheimer, Patrick
See Live
Daisley, Bob
See Black Sabbath
Dale, Dick **13**
Daley, Richard
See Third World
Dall, Bobby
See Poison
Dallin, Sarah
See Bananarama
Dalton, John
See Kinks, The
Dalton, Nic
See Lemonheads, The
Daltrey, Roger **3**
Also see Who, The
Dammers, Jerry
See Specials, The
Dando, Evan
See Lemonheads, The
Dandy Warhols **22**
Danell, Dennis
See Social Distortion
D'Angelo, Greg
See Anthrax
Daniels, Charlie **6**
Daniels, Jack
See Highway 101
Danko, Rick
See Band, The
Danny Boy
See House of Pain
Danzig **7**
Danzig, Glenn
See Danzig
D'Arby, Terence Trent **3**
Darin, Bobby **4**
Darling, Eric
See Weavers, The
Darriau, Matt
See Klezmatics, The
Darvill, Benjamin
See Crash Test Dummies
Das EFX **14**
Daugherty, Jay Dee
See Church, The
Daulne, Marie
See Zap Mama
Dave, Doggy
See Lords of Acid
Dave Clark Five, The **12**
Dave Matthews Band **18**
Davenport, N'Dea
See Brand New Heavies, The
Davidson, Lenny
See Dave Clark Five, The
Davies, Dave
See Kinks, The
Davies, James
See Jimmie's Chicken Shack
Davies, Ray **5**
Also see Kinks, The
Davies, Saul
See James
Davis, Anthony **17**
Davis, Brad
See Fu Manchu
Davis, Chip **4**
Davis, Clive **14**
Davis, Jonathan
See Korn
Davis, Linda **21**
Davis, Michael
See MC5, The
Davis, Miles **1**
Davis, Reverend Gary **18**
Davis, Sammy, Jr. **4**
Davis, Skeeter **15**
Davis, Spencer
See Spencer Davis Group
Davis, Steve
See Mystic Revealers
Davis, Zelma
See C + C Music Factory
Dawdy, Cheryl
See Chenille Sisters, The
Dayne, Taylor **4**
dc Talk **18**
de Albuquerque, Michael
See Electric Light Orchestra
Deacon, John
See Queen

Dead Can Dance **16**
Dead Milkmen **22**
Deakin, Paul
See Mavericks, The
Deal, Kelley
See Breeders
Deal, Kim
See Breeders
Also see Pixies, The
Dean, Billy **19**
DeBarge, El **14**
de Burgh, Chris **22**
de Coster, Jean Paul
See 2 Unlimited
Dee, Mikkey
See Dokken
Also see Motörhead
Deee-lite **9**
Deep Forest **18**
Deep Purple **11**
Def Leppard **3**
Deftones **22**
DeGarmo, Chris
See Queensryche
de Grassi, Alex **6**
Deibert, Adam Warren
See Aquabats
Deily, Ben
See Lemonheads, The
DeJohnette, Jack **7**
Del Rubio Triplets **21**
Delaet, Nathalie
See Lords of Acid
De La Soul **7**
DeLeo, Dean
See Stone Temple Pilots
DeLeo, Robert
See Stone Temple Pilots
De La Luna, Shai
See Lords of Acid
de la Rocha, Zack
See Rage Against the Machine
DeLorenzo, Victor
See Violent Femmes
Del Amitri **18**
Del Mar, Candy
See Cramps, The
Delp, Brad
See Boston
de Lucia, Paco **1**
DeMent, Iris **13**
Demeski, Stanley
See Luna
De Meyer, Jean-Luc
See Front 242
Demos, Greg
See Guided By Voices
Dempsey, Michael
See Cure, The
Denison, Duane
See Jesus Lizard
Dennis, Garth
See Black Uhuru
Denny, Sandy
See Fairport Convention
Densmore, John
See Doors, The
Dent, Cedric
See Take 6
Denton, Sandy
See Salt-N-Pepa
Denver, John **22**
Earlier sketch in CM **1**
De Oliveria, Laudir
See Chicago
Depeche Mode **5**
de Prume, Ivan
See White Zombie
Derosier, Michael
See Heart
Desaulniers, Stephen
See Scud Mountain Boys
Deschamps, Kim
See Blue Rodeo
Desert Rose Band, The **4**
Des'ree **15**
Destri, Jimmy
See Blondie
Deupree, Jerome
See Morphine
Deutrom, Mark
See Melvins
DeVille, C. C.
See Poison
Devo **13**
Devoto, Howard
See Buzzcocks, The
DeWitt, Lew C.
See Statler Brothers, The
de Young, Joyce
See Andrews Sisters, The
Dexter X
See Man or Astroman?
Diagram, Andy
See James
Diamond "Dimebag" Darrell
See Pantera
Diamond, Mike
See Beastie Boys, The
Diamond, Neil **1**
Diamond Rio **11**
Di'anno, Paul
See Iron Maiden
Dibango, Manu **14**
Dickens, Little Jimmy **7**
Dickerson, B.B.
See War
Dickinson, Paul Bruce
See Iron Maiden
Dickinson, Rob
See Catherine Wheel
Diddley, Bo **3**
Diffie, Joe **10**
Difford, Chris
See Squeeze
DiFranco, Ani **17**
Digable Planets **15**
Diggle, Steve
See Buzzcocks, The
Digital Underground **9**
DiMant, Leor
See House of Pain
Di Meola, Al **12**
DiMucci, Dion
See Dion
DiNizo, Pat
See Smithereens, The
Dilworth, Joe
See Stereolab
Dinning, Dean
See Toad the Wet Sprocket
Dinosaur Jr. **10**
Dio, Ronnie James
See Black Sabbath
Dion **4**
Dion, Céline **12**
Dire Straits **22**
Dirks, Michael
See Gwar
Dirnt, Mike
See Green Day
Dittrich, John
See Restless Heart
Dixon, George W.
See Spinners , The
Dixon, Jerry
See Warrant
Dixon, Willie **10**
DJ Domination
See Geto Boys, The
DJ Fuse
See Digital Underground
DJ Jazzy Jeff and the Fresh Prince **5**
D.J. Lethal
See House of Pain
D.J. Minutemix
See P.M. Dawn
DJ Muggs
See Cypress Hill
DJ Premier
See Gang Starr
DJ Ready Red
See Geto Boys, The
DJ Terminator X
See Public Enemy
Doc Pomus **14**
Doe, John
See X
Dogbowl
See King Missile
Dog's Eye View **21**
Doherty, Denny
See Mamas and the Papas
Dokken **16**
Dokken, Don
See Dokken
Dolby, Monica Mimi
See Brownstone
Dolby, Thomas **10**
Dolenz, Micky
See Monkees, The
Dombroski, Vinnie
See Sponge
Domingo, Placido **20**
Earlier sketch in CM **1**

Domino, Fats **2**
Donahue, Jerry
See Fairport Convention
Donahue, Jonathan
See Flaming Lips
Donald, Tony
See Simple Minds
Donelly, Tanya
See Belly
Also see Breeders
Also see Throwing Muses
Donovan **9**
Donovan, Bazil
See Blue Rodeo
Don, Rasa
See Arrested Development
Doobie Brothers, The **3**
Doodlebug
See Digable Planets
Doors, The **4**
Dorge, Michel (Mitch)
See Crash Test Dummies
Dorney, Tim
See Republica
Dorough, Howie
See Backstreet Boys
Dorsey, Jimmy
See Dorsey Brothers, The
Dorsey, Thomas A. **11**
Dorsey, Tommy
See Dorsey Brothers, The
Dorsey Brothers, The **8**
Doth, Anita
See 2 Unlimited
Doucet, Michael **8**
Doughty, M.
See Soul Coughing
Douglas, Jerry
See Country Gentlemen, The
Dowd, Christopher
See Fishbone
Dowling, Dave
See Jimmie's Chicken Shack
Downes, Geoff
See Yes
Downey, Brian
See Thin Lizzy
Downie, Gordon
See Tragically Hip, The
Downing, K. K.
See Judas Priest
Doyle, Candida
See Pulp
Dozier, Lamont
See Holland-Dozier-Holland
Drake, Nick **17**
Drake, Steven
See Odds
Drayton, Leslie
See Earth, Wind and Fire
Dr. Dre **15**
Also see N.W.A.
Dreja, Chris
See Yardbirds, The
Drew, Dennis
See 10,000 Maniacs
Dr. John **7**
Drozd, Stephen
See Flaming Lips
Drumbago,
See Skatalites, The
Drumdini, Harry
See Cramps, The
Drummond, Don
See Skatalites, The
Drummond, Tom
See Better Than Ezra
Dryden, Spencer
See Jefferson Airplane
Dubbe, Berend
See Bettie Serveert
Dube, Lucky **17**
Dubstar **22**
Dudley, Anne
See Art of Noise
Duffey, John
See Country Gentlemen, The
Also see Seldom Scene, The
Duffy, Billy
See Cult, The
Duffy, Martin
See Primal Scream
Dukowski, Chuck
See Black Flag
Dulli, Greg
See Afghan Whigs
Dumont, Tom
See No Doubt
Dunbar, Aynsley
See Jefferson Starship
Also see Journey
Also see Whitesnake
Dunbar, Sly
See Sly and Robbie
Duncan, Bryan **19**
Duncan, Steve
See Desert Rose Band, The
Duncan, Stuart
See Nashville Bluegrass Band
Dunlap, Slim
See Replacements, The
Dunn, Holly **7**
Dunn, Larry
See Earth, Wind and Fire
Dunn, Ronnie
See Brooks & Dunn
Dunning, A.J.
See Verve Pipe, The
Dupree, Champion Jack **12**
Duran Duran **4**
Durante, Mark
See KMFDM
Duritz, Adam
See Counting Crows
Durrill, Johnny
See Ventures, The
Dutt, Hank
See Kronos Quartet
Dyble, Judy
See Fairport Convention
Dylan, Bob **21**
Earlier sketch in CM **3**
Dylan, Jakob
See Wallflowers, The
D'Amour, Paul
See Tool
E., Sheila
See Sheila E.
Eacrett, Chris
See Our Lady Peace
Eagles, The **3**
Earl, Ronnie **5**
Also see Roomful of Blues
Earle, Steve
See Afghan Whigs
Earle, Steve **16**
Earth, Wind and Fire **12**
Easton, Elliot
See Cars, The
Easton, Sheena **2**
Eazy-E **13**
Also see N.W.A.
Echeverria, Rob
See Helmet
Echobelly **21**
Eckstine, Billy **1**
Eddy, Duane **9**
Eden, Sean
See Luna
Edge, Graeme
See Moody Blues, The
Edge, The
See U2
Edmonds, Kenneth "Babyface" **12**
Edmonton, Jerry
See Steppenwolf
Edwards, Dennis
See Temptations, The
Edwards, Edgar
See Spinners, The
Edwards, Gordon
See Kinks, The
Edwards, John
See Spinners , The
Edwards, Johnny
See Foreigner
Edwards, Leroy "Lion"
See Mystic Revealers
Edwards, Mark
See Aztec Camera
Edwards, Mike
See Electric Light Orchestra
Edwards, Nokie
See Ventures, The
Ehran
See Lords of Acid
Einheit
See Einstürzende Neubauten
Einheit, F.M.
See KMFDM
Einstürzende Neubauten **13**

Eisenstein, Michael
See Letters to Cleo
Eitzel, Mark
See American Music Club
Ekberg, Ulf
See Ace of Base
Eklund, Greg
See Everclear
El-Hadi, Sulieman
See Last Poets
Eldon, Thór
See Sugarcubes, The
Eldridge, Ben
See Seldom Scene, The
Eldridge, Roy **9**
Also see McKinney's Cotton Pickers
Electric Light Orchestra **7**
Elfman, Danny **9**
Elias, Manny
See Tears for Fears
Ellefson, Dave
See Megadeth
Ellington, Duke **2**
Elliot, Cass **5**
Elliot, Joe
See Def Leppard
Elliott, Cass
See Mamas and the Papas
Elliott, Dennis
See Foreigner
Elliott, Doug
See Odds
Ellis, Bobby
See Skatalites, The
Ellis, Herb **18**
Ellis, Terry
See En Vogue
ELO
See Electric Light Orchestra
Ely, John
See Asleep at the Wheel
Ely, Vince
See Cure, The
Emerson, Bill
See Country Gentlemen, The
Emerson, Keith
See Emerson, Lake & Palmer/Powell
Emerson, Lake & Palmer/Powell **5**
Emery, Jill
See Hole
Emmanuel, Tommy **21**
English, Richard
See Flaming Lips
English Beat, The **9**
Enigma **14**
Eno, Brian **8**
Enos, Bob
See Roomful of Blues
Enright, Pat
See Nashville Bluegrass Band
Entwistle, John
See Who, The
En Vogue **10**
Enya **6**
EPMD **10**
Erasure **11**
Eric B.
See Eric B. and Rakim
Eric B. and Rakim **9**
Erickson, Roky **16**
Erlandson, Eric
See Hole
Erskine, Peter
See Weather Report
Ertegun, Ahmet **10**
Esch, En
See KMFDM
Escovedo, Alejandro **18**
Eshe, Montsho
See Arrested Development
Eskelin, Ian **19**
Esler-Smith, Frank
See Air Supply
Esquivel, Juan **17**
Estefan, Gloria **15**
Earlier sketch in CM **2**
Estrada, Roy
See Little Feat
Etheridge, Melissa **16**
Earlier sketch in CM **4**
Eurythmics **6**
Evan, John
See Jethro Tull
Evans, Bill **17**
Evans, Dick
See U2
Evans, Gil **17**
Evans, Mark
See AC/DC
Evans, Shane
See Collective Soul
Everclear **18**
Everlast
See House of Pain
Everly Brothers, The **2**
Everly, Don
See Everly Brothers, The
Everly, Phil
See Everly Brothers, The
Everman, Jason
See Soundgarden
Everything But The Girl **15**
Evora, Cesaria **19**
Ewen, Alvin
See Steel Pulse
Exkano, Paul
See Five Blind Boys of Alabama
Exposé **4**
Extreme **10**
Ezell, Ralph
See Shenandoah
Fabian **5**
Fabulous Thunderbirds, The **1**
Faces, The **22**
Fadden, Jimmie
See Nitty Gritty Dirt Band, The
Fagan, Don
See Steely Dan
Fahey, John **17**
Fahey, Siobhan
See Bananarama
Fairport Convention **22**
Faithfull, Marianne **14**
Faith No More **7**
Fakir, Abdul "Duke"
See Four Tops, The
Falconer, Earl
See UB40
Fall, The **12**
Fallon, David
See Chieftains, The
Fältskog, Agnetha
See Abba
Fambrough, Henry
See Spinners, The
Farley, J. J.
See Soul Stirrers, The
Farndon, Pete
See Pretenders, The
Farrar, Jay
See Son Volt
Farrar, John
See Shadows, The
Farrell, Perry
See Jane's Addiction
Farris, Dionne
See Arrested Development
Farris, Tim
See Israel Vibration
Farriss, Andrew
See INXS
Farriss, Jon
See INXS
Farriss, Tim
See INXS
Fatboy Slim **22**
Fay, Johnny
See Tragically Hip, The
Fay, Martin
See Chieftains, The
Fearnley, James
See Pogues, The
Fehlmann, Thomas
See Orb, The
Feinstein, Michael **6**
Fela
See Kuti, Fela
Felber, Dean
See Hootie and the Blowfish
Felder, Don
See Eagles, The
Feldman, Eric Drew
See Pere Ubu
Feliciano, José **10**
Fender, Freddy
See Texas Tornados, The
Fender, Leo **10**
Fennell, Kevin
See Guided By Voices
Fennelly, Gere
See Redd Kross

Fenwick, Ray
See Spencer Davis Group
Ferguson, Jay
See Spirit
Ferguson, Keith
See Fabulous Thunderbirds, The
Ferguson, Maynard **7**
Ferguson, Neil
See Chumbawamba
Ferguson, Steve
See NRBQ
Ferrell, Rachelle **17**
Ferrer, Frank
See Love Spit Love
Ferry, Bryan **1**
Ficca, Billy
See Television
Fiedler, Arthur **6**
Fielder, Jim
See Blood, Sweat and Tears
Fields, Johnny
See Five Blind Boys of Alabama
Fier, Anton
See Pere Ubu
Finch, Jennifer
See L7
Finer, Jem
See Pogues, The
Fine Young Cannibals **22**
Finn, Micky
See T. Rex
Finn, Neil
See Crowded House
Finn, Tim
See Crowded House
fIREHOSE **11**
Fishbone **7**
Fisher, Eddie **12**
Fisher, Jerry
See Blood, Sweat and Tears
Fisher, John "Norwood"
See Fishbone
Fisher, Phillip "Fish"
See Fishbone
Fisher, Roger
See Heart
Fishman, Jon
See Phish
Fitzgerald, Ella **1**
Fitzgerald, Kevin
See Geraldine Fibbers
Five Blind Boys of Alabama **12**
Flack, Roberta **5**
Flaming Lips **22**
Flanagan, Tommy **16**
Flansburgh, John
See They Might Be Giants
Flatt, Lester **3**
Flavor Flav
See Public Enemy
Flea
See Red Hot Chili Peppers, The
Fleck, Bela **8**
Also see New Grass Revival, The
Fleetwood, Mick
See Fleetwood Mac
Fleetwood Mac **5**
Fleischmann, Robert
See Journey
Flemons, Wade
See Earth, Wind and Fire
Flesh-N-Bone
See Bone Thugs-N-Harmony
Fletcher, Andy
See Depeche Mode
Fletcher, Guy
See Dire Straits
Flint, Keith
See Prodigy
Flores, Rosie **16**
Floyd, Heather
See Point of Grace
Flür, Wolfgang
See Kraftwerk
Flynn, Pat
See New Grass Revival, The
Fogelberg, Dan **4**
Fogerty, John **2**
Also see Creedence Clearwater Revival
Fogerty, Thomas
See Creedence Clearwater Revival
Folds, Ben
See Ben Folds Five
Foley
See Arrested Development
Foo Fighters **20**
Forbes, Derek
See Simple Minds
Ford, Lita **9**
Ford, Mark
See Black Crowes, The
Ford, Penny
See Soul II Soul
Ford, Tennessee Ernie **3**
Fordham, Julia **15**
Foreigner **21**
Fortune, Jimmy
See Statler Brothers, The
Fortus, Richard
See Love Spit Love
Fossen, Steve
See Heart
Foster, David **13**
Foster, Malcolm
See Pretenders, The
Foster, Paul
See Soul Stirrers, The
Foster, Radney **16**
Fountain, Clarence
See Five Blind Boys of Alabama
Fountain, Pete **7**
Four Tops, The **11**
Fox, Lucas
See Motörhead
Fox, Oz
See Stryper
Fox, Samantha **3**
Frame, Roddy
See Aztec Camera
Frampton, Peter **3**
Francis, Black
See Pixies, The
Francis, Connie **10**
Francis, Mike
See Asleep at the Wheel
Franke, Chris
See Tangerine Dream
Franklin, Aretha **17**
Earlier sketch in CM **2**
Franklin, Elmo
See Mighty Clouds of Joy, The
Franklin, Kirk **22**
Franklin, Larry
See Asleep at the Wheel
Franklin, Melvin
See Temptations, The
Franti, Michael **16**
Frantz, Chris
See Talking Heads
Fraser, Elizabeth
See Cocteau Twins, The
Frater, Shaun
See Fairport Convention
Frazier, Stan
See Sugar Ray
Freese, Josh
See Suicidal Tendencies
Frehley, Ace
See Kiss
Freiberg, David
See Jefferson Starship
French, Mark
See Blue Rodeo
Freni, Mirella **14**
Frey, Glenn **3**
Also see Eagles, The
Fricker, Sylvia
See Ian and Sylvia
Friedman, Marty
See Megadeth
Friel, Tony
See Fall, The
Fripp, Robert **9**
Also see King Crimson
Frisell, Bill **15**
Frishmann, Justine
See Suede
Frith, Fred **19**
Frizzell, Lefty **10**
Froese, Edgar
See Tangerine Dream
Front 242 **19**
Front Line Assembly **20**
Froom, Mitchell **15**
Frusciante, John
See Red Hot Chili Peppers, The
Fugazi **13**
Fugees, The **17**
Fulber, Rhys
See Front Line Assembly
Fuller, Blind Boy **20**
Fulson, Lowell **20**
Fu Manchu **22**
Fun Lovin' Criminals **20**

Furr, John
See Treadmill Trackstar
Furuholmen, Magne
See A-ha
Futter, Brian
See Catherine Wheel
Gabay, Yuval
See Soul Coughing
Gabriel, Peter **16**
Earlier sketch in CM **2**
Also see Genesis
Gadler, Frank
Gagliardi, Ed
See Foreigner
Gahan, Dave
See Depeche Mode
Gaines, Steve
See Lynyrd Skynyrd
Gaines, Timothy
See Stryper
Galea, Darren
See Jamiroquai
Galás, Diamanda **16**
Gale, Melvyn
See Electric Light Orchestra
Gallagher, Liam
See Oasis
Gallagher, Noel
See Oasis
Gallup, Simon
See Cure, The
Galore, Lady
See Lords of Acid
Galway, James **3**
Gambill, Roger
See Kingston Trio, The
Gamble, Cheryl "Coko"
See SWV
Gane, Tim
See Stereolab
Gang of Four **8**
Gang Starr **13**
Gannon, Craig
See Aztec Camera
Gano, Gordon
See Violent Femmes
Garcia, Dean
See Curve
Garcia, Jerry **4**
Also see Grateful Dead, The
Garcia, Leddie
See Poi Dog Pondering
Gardner, Carl
See Coasters, The
Gardner, Suzi
See L7
Garfunkel, Art **4**
Garland, Judy **6**
Garrett, Peter
See Midnight Oil
Garrett, Scott
See Cult, The
Garvey, Steve
See Buzzcocks, The
Gaskill, Jerry
See King's X
Gatton, Danny **16**
Gaudreau, Jimmy
See Country Gentlemen, The
Gaugh, "Bud" Floyd, IV
See Sublime
Gavurin, David
See Sundays, The
Gaye, Marvin **4**
Gaynor, Mel
See Simple Minds
Gayol, Rafael "Danny"
See BoDeans
Gayle, Crystal **1**
Geary, Paul
See Extreme
Gee, Rosco
See Traffic
Geffen, David **8**
Geldof, Bob **9**
Genesis **4**
Gentling, Matt
See Archers of Loaf
Gentry, Teddy Wayne
See Alabama
George, Lowell
See Little Feat
George, Rocky
See Suicidal Tendencies
Georges, Bernard
See Throwing Muses
Georgiev, Ivan
See Tuxedomoon
Geraldine Fibbers **21**
Germano, Lisa **18**
Gerrard, Lisa
See Dead Can Dance
Gershwin, George and Ira **11**
GetoBoys, The **11**
Getz, Stan **12**
Giammalvo, Chris
See Madder Rose
Gianni, Angelo
See Treadmill Trackstar
Gibb, Barry
See Bee Gees, The
Gibb, Maurice
See Bee Gees, The
Gibb, Robin
See Bee Gees, The
Gibbons, Beth
See Portishead
Gibbons, Billy
See ZZ Top
Gibbons, Ian
See Kinks, The
Giblin, John
See Simple Minds
Gibson, Debbie **1**
Gibson, Wilf
See Electric Light Orchestra
Gifford, Katharine
See Stereolab
Gifford, Peter
See Midnight Oil
Gift, Roland **3**
Also see Fine Young Cannibals
Gilbert, Gillian
See New Order
Gilbert, Nicole Nicci
See Brownstone
Gilbert, Ronnie
See Weavers, The
Gilbert, Simon
See Suede
Giles, Michael
See King Crimson
Gilkyson, Tony
See X
Gill, Andy
See Gang of Four
Gill, Janis
See Sweethearts of the Rodeo
Gill, Johnny **20**
Gill, Pete
See Motörhead
Gill, Vince **7**
Gillan, Ian
See Deep Purple
Gillespie, Bobby
See Primal Scream
Gillespie, Dizzy **6**
Gilley, Mickey **7**
Gillian, Ian
See Black Sabbath
Gillies, Ben
See Silverchair
Gillingham, Charles
See Counting Crows
Gilmore, Jimmie Dale **11**
Gilmour, David
See Pink Floyd
Gin Blossoms **18**
Gingold, Josef **6**
Ginn, Greg
See Black Flag
Gioia
See Exposé
Gipsy Kings, The **8**
Gittleman, Joe
See Mighty Mighty Bosstones
Glass, Eddie
See Fu Manchu
Glass, Philip **1**
Glasscock, John
See Jethro Tull
Glennie, Jim
See James
Glitter, Gary **19**
Glover, Corey
See Living Colour
Glover, Roger
See Deep Purple
Gobel, Robert
See Kool & the Gang
Godchaux, Donna
See Grateful Dead, The

Godchaux, Keith
See Grateful Dead, The
Goettel, Dwayne Rudolf
See Skinny Puppy
Gogin, Toni
See Sleater-Kinney
Goh, Rex
See Air Supply
Gold, Julie **22**
Golden, William Lee
See Oak Ridge Boys, The
Golding, Lynval
See Specials, The
Goldsmith, William
See Foo Fighters
Goldstein, Jerry
See War
Golson, Benny **21**
Goo Goo Dolls, The **16**
Gooden, Ramone Pee Wee
See Digital Underground
Goodman, Benny **4**
Goodman, Jerry
See Mahavishnu Orchestra
Goodridge, Robin
See Bush
Gordon, Dexter **10**
Gordon, Dwight
See Mighty Clouds of Joy, The
Gordon, Jim
See Traffic
Gordon, Kim
See Sonic Youth
Gordon, Mike
See Phish
Gordon, Nina
See Veruca Salt
Gordy, Berry, Jr. **6**
Gordy, Emory, Jr. **17**
Gore, Martin
See Depeche Mode
Gorham, Scott
See Thin Lizzy
Gorka, John **18**
Gorman, Christopher
See Belly
Gorman, Steve
See Black Crowes, The
Gorman, Thomas
See Belly
Gosling, John
See Kinks, The
Gossard, Stone
See Brad
Also see Pearl Jam
Gott, Larry
See James
Goudreau, Barry
See Boston
Gould, Billy
See Faith No More
Gould, Glenn **9**
Gould, Morton **16**
Goulding, Steve
See Poi Dog Pondering
Gracey, Chad
See Live
Gradney, Ken
See Little Feat
Graffety-Smith, Toby
See Jamiroquai
Graham, Bill **10**
Graham, Glen
See Blind Melon
Graham, Johnny
See Earth, Wind and Fire
Gramm, Lou
See Foreigner
Gramolini, Gary
See Beaver Brown Band, The
Grandmaster Flash **14**
Grant, Amy **7**
Grant, Bob
See The Bad Livers
Grant Lee Buffalo **16**
Grant, Lloyd
See Metallica
Grappelli, Stephane **10**
Grateful Dead, The **5**
Gravatt, Eric
See Weather Report
Graves, Denyce **16**
Gray, Del
See Little Texas
Gray, Ella
See Kronos Quartet
Gray, F. Gary **19**
Gray, James
See Blue Rodeo
Gray, James
See Spearhead
Gray, Luther
See Tsunami
Gray, Tom
See Country Gentlemen, The
Also see Seldom Scene, The
Gray, Walter
See Kronos Quartet
Gray, Wardell
See McKinney's Cotton Pickers
Grebenshikov, Boris **3**
Grech, Rick
See Traffic
Greco, Paul
See Chumbawamba
Green, Al **9**
Green, Benny **17**
Green, Charles
See War
Green, David
See Air Supply
Green Day **16**
Green, Grant **14**
Green, Karl Anthony
See Herman's Hermits
Green, Peter
See Fleetwood Mac
Green, Susaye
See Supremes, The
Green, Willie
See Neville Brothers, The
Greenhalgh, Tom
See Mekons, The
Greenspoon, Jimmy
See Three Dog Night
Greenwood, Al
See Foreigner
Greenwood, Gail
See Belly
Greenwood, Lee **12**
Greer, Jim
See Guided By Voices
Gregg, Paul
See Restless Heart
Gregory, Bryan
See Cramps, The
Gregory, Dave
See XTC
Grey, Charles Wallace
See Aquabats
Griffin, Bob
See BoDeans, The
Griffin, Kevin
See Better Than Ezra
See NRBQ
Griffin, Mark
See MC 900 Ft. Jesus
Griffith, Nanci **3**
Grigg, Chris
See Treadmill Trackstar
Grisman, David **17**
Grohl, Dave
See Nirvana
Grohl, David
See Foo Fighters
Grotberg, Karen
See Jayhawks, The
Groucutt, Kelly
See Electric Light Orchestra
Grove, George
See Kingston Trio, The
Grover, Charlie
See Sponge
Grusin, Dave **7**
Guaraldi, Vince **3**
Guard, Dave
See Kingston Trio, The
Gudmundsdottir, Björk
See Björk
Also see Sugarcubes, The
Guerin, John
See Byrds, The
Guest, Christopher
See Spinal Tap
Guided By Voices **18**
Gunn, Trey
See King Crimson
Guns n' Roses **2**
Gunther, Cornell
See Coasters, The

Guru
See Gang Starr
Guss, Randy
See Toad the Wet Sprocket
Gustafson, Steve
See 10,000 Maniacs
Gut, Grudrun
See Einstürzende Neubauten
Guthrie, Arlo **6**
Guthrie, Robin
See Cocteau Twins, The
Guthrie, Woody **2**
Guy, Billy
See Coasters, The
Guy, Buddy **4**
Gwar **13**
Hacke, Alexander
See Einstürzende Neubauten
Hackett, Bobby **21**
Hackett, Steve
See Genesis
Haden, Charlie **12**
Hadjopulos, Sue
See Simple Minds
Hagar, Regan
See Brad
Hagar, Sammy **21**
Also see Van Halen
Haggard, Merle **2**
Hakim, Omar
See Weather Report
Hakmoun, Hassan **15**
Hale, Simon
See Incognito
Haley, Bill **6**
Haley, Mark
See Kinks, The
Halford, Rob
See Judas Priest
Hall, Daryl
See Hall & Oates
Hall, John S.
See King Missile
Hall, Lance
See Inner Circle
Hall, Randall
See Lynyrd Skynyrd
Hall, Terry
See Specials, The
Hall, Tom T. **4**
Hall, Tony
See Neville Brothers, The
Hall & Oates **6**
Halliday, Toni
See Curve
Halliwell, Geri
See Spice Girls
Hamer, Harry
See Chumbawamba
Hamilton, Frank
See Weavers, The
Hamilton, Katie
See Treadmill Trackstar
Hamilton, Milton
See Third World
Hamilton, Page
See Helmet
Hamilton, Tom
See Aerosmith
Hamilton, Tom
See Aerosmith
Hamlisch, Marvin **1**
Hammer, Jan **21**
Also see Mahavishnu Orchestra
Hammer, M.C. **5**
Hammerstein, Oscar
See Rodgers, Richard
Hammett, Kirk
See Metallica
Hammon, Ron
See War
Hammond, John **6**
Hammond-Hammond, Jeffrey
See Jethro Tull
Hampson, Sharon
See Sharon, Lois & Bram
Hampson, Thomas **12**
Hampton, Lionel **6**
Hancock, Herbie **8**
Handy, W. C. **7**
Hanley, Kay
See Letters to Cleo
Hanley, Steve
See Fall, The
Hanna, Jeff
See Nitty Gritty Dirt Band, The
Hanneman, Jeff
See Slayer
Hannon, Frank
See Tesla
Hannan, Patrick
See Sundays, The
Hansen, Mary
See Stereolab
Hanson **20**
Hanson, Isaac
See Hanson
Hanson, Taylor
See Hanson
Hanson, Zachary
See Hanson
Hardcastle, Paul **20**
Hardin, Eddie
See Spencer Davis Group
Hardin, Tim **18**
Harding, John Wesley **6**
Hardson, Tre "Slimkid"
See Pharcyde, The
Hargrove, Kornell
See Poi Dog Pondering
Hargrove, Roy **15**
Harket, Morten
See A-ha
Harley, Bill **7**
Harper, Ben **17**
Harper, Raymond
See Skatalites, The
Harrell, Andre **16**
Harrell, Lynn **3**
Harrington, Carrie
See Sounds of Blackness
Harrington, David
See Kronos Quartet
Harris, Addie "Micki"
See Shirelles, The
Harris, Damon Otis
See Temptations, The
Harris, Eddie **15**
Harris, Emmylou **4**
Harris, Evelyn
See Sweet Honey in the Rock
Harris, Gerard
See Kool & the Gang
Harris, James
See Echobelly
Harris, Jet
See Shadows, The
Harris, Lee
See Talk Talk
Harris, Mary
See Spearhead
Harris, R. H.
See Soul Stirrers, The
Harris, Steve
See Iron Maiden
Harris, Teddy **22**
Harrison, George **2**
Also see Beatles, The
Harrison, Jerry
See Talking Heads
Harrison, Nigel
See Blondie
Harrison, Richard
See Stereolab
Harry, Deborah **4**
Also see Blondie
Hart, Lorenz
See Rodgers, Richard
Hart, Mark
See Crowded House
Hart, Mickey
See Grateful Dead, The
Hart, Robert
See Bad Company
Hart, Tim
See Steeleye Span
Hartford, John **1**
Hartke, Stephen **5**
Hartley, Matthieu
See Cure, The
Hartman, Bob
See Petra
Hartman, John
See Doobie Brothers, The
Hartnoll, Paul
See Orbital
Hartnoll, Phil
See Orbital
Harvey, Bernard "Touter"
See Inner Circle
Harvey, Philip "Daddae"
See Soul II Soul
Harvey, Polly Jean **11**

Harvie, Iain
See Del Amitri
Harwood, Justin
See Luna
Haseltine, Dan
See Jars of Clay
Hashian
See Boston
Haskell, Gordon
See King Crimson
Haskins, Kevin
See Love and Rockets
Haslinger, Paul
See Tangerine Dream
Hassan, Norman
See UB40
Hatfield, Juliana **12**
Also see Lemonheads, The
Hauser, Tim
See Manhattan Transfer, The
Havens, Richie **11**
Hawes, Dave
See Catherine Wheel
Hawkes, Greg
See Cars, The
Hawkins, Coleman **11**
Hawkins, Erskine **19**
Hawkins, Nick
See Big Audio Dynamite
Hawkins, Roger
See Traffic
Hawkins, Screamin' Jay **8**
Hawkins, Sophie B. **21**
Hawkins, Taylor
See Foo Fighters
Hawkins, Tramaine **17**
Hay, George D. **3**
Hayes, Isaac **10**
Hayes, Roland **13**
Haynes, Gibby
See Butthole Surfers
Haynes, Warren
See Allman Brothers, The
Hays, Lee
See Weavers, The
Hayward, David Justin
See Moody Blues, The
Hayward, Richard
See Little Feat
Headliner
See Arrested Development
Headon, Topper
See Clash, The
Healey, Jeff **4**
Heard, Paul
See M People
Hearn, Kevin
See Barenaked Ladies
Heart **1**
Heaton, Paul
See Beautiful South
Heavy D **10**
Hecker, Robert
See Redd Kross
Hedford, Eric
See Dandy Warhols, The
Hedges, Eddie
See Blessid Union of Souls
Hedges, Michael **3**
Heggie, Will
See Cocteau Twins, The
Heidorn, Mike
See Son Volt
Helfgott, David **19**
Hell, Richard
See Television
Hellerman, Fred
See Weavers, The
Helm, Levon
See Band, The
Also see Nitty Gritty Dirt Band, The
Helmet **15**
Hemingway, Dave
See Beautiful South
Hemmings, Paul
See Lightning Seeds
Henderson, Andy
See Echobelly
Henderson, Billy
See Spinners, The
Henderson, Fletcher **16**
Henderson, Joe **14**
Hendricks, Barbara **10**
Hendrix, Jimi **2**
Henley, Don **3**
Also see Eagles, The
Henrit, Bob
See Kinks, The
Henry, Bill
See Northern Lights
Henry, Joe **18**
Henry, Kent
See Steppenwolf
Henry, Nicholas "Drummie"
See Mystic Revealers
Hensley, Ken
See Uriah Heep
Herdman, Bob
See Audio Adrenaline
Herman, Maureen
See Babes in Toyland
Herman, Tom
See Pere Ubu
Herman, Woody **12**
Herman's Hermits **5**
Herndon, Mark Joel
See Alabama
Herndon, Ty **20**
Herrera, R. J.
See Suicidal Tendencies
Herrmann, Bernard **14**
Herron, Cindy
See En Vogue
Hersh, Kristin
See Throwing Muses
Hester, Paul
See Crowded House
Hetfield, James
See Metallica
Hetson, Greg
See Circle Jerks, The
Hewson, Paul
See U2
Hexum, Nick
See 311
Hiatt, John **8**
Hickman, Johnny
See Cracker
Hicks, Chris
See Restless Heart
Hicks, Sheree
See C + C Music Factory
Hidalgo, David
See Los Lobos
Higgins, Jimmy
See Altan
Highway 101 **4**
Hijbert, Fritz
See Kraftwerk
Hill, Brendan
See Blues Traveler
Hill, Dusty
See ZZ Top
Hill, Faith **18**
Hill, Ian
See Judas Priest
Hill, Lauryn "L"
See Fugees, The
Hill, Scott
See Fu Manchu
Hill, Stuart
See Shudder to Think
Hillage, Steve
See Orb, The
Hillier, Steve
See Dubstar
Hillman, Bones
See Midnight Oil
Hillman, Chris
See Byrds, The
Also see Desert Rose Band, The
Hinderas, Natalie **12**
Hinds, David
See Steel Pulse
Hines, Earl "Fatha" **12**
Hines, Gary
See Sounds of Blackness
Hinojosa, Tish **13**
Hirst, Rob
See Midnight Oil
Hirt, Al **5**
Hitchcock, Robyn **9**
Hitchcock, Russell
See Air Supply
Hodo, David
See Village People, The
Hoenig, Michael
See Tangerine Dream
Hoffman, Guy
See BoDeans, The
Also see Violent Femmes
Hoffman, Kristian
See Congo Norvell

Hoffs, Susanna
See Bangles
Hogan, Mike
See Cranberries, The
Hogan, Noel
See Cranberries, The
Hoke, Jim
See NRBQ
Hole **14**
Holiday, Billie **6**
Holland, Brian
See Holland-Dozier-Holland
Holland, Bryan "Dexter"
See Offspring
Holland, Dave
See Judas Priest
Holland, Eddie
See Holland-Dozier-Holland
Holland, Julian "Jools"
See Squeeze
Holland-Dozier-Holland **5**
Hollis, Mark
See Talk Talk
Holly, Buddy **1**
Holmes, Malcolm
See Orchestral Manoeuvres in the Dark
Holmstrom, Peter
See Dandy Warhols, The
Holt, David Lee
See Mavericks, The
Honeyman, Susie
See Mekons, The
Honeyman-Scott, James
See Pretenders, The
Hood, David
See Traffic
Hook, Peter
See Joy Division
Also see New Order
Hooker, John Lee **1**
Hoon, Shannon
See Blind Melon
Hooper, Nellee
See Soul II Soul
Also see Massive Attack
Hooters **20**
Hootie and the Blowfish **18**
Hope, Gavin
See Nylons, The
Hopkins, Doug
See Gin Blossoms
Hopkins, Lightnin' **13**
Hopwood, Keith
See Herman's Hermits
Horn, Shirley **7**
Horn, Trevor
See Yes
Horne, Lena **11**
Horne, Marilyn **9**
Horner, Jessica
See Less Than Jake
Hornsby, Bruce **3**
Horovitz, Adam
See Beastie Boys, The
Horowitz, Vladimir **1**
Horton, Jeff
See Northern Lights
Horton, Walter **19**
Hossack, Michael
See Doobie Brothers, The
House, Son **11**
House of Pain **14**
Houston, Cissy **6**
Houston, Whitney **8**
Howard, Harlan **15**
Howe, Brian
See Bad Company
Howe, Steve
See Yes
Howell, Porter
See Little Texas
Howlett, Liam
See Prodigy
Howlin' Wolf **6**
H.R.
See Bad Brains
Hubbard, Greg "Hobie"
See Sawyer Brown
Hubbard, Preston
See Fabulous Thunderbirds, The
Also see Roomful of Blues
Huber, Connie
See Chenille Sisters, The
Hudson, Earl
See Bad Brains
Hudson, Garth
See Band, The
Huffman, Doug
See Boston
Hughes, Bruce
See Cracker
Hughes, Glenn
See Black Sabbath
Hughes, Glenn
See Village People, The
Hughes, Leon
See Coasters, The
Human League, The **17**
Humes, Helen **19**
Humperdinck, Engelbert **19**
Humphreys, Paul
See Orchestral Manoeuvres in the Dark
Hunt, Darryl
See Pogues, The
Hunter, Alberta **7**
Hunter, Mark
See James
Hunter, Shepherd "Ben"
See Soundgarden
Hurley, George
See fIREHOSE
Hurst, Ron
See Steppenwolf
Hutchence, Michael
See INXS
Hutchings, Ashley
See Fairport Convention
Also see Steeleye Span
Huth, Todd
See Primus
Hyatt, Aitch
See Specials, The
Hyman, Rob
See Hooters
Hyslop, Kenny
See Simple Minds
Hütter, Ralf
See Kraftwerk
Hutton, Danny
See Three Dog Night
Huxley, Rick
See Dave Clark Five, The
Hyman, Jerry
See Blood, Sweat and Tears
Hynde, Chrissie
See Pretenders, The
Ian, Janis **5**
Ian, Scott
See Anthrax
Ian and Sylvia **18**
Ibbotson, Jimmy
See Nitty Gritty Dirt Band, The
Ibold, Mark
See Pavement
Ice Cube **10**
Also see N.W.A
Ice-T **7**
Idol, Billy **3**
Iglesias, Julio **20**
Earlier sketch in CM **2**
Iha, James
See Smashing Pumpkins
Illsley, John
See Dire Straits
Incognito **16**
Indigo Girls **20**
Earlier sketch in CM **3**
Inez, Mike
See Alice in Chains
Infante, Frank
See Blondie
Ingram, James **11**
Inner Circle **15**
Innes, Andrew
See Primal Scream
Innis, Dave
See Restless Heart
Insane Clown Posse **22**
Interior, Lux
See Cramps, The
INXS **21**
Earlier sketch in CM **2**
Iommi, Tony
See Black Sabbath
Iron Maiden **10**
Irons, Jack
See Red Hot Chili Peppers, The
Isaak, Chris **6**
Isham, Mark **14**
Isles, Bill
See O'Jays, The
Isley, Ernie
See Isley Brothers, The
Isley, Marvin
See Isley Brothers, The

Isley, O'Kelly, Jr.
See Isley Brothers, The
Isley, Ronald
See Isley Brothers, The
Isley, Rudolph
See Isley Brothers, The
Isley Brothers, The **8**
Israel Vibration **21**
Ives, Burl **12**
Ivey, Michael
See Basehead
Ivins, Michael
See Flaming Lips
J.
See White Zombie
J, David
See Love and Rockets
Jabs, Matthias
See Scorpions, The
Jackson, Alan **7**
Jackson, Eddie
See Queensryche
Jackson, Freddie **3**
Jackson, Jackie
See Jacksons, The
Jackson, Janet **16**
Earlier sketch in CM **3**
Jackson, Jermaine
See Jacksons, The
Jackson, Joe **22**
Earlier sketch in CM **4**
Jackson, Karen
See Supremes, The
Jackson, Mahalia **8**
Jackson, Marlon
See Jacksons, The
Jackson, Michael **17**
Earlier sketch in CM **1**
Also see Jacksons, The
Jackson, Millie **14**
Jackson, Milt **15**
Jackson, Pervis
See Spinners , The
Jackson, Randy
See Jacksons, The
Jackson, Tito
See Jacksons, The
Jackson 5, The
See Jacksons, The
Jacksons, The **7**
Jacobs, Christian Richard
See Aquabats
Jacobs, Jeff
See Foreigner
Jacobs, Parker
See Aquabats
Jacobs, Walter
See Little Walter
Jacox, Martin
See Soul Stirrers, The
Jacquet, Illinois **17**
Jade 4U
See Lords of Acid
Jaffee, Rami
See Wallflowers, The
Jagger, Mick **7**
Also see Rolling Stones, The
Jairo T.
See Sepultura
Jalal
See Last Poets
Jam, Jimmy
See Jam, Jimmy, and Terry Lewis
Jam, Jimmy, and Terry Lewis **11**
Jam Master Jay
See Run-D.M.C.
James **12**
James, Alex
See Blur
James, Andrew "Bear"
See Midnight Oil
James, Boney **21**
James, Cheryl
See Salt-N-Pepa
James, David
See Spearhead
James, Doug
See Roomful of Blues
James, Elmore **8**
James, Etta **6**
James, Harry **11**
James, Onieda
See Spearhead
James, Richard
See Aphex Twin
James, Rick **2**
James, Ruby
See Aztec Camera
James, Sylvia
See Aztec Camera
Jamiroquai **21**
Jamison, Le Le
See Spearhead
Jane's Addiction **6**
Janovitz, Bill
See Buffalo Tom
Jansch, Bert
See Pentangle
Jardine, Al
See Beach Boys, The
Jarobi
See Tribe Called Quest, A
Jarre, Jean-Michel **2**
Jarreau, Al **1**
Jarrett, Irwin
See Third World
Jarrett, Keith **1**
Jars of Clay **20**
Jasper, Chris
See Isley Brothers, The
Jay, Miles
See Village People, The
Jayhawks, The **15**
Jayson, Mackie
See Bad Brains
Jazzie B
See Soul II Soul
Jean, Wyclef **22**
Also see Fugees, The
Jeanrenaud, Joan Dutcher
See Kronos Quartet
Jeczalik, Jonathan
See Art of Noise
Jefferson, Blind Lemon **18**
Jefferson Airplane **5**
Jefferson Starship
See Jefferson Airplane
Jenifer, Darryl
See Bad Brains
Jenkins, Barry
See Animals
Jennings, Greg
See Restless Heart
Jennings, Waylon **4**
Jensen, Ingrid **22**
Jerry, Jah
See Skatalites, The
Jessee, Darren
See Ben Folds Five
Jessie, Young
See Coasters, The
Jesus and Mary Chain, The **10**
Jesus Lizard **19**
Jethro Tull **8**
Jett, Joan **3**
Jimenez, Flaco
See Texas Tornados, The
Jimmie's Chicken Shack **22**
Joannou, Chris
See Silverchair
Jobim, Antonio Carlos **19**
Jobson, Edwin
See Jethro Tull
Jodeci **13**
Joel, Billy **12**
Earlier sketch in CM **2**
Johansen, David
See New York Dolls
Johansen, David **7**
Johanson, Jai Johanny
See Allman Brothers, The
Johansson, Glenn
See Echobelly
Johansson, Lars-Olof
See Cardigans
John, Elton **20**
Earlier sketch in CM **3**
Johns, Daniel
See Silverchair
Johnson, Alphonso
See Weather Report
Johnson, Bob
See Steeleye Span
Johnson, Brian
See AC/DC
Johnson, Courtney
See New Grass Revival, The
Johnson, Danny
See Steppenwolf
Johnson, Daryl
See Neville Brothers, The
Johnson, Eric
See Archers of Loaf
Johnson, Eric **19**
Johnson, Gene
See Diamond Rio

Johnson, Gerry
See Steel Pulse
Johnson, James P. **16**
Johnson, Lonnie **17**
Johnson, Matt
See The The
Johnson, Mike
See Dinosaur Jr.
Johnson, Ralph
See Earth, Wind and Fire
Johnson, Robert **6**
Johnson, Scott
See Gin Blossoms
Johnson, Shirley Childres
See Sweet Honey in the Rock
Johnson, Tamara "Taj"
See SWV
Johnston, Bruce
See Beach Boys, The
Johnston, Freedy **20**
Johnston, Howie
See Ventures, The
Johnston, Tom
See Doobie Brothers, The
JoJo
See Jodeci
Jolly, Bill
See Butthole Surfers
Jolson, Al **10**
Jon Spencer Blues Explosion **18**
Jones, Adam
See Tool
Jones, Booker T. **8**
Jones, Brian
See Rolling Stones, The
Jones, Busta
See Gang of Four
Jones, Claude
See McKinney's Cotton Pickers
Jones, Davy
See Monkees, The
Jones, Denise
See Point of Grace
Jones, Elvin **9**
Jones, Geoffrey
See Sounds of Blackness
Jones, George **4**
Jones, Grace **9**
Jones, Hank **15**
Jones, Jamie
See All-4-One
Jones, Jim
See Pere Ubu
Jones, John Paul
See Led Zeppelin
Jones, Kendall
See Fishbone
Jones, Kenny
See Faces, The
Jones, Kenny
See Who, The
Jones, Marshall
See Ohio Players
Jones, Maxine
See En Vogue
Jones, Michael
See Kronos Quartet
Jones, Mic
See Big Audio Dynamite
Also see Clash, The
Jones, Mick
See Foreigner
Jones, Philly Joe **16**
Jones, Quincy **20**
Earlier sketch in CM **2**
Jones, Rickie Lee **4**
Jones, Robert "Kuumba"
See Ohio Players
Jones, Ronald
See Flaming Lips
Jones, Sandra "Puma"
See Black Uhuru
Jones, Simon
See Verve, The
Jones, Spike **5**
Jones, Stacy
See Veruca Salt
Jones, Stacy
See Letters to Cleo
Jones, Steve
See Sex Pistols, The
Jones, Terry
See Point of Grace
Jones, Thad **19**
Jones, Tom **11**
Jones, Will "Dub"
See Coasters, The
Joplin, Janis **3**
Joplin, Scott **10**
Jordan, Lonnie
See War
Jordan, Louis **11**
Jordan, Stanley **1**
Jorgensor, John
See Desert Rose Band, The
Joseph-I, Israel
See Bad Brains
Jourgensen, Al
See Ministry
Journey **21**
Joyce, Mike
See Buzzcocks, The
Also see Smiths, The
Joy Division **19**
Judas Priest **10**
Judd, Naomi
See Judds, The
Judd, Wynonna
See Judds, The
Also see Wynonna
Judds, The **2**
Juhlin, Dag
See Poi Dog Pondering
Jukebox
See Geto Boys, The
Jungle DJ "Towa" Towa
See Deee-lite
Jurado, Jeanette
See Exposé
Kabongo, Sabine
See Zap Mama
Kahlil, Aisha
See Sweet Honey in the Rock
Kain, Gylan
See Last Poets
Kakoulli, Harry
See Squeeze
Kalligan, Dick
See Blood, Sweat and Tears
Kaminski, Mik
See Electric Light Orchestra
Kamomiya, Ryo
See Pizzicato Five
Kanal, Tony
See No Doubt
Kanawa, Kiri Te
See Te Kanawa, Kiri
Kane, Arthur
See New York Dolls
Kane, Big Daddy **7**
Kane, Nick
See Mavericks, The
Kannberg, Scott
See Pavement
Kanter, Paul
See Jefferson Airplane
Karajan, Herbert von
See von Karajan, Herbert
Karges, Murphy
See Sugar Ray
Kath, Terry
See Chicago
Kato, Nash
See Urge Overkill
Katz, Simon
See Jamiroquai
Katz, Steve
See Blood, Sweat and Tears
Kaukonen, Jorma
See Jefferson Airplane
Kavanagh, Chris
See Big Audio Dynamite
Kay, Jason
See Jamiroquai
Kay, John
See Steppenwolf
Kaye, Carol **22**
Kaye, Tony
See Yes
Kay Gee
See Naughty by Nature
K-Ci
See Jodeci
Kean, Martin
See Stereolab
Keane, Sean
See Chieftains, The
Kee, John P. **15**
Keelor, Greg
See Blue Rodeo
Keenan, Maynard James
See Tool
Keene, Barry
See Spirit

Keifer, Tom
See Cinderella
Keitaro
See Pizzicato Five
Keith, Jeff
See Tesla
Keith, Toby **17**
Kelly, Charlotte
See Soul II Soul
Kelly, Kevin
See Byrds, The
Kelly, Rashaan
See US3
Kemp, Rick
See Steeleye Span
Kendrick, David
See Devo
Kendricks, Eddie
See Temptations, The
Kennedy, Delious
See All-4-One
Kennedy, Frankie
See Altan
Kennedy, Nigel **8**
Kenner, Doris
See Shirelles, The
Kenny, Clare
See Aztec Camera
Kenny G **14**
Kenton, Stan **21**
Kentucky Headhunters, The **5**
Kern, Jerome **13**
Kerr, Jim
See Simple Minds
Kershaw, Sammy **15**
Ketchum, Hal **14**
Key, Cevin
See Skinny Puppy
Keyser, Alex
See Echobelly
Khan, Chaka **19**
Earlier sketch in CM **9**
Khan, Nusrat Fateh Ali **13**
Khan, Praga
See Lords of Acid
Kibble, Mark
See Take 6
Kibby, Walter
See Fishbone
Kick, Johnny
See Madder Rose
Kid 'n Play **5**
Kidjo, Anjelique **17**
Kiedis, Anthony
See Red Hot Chili Peppers, The
Kilbey, Steve
See Church, The
Killian, Tim
See Kronos Quartet
Kimball, Jennifer
See Story, The
Kimball, Jim
See Jesus Lizard
Kimble, Paul
See Grant Lee Buffalo
Kincaid, Jan
See Brand New Heavies, The
Kinchla, Chan
See Blues Traveler
King, Albert **2**
King, B.B. **1**
King, Andy
See Hooters
King, Ben E. **7**
King, Bob
See Soul Stirrers, The
King, Carole **6**
King, Ed
See Lynyrd Skynyrd
King, Freddy **17**
King, Jon
See Gang of Four
King, Kerry
See Slayer
King, Philip
See Lush
King Ad-Rock
See Beastie Boys, The
King Crimson **17**
King Missile **22**
Kingston Trio, The **9**
King's X **7**
Kinks, The **15**
Kinney, Sean
See Alice in Chains
Kirk, Rahsaan Roland **6**
Kirk, Richard H.
See Cabaret Voltaire
Kirke, Simon
See Bad Company
Kirkwood, Cris
See Meat Puppets, The
Kirkwood, Curt
See Meat Puppets, The
Kirtley, Peter
See Pentangle
Kirwan, Danny
See Fleetwood Mac
Kiss **5**
Kisser, Andreas
See Sepultura
Kissin, Evgeny **6**
Kitaro **1**
Kitsos, Nick
See BoDeans
Kitt, Eartha **9**
Klein, Jon
See Siouxsie and the Banshees
Klezmatics, The **18**
Klugh, Earl **10**
Kmatsu, Bravo
See Pizzicato Five
KMFDM **18**
Knight, Gladys **1**
Knight, Jon
See New Kids on the Block
Knight, Jordan
See New Kids on the Block
Knight, Larry
See Spirit
Knight, Peter
See Steeleye Span
Knight, Suge **15**
Knopfler, David
See Dire Straits
Knopfler, Mark **3**
See Dire Straits
Know, Dr.
See Bad Brains
Knowledge
See Digable Planets
Knox, Nick
See Cramps, The
Knudsen, Keith
See Doobie Brothers, The
Konietzko, Sascha
See KMFDM
Konishi, Yasuharu
See Pizzicato Five
Konto, Skip
See Three Dog Night
Kool & the Gang **13**
Kool Moe Dee **9**
Kooper, Al
See Blood, Sweat and Tears
Koppelman, Charles **14**
Koppes, Peter
See Church, The
Korn **20**
Kottke, Leo **13**
Kotzen, Richie
See Poison
Kowalczyk, Ed
See Live
Kraftwerk **9**
Krakauer, David
See Klezmatics, The
Kramer, Joey
See Aerosmith
Kramer, Wayne
See MC5, The
Krasnow, Bob **15**
Krause, Bernie
See Weavers, The
Krauss, Alison **10**
Krauss, Scott
See Pere Ubu
Kravitz, Lenny **5**
Krayzie Bone
See Bone Thugs-N-Harmony
Krazy Drayz
See Das EFX
Kretz, Eric
See Stone Temple Pilots
Kreutzman, Bill
See Grateful Dead, The
Krieger, Robert
See Doors, The
Kriesel, Greg
See Offspring
Kris Kross **11**
Kristofferson, Kris **4**
Krizan, Anthony
See Spin Doctors
Kronos Quartet **5**

Kropp, Mike
See Northern Lights
KRS-One **8**
Krupa, Gene **13**
Krusen, Dave
See Pearl Jam
Kulak, Eddie
See Aztec Camera
Kulick, Bruce
See Kiss
Kunkel, Bruce
See Nitty Gritty Dirt Band, The
Kunzel, Erich **17**
Kurdziel, Eddie
See Redd Kross
Kuti, Fela **7**
LaBar, Jeff
See Cinderella
LaBelle, Patti **8**
Lack, Steve
See Veruca Salt
Lady Miss Kier
See Deee-lite
Ladybug
See Digable Planets
Ladysmith Black Mambazo **1**
Lafalce, Mark
See Mekons, The
Lagerburg, Bengt
See Cardigans, The
Laine, Cleo **10**
Laine, Denny
See Moody Blues, The
Laird, Rick
See Mahavishnu Orchestra
Lake, Greg
See Emerson, Lake & Palmer/Powell
Also see King Crimson
LaLonde, Larry "Ler"
See Primus
Lally, Joe
See Fugazi
Lamble, Martin
See Fairport Convention
Lamm, Robert
See Chicago
Landreth, Sonny **16**
Lane, Jani
See Warrant
Lane, Jay
See Primus
Lane, Ronnie
See Faces, The
lang, k. d. **4**
Langan, Gary
See Art of Noise
Langford, Jon
See Mekons, The
Langley, John
See Mekons, The
Langlois, Paul
See Tragically Hip, The
Langston, Leslie
See Throwing Muses
Lanier, Allen
See Blue Oyster Cult
Lanois, Daniel **8**
Larkin, Patty **9**
Larson, Chad Albert
See Aquabats
Larson, Nathan
See Shudder to Think
Last Poets **21**
Laswell, Bill **14**
Lataille, Rich
See Roomful of Blues
Lateef, Yusef **16**
Latimer, Andrew
See Camel
Laughner, Peter
See Pere Ubu
Lauper, Cyndi **11**
Laurence, Lynda
See Supremes, The
Lavin, Christine **6**
Lavis, Gilson
See Squeeze
Lawlor, Feargal
See Cranberries, The
Lawrence, Tracy **11**
Lawry, John
See Petra
Laws, Roland
See Earth, Wind and Fire
Lawson, Doyle
See Country Gentlemen, The
Layzie Bone
See Bone Thugs-N-Harmony
Leadbelly **6**
Leadon, Bernie
See Eagles, The
Also see Nitty Gritty Dirt Band, The
Leary, Paul
See Butthole Surfers
Leavell, Chuck
See Allman Brothers, The
LeBon, Simon
See Duran Duran
Leckenby, Derek "Lek"
See Herman's Hermits
Ledbetter, Huddie
See Leadbelly
LeDoux, Chris **12**
Led Zeppelin **1**
Lee, Beverly
See Shirelles, The
Lee, Brenda **5**
Lee, Buddy
See Less Than Jake
Lee, Geddy
See Rush
Lee, Peggy **8**
Lee, Pete
See Gwar
Lee, Sara
See Gang of Four
Lee, Tommy
See Mötley Crüe
Lee, Tony
See Treadmill Trackstar
Leeb, Bill
See Front Line Assembly
Leen, Bill
See Gin Blossoms
Leese, Howard
See Heart
Legg, Adrian **17**
Lehrer, Tom **7**
Leiber and Stoller **14**
Leiber, Jerry
See Leiber and Stoller
Lemmy
See Motörhead
Lemonheads, The **12**
Lemper, Ute **14**
Le Mystère des VoixBulgares
See Bulgarian State Female Vocal Choir, The
Lenear, Kevin
See Mighty Mighty Bosstones
Lenners, Rudy
See Scorpions, The
Lennon, John **9**
Also see Beatles, The
Lennon, Julian **2**
Lennox, Annie **18**
Also see Eurythmics
Leonard, Glenn
See Temptations, The
Lerner, Alan Jay
See Lerner and Loewe
Lerner and Loewe **13**
Lesh, Phil
See Grateful Dead, The
Leslie, Chris
See Fairport Convention
Lessard, Stefan
See Dave Matthews Band
Less Than Jake **22**
Letters to Cleo **22**
Levene, Keith
See Clash, The
Levert, Eddie
See O'Jays, The
Levin, Tony
See King Crimson
Levine, James **8**
Levy, Andrew
See Brand New Heavies, The
Levy, Ron
See Roomful of Blues
Lewis, Huey **9**
Lewis, Ian
See Inner Circle
Lewis, Jerry Lee **2**
Lewis, Marcia
See Soul II Soul
Lewis, Otis
See Fabulous Thunderbirds, The
Lewis, Peter
See Moby Grape
Lewis, Ramsey **14**

Lewis, Roger
See Inner Circle
Lewis, Roy
See Kronos Quartet
Lewis, Samuel K.
See Five Blind Boys of Alabama
Lewis, Terry
See Jam, Jimmy, and Terry Lewis
Lhote, Morgan
See Stereolab
Li Puma, Tommy **18**
Libbea, Gene
See Nashville Bluegrass Band
Liberace **9**
Licht, David
See Klezmatics, The
Lifeson, Alex
See Rush
Lightfoot, Gordon **3**
Lightning Seeds **21**
Ligon, Willie Joe
See Mighty Clouds of Joy, The
Liles, Brent
See Social Distortion
Lilienstein, Lois
See Sharon, Lois & Bram
Lilker, Dan
See Anthrax
Lilley, John
See Hooters
Lillywhite, Steve **13**
Lincoln, Abbey **9**
Lindley, David **2**
Lindes, Hal
See Dire Straits
Linna, Miriam
See Cramps, The
Linnell, John
See They Might Be Giants
Lipsius, Fred
See Blood, Sweat and Tears
Little, Keith
See Country Gentlemen, The
Little Feat **4**
Little Richard **1**
Little Texas **14**
Little Walter **14**
Littrell, Brian
See Backstreet Boys
Live **14**
Living Colour **7**
Llanas, Sam
See BoDeans
Llanas, Sammy
See BoDeans, The
L.L. Cool J. **5**
Lloyd, Charles **22**
Lloyd, Richard
See Television
Lloyd Webber, Andrew **6**
Locke, John
See Spirit
Locking, Brian
See Shadows, The
Lockwood, Robert, Jr. **10**
Lodge, John
See Moody Blues, The
Loewe, Frederick
See Lerner and Loewe
Loggins, Kenny **20**
Earlier sketch in CM **3**
Lombardo, Dave
See Slayer
London, Frank
See Klezmatics, The
Lopes, Lisa "Left Eye"
See TLC
Lopez, Israel "Cachao" **14**
Lord, Jon
See Deep Purple
Lords of Acid **20**
Loria, Steve
See Spirit
Lorson, Mary
See Madder Rose
Los Lobos **2**
Los Reyes
See Gipsy Kings, The
Loughnane, Lee
See Chicago
Louison, Steve
See Massive Attack
Louris, Gary
See Jayhawks, The
Louvin Brothers, The **12**
Louvin, Charlie
See Louvin Brothers, The
Louvin, Ira
See Louvin Brothers, The
Lovano, Joe **13**
Love and Rockets **15**
Love, Courtney
See Hole
Love, Gerry
See Teenage Fanclub
Love, Laura **20**
Love, Mike
See Beach Boys, The
Loveless, Patty **21**
Earlier sketch in CM **5**
Lovering, David
See Cracker
Also see Pixies, The
Love Spit Love **21**
Lovett, Lyle **5**
Lowe, Chris
See Pet Shop Boys
Lowe, Nick **6**
Lowell, Charlie
See Jars of Clay
Lowery, David
See Cracker
Lozano, Conrad
See Los Lobos
L7 **12**
Lucas, Trevor
See Fairport Convention
Luccketta, Troy
See Tesla
Lucia, Paco de
See de Lucia, Paco
Luciano, Felipe
See Last Poets
Luke
See Campbell, Luther
Lukin, Matt
See Mudhoney
Luna **18**
Lupo, Pat
See Beaver Brown Band, The
LuPone, Patti **8**
Lush **13**
Lydon, John **9**
Also see Sex Pistols, The
Lynch, Dermot
See Dog's Eye View
Lynch, George
See Dokken
Lyngstad, Anni-Frid
See Abba
Lynn, Loretta **2**
Lynne, Jeff **5**
Also see Electric Light Orchestra
Lynne, Shelby **5**
Lynott, Phil
See Thin Lizzy
Lynyrd Skynyrd **9**
Lyons, Leanne "Lelee"
See SWV
Ma, Yo-Yo **2**
MacColl, Kirsty **12**
MacDonald, Eddie
See Alarm
Macfarlane, Lora
See Sleater-Kinney
MacGowan, Shane
MacIsaac, Ashley **21**
MacKaye, Ian
See Fugazi
Mack Daddy
See Kris Kross
Mackey, Steve
See Pulp
MacNeil, Michael
See Simple Minds
MacPherson, Jim
See Breeders
Madan, Sonya Aurora
See Echobelly
Madder Rose **17**
Madonna **16**
Earlier sketch in CM **4**
Mael, Ron
See Sparks
Mael, Russell
See Sparks
Maginnis, Tom
See Buffalo Tom
Magnie, John
See Subdudes, The
Magoogan, Wesley
See English Beat, The
Maher, John
See Buzzcocks, The

Mahoney, Tim
See 311
Maida, Raine
See Our Lady Peace
Maimone, Tony
See Pere Ubu
Makeba, Miriam **8**
Malcolm, Hugh
See Skatalites, The
Malcolm, Joy
See Incognito
Male, Johnny
See Republica
Malins, Mike
See Goo Goo Dolls, The
Malkmus, Stephen
See Pavement
Malley, Matt
See Counting Crows
Mallinder, Stephen
See Cabaret Voltaire
Malo, Raul
See Mavericks, The
Malone, Tom
See Blood, Sweat and Tears
Malone, Tommy
See Subdudes, The
Mamas and the Papas **21**
Mancini, Henry **20**
Earlier sketch in CM **1**
Mandrell, Barbara **4**
Maness, J. D.
See Desert Rose Band, The
Manhattan Transfer, The **8**
Manilow, Barry **2**
Mann, Aimee **22**
Mann, Herbie **16**
Man or Astroman? **21**
Manuel, Richard
See Band, The
Manzarek, Ray
See Doors, The
March, Kevin
See Shudder to Think
Marie, Buffy Sainte
See Sainte-Marie, Buffy
Marilyn Manson **18**
Marini, Lou, Jr.
See Blood, Sweat and Tears
Marley, Bob **3**
Marley, Rita **10**
Marley, Ziggy **3**
Marr, Johnny
See Smiths, The
Also see The The
Marriner, Neville
Mars, Chris
See Replacements, The
Mars, Derron
See Less Than Jake
Mars, Mick
See Mötley Crüe
Marsalis, Branford **10**
Marsalis, Ellis **13**
Marsalis, Wynton **20**
Earlier sketch in CM **6**
Marsh, Ian Craig
See Human League, The
Marshal, Cornel
See Third World
Martin, Barbara
See Supremes, The
Martin, Christopher
See Kid 'n Play
Martin, Dean **1**
Martin, George **6**
Martin, Greg
See Kentucky Headhunters, The
Martin, Jim
See Faith No More
Martin, Jimmy **5**
Also see Osborne Brothers, The
Martin, Johnney
See Mighty Clouds of Joy, The
Martin, Phonso
See Steel Pulse
Martin, Sennie
See Kool & the Gang
Martin, Tony
See Black Sabbath
Martinez, Anthony
See Black Flag
Martinez, S. A.
See 311
Martino, Pat **17**
Marvin, Hank B.
See Shadows, The
Marx, Richard **21**
Earlier sketch in CM **3**
Mascis, J
See Dinosaur Jr.
Masdea, Jim
See Boston
Masekela, Hugh **7**
Maseo, Baby Huey
See De La Soul
Mason, Dave
See Traffic
Mason, Nick
See Pink Floyd
Mason, Steve
See Jars of Clay
Mason, Terry
See Joy Division
Masse, Laurel
See Manhattan Transfer, The
Massey, Bobby
See O'Jays, The
Massive Attack **17**
Mastelotto, Pat
See King Crimson
Master P **22**
Masur, Kurt **11**
Material
See Laswell, Bill
Mathis, Johnny **2**
Mathus, Jim
See Squirrel Nut Zippers
Matlock, Glen
See Sex Pistols, The
Mattacks, Dave
See Fairport Convention
Mattea, Kathy **5**
Matthews, Chris
See Shudder to Think
Matthews, Dave
See Dave Matthews Band
Matthews, Eric **22**
Matthews, Ian
See Fairport Convention
Matthews Band, Dave
See Dave Matthews Band
Matthews, Quinn
See Butthole Surfers
Matthews, Scott
See Butthole Surfers
Maunick, Bluey
See Incognito
Maurer, John
See Social Distortion
Mavericks, The **15**
Maxwell **22**
Maxwell, Charmayne
See Brownstone
Maxwell, Tom
See Squirrel Nut Zippers
May, Brian
See Queen
Mayall, John **7**
Mayfield, Curtis **8**
Mays, Odeen, Jr.
See Kool & the Gang
Mazelle, Kym
See Soul II Soul
Mazibuko, Abednigo
See Ladysmith Black Mambazo
Mazibuko, Albert
See Ladysmith Black Mambazo
Mazzola, Joey
See Sponge
Mazzy Star **17**
MCA
See Yauch, Adam
McAloon, Martin
See Prefab Sprout
McAloon, Paddy
See Prefab Sprout
McArthur, Keith
See Spearhead
McBrain, Nicko
See Iron Maiden
MCBreed **17**
McBride, Christian **17**
McBride, Martina **14**
McCabe, Nick
See Verve, The
McCabe, Zia
See Dandy Warhols, The
McCall, Renee
See Sounds of Blackness
McCarrick, Martin
See Siouxsie and the Banshees

McCarroll, Tony
See Oasis
McCartney, Paul **4**
Also see Beatles, The
McCarty, Jim
See Yardbirds, The
MC Clever
See Digital Underground
McCary, Michael S.
See Boyz II Men
McClinton, Delbert **14**
McCluskey, Andy
See Orchestral Manoeuvres in the Dark
McCollum, Rick
See Afghan Whigs
McConnell, Page
See Phish
McCook, Tommy
See Skatalites, The
McCoury, Del **15**
McCowin, Michael
See Mighty Clouds of Joy, The
McCoy, Neal **15**
McCracken, Chet
See Doobie Brothers, The
McCready, Mike
See Pearl Jam
McCready, Mindy **22**
McCulloch, Andrew
See King Crimson
McCullough, Danny
See Animals
McD, Jimmy
See Jimmie's Chicken Shack
McDaniels, Darryl "D"
See Run-D.M.C.
McDermott, Brian
See Del Amitri
McDonald, Barbara Kooyman
See Timbuk 3
McDonald, Ian
See Foreigner
Also see King Crimson
McDonald, Jeff
See Redd Kross
McDonald, Michael
See Doobie Brothers, The
McDonald, Pat
See Timbuk 3
McDonald, Steven
See Redd Kross
McDorman, Joe
See Statler Brothers, The
McDowell, Hugh
See Electric Light Orchestra
McDowell, Mississippi Fred **16**
McEntire, Reba **11**
MC Eric
See Technotronic
McEuen, John
See Nitty Gritty Dirt Band, The
McFarlane, Elaine
See Mamas and the Papas
McFee, John
See Doobie Brothers, The
McFerrin, Bobby **3**
MC5, The **9**
McGee, Brian
See Simple Minds
McGee, Jerry
See Ventures, The
McGeoch, John
See Siouxsie and theBanshees
McGinley, Raymond
See Teenage Fanclub
McGinniss, Will
See Audio Adrenaline
McGrath, Mark
See Sugar Ray
McGraw, Tim **17**
McGuigan, Paul
See Oasis
McGuinn, Jim
See McGuinn, Roger
McGuinn, Roger
See Byrds, The
M.C. Hammer
See Hammer, M.C.
McGuire, Mike
See Shenandoah
McIntosh, Robbie
See Pretenders, The
McIntyre, Joe
See New Kids on the Block
McJohn, Goldy
See Steppenwolf
McKagan, Duff
See Guns n' Roses
McKay, Al
See Earth, Wind and Fire
McKay, John
See Siouxsie and the Banshees
McKean, Michael
See Spinal Tap
McKee, Maria **11**
McKeehan, Toby
See dc Talk
McKenna, Greg
See Letters to Cleo
McKenzie, Derrick
See Jamiroquai
McKenzie, Scott
See Mamas and the Papas
McKernarn, Ron "Pigpen"
See Grateful Dead, The
McKinney, William
See McKinney's Cotton Pickers
McKinney's Cotton Pickers **16**
McKnight, Brian **22**
McKnight, Claude V. III
See Take 6
McLachlan, Sarah **12**
McLagan, Ian
See Faces, The
McLaughlin, John **12**
Also see Mahavishnu Orchestra
McLean, A. J.
See Backstreet Boys
McLean, Don **7**
McLennan, Grant **21**
McLeod, Rory
See Roomful of Blues
MC Lyte **8**
McLoughlin, Jon
See Del Amitri
McMeel, Mickey
See Three Dog Night
McMurtry, James **10**
McNabb, Travis
See Better Than Ezra
McNair, Sylvia **15**
McNeilly, Mac
See Jesus Lizard
MC 900 Ft. Jesus **16**
McPartland, Marian **15**
McQuillar, Shawn
See Kool & the Gang
McRae, Carmen **9**
M.C. Ren
See N.W.A.
McReynolds, Jesse
See McReynolds, Jim and Jesse
McReynolds, Jim
See McReynolds, Jim and Jesse
McReynolds, Jim and Jesse **12**
MC Serch **10**
McShane, Ronnie
See Chieftains, The
McShee, Jacqui
See Pentangle
McTell, Blind Willie **17**
McVie, Christine
See Fleetwood Mac
McVie, John
See Fleetwood Mac
Mdletshe, Geophrey
See Ladysmith Black Mambazo
Meat Loaf **12**
Meat Puppets, The **13**
Medley, Bill **3**
Medlock, James
See Soul Stirrers, The
Meehan, Tony
See Shadows, The
Megadeth **9**
Mehta, Zubin **11**
Meine, Klaus
See Scorpions, The
Meisner, Randy
See Eagles, The
Mekons, The **15**
Melanie **12**
Melax, Einar
See Sugarcubes, The
Mellencamp, John **20**
Earlier sketch in CM **2**
Melvins **21**
Mendel, Nate
See Foo Fighters
Mengede, Peter
See Helmet
Menken, Alan **10**
Menuhin, Yehudi **11**
Menza, Nick
See Megadeth

Mercer, Johnny **13**
Merchant, Natalie
See 10,000 Maniacs
Mercier, Peadar
See Chieftains, The
Mercury, Freddie
See Queen
Mertens, Paul
See Poi Dog Pondering
Mesaros, Michael
See Smithereens, The
Metallica **7**
Meters, The **14**
Methembu, Russel
See Ladysmith Black Mambazo
Metheny, Pat **2**
Meyer, Eric
See Charm Farm
Meyers, Augie
See Texas Tornados, The
Mhaonaigh, Mairead Ni
See Altan
Michael, George **9**
Michaels, Bret
See Poison
Michel, Prakazrel "Pras"
See Fugees, The
Middlebrook, Ralph "Pee Wee"
See Ohio Players
Midler, Bette **8**
Midnight Oil **11**
Midori **7**
Mighty Clouds of Joy, The **17**
Mighty Mighty Bosstones **20**
Mike & the Mechanics **17**
Mike D
See BeastieBoys, The
Mikens, Dennis
See Smithereens, The
Mikens, Robert
See Kool & the Gang
Milchem, Glenn
See Blue Rodeo
Miles, Chris
See Northern Lights
Miles, Richard
See Soul Stirrers, The
Miles, Ron **22**
Millar, Deborah
See Massive Attack
Miller, Charles
See War
Miller, Glenn **6**
Miller, Jacob "Killer" Miller
See Inner Circle
Miller, Jerry
See Moby Grape
Miller, Mark
See Sawyer Brown
Miller, Mitch **11**
Miller, Rice
See Williamson, Sonny Boy
Miller, Roger **4**
Miller, Steve **2**
Milli Vanilli **4**
Mills Brothers, The **14**
Mills, Donald
See Mills Brothers, The
Mills, Fred
See Canadian Brass, The
Mills, Harry
See Mills Brothers, The
Mills, Herbert
See Mills Brothers, The
Mills, John, Jr.
See Mills Brothers, The
Mills, John, Sr.
See Mills Brothers, The
Mills, Sidney
See Steel Pulse
Mills, Stephanie **21**
Milsap, Ronnie **2**
Mingus, Charles **9**
Ministry **10**
Miss Kier Kirby
See Lady Miss Kier
Mitchell, Alex
See Curve
Mitchell, John
See Asleep at the Wheel
Mitchell, Joni **17**
Earlier sketch in CM **2**
Mitchell, Keith
See Mazzy Star
Mitchell, Mitch
See Guided By Voices
Mittoo, Jackie
See Skatalites, The
Mize, Ben
See Counting Crows
Mizell, Jay
See Run-D.M.C.
Moby **17**
Moby Grape **12**
Modeliste, Joseph "Zigaboo"
See Meters, The
Moffatt, Katy **18**
Moginie, Jim
See Midnight Oil
Mohr, Todd
See Big Head Todd and the Monsters
Mo', Keb' **21**
Molloy, Matt
See Chieftains, The
Moloney, Paddy
See Chieftains, The
Monarch, Michael
See Steppenwolf
Money B
See Digital Underground
Money, Eddie **16**
Monk, Meredith **1**
Monk, Thelonious **6**
Monkees, The **7**
Monroe, Bill **1**
Montand, Yves **12**
Montenegro, Hugo **18**
Montgomery, John Michael **14**
Montgomery, Wes **3**
Monti, Steve
See Curve
Montoya, Craig
See Everclear
Montrose, Ronnie **22**
Moody Blues, The **18**
Moon, Keith
See Who, The
Mooney, Tim
See American Music Club
Moore, Alan
See Judas Priest
Moore, Angelo
See Fishbone
Moore, Chante **21**
Moore, Johnny "Dizzy"
See Skatalites, The
Moore, LeRoi
See Dave Matthews Band
Moore, Melba **7**
Moore, Sam
See Sam and Dave
Moore, Thurston
See Sonic Youth
Morand, Grace
See Chenille Sisters, The
Moraz, Patrick
See Moody Blues, The
Also see Yes
Moreira, Airto
See Weather Report
Morello, Tom
See Rage Against the Machine
Moreno, Chino
See Deftones
Moreve, Rushton
See Steppenwolf
Morgan, Frank **9**
Morgan, Lorrie **10**
Morley, Pat
See Soul Asylum
Morphine **16**
Morricone, Ennio **15**
Morris, Keith
See Circle Jerks, The
Morris, Kenny
See Siouxsie and the Banshees
Morris, Nate
See Boyz II Men
Morris, Stephen
See Joy Division
Also see New Order
Also see Pogues, The
Morris, Wanya
See Boyz II Men
Morrison, Bram
See Sharon, Lois & Bram
Morrison, Claude
See Nylons, The
Morrison, Jim **3**
Also see Doors, The
Morrison, Sterling
See Velvet Underground, The

Morrison, Van **3**
Morrissett, Paul
See Klezmatics, The
Morrissey **10**
Also see Smiths, The
Morrissey, Bill **12**
Morrissey, Steven Patrick
See Morrissey
Morton, Everett
See English Beat, The
Morton, Jelly Roll **7**
Morvan, Fab
See Milli Vanilli
Mosbaugh, Garth
See Nylons, The
Mosely, Chuck
See Faith No More
Moser, Scott "Cactus"
See Highway 101
Mosher, Ken
See Squirrel Nut Zippers
Mosley, Bob
See Moby Grape
Mothersbaugh, Bob
See Devo
Mothersbaugh, Mark
See Devo
Mouzon, Alphonse
See Weather Report
Moyse, David
See Air Supply
Mötley Crüe **1**
Motörhead **10**
Motta, Danny
See Roomful of Blues
Mould, Bob **10**
Moulding, Colin
See XTC
Mounfield, Gary
See Stone Roses, The
Mouquet, Eric
See Deep Forest
Mouskouri, Nana **12**
Moyet, Alison **12**
M People **15**
Mr. Dalvin
See Jodeci
Mudhoney **16**
Mueller, Karl
See Soul Asylum
Muir, Jamie
See King Crimson
Muir, Mike
See Suicidal Tendencies
Muldaur, Maria **18**
Mulholland, Dave
See Aztec Camera
Mullen, Larry, Jr.
See U2
Mullen, Mary
See Congo Norvell
Mulligan, Gerry **16**
Murcia, Billy
See New York Dolls
Murdock, Roger
See King Missile
Murph
See Dinosaur Jr.
Murphy, Brigid
See Poi Dog Pondering
Murphy, Dan
See Soul Asylum
Murphy, Peter **22**
Murphey, Michael Martin **9**
Murray, Anne **4**
Murray, Dave
See Iron Maiden
Murray, Dee
See Spencer Davis Group
Mushroom
See Massive Attack
Musselwhite, Charlie **13**
Mustaine, Dave
See Megadeth
Also see Metallica
Mwelase, Jabulane
See Ladysmith Black Mambazo
Mydland, Brent
See Grateful Dead, The
Myers, Alan
See Devo
Myles, Alannah **4**
Mystic Revealers **16**
Nadirah
See Arrested Development
Nagler, Eric **8**
Najee **21**
Nakamura, Tetsuya "Tex"
See War
Nakatami, Michie
See Shonen Knife
Narcizo, David
See Throwing Muses
Nascimento, Milton **6**
Nashville Bluegrass Band **14**
Nastanovich, Bob
See Pavement
Naughty by Nature **11**
Navarro, David
See Jane's Addiction
Nawasadio, Sylvie
See Zap Mama
N'Dour, Youssou **6**
Ndegéocello, Me'Shell **18**
Ndugu
See Weather Report
Near, Holly **1**
Neel, Johnny
See Allman Brothers, The
Negron, Chuck
See Three Dog Night
Neil, Chris
See Less Than Jake
Neil, Vince
See Mötley Crüe
Nelson, David
See Last Poets
Nelson, Errol
See Black Uhuru
Nelson, Rick **2**
Nelson, Shara
See Massive Attack
Nelson, Willie **11**
Earlier sketch in CM **1**
Nesbitt, John
See McKinney's Cotton Pickers
Nesmith, Mike
See Monkees, The
Ness, Mike
See Social Distortion
Neufville, Renee
See Zhane
Neumann, Kurt
See BoDeans
Nevarez, Alfred
See All-4-One
Neville, Aaron **5**
Also see Neville Brothers, The
Neville, Art
See Meters, The
Also see Neville Brothers, The
Neville, Charles
See Neville Brothers, The
Neville, Cyril
See Meters, The
Also see Neville Brothers, The
Neville Brothers, The **4**
Nevin, Brian
See Big Head Todd and the Monsters
New Grass Revival, The **4**
New Kids on the Block **3**
Newman, Randy **4**
Newmann, Kurt
See BoDeans, The
New Order **11**
New Rhythm and Blues Quartet
See NRBQ
Newson, Arlene
See Poi Dog Pondering
Newton, Paul
See Uriah Heep
Newton, Wayne **2**
Newton-Davis, Billy
See Nylons, The
Newton-John, Olivia **8**
New York Dolls **20**
Nibbs, Lloyd
See Skatalites, The
Nicholls, Geoff
See Black Sabbath
Nichols, Todd
See Toad the Wet Sprocket
Nicks, Stevie **2**
Also see Fleetwood Mac
Nico
See Velvet Underground, The
Nicol, Simon
See Fairport Convention
Nicolette
See Massive Attack
Nielsen, Rick
See Cheap Trick
Nilija, Robert
See Last Poets
Nilsson **10**

Nilsson, Harry
See Nilsson
Nirvana **8**
Nisbett, Steve "Grizzly"
See Steel Pulse
Nitty Gritty Dirt Band, The **6**
Nobacon, Danbert
See Chumbawamba
Nocentelli, Leo
See Meters, The
No Doubt **20**
Nolan, Jerry
See New York Dolls
Nomiya, Maki
See Pizzicato Five
Noone, Peter
See Herman's Hermits
Norica, Sugar Ray
See Roomful of Blues
Norman, Jessye **7**
Norman, Jimmy
See Coasters, The
Norris, Jean
See Zhane
Northey, Craig
See Odds
Norum, John
See Dokken
Norvell, Sally
See Congo Norvell
Norvo, Red **12**
Notorious B.I.G. **20**
Novoselic, Chris
See Nirvana
Nowell, Bradley James
See Sublime
NRBQ **12**
Nugent, Ted **2**
Nunn, Bobby
See Coasters, The
N.W.A. **6**
Nutter, Alice
See Chumbawamba
Nylons, The **18**
Nyman, Michael **15**
Nyolo, Sally
See Zap Mama
Nyro, Laura **12**
Oakes, Richard
See Suede
Oakey, Philip
See Human League, The
Oakley, Berry
See Allman Brothers, The
Oak Ridge Boys, The **7**
Oasis **16**
Oates, John
See Hall & Oates
O'Brien, Derek
See Social Distortion
O'Brien, Dwayne
See Little Texas
O'Bryant, Alan
See Nashville Bluegrass Band
Ocasek, Ric
See Cars, The
Ocasek, Ric **5**
Ocean, Billy **4**
Oceans, Lucky
See Asleep at the Wheel
Ochs, Phil **7**
O'Connell, Chris
See Asleep at the Wheel
O'Connor, Billy
See Blondie
O'Connor, Daniel
See House of Pain
O'Connor, Mark **1**
O'Connor, Sinead **3**
O'Day, Anita **21**
Odds **20**
Odetta **7**
O'Donnell, Roger
See Cure, The
Odmark, Matt
See Jars of Clay
Ogletree, Mike
See Simple Minds
Ogre, Nivek
See Skinny Puppy
O'Hagan, Sean
See Stereolab
Ohanian, David
See Canadian Brass, The
O'Hare, Brendan
See Teenage Fanclub
Ohio Players **16**
O'Jays, The **13**
Oje, Baba
See Arrested Development
Olafsson, Bragi
See Sugarcubes, The
Olander, Jimmy
See Diamond Rio
Oldfield, Mike **18**
Olds, Brent
See Poi Dog Pondering
Oliver, Joe
See Oliver, King
Oliver, King **15**
Olson, Jeff
See Village People, The
Olson, Mark
See Jayhawks, The
Olsson, Nigel
See Spencer Davis Group
Onassis, Blackie
See Urge Overkill
Ono, Yoko **11**
Orb, The **18**
Orbison, Roy **2**
Orbital **20**
Orchestral Manoeuvres in the Dark **21**
O'Reagan, Tim
See Jayhawks, The
Orff, Carl **21**
Orlando, Tony **15**
O'Riordan, Cait
See Pogues, The
O'Riordan, Dolores
See Cranberries, The
Örn, Einar
See Sugarcubes, The
Örnolfsdottir, Margret
See Sugarcubes, The
Orr, Benjamin
See Cars, The
Orr, Casey
See Gwar
Orrall, Frank
See Poi Dog Pondering
Orzabal, Roland
See Tears for Fears
Osborne, Bob
See Osborne Brothers, The
Osborne, Buzz
See Melvins
Osborne, Sonny
See Osborne Brothers, The
Osborne Brothers, The **8**
Osbourne, Ozzy **3**
Also see Black Sabbath
Osby, Greg **21**
Oskar, Lee
See War
Oslin, K. T. **3**
Osman, Mat
See Suede
Osmond, Donny **3**
Ostin, Mo **17**
Otis, Johnny **16**
Ott, David **2**
Our Lady Peace **22**
Outler, Jimmy
See Soul Stirrers, The
Owen, Randy Yueull
See Alabama
Owens, Buck **2**
Owens, Campbell
See Aztec Camera
Owens, Ricky
See Temptations, The
Oyewole, Abiodun
See Last Poets
Page, Jimmy **4**
Also see Led Zeppelin
Also see Yardbirds, The
Page, Patti **11**
Page, Steven
See Barenaked Ladies
Paice, Ian
See Deep Purple
Palmer, Carl
See Emerson, Lake & Palmer/Powell
Palmer, David
See Jethro Tull
Palmer, Jeff **20**
Palmer, Keeti
See Prodigy
Palmer, Phil
See Dire Straits

Palmer, Robert **2**
Palmer-Jones, Robert
See King Crimson
Palmieri, Eddie **15**
Paluzzi, Jimmy
See Sponge
Pamer, John
See Tsunami
Pankow, James
See Chicago
Panter, Horace
See Specials, The
Pantera **13**
Papach, Leyna
See Geraldine Fibbers
Parazaider, Walter
See Chicago
Paris, Twila **16**
Park, Cary
See Boy Howdy
Park, Larry
See Boy Howdy
Parkening, Christopher **7**
Parker, Charlie **5**
Parker, Graham **10**
Parker, Kris
See KRS-One
Parker, Maceo **7**
Parker, Tom
See Animals
Parkin, Chad
See Aquabats
Parks, Van Dyke **17**
Parnell, Lee Roy **15**
Parsons, Alan **12**
Parsons, Dave
See Bush
Parsons, Gene
See Byrds, The
Parsons, Gram **7**
Also see Byrds, The
Parsons, Tony
See Iron Maiden
Parton, Dolly **2**
Partridge, Andy
See XTC
Pasemaster, Mase
See De La Soul
Pass, Joe **15**
Pastorius, Jaco
See Weather Report
Paterson, Alex
See Orb, The
Patinkin, Mandy **20**
Earlier sketch CM **3**
Patti, Sandi **7**
Patton, Charley **11**
Patton, Mike
See Faith No More
Paul, Alan
See Manhattan Transfer, The
Paul, Les **2**
Paul, Vinnie
See Pantera
Paul III, Henry
See BlackHawk
Paulo, Jr.
See Sepultura
Pavarotti, Luciano **20**
Earlier sketch in CM **1**
Pavement **14**
Paxton, Tom **5**
Payne, Bill
See Little Feat
Payne, Scherrie
See Supremes, The
Payton, Denis
See Dave Clark Five, The
Payton, Lawrence
See Four Tops, The
Pearl, Minnie **3**
Pearl Jam **12**
Pearson, Dan
See American Music Club
Peart, Neil
See Rush
Pedersen, Herb
See Desert Rose Band, The
Peduzzi, Larry
See Roomful of Blues
Peek, Dan
See America
Peeler, Ben
See Mavericks, The
Pegg, Dave
See Fairport Convention
Also see Jethro Tull
Pegrum, Nigel
See Steeleye Span
Pence, Jeff
See Blessid Union of Souls
Pendergrass, Teddy **3**
Pengilly, Kirk
See INXS
Peniston, CeCe **15**
Penn, Michael **4**
Penner, Fred **10**
Pentangle **18**
Pepper, Art **18**
Perahia, Murray **10**
Pere Ubu **17**
Peretz, Jesse
See Lemonheads, The
Perez, Louie
See Los Lobos
Perkins, Carl **9**
Perkins, John
See XTC
Perkins, Percell
See Five Blind Boys of Alabama
Perkins, Steve
See Jane's Addiction
Perlman, Itzhak **2**
Perlman, Marc
See Jayhawks, The
Pernice, Joe
See Scud Mountain Boys
Perry, Brendan
See Dead Can Dance
Perry, Doane
See Jethro Tull
Perry, Joe
See Aerosmith
Perry, Steve
See Journey
Persson, Nina
See Cardigans
Peter, Paul & Mary **4**
Peters, Bernadette **7**
Peters, Dan
See Mudhoney
Peters, Joey
See Grant Lee Buffalo
Peters, Mike
See Alarm
Petersen, Chris
See Front Line Assembly
Peterson, Debbi
See Bangles
Peterson, Oscar **11**
Peterson, Vicki
See Bangles
Petersson, Tom
See Cheap Trick
Petra **3**
Pet Shop Boys **5**
Petty, Tom **9**
Pfaff, Kristen
See Hole
Phair, Liz **14**
Phantom, Slim Jim
See Stray Cats, The
Pharcyde, The **17**
Phelps, Doug
See Kentucky Headhunters, The
Phelps, Ricky Lee
See Kentucky Headhunters, The
Phife
See Tribe Called Quest, A
Phil, Gary
See Boston
Philips, Anthony
See Genesis
Phillips, Chris
See Squirrel Nut Zippers
Phillips, Chynna
See Wilson Phillips
Phillips, Glenn
See Toad the Wet Sprocket
Phillips, Grant Lee
See Grant Lee Buffalo
Phillips, Harvey **3**
Phillips, John
See Mamas and the Papas
Phillips, Mackenzie
See Mamas and the Papas
Phillips, Michelle
See Mamas and the Papas
Phillips, Sam **5**
Phillips, Sam **12**
Phillips, Shelley
See Point of Grace
Phillips, Simon
See Judas Priest
Phish **13**

Phungula, Inos
See Ladysmith Black Mambazo
Piaf, Edith **8**
Piazzolla, Astor **18**
Picciotto, Joe
See Fugazi
Piccolo, Greg
See Roomful of Blues
Pickering, Michael
See M People
Pickett, Wilson **10**
Pierce, Marvin "Merv"
See Ohio Players
Pierce, Webb **15**
Pierson, Kate
SeeB-52's, The
Pilatus, Rob
See Milli Vanilli
Pilson, Jeff
See Dokken
Pinder, Michael
See Moody Blues, The
Pine, Courtney
See Soul II Soul
Pink Floyd **2**
Pinkus, Jeff
See Butthole Surfers
Pinnick, Doug
See King's X
Pirner, Dave
See Soul Asylum
Pirroni, Marco
See Siouxsie and the Banshees
Pixies, The **21**
Pizzicato Five **18**
Plakas, Dee
See L7
Plant, Robert **2**
Also see Led Zeppelin
Ploog, Richard
See Church, The
P.M. Dawn **11**
Pogues, The **6**
Poi Dog Pondering **17**
Poindexter, Buster
See Johansen, David
Point of Grace **21**
Pointer, Anita
See Pointer Sisters, The
Pointer, Bonnie
See Pointer Sisters, The
Pointer, June
See Pointer Sisters, The
Pointer, Ruth
See Pointer Sisters, The
Pointer Sisters, The **9**
Poison **11**
Poison Ivy
See Rorschach, Poison Ivy
Poland, Chris
See Megadeth
Polce, Tom
See Letters to Cleo
Police, The **20**
Pollard, Jim
See Guided By Voices
Pollard, Robert, Jr.
See Guided By Voices
Pollock, Courtney Adam
See Aquabats
Polygon Window
See Aphex Twin
Pomus, Doc
See Doc Pomus
Ponty, Jean-Luc **8**
Also see Mahavishnu Orchestra
Pop, Iggy **1**
Popper, John
See Blues Traveler
Porter, Cole **10**
Porter, George, Jr.
See Meters, The
Porter, Tiran
See Doobie Brothers, The
Portishead **22**
Portman-Smith, Nigel
See Pentangle
Posdnuos
See De La Soul
Post, Louise
See Veruca Salt
Post, Mike **21**
Potts, Sean
See Chieftains, The
Powell, Billy
See Lynyrd Skynyrd
Powell, Bud **15**
Powell, Cozy
See Emerson, Lake & Palmer/Powell
Powell, Kobie
See US3
Powell, Paul
See Aztec Camera
Powell, William
See O'Jays, The
Powers, Congo
See Cramps, The
Powers, Kid Congo
See Congo Norvell
Prater, Dave
See Sam and Dave
Prefab Sprout **15**
Presley, Elvis **1**
Pretenders, The **8**
Previn, André **15**
Price, Alan
See Animals
Price, Leontyne **6**
Price, Louis
See Temptations, The
Price, Mark
See Archers of Loaf
Price, Ray **11**
Price, Rick
See Electric Light Orchestra
Pride, Charley **4**
Priest, Maxi **20**
Prima, Louis **18**
Primal Scream **14**
Primettes, The
See Supremes, The
Primus **11**
Prince **14**
Earlier sketch in CM **1**
Prince Be
See P.M. Dawn
Prince, Prairie
See Journey
Prine, John **7**
Prior, Maddy
See Steeleye Span
Proclaimers, The **13**
Prodigy **22**
Professor Longhair **6**
Propes, Duane
See Little Texas
Prout, Brian
See Diamond Rio
Public Enemy **4**
Puente, Tito **14**
Pullen, Don **16**
Pulp **18**
Pulsford, Nigel
See Bush
Pusey, Clifford "Moonie"
See Steel Pulse
Pyle, Andy
See Kinks, The
Pyle, Artemis
See Lynyrd Skynyrd
Q-Tip
See Tribe Called Quest, A
Quaife, Peter
See Kinks, The
Queen **6**
Queen Ida **9**
Queen Latifah **6**
Queensryche **8**
Querfurth, Carl
See Roomful of Blues
Rabbitt, Eddie **5**
Rabin, Trevor
See Yes
Raffi **8**
Rage Against the Machine **18**
Raheem
See GetoBoys, The
Rainey, Ma **22**
Raitt, Bonnie **3**
Rakim
See Eric B. and Rakim
Raleigh, Don
See Squirrel Nut Zippers
Ralphs, Mick
See Bad Company
Ramone, C. J.
See Ramones, The
Ramone, Dee Dee
See Ramones, The
Ramone, Joey
See Ramones, The

Ramone, Johnny
See Ramones, The
Ramone, Marky
See Ramones, The
Ramone, Ritchie
See Ramones, The
Ramone, Tommy
See Ramones, The
Ramones, The **9**
Rampal, Jean-Pierre **6**
Ramsay, Andy
See Stereolab
Ranaldo, Lee
See Sonic Youth
Randall, Bobby
See Sawyer Brown
Ranglin, Ernest
See Skatalites, The
Ranken, Andrew
See Pogues, The
Ranking Roger
See English Beat, The
Rarebell, Herman
See Scorpions, The
Ray, Amy
See Indigo Girls
Raybon, Marty
See Shenandoah
Raye, Collin **16**
Raymonde, Simon
See Cocteau Twins, The
Rea, Chris **12**
Read, John
See Specials, The
Reagon, Bernice Johnson
See Sweet Honey in the Rock
Redding, Otis **5**
Redd Kross **20**
Reddy, Helen **9**
Red Hot Chili Peppers, The **7**
Redman, Don
See McKinney's Cotton Pickers
Redman, Joshua **12**
Redpath, Jean **1**
Reece, Chris
See Social Distortion
Reed, Jimmy **15**
Reed, Lou **16**
Earlier sketch in CM **1**
Also see Velvet Underground, The
Reese, Della **13**
Reeves, Dianne **16**
Reeves, Jim **10**
Reeves, Martha **4**
Reich, Steve **8**
Reid, Charlie
See Proclaimers, The
Reid, Christopher
See Kid 'n Play
Reid, Craig
See Proclaimers, The
Reid, Delroy "Junior"
See Black Uhuru
Reid, Don
See Statler Brothers, The
Reid, Ellen Lorraine
See Crash Test Dummies
Reid, Harold
See Statler Brothers, The
Reid, Janet
See Black Uhuru
Reid, Jim
See Jesus and Mary Chain, The
Reid, Vernon **2**
Also see Living Colour
Reid, William
See Jesus and Mary Chain, The
Reifman, William
See KMFDM
Reinhardt, Django **7**
Reitzell, Brian
See Redd Kross
Relf, Keith
See Yardbirds, The
R.E.M. **5**
Renbourn, John
See Pentangle
Reno, Ronnie
See Osborne Brothers, The
Replacements, The **7**
Republica **20**
Residents, The **14**
Restless Heart **12**
Revell, Adrian
See Jamiroquai
Rex
See Pantera
Reyes, Andre
See Gipsy Kings, The
Reyes, Canut
See Gipsy Kings, The
Reyes, Nicolas
See Gipsy Kings, The
Reynolds, Nick
See Kingston Trio, The
Reynolds, Robert
See Mavericks, The
Reynolds, Sheldon
See Earth, Wind and Fire
Reznor, Trent **13**
Rhodes, Nick
See Duran Duran
Rhodes, Philip
See Gin Blossoms
Rhodes, Todd
See McKinney's Cotton Pickers
Rhone, Sylvia **13**
Rich, Buddy **13**
Rich, Charlie **3**
Richard, Cliff **14**
Richard, Zachary **9**
Richards, Keith **11**
Also see Rolling Stones, The
Richardson, Kevin
See Backstreet Boys
Richey, Kim **20**
Richie, Lionel **2**
Richling, Greg
See Wallflowers, The
Richman, Jonathan **12**
Rick, Dave
See King Missile
Riebling, Scott
See Letters to Cleo
Rieckermann, Ralph
See Scorpions, The
Rieflin, William
See Ministry
Riley, Teddy **14**
Riley, Timothy Christian
See Tony! Toni! Toné!
Rippon, Steve
See Lush
Ritchie, Brian
See Violent Femmes
Ritchie, Jean **4**
Ritenour, Lee **7**
Roach, Max **12**
Roback, David
See Mazzy Star
Robbins, Charles David
See BlackHawk
Robbins, Marty **9**
Roberts, Brad
See Crash Test Dummies
Roberts, Brad
See Gwar
Roberts, Dan
See Crash Test Dummies
Roberts, Ken
See Charm Farm
Roberts, Marcus **6**
Roberts, Nathan
See Flaming Lips
Robertson, Brian
See Motörhead
Also see Thin Lizzy
Robertson, Ed
See Barenaked Ladies
Robertson, Robbie **2**
Also see Band, The
Robeson, Paul **8**
Robillard, Duke **2**
Also see Roomful of Blues
Robinson, Arnold
See Nylons, The
Robinson, Chris
See Black Crowes, The
Robinson, David
See Cars, The
Robinson, Dawn
See En Vogue
Robinson, R.B.
See Soul Stirrers, The
Robinson, Rich
See Black Crowes, The
Robinson, Romye "Booty Brown"
See Pharcyde, The
Robinson, Smokey **1**
Roche, Maggie
See Roches, The
Roche, Suzzy
See Roches, The
Roche, Terre
See Roches, The

Roches, The **18**
Rockenfield, Scott
See Queensryche
Rocker, Lee
See Stray Cats, The
Rockett, Rikki
See Poison
Rockin' Dopsie **10**
Rodford, Jim
See Kinks, The
Rodgers, Jimmie **3**
Rodgers, Nile **8**
Rodgers, Paul
See Bad Company
Rodgers, Richard **9**
Rodney, Red **14**
Rodriguez, Rico
See Skatalites, The
Also see Specials, The
Rodriguez, Sal
See War
Roe, Marty
See Diamond Rio
Roeder, Klaus
See Kraftwerk
Roeser, Donald
See Blue Oyster Cult
Roeser, Eddie "King"
See Urge Overkill
Roessler, Kira
See Black Flag
Rogers, Dan
See Bluegrass Patriots
Rogers, Kenny **1**
Rogers, Norm
See Jayhawks, The
Rogers, Roy **9**
Rogers, Willie
See Soul Stirrers, The
Roland, Dean
See Collective Soul
Roland, Ed
See Collective Soul
Rolie, Gregg
See Journey
Rolling Stones, The **3**
Rollins, Henry **11**
Also see Black Flag
Rollins, Sonny **7**
Rollins, Winston
See Jamiroquai
Romano, Ruben
See Fu Manchu
Romm, Ronald
See Canadian Brass, The
Ronstadt, Linda **2**
Roomful of Blues **7**
Roper, De De
See Salt-N-Pepa
Rorschach, Poison Ivy
See Cramps, The
Rosas, Cesar
See Los Lobos
Rose, Axl
See Guns n' Roses
Rose, Michael
See Black Uhuru
Rosen, Gary
See Rosenshontz
Rosen, Peter
See War
Rosenshontz **9**
Rosenthal, Jurgen
See Scorpions, The
Rosenthal, Phil
See Seldom Scene, The
Ross, Diana **1**
Also see Supremes, The
Ross, Malcolm
See Aztec Camera
Rossdale, Gavin
See Bush
Rossi, John
See Roomful of Blues
Rossington, Gary
See Lynyrd Skynyrd
Rostill, John
See Shadows, The
Rostropovich, Mstislav **17**
Rota, Nino **13**
Roth, C. P.
See Blessid Union of Souls
Roth, David Lee **1**
Also see Van Halen
Roth, Ulrich
See Scorpions, The
Rotheray, Dave
See Beautiful South
Rotsey, Martin
See Midnight Oil
Rotten, Johnny
See Lydon, John
Also see Sex Pistols, The
Rourke, Andy
See Smiths, The
Rowberry, Dave
See Animals
Rowe, Dwain
See Restless Heart
Rowlands, Bruce
See Fairport Convention
Rowlands, Tom
See Chemical Brothers
Rowntree, Dave
See Blur
Rubin, Mark
See Bad Livers, The
Rubin, Rick **9**
Rubinstein, Arthur **11**
Rucker, Darius
See Hootie and the Blowfish
Rudd, Phillip
See AC/DC
Rue, Caroline
See Hole
Ruffin, David **6**
Also see Temptations, The
Ruffy, Dave
See Aztec Camera
Rundgren, Todd **11**
Run-D.M.C. **4**
RuPaul **20**
Rush **8**
Rush, Otis **12**
Rushlow, Tim
See Little Texas
Russell, Alecia
See Sounds of Blackness
Russell, Graham
See Air Supply
Russell, John
See Steppenwolf
Russell, Mark **6**
Russell, Mike
See Shudder to Think
Rutherford, Mike
See Genesis
Also see Mike & the Mechanics
Rutsey, John
See Rush
Ryan, David
See Lemonheads, The
Ryan, Mick
See Dave Clark Five, The
Ryder, Mitch **11**
Ryland, Jack
See Three Dog Night
Rzeznik, Johnny
See Goo Goo Dolls, The
Sabo, Dave
See Bon Jovi
Sade **2**
Sadier, Laetitia
See Stereolab
Saffron,
See Republica
Sager, Carole Bayer **5**
Sahm, Doug
See Texas Tornados, The
St. Hubbins, David
See Spinal Tap
St. John, Mark
See Kiss
St. Marie, Buffy
See Sainte-Marie, Buffy
St. Nicholas, Nick
See Steppenwolf
Sainte-Marie, Buffy **11**
Sakamoto, Ryuichi **19**
Salerno-Sonnenberg, Nadja **3**
Saliers, Emily
See Indigo Girls
Salisbury, Peter
See Verve, The
Also see Pizzicato Five
Salmon, Michael
See Prefab Sprout
Salonen, Esa-Pekka **16**
Salt-N-Pepa **6**
Sam and Dave **8**
Sambora, Richie
See Bon Jovi
Sampson, Doug
See Iron Maiden
Samuelson, Gar
See Megadeth

Samwell-Smith, Paul
See Yardbirds, The
Sanborn, David **1**
Sanchez, Michel
See Deep Forest
Sanctuary, Gary
See Aztec Camera
Sanders, Ric
See Fairport Convention
Sanders, Steve
See Oak Ridge Boys, The
Sandman, Mark
See Morphine
Sandoval, Arturo **15**
Sandoval, Hope
See Mazzy Star
Sands, Aaron
See Jars of Clay
Sanford, Gary
See Aztec Camera
Sangare, Oumou **22**
Sanger, David
See Asleep at the Wheel
Santana, Carlos **20**
Earlier sketch in CM 1
Santiago, Joey
See Pixies, The
Saraceno, Blues
See Poison
Sasaki, Mamiko
See PulpSanders, Pharoah **16**
Satchell, Clarence "Satch"
See Ohio Players
Satriani, Joe **4**
Savage, Rick
See Def Leppard
Savage, Scott
See Jars of Clay
Sawyer Brown **13**
Sawyer, Phil
See Spencer Davis Group
Saxa
See English Beat, The
Saxon, Stan
See Dave Clark Five, The
Scaccia, Mike
See Ministry
Scaggs, Boz **12**
Scanlon, Craig
See Fall, The
Scarface
See Geto Boys, The
Schelhaas, Jan
See Camel
Schemel, Patty
See Hole
Schenker, Michael
See Scorpions, The
Schenker, Rudolf
See Scorpions, The
Schenkman, Eric
See Spin Doctors
Schermie, Joe
See Three Dog Night
Scherpenzeel, Ton
See Camel
Schickele, Peter **5**
Schlitt, John
See Petra
Schloss, Zander
See Circle Jerks, The
Schmelling, Johannes
See Tangerine Dream
Schmit, Timothy B.
See Eagles, The
Schmoovy Schmoove
See Digital Underground
Schneider, Florian
See Kraftwerk
Schneider, Fred III
See B-52's, The
Schnitzler, Conrad
See Tangerine Dream
Scholten, Jim
See Sawyer Brown
Scholz, Tom
See Boston
Schon, Neal
See Journey
Schrody, Erik
See House of Pain
Schroyder, Steve
See Tangerine Dream
Schulman, Mark
See Foreigner
Schulze, Klaus
See Tangerine Dream
Schuman, William **10**
Schuur, Diane **6**
Sclavunos, Jim
See Congo Norvell
Scofield, John **7**
Scorpions, The **12**
Scott, Ronald Belford "Bon"
See AC/DC
Scott, George
See Five Blind Boys of Alabama
Scott, Howard
See War
Scott, Jimmy **14**
Scott, Sherry
See Earth, Wind and Fire
Scott-Heron, Gil **13**
Scruggs, Earl **3**
Schulz, Guenter
See KMFDM
Scud Mountain Boys **21**
Seal **14**
Seales, Jim
See Shenandoah
Seals, Brady
See Little Texas
Seals, Dan **9**
Seals, Jim
See Seals & Crofts
Seals & Crofts **3**
Seaman, Ken
See Bluegrass Patriots
Sears, Pete
See Jefferson Starship
Secada, Jon **13**
Sedaka, Neil **4**
Seeger, Pete **4**
Also see Weavers, The
Seger, Bob **15**
Segovia, Andres **6**
Seldom Scene, The **4**
Selena **16**
Sen Dog
See Cypress Hill
Senior, Milton
See McKinney's Cotton Pickers
Senior, Russell
See Pulp
Sensi
See Soul II Soul
Sepultura **12**
Seraphine, Daniel
See Chicago
Sermon, Erick
See EPMD
Setzer, Brian
See Stray Cats, The
Severin, Steven
See Siouxsie and the Banshees
Severinsen, Doc **1**
Sex Pistols, The **5**
Sexton, Chad
See 311
Seymour, Neil
See Crowded House
Shabalala, Ben
See Ladysmith Black Mambazo
Shabalala, Headman
See Ladysmith Black Mambazo
Shabalala, Jockey
See Ladysmith Black Mambazo
Shabalala, Joseph
See Ladysmith Black Mambazo
Shadows, The **22**
Shaffer, Paul **13**
Shakespeare, Robbie
See Sly and Robbie
Shakur, Tupac
See 2Pac
Shallenberger, James
See Kronos Quartet
Shane, Bob
See Kingston Trio, The
Shanice **14**
Shankar, Ravi **9**
Shannon, Del **10**
Shanté **10**
Shapiro, Jim
See Veruca Salt
Shapps, Andre
See Big Audio Dynamite
Sharon, Lois & Bram **6**
Sharp, Dave
See Alarm
Sharpe, Matt
See Weezer
Sharrock, Chris
See Lightning Seeds

Sharrock, Sonny **15**
Shaw, Artie **8**
Shaw, Martin
See Jamiroquai
Shea, Tom
See Scud Mountain Boys
Shearer, Harry
See Spinal Tap
Sheehan, Bobby
See Blues Traveler
Sheehan, Fran
See Boston
Sheila E. **3**
Shelley, Peter
See Buzzcocks, The
Shelley, Steve
See Sonic Youth
Shenandoah **17**
Shepherd, Kenny Wayne **22**
Sheppard, Rodney
See Sugar Ray
Sherba, John
See Kronos Quartet
Sherman, Jack
See Red Hot Chili Peppers, The
Shines, Johnny **14**
Shirelles, The **11**
Shocked, Michelle **4**
Shock G
See Digital Underground
Shocklee, Hank **15**
Shogren, Dave
See Doobie Brothers, The
Shonen Knife **13**
Shontz, Bill
See Rosenshontz
Shorter, Wayne **5**
Also see Weather Report
Shovell
See M People
Shudder to Think **20**
Siberry, Jane **6**
Sice
See Boo Radleys, The
Sidelnyk, Steve
See Aztec Camera
Siegal, Janis
See Manhattan Transfer, The
Sikes, C. David
See Boston
Sills, Beverly **5**
Silva, Kenny Jo
See Beaver Brown Band, The
Silverchair **20**
Simien, Terrance **12**
Simmons, Gene
See Kiss
Simmons, Joe "Run"
See Run-D.M.C.
Simmons, Patrick
See Doobie Brothers, The
Simmons, Russell **7**
Simmons, Trinna
See Spearhead
Simon, Carly **22**
Earlier sketch in CM **4**
Simon, Paul **16**
Earlier sketch in CM **1**
Simone, Nina **11**
Simonon, Paul
See Clash, The
Simons, Ed
See Chemical Brothers
Simins, Russell
See Jon Spencer Blues Explosion
Simple Minds **21**
Simpson, Denis
See Nylons, The
Simpson, Derrick "Duckie"
See Black Uhuru
Simpson, Mel
See US3
Simpson, Ray
See Village People, The
Sims, David William
See Jesus Lizard
Sims, Neil
See Catherine Wheel
Sinatra, Frank **1**
Sinclair, David
See Camel
Sinclair, Gord
See Tragically Hip, The
Sinclair, Richard
See Camel
Sinfield, Peter
See King Crimson
Singer, Eric
See Black Sabbath
Singh, Talvin
See Massive Attack
Sioux, Siouxsie
See Siouxsie and the Banshees
Siouxsie and the Banshees **8**
Sir Mix-A-Lot
Sir Rap-A-Lot
See Geto Boys, The
Sirois, Joe
See Mighty Mighty Bosstones
Siverton
See Specials, The
Sixx, Nikki
See Mötley Crüe
Sixx, Roger
See Less Than Jake
Skaggs, Ricky **5**
Also see Country Gentlemen, The
Skatalites, The **18**
Skeoch, Tommy
See Tesla
Skillings, Muzz
See Living Colour
Skinny Puppy **17**
Sklamberg, Lorin
See Klezmatics, The
Skoob
See Das EFX
Slash
See Guns n' Roses
Slayer **10**
Sleater-Kinney **20**
Sledd, Dale
See Osborne Brothers, The
Sledge, Percy **15**
Sledge, Robert
See Ben Folds Five
Slick, Grace
See Jefferson Airplane
Slijngaard, Ray
See 2 Unlimited
Sloan, Eliot
See Blessid Union of Souls
Slovak, Hillel
See Red Hot Chili Peppers, The
Sly and Robbie **13**
Small, Heather
See M People
Smalls, Derek
See Spinal Tap
Smart, Terence
See Butthole Surfers
Smashing Pumpkins **13**
Smear, Pat
See Foo Fighters
Smith, Adrian
See Iron Maiden
Smith, Bessie **3**
Smith, Brad
See Blind Melon
Smith, Chad
See Red Hot Chili Peppers, The
Smith, Charles
See Kool & the Gang
Smith, Curt
See Tears for Fears
Smith, Debbie
See Curve
Smith, Debbie
See Echobelly
Smith, Fran
See Hooters
Smith, Fred
See Blondie
Smith, Fred
See MC5, The
Smith, Fred
See Television
Smith, Garth
See Buzzcocks, The
Smith, Joe
See McKinney's Cotton Pickers
Smith, Kevin
See dc Talk
Smith, Mark E.
See Fall, The
Smith, Michael W. **11**
Smith, Mike
See Dave Clark Five, The
Smith, Parrish
See EPMD

Smith, Patti **17**
Earlier sketch in CM **1**
Smith, Robert
See Cure, The
Also see Siouxsie and the Banshees
Smith, Robert
See Spinners, The
Smith, Shawn
See Brad
Smith, Smitty
See Three Dog Night
Smith, Steve
See Journey
Smith, Tweed
See War
Smith, Wendy
See Prefab Sprout
Smith, Willard
See DJ Jazzy Jeff and the Fresh Prince
Smithereens, The **14**
Smiths, The **3**
Smyth, Joe
See Sawyer Brown
Sneed, Floyd Chester
See Three Dog Night
Snoop Doggy Dogg **17**
Snow, Don
See Squeeze
Snow, Phoebe **4**
Soan, Ashley
See Del Amitri
Sobule, Jill **20**
Solal, Martial **4**
Soloff, Lew
See Blood, Sweat and Tears
Solti, Georg **13**
Sondheim, Stephen **8**
Sonefeld, Jim
See Hootie and the Blowfish
Sonic Youth **9**
Sonnenberg, Nadja Salerno
See Salerno-Sonnenberg, Nadja
Sonni, Jack
See Dire Straits
Sonnier, Jo-El **10**
Son Volt **21**
Sorum, Matt
See Cult, The
Sosa, Mercedes **3**
Soul Asylum **10**
Soul Coughing **21**
Soul Stirrers, The **11**
Soul II Soul **17**
Soundgarden **6**
Sounds of Blackness **13**
Sousa, John Philip **10**
Spampinato, Joey
See NRBQ
Spampinato, Johnny
See NRBQ
Spann, Otis **18**
Sparks **18**
Sparks, Donita
See L7
Special Ed **16**
Specials, The **21**
Spector, Phil **4**
Speech
See Arrested Development
Spence, Alexander "Skip"
See Jefferson Airplane
Also see Moby Grape
Spence, Cecil
See Israel Vibration
Spence, Skip
See Spence, Alexander "Skip"
Spencer, Jeremy
See Fleetwood Mac
Spencer, Jim
See Dave Clark Five, The
Spencer, Jon
See Jon Spencer Blues Explosion
Spencer, Thad
See Jayhawks, The
Spice Girls **22**
Spinal Tap **8**
Spin Doctors **14**
Spinners, The **21**
Spirit **22**
Spitz, Dan
See Anthrax
Spitz, Dave
See Black Sabbath
Sponge **18**
Spring, Keith
See NRBQ
Springfield, Dusty **20**
Springfield, Rick **9**
Springsteen, Bruce **6**
Sproule, Daithi
See Altan
Sprout, Tobin
See Guided By Voices
Squeeze **5**
Squire, Chris
See Yes
Squire, John
See Stone Roses, The
Squires, Rob
See Big Head Todd and the Monsters
Squirrel Nut Zippers **20**
Stacey, Peter "Spider"
See Pogues, The
Stacy, Jeremy
See Aztec Camera
Staehely, Al
See Spirit
Staehely, J. Christian
See Spirit
Staley, Layne
See Alice in Chains
Staley, Tom
See NRBQ
Stanier, John
See Helmet
Stanley, Ian
See Tears for Fears
Stanley, Paul
See Kiss
Stanley, Ralph **5**
Stansfield, Lisa **9**
Staples, Mavis **13**
Staples, Neville
See Specials, The
Staples, Pops **11**
Starcrunch
See Man or Astroman?
Starling, John
See Seldom Scene, The
Starr, Mike
See Alice in Chains
Starr, Ringo **10**
Also see Beatles, The
Starship
See Jefferson Airplane
Statler Brothers, The **8**
Stead, David
See Beautiful South
Steel, John
See Animals
Steele, Billy
See Sounds of Blackness
Steele, David
See English Beat, The
Also see Fine Young Cannibals
Steel Pulse **14**
Steele, Jeffrey
See Boy Howdy
Steele, Michael
See Bangles
Steely Dan **5**
Stefani, Gwen
See No Doubt
Steier, Rick
See Warrant
Stein, Chris
See Blondie
Steinberg, Sebastian
See Soul Coughing
Stephenson, Van Wesley
See BlackHawk
Steppenwolf **20**
Sterban, Richard
See Oak Ridge Boys, The
Stereolab **18**
Sterling, Lester
See Skatalites, The
Stern, Isaac **7**
Stevens, Cat **3**
Stevens, Ray **7**
Stevens, Roger
See Blind Melon
Stevenson, Bill
See Black Flag
Stevenson, Don
See Moby Grape
Steward, Pat
See Odds
Stewart, Dave
See Eurythmics

Stewart, Derrick "Fatlip"
See Pharcyde, The
Stewart, Ian
See Rolling Stones, The
Stewart, Jamie
See Cult, The
Stewart, John
See Kingston Trio, The
Stewart, Larry
See Restless Heart
Stewart, Rod **20**
Earlier sketch in CM **2**
Also see Faces, The
Stewart, Tyler
See Barenaked Ladies
Stewart, William
See Third World
Stewart, Winston "Metal"
See Mystic Revealers
Stills, Stephen **5**
Sting **19**
Earlier sketch in CM **2**
Also see Police, The
Stinson, Bob
See Replacements, The
Stinson, Tommy
See Replacements, The
Stipe, Michael
See R.E.M.
Stockman, Shawn
See Boyz II Men
Stoller, Mike
See Leiber and Stoller
Stoltz, Brian
See Neville Brothers, The
Stonadge, Gary
See Big Audio Dynamite
Stone, Curtis
See Highway 101
Stone, Doug **10**
Stone Roses, The **16**
Stone, Sly **8**
Stone Temple Pilots **14**
Stookey, Paul
See Peter, Paul & Mary
Story, Liz **2**
Story, The **13**
Stradlin, Izzy
See Guns n' Roses
Strain, Sammy
See O'Jays, The
Strait, George **5**
Stratton, Dennis
See Iron Maiden
Stravinsky, Igor **21**
Straw, Syd **18**
Stray Cats, The **11**
Strayhorn, Billy **13**
Street, Richard
See Temptations, The
Streisand, Barbra **2**
Strickland, Keith
See B-52's, The
Strummer, Joe
See Clash, The
Stryper **2**
Stuart, Mark
See Audio Adrenaline
Stuart, Marty **9**
Stuart, Peter
See Dog's Eye View
Stubbs, Levi
See Four Tops, The
Styne, Jule **21**
Subdudes, The **18**
Sublime **19**
Such, Alec Jon
See Bon Jovi
Suede **20**
Sugar Ray **22**
Sugarcubes, The **10**
Suicidal Tendencies **15**
Sulley, Suzanne
See Human League, The
Sullivan, Jacqui
See Bananarama
Summer, Donna **12**
Summer, Mark
See Turtle Island String Quartet
Summers, Andy **3**
Also see Police, The
Sumner, Bernard
See Joy Division
Also see New Order
Sundays, The **20**
Sun Ra **5**
Sunnyland Slim **16**
Super DJ Dmitry
See Deee-lite
Supremes, The **6**
Sure!, AlB. **13**
Sutcliffe, Stu
See Beatles, The
Sutherland, Joan **13**
Svenigsson, Magnus
See Cardigans
Svensson, Peter
See Cardigans
Svigals, Alicia
See Klezmatics, The
Swarbrick, Dave
See Fairport Convention
Sweat, Keith **13**
Sweet, Matthew **9**
Sweet, Michael
See Stryper
Sweet, Robert
See Stryper
Sweethearts of the Rodeo **12**
Sweet Honey in the Rock **1**
Swing, DeVante
See Jodeci
SWV **14**
Sykes, John
See Whitesnake
Sykes, Roosevelt **20**
Sylvain, Sylvain
See New York Dolls
Tabac, Tony
See Joy Division
Tabor, Ty
See King's X
TAFKAP (The Artist Formerly Known as Prince)
See Prince
Taggart, Jeremy
See Our Lady Peace
Tait, Michael
See dc Talk
Taj Mahal **6**
Tajima, Takao
See Pizzicato Five
Takac, Robby
See Goo Goo Dolls, The
Takanami
See Pizzicato Five
Takemitsu, Toru **6**
Take 6 **6**
Talbot, John Michael **6**
Talcum, Joe Jack
See Dead Milkmen
Talking Heads **1**
Tandy, Richard
See Electric Light Orchestra
Tangerine Dream **12**
Taree, Aerle
See Arrested Development
Tate, Geoff
See Queensryche
Tatum, Art **17**
Taupin, Bernie **22**
Taylor, Andy
See Duran Duran
Taylor, Billy **13**
Taylor, Cecil **9**
Taylor, Chad
See Live
Taylor, Courtney
See Dandy Warhols, The
Taylor, Dave
See Pere Ubu
Taylor, Dick
See Rolling Stones, The
Taylor, Earl
See Country Gentlemen, The
Taylor, James **2**
Taylor, James "J.T."
See Kool & the Gang
Taylor, John
See Duran Duran
Taylor, Johnnie
See Soul Stirrers, The
Taylor, Koko **10**
Taylor, Leroy
See Soul Stirrers, The
Taylor, Melvin
See Ventures, The
Taylor, Mick
See Rolling Stones, The
Taylor, Philip "Philthy Animal"
See Motörhead
Taylor, Roger
See Duran Duran
Taylor, Roger Meadows
See Queen

Taylor, Teresa
See Butthole Surfers
Teagarden, Jack **10**
Tears for Fears **6**
Technotronic **5**
Teenage Fanclub **13**
Te Kanawa, Kiri **2**
Television **17**
Teller, Al **15**
Tempesta, John
See White Zombie
Temple, Michelle
See Pere Ubu
Temptations, The **3**
Tennant, Neil
See Pet Shop Boys
10,000 Maniacs **3**
Terminator X
See Public Enemy
Terrell, Jean
See Supremes, The
Terry, Boyd
See Aquabats
Tesh, John **20**
Tesla **15**
Texas Tornados, The **8**
Thacker, Rocky
See Shenandoah
Thain, Gary
See Uriah Heep
Thayil, Kim
See Soundgarden
The The **15**
They Might Be Giants **7**
Thielemans, Toots **13**
Thin Lizzy **13**
Third World **13**
Thomas, Alex
See Earth, Wind and Fire
Thomas, David
See Pere Ubu
Thomas, David
See Take 6
Thomas, David Clayton
See Clayton-Thomas, David
Thomas, Dennis "D.T."
See Kool & the Gang
Thomas, George "Fathead"
See McKinney's Cotton Pickers
Thomas, Irma **16**
Thomas, Mickey
See Jefferson Starship
Thomas, Olice
See Five Blind Boys of Alabama
Thomas, Ray
See Moody Blues, The
Thomas, Rozonda "Chilli"
See TLC
Thompson, Chester
See Weather Report
Thompson, Danny
See Pentangle
Thompson, Dennis
See MC5, The
Thompson, Les
See Nitty Gritty Dirt Band, The
Thompson, Mayo
See Pere Ubu
Thompson, Porl
See Cure, The
Thompson, Richard
See Fairport Convention
Thompson, Richard **7**
Thomson, Kristin
See Tsunami
Thorn, Christopher
See Blind Melon
Thorn, Stan
See Shenandoah
Thorn, Tracey
See Everything But The Girl
Also see Massive Attack
Thornalley, Phil
See Cure, The
Thornhill, Leeroy
See Prodigy
Thornton, Big Mama **18**
Thornton, Willie Mae
See Thornton, Big Mama
Threadgill, Henry **9**
311 **20**
3-D
See Massive Attack
Three Dog Night **5**
Throwing Muses **15**
Thunders, Johnny
See New York Dolls
Tickner, George
See Journey
Tiffany **4**
Tikaram, Tanita **9**
Tilbrook, Glenn
See Squeeze
Tiller, Mary
See Anointed
Tillis, Mel **7**
Tillis, Pam **8**
Timbuk 3 **3**
Timmins, Margo
See Cowboy Junkies, The
Timmins, Michael
See Cowboy Junkies, The
Timmins, Peter
See Cowboy Junkies, The
Timms, Sally
See Mekons, The
Tinsley, Boyd
See Dave Matthews Band
Tippin, Aaron **12**
Tipton, Glenn
See Judas Priest
TLC **15**
Toad the Wet Sprocket **13**
Toback, Jeremy
See Brad
Todd, Andy
See Republica
Tolhurst, Laurence
See Cure, The
Tolland, Bryan
See Del Amitri
Toller, Dan
See Allman Brothers, The
Tone-L c **3**
Tontoh, Frank
See Aztec Camera
Tony K
See Roomful of Blues
Tony! Toni! Toné! **12**
Too $hort **16**
Toohey, Dan
See Guided By Voices
Took, Steve Peregrine
See T. Rex
Tool **21**
Toomey, Jenny
See Tsunami
Topham, Anthony "Top"
See Yardbirds, The
Tork, Peter
See Monkees, The
Torme, Mel **4**
Torres, Hector "Tico"
See Bon Jovi
Toscanini, Arturo **14**
Tosh, Peter **3**
Toure, Ali Farka **18**
Tourish, Ciaran
See Altan
Toussaint, Allen **11**
Towner, Ralph **22**
Townes, Jeffery
See DJ Jazzy Jeff and the Fresh Prince
Townshend, Pete **1**
Also see Who, The
Tragically Hip, The **18**
Travers, Brian
See UB40
Travers, Mary
See Peter, Paul & Mary
Travis, Merle **14**
Travis, Randy **9**
Treach
See Naughty by Nature
T. Rex **11**
Treadmill Trackstar **21**
Tribe Called Quest, A **8**
Tricky
See Massive Attack
Tricky **18**
Tritt, Travis **7**
Trotter, Kera
See C + C Music Factory
Trucks, Butch
See Allman Brothers, The
Trugoy the Dove
See De La Soul
Trujillo, Robert
See Suicidal Tendencies
Truman, Dan
See Diamond Rio
Trynin, Jen **21**
Tsunami **21**

Tubb, Ernest **4**
Tubridy, Michael
See Chieftans, The
Tucker, Corin
See Sleater-Kinney
Tucker, Moe
See Velvet Underground, The
Tucker, Sophie **12**
Tucker, Tanya **3**
Tufnel, Nigel
See Spinal Tap
Tull, Bruce
See Scud Mountain Boys
Turbin, Neil
See Anthrax
Turgon, Bruce
See Foreigner
Turner, Big Joe **13**
Turner, Erik
See Warrant
Turner, Joe Lynn
See Deep Purple
Turner, Mike
See Our Lady Peace
Turner, Steve
See Mudhoney
Turner, Tina **1**
Turpin, Will
See Collective Soul
Turre, Steve **22**
Turtle Island String Quartet **9**
Tutton, Bill
See Geraldine Fibbers
Tutuska, George
See Goo Goo Dolls, The
Tuxedomoon **21**
Twain, Shania **17**
Twist, Nigel
See Alarm
Twitty, Conway **6**
2 Unlimited **18**
23, Richard
See Front 242
2Pac **17**
Also see Digital Underground
Tyagi, Paul
See Del Amitri
Tyler, Steve
See Aerosmith
Tyner, McCoy **7**
Tyner, Rob
See MC5, The
Tyson, Ian
See Ian and Sylvia
Tyson, Ron
See Temptations, The
UB40 **4**
US3 **18**
Ulmer, James Blood **13**
Ulrich, Lars
See Metallica
Ulvaeus, Björn
See Abba
Um Romao, Dom
See Weather Report
Unruh, N. U.
See Einstürzende Neubauten
Uosikkinen, David
See Hooters
Upshaw, Dawn **9**
Urge Overkill **17**
U2 **12**
Earlier sketch in CM **2**
Utley, Adrian
See Portishead
Vaché, Jr., Warren **22**
Vachon, Chris
See Roomful of Blues
Vai, Steve **5**
Also see Whitesnake
Valentine, Gary
See Blondie
Valentine, Hilton
See Animals
Valentine, Rae
See War
Valenzuela, Jesse
See Gin Blossoms
Valli, Frankie **10**
Valory, Ross
See Journey
van Dijk, Carol
See Bettie Serveert
Van Gelder, Nick
See Jamiroquai
Van Hook, Peter
See Mike & the Mechanics
Vandenburg, Adrian
See Whitesnake
Vander Ark, Brad
See Verve Pipe, The
Vander Ark, Brian
See Verve Pipe, The
Vandross, Luther **2**
Van Halen **8**
Van Halen, Alex
See Van Halen
Van Halen, Edward
See Van Halen
Vanilla Ice **6**
Van Ronk, Dave **12**
Van Shelton, Ricky **5**
Van Vliet, Don
See Captain Beefheart
Van Zandt, Townes **13**
Van Zant, Johnny
See Lynyrd Skynyrd
Van Zant, Ronnie
See Lynyrd Skynyrd
Vasquez, Junior **16**
Vaughan, Jimmie
See Fabulous Thunderbirds, The
Vaughan, Sarah **2**
Vaughan, Stevie Ray **1**
Vedder, Eddie
See Pearl Jam
Vega, Suzanne **3**
Velvet Underground, The **7**
Ventures, The **19**
Verlaine, Tom
See Television
Verta-Ray, Matt
See Madder Rose
Veruca Salt **20**
Verve, The **18**
Verve Pipe, The **20**
Vettese, Peter-John
See Jethro Tull
Vicious, Sid
See Sex Pistols, The
Also see Siouxsie and the Banshees
Vickrey, Dan
See Counting Crows
Vig, Butch **17**
Village People, The **7**
Vincent, Vinnie
See Kiss
Vincent, Gene **19**
Vinnie
See Naughty by Nature
Vinton, Bobby **12**
Violent Femmes **12**
Virtue, Michael
See UB40
Visser, Peter
See Bettie Serveert
Vito, Rick
See Fleetwood Mac
Vitous, Mirslav
See Weather Report
Voelz, Susan
See Poi Dog Pondering
Volz, Greg
See Petra
Von, Eerie
See Danzig
von Karajan, Herbert **1**
Vox, Bono
See U2
Vudi
See American Music Club
Waaktaar, Pal
See A-ha
Wade, Adam
See Shudder to Think
Wadenius, George
See Blood, Sweat and Tears
Wadephal, Ralf
See Tangerine Dream
Wagoner, Faidest
See Soul Stirrers, The
Wagoner, Porter **13**
Wahlberg, Donnie
See New Kids on the Block
Wailer, Bunny **11**
Wainwright III, Loudon **11**
Waits, Tom **12**
Earlier sketch in CM **1**
Wakeling, David
See English Beat, The
Wakeman, Rick
See Yes
Walden, Narada Michael **14**

Walford, Britt
See Breeders
Walker, Clay **20**
Walker, Colin
See Electric Light Orchestra
Walker, Ebo
See New Grass Revival, The
Walker, Jerry Jeff **13**
Walker, T-Bone **5**
Wallace, Ian
See King Crimson
Wallace, Richard
See Mighty Clouds of Joy, The
Wallace, Sippie **6**
Waller, Charlie
See Country Gentlemen, The
Waller, Fats **7**
Wallflowers, The **20**
Wallinger, Karl **11**
Wallis, Larry
See Motörhead
Walls, Chris
See Dave Clark Five, The
Walls, Denise "Nee-C"
See Anointed
Walls, Greg
See Anthrax
Walsh, Joe **5**
Also see Eagles, The
Walters, Robert "Patch"
See Mystic Revealers
War **14**
Ward, Andy
See Camel
Ward, Andy
See Chumbawamba
Ward, Bill
Ward, Michael
See Wallflowers, The
See Black Sabbath
Ware, Martyn
See Human League, The
Wareham, Dean
See Luna
Wariner, Steve **18**
Warner, Les
See Cult, The
Warnes, Jennifer **3**
Warrant **17**
Warren, George W.
See Five Blind Boys of Alabama
Warren, Mervyn
See Take 6
Warwick, Clint
See Moody Blues, The
Warwick, Dionne **2**
Was, David
See Was (Not Was)
Was, Don **21**
Also see Was (Not Was)
Wash, Martha
See C + C Music Factory
Washington, Chester
See Earth, Wind and Fire
Washington, Dinah **5**
Washington, Grover, Jr. **5**
Was (Not Was) **6**
Wasserman, Greg
See Offspring
Waters, Crystal **15**
Waters, Ethel **11**
Waters, Muddy **4**
Waters, Roger
See Pink Floyd
Watkins, Christopher
See Cabaret Voltaire
Watkins, Tionne "T-Boz"
See TLC
Watley, Jody **9**
Watson, Doc **2**
Watt, Ben
See Everything But The Girl
Watt, Mike **22**
Also see fIREHOSE
Watts, Charlie
See Rolling Stones, The
Watts, Eugene
See Canadian Brass, The
Watts, Lou
See Chumbawamba
Watts, Raymond
See KMFDM
Weaver, Louie
See Petra
Weavers, The **8**
Webb, Chick **14**
Webb, Jimmy **12**
Webb, Paul
See Talk Talk
Webber, Andrew Lloyd
See Lloyd Webber, Andrew
Webber, Mark
See Pulp
Webster, Andrew
See Tsunami
Wedren, Craig
See Shudder to Think
Weezer **20**
Weider, John
See Animals
Weiland, Scott
See Stone Temple Pilots
Weill, Kurt **12**
Weir, Bob
See Grateful Dead, The
Weiss, Janet
See Sleater-Kinney
Welch, Bob
Welch, Bruce
See Shadows, The
Welch, Mcguinness
See Fleetwood Mac
Also see Lords of Acid
Welch, Sean
See Beautiful South
Welk, Lawrence **13**
Weller, Paul **14**
Wells, Cory
See Three Dog Night
Wells, Junior **17**
Wells, Kitty **6**
Welnick, Vince
See Grateful Dead, The
Welty, Ron
See Offspring
West, Dottie **8**
West, Steve
See Pavement
Westerberg, Paul
See Replacements, The
Weston
See Orb, The
Weston, Randy **15**
Wetton, John
See King Crimson
Wexler, Jerry **15**
Weymouth, Tina
See Talking Heads
Whalen, Katharine
See Squirrel Nut Zippers
Wheat, Brian
See Tesla
Wheeler, Audrey
See C + C Music Factory
Wheeler, Caron
See Soul II Soul
Wheeler, Harriet
See Sundays, The
Wheeler, Robert
See Pere Ubu
Whelan, Bill **20**
Whelan, Gavan
See James
Whitaker, Rodney **20**
White, Alan
See Oasis
White, Alan
See Yes
White, Barry **6**
White, Billy
White, Chris
See Dire Straits
White, Dennis
See Charm Farm
See Dokken
White, Clarence
See Byrds, The
White, Dave
See Warrant
White, Freddie
See Earth, Wind and Fire
White, Lari **15**
White, Mark
See Mekons, The
White, Mark
See Spin Doctors
White, Maurice
See Earth, Wind and Fire
White, Ralph
See Bad Livers, The
White, Roland
See Nashville Bluegrass Band
White, Verdine
See Earth, Wind and Fire

Whitehead, Donald
See Earth, Wind and Fire
Whiteman, Paul **17**
Whitesnake **5**
White Zombie **17**
Whitfield, Mark **18**
Whitford, Brad
See Aerosmith
Whitley, Chris **16**
Whitley, Keith **7**
Whittaker, Hudson **20**
Whitten, Chris
See Dire Straits
Whitwam, Barry
See Herman's Hermits
Who, The **3**
Widenhouse, Je
See Squirrel Nut Zippers
Wiggins, Dwayne
See Tony! Toni! Toné!
Wiggins, Raphael
See Tony! Toni! Toné!
Wiggs, Josephine
See Breeders
Wikso, Ron
See Foreigner
Wilborn, Dave
See McKinney's Cotton Pickers
Wilburn, Ishmael
See Weather Report
Wilcox, Imani
See Pharcyde, The
Wilde, Phil
See 2 Unlimited
Wilder, Alan
See Depeche Mode
Wilk, Brad
See Rage Against the Machine
Wilkeson, Leon
See Lynyrd Skynyrd
Wilkie, Chris
See Dubstar
Wilkinson, Geoff
See US3
Wilkinson, Keith
See Squeeze
Williams, Andy **2**
Williams, Boris
See Cure, The
Williams, Cliff
See AC/DC
Williams, Dana
See Diamond Rio
Williams, Deniece **1**
Williams, Don **4**
Williams, Fred
See C + C Music Factory
Williams, Hank, Jr. **1**
Williams, Hank, Sr. **4**
Williams, James "Diamond"
See Ohio Players
Williams, Joe **11**
Williams, John **9**
Williams, Lamar
See Allman Brothers, The
Williams, Lucinda **10**
Williams, Marion **15**
Williams, Otis
See Temptations, The
Williams, Paul **5**
See Temptations, The
Williams, Phillard
See Earth, Wind and Fire
Williams, Terry
See Dire Straits
Williams, Vanessa **10**
Williams, Victoria **17**
Williams, Walter
See O'Jays, The
Williams, Wilbert
See Mighty Clouds of Joy, The
Williamson, Sonny Boy **9**
Willie D.
See Geto Boys, The
Willis, Clarence "Chet"
See Ohio Players
Willis, Kelly **12**
Willis, Larry
See Blood, Sweat and Tears
Willis, Pete
See Def Leppard
Willis, Rick
See Foreigner
Willis, Victor
See Village People, The
Willner, Hal **10**
Wills, Bob **6**
Wills, Aaron (P-Nut)
See 311
Wills, Rick
See Bad Company
Willson-Piper, Marty
See Church, The
Wilmot, Billy "Mystic"
See Mystic Revealers
Wilson, Anne
See Heart
Wilson, Brian
See Beach Boys, The
Wilson, Carl
See Beach Boys, The
Wilson, Carnie
See Wilson Phillips
Wilson, Cassandra **12**
Wilson, Chris
See Love Spit Love
Wilson, Cindy
See B-52's, The
Wilson, Don
See Ventures, The
Wilson, Dennis
See Beach Boys, The
Wilson, Eric
See Sublime
Wilson, Jackie **3**
Wilson, Kim
See Fabulous Thunderbirds, The
Wilson, Mary
See Supremes, The
Wilson, Nancy **14**
See Heart
Wilson, Patrick
See Weezer
Wilson, Ransom **5**
Wilson, Ricky
See B-52's, The
Wilson, Robin
See Gin Blossoms
Wilson, Shanice
See Shanice
Wilson, Wendy
See Wilson Phillips
Wilson Phillips **5**
Wilton, Michael
See Queensryche
Wimpfheimer, Jimmy
See Roomful of Blues
Winans, Carvin
See Winans, The
Winans, Marvin
See Winans, The
Winans, Michael
See Winans, The
Winans, Ronald
See Winans, The
Winans, The **12**
Winbush, Angela **15**
Winfield, Chuck
See Blood, Sweat and Tears
Winston, George **9**
Winter, Johnny **5**
Winter, Paul **10**
Winwood, Muff
See Spencer Davis Group
Winwood, Steve **2**
Also see Spencer Davis Group
Also see Traffic
Wiseman, Bobby
See Blue Rodeo
WishBone
See Bone Thugs-N-Harmony
Withers, Pick
See Dire Straits
Wolstencraft, Simon
See Fall, The
Womack, Bobby **5**
Wonder, Stevie **17**
Earlier sketch in CM **2**
Wood, Chris
See Traffic
Wood, Danny
See New Kids on the Block
Wood, Ron
See Faces, The
Also see Rolling Stones, The
Wood, Roy
See Electric Light Orchestra
Woods, Gay
See Steeleye Span
Woods, Terry
See Pogues, The

Woodson, Ollie
See Temptations, The
Woodward, Keren
See Bananarama
Woody, Allen
See Allman Brothers, The
Woolfolk, Andrew
See Earth, Wind and Fire
Worrell, Bernie **11**
Wray, Link **17**
Wreede, Katrina
See Turtle Island String Quartet
Wren, Alan
See Stone Roses, The
Wretzky, D'Arcy
See Smashing Pumpkins
Wright, Adrian
See Human League, The
Wright, David "Blockhead"
See English Beat, The
Wright, Hugh
See Boy Howdy
Wright, Jimmy
See Sounds of Blackness
Wright, Norman
See Country Gentlemen, The
Wright, Rick
See Pink Floyd
Wright, Simon
See AC/DC
Wright, Tim
See Pere Ubu
Wurzel
See Motörhead
Wyman, Bill
See Rolling Stones, The
Wynette, Tammy **2**
Wynne, Philippe
See Spinners, The
Wynonna **11**
Also see Judds, The
X **11**
XTC **10**
Xefos, Chris
See King Missile
Ya Kid K
See Technotronic
Yamamoto, Hiro
See Soundgarden
Yamano, Atsuko
See Shonen Knife
Yamano, Naoko
See Shonen Knife
Yamashita, Kazuhito **4**
Yamauchi, Tetsu
See Faces, The
Yankovic, "Weird Al" **7**
Yanni **11**
Yardbirds, The **10**
Yarrow, Peter
See Peter, Paul & Mary
Yates, Bill
See Country Gentlemen, The
Yauch, Adam
See Beastie Boys, The
Yearwood, Trisha **10**
Yella
See N.W.A.
Yes **8**
Yeston, Maury **22**
Yoakam, Dwight **21**
Earlier sketch in CM 1
Yoot, Tukka
See US3
York, Andrew **15**
York, John
See Byrds, The
York, Pete
See Spencer Davis Group
Young, Adrian
See No Doubt
Young, Angus
See AC/DC
Young, Faron **7**
Young, Fred
See Kentucky Headhunters, The
Young, Gary
See Pavement
Young, Grant
See Soul Asylum
Young, Jeff
See Megadeth
Young, La Monte **16**
Young, Lester **14**
Young, Malcolm
See AC/DC
Young, Neil **15**
Earlier sketch in CM **2**
Young, Paul
See Mike & the Mechanics
Young, Richard
See Kentucky Headhunters, The
Young, Robert "Throbert"
See Primal Scream
Young M.C. **4**
Yo Yo **9**
Yow, David
See Jesus Lizard
Yseult, Sean
See White Zombie
Yule, Doug
See Velvet Underground, The
Zander, Robin
See Cheap Trick
Zankey, Glen
See Bluegrass Patriots
Zap Mama **14**
Zappa, Frank **17**
Earlier sketch in CM **1**
Zawinul, Josef
See Weather Report
Zender, Stuart
See Jamiroquai
Zevon, Warren **9**
Zhane **22**
Zilinskas, Annette
See Bangles
Zimmerman, Udo **5**
Zombie, Rob
See White Zombie
Zoom, Billy
See X
Zorn, John **15**
Zoyes, Dino
See Charm Farm
Zuccaro, Steve
See Charm Far
Zukerman, Pinchas **4**
Zulu, Ras I
See Spearhead
ZZ Top **2**